W. Greene, L.E. Schmidt

Labor Laws of Mauritius

Salzwasser

W. Greene, L.E. Schmidt

Labor Laws of Mauritius

1. Auflage | ISBN: 978-3-84605-188-7

Erscheinungsort: Frankfurt, Deutschland

Erscheinungsjahr: 2020

Salzwasser Verlag GmbH

Reprint of the original, first published in 1869.

LABOR LAWS

OF

MAURITIUS

OR

A COLLECTION OF THE LAWS

SPECIALLY RELATING TO MASTERS AND SERVANTS AT MAURITIUS

INCLUDING

THE ACTS OF THE GOVERNMENT OF INDIA

ON EMIGRATION TO THAT COLONY

COMPILED

IN THE FORM OF A CODE

BY

W. GREENE,

ACTING CROWN SOLICITOR.

AND

L. E. SCHMIDT,

REGISTRAR, COLONIAL SECRETARY'S DEPARTMENT
MAURITIUS.

MAURITIUS.

L. CHANNELL'S STEAM PRINTING ESTABLISHMENT, POUDRIÈRE STREET.

1869.

LOIS SUR LE TRAVAIL

A

MAURICE

OU

RECUEIL DES LOIS SE RAPPORTANT SPÉCIALEMENT AUX MAITRES ET SERVITEURS A MAURICE

COMPRENANT

LES ACTES DU GOUVERNEMENT DE L'INDE SUR L'EMIGRATION A CETTE COLONIE

PUBLIÉ

SOUS LA FORME D'UN CODE

PAR

W. GREENE,

CROWN SOLICITOR PAR INTÉRIM.

ET

L. E. SCHMIDT

REGISTRAR, SECRÉTARIAT COLONIAL
MAURICE.

MAURICE.

IMPRIMERIE A VAPEUR DE L. CHANNELL, RUE DE LA POUDRIÈRE.

1869.

PREFACE.

The respective rights and obligations of Masters and Servants are matters which affect so intimately the daily occupations of every one in Mauritius, that there is little need of justifying the publication of a work intended to popularize a knowledge of that section of the laws of the Colony which relates to Labor.

Hitherto, the acquisition of anything like a complete knowledge of the legislation on this subject has been a task from which the majority of employers have shrunk. The startling number of the enactments of different dates and origin; the uncertainty as to which of these laws had really ceased to be in force or were still in operation; the time, research, perseverance, and judgment, requisite to group together and compare the widely scattered provisions;—were difficulties indeed that few persons out of the legal profession could be expected to grapple with and overcome.

A book was needed which should contain all the existing legislation on Labor, classified for the use of persons unfamiliar with the study of the law. The present volume has been compiled to meet that want.

It is a reprint of the laws in English and French, in the form of a Code. It is divided into sections in each of which all the provisions on the same subject are ranged in their most natural order, irrespective of date etc. The provisions are numbered *seriatim* throughout, and the law to which each provision belongs is noted in the margin. A few articles such as declaratory and repealing clauses etc., which could not be said properly to belong to any particular section, have been placed in the Appendix.—The clearness with which each subject is shewn by this system (now employed for the first time) is much greater than could have been obtained by any other arrangement.

Explanatory notes have been given whenever these seemed to be useful; and all the decisions of the Supreme Court concerning the laws contained in the work have been indicated by references to Piston's Reports.

While the last pages were in the hands of the printer, an amending Act on the Emigration of Laborers was passed by the Indian Government; and, at the same time, a few additional Regulations, (chiefly for the prevention of Vagrancy) were made by the legislature of Mauritius. These laws have been placed at the end of the work in the section of " Supplementary Laws "; but it is believed that the references thereto, which have been inserted in the Index and at the several places in the volume which the new provisions should have occupied, will in practise be found to have counteracted the inconvenience which might have been caused by this unavoidable departure from the general plan of the work.

Having thus said all that is needful concerning the arrangement of our materials, we have now only to add a few words in explanation of the delay which has ensued since the intended publication of the work was first announced.

It was in 1866 that we brought our undertaking to the notice of the Public and that the first pages of the book were printed: almost at the outset, however, our progress was interrupted for many months by the fever-epidemic of 1867; and, when this affliction had somewhat diminished, a new difficulty arose by the passing of a law which consolidated many enactments, and which necessitated the re-casting of our manuscript. Later on, the completion of the work met with numerous other obstacles which we regret we have not been able sooner to remove.

We have spared no pains to make the volume really useful to all employers of labor, and in laying it now before the Public we venture to express the hope that we have done so successfully.

Port Louis, October 1869.

W. G.
L. E. S.

PRÉFACE.

Les questions qui se rattachent à la situation respective des Maîtres et des Serviteurs, à leurs droits et à leurs obligations réciproques, occupent une si large place dans les affaires particulières des uns et des autres, à Maurice, qu'il serait superflu de notre part de chercher à prouver l'utilité d'un ouvrage destiné à rendre facilement accessible à tout le monde cette partie de nos lois qui a trait au Travail.

Nous croyons pouvoir dire que jamais personne, à part les hommes de la profession légale, n'a cherché, jusqu'à présent, à avoir des notions exactes et complètes sur le sujet dont nous parlons. Il n'est pas étonnant du reste qu'il en soit ainsi, car une pareille tâche présente des difficultés d'une nature si rebutante que nous comprenons parfaitement qu'on ne les affronte pas de gaieté de cœur et sans y être obligé. Nous ne voulons pas parler du nombre surprenant de mesures législatives, promulguées à diverses époques et provenant de sources différentes, qu'il est nécessaire d'examiner, ni de l'incertitude dans laquelle on se trouve à chaque instant lorsqu'il s'agit de savoir lesquelles de ces lois sont encore en vigueur dans notre colonie, mais il faut du temps, des recherches, de la patience, et une certaine habitude de ce genre de travail pour grouper et comparer les dispositions éparses çà et là dans notre amas d'Ordonnances.

On avait besoin d'un livre contenant toutes les lois sur le Travail, classées de manière que l'on pût facilement les consulter. L'ouvrage que nous publions aujourd'hui a été entrepris dans le but de combler cette lacune.

Ce volume n'est qu'une reproduction textuelle, en Anglais et en Français, sous la forme d'un Code, des lois dont nous venons de parler. Il est divisé en Sections, et nous avons réuni dans chacune de ces Sections toutes les dispositions

existant sur la même matière suivant l'ordre qui nous a semblé le plus logique et le plus naturel et sans tenir compte de la date de leur promulgation. Ces dispositions sont elles-mêmes séparées les unes des autres par des numéros successifs, et nous avons indiqué en marge la loi à laquelle appartient chacune d'elles. Quelques articles—tels que les clauses déclaratives et abrogatives—qui ne pouvaient être considérés comme appartenant à une Section particulière de l'ouvrage plutôt qu'à une autre, ont été insérés dans l'Appendice. Nous croyons avoir atteint par ce système (qui est employé pour la première fois) un degré de clarté que nous n'aurions pu obtenir autrement.

Nous avons donné des notes explicatives toutes les fois que nous avons jugé qu'elles pouvaient être utiles, et nous avons également indiqué, par des renvois au Recueil de Piston, les jugements de la Cour Suprême sur les points soumis à sa décision.

Tandis que l'on imprimait les dernières pages de notre ouvrage, le Gouvernement de l'Inde promulguait un Acte qui modifie la loi sur l'Emigration des Travailleurs, et notre propre Législature décrétait en même temps quelques dispositions qui ont principalement pour but la répression du Vagabondage. En plaçant ces nouvelles mesures à la fin du volume, sous le titre de "Lois Additionnelles," nous avons dû dévier du plan général de l'ouvrage, mais nous nous sommes efforcés d'obvier autant que possible à cet inconvénient en donnant, dans notre Table Alphabétique les indications les plus complètes sur ces dispositions, et en ajoutant des renvois aux endroits mêmes du volume où elles eussent figuré si elles avaient paru plus tôt.

Avant de terminer, nous croyons devoir expliquer les raisons qui ont retardé la publication de notre ouvrage.

Nous fîmes part de notre projet au Public en 1866, et aussitôt après nous livrâmes nos premières pages à l'impression. La Fièvre Epidémique qui éclata en 1867 vint interrompre notre travail pendant plusieurs mois. Cependant nous aurions pu le reprendre vers la fin de cette année, lorsqu'un nouveau contre-temps vint à surgir : la promulgation par le Gouvernement d'une loi qui en consolidait plusieurs

autres. Force nous fut alors de remanier notre manuscrit. Plus tard encore nous avons rencontré dans la publication de ce volume bien d'autres obstacles que nous regrettons de n'avoir pu surmonter plus tôt.

Nous ne nous sommes épargnés aucunes peines pour rendre cet ouvrage réellement utile aux personnes qui emploient des Travailleurs, et en le livrant aujourd'hui au Public nous osons espérer que nous avons atteint le but que nous avions en vue.

Port-Louis, Octobre 1869.

W. G.
L. E. S.

TABLE OF CONTENTS.

	Page.
INTRODUCTION OF LABOR.	
Ch. I.—Introduction of Labor from British India ...	2
II.—Illegal introduction of Labor from British India	96
III.—Introduction of Labor from elsewhere than British India	100
IV.—Liberated African Slaves...	120
INDUSTRIAL RESIDENCE AND STAMP DUTY.	
Ch. I.—Definition.—Release and Exemption	130
II.—Redemption-Money and Stamp-duty	136
CONTRACTS OF SERVICE.	
Ch. I.—Engagements and Discharges...	148
II.—Duration &c. of Labor ... ... / Effect on Contract, of imprisonment ... ... / „ „ of transfer &c. of estate.	178
III.—Ill-usage	182
IV.—Breach of Contract by the Master...	184
V.— „ „ by the Servant	186
VI.—Causes of premature termination of Contracts.	188
VII.—Illegal employment and harbouring	194
VIII.—Apprenticeship of children	200
TICKETS, POLICE PASSES AND OTHER PAPERS ...	206
JOB-CONTRACTORS...	232
WAGES, RATIONS AND LODGING.	
Ch. I.—Wages and Rations...	244
II.—Lodging	268
MEDICAL CARE AND BURIAL.	
Ch. I.—Medical care	266
II.—Burial	300
DESERTION AND VAGRANCY.	
Ch. I.—Unlawful absence and Desertion	302
II.—Vagrancy	310
COALITION	338

Page.

STIPENDIARY COURTS.

Ch. I.—Jurisdiction, Procedure, &c. 354

II.—Tariff of Costs 368

III.—Prise à partie 372

IV.—Appeals 376

PROTECTOR AND IMMIGRATION DEPOT 382

MARRIAGES.

Ch. I.—Of Immigrants in India 392

II.—Of Immigrants in Mauritius 398

DEPARTURES AND DEPORTATION... 402

VACANT ESTATES 404

DEFINITION OF TERMS... 410

SUPPLEMENTARY LAWS 416

APPENDIX 432

TABLE OF CONTENTS I

ALPHABETICAL INDEX... III

CHRONOLOGICAL INDEX XIX

TABLE OF DECISIONS XXVI

ALPHABETICAL INDEX.

(The numbers refer to the paragraphs.)

ABSENCE.—*see* UNLAWFUL ABSENCE AND DESERTION.

AFRICAN SLAVES.—*see* INTRODUCTION OF LABOR.

APPEALS.—*see* STIPENDIARY COURTS.

APPRENTICESHIP.
- Children between 10 and 16. Consent. 264. 266.
- Certain labor prohibited. 265.
- Youths of sixteen years. 267.
- Illegal employment, &c. 260.
- Law of England applicable. 268—270.
- Master becoming Bankrupt. 272.
- *See also* MINORS.

ARBITRATION.
- Magistrate acting as Arbitrator. 459.

BADGES.—*see* JOB-MEN.

BOOKS.—*see* REGISTERS.

BREACH OF CONTRACT.—*see* CONTRACTS OF SERVICE.

BURIAL.
- Burial expenses of servants. 398.

CANCELLATION OF CONTRACTS.
- Immigrants not claimed on arrival. 129.
- Release by mutual consent. 180. 182.
- On exceptional grounds shewn by new Immigrant. 255.
- On failure to provide lodging or hospital. 358. 361.
- On account of sickness, &c., of Immigrant. 256.
- Female Immigrants. 220.
- For breach of contract by master. 251.
- For wages being in arrear. 329.
- Against job-contractors. 305—309.
- On account of minority of servant. 224.
- Fictitious engagement with old Immigrant. 257. 258. 563.
- For negligence, &c., by servant. 252.
- For breach of law on Sunday labor. 242. 243.
- Misdemeanor or felony committed by servant. 259.
- On expulsion from the Colony by Governor. 544.

CERTIFICATES.
- Indian passengers' certificate. 208.
- Forged certificates. 296. 297.
- Unlawful issue of certificates. 298.
- Unlawful retention of papers. 284. 300.

CERTIFICATES.—(*Continued.*)

Certificate of Engagement.

Certificate of newly arrived Immigrants. 128.
Fee payable to Protector. 525.
Certificate to laborers in written contract. 232—234.
Fee payable to Stipendiary Court. 487.
Clerks may sign certificates. 222
Unlawful retention by Master. 234.
On re-engagement certificate or duplicate required. 235.
Stamp-fee for duplicate. 487.
Production by laborer on demand. 291.

Certificate of Discharge.

Certificate given by Master at close of contract. 238.
Clerks may sign certificates. 228.
Stamp-fee. 487.
Issue free of charge by Magistrate. 239.
Duplicate certificate. Cost. 273, 487.
Certificate to be produced on engagement. 227. 232.
When retained by Magistrate. 232. 238.
Withdrawal on departure from the Colony. 541.

Certificate of Protector.

In lieu of certificate of discharge. 278. 408.
Fee payable to Protector. 525.
Exemption from fee. 525 bis.
Certificate to be produced on engagement. 227.
See also MARRIAGES.

CHIEF CIVIL JUDGE.

Meaning of the term. 549.

CHILDREN.—*see* APPRENTICESHIP.—MINORS.

COALITION.

By Masters or Servants. 440—442. 444.
British Statute applicable to Mauritius. 443.
Meetings, for what object lawful. 445. 446.
Queen's evidence. Indemnity. 447.
Summons &c.. of offenders or witnesses. 448. 449.
Forms of conviction. 450.
Appeals. 451. 452.

CONTEMPT OF COURT.

Penalty. 478.

CONTRACTS OF SERVICE.

Meaning of the term. 549.
Engagements and discharges. 205—240.
Duration &c., of labor. Task-work. 241—244.
Effect of imprisonment on contract. 245.
Effect of sale &c., of estate. 246—248.
Ill-usage. 249. 250.
Breach of contract by Master. 251.
Breach of contract by Servant. 252.
Causes of premature termination of the contract. 255—259.
Illegal employment and harboring of laborers. 260—263.
Apprenticeship of children. 264. 272.
Contract to be produced by Master on demand. 299.

COSTS.— *see* STIPENDIARY COURTS.

DAY-LABORERS.— *see* JOB-MEN.

DEPARTURES.

Formalities on leaving Colony.—Passport. 540.
Form of Passport. Withdrawal of papers. 541.
Fee for passport. 525.
Delivery of passport gratis. 525 bis.
Illegal embarkation. Penalty against master of vessel. 542.
Illegal embarkation. Penalty against Immigrant. 543.
Free return-passages granted. 183.

DEPORTATION.

Deportation to India of Immigrant Offenders. 544. 545.

DEPOT.— *see* IMMIGRATION DEPOT.

DESERTION.— *see* UNLAWFUL ABSENCE AND DESERTION.

DISCHARGES.— *see* ENGAGEMENTS AND DISCHARGES.

DUPLICATES.— *see* CERTIFICATES.—PASSES AND PERMITS. TICKETS.

ENGAGEMENTS AND DISCHARGES.

All Contracts to be made in Mauritius. 205.
Exceptions to the rule. 109. 206.

Verbal Contracts.

Duration not to be exceed 4 weeks. 207.
Renewal. Notice to quit. 208.
Note on Police Pass of termination. 573.
New Immigrant. Verbal employment. Penalty. 263.
Verbal employment by Job-Planters. Penalty. 567.
Fictitions verbal Contracts. 209.

Written Contracts.

New Immigrants' Contracts must be written. 210.
Duration. 211. 212.
General conditions and form. 214—218. 301.
Female Immigrants' contracts. 219. 220.
Formalities on passing engagements. 221.
Clerks may pass engagements. 222.
Contract signed by Proxy. 223.
Engagement of laborers by Job-Contractors. 303—307. 567. 568.
Minors. Conditions of engagement. Age. 224.
Right of Magistrate to refuse to pass Contracts. 225. 226.
Papers to be produced on engaging Immigrants. 227. 229—231. 235.
Papers to be produced in ordinary engagements. 232.
Certificate of Discharge,—when retained by Magistrate. 232. 233.
Certificate of Engagement issued to servant. 232—234.
Stamp-fee for certificate of engagement. 487.
Unlawful retention of certificate. 234. 300.
Ticket of servant delivered to Master. Liability. 227. 228.
Cancellation of Contract by mutual consent. 180—182.
Notice of termination of engagement not needed. 213.

ENGAGEMENTS AND DISCHARGES.—(*Continued.*)
Certificate of discharge. Note of wages due. Penalty. 238.
Stamp-fee for certificate of discharge. 487.
Discharges may be made by clerks. 222.
Duplicate certificate of discharge. Cost. 239. 487.
Duty of New Immigrants on being discharged. 240.
Duty of Old Immigrants ,, ,, 278. 280. 564.
Transfer of Immigrants' contracts. Cost. 132. 236. 237.
Stamp-fee on transfers. 487. 525.
See also CANCELLATION OF CONTRACTS.—JOB-CONTRACTORS.

ESTATE-HOSPITALS.— *see* MEDICAL CARE.

EXPULSION FROM THE COLONY.— *see* DEPORTATION.

FALSE COMPLAINTS.
Penalty. 471.

FALSE EVIDENCE.
Perjury at Stipendiary Courts. 470.

FALSE PAPERS.— *see* CERTIFICATES.—PASSES & PERMITS.—TICKETS.

FEES.— *see* PROTECTOR OF IMMIGRANTS.—STIPENDIARY COURTS.

FEMALE IMMIGRANTS.
Proportion of women to be brought from India. 86. 122. 557.
Contracts of service.—Conditions and form. 212. 219.
Suspension, &c., of contract. 220.

FICTITIOUS CONTRACTS.
Verbal engagements. 209. 282.
Magistrate may refuse to pass contracts. 226.
Cancellation by Magistrate.—Penalty. 257. 258. 563.

FINES.— *see* STIPENDIARY COURTS.

GOVERNOR.
Meaning of the term. 549.

GUARANTEE.— *see* JOB-CONTRACTORS.

GUARDIANS.— *see* MINORS.

HOSPITALS.— *see* MEDICAL CARE.

HOURS FOR LABOR.
Duration of field-labor. 241.
Labor on Sunday. 242. 243.

ILLEGAL EMPLOYMENT, &c.
Harboring, employing, &c., Servant. 260. 261.
Employing Immigrant with expired permit. Penalty. 571.
Harboring vagrants. 262.
Employing &c., New Immigrant verbally. 263.
Penalties against job-contractors. 311—312. 567. 568.
Fictitious contracts. 258. 563. 209.

ILL-USAGE.
Penalty against Master. 251. 328.
Representatives of Master. Liability. 249.
Cases referred to the ordinary Courts. 250.

IMMIGRATION DEPOT.
Reception of Immigrants without employment. 240. 516.
Reception of liberated african slaves. 168.
Disposal of pauper immigrants. 517.
Disposal of vagrant immigrants. 415.
Immigrants arrested as vagrants. 291. 408—413.
Diet and medical care at Depot. 518.
Immigrants at Depot bound to work. 519.
Wages for work done at Depot. 520.
Recovery of cost of maintenance. 521.
Conditions of quitting Depot. 523.
Surrender of expired permit. 571.
Escape from Depot. 524.
Admission of Public to the Depot. 522.
See also PROTECTOR OF IMMIGRANTS.

IMMIGRANTS.— *see* INTRODUCTION OF LABOR.

IMPRISONMENT.
Effect on contracts of service. 245.

INDUSTRIAL RESIDENCE.
Definition. 178.
How to be completed. 179.
Release by employers. 180.
" " on arrrival. 181.
" " after arrival. 182.
Fee payable on release. 487. 525.
Exemption by Governor. 183.
Residence of children under 10 years. 123.
Re-registration of new Immigrants. 274. 184. 185.
On completion of residence.—Duty of laborer. 280. 281. 564.
Proof of completion before leaving Colony. 540.

Redemption of Residence.
By laborer free from contract. 186. 187.
Exceptional redemption during contract. 188.
Payment by laborer. Receipt. 189.
Note on ticket of redemption-money due. 194.
Right of introducer to redemption-money. 196.
Forfeiture of the right. 197. 198.
Lists published of persons entitled to payment. 200.
Payment of redemption-money to employers. 199.
Transfer to, and payment from Treasury. 201. 202.
Keeping of accounts. Receipt. 203.

INTERPLEADER.
By wife of employer, on seizure for wages. 335.

INTRODUCTION OF LABOR.

FROM BRITISH INDIA.

Emigration authorised.
Emigration of laborers, lawful. 27—29.
Ports for emigration. 30.
Seasons. 8—68. 554.
Rules to be observed. 1.

INTRODUCTION OF LABOR.—(*Continued.*)
Emigration to be subject to the Indian law. 26. 86. 557. 92. 133. 135.
Suspension of Emigration. 87—90. 556.

Appointment, &c., of Officers.
Protector of Immigrants at Mauritius. 2.
Emigration Agents in India. 2. 3. 33—35.
Protector of Emigrants in India. 36—38. 45.
Medical Inspector of Emigrants in India. 40. 45.

Application for Laborers.
Requisitions. Form, &c. 109. 110.
Wages and allowances offered. 111—113.
Duration and cancellation of Requisitions. 115. 116.
Security bond for introduction—expenses. 114.

Recruiting.
Licensing of Recruiters. 48—50. 552. 559.
Recruiter's badge. 51.
Production of license. 52.
Registration of Emigrants by Magistrate. 53. 55. 558.
Registration of Town Emigrants by Protector. 56—58. 559.
Transport of Emigrants to Depot. 59.
Penalties against Recruiters. 93—96.

Emigration Depots.
Depots to be established and licensed. 41. 42. 559.
Inspection. 43. 44. 46.
Report of arrivals. 60.

Protective measures.
Explanations advice &c., by Emigration Agents. 4. 64. 120.
" " " Protector. 39. 66. 74. 75.
Certificate of Medical Inspector. 61.
Disposal of laborers recruited irregularly, or rejected. 62. 63. 64.
Laborers refusing to embark. 67.

Contracts of Service.
Laborers to enter into contract in India. 117.
Contracts not to differ from contracts made by other laborers. 21.
Form of contract for male laborers. 118.
" " females. 219.
Additional clause for advances of wages. 119.

Embarkation.
Despatch of laborers with necessary papers. 121.
Proportion of females to accompany each gang. 122.
Pass issued to emigrants. 65.
Presentation of pass on board. 76.
Measures to prevent illegal embarkation. 12. 77. 81. 102

Voyage.
Inspection and licensing of vessels. 46. 69.
Accommodation. Number of passengers. 5. 7. 70. 555. Appendix 12.
Estimated length of voyage. 8. 31. 551. 32.

INTRODUCTION OF LABOR.—(*Continued.*)

Supply of provisions. Medical attendance. 7. 10. 71.
Winter clothing for passengers. 72.
Copies of Emigration regulations to be on board. 11. 84.
Certificate of compliance by vessel with regulations. 9. 73.
Departure of vessels from Calcutta. 82. 83.
Sickness on vessel bound to Seychelles. 85.
Penalties against vessels. 16. 17. 97—101. 134.
Vessels of Admiralty or Navy not subject to emigration rules. 18. 108.

Arrival at Mauritius.

Vessel to ration Immigrants for 48 hours after arrival. 10. 16.
Master to deliver passes to Emigrants. 76.
Notice of arrival. Lists. Inspection. 12. 18. 77.
Payment of passage-money by Treasurer. 14. 22.
Register of Immigrants. 15.
Public notice of arrival of Immigrants. 124.
Delay for engagements. Previous contracts. 19. 20.
Liability for expenses of introduction. 125. 127.
Recovery of „ „ 126.
Delivery of laborers to their Masters. Papers. 127. 128. 307.
Immigrants not claimed on arrival. 129. 131.
Transfer of contract on arrival. 132.
Disposal of Immigrants unlawfully introduced. 136.

Illegal Introduction.

From unauthorized Ports. 133.
Licence of vessel. 134.
Seamen and others exempted. 135.
Disposal of laborers unlawfully introduced. 136.

FROM ELSEWHERE THAN BRITISH INDIA.

Immigration, when lawful. 137.
Licensing of vessels. 138.
Inspection on arrival of vessel. 141.
Ill-treatment during voyage. Penalty. 150.
Landing of Immigrants. Rations. 142.
Unlawful introduction. Penalty. 139.
Disposal of laborers unlawfully introduced. 140. 145.
Rate of passage-money. 147. 148.
Payment of passage-money before delivery of laborers. 145.
Employer's liability for passage-money. 149.
Laborers brought for one person but engaging with another. 146.
Delay for engagements. Previous contracts. 143.
Registration and Ticket. 144.
Proofs of marriage. 153—157.
Safe-keeping of marriage-registers. 158.
Labor-laws applicable. 152.
Unlawful sequestration of Immigrants. 151.
Enticing immigrant's wives. 159.
Prosecutions. 161.
Regulations to be made. 160.
Repeal. 162.

LIBERATED AFRICAN SLAVES.
Contracts lawful. 163.
Maintenance, &c., at Seychelles. 167.
Transfer of laborers from Seychelles. 166.
Maintenance pending engagement. 168.
Refund of expenses by Master. 169. 170.
Engagement on allotment. 171.
Duration and terms of contract. 164. 165.
Allotment certificate. Wages and rations. 175. 176.
Ticket issued on engagement. 177.
Special sections of labor laws applicable. 172.
Appointment of guardians. 173.
Regulations to be made. 174.

JOB-CONTRACTORS.
License. Duration. Production of license on engagement. 303. 304.
Verbal contracts unlawful. 567.
Written contracts limited to the District. 567.
General engagements for no specified estate. 568.
Laborers engaged for one estate. Guarantee of owner. 305.
Immigrants engaged for agricultural labor. Guarantee. 307.
Signing of guarantee. Terms and conditions. 308. 223.
Cessation of guarantee. Breaking of contract. Exception. 305. 309.
New guarantee on removal to another estate. 310.
Employment without guarantee or licence. Penalty. 311. 312.
Recovery of penalty. Appeal. 313.
Mode of paying wages guaranteed. Pay-book. 315.
Laborer's rights not affected by settlements between owner and job-contractor. 316.
Recovery of wages from guarantee. 317.
Privilege of Immigrants over estates. 318.
Contract made before passing of ordinance. 314.
Special law on guarantee applicable to all Immigrants. 306.
" applicable to Mauritius and Dependencies. 319.
Hospital accommodation for laborers. 355. 356.

JOB-MEN.
License to be taken out before getting a pass. 283.
Stamp-fee for License. 487. 572.
Production and renewal of license. 284.
Badge to be worn. 285.
Limited number of Job-men. Tariff. 569.
Forfeiture of License for not working as Job-man. 570.
Penalty for contravention of Regulations. 570.

LEGISLATION.
Order in Council of 7th Sept. 1838,—Preamble, Promulgation, &c. Appendix Nos. 1. 2. 3. 4. 5. 6. 7.
Repeal of local laws inconsistent with O. C. of 7th September 1838. Appendix 8.
Authority to amend the O. C. of 7th Sept. 1838. Appendix 11.
Ordinance No. 16 of 1862 declared not to have lapsed.—Appendix 20—22.
Repeal of certain laws. Appendix Nos. 14. 16. 18. 19. 23. 24. 25, 28.

LIBERATED AFRICAN SLAVES.— *See* INTRODUCTION OF LABOR.

LICENSES.— *see* JOB CONTRACTORS.—JOB-MEN.

LODGING.

Proper lodging to be furnished. Penalties. 353.
Inspections by Medical Inspecting Officers. 378.
Inspection by Protector of Immigrants. 510.

MALICIOUS COMPLAINTS.

Penalty. 471.

MARRIAGES.

Proof of marriages of Immigrants from elsewhere than British India. 153—159.
Proof of marriages of Immigrants from British India. 526—532.
Fee to Protector for certificate of marriage. 525.
Enticing away wives of Immigrants. Penalty. 159. 533. 534.
Formalities for marriages of Immigrants in the colony. 536.
Consent of Protector to marriages of orphan Immigrants. 537—539.

MASTER.

Meaning of the term. 549.

MEDICAL CARE.

Masters to have Hospital. Civil Hospital, Port Louis. 354. 356.
Regulations as to use of Civil Hospital. 391. 392.
Job-contractors. Hospital accommodation. Notice to Magistrate. 355. 356.
Site. Structure. Beds. Medicines. Attendants &c. 357.
Hospitals built under former law. 358. 360.
During epidemic, additional hospitals. 359.
Delays for providing hospital. Penalty 360.
Failure to have hospital. Contract cancelled. 361.
Sick laborers bound to go to hospital. 362.
Union-hospitals for servants indifferent places. 363. 392. 393.
Master to engage medical man and notify to Magistrate. 364.
Rights of Indian Immigrants during sickness. 321.
Failure to give notice, after warning. Penalty. 364. 366.
Penalties against parties for false notice. 365.
Cessation, &c., of med. man's services. Substitution. 367.
Number of visits obligatory. 368.
Register of med. man. Certificate. 369.
Register not provided or produced by Master. 370.
False entry or certificate by med. man. 370.
Interdiction of med. man for failing to keep up register. 371.
Rate of salary of med. man. 372.
Wives and children of servants. Medical care. 373.
Recovery of med. man's salary. Return of arrears. 374.
Privilege for salary. Payment on sale of estate. 375.
Inspecting Medical Officers. Appointment. Duties, &c. 376. 377. 382. 390.
Right to visit hospitals and camps. Obstruction. 378. 510.
Quarterly visits to hospitals. 386.
Report of Inspecting Officers. 387.
Information to be given by Stipend. Magistrates. 394, 395.

MEDICAL CARE.—(*Continued.*)
Contraventions of the law. Jurisdiction. 379.
Appeal. 380.
Regulation to be made under Ord. No. 29 of 1865. 381.
Poor Relief hospitals open to Masters. 396.

MINORS.
Infancy of employer. Plea inadmissible. 383.
Industrial residence of immigrant children. 123.
Contracts of service with minors. 224.
Guardianship of minors. 271. 537—539.
Apprenticeship. 264—272.
Scale of wages for minors. Appendix No. 26.

NEGLECT OF WORK.— *see* CONTRACTS OF SERVICE.—UNLAWFUL ABSENCE AND DESERTION.

NEW IMMIGRANT.
Meaning of the term, 550.

OATH (Decisory).— *see* WAGES ET RATIONS.

OLD IMMIGRANT.
Meaning of the term. 550.

OPPOSITIONS.— *see* WAGES AND RATIONS.

ORPHANS.— *see* MINORS.

PAPERS.— *see* CERTIFICATES. PASSES AND PERMITS. TICKETS.

PASSES AND PERMITS.

Police-Passes.
Application for pass within delay. Declaration. 279. 281.
Penalty for non-application. 564.
Verification of declarations. 292.
Form of pass. 289. 301.
Pass withdrawn on written engagement. 230. 231.
Obtaining pass by fictitious verbal engagement. 209.
Note on pass of termination of verbal engagement. Penalty. 573.
Job-men to take out license before getting pass. 283.
Production and renewal of Job-men's license. 284.
Badge worn by Job-men 285.
Verification of condition of holders of passes. 293.
Pass to be produced on demand. 291.
Change of district. Notice. Penalty. 286—288. 566. 413.
Change of abode, &c. Notice. Penalty. 287. 565.
Pass for foreign districts. 575.
Duplicate pass. Fee. False statement. 290. 487.
Free duplicate pass. 290 (bis). 525 (bis).
Fraudulent use of pass. 294.
Unlawful retention of pass. 300.
Withdrawal of pass on departure from colony. 541.

Depot Passes and Permits.
Issue of permits to work. Visà. 279. 522.
Expired permits. Penalty against employer and Immigrant. 571.
Permit in lieu of certificate of discharge. 227. 273. 408.
Fees for pass or permit. 525.
Free Pass or permit. 525 bis,

PASSES AND PERMITS.—(*Continued.*)

False Passes and Permits.
Forged Immigrants pass. 296.
Forged permit. 297.
Unlawful issue of passes. 298.

PASSPORTS.— *see* DEPARTURES.

PAY-BOOK.— *see* REGISTERS.—WAGES AND RATIONS.

PERJURY.
False evidence in Stipendiary Courts. 470.

PERMITS.—*see* PASSES & PERMITS.

PETTY-SESSIONS.— *see* STIPENDIARY COURTS.

POLICE PASS.— *see* PASSES & PERMITS.

PORTRAIT-TICKET.— *see* TICKETS.

PRISE A PARTIE.
Citing of Stipendiary Magistrates. 489—501.

PRIVILEGE.— *see* WAGES & RATIONS.

PROTECTOR OF IMMIGRANTS.
Appointment by Governor. 2.
Chief Clerk of the Department may act for Protector. 513. 514.
Arrival of immigrant-ships. Inspection. Lists. 12—14. 77. 81.
Register of Immigrants. 15.
Introduction of laborers from India. 109—130.
Transfer of Immigrant's contract on arrival. 132.
Laborers illegally brought from British India. 136.
Laborers from elsewhere than British India. 141—158.
Liberated African slaves. 168—177.
Industrial residence, &c., of Immigrants. 181—200.
Re-registration of Immigrants. 274. 184. 204.
Contracts of female Immigrants. 220.
New Immigrants without employment. 240.
Cancellation of contracts for special causes. 255. 256.
Issue of tickets, &c., to Immigrants. 273—281. 571.
Fees payable on papers issued by Protector. 525.
Issue of papers free of charge. 525 bis.
Tariff and number of job-men. 569.
Job-contractors' guarantee. 307. 308.
Visits to estates, camps, &c. 510.
Suspension of medical attendant of estate hospitals. 371.
Deserters Book. Notice to master. Certificate. 408.
Visits to Vagrant Depots. 511.
Disposal of vagrants after expiry of sentence. 436.
Intervention in cases of appeal. 508.
,, in actions for damages. 512.
Marriages of Immigrants. 526—537.
Guardianship of orphans and lunatics. 538. 539.
Departure of immigrants from Mauritius. 540. 542.
Vacant estates of deceased immigrants. 548.
See also IMMIGRATION DEPOT.

RATIONS.— *see* WAGES AND RATIONS.

REDEMPTION-MONEY.— *see* INDUSTRIAL RESIDENCE.

REGISTERS.

Wages-Book.—in what language admissible. 326.
Registers of laborers exempted from stamp duty. 488.
Penalty for refusal to produce books &c. in evidence. 469.
See also MEDICAL CARE.

REGULATIONS.

Authority to make them. 486.

RELEASE FROM PRISON.

Immigrant laborers imprisoned by employers. 254.
Liberated African slaves „ „ 172. 254.

REQUISITIONIST.

Meaning of the term. 550.

RETURN TO INDIA.— *see* DEPARTURES. DEPORTATION.

SAISIE-BRANDON.

Seizure of crop for wages. 336. 337.

SALE &c. OF ESTATE.

Immigrants to serve new owner of estate. 246. 248.
Freedom of former employer from liability. 247.
Provisions applicable to liberated African slaves. 172.

SCALE OF WAGES.— *See* WAGES AND RATIONS.

SERVANT.

Meaning of the term. 549.

SERVICE OF PROCESS.— *see* STIPENDIARY COURTS.

SIGNATURES.

Proof of genuineness of signatures, not requisite. 302.

SPECIAL CONSTABLES.— *see* VAGRANTS.

STAMP-DUTY.

On New Immigrants' Contracts.

Duty on new Immigrants' contracts.—Exemption by Protectector. 191.
From whom not claimable. 190.
Not payable twice for the same period. Exception. 192. 193.
Note on ticket of duty claimable. 194.
Where payable. 195.
Return of duty in certain cases. 188. 204.
Right of introducer to stamp duty. 196.
Forfeiture of the right. 197. 198.
Lists published of persons having the right. 200.
Payment by cashiers of stamp-duty to employers. 199.
Transfer to, and payment from Treasury. 201. 202.
Keeping of accounts. Receipt. 203.

On divers papers.

Fees levied by stamps on documents concerning laborers. 487. 572.
Proceedings in Stipendiary Courts. Register of Masters. General law on stamps not applicable. 488.

STIPENDIARY COURTS.

Jurisdiction, Procedure, &c.

Appointment of Magistrate. Suspension. 454.
Meaning of the words "Stipendiary Magistrate." 549.
Subordination to Governor. Reports. 455.
Jurisdiction. 456. 457. 462.
Court of jurisdiction determined by residence. 460. 461.
Arbitration. 459.
Cases of ill-usage sent to ordinary tribunals. 458.
Warrants, &c., to be executed by Police. 466.
Process served by District Court usher. 467.
Appearance of defendant before issue of process. 468.
Refusal to attend Court or give evidence. 469.
Perjury. 470.
Frivolous or malicious complaints. 471.
Contempt of Court. Insults. 478.
Assault upon officers. Rescue of seizures. 479.
Warrants of commitment may include several persons. 476. 477.
Non-payment of fines, &c. Remedy. 474. 475.
Indemnity of Magistrates. 480.
Dist. and Stip. Magistrates (Rural) to act for one another. 481.
Actions in damages against Magistrates. 482. 483.
Petty Sessions. 484. 485.

Fees of Court.

Authority to establish tariff of costs. 486.
Table of fees. 487. 572.
Documents exempted from general stamp-law. 488.
Prepayment of fees. 463.
Exemption from pre-payment. 463. 465.
Refund of fees prepaid. 473.
Costs to be paid by the losing side. 472.

Prise à partie.

Citing of Stipendiary Magistrates. 489—501.

Appeals.

Judgments appealable on points of law. 502.
Proceedings not vitiated by error, &c. 503.
Decisions in arbitration not appealable. 459.
Conditions, &c., of ordinary appeals. 504. 505.
" of appeals by job-contractors. 313.
" " as to Hospital law. 380.
" " by vagrants. 422.
" " as to coalition. 452.
Record to be transmitted to Supreme Court. 506.
Notice to Procureur General. Delay for hearing. 507.
Intervention of Protector of Immigrants. 508.

STRIKES.—*see* COALITION.

SUBROGATION.—*see* WAGES AND RATIONS.

SUBSTITUTED EMPLOYER.

Meaning of the term. 550.

SUNDAY-LABOR.
Duration, &c., on rural estates. 242. 243.

TASK-WORK.
Field-labor by Task-work. 244.

TERMS.
Meaning of words. 549. 550.

TICKETS.
Of laborers not from British India. 144.
Of liberated african slaves. 177.
Of New Immigrants. 128. also Page 208.
Of re-registered New Immigrants. 274.
Old Immigrants' Portrait-Tickets. 275.
Abolition of Tickets without Portrait. 278.
Immigrants' Tickets produced on engagement. 227. 229.
Note of engagement on Ticket. 227.
Endorsement of stamp-duty or redemption money. 194. 198.
Prolongation for Desertion. Note on Ticket. 402.
Liability of Master for Ticket. 227. 228.
Production and surrender of Ticket by Master. 299. 300.
Non-production of Ticket by Immigrant not under written contract. Penalty. 574.
Production of Ticket by servant on redeeming residence 187.
" " " on applying for Pass. 280.
Exemption by Protector of fee for Portrait. 276.
Issue of Duplicate Tickets. Fee. 279. 525.
Fraudulent use &c., of genuine Tickets. 295.
Forged Tickets. 296.
Forms of Tickets may be altered. 301.
Surrender of Ticket on quitting the Colony. 541.

UNFOUNDED COMPLAINTS.
Penalty. 471.

UNLAWFUL ABSENCE AND DESERTION.
Unlawful absence defined. 399.
Refusal to go to Hospital held to be unlawful absence. 362,
Punishments for unlawful absence. 400—402.
Imprisonment to reckon as part of contract. 245.
Desertion defined. Punishments. 403.
Arrest of deserters by Master, &c., or Police. 404. 405.
Wrongful arrest. Penalty. Damages. 406.
Declaration of deserters to Protector. 407.
Publication of names of deserters at Depot. Disposal. 408.
See also VAGRANTS.

VACANT ESTATES.
Administration of property of Immigrants dying intestate. 546.
" " liberated African slaves " 172.
Non-declaration of property by employer. Penalty. 547.
Publication of inventories. 548.

VAGRANTS.
False declarations to obtain pass. Enquiry. 409.
Non-production of pass or cert. of engagement. Arrest. 410.

VAGRANTS.—(*Continued.*)
Holders of passes. Verification of status. 411.
Immigrant found out of his district. 413.
Entry with warrant in search of vagrant Immigrants. 412.
Harbouring vagrants. Penalty. 414.
Penalties for vagrancy. 416.
Deserters refusing work at Immigration Depot punished as vagrants. 415.
Warrants of conviction may include several parties. 476.
Sentences to be undergone in Vagrant Depots. 429.
Publication of names, &c., of vagrants. 430. 431.
Notice to master of servant condemned as vagrant. 431.
Visits of masters, &c, to Vagrant Depot. 433.
Visits of Protector do. do. 511.
Disposal of vagrants at expiry of sentence. 432. 434—437.
Special constables for escort of vag. laborers. 434. 437—439.
Idle and disorderly persons. Penalty. 417.
Rogue and vagabond. Penalty. 418.
Incorrigible rogues. 419. 423.
Arrest of offenders. 420. 421. 425.
Neglect of duty by Police. 424.
Form of conviction. 426.
Mode of appeal. 427.
Recognizance of witnesses in appeals. 422.
Repeal of former vagrancy laws. 428.

VERBAL CONTRACTS.— *see* ENGAGEMENTS AND DISCHARGES.

VISITS TO ESTATES.— *see* LODGING.

WAGES AND RATIONS.
Wages &c., offered in requisitions for laborers from British India. 109—112.
Government scale. *Appendix No.* 26.
Scale may be altered. 113.
Remuneration specified in contract. 215—219.
Remuneration to be paid as stipulated. 320.
Rights of Immigrants during sickness. 321.
Unlawful absence. Forfeiture. Deduction. 399—401.
Shop-debts of laborer. 322.
Promissory-notes for wages. Recovery. 325.
Non-payment of wages, &c. Recovery. 323. 328.
Three months arrears. Cancellation of contract. 329.
Claims against Job-contractor's guarantee. 317.
Proof of payment by Job-contractor's guarantee. 568.
Salaries of manager, &c. Jurisdiction. 324.
Decisory oath of Master abolished. 327.
Wages-book. In what language admissible. 326.
Wages noted on certificate of discharge. 330.
Notice to Master, of judgment. Stamp-fee. 331. 487.
Execution of judgment after delay. 332.
Employers being minors. Liability. 333.
" Tierce opposition." When available. 334.
Goods claimed on seizure by employer's wife. 335.
Seizure of crop. (*Saisie brandon.*) 336. 337.
Sale of goods seized. 338.

WAGES AND RATIONS.—(*Continued*)
Oppositions to goods seized or proceeds. 339: 340.
Subrogation in wages. Stamp-fee. 341. 487.
Seizure of real property. Subrogation. 342.
Sale of estate. Judge's Order. Delay. Limit of privilege. 343.
" Laborers " and " Gens de Service " defined. 344. 348.
Privilege of Immigrants working for Job-contractors. 318.
Medical attendants, salary and privilege. 372—375.
Claims by managers &c., privilege and rank. 351.
Rank of claims for wages. 345—347.
Extent of privilege. How computed. 349.
Collocation. Due diligence. Claim under divers judgments. 350.
Clerk, servant or laborer of Bankrupt. Payment by Court. 352. 352 bis.
Wages of deceased Immigrants or liberated african slaves. 546.

WRITTEN CONTRACTS.—see CONTRACTS OF SERVICE.

CHRONOLOGICAL INDEX

OF THE

LAWS AND PARTS OF LAWS

CONTAINED IN THE WORK.

(The numbers refer to the paragraphs.—The numbers preceded by the letter A form the Appendix.)

No.

1. ORDER IN COUNCIL 7TH SEPTEMBER 1838. — Published 11th March 1839. Came into force on 31st March 1839.

Preamble. Par. 1 A. 1
„ 2 A. 2
„ 3 A. 3
„ 4 } 549
„ 5 }
„ 6 A. 4
„ 7 A. 5
Chap. 1 Sect. 1 A. 6
„ 2 A. 7
„ 3 A. 8
Chap. 2 Sect. 1 .. 205
„ 2 .. 207
„ 3 .. 221
„ 4 .. 211
„ 5 .. 213
„ 6 .. 214
„ 7 .. 216
„ 8 .. 215
„ 9 .. 320
„ 10 .. 217
Chap. 3 Sect. 1 .. 264
„ 2 .. 265
„ 3 .. 266
„ 4 .. 267

No.

Chap. 3 Sect. 5 .. 268
„ 6 .. 269
Chap. 4 Sect. 1 .. 456
„ 2 .. 457
„ 3 A. 9
„ 4 A. 10
„ 5 .. 502
„ 6 .. 480
„ 7 .. 252
„ 8 { 251 / 328
„ 9 { 250 / 458
„ 10 .. 459
Chap. 5 Sect. 1 .. 454
„ 2 .. 455
„ 3 .. 484
„ 4 .. 466
Chap. 6, Sect. 1, Par. 1 .. 443
„ 2 A. 29

2. ORDINANCE No. 6 OF 1838.—(*Colonial Penal Code.*)—Came into force on 29th December 1838.

Art. 323 .. 260
„ 340 .. 440
„ 341 .. 441
„ 342 .. 442

No.

3. Government Notice 16th January 1840. .. 270

4. Order in Council 23rd June 1841. — Published on 7th Dec. 1841. .. 206

5. Ordinance No. 17 of 1841.— Came into force on 5th July 1841. Confirmed. — Proclamation of 8th March 1842.
Art. 1 .. 242
„ 2 .. 243
„ 3 A. 29

6. Order in Council 15th January 1842.— Published on 5th May 1842. Came into force on 28th January 1843. .. 1 et seq.

7. Order in Council 10th June 1843. A. 11

8. Ordinance No. 42 of 1844.— Came into force on 10th June 1844. Confirmed. — Proclamation of 5th March 1845.
Art. 1 .. 417
„ 2 .. 418
„ 3 .. 419
„ 4 .. 420
„ 5 .. 421
„ 6 .. 422
„ 7 .. 423
„ 8 .. 424
„ 9 .. 425
„ 10 .. 426
„ 11 .. 427
„ 12 .. 428
„ 13 A. 29

9. Proclamation of 24th April 1851. A. 12

10. Ordinance No. 15 of 1852.— Came into force on 1st May 1852. Confirmed. Proclamation 15th April 1853.
Art. 1 .. 471
„ 2 .. 208
„ 3 .. 259
„ 4 .. 238
„ 5 .. 232
„ 6 .. 297
„ 7 .. 261
„ 8 .. 460
„ 9 .. 470
„ 10 .. 328

No.

Art. 11 .. 329
„ 12 .. 325
„ 13 .. 322
„ 14 .. 249
„ 15 .. 338
„ 16 .. 339
„ 17 .. 343
„ 18 .. 485
„ 19 .. 504
„ 20 .. 506
„ 21 .. 507
„ 22 .. 503
„ 23 .. 489
„ 24 A. 13
„ 25 A. 14
„ 26 A. 29

11. Ordinance No. 35 of 1852.— Came into force on 1st February 1853. Confirmed. Proclamation 16th April 1853.
Art. 129 .. 483

12. Ordinance No. 21 of 1853.— Came into force on 1st January 1855. Confirmed. Proclamation of 16th November 1855.
Art 8 .. 536
„ 12 .. 271
„ 13 .. 538
„ 14 .. 537

13. Ordinance No. 33 of 1853.
Art. 107 .. 352
„ 108 .. 352 (bis.)
„ 109 .. 272 (bis.)

14. Ordinance No. 3 of 1856.— Came into force on 5th April 1856. Confirmed. Proclamation of 22nd October 1856. .. 526 et seq.

15. Ordinance No. 13 of 1857.— Came into force on 1st January 1859. Confirmed. Proclamation 27th Dec. 1858.
Art. 29 .. 546

16. Ordinance No. 18 of 1857.— Camo into force on 1st July 1857. Confirmed. Proclamation of 4 December 1857.
Art. 1 .. 481
„ 4 .. 482

No.

17. ORDINANCE No. 23 OF 1857.—Came into force on 12th January 1860. Confirmed. Proclamation of 12th January 1860. .. 137 et seq.

18. ORDINANCE No. 26 OF 1857.—Came into force on 5th September 1857. Confirmed. Proclamation of 8th April 1858... 133 et seq.

19. ORDINANCE No. 7 OF 1858.—Came into force on 24th April 1858. Confirmed. Proclamation 4th November 1858.

Art. 1 .. 192
„ 2 A. 15
„ 3 .. 193
„ 4 A. 16
„ 5 A. 29

20. ORDINANCE No. 18 OF 1860.—Came into force on 1st January 1861. Confirmed. Proclamation of 28th January 1861.

Art. 90 .. 398

21. ORDINANCE No. 16 OF 1862.—Came into force on 6th April 1863. Confirmed. See Ordinance No. 28 of 1865.

Art. 1 .. 109
„ 2 .. 114
„ 3 .. 115
„ 4 .. 125
„ 5 .. 117
„ 6 .. 118
„ 7 .. 246
„ 8 .. 247
„ 9 .. 248
„ 10 .. 236
„ 11 .. 219
„ 12 .. 220
„ 13 .. 321
„ 14 A. 28
„ 15 .. 274
„ 16 .. 184
„ 17 .. 510
„ 18 .. 400
„ 19 .. 401
„ 20 .. 402

No.
„ 21 .. 295
„ 22 .. 126
„ 23 .. 254
„ 24 A. 17
„ 25 A. 18
„ 26 A. 29

22. ORDINANCE No. 28 OF 1863—Came into force on 17th Ocber 1863. Confirmed. Proclamation of 15th April 1864.

Art. 1 A. 19
„ 2 .. 508
„ 3 .. 512
„ 4 A. 29

23. ORDINANCE No. 4 OF 1864.—Came into force on 15th March 1864. Confirmed. Proclamation of 1st Sept. 1864.

Art. 8 .. 511
„ 10 .. 429
Art. 12, Sect. 1, 2, 3 .. 434
„ 12, „ 4, 5 .. 436
„ 13 .. 416
„ 14 .. 430
„ 17 .. 253

24. PROCLAMATION OF 24TH MARCH 1864.—Came into force on 2nd April 1864.

Art. 37 .. 433
„ 38 .. 437
„ 39 .. 439
„ 40 .. 431
„ 41 .. 432
„ 48 .. 438

25. GOVERNMENT NOTICE No. 86 4TH AUGUST 1864. — Came into force on 13th Aug. 1864.

Art. 5 .. 435

26. ORDINANCE No. 5 OF 1865.—Came into operation on 18th February 1865. Confirmed. Proclamation of 28th July 1865.

Art. 1 .. 513
„ 2 .. 514
„ 3 .. 515
„ 4 A. 29

No.

27. Ordinance No. 7 of 1865.— Came into force on 18th March 1865. Confirmed. Proclamation of 25th Aug. 1865.

Art. 1 .. 307
„ 2 .. 308
„ 3 .. 309
„ 4 .. 310
„ 5 .. 311
„ 6 .. 313
„ 7 .. 314
„ 8 .. 316
„ 9 .. 317
„ 10 .. 318
„ 11 .. 319
„ 12 A. 29

28. Ordinance No. 18 of 1865.— Came into force on 5th June 1865. Confirmed. Proclamation of 24th November 1865.

Art. 1 .. 163
„ 2 .. 164
„ 3 .. 165
„ 4 .. 166
„ 5 .. 167
„ 6 .. 168
„ 7 . 169
„ 8 .. 171
„ 9 .. 172
„ 10 { 173, 272 }
„ 11 .. 174
„ 12 A. 29

29. Government Notice No. 111 of 4th Nov. 1865. Came into force on 4th Nov. 1865.

Art. 1 .. 175
„ 2 .. 176
„ 3 .. 28
„ 4 A. 177
„ 5 A. 29

30. Ordinance No. 28 of 1865.— Came into force on 18th November 1865. Confirmed. Proclamation of 2nd March 1866.

Preamble A. 20
Art. 1 A. 21
„ 2 A. 22
„ 3 A. 29

No.

31. Ordinance No. 29 of 1865.— Came into force on 1st January 1866. Confirmed. Proclamation of 1st June 1866.

Art. 1 A. 23
„ 2 .. 354
„ 3 .. 355
„ 4 . 356
„ 5 .. 357
„ 6 .. 358
„ 7 .. 359
„ 8 .. 360
„ 9 .. 361
„ 10 .. 362
„ 11 .. 363
„ 12 .. 364
„ 13 .. 366
„ 14 .. 367
„ 15 .. 368
„ 16 .. 369
„ 17 .. 370
„ 18 .. 371
„ 19 .. 372
„ 20 .. 373
„ 21 .. 374
„ 22 .. 375
„ 23 .. 376
„ 24 .. 377
„ 25 .. 378
„ 26 A. 28
„ 27 .. 380
„ 28 .. 381
„ 29 A. 29

32. Ordinance No. 31 of 1865.— Came into force on 1st January 1866. Confirmed. Proclamation of 1st June 1866.

Art. 1 .. 304

33. Proclamation of 5th January 1866.— Came into force on 6th January 1866. .. 382 et seq.

34. Government Notice of 9th August 1867. — Came into force 17th August 1867. .. 170

35. Ordinance No. 31 of 1867.— Came into force 2nd May 1868. Confirmed. Proclamation of 9th July 1868.

Art. 1 .. 550
„ 2 .. 129

No.

Ordinance No. 31 of 1867. — (*Continued.*)

Art. 3 .. 212
„ 4 .. 210
„ 5 .. 263
„ 6 .. 227
„ 7 .. 234
„ 8 .. 224
„ 9 .. 123
„ 10 .. 190
„ 11 .. 191
„ 12 .. 186
„ 13 .. 187
„ 14 { 188, 255
„ 15 .. 197
„ 16 .. 196
„ 17 .. 180
„ 18 .. 183
„ 19 .. 256
„ 20 .. 226
„ 21 .. 257
„ 22 .. 241
„ 23 .. 244
„ 24 .. 353
„ 25 .. 333
„ 26 .. 344
„ 27 .. 348
„ 28 .. 349
„ 29 ... 350
„ 30 .. 351
„ 31 .. 324
„ 32 .. 327
„ 33 .. 334
„ 34 .. 340
„ 35 .. 335
„ 36 .. 330
„ 37 .. 341
„ 38 .. 342
„ 39 .. 275
„ 40 .. 277
„ 41 .. 229
„ 42 .. 278
„ 43 .. 280
„ 44 .. 286
„ 45 .. 230
„ 46 { 291, 410
„ 47 { 293, 411
„ 48 .. 413
„ 49 .. 399
„ 50 .. 403
„ 51 .. 404

No.

Art. 52 .. 405
„ 53 .. 406
„ 54 .. 245
„ 55 .. 412
„ 56 .. 299
„ 57 .. 298
„ 58 .. 296
„ 59 .. 516
„ 60 .. 524
Art. 61, Sect. 1 .. 540
„ 61, „ 2 .. 542
„ 62 .. 544
„ 63 .. 547
„ 64 .. 306
„ 65 .. 365
„ 66 { 509, 539
„ 67 .. 469
„ 68 .. 478
„ 69 .. 479
„ 70 .. 467
„ 71 .. 474
„ 72 .. 505
„ 73 .. 301
„ 74 .. 222
Art. 75, Sect. 1, 2, 3 .. 486
„ 75, „ 4, 5 .. 463
„ 76 { 379, 461
„ 77 .. 462
„ 78 A. 24
„ 79 A. 29

36. Government Notice No. 166 of 11th Nov. 1868. (*Regulations made under Ord. No. 31 of* 1867.) Came into force on 10th November 1868.

Art. 1 .. 110
„ 2 .. 116
„ 3 .. 111
„ 4 .. 112
„ 5 .. 118
„ 6 .. 120
„ 7 .. 119
„ 8 .. 121
„ 9 .. 122
„ 10 .. 124
„ 11 .. 127
„ 12 ... 128
„ 13 .. 130
„ 14 .. 131
„ 15 .. 218
„ 16 .. 181

No.

Government Notice No. 166 of 11th Nov. 1868.—(*Continued.*)

Art. 17 .. 182
„ 18 .. 132
„ 19 .. 237
„ 20 .. 189
„ 21 .. 195
„ 22 .. 194
„ 23 .. 198
„ 24 .. 199
„ 25 .. 200
„ 26 .. 201
„ 27 .. 202
„ 28 .. 203
„ 29 .. 240
„ 30 .. 204
„ 31 .. 185
„ 32 .. 235
„ 33 .. 233
„ 34 .. 231
„ 35 .. 225
„ 36 .. 258
„ 37 .. 273
„ 38 .. 331
„ 39 .. 332
„ 40 .. 289
„ 41 { 292 / 409
„ 42 .. 281
„ 43 .. 287
„ 44 .. 288
„ 45 .. 209
„ 46 .. 290
„ 47 .. 294
„ 48 .. 290 (bis)
„ 49 .. 282
„ 50 .. 303
„ 51 .. 305
„ 52 .. 312
„ 53 .. 315
„ 54 .. 283
„ 55 .. 284
„ 56 .. 285
„ 57 .. 518
„ 58 .. 519
„ 59 .. 517
„ 60 .. 415
„ 61 .. 407
„ 62 .. 408
„ 63 .. 522
„ 64 .. 523

No.

Art. 65 .. 520
„ 66 .. 521
„ 67 .. 279
„ 68 .. 228
„ 69 .. 541
„ 70 .. 543
„ 71 .. 545
„ 72 .. 548
„ 73 .. 300
„ 74 { 262 / 414
„ 75 { 525 / 487
„ 76 .. 464
„ 77 .. 465
„ 78 .. 468
„ 79 .. 472
„ 80 .. 473
„ 81 .. 525 (bis)
„ 82 .. 276
„ 83 .. 239
„ 84 .. 476
„ 85 .. 477
„ 86 .. 475
„ 87 .. 223
„ 88 .. 326
„ 89 .. 302
„ 90 A. 25
„ 91 A. 29

37. Ordinance No. 20 of 1868.—Came into force on 16th Nov. 1868. Confirmed. Proclamation of 18th May 1869.

Art. 4, Sect. 3 .. 396
„ 4 .. 397

38. Government Notice No. 187 of 8th December 1868. A. 26

39. Ordinance No. 2 of 1869.—Came into force on 18th March 1869.

Art. 9 .. 488

40. Government Notice No. 142 of 25th Aug. 1869, (*amended Regulations made under Ord. No.* 31 *of* 1867.) Came into force on 1st Sept. 1869. .. 562 et seq.

No.

41. Civil Code.

Art. 2101 .. 345
„ 2104 .. 346
„ 2105 .. 347

42. Code of Civil Procedure.

Art. 505 .. 490
„ 506 .. 491
„ 507 .. 492
„ 508 .. 493
„ 509 .. 494
„ 510 .. 495
„ 511 .. 496
„ 512 .. 497
„ 513 .. 498
„ 514 .. 499
„ 515 .. 500
„ 516 .. 501
„ 626 .. 336
„ 627 .. 337

No.

43. Imperial Statute 6 Geo. 4 Cap. 129.—Published on 6th August 1840.

Art. 1 A. 27
„ 2 A. 27
„ 3 .. 444
„ 4 .. 445
„ 5 .. 446
„ 6 .. 447
„ 7 .. 448
„ 8 .. 449
„ 9 .. 450
„ 10 .. 451
„ 11 A. 27
„ 12 .. 452
„ 13 .. 453

44. Indian Act No. 13 of 1864 .. 24 et seq.

45. Indian Act No. 6 of 1869. .. 551 et seq.

TABLE OF THE DECISIONS OF THE SUPREME COURT

NOTED IN THE WORK.

	Page.
Thamun and ors *v.* Widow d'Emmerez...	180
Pandoo and ors *v.* Reid, Irving & Co....	181
Montille *v.* Regina	184
Saïsse *v.* Sérendat	186
Pillay *v.* Eroolapen	232
Boullé *v.* Arbuthnot	246
Montille *v.* Goburdhun and ors	250
Piat, Allandy and ors *v.* Creditors of F. Tonnet and H. Nina and ors	256
Dioré *v.* Beeharry and ors	258
The Ceylon Company Limited *v.* Hardy	258
Mohabut and ors *v.* De Courson and Kyvern	260
Lamarre *v.* Joly and ors	260
Montille *v.* Goburdhun and ors	262
The Credit Foncier of Mauritius Limited *v.* Geraudflé and another	262
Itoo and ors *v* Barron, Moon, and ors	302
Dupont *v.* Pellereau	354
Renne and ors *v.* Rondeaux	354
Duval *v.* Gogun	376
Seik-Ibrahim *v.* Lablache and De Chazal	376
Teeluck *v.* Heirs Trébuchet	378
Inguy *v.* Ministère Public	378

LABOR LAWS

OF

MAURITIUS.

LOIS SUR LE TRAVAIL

A

MAURICE.

INTRODUCTION OF LABOR.

CHAPTER I.

Introduction of Labor from British India.

Order in Council, 15th January 1842.

1.—Whereas it is probable that the Laws now in force in British India for preventing the Emigration of the Inhabitants thereof to Her Majesty's Colonial Possessions will be shortly repealed so far as respects Emigration to the Island of Mauritius, and that such last mentioned Emigration will be sanctioned by Laws to be for that purpose enacted in India subject to various provisions to be in such Laws made for the protection of such Emigrants and for the prevention of abuses. And whereas it is probable that amongst the provisions so to be made, as last aforesaid will be a provision for enabling the Governor General of India to appoint at Ports or Places in India Officers charged with the care, protection, and superintendence of all persons proposing to Emigrate as Labourers from India to Mauritius. And whereas it is probable that provision will be made by Law at Mauritius for defraying from the Public Revenue of that Island the expense of introducing Immigrants thither from British India and whereas it is necessary that effectual provision should be made by Law at Mauritius for regulating any such expenditure, and for the prevention of abuses in the introduction of Immigrants from British India into that Island. It is thereof hereby ordered by the Queen's Most Excellent Majesty by and with the advice of Her Majesty's Privy Council, that in the event of any Law being made in British India authorizing the Immigration to Mauritius of the Natives of India and repealing the restrictions now in force there in regard to such Immigration and in the event of any such Law containing provi-

DE L'INTRODUCTION DES TRAVAILLEURS.

CHAPITRE 1.

De l'introduction des Travailleurs de l'Inde Anglaise.

Ordre en Conseil, 15 Janvier 1842.

1.—Attendu qu'il est probable que les lois actuellement en vigueur dans l'Inde Britannique, à l'effet d'empêcher l'émigration des habitants de cette contrée pour les possessions coloniales de Sa Majesté seront bientôt rapportées en ce qu'elles concernent l'émigration pour l'Ile Maurice, et que cette dernière émigration sera sanctionnée par des lois qui devront être passés dans l'Inde à cet effet, et contenir des mesures propres à protéger les dits émigrants et à prévenir tous abus. Et attendu qu'il est probable que par une des clauses des dites lois, le Gouverneur-Général de l'Inde sera autorisé à nommer dans les différents ports ou places de l'Inde, des officiers chargés de soigner, de protéger et surveiller toutes personnes se proposant d'émigrer comme laboureurs, de l'Inde à Maurice. Et attendu qu'il est probable qu'il sera passé une loi à Maurice à l'effet de pourvoir, au moyen des revenus publics de cette île, aux frais d'introduction, dans cette colonie, des Immigrants de l'Inde Britannique. Et attendu qu'il est nécessaire que des dispositions particulières et efficaces soient légalement prises à Maurice pour régler les dépenses susdites et pour prévenir les abus qui pourraient résulter de l'introduction des Émigrants de l'Inde Britannique en la dite île. Il est en conséquence ordonné par ces présentes, par Sa Très-Excellente Majesté la Reine, de l'avis de son Conseil Privé que dans le cas où une loi serait faite dans l'Inde Britannique á l'effet d'autoriser l'Émigration pour Maurice de Natifs de l'Inde et d'annuler les restrictions qui sont en vigueur dans cette contrée au sujet de la dite Émigration, et dans le cas où cette dite loi

sions enabling the Governor General of India to appoint at the several Ports of Embarkation in India, officers charged with the protection of persons emigrating from such Ports to Mauritius, the various Rules and Regulations comprised and set forth in the Schedule to this present order subjoined, shall, within the Island of Mauritius, have the force and effect of law, and shall be observed and carried into effect by all Her Majesty's Officers, Civil and Military, in Mauritius; and by all Her Majesty's subjects within the said Island, as to them may respectively appertain. And the Right Honorable Lord Stanley, one of Her Majesty's Principal Secretaries of State, is to give the necessary instructions herein accordingly.

As foreseen above, the Indian law prohibiting Emigration from India to Mauritius, was repealed shortly after the passing of the Order in Council. The Regulations which it introduced, were adopted by the Indian Government, as the basis of the system of Emigration established by the Act No. 21 of 1843, which has since been repealed by the Act No. 13 of 1864. See No. 24 et seq.) The latter law contains many new provisions on the details of Emigration, and reproduces several of the Articles of the Order in Council, but it also enacts certain clauses which are repugnant thereto. The notes which follow certain Articles of the Order in Council will facilitate a comparison between its provisions and those of the Indian Act, whenever both these laws treat of the same matter.

SCHEDULE.

Idem Schedule Art. I. 2.—The Governor of Mauritius may from time to time nominate such persons as he shall see fit to act as Emigration Agents at any port or place in India, which the Governor-General of India may designate as a port or place for the embarkation of Emigrants to Mauritius and may also from time to time nominate a proper person to act as Protector of Immigrants at Mauritius.—(*See Nos.* 30, 33 *and* 34.)

Idem, Art. 2. 3.—The remuneration to be given to any such Agent in India, shall not depend upon or be regulated by the number of the Emigrants sent to Mauritius by him, but shall be in the nature of an annual salary.—(*See No.* 35.)

Idem, Art. 3. 4.—Every such Emigration Agent shall ascertain by personal communication with every Emigrant previously to his or her em-

contiendrait des dispositions pour autoriser le Gouverneur-Général de l'Inde à nommer dans les différens ports d'embarquement dans l'Inde, des officiers chargés de protéger les personnes qui émigrent des dits ports pour Maurice, les divers règlemens compris dans la cédule jointe au présent ordre, auront à l'île Maurice force de loi, et seront observés et mis à exécution par tous les officiers de Sa Majesté, civils et militaires, et par tous les sujets de Sa Majesté en ladite île en ce qui leur appartiendra respectivement. Et le Très-Honorable Lord Stanley, l'un des principaux Secrétaires d'État de Sa Majesté, donnera les instructions nécessaires à l'effet des présentes.

La loi indienne prohibant l'Emigration de l'Inde à Maurice fut ainsi qu'il avait été prévu plus haut, abrogée peu de temps après la promulgation de cet Ordre en Conseil. Les règlements qu'il avait institués furent adoptés par le Gouvernement de l'Inde comme base du système d'Émigration mis en vigueur par l'acte 21 de 1843 qui a depuis été abrogé par l'acte 13 de 1864. (Voir le No. 24 et seq.) Cette dernière loi contient de nouvelles dispositions se rapportant aux détails de l'Emigration et reproduit plusieurs des articles de l'Ordre en Conseil, en même temps qu'il décrète des clauses qui sont contraires à cet Ordre. Les notes qui suivent certains articles de l'Ordre en Conseil rendront facile une comparaison des dispositions de cet Ordre avec celles de l'Acte du Gouvernement de l'Inde, toutes les fois que ces deux lois traitent des mêmes matières.

CÉDULE.

2.—Le Gouverneur de Maurice pourra de temps à autre nommer telles personnes qu'il jugera propres à agir comme Agents d'émigration dans aucun port ou place de l'Inde désigné par le Gouverneur-Général de l'Inde comme port ou lieu d'embarquement des émigrants pour Maurice, et pourra aussi de temps à autre nommer une personne convenable pour agir comme Protecteur des Immigrants à Maurice.—(*Voir les Nos.* 30, 33, *et* 34.) **Idem, Cédule, Art. 1.**

3.—La rémunération à allouer à un tel agent dans l'Inde ne sera pas basée et réglée sur le nombre des émigrants qu'il enverra à Maurice ; mais sera d'un salaire annuel.—(*Voir le No.* 35.) **Idem, Art 2.**

4.—Tout agent d'émigration devra s'assurer par une communication personnelle avec chaque émigrant avant son embarquement **Idem, Art. 3.**

embarkation from the port or place for which such Agent shall be appointed, that such Emigrant has not been induced to emigrate by any fraud, false or unreasonable representation, and is aware of the distance of Mauritius from the place where he or she is about to emigrate ; and such Agent shall explain the real advantages likely to be derived by such Emigrant from a removal to Mauritius, at the same time cautioning such Emigrant against unreasonable and unwarranted expectations, and such Agent shall also ascertain that every such Emigrant is in good health and not incapacitated for labor by old age, bodily infirmity or disease.—(*See Nos.* 61 *to* 66, *and Nos.* 74 *and* 75.)

Idem, Art. 4. 5.—It shall not be lawful to ship on board of any ship or vessel carrying Emigrants from India to Mauritius, any number of passengers exceeding the proportion of one person for every two tons of the registered burden of such ship or vessel, and no such ship or vessel carrying Emigrants, and having more than one Deck, shall have less than the height of six feet at the least, between Decks, and in case such ship or vessel shall have only one Deck, a platform shall be laid beneath such Deck, and in such manner, as to afford a space of the height of six feet at the least; and such platform shall not be so laid as that the lower beams shall project above the same and no such ship or vessel shall have more than two tiers of Berths, and no such ship or vessel shall carry passengers on any such voyage to Mauritius unless there shall be an interval of six inches at the least between the Deck or platform and the floor of the lower tiers throughout the whole extent thereof ; and whatever may be the tonnage of the ship or vessel, no greater number of passengers shall be taken on board of such ship or vessel than shall be after the rate of one such person for every twelve superficial feet of the lower Deck or platform, unoccupied by goods or stores not being the personal baggage of such persons —(*See No.* 70.—*See also in Appendix, Proclamation of 24th April* 1851.)

Idem, Art. 5. 6.—In the computation of the number of passengers within the meaning of these regulations, two children under the age of ten years shall be considered as equal to and shall be reckoned as one person only —(*See Note to No.* 5.)

[Ide]m, Art. 6. 7.—There shall be actually laden and on board of every ship

dans le port ou lieu pour lequel le dit agent aura été nommé que l'émigrant n'a pas été induit à émigrer par fraude, ni par des descriptions fausses ou déraisonnables, et que le dit émigrant connaît la distance qui sépare Maurice de l'endroit d'où il est au moment d'émigrer, et le dit agent expliquera aux émigrants les avantages réels qu'ils pourront retirer de leur séjour à Maurice en les prémunissant en même temps contre des espérances déraisonnables et sans fondement. Et le dit agent s'assurera aussi que les émigrants jouissent d'une bonne santé et ne sont pas rendus incapables de travail par la vieillesse, les infirmités ou la maladie.—(*Voir les Nos.* 61 *à* 66 *et les Nos.* 74 *et* 75.)

5.—Il ne sera pas permis d'embarquer à bord d'un navire portant des émigrants de l'Inde à Maurice un nombre de passagers excédant la proportion d'une personne par deux tonneaux selon le tonnage porté au registre du dit navire, et aucun navire portant des émigrants et ayant plus d'un pont n'aura moins de six pieds de hauteur, dans l'entrepont; et dans le cas où le dit navire n'aurait qu'un pont, une plate-forme sera placée sous le dit pont de manière à laisser un espace de six pieds de haut au moins entre la dite plateforme et le pont; et la plate-forme sera faite de manière à ce que les poutres ou solives inférieures ne projettent pas au-dessus de la plate-forme. Et aucun dit navire n'aura plus de deux rangées de couchettes et ne portera des passagers pour se rendre à Maurice, à moins qu'il n'y ait un espace de six pouces au moins entre le pont ou la plate-forme et le plancher de la rangée inférieure dans toute son étendue; et quel que soit le tonnage du dit navire, il ne pourra y être pris un plus grand nombre de passagers qu'à raison d'une personne par onze pieds de superficie du pont inférieur ou de la plate-forme non occupée par des marchandises ou provisions n'étant pas le bagage des dites personnes.—(*Voir le No.* 70.—*Voir aussi à l'Appendice la Proclamation du* 24 *Avril* 1851.) **Idem, Art. 4.**

6.—Dans le calcul des passagers d'après le sens des présents règlements, deux enfans au-dessous de 10 ans seront comptés pour une seule personne.—(*Voir la note au No.* 5.) **Idem, Art. 5.**

7.—Il sera embarqué à bord de chaque navire portant des émi- **Idem, Art. 6.**

or vessel bringing Emigrants into Mauritius, at the time of the departure of such ship or vessel from the Port or Place at which such Labourers shall be embarked, good and wholesome provisions for the use and consumption of the said passengers over and above the victualling of the crew to the amount or in the proportion following, that is to say : a supply of water to the amount of five gallons to every week of the computed voyage for every passenger on board such ship or vessel, such water being carried in tanks or sweet casks, and a supply of rice, bread, biscuit, flour, oatmeal, or bread stuffs, to the amount of seven pounds weight to every week of the computed voyage for every such passenger. Provided always, that when any such ship or vessel shall be destined to call at a Port or Place in the course of her voyage, for the purpose of filling up her water casks, a supply of water at the rate before mentioned for every week of an average voyage to such Port or Place of calling shall be deemed to be a compliance with this regulation. And provided that the preceding regulation regarding food shall be deemed to have been complied with in any case where it shall be made to appear that by the special Authority of the Governor General of India any other articles of food were substituted for the articles above enumerated as being in his judgment equivalent thereto.—(*See No.* 71.)

Idem, Art. 7. 8.—The number of weeks which shall be deemed necessary for the voyage to Mauritius from any Port or Ports in India shall be such as shall from time to time be determined by any Law or Ordinance to be promulgated for that purpose by the Governor General of India in Council, and, according to any such Law or Ordinance shall and may be further determined whether at different periods of the year different estimations are to be made of the probable length of any such voyage, and if by any such Law or Ordinance the removal of Emigrants should during any particular period of the year be prohibited altogether, then any such removal during such prohibited period shall in Mauritius be regarded, dealt with, and punished as an infringement of the present regulations.—(*See Nos.* 31 *and* 68.)

Idem, Art. 8. 9.—Before any such Ship or Vessel shall be cleared out on any such voyage, the Agent appointed under this Ordinance, for the Port or place from which such ship or vessel shall be cleared

grants à Maurice, au moment du départ dudit navire du port ou de l'endroit où seront embarqués lesdits laboureurs, des provisions bonnes et saines pour l'usage et la consommation desdits passagers indépendamment des provisions de l'équipage, dans les quantité et proportion suivantes : c'est-à-dire, un approvisionnement d'eau dans la proportion de cinq gallons par semaine pour chaque passager pendant le voyage dudit navire—l'eau étant contenue dans des citernes ou des barriques.—Et un approvisionnement de riz, pain, biscuits, farine, gruau, ou autres substances farineuses dans la proportion de sept livres pesant par semaine pour chaque passager pendant le voyage dudit navire. Pourvu toutefois que lorsque ledit navire devra toucher à un port ou lieu intermédiaire dans le cours de son voyage afin de remplir ses barriques à eau, un approvisionnement d'eau dans la proportion mentionnée ci-dessus, par semaine, pour le voyage dudit navire au port ou à l'endroit de relâche, sera considéré comme l'exécution du présent règlement. Et le règlement ci-dessus concernant la nourriture sera considéré comme ayant été exécuté dans tous les cas où il sera prouvé qu'avec l'autorisation spéciale du Gouverneur-Général de l'Inde tous autres comestibles auront été substitués à ceux énumérés ci-dessus et qu'il aura jugé leur être équivalent.—(*Voir le No.* 71.)

8.—Le nombre de semaines qui sera jugé nécessaire pour effec- **Idem, Art. 7.**
tuer le voyage d'un des ports de l'Inde à Maurice sera de temps à autre déterminé par une loi ou ordonnance, qui sera promulguée à cet effet par le Gouverneur-Général de l'Inde en Conseil ; et par ladite loi ou ordonnance il sera de plus déterminé si à différentes époques de l'année, il convient d'estimer différemment la longueur présumée dudit voyage, et si par ladite loi ou ordonnance le transport des émigrants se trouvait pendant une époque particulière de l'année entièrement prohibé, dans ce cas tout transport d'émigrants pendant la durée de ladite prohibition, sera, à Maurice, considéré, traité et puni comme une violation des présents règlements.—(*Voir les Nos.* 31 *et* 68.)

9.—Avant qu'aucun dit navire soit expédié pour un tel voyage, **Idem, Art. 8.**
l'agent nommé en vertu de la présente ordonnance pour le port ou l'endroit d'où ledit navire devra être expédié, examinera ou fera exa-

out, shall survey or cause to be surveyed by some competent person, the provisions and water hereinbefore required to be on board for the consumption of the passengers and shall ascertain that the same are in good and sweet condition, and also that over and above the same there is on board an ample supply of water and stores for the victualling of the crew of the ship or vessel, and shall also ascertain that such ship or vessel is generally reputed sea-worthy, and that the directions hereinbefore contained for ensuring the health and safety of the passengers have been complied with, and shall grant a certificate thereof under his hand to the master of such ship or vessel.—(*See Nos.* 69, 71 *and* 73.)

Idem, Art. 9. 10.—The master of every ship or vessel bringing emigrants to Mauritius, shall be bound to provide for and furnish to every such emigrant, and his wife, and children a sufficient quantity of good and wholesome provisions, for his, her, and their daily maintenance during such voyage and during the space of 48 hours next after the arrival of such ship or vessel in Mauritius.

Idem, Art. 10. 11.—Two copies of these regulations, authenticated by the signature of the agent at the port or place from which such emigrants shall come shall be delivered to the master by such agent on demand at the time of clearance, and shall be kept on board of every ship or vessel carrying such emigrants as aforesaid, and one of such copies shall upon request made at reasonable times to the master of the ship or vessel be produced to any passenger for his perusal.—(*See No.* 84.)

Idem, Art. 11. 12.—The master of every ship or vessel carrying Emigrants from India to Mauritius, shall before clearing out such ship or vessel deliver to such agent at the Port or place from which such ship or vessel shall be cleared out a List in writing together with a Duplicate of the same specifying as accurately as may be, the names, ages, aud occupations of all and every, the emigrants on board such ship or vessel ; and such agent shall thereupon deliver to the said Master the counterpart of such list signed by such agent ; and the said master shall on the arrival of such ship or vessel at Mauritius, and previous to the disembarkation of any such Emigrants, give notice of the arrival of such ship or vessel and deliver the said counterpart of such list to the Protector of Immi-

miner par une personne compétente les provisions et l'eau qui doivent, par ces présentes, être embarquées pour la consommation des passagers, et s'assurera de la bonne qualité desdites provisions, et s'assurera aussi qu'indépendamment de ces mêmes provisions, il se trouve à bord une provision d'eau et des aliments suffisans pour l'équipage du navire, et de plus que ledit navire est généralement reconnu comme étant en état de navigabilité, et que les instructions ci-dessus contenues, pour assurer la santé et la sûreté des passagers, ont été exécutées, et il en devra délivrer un certificat de sa main au capitaine dudit navire.—(*Voir les Nos.* 69, 71 *et* 73.)

10.—Le capitaine de tout navire transportant des émigrants à Maurice sera tenu de fournir à chaque émigrant ainsi qu'à sa femme et à ses enfants une quantité suffisante de provisions bonnes et saines pour leur entretien journalier pendant le dit voyage et pendant les 48 heures qui suivront l'arrivée du dit navire à Maurice. Idem, Art. 9.

11.—Il sera délivré au capitaine sur sa demande, lors de l'expédition du dit navire, deux copies des présents réglements signées et certifiées par l'agent du port ou de l'endroit d'où viendront les émigrants : ces copies seront conservées à bord de chaque navire transportant les dits émigrants, et l'une de ces copies sera produite à tout passager, sur la demande qu'il en fera en temps convenable, pour qu'il en prenne connaissance.—(*Voir le No.* 84.) Idem, Art. 10.

12.—Le capitaine de tout navire transportant des émigrants de l'Inde à Maurice remettra, avant d'expédier son navire, à l'agent du port ou de l'endroit d'où le dit navire sera expédié, une liste en duplicata dans laquelle seront spécifiés aussi exactement que possible les noms, âges et emplois de tous les émigrants embarqués à bord de son navire, et le dit agent remettra alors au dit capitaine une des copies de cette liste signée de lui et le dit capitaiue, à l'arrivée du navire à Maurice et avant le débarquement des dits émigrants, devra donner avis de l'arrivée du dit navire et remettre la copie de la liste mentionnée ci-dessus au Protecteur des Emigrants, lequel se rendra immédiatement à bord du dit navire, et s'assurera autant que possible par une inspection personnelle du navire, et des pas- Idem, Art. 11.

grants hereinbefore mentioned.—And such Protector of Immigrants shall forthwith proceed on board of such ship or vessel and shall ascertain as far as possible by personal inspection of the ship or vessel and passengers whether the directions hereinbefore contained with regard to the situation of the berths of such ship or vessel, the proportion of the passengers to the burthen and measurement of such ship or vessel and the maintenance of the emigrants, during such passage have been complied with, and such Protector of Immigrants shall personally muster such emigrants and compare the numbers and names of such emigrants with the said counterpart of such lists and shall certify in writing under his hand upon such counterpart the total number of emigrants then living and being on board of such vessel ; and in case any such emigrants shall have died during the passage, or the number or names of the emigrants shall differ from the number or names stated in such counterpart the Protector of Immigrants shall note such death or difference upon such counterpart and thereupon shall grant a licence under his hand for the disembarkation and landing of such emigrants.—(*See Nos.* 76 *to* 81.)

Idem, Art. 12. 13.—If the Protector of Immigrants on such personal inspection of the ship or vessel, and emigrants, shall be satisfied that the preceding regulations have been complied with, he shall grant a certificate under his hand of the arrival in Mauritius of such immigrants respectively and the place from which, and the ship or vessel in which such Immigrants shall have arrived.

Idem, Art. 13. 14.—No money shall be payable by the Colonial Treasurer of Mauritius in respect of any such Immigrants as aforesaid except on the warrant of the Governor of that Island, which warrant shall not be issued except on such certificate as aforesaid of the said Protector of Immigrants.

Idem, Art. 14. 15.—The Protector of Immigrants shall keep a register of all persons in respect of whom any such certificate as aforesaid shall be granted and of the ship or vessel in which, the port from which, and the time at which such persons shall have arrived in this Colony ; a copy of which registry shall be laid before the Council of Government on the 31st day of March, the 30th day of June, the 30th day of September, and the 31st day of December in each year.

sagers si les ordres contenus ci-dessus relativement à la situation des couchettes du dit navire, au nombre des passagers proportionnellement au tonnage et au mesurage du dit navire, et au traitement des émigrants pendant le dit voyage, ont été exécutés ; et le dit Protecteur fera assembler en sa présence les dits émigrants, et comparera le nombre et les noms des dits émigrants avec le nombre et les noms de ceux portés dans le double de la dite liste, et certifiera par écrit sur le double de la dite liste le nombre total des émigrants alors vivans et se trouvant à bord du dit navire, et, en cas de mort de l'un ou de plusieurs des dits émigrants pendant le voyage, ou dans le cas où le nombre ou les noms des émigrants différeraient du nombre ou des noms portés dans le double de la dite liste, le Protecteur des Immigrants prendra note des mortalités ou des différences sur le double de la dite liste et accordera ensuite un permis de sa main pour le débarquement des dits émigrants.—(*Voir les Nos*. 76 *à* 81.)

13.—Si le Protecteur des Immigrants, d'après l'inspection personnelle qu'il aura faite du navire et des Emigrants, reconnaît qu'il a été satisfait aux réglemens ci-dessus, il donnera un certificat de sa main de l'arrivée desdits Emigrants à Maurice, mentionnant le lieu de leur départ et le nom du navire sur lequel ils seront arrivés. **Idem, Art. 12.**

14.—Aucune somme ne sera payée par le Trésorier Colonial de Maurice pour aucun des dits Emigrants, si ce n'est sur l'ordre du Gouverneur de cette Ile, lequel ordre ne sera délivré que sur le certificat du Protecteur des Immigrants, dont il est fait mention plus haut. **Idem, Art. 13.**

15—Le Protecteur des Immigrants tiendra un registre de toutes personnes à l'égard desquelles le certificat mentionné ci-dessus aura été accordé, ainsi que du navire sur lequel ces personnes seront arrivées, du lieu de leur départ, et de la date de leur arrivée à Maurice. Copie de ce registre sera les 31 Mars, 30 Juin, 30 Septembre et 31 Décembre de chaque année soumise au Conseil du Gouvernement. **Idem, Art. 14.**

Idem, Art. 15. 16.—If any ship or vessel bringing Emigrants from India to Mauritius shall carry any number of passengers exceeding the proportion authorized and allowed by these regulations a penalty of Five pounds per head shall be payable in respect of each passenger so carried in excess of such proportion ; or if such ship or vessel shall not be of the height between Decks hereinbefore required ; or if such a platform as hereinbefore directed shall not be laid and continued throughout the whole duration of any such voyage, in such manner as is hereinbefore required ; or if there shall be more than two tiers of berths ; or if there shall not be throughout the whole duration of any such voyage such an interval as is hereinbefore prescribed between the Deck and the floor of the lower tier of berths ; or if any such ship or vessel shall clear out and put to sea not having on board such water and provisions as aforesaid for the use and consumption of the passengers, of the kind and to the amount, and in the proportion hereinbefore directed ; or if any such ship or vessel shall be cleared out before such lists of Emigrants shall have been delivered in manner and form aforesaid ; or if any such lists shall be wilfully false ; or if the copy of these regulations be not produced as hereinbefore required ; or if any Emigrant shall not be maintained during such voyage and for 48 hours after his arrival ; the master of any such ship or vessel shall for and in respect of each and every such offence be liable on summary conviction before any Stipendiary Magistrate at any time within the space of 12 calendar months next after the arrival of such Master within the Colony of Mauritius to the payment of a fine not less than £ 5 nor more than £ 20 British sterling, and in default of payment of the fine above mentioned, either immediately or at the time fixed by such Stipendiary Magistrate at the time of making such conviction, to imprisonment for any time not less than one nor more than three calendar months.

Idem, Art. 16. 17.—Provided nevertheless that nothing herein contained shall take away or abridge any right of suit or action which may accrue to any Emigrant in any such ship or vessel, or to any other person in respect of the breach or non-performance of any contract made or entered into between, or on the behalf of any such Emigrant or other person and the Master, owner or owners of any such ship or vessel.

16.—Dans le cas où un navire transportant des Emigrants de l'Inde à Maurice porterait un nombre de passagers excédant la proportion autorisée par ces réglements, il y aura lieu à une amende de cinq livres sterling par personne, pour chaque passager transporté au-delà du nombre permis ; ou dans le cas où le dit navire n'aurait pas dans l'entrepont la hauteur mentionnée ci-dessus, ou que la plate-forme requise ne serait pas placée et maintenue pendant toute la durée du dit voyage de la manière voulue par ces présentes, ou qu'il y aurait plus de deux rangées de couchettes, ou que pendant toute la durée du dit voyage il n'y aurait pas eu l'espace prescrit entre le pont et le plancher de la rangée inférieure des couchettes, ou que le dit navire serait expédié et ferait voile n'ayant pas à bord l'eau et les provisions mentionnées ci-dessus, pour l'usage et la consommation des passagers, de la qualité et dans les proportions voulues plus haut, ou que le dit navire serait expédié avant que la liste des Emigrants n'ait été remise de la manière et dans la forme indiquées ci-dessus, ou que la dite liste serait fausse, ou que copie de ces réglements ne serait pas produite ainsi qu'il est mentionné dans ces présentes, ou que l'un ou plusieurs des dits Emigrants ne seraient pas maintenus et entretenus pendant le dit voyage et durant les 48 heures qui suivront l'arrivée du navire, le Capitaine du dit navire sera passible, pour chacune des contraventions ci-dessus, dont il pourra être convaincu d'une manière sommaire devant un Magistrat Stipendiaire, dans les 12 mois qui suivront l'arrivée du dit navire à Maurice, d'une amende qui ne sera pas moindre de cinq livres sterling et qui n'excèdera pas 20 livres sterling ; et, en cas de non-paiement de l'amende mentionnée ci-dessus, soit immédiatement, soit à l'époque fixée par le dit Magistrat Stipendié, lors de la prononciation de son jugement, le dit capitaine sera passible d'un emprisonnement qui ne sera pas moindre d'un mois et qui n'excèdera pas trois mois. Idem, Art. 15.

17.—Pourvu toutefois, et il est bien entendu que rien de ce qui est contenu dans les présentes n'empêchera et n'abrégera aucun droit d'action ou de poursuite que pourrait avoir un Emigrant ou toute autre personne, relativement à la violation ou à la non exécution d'un contrat quelconque qui aurait été fait et passé entre un Emigrant ou une autre personne, ou en leur nom, et le capitaine ou le propriétaire du dit navire. Idem, Art. 16.

Idem, Art. 17. 18.—Provided always that nothing in these regulations contained shall apply to any ship or vessel in the service of the Lords Commissioners of the Admiralty or to any of Her Majesty's ships of war.—(*See No.* 108.)

Idem, Art. 18. 19.—No Emigrant arriving from India at Mauritius shall be capable of entering into any contract of service to be performed in that Island, until he shall have been at least 48 hours on shore there, and every such contract of service made before that time shall be null and void to all intents and purposes.

Laborers before leaving India may now enter into Five Years' Contracts to be performed in Mauritius.

Idem, Art. 19. 20.—No Emigrants arriving from India at Mauritius and engaging to labour in that island shall, within Mauritius, be liable to any action, suit, or demand for or in respect of any debt contracted, or any contract made by such Emigrant before his arrival in the said island.—(*Contracts.—See Note to No.* 19.)

Idem, Art. 20. 21.—No Emigrant arriving from India at Mauritius shall in Mauritius be capable of entering into any contract for service, except for the period, in the manner, and under the superintendence which, by a law in force there, is required in the case of contracts for service made by other labourers in agriculture or manufactures within the said island.

Idem, Art. 21. 22.—No payment shall be made from the Treasury of the said island in respect of any Emigrants introduced there from India, unless on proof, to the satisfaction of the Governor of Mauritius that all rules and regulations which may be established by Law in India for the advantage and protection of such Emigrants have been duly complied with, such rules and regulations not being repugnant to any thing in these regulations contained.

Idem, Art. 22. 23.—In every case in which the penalties hereby denounced against offences, are imposed by the use of words in the masculine gender or in the singular person, such words shall be understood as extending to the feminine gender also, and to any number of persons, unless when the opposite construction is required in order to meet the object and to accomplish the ends with a view to which these regulations are established and made.

18.—Pourvu aussi que rien de ce qui est contenu dans ces réglements ne s'applique à aucun navire au service des Lords Commissaires de l'Amirauté ou à aucun des navires de guerre de Sa Majesté.—(*Voir le No.* 108.) Idem, Art. 17.

19.—Aucun Emigrant arrivant de l'Inde à Maurice ne pourra passer un contrat de service pour être exécuté dans cette île, à moins qu'il n'ait été 48 heures à terre. Et tout contrat de service fait et passé avant ce temps, sera nul et de nul effet sous tous les rapports. Idem, Art. 18.

Les laboureurs, avant de quitter l'Inde, peuvent maintenant passer un contrat pour travailler pendant 5 ans dans la Colonie.

20.—Aucun Emigrant arrivant de l'Inde à Maurice et s'engageant à travailler dans cette île, ne pourra être poursuivi à Maurice pour aucune dette qu'il aurait contractée ou pour aucun contrat qu'il aurait passé avant son arrivée en la dite île.—(*Des Contrats.—Voir la note au No.* 19.) Idem, Art. 19.

21.—Aucun Emigrant arrivant de l'Inde à Maurice ne pourra passer dans cette Ile un engagement de service, si ce n'est pour le temps autorisé, et de la manière prescrite, par la loi qui y est en vigueur à l'égard des contrats de service faits par d'autres laboureurs ou ouvriers, pour l'agriculture et les manufactures dans la dite île. Idem, Art. 20.

22.—Il ne sera fait aucun paiement du Trésor de la dite île au sujet des Emigrants qui y seront introduits de l'Inde, à moins que ce ne soit sur la preuve satisfaisante qui aura été donnée au Gouverneur de Maurice, que tous les réglements établis dans l'Inde dans l'intérêt et pour la protection des dits Emigrants, ont été dûment suivis et observés, les dits réglements n'étant pas contraires à ce qui est contenu dans ces présentes. Idem, Art. 21.

23.—Dans tous les cas où les peines et les amendes mentionées dans ces présentes sont imposées par l'emploi de mots du genre masculin ou au singulier, les dits mots seront compris comme devant s'étendre au genre féminin aussi, et à tout nombre de personnes, à moins que le sens contraire ne soit nécessaire afin de remplir le but et les fins pour lesquels les présents réglements ont été faits. Idem, Art. 22.

Indian Act. No. 13 of 1864, Art. 1.

24.—From the date on which this Act shall come into operation, the Acts or parts of Acts set forth in the Schedule (A) annexed to this Act, shall be held to be and are hereby repealed to the extent mentioned in the said Schedule, except so far as they repeal any other Act or Regulation, or part of any other Act or Regulation.

SCHEDULE A.

NUMBER AND DATE OF ACTS.		TITLE.	EXTENT OF REPEAL
Act	XIV. 1839	Relating to contracts for labor in British or Foreign Colonies	The whole Act.
„	XV. 1842	For regulating the Emigration of the Native Inhabitants of the Territories under the Government of the East India Company to the Island of Mauritius	Ditto.
„	XXI. 1843	For regulating the Emigration of laborers from India to Mauritius.	Ditto.
„	XXI. 1844	For regulating the Emigration of the Native Inhabitants of the Territories under the Government of the East India Company to Jamaica, British Guiana, and Trinidad. .	Ditto.
„	XXV. 1845	For regulating the time of sailing of ships carrying Emigrants from Madras to Jamaica, British Guiana and Trinidad	Ditto.
„	VIII. 1847	For rendering lawful the Emigration of Laborers from the Port of Madras, in the Presidency of Fort St. George to Mauritius . .	Ditto.
„	XIII. 1847	For regulating Act XIV of 1839, so far as it relates to the Emigration of Natives of India to the Island of Ceylon	Ditto.
„	IV. 1852	To amend the law relating to Emigrant Vessels and the Emigration of laborers	Ditto.
„	XXIV. 1852	For amending and explaining Act XIV of 1839 and for the better prevention of crimping.	Ditto.
„	XXXI. 1855	Relating to the Emigration of Native Laborers to the British Colonies of St. Lucia and Grenada	Ditto.
„	XIX. 1856	To enable the Governor-General of India in Council to suspend the operation of certain Acts relating to the Emigration of Native Laborers.	So much of the Act as is not incorporated in Acts XLVI of 1860 and VII of 1862.
„	XII. 1860	Relating to the Emigration of Native Laborers to the British Colony of Saint Vincent . .	The whole Act.
„	XXXIII. 1860	Relating to Emigration to the British Colony of Natal	Ditto.
„	XLI. 1860	Relating to the Emigration of Native Laborers to the British Colony of Saint Kitts . . .	Ditto.
„	XLIX. 1860	Relating to Vessels carrying Emigrant Passengers to the British Colonies.	Ditto.
„	XXII. 1862	Relating to Emigration to the British Colonial Dependency of Seychelles	Ditto.
„	VII. 1863	Relating to the Emigration of Native Laborers to the Danish Colony of Saint Croix. . .	Ditto.

24.—A partir de la date de la mise en vigueur de cet acte, les Acte du Gouvt No. 4,

24.

Pour les modifications de cet Acte.—Voir les Nos. 551 et suiv :

- - -

CÉDULE A.

NUMÉRO ET DATE DES ACTES.	TITRE.	PARTIES ABROGÉES.
Acte XIV. 1839	Se rapportant aux Contrats de Service dans les Colonies Anglaises ou étrangères. . .	L'Acte entier.
„ XV. 1842	Pour régler l'émigration à Maurice des habitants indigènes des Territoires sous le Gouvernement de la Compagnie des Indes Orientales.	Ditto.
„ XXI. 1843	Pour régler l'émigration des laboureurs de l'Inde à Maurice	Ditto.
„ XXI. 1844	Pour régler l'émigration à la Jamaïque, à la Guiane Anglaise, et à Trinidad des habitants indigènes des Territoires sous le Gouvernement de la Compagnie des Indes Orientales.	Ditto.
„ XXV. 1845	Pour régler l'époque du départ des navires transportant des Emigrants de Madras à la Jamaïque, à la Guiane Anglaise et à Trinidad.	Ditto.
„ VIII. 1847	Pour rendre légale l'émigration à Maurice des laboureurs du port de Madras dans la Presidence du Fort de St.-George.	Ditto.
„ XIII. 1847	Pour modifier l'Acte XIV de 1839 en autant qu'il se rapporte à l'émigration des Indiens à l'Ile de Ceylan.	Ditto.
„ VI. 1852	Pour modifier la loi sur les navires à émigrants et l'émigration des laboureurs.	Ditto.
„ XXIV. 1852	Pour modifier et expliquer l'Acte XIV de 1839 et pour mieux empêcher le racolage. . .	Ditto.
„ XXXI. 1855	Réglant l'émigration des laboureurs indigènes aux Colonies Anglaises de St.-Lucie et de Grenade.	Ditto.
„ XIX. 1856	Pour permettre au Gouverneur-Général de l'Inde en Conseil de suspendre l'effet de certains Actes se rapportant à l'émigration des laboureurs indigènes	Telles parties qui ne se trouvent pas reproduites dans les Actes 46 de 1860 et 7 de 1862.
„ XII. 1860	Se rapportant à l'émigration des laboureurs indigènes à la Colonie Anglaise de St.-Vincent	L'Acte entier.
„ XXXIII. 1860	Se rapportant à l'émigration à la Colonie Anglaise de Natal	Ditto.
„ XLI. 1860	Se rapportant à l'émigration des laboureurs indigènes à la Colonie Anglaise de St.-Kitts.	Ditto.
„ XLIX. 1860	Se rapportant aux navires transportants des émigrants aux Colonies. Anglaises . . .	Ditto.
„ XXII. 1862	Se rapportant à l'émigration aux Seychelles, Dépendance d'une Colonie Anglaise. . .	Ditto.
„ VII. 1863	Se rapportant à l'émigration des laboureurs indigènes à la Colonie Danoise de Ste.-Croix.	Ditto.

Idem, Art. 2. 25.—The following words and expressions in this Act shall have the meanings hereby assigned to them, unless there be something in the subject or context repugnant to such construction, that is to say :—

The word "Emigrate" shall denote the departure of any Native of India out of British India for the purpose of laboring for hire in some other place, and the word *Emigrant* shall denote any Native of India under engagement to emigrate.

The words "The Magistrate of the District" shall denote the Chief Officer charged with the Executive Administration of a District and exercising the powers of a Magistrate, by whatever designation the Chief Officer charged with such Executive Administration is styled, or in the absence of such Officer from the station at which his Court is ordinarily held, the Senior Officer at the station exercising the powers of a Magistrate, as defined in the Code of *Criminal Procedure.*

The words "British India" shall denote the territories vested in Her Majesty by the Statute 21 and 22 Vic., Cap. 106, entitled "An Act for the better Government of India," except the settlement of Prince of Wales' Island, Singapore and Malacca.

The words "Local Government" shall denote the person authorized by law to administer Executive Government in any part of British India.

The word "Section" shall denote a section of this Act.

The word "Vessel" shall include anything made for the conveyance by water of human beings and property.

Words importing the singular number shall include the plural number, and words importing the plural number shall include the singular.

Words importing the masculine gender shall include females.

Idem, Art. 3. 26.—Except under and in conformity with the provisions of this Act, it shall not be lawful to make any contract with any native of India for labor to be performed in any place beyond Bri-

25.—Les mots et expressions qui suivent dans cet acte auront la signification qui leur est ici assignée, à moins qu'il ne se trouve quelque chose dans le sujet ou dans l'expression qui soit contraire à cette interprétation, c'est-à-dire :— Idem, Art. 2.

Le mot "émigrer" indiquera le départ de l'Inde Anglaise de tout indigène dans le but d'aller travailler à gages dans quelqu'autre lieu ; et le mot *Emigrant* indiquera tout natif de l'Inde qui se sera engagé à émigrer.

Les mots "Le Magistrat du District" indiqueront l'officier principal chargé de l'administration Exécutive d'un district et exerçant les fonctions de Magistrat, quelle que soit la désignation sous laquelle cet officier est connu, ou en son absence de la station où se trouve ordinairement le siège de sa Cour, le plus ancien officier de la Cour exerçant les fonctions de Magistrat ainsi qu'elles sont définies dans le Code de *Procédure Criminelle.*

Les mots "Inde Anglaise" indiqueront les territoires dont Sa Majesté a été investie par le Statut 21 et 22, Vict. Cap. 106, intitulé "Un Acte pour le meilleur Gouvernement de l'Inde," excepté la colonie de "Prince of Wales' Island," Singapore et les Iles Malacques.

Les mots "Gouvernement Local" indiqueront la personne autorisée par la loi à administrer le Gouvernement Exécutif dans une partie quelconque de l'Inde Anglaise.

Le mot "Section" indiquera une Section de cet Acte.

Le mot "Bâtiment" comprendra toute chose faite pour le transport par eau de choses ou d'êtres humains.

Les mots indiquant le singulier comprendront le pluriel et les mots indiquant le pluriel comprendront le singulier.

Les mots indiquant le masculin comprendront le féminin.

26.—Aucun contrat avec un natif de l'Inde par lequel il s'engagera à travailler dans un endroit quelconque hors de l'Inde Anglaise ne sera valable que tout autant qu'il sera passé conformé- Idem, Art. 3.

tish India, or to enable any native of India to emigrate, or to assist any native of India in emigrating. Provided that nothing in this Act shall apply to any contract with any Native of India for labor to be performed in any Foreign Settlement on the main land of India, or in any Native State of India, or to emigration to any such Settlement or State; or shall apply to any contract for labor to be performed in or to emigration to the Island of Ceylon; or shall apply to any contract with or the emigration of any Native Seaman or other person who, of his own free will, shall contract to navigate or serve on board of any vessel, or who shall embark on board such vessel in pursuance of such contract, or any person who shall contract to serve as a menial servant only, and who shall embark as such menial servant.

Idem, Art. 4. 27.—Contracts may be made with Natives of India to emigrate to any of the British Colonies of

Mauritius.
Jamaica.
British Guiana.
Trinidad.
St. Lucia.
Grenada.
St. Vincent.
Natal.
St. Kitts, and
Seychelles,

and to the Danish Colony of St. Croix; and it shall be lawful to enable or assist any Native of India to emigrate to any such Colony.

Idem, Art. 5. 28.—The Governor-General of India in Council may from time to time, by notification published in the Gazette of India, declare that the emigration of Natives of India shall be lawful to any place other than the places mentioned in the last preceding Section; provided that every such notification shall contain also a declaration that the Governor-General of India in Council has been duly certified that the Government of the place to which the

ment aux dispositions de cet acte, et il ne sera pas permis à qui que ce soit de procurer à un natif de l'Inde les moyens d'émigrer à moins qu'il n'agisse en vertu des dispositions de cet acte ; mais aucune des dispositions de cet acte ne pourra s'appliquer à un contrat passé avec un natif de l'Inde par lequel il s'engagera à travailler soit dans une colonie étrangère sur le continent de l'Inde, soit dans un Etat de l'Inde indépendant de la domination anglaise, ni à l'émigration dans cette colonie ou dans cet Etat ; aucune de ces dispositions ne pourra s'appliquer non plus à un contrat par lequel le laboureur s'engagera à travailler ou à émigrer dans l'Ile de Ceylan ; ni à un contrat passé avec un marin natif ou toute autre personne qui, de sa propre volonté, s'obligera à naviguer ou à servir à bord d'un navire quelconque, ou qui s'embarquera à bord du dit navire en vertu de cet engagement, ni à un contrat passé avec une personne qui s'engagera à servir comme domestique seulement et qui s'embarquera comme tel.

27.—Il sera permis de passer des contrats avec des natifs de l'Inde par lesquels ils s'obligeront à émigrer dans une des Colonies Anglaises Idem, Art. 4.

de Maurice,
de la Jamaïque,
de la Guiane Anglaise,
de Trinidad,
de St. Lucie,
de Grenade,
de St. Vincent,
de Natal,
de St. Kitts,
et des Seychelles,

et dans la Colonie Danoise de St. Croix, et il sera permis d'aider un natif de l'Inde quelconque à émigrer dans une des dites Colonies.

28.—Le Gouverneur Général de l'Inde en Conseil pourra de temps à autre au moyen d'avis publiés dans la Gazette de l'Inde, proclamer légale l'émigration des natifs de l'Inde pour un endroit quelconque autre que ceux qui sont énumérés dans la Section précédente, pourvu que chacun de ces avis contienne aussi une déclaration établissant que le Gouverneur Général de l'Inde en Conseil s'est dûment assuré que le Gouvernement de l'endroit auquel Idem, Art. 5.

notification refers has made such laws and other provisions as the Governor-General of India in Council thinks sufficient for the protection of Natives of India emigrating to such place.

Idem, Art. 6. 29.—From the date of any such notification by the Governor-General of India in Council, Contracts may be made with any Native of India for labor to be performed in any place to which Emigration is authorized in the Notification, and it shall be lawful to enable or assist any Native of India to emigrate to such place; but all Contracts and Emigration under any such Notification, shall be made and conducted subject to the provisions of this Act.

Idem, Art. 7. 30.—Emigration shall not be lawful except from the port of Calcutta, the port of Madras, or the port of Bombay.

Idem, Art. 8. 31.—The probable length of the voyages to the places enumerated in Section IV from Calcutta, Madras or Bombay, respectively, shall, for the purposes of this Act, be deemed to be as follows :—

From Calcutta	To Mauritius and Seychelles	Between the months of April and October inclusive, 10 weeks; and between the months of November and March inclusive, 8 weeks.
	To Jamaica, British Guiana, Trinidad, St. Lucia, Grenada, St. Vincent, St. Kitts and St. Croix ...	20 weeks.
	To Natal.	12 "
From Madras	To Mauritius and Seychelles	Between the months of April and October inclusive, 7 weeks; and between the months of November and March, inclusive, 5 weeks.
	To Jamaica, British Guiana, Trinidad, St. Lucia, Grenada, St. Vincent, St. Kitts and St. Croix ..	19 weeks.
	To Natal.	10 "
From Bombay	To Mauritius and Seychelles	Between the months of April and September inclusive, 5 weeks; and between the months of October and March inclusive, 6 weeks.
	To Jamaica, British Guiana, Trinidad, St. Lucia, Grenada, St. Vincent, St. Kitts and St. Croix ..	19 weeks.
	To Natal.	10 "

(*Sect* : 4. *See No.* 27.)

Idem. Art. 9. 32.—In every Notification issued under Section V, there shall be stated the probable length of the voyages, from Calcutta, Madras & Bombay respectively, to every place to which Emigration is by such Notification authorized and thereupon such period shall, for the purposes of this Act, be taken to be the probable length of such voyage.—(*Sect*: 5. *See No.* 28.)

l'avis se rapporte, a promulgué telles lois et tels réglements que le Gouverneur Général de l'Inde en Conseil croira suffisants pour la protection des natifs de l'Inde émigrant au dit endroit.

29.—A partir de la date de la publication du dit avis par le Gouverneur Général de l'Inde en Conseil, il sera permis de passer avec des natifs de l'Inde des contrats de service pour être exécutés dans un endroit auquel l'émigration est permise par cet avis ; et il sera permis d'aider un natif de l'Inde quelconque à émigrer au dit endroit ; mais les termes et l'exécution de tous contrats passés en vertu du dit avis ainsi que l'émigration qui s'ensuivra seront soumis aux dispositions du présent acte. Idem, Art. 6.

30.—L'Emigration ne sera légale que des Ports de Calcutta, de Madras ou de Bombay. Idem, Art. 7.

31.—La durée probable des voyages aux lieux énumérés dans la Section IV, de Calcutta, de Madras ou de Bombay, respectivement, sera pour les besoins de cet acte considérée être comme suit : Idem, Art. 8.

De Calcutta.	A Maurice et aux Seychelles.	Entre les mois d'Avril et d'Octobre inclusivement, 10 semaines ; et entre les mois de Novembre et de Mars inclusivement, 8 semaines.
	A la Jamaïque, la Guiane Anglaise, Trinidad, Ste.Lucie, Grenade, St. Vincent, St. Kitts et Ste. Croix	20 semaines.
	A Natal	12 do.
De Madras.	A Maurice et aux Seychelles.	Entre les mois d'Avril et d'Octobre inclusivement, 7 semaines ; et entre les mois de Novem- et de Mars inclusivement ; 5 semaines.
	A la Jamaïque, la Guiane Anglaise, Trinidad, Ste. Lucie, Grenade, St. Vincent, St. Kitts et Ste. Croix	19 Semaines.
	A Natal	10 do.
De Bombay.	A Maurice et aux Seychelles.	Entre les mois d'Avril et de Septembre, inclusivement, 5 semaines ; et entre les mois d'Octobre et de Mars inclusivement, 6 semaines.
	A la Jamaïque, la Guiane Anglaise, Trinidad, Grenade, Ste. Lucie, St. Vincent, St. Kitts et Ste. Croix	19 semaines.
	A Natal	10 do.

(*Section* 4 : *Voir le No.* 27.)

32.—Dans chaque notification aux termes de la Section V sera stipulée la durée probable des voyages de Calcutta, de Madras ou de Bombay, respectivement, à tout lieu auquel l'émigration sera permise par la dite notification, et l'espace de temps ainsi déterminée sera, pour les besoins de cet acte, considéré être la durée probable de ces voyages.—(*Section* 5 : *voir le No.* 28.) Idem, Art. 9.

Idem, Art. 10. 33.—The Government of every place to which Emigration shall be lawful under this Act, may, from time to time, nominate a person to act as Emigration Agent in Calcutta, Madras and Bombay, respectively. But such nomination shall be subject to the approval of the local Government. Every Emigration Agent shall be liable to removal by the Government which nominated him.

Idem, Art. 11. 34.—Every Emigration Agent who, at the time when this Act shall come into operation, shall have been nominated by the Government of any of the Colonies enumerated in Section IV, shall be deemed to have been nominated under this Act.—(*Sect*: 4. *See No.* 27.)

Idem, Art. 12. 35.—The remuneration to be given to Emigration Agents shall not depend upon, or be regulated by the number of Emigrants sent by such Agents but shall be in the nature of a fixed annual salary.

Idem, Art. 13. 36.—It shall be lawful for the local Government to nominate a proper person to act as Protector of Emigrants at each of the three ports aforesaid, and with the sanction of the Governor-General of India in Council to assign to such person such salary and establishment as shall be deemed proper. Every Protector of Emigrants shall be subject to removal by the local Government to which he is subordinate.

Idem, Art. 14. 37.—No Protector of Emigrants nominated under this Act shall except with the permission of the local Government hold any other office under Government, or follow any other profession or occupation.

Idem, Art. 15. 38.—Every Protector of Emigrants who at the time when this Act shall come into operation, shall have been nominated by the local Government, shall be deemed to have been nominated under this Act.

Idem, Art. 16. 39.—Every Protector of Emigrants in addition to any special duties assigned to him by this Act, shall so far as in his power, generally protect and aid with his advice, or otherwise, all Emigrants, and shall cause all the provisions of this Act to be duly

33.—Le Gouvernement de tout lieu auquel l'émigration sera permise aux termes de cet acte, pourra, de temps à autre, nommer une personne pour remplir les fonctions d'Agent d'Emigration à Calcutta, à Madras, et à Bombay, respectivement, mais cette nomination sera sujette à l'approbation du Gouvernement Local. Tout Agent d'Emigration pourra être destitué par le Gouvernement qui l'aura nommé. Idem, Art. 10.

34.—Tout Agent d'Emigration qui à l'époque de la mise en vigueur de cet acte aura été nommé par le Gouvernement d'une des colonies énumérées dans la Section IV sera considéré avoir été nommé en vertu de cet acte.—(*Section 4 : voir le No. 27.*) Idem, Art. 11.

35.—La rémunération qui sera allouée aux Agents d'Emigration ne dépendra pas du nombre des Émigrants envoyés par les dits Agents et ne sera pas déterminée par ce nombre, mais devra être de la nature d'un salaire annuel fixe. Idem, Art. 12.

36.—Le Gouvernement Local pourra nommer une personne convenable pour remplir les fonctions de Protecteur des Emigrants à chacun des trois ports ci-dessus mentionnés, et avec le consentement du Gouverneur Général de l'Inde en Conseil, lui assigner tout salaire et toute assistance qui lui paraitront convenable. Tout Protecteur des Emigrants pourra être destitué par le Gouvernement Local dont il relèvera. Idem, Art. 13.

37.—Aucun Protecteur des Emigrants nommé en vertu de cet acte ne pourra, sauf la permission du Gouvernement Local, occuper aucune autre place du Gouvernement, ou exercer aucune autre profession ou état. Idem, Art. 14.

38.—Tout Protecteur des Emigrants qui à l'époque de la mise en vigueur de cet acte aura été nommé par le Gouvernement Local sera considéré avoir été nommé en vertu de cet acte. Idem, Art. 15.

39.—Tout Protecteur des Emigrants, en outre des devoirs speciaux qui lui sont assignés par cet acte, devra autant que cela sera en son pouvoir protéger en général et aider de ses conseils ou autrement tous les Emigrants, et devra veiller à ce que toutes les Idem. Art. 16.

complied with; he shall also inspect on arrival, all vessels bringing return Emigrants to the Port at which he is Protector, and enquire into the treatment received by such Emigrants, both during the period of their service in the place to which they emigrated, and also during the voyage, and shall make a report thereon to the local Government, and he shall aid and advise such return Emigrants so far as he reasonably can, when called upon by them to do so.

Idem, Art. 17. 40.—At each of the three ports aforesaid, it shall be lawful for the local Government to nominate a competent person to be Medical Inspector of Emigrants; and with the sanction of the Governor-General of India in Council to assign to the Medical Inspector so nominated such salaries as shall be deemed proper.

Idem, Art. 18. 41.—In each of the Towns of Calcutta, Madras and Bombay, or in the suburbs of those towns, a suitable depot shall be established by the Emigration Agent of every place to which Emigration shall be lawful under this Act, for the persons who shall be engaged as laborers for such place; and by the Emigration Agent nominated by the French Government under Act XLVI of 1860 "To authorize and regulate the Emigration of Native laborers to the French Colonies," and Act VII of 1862 "To amend Act XLVI of 1860" for the persons who shall be engaged as laborers for the French Colonies.

Idem, Art. 19. 42.—Every Depot shall be licensed by the Protector of Emigrants after being inspected and approved of by him and by the Medical Inspector of Emigrants. No license shall be enforced for a longer period than a year, and any license may be cancelled by the Protector of Emigrants if he shall consider that the depot for which it was granted is unhealthy, or in any respect has become unsuitable for the purpose for which the depot was established. For every license granted under this Section there shall be paid to the Protector a fee of Ten Rupees.

Idem, Art. 20. 43.—Every Protector of Emigrants, and every Medical Inspector of Emigrants shall from time to time and at least once in

formalités requises par cet acte soient dûment remplies : il devra de même inspecter à l'arrivée tous navires ramenant des Emigrants au Port où il remplit les fonctions de Protecteur, s'enquérir de la manière dont les dits Emigrants ont été traités non-seulement pendant la durée de leur service dans le pays où ils ont émigré mais aussi pendant le voyage, et il en fera un rapport au Gouvernement Local, et il aidera et conseillera ces dits Emigrants autant qu'il pourra raisonablement le faire lorsqu'ils l'en requérront.

40.—A chacun des trois ports ci-dessus mentionnés le Gouvernement Local pourra nommer une personne compétente pour remplir les fonctions d'Inspecteur Médical des Emigrants et, avec le consentement du Gouverneur Général de l'Inde en Conseil, assigner à l'Inspecteur Médical ainsi nommé tel salaire qu'il jugera convenable. Idem, Art. 17.

41.—Dans chacune des villes de Calcutta, de Madras, et de Bombay, ou dans les faubourgs de ces villes, il sera établi un Dépôt convenable par l'agent d'Emigration de tout endroit auquel l'Emigration sera permise en vertu de cet acte pour les personnes qui seront engagées comme laboureurs pour le dit endroit : et par l'Agent d'Emigration nommé par le Gouvernement Français en vertu de l'acte XLVI de 1860 (pour autoriser et régler l'émigration des laboureurs indigènes aux Colonies Françaises) et en vertu de l'acte VII de 1862 (pour amender l'acte XLVI de 1860) pour les personnes qui seront engagées comme laboureurs pour les Colonies Françaises. Idem, Art. 18.

42.—Tout Dépôt sera autorisé par le Protecteur des Emigrants après qu'il aura été inspecté et trouvé convenable par l'Inspecteur Médical des Emigrants. Aucune autorisation ne pourra être accordée pour plus d'une année et toute autorisation pourra être révoquée par le Protecteur des Emigrants, s'il est d'opinion que le Dépôt pour lequel l'autorisation a été accordée est malsain ou est devenu sous un rapport quelconque impropre au but pour lequel il a été établi. Pour chaque autorisation accordée en vertu de cette Section, il sera payé au Protecteur un droit de Dix Roupies. Idem, Art. 19.

43.—Chaque Protecteur des Emigrants et chaque Inspecteur Médical des Emigrants devra de temps en temps, et au moins une Idem, Art. 20.

every week inspect the Emigrants in the various Depots for the reception of Emigrants about to embark from the Port at which they are Protector and Medical Inspector respectively, and examine into the state of the Depots, and the manner in which the Emigrants are therein lodged, fed, clothed, and otherwise provided for and attended to.

Idem, Art. 21. **44.**—It shall be the duty of the Medical Inspector to report to the Protector of Emigrants any circumstance which may come to his knowledge, shewing that the Depot is not suitable for its purpose or that the Emigrants are treated with any neglect or oppression.

Idem, Art. 22. **45.**—Every Protector of Emigrants and every Medical Inspector of Emigrants shall be held to be a *Public Servant*, within the meaning of the Indian Penal Code.

Idem, Art. 23. **46.**—It shall be the duty of every Emigration Agent and of all persons in charge of or employed in any Depot or in any vessel licensed to carry Emigrants as hereinafter provided to give the Protector and the Medical Inspector every facility for making such inspections, examinations, and surveys as may be necessary or proper under this Act, and to afford them all such information as may be reasonably required by them.

Idem, Art. 24. **47.**—The Protector of Emigrants at each of the three ports aforesaid, shall license so many fit persons as shall to him seem necessary to be Recruiters of laborers, and no person shall act or be employed as a Recruiter of laborers, except under a licence from a Protector of Emigrants.

Idem, Art. 25. **48.**—Every Recruiter shall be licensed to obtain laborers, for some particular place, to which Emigration shall be lawful under this Act, and no license to obtain laborers for any place shall be granted, except on the application of the Emigration Agent of such place.

Idem, Art. 26. **49.**—No license shall be enforced for a longer period than one

fois par semaine, inspecter les Emigrants dans les divers Dépôts où sont logés les Emigrants sur le point de quitter le Port où ces fonctionnaires remplissent respectivement les fonctions de Protecteur et d'Inspecteur Médical, et ils devront aussi examiner les Dépôts et s'enquérir de la manière dont les Emigrants y sont logés, nourris et vêtus ainsi que des soins qu'ils y reçoivent.

44.—L'Inspecteur Médical devra donner avis au Protecteur des Emigrants de toute circonstance qui pourra être portée à sa connaissance et qui tendra à prouver que le Dépôt ne répond pas à son but ou que les Emigrants sont traités avec négligence ou avec rigueur. Idem, Art. 21.

45.—Tout Protecteur des Emigrants et tout Inspecteur Médical des Emigrants devra être considéré comme un *fonctionnaire public*, d'après le sens donné à ces mots par le Code Pénal. Idem, Art. 22.

46.—Chaque Agent d'Emigration ainsi que tous les individus qui seront chargés d'un Dépôt, ou qui seront employés dans un Dépôt, ou à bord d'un navire ayant une autorisation pour le transport des Emigrants comme il est prévu ci-après, devront donner au Protecteur et à l'Inspecteur Médical toutes les facilités en leur pouvoir pour les inspections et les examens qui seront nécessaires ou conformes au présent Acte, et leur fournir tous les renseignements qu'ils pourront raisonnablement demander. Idem, Art. 23.

47.—Le Protecteur des Emigrants à chacun des trois ports ci-dessus mentionnés autorisera autant de personnes convenables qu'il jugera nécessaire à agir comme recruteurs des laboureurs, et nul ne pourra agir ni être employé comme recruteur des laboureurs s'il n'est muni d'une autorisation du Protecteur des Emigrants. Idem, Art. 24.

48.—Chaque recruteur sera autorisé à recruter des laboureurs pour quelque endroit particulier auquel l'Emigration sera permise d'après le présent Acte, et aucune autorisation pour le recrutement de laboureurs pour un endroit quelconque ne sera accordée à moins que ce ne soit sur la demande de l'Agent d'Emigration de l'endroit. Idem, Art. 25.

49.—Aucune autorisation ne devra être accordée pour plus Idem, Art. 26.

year; and, in cases of misconduct on the part of any Recruiter, the Protector of Emigrants may cancel his license, before the expiration of the period for which it was granted.

Idem, Art. 27. 50.—Every license shall be in the form set forth in the Schedule (B) to this Act annexed. For every license, there shall be paid to the Protector a fee of ten Rupees.

SCHEDULE B.

Office of the Protector of Emigrants at the Port of

A. B. is hereby licensed under Act of 186 of the Governor-General of India in Council, to be a Recruiter for engaging persons to proceed to for the purpose of labouring for hire.

This license will be in force for one year from this date.

Dated the day of (Signed) C. D.
Protector of Emigrants.

Idem, Art. 28. 51.—Every person holding a license as a Recruiter of laborers, shall wear a badge bearing the following inscription in English and in the vernacular language of the Town, District or Districts in which he is licensed to engage laborers. (*Recruiter of Emigrants for the Mauritius*) [*or other place, as the case may be.*]

Idem, Art. 29. 52.—No Recruiter shall engage or attempt to engage laborers in any Districts, or in the towns of Calcutta, Madras or Bombay, without having first exhibited his license to the Magistrate of such District or a Magistrate of such Town, and obtained the countersignature of such Magistrate thereupon. Such countersignature shall be given, provided that the license be in force at the time.

Idem, Art. 30. 53.—Every Native of India who shall, in any place other than the Towns of Calcutta, Madras or Bombay, enter into any engagement with a Recruiter to emigrate, shall, prior to leaving the District, within which the engagement was entered into, appear with the Recruiter before the Magistrate of such District, and no Recruiter shall remove such Emigrant from the said District, until he shall have so appeared. Upon so appearing, the Magistrate shall examine the intending Emigrant with reference to his engagement; and if it appears that he comprehends the nature of the

d'une année, et en cas d'inconduite de la part du Recruteur, le Protecteur des Emigrants pourra annuler l'autorisation qui lui aura été accordé avant l'expiration de l'époque pour laquelle elle aura été accordée.

50.—Chaque autorisation sera faite dans la forme de la Cédule B annexée au présent acte. Il sera payé pour chaque autorisation un droit de Dix Roupies. Idem, Art. 27.

CÉDULE B.

Bureau du Protecteur des Emigrants au Port de

A. B. est par ces présentes autorisé en vertu de l'acte de 186 du Gouverneur Général de l'Inde en Conseil, à agir comme Recruteur pour passer des engagements avec des travailleurs qui voudraient se rendre à pour y travailler à gages.

Cette autorisation ne sera valable que pour un an à partir de cette date.

Ce jour de (Signé) C. D.
Protecteur des Emigrants.

51.—Toute personne munie d'une autorisation d'agir comme Recruteur de laboureurs devra être muni d'une plaque portant l'inscription suivante écrite en anglais et dans le dialecte de la ville, du District ou des Districts dans lesquels il est autorisé à engager des laboureurs. (*Recruteur d'Emigrants pour Maurice*) [*ou tout autre endroit, selon le cas.*] Idem, Art. 28.

52.—Aucun recruteur ne devra engager ou chercher à engager des laboureurs dans un District quelconque, ou dans les villes de Calcutta, de Madras ou de Bombay, avant d'avoir exhibé son autorisation au Magistrat du dit District ou à un Magistrat d'une de ces villes et l'avoir fait viser par ce Magistrat. Ce visa sera accordé pourvu que l'autorisation soit alors en vigueur. Idem, Art. 29.

53.—Tout natif de l'Inde qui, hors des villes de Calcutta, de Madras ou de Bombay, passera avec un Recruteur, un engagement pour émigrer devra, avant de quitter le District où l'engagement aura été passé, comparaitre avec le Recruteur devant le Magistrat du dit District, et jusqu'à ce qu'il ait ainsi comparu, aucun Recruteur ne pourra emmener le dit Emigrant hors de ce District. Lorsque l'Emigrant comparaitra devant le Magistrat, celui-ci devra le questionner au sujet de son Engagement, et s'il lui semble qu'il comprend la nature de l'Engagement qu'il a contracté, et qu'il est Idem, Art. 30.

engagement he has entered into, and that he is willing to fulfil the same, the Magistrate shall register in a book to be kept for the purpose in such form as the Local Government shall prescribe, the name, name of the father, and the age of such Emigrant and the name of the village or place of which such Emigrant is a resident, the Immigration Depot to which it is intended he shall proceed, and the rate of wages and period of service, if any, agreed upon between the Emigrant and the Recruiter. If the Magistrate shall be of opinion that the intending Emigrant does not comprehend the nature of the engagement, or has been induced to enter into the engagement by fraud or misrepresentation, he shall refuse to register his name, a copy of every registration under this Section, written on substantial paper, which shall not require a stamp, shall be furnished by the Magistrate to the Emigrant registered.

Idem, Art. 31. 54.—For the registration of every Emigrant, the Recruiter shall pay to the Magistrate a fee of One Rupee. On proof of the desertion of any Emigrant before reaching the Depot for which he was registered, the fee paid in respect of such Emigrant, may be refunded by the Magistrate to the Recruiter, by whom it was paid, under such rules, as shall, from time to time, be made in that behalf, by the Governor-General of India in Council.

Idem, Art. 32. 55.—Authentic copies of every registration shall be forthwith forwarded by the Magistrate to the Emigration Agent at the Depot to which the person named therein shall have been engaged to proceed, and the Protector of Emigrants, at the intended port of embarkation.

Idem, Art. 33. 56.—Every Native of India who shall, in the Towns of Calcutta, Madras or Bombay, enter into any engagement with a Recruiter to emigrate, shall, within forty eight hours of making such engagement, appear with the Recruiter before the Protector of Emigrants in such Town, and no Recruiter shall remove such Emigrant from the said Town, or to any Emigration Depot, until he shall have so appeared. Upon his so appearing, the Protector of Emigrants shall examine the intending Emigrant with reference to his engagement; and if it appears that he comprehends the nature of the engagement he has entered into, and that he is willing to fulfil the same, the Protector of Emigrants shall register in a book to be kept

disposé à le remplir, le Magistrat enregistrera, dans un livre qui sera tenu à cet effet dans la forme que le gouvernement local désignera, le nom, le nom du père, et l'âge du dit Emigrant, le nom du village ou de l'endroit que le dit Emigrant habite, le Dépot d'Emigration vers lequel il doit se diriger, et le taux des gages et le temps de service, s'ils ont été déterminés, convenus entre l'Emigrant et le Recruteur. Si le Magistrat est d'opinion que l'Emigrant ne comprend pas la nature de l'Engagement ou qu'il a été induit à contracter l'Engagement par fraude ou par de fausses représentations, il refusera d'enregistrer son nom. Une copie de chaque enregistrement en vertu de cette section, transcrite sur de fort papier, qui n'aura pas besoin d'être timbré, sera délivré par le Magistrat à l'Emigrant qui aura été enregistré.

54.—Pour l'enregistrement de chaque Emigrant, le Recruteur Idem, Art. 31.
paiera au Magistrat un droit d'une Roupie. Sur la preuve qui lui sera fournie qu'un Emigrant a déserté avant d'arriver au Dépot pour lequel il a été enregistré, le droit payé pour le dit Emigrant pourra être remboursé par le Magistrat au Recruteur qui l'aura payé, en vertu des Réglements qui pourront de temps à autre être faits dans ce but par le Gouverneur Général de l'Inde en Conseil.

55.—Des copies authentiques de chaque enregistrement seront Idem, Art. 32.
envoyées immédiatement par le Magistrat à l'Agent d'Emigration au Dépôt auquel la personne qui sera nommée dans le dit enregistrement se sera engagée à se rendre, et au Protecteur des Emigrants du Port où la dite personne doit s'embarquer.

56.—Tout natif de l'Inde qui, dans une des villes de Calcutta, Idem, Art. 33.
de Madras ou de Bombay, passera avec un Recruteur un engagement pour émigrer, devra dans les 48 heures qui suivront le dit engagement, comparaître avec le Recruteur devant le Protecteur des Emigrants de la dite ville, et avant qu'il n'ait ainsi comparu, aucun Recruteur ne pourra emmener le dit Emigrant hors de la dite ville ou dans aucun Dépôt d'Emigration. Le Protecteur des Emigrants devra, lorsque l'Emigrant se présentera devant lui, le questionner relativement à son engagement et s'il y a lieu de croire qu'il comprend la nature de l'engagement qu'il a contracté et qu'il est disposé à le remplir, le Protecteur des Emigrants en-

for the purpose, in such form as the Local Government shall prescribe, the name, the name of the father, and the age of such Emigrant and the name of the village or place of which such Emigrant is a resident, the Emigration Depot to which it is intended he shall proceed, and the rate of wages and period of service, if any, agreed upon between the Emigrant and the Recruiter. If the Protector of Emigrants shall be of opinion that the intending Emigrant does not comprehend the nature of the engagement or has been induced to enter into the engagement by fraud or misrepresentation, he shall refuse to register his name. A copy of every registration under this section, written on substantial paper, which shall not require a stamp, shall be furnished by the Protector to the Emigrant registered.

Idem, Art. 34. 57.—For the registration of every Emigrant under the last preceding Section, the Recruiter shall pay to the Protector of Emigrants a fee of One Rupee. On proof of the desertion of any Emigrant before reaching the Depot for which he was registered, the fee paid in respect to such Emigrant may be refunded by the Protector to the Recruiter, by whom it was paid, under such rules as shall, from time to time, be made in that behalf by the Governor-General of India in Council.

Idem, Art. 35. 58.—An authentic copy of every registration by a Protector of Emigrants, shall be forthwith forwarded by the Protector to the Emigration Agent of the place for which the person named therein shall have been engaged.

Idem, Art. 36. 59.—Every Emigrant recruited under the provisions of this Act, shall be conveyed by land or river with all convenient despatch to the Depot at the Port of embarkation, established by the Emigration Agent of the place to which such Emigrant has contracted to emigrate.

The registered Emigrants engaged by any Recruiter shall, while proceeding to a Depot, be accompanied throughout the journey either by the Recruiter himself or by a competent person appointed by him, with the approval of the Magistrate by whom the Emigrants may have been registered. The Magistrate shall give to the person so appointed a certificate under his signature, stating that he has been appointed for the journey to the Depot.

registrera dans un livre qui sera tenu à cet effet, dans la forme que le Gouvernement Local prescrira, le nom, le nom du père, et l'âge du dit Emigrant, ainsi que le nom du village ou de l'endroit où le dit Emigrant habite, le Dépôt auquel il doit se rendre, et le taux des gages et le temps de service, s'ils ont été déterminés, convenus entre l'Emigrant et le Recruteur. Si le Protecteur des Emigrants est d'opinion que l'Emigrant ne comprend pas la nature de l'engagement, ou qu'il a été induit par fraude ou de fausses représentations à contracter l'engagement, il refusera d'enregistrer son nom. Une copie de chaque enregistrement en vertu de cette Section, transcrite sur de fort papier, qui n'aura pas besoin d'être timbré, sera fournie par le Protecteur des Emigrants à l'Emigrant qui aura été enregistré.

57.—Pour l'enregistrement de chaque Emigrant en vertu de la Section précédente, le Recruteur paiera au Protecteur des Emigrants un droit d'une Roupie. Quand il sera prouvé qu'un Emigrant a déserté avant d'arriver au Dépôt pour lequel il aura été enregistré, le droit qui aura été payé pour le dit Emigrant pourra être remboursé par le Protecteur au Recruteur qui l'aura payé, d'après tels réglements qui pourront de temps à autre être faits par le Gouverneur Général de l'Inde en Conseil. Idem, Art. 34.

58.—Une copie authentique de chaque enregistrement par un Protecteur des Emigrants devra être transmise sur le champ par le Protecteur à l'Agent d'Emigration de l'endroit pour lequel la personne dénommée dans le dit enregistrement se sera engagée. Idem, Art. 35.

59.—Tout Emigrant recruté en vertu des dispositions de cet Acte, sera transporté par terre ou par rivière avec toute la célérité convenable au Dépôt établi au Port d'embarquement par l'Agent d'Emigration de l'endroit auquel le dit Emigrant se sera engagé à émigrer. Idem, Art. 36.

Les Emigrants enregistrés qui auront été engagés par un Recruteur, devront, en se rendant au Dépôt, être accompagnés pendant tout le voyage soit par le Recruteur lui-même, soit par une personne compétente nommée par lui qui aura été acceptée par le Magistrat par lequel les Emigrants auront été enregistrés. Le Magistrat donnera à la personne ainsi nommée un certificat signé de lui déclarant qu'il a été nommé pour le voyage jusqu'au Dépôt.

Every Recruiter by or through whom Emigrants may be forwarded to a Depot, shall throughout their journey provide them with suitable lodging and food.

Idem, Art. 37. 60.—The arrival of each Emigrant at a Depot shall immediately be reported by the person in charge of the Depot to the Emigration Agent and by such Agent to the Protector of Emigrants.

Idem, Art. 38. 61.—The copy of the registration of every Emigrant received by the Emigration Agent from the Magistrate, or from the Protector of Emigrants, shall, as soon as conveniently may be after the arrival of the Emigrant, be exhibited to the Medical Inspector of Emigrants, and the Emigrant shall be examined by the Medical Inspector to ascertain if he is in a fit state of health to emigrate to the place to which he has contracted to proceed. The Medical Inspector, if satisfied of his fitness, shall give a certificate thereof to the Emigration Agent : if satisfied of his unfitness, he shall give a certificate thereof to the Protector of Emigrants.

Idem, Art. 39. 62.—If the Medical Inspector shall certify that any Emigrant is not in a fit state of health to emigrate to the place to which he has contracted to proceed, or if any irregularity shall have occurred in the recruitment of any Emigrant, it shall be lawful for the Protector of Emigrants to order the Emigration Agent in whose Depot such Emigrant may be, forthwith to pay to him, the Protector of Emigrants, such reasonable sum as shall be necessary, to enable the laborer to return to the place where he was registered, and the Protector of Emigrants may take any steps he thinks necessary for the conveyance of the laborer to such place.

Idem, Art. 40. 63.—On failure of the Emigration Agent, for twenty-four hours, to comply with an order of the Protector for the payment of any such sum of money as in the last preceding section mentioned, it shall be lawful for the Protector to pay the same to or on behalf of the Emigrant, and every sum so disbursed shall be recoverable by the Protector, with six per cent interest from the date of disbursement, from the Emigration Agent on whose default it may be paid, as money paid to the use of such Emigration Agent.

Chaque Recruteur qui accompagnera ou fera accompagner des Emigrants à un Dépôt, devra, pendant tout le voyage, leur fournir un logement et une nourriture convenables.

60.—La personne chargée du Dépôt donnera connaissance de l'arrivée de chaque Emigrant au Dépôt à l'Agent de l'Emigration qui, à son tour, en informera le Protecteur. Idem, Art. 37.

61.—Après l'arrivée de chaque Emigrant, et aussitôt qu'on pourra le faire, on soumettra à l'Inspecteur Médical l'extrait du Registre des Emigrants tenu par le Magistrat de District ou par le Protecteur des Emigrants, et expédié par l'un ou par l'autre selon le cas, à l'Agent de l'Emigration. L'Inspecteur Médical examinera l'Emigrant pour s'assurer si son état de santé lui permet d'émigrer à l'endroit où il s'est engagé à se rendre; et dans le cas où son état de santé lui paraîtra satisfaisant, il délivrera un certificat à cet effet à l'Agent de l'Emigration; si, au contraire, il croit que la santé de l'émigrant est mauvaise, il délivrera un certificat constatant ce fait. Idem, Art. 38.

62.—Si l'Inspecteur Médical certifie que la santé d'un Emigrant ne lui permet pas de partir pour l'endroit où il s'est engagé à émigrer, ou si une irrégularité quelconque a eu lieu dans le recrutement d'un émigrant, le Protecteur des Emigrants aura le droit d'ordonner à l'Agent d'Emigration préposé au Dépôt où cet émigrant se trouvera, de payer à lui, le Protecteur des Emigrants, telle somme qui sera jugée raisonnable et nécessaire pour mettre le laboureur à même de retourner dans l'endroit où il a été enregistré, et le Protecteur des Emigrants pourra prendre toutes les mesures qui lui paraîtront nécessaires pour le repatriement de ce laboureur. Idem, Art. 39.

63.—Dans le cas où l'Agent d'Emigration n'aurait pas obtempéré à l'ordre du Protecteur des Emigrants de payer dans les 24 heures la somme mentionnée dans la Section précédente, le Protecteur aura le droit de remettre cette somme à l'Emigrant lui-même ou de la payer pour qu'elle soit employée pour le dit Emigrant; et toute somme qui aura été payée dans ces conditions pourra être recouvrée par le Protecteur, avec 6 0[0 d'intérêts à partir de la date du paiement, de l'Agent d'Emigration Idem, Art. 40.

No further proof shall be required by any Court in any such case than that the Protector gave the Emigration Agent an order to pay the same, and that the Emigration Agent for a space of twenty-four hours made default in complying therewith. Provided that any Emigrant who, from his state of health is, in the opinion of the Medical Inspector, unfit to undertake the journey back to the place where he was registered, shall, in addition to his being conveyed back at the expense of the Emigration Agent, be entitled to continue in the Depot, and to be fed, clothed, lodged and attended to there, by and at the expense of the Emigration Agent until such time as the Protector shall otherwise order.

Idem, Art. 41. 64.—The Emigration Agent, in the presence of the Protector of Emigrants, and within forty-eight hours after the arrival of each Emigrant at the Depot, shall ascertain by personal communication with such Emigrant, whether or not he has been properly fed, and otherwise properly treated on his journey to the Depot. The Emigration Agent shall also, in the presence of the Protector and within such time as aforesaid, examine the copy of the registration furnished to the Emigrant under Sec. XXX or Sec. XXXIII. If, for any reason, further enquiry be necessary, such enquiry shall be made forthwith, unless the Emigration Agent shall, with the consent of the Protector, refuse to recognize or to be bound by the contract entered into by the Recruiter with the Emigrant, as shewn by the copy of the registration produced by the Emigrant, such copy, if it be a copy furnished under Section XXX, shall be countersigned by both the Emigration Agent and the Protector, and if it be a copy furnished under Sect. XXXIII, shall be countersigned by the Emigration Agent alone, and the copy so countersigned under whichever Section it may have been furnished, shall be delivered back to the Emigrant. If the Emigration Agent shall, without the consent of the Protector, refuse to be bound by the contract entered into by the Recruiter with the Emigrant, the Protector may thereupon order the Emigration Agent forthwith to pay to him, the Protector of Emigrants, such reasonable sum as shall be necessary to enable the Emigrant to return to the place where he was registered; and, on failure of the Emigration Agent, to pay such sum within twenty-four hours of his being ordered so to do, the Protector may pay the

qui aura négligé de la payer, comme si cet argent avait été versé à l'Agent d'Emigration pour son propre usage. Il suffira de prouver devant n'importe quelle Cour dans un cas pareil que le Protecteur a donné l'ordre à l'Agent d'Emigration de payer cette somme et que ce dernier n'y a pas obtempéré dans les 24 heures. Toutefois tout Emigrant qui en raison de son état de santé, sera considéré, par l'Inspecteur Médical, incapable d'entreprendre le voyage de retour dans l'endroit où il aura été enregistré, aura droit, nonseulement à être reconduit dans cet endroit aux frais de l'Agent d'Emigration, mais encore de rester au Dépôt, et d'y être logé, nourri, habillé et soigné aux frais de l'Agent d'Emigration jusqu'à ce que le Protecteur en ordonne autrement.

64.—L'Agent d'Emigration en présence du Protecteur des Emigrants, et dans les 48 heures qui suivront l'arrivée de chaque Emigrant au Dépôt, s'informera en se mettant en communication directe avec cet émigrant, s'il a été convenablement nourri et bien traité sous tous les rapports pendant son trajet au Dépôt. L'Agent d'Emigration dans le même délai et en présence du Protecteur examinera la copie de l'enregistrement remise à l'émigrant conformément aux dispositions des Sections 30 et 33.—Si pour une raison quelconque il était nécessaire de pousser l'enquête plus loin, on le fera immédiatement à moins que l'Agent d'Emigration, du consentement du Protecteur, ne se refuse à reconnaître le contrat passé entre le recruteur et l'émigrant et à être lié par ce contrat ainsi qu'il appert de la copie du registre produite par l'Emigrant ; cette copie, si elle a été donnée conformément à la Section 30, sera contre-signée par l'Agent d'Emigration et par le Protecteur ; et dans le cas où elle aurait été délivrée conformément à la Section 33, elle ne sera contre-signée que par l'Agent d'Emigration, et cette copie, quelle que soit la section en vertu de laquelle elle a été délivrée, sera rendue à l'Emigrant. Si l'Agent d'Emigration refuse, sans le consentement du Protecteur, d'être lié par le contrat passé entre le Recruteur et l'Emigrant, le Protecteur pourra ordonner au dit Agent de payer à l'Emigrant telle somme qu'il jugera raisonnable et nécessaire pour lui procurer les moyens de retourner à l'endroit où il a été enregistré, et dans le cas où l'Agent d'Emigration n'aurait pas payé cette somme dans les 24 heures qui suivront l'ordre du Protecteur, ce dernier pourra la payer à l'Emigrant en personne Idem, Art. 41.

same to or on behalf of the Emigrant, and all the provisions of the last preceding Section as to sums paid by the Protector, shall be applicable so far as the circumstances of the case will permit, to sums paid by him under this Section. The Protector shall also in every case in which it shall seem proper to him to do so, institute a suit on behalf of the Emigrant against the Emigration Agent for the recovery of damages for the breach of Contract committed by the Emigration Agent. In every such suit, the contract entered into by the Recruiter, shall be deemed to have been entered into by, and to be binding on the Emigration Agent. (*Sect* : 30. *See No.* 53.—*Sect* : 33. *See No.* 56.)

Idem, Art. 42. 65.—After the examination in the last preceding Section provided, and if the Medical Inspector shall have given a certificate of the fitness of the Emigrant to emigrate, the Emigration Agent shall deliver to the Emigrant a pass countersigned by the Protector of Emigrants, as hereinafter provided, stating the name and age of the Emigrant, and the name of his father, and certifying that he is in a fit state of health to emigrate to the place to which he has contracted to go.

Idem, Art. 43. 66.—The Protector of Emigrants shall attend personally at the examination and passing of Emigrants by the Emigration Agent under Sections XLI and XLII, and shall see that the Emigration Agent makes all such enquiries of the Emigrant as it may be his duty to make, and if such Protector is satisfied with such enquiries, but not otherwise, he shall countersign the Pass granted by the Emigration Agent. (*Sect* : 41. *See No.* 64.—*Sect* : 42. *See No.* 65.)

Idem, Art. 44. 67.—If any Emigrant shall, without good and sufficient cause, refuse or neglect to embark, when called upon by the Emigration Agent so to do, it shall not be lawful to compel such Emigrant to embark or to put him on board ship against his will, or to detain him against his will at the depot or elsewhere; but nothing in this Section shall be taken to diminish or affect, in any way, the legal liabilities, civil or criminal, of such Emigrant incurred by him, by reason or in respect of his refusal or neglect aforesaid. Every case in which an Emigrant is charged before a

ou pour l'usage du dit Emigrant, et toutes les dispositions de la section précédente quant aux sommes payées par le Protecteur, seront applicables, autant que le cas le permettra, aux sommes payées par le Protecteur conformément aux dispositions de la présente Section. Le Protecteur dans tous les cas où il croira nécessaire de le faire, pourra intenter une action au nom de l'Emigrant contre l'Agent d'Emigration afin d'obtenir des dommages et intérêts pour la violation du contrat par l'Agent d'Emigration. Dans toute affaire de ce genre, le contrat passé par le Recruteur sera réputé passé par l'Agent d'Emigration qui sera tenu de l'exécuter. (*Section* 30 : *voir le No.* 53.—*Section* 33 : *voir le No.* 56.)

65.—Après l'examen exigé par la section précédente, et lorsque l'Inspecteur Médical aura délivré un certificat constatant que l'état de santé de l'Emigrant lui permet d'émigrer, l'Agent d'Emigration délivrera à l'Emigrant une autorisation, contre-signée par le Protecteur des Emigrants comme il est dit plus loin, énumérant le nom et l'âge de l'émigrant, le nom de son père, et certifiant que son état de santé lui permet d'émigrer à l'endroit où il s'est engagé à se rendre. Idem, Art. 42.

66.—Le Protecteur des Emigrants assistera en personne à l'examen des Emigrants ainsi qu'à la distribution des autorisations aux émigrants par l'Agent d'Emigration, conformément aux Sections 41 et 42, et il veillera à ce que l'Agent d'Emigration prenne tous les renseignements nécessaires auprès des Emigrants ainsi que son devoir l'exige, et dans le cas seulement où le Protecteur sera satisfait de l'enquête faite en sa présence, il contresignera l'autorisation accordée par l'Agent d'Emigration. (*Section* 41 : *voir le No.* 64.—*Section* 42 : *voir le No.* 65.) Idem, Art. 43.

67.—Tout Emigrant qui, sans une raison valable et suffisante, refusera ou négligera de s'embarquer lorsque l'Agent d'Emigration le requerra de le faire, ne pourra être forcé à s'embarquer, ni être mis à bord du navire contre son gré ni être détenu contre son gré au Dépôt ou ailleurs ; mais rien de ce qui est contenu dans cette section ne pourra diminuer ou modifier les obligations, civiles et criminelles, auxquelles le dit Emigrant pourra s'exposer par suite de son refus ou de sa négligence comme il est dit plus haut. Toute plainte qui sera portée devant un Magistrat de Cal- Idem, Art. 44.

Magistrate of a Presidency Town with refusing or neglecting to embark without good or sufficient cause, shall be heard and determined by such Magistrate in a summary manner, and every such laborer shall, on conviction, be punished in the manner provided in Section CCCCXCII of the Indian Penal Code for the punishment of offences under that Section.

Idem, Art. 45. 68.—Emigrants may leave India for any place East of the Cape of Good Hope, to which Emigration may be lawful under this Act, at all times of the year. For any place West of the Cape of Good Hope, Emigrants may leave only between the 31st of July and the 16th of March, unless they embark in vessels using steam power, in which case they may leave at any time of the year.

Idem, Art. 46. 69.—It shall not be lawful to receive any Emigrant on board any vessel unless a license to carry Emigrants in such vessel shall have been obtained from the local Government, and the granting or withholding any such license shall be entirely discretionary with the local Government.

The Master or owner of any vessel who is desirous of obtaining a license to carry Emigrants in such vessel, shall apply in writing through the Protector of Emigrants to the local Government for such license.

Every application for a license shall state the number of men, women and children proposed to be carried, and the tonnage and other particulars respecting the vessel.

The Protector of Emigrants shall cause the vessel to be carefully surveyed by a competent person, with a view to ascertain her sea-worthiness and the extent and nature of her accommodation for Emigrants, and to ascertain that she is properly ventilated and is supplied with all the requisite tackle for her voyage.

The Protector of Emigrants shall make a full report on the survey to the local Government; and if he is of opinion that the vessel is in all respects suitable for the carrying of Emigrants

cutta, de Madras ou de Bombay contre un Emigrant pour avoir, sans une raison valable et suffisante, refusé ou négligé de s'embarquer, sera entendue et jugée par le dit Magistrat d'une manière sommaire, et l'Emigrant sera, s'il est trouvé coupable, passible des peines décrétées par l'Article CCCCXCII du Code Pénal de l'Inde pour les délits énumérés dans cette section.

68.—Les Emigrants pourront quitter l'Inde pour un endroit quelconque à l'Est du Cap de Bonne Espérance auquel l'émigration sera permise à n'importe quelle époque de l'année Pour tout endroit à l'Ouest du Cap de Bonne Espérance les Emigrants ne pourront quitter l'Inde que du 31 Juillet au 16 Mars à moins qu'ils ne s'embarquent à bord de bateaux à vapeur et dans ce cas ils pourront partir à n'importe quelle époque de l'année. Idem, Art. 45.

69.—Aucun Emigrant ne pourra être embarqué à bord d'un navire quelconque si le Gouvernement local n'a, au préalable, accordé une autorisation pour le transport des Emigrants par le dit navire, et le Gouvernement Local pourra à sa discrétion accorder ou refuser cette autorisation. Idem, Art. 46.

Le Capitaine ou l'Armateur d'un navire qui désirerait obtenir une autorisation pour le transport des Emigrants par le dit navire devra en faire la demande par écrit au Gouvernement Local par l'intermédiaire du Protecteur des Emigrants.

Toute demande pour une autorisation de cette nature devra énumérer le nombre d'hommes, de femmes et d'enfants qu'on se propose de transporter, ainsi que le tonnage du navire et tous autres détails se rapportant au navire.

Le Protecteur des Emigrants devra ordonner une visite minutieuse du navire par une personne compétente, afin de s'assurer de son état de navigabilité ainsi que de l'étendue et de la nature de ses emménagements pour des Emigrants, et afin de s'assurer que le navire est pourvu de ventilateurs suffisants ainsi que de tout le gréement qui lui est nécessaire pour le voyage.

Le Protecteur devra faire au Gouvernement Local un rapport détaillé de la visite, et, dans le cas seulement où il sera d'opinion que le navire est sous tous les rapports convenable pour le trans-

under this Act, but not otherwise, he shall give a certificate to that effect to the Master of the vessel.

In consideration of his obtaining a license to carry Emigrants, the Master of every vessel intended to carry Emigrants shall, upon the requisition of the Protector of Emigrants and before any Emigrant shall embark on board of such vessel, execute in duplicate a bond, in such form as the local Government shall prescribe, binding himself and his owners in a penal sum of ten thousand Rupees to conform to the several conditions in this Act provided. It shall be the duty of the Protector of Emigrants to require the Master to execute such bond as aforesaid in duplicate, and to forward one copy of it to the Government of the place to which the Emigrants are to be carried, and the other copy of it to the local Government.

Idem, Art. 47. 70.—1o. No certificate under the last preceding Section shall be granted unless there shall be provided for the Emigrants, either between decks or in cabins, on the upper deck, firmly secured and entirely covered in, a space devoted to their exclusive use. Such cabins and space between decks shall, in every part, have a height of not less than five feet and a half.

2o. No compartment shall take more than one adult Emigrant for every ten superficial feet on deck and for every cubic space of seventy two feet.

3o. A distinct and separate place shall be fitted up for a hospital in every Emigrant Ship.

4o. Women and children shall occupy a compartment of the vessel, distinct and separate from the compartments of the single men.

5o. An Emigrant above the age of ten years shall, for the purposes of this Act, count as an adult, and two children from one to ten years of age, shall count as one adult.

Idem, Art. 48. 71.—There shall be actually laden and on board of every vessel carrying Emigrants at the time of the departure of such vessel from the port at which the Emigrants shall embark, in

port des Emigrants d'après cet Acte, il délivrera un certificat à cet effet au Capitaine du navire.

Le Capitaine de tout navire destiné au transport des Emigrants qui aura obtenu une autorisation à cet effet, devra, sur la demande du Protecteur des Emigrants et avant qu'aucun Emigrant ne soit embarqué à bord du dit navire, signer, en duplicata, une obligation, dans telle forme qui sera prescrite par le Gouvernement Local, par laquelle il s'engagera lui et ses armateurs, sous peine d'une amende de dix mille roupies, à se conformer aux diverses conditions exigées par cet Acte. Il sera du devoir de l'Agent d'Emigration d'exiger que le Capitaine fournisse cette obligation en duplicata, et d'en envoyer une copie au Gouvernement de l'endroit auquel les Emigrants doivent être transportés, et l'autre copie au Gouvernement Local.

70.—1o. Aucun certificat d'après la section précédente ne sera délivré à moins qu'il ne soit réservé pour les Emigrants, soit dans l'entrepont soit dans des cabanes sur le Pont qui soient fortement assujetties au navire et entièrement recouvertes, un espace pour leur usage exclusif. La hauteur des dites cabanes ou du dit espace dans l'entrepont devra être partout de cinq pieds et demi au moins. Idem, Art. 47.

2o. Aucun compartiment ne pourra contenir plus d'un Emigrant par chaque dix pieds de superficie sur le pont et par chaque espace cubique de soixante douze pieds.

3o. Un endroit distinct et séparé sera préparé pour servir d'hôpital à bord de chaque navire à Emigrants.

4o. Les femmes et les enfants occuperont un compartiment du navire qui sera distinct et séparé des compartiments occupés par les hommes non-mariés.

5o. Un Emigrant au-dessus de dix ans sera, d'après le sens de cet Acte considéré comme un adulte, et deux enfants de un à dix ans seront comptés pour un adulte.

71.—Il sera mis à bord de chaque navire qui transportera des Emigrants, au moment du départ du dit navire du Port où les Emigrants s'embarqueront, en telle quantité et de telle nature et Idem, Art. 48.

such quantity and of such description and quality as may be prescribed by any rule, framed by the Governor-General of India in Council, under Section LXIII, good and wholesome provisions for the use and consumption of the said Emigrants, with fuel for cooking the same, over and above the victualling of the Captain, Officers and of the cabin and other passengers, if any, and a supply of water, which shall be carried in tanks or casks, to be approved by the Protector of Emigrants, to the amount of seven gallons for every week of the computed voyage for every Emigrant on board such ship or vessel. When casks are used, they shall be sweet and tight, of sufficient strength, and, if of wood, properly charred inside, and shall not be capable severally of containing more than three hundred gallons each; the staves of the water-casks shall not be made of fir, pine or soft wood.

Every such vessel shall, at the time of departure aforesaid, have actually on board and shall carry with her a properly qualified European or Native Surgeon, and such Medicines and other stores in such quantity and of such quality as may be prescribed by any rules made under Section LXIII.

When any vessel shall be destined to call at a port or place in the course of her voyage for the purpose of filling up her tanks or casks, a supply of water at the rate hereinbefore mentioned, for every week of the proposed voyage to such port or place of calling, shall be deemed to be a compliance with this Section. The probable length of the voyage to such port or place of calling shall be determined from time to time by the Protector of Emigrants, subject to the approval of the local Government.

When any such vessel is fitted with Normandy's apparatus, or other apparatus approved by the Protector of Emigrants, for distilling sea-water, and with proper and sufficient means for working the same, a reduction shall be allowed of one third in the quantity of water required under this Section.

It shall be the duty of the Protector of Emigrants and of the Medical Inspector of Emigrants to see personally that all the provisions of this Section are complied with. (*Sect* : 63. *See No.* 86.)

qualité qu'il pourra être prescrit par un réglement passé par le Gouverneur Général de l'Inde en Conseil, en vertu de la Section LXIII, des provisions bonnes et saines à l'usage et pour la consommation des dits Emigrants, avec le combustible nécessaire pour les cuire, indépendamment des provisions du Capitaine, des Officiers et des Passagers de chambre ou autres, s'il y en a ; et un approvisionnement d'eau, qui sera contenu dans des citernes ou des barriques et dont le Protecteur des Emigrants devra être satisfait, dans la proportion de sept gallons par semaine pour chaque Emigrant pendant le voyage du dit navire. Lorsqu'on emploiera des barriques, elles devront être bien conditionnées, d'une force suffisante, et si elles sont faites de bois, l'intérieur devra être convenablement passé au feu, et ces pièces à eau ne pourront contenir chacune plus de trois cents gallons ; les douves des barriques en bois ne devront pas être faites de sapin, de pin ou d'un bois mou.

Chaque navire à Emigrants devra, au moment de son départ, avoir à son bord un Docteur Européen ou natif possédant les connaissances requises, ainsi que des médicaments et autres provisions, en telle quantité et de telle qualité que pourront l'exiger des réglements passés en vertu de la Section LXIII.

Lorsqu'un navire devra toucher à un Port ou lieu intermédiaire pendant le cours de son voyage afin de remplir ses citernes ou ses barriques à eau, un approvisionnement d'eau dans la proportion mentionnée ci-dessus, par semaine, pour le voyage du dit navire au Port ou à l'endroit de relache sera considéré comme l'exécution de la présente Section. La durée probable du voyage au dit Port ou lieu de relâche sera, de temps à autres, fixée par le Protecteur des Emigrants, sauf l'approbation du Gouvernement Local.

Lorsqu'un navire à Emigrants sera pourvu de l'appareil de Normandy, ou tout autre appareil accepté par le Protecteur des Emigrants, pour distiller l'eau de mer, et des moyens nécessaires pour les faire mouvoir, il sera accordé une réduction d'un tiers de la quantité d'eau exigée par cette Section.

Le Protecteur des Emigrants et l'Inspecteur Médical devront s'assurer personnellement qu'on se conforme à toutes les dispositions de cette Section. (*Section* 63 : *voir le No.* 86.)

Idem, Art. 49. 72.—Before any vessel carrying Emigrants clears out for any place westward of the Cape of Good Hope, between the 1st day of March and the 15th day of September, the Protector of Emigrants shall personally see that every Emigrant is supplied with at least one extra double blanket, and that the same is placed with his other clothes and luggage. Every Emigrant shall be allowed to make use of such double blanket so long as the vessel is outside of the Tropics.

Idem, Art. 50. 73.—Before any vessel licensed to carry Emigrants shall be cleared out from the port of Calcutta, Madras or Bombay, it shall be necessary for the Master of such vessel to obtain from the Protector of Emigrants at the port of clearance and from the Emigration Agent for the place to which the Emigrants are intended to proceed, certificates under the hands of such Protector and Emigration Agent respectively, to the effect following, that is to say,—that such Protector and Emigration Agent have, in respect of the Emigrant proceeding in such vessel, done all which is hereinbefore by this Act required to be done on the part of such Protector and Emigration Agent respectively; and that all the directions contained in this Act, for ensuring the health, comfort and safety of the Emigrants, have been duly complied with, as well as all such rules as the Governor General of India in Council shall, from time to time, frame under Section LXIII. (*Sect* : 63. *See No.* 86.)

Idem, Art. 51. 74.—The Protector of Emigrants shall, from the Report of the Medical Inspector and by personal communication with every Emigrant before embarkation, ascertain that the Emigrant is in good health and not incapacitated from labor, by old age, bodily infirmity or disease. If the Protector of Emigrants shall be of opinion that every Emigrant is in a state of health, which makes him unfit to undertake the voyage on which he is about to embark, the Protector shall refuse to permit the embarkation of such Emigrant. The Protector of Emigrants shall also, before the embarkation of any Emigrant, ascertain that such Emigrant has, in his possession, the copy of the registration provided under Section XXX or Section XXXIII. If it shall appear to the satisfaction of the Protector of Emigrants that any Emigrant has lost the copy of the registration aforesaid, the Protector may fur-

72.—Avant qu'aucun navire transportant des Emigrants soit expédié pour un Port quelconque à l'Ouest du Cap de Bonne Espérance entre le 1er jour de Mars et le 15me jour de Septembre, le Protecteur des Emigrants devra en personne s'assurer que chaque Emigrant a reçu au moins une couverture de rechange et qu'elle a été mise avec ses autres vêtements et son bagage. Chaque Emigrant pourra se servir de cette couverture tant que le navire sera en dehors des Tropiques. Idem, Art. 49.

73.—Avant qu'aucun navire qui aura obtenu une autorisation pour le transport des Emigrants soit expédié du Port de Calcutta, de Madras ou de Bombay, le Capitaine du dit navire sera tenu d'obtenir du Protecteur des Emigrants à son Port d'expédition et de l'Agent d'Emigration pour l'endroit auquel les Emigrants doivent se rendre, des certificats signés de leur main et de la teneur suivante : c'est à dire que le dit Protecteur des Emigrants et que le dit Agent d'Emigration ont, en ce qui concerne les Emigrants embarqués à bord du dit navire, rempli toutes les formalités ci-dessus énumérées et qu'ils sont d'après cet acte tenus de remplir comme Protecteur des Emigrants et Agent d'Emigration respectivement ; et que toutes les instructions ci-dessus contenues pour assurer la santé, le bien-être et la sureté des Emigrants ont été exécutées, ainsi que tous les réglements que le Gouverneur Général de l'Inde en Conseil pourra de temps à autre passer en vertu de la section LXIII. (*Section* 63 : *voir le No.* 86.) Idem, Art. 50.

74.—Le Protecteur des Emigrants devra s'assurer, par le rapport de l'Inspecteur Médical et par une communication personnelle avec chaque émigrant avant son embarquement, que l'émigrant jouit d'une bonne santé et qu'il n'est pas rendu incapable de travail par la vieillesse, les infirmités ou la maladie. Si le Protecteur des Emigrants est d'opinion que l'état de santé de quelqu' émigrant le rend incapable de faire le voyage qu'il est sur le point d'entreprendre, le Protecteur refusera le permis d'embarquement du dit Emigrant. Le Protecteur devra aussi s'assurer, avant l'embarquement de chaque émigrant, que le dit émigrant est muni d'une copie du registre requis par la Section 30 ou la Section 33. S'il est prouvé à la satisfaction du Protecteur des Emigrants que quelqu' Emigrant a perdu la copie de son registre, le Protecteur pourra en donner une copie à l'Emigrant, laquelle copie devra être Idem, Art. 51.

nish such Emigrant with a copy of such registration, to be made from the copy received by the Protector from the Magistrate under Section XXXII, or from the Register kept by himself under Section XXXIII, and shall thereupon allow such Emigrant to embark.—(*Sect*: 30. *See No.* 53.—*Sect*: 32. *See No.* 55.—*Sect*: 33. *See No.* 56.)

Idem, Art. 52. 75.—The provisions of this Act so far as they are likely more immediately to affect them, shall be explained in a general manner by the Protector of Emigrants to all Emigrants prior to their embarkation.

Idem, Art. 53. 76.—1o. When any Emigrants are about to embark in any Vessel, the Emigration Agent, for the place to which they are intended to proceed, shall furnish the Master of the Vessel with five copies of a list, specifying as accurately as may be, the names, ages and occupations, and the names of the fathers of the Emigrants about to embark on board such vessel.

2o. On embarkation every Emigrant shall deliver to the Master of the Vessel the pass granted to him under Section XLII, and it shall not be lawful for the Master to receive any Emigrant on board, unless he delivers up such pass. The Master shall compare the Emigrants who embark, and the passes delivered by them, with the list furnished by the Emigration Agent, and if the list appear to be correct and to correspond with the passes delivered and with the Emigrants embarked, the Master shall sign the five copies of the list.—(*Sect*: 42. *See No.* 65.)

3o. It shall be the duty of the Protector of Emigrants to be personally present at the embarkation of all Emigrants, and to see that the Master duly compares the list with the passes and Emigrants, and he shall himself also compare the passes and Emigrants.

4o. When the copies of the list have been signed, the Master shall give two copies to the Protector of Emigrants who shall sign such copies if he believes them to be correct, and shall return one

faite sur la copie reçue du Magistrat par le Protecteur en vertu de la Section 32, ou sur le Registre tenu par lui-même en vertu de la Section 33, et permettra ensuite à l'Emigrant de s'embarquer.—(*Section* 30 : *voir le No.* 53.—*Section* 32 : *voir le No.* 55.—*Section* 33 : *voir le No.* 56.)

75.—Le Protecteur des Emigrants expliquera d'une manière générale aux Emigrants avant leur embarquement autant des dispositions de cet acte qu'il croira devoir les concerner plus particulièrement. **Idem, Art. 52.**

76.—1o. Lorsque des Emigrants seront sur le point de s'embarquer à bord d'un navire, l'Agent d'Emigration du lieu où ils doivent se rendre remettra au capitaine du navire cinq copies d'une liste dans laquelle seront spécifiés, aussi exactement que possible, les noms, âges et emplois de tous les Emigrants qui sont sur le point de s'embarquer à bord du dit navire, ainsi que les noms de leurs pères. **Idem, Art. 53.**

2o. Lors de son embarquement, chaque Emigrant remettra au capitaine du navire le permis qui lui a été accordé en vertu de la Section 42, et il ne sera pas permis au capitaine de recevoir à son bord aucun Emigrant à moins que celui-ci ne lui remette le dit permis. Le capitaine comparera les Emigrants qui s'embarquent et les permis qu'ils lui remettent, avec la liste fournie par l'Agent d'Emigration, et s'il lui semble que la liste est correcte, et qu'elle correspond avec les permis qui lui ont été remis et les Emigrants qui se sont embarqués, le capitaine signera les cinq copies de la liste. —(*Section* 42 : *voir le No.* 65.)

3o. Il sera du devoir du Protecteur des Emigrants d'assister à l'embarquement de tous les Emigrants et de s'assurer que le capitaine a soigneusement comparé la liste des Emigrants avec les permis, et avec les Emigrants eux-mêmes, et il devra aussi comparer la liste des Emigrants avec les permis et avec les Emigrants.

4o. Lorsque les copies de la liste auront été signées, le capitaine en remettra deux au Protecteur des Emigrants qui les signera s'il les croit correctes et en rendra une au capitaine du navire.

copy to the Master of the Vessel; the other copy shall be filed in the office of the Protector of Emigrants.

5o. The Protector of Emigrants shall not permit any Emigrant to remain on board who has not a pass, or who is not mentioned in the list aforesaid.

6o. Every pass delivered up to the Master of a Vessel under this Section, shall be returned by him to the Emigrant by whom the same was delivered up, prior to such Emigrant disembarking on the arrival of the Vessel at her place of destination.

Idem, Art. 54. 77.—The Master of every Vessel carrying Emigrants shall, after the embarkation of the Emigrants, and before the departure of the vessel, give the Emigration Agent at the Port from which such vessel is cleared out, two others of the five copies of the list of Emigrants mentioned in the last preceding Section, duly signed by the Master. The Emigration Agent shall thereupon sign such copies, and shall return to the Master one of the said copies, which shall, on the arrival of the vessel at the place of destination, and previous to the disembarkation of any Emigrant, be delivered by the Master to the Protector of Emigrants or other, the proper officer at such place.

Idem, Art. 55. 78.—Whenever a vessel carrying Emigrants shall have cleared and shall be proceeding to sea, the Officer of Customs or the Pilot, whichever of these Officers shall remain last on board of the vessel, shall as shortly as conveniently can be, before his leaving the vessel, make a muster of the Crew and Passengers and Emigrants. Such Officer of Customs or Pilot shall use as a Muster-Roll a copy of the list signed by the Master and by the Protector of Emigrants, under Section LIII, which copy shall be furnished to him by the Master; and after the muster he shall sign such Muster-Roll noting upon it such discrepancies (if any) as he may have observed. —(*Sect* : 53. *See No.* 76.)

Idem, Art. 56. 79.—Every Officer of Customs and Pilot who shall make a muster under the last preceding Section, shall make a declaration stating according to the best of his belief that no additional Emigrant has been received on board since the list was signed by the

L'autre copie sera placée dans les archives du bureau du Protecteur des Emigrants.

5o. Le Protecteur des Emigrants ne devra permettre à aucun Emigrant de rester à bord du navire à moins qu'il ne soit muni d'un permis et que son nom ne soit porté sur la liste ci-dessus mentionnée.

6o. Chaque permis qui aura été remis au capitaine d'un navire en vertu de cette Section, devra être rendu par lui à l'Emigrant qui le lui aura remis, avant le débarquement du dit Emigrant, à l'arrivée du navire à son port de destination.

77.—Le capitaine de chaque navire transportant des Emigrants, Idem, Art. 54.
devra, après l'embarquement des Emigrants et avant le départ du navire, remettre à l'Agent d'Emigration du port d'où le navire est expédié deux autres des cinq copies de la liste des Emigrants mentionée dans les deux Sections précédentes, et ces copies devront être signées par le capitaine. L'Agent d'Emigration devra alors signer les dites copies et en rendre une au capitaine, qui devra, à l'arrivée du navire dans son port de destination, et avant qu'aucun Emigrant n'ait débarqué, la remettre au Protecteur des Emigrants ou à tout autre fonctionnaire remplissant des fonctions analogues dans le dit Port.

78.—Lorsque un navire transportant des Emigrants aura été Idem, Art. 55.
expédié et prendra la mer, l'Officier de Douane ou le Pilote, suivant que l'un ou l'autre de ces fonctionnaires restera le dernier à bord du navire, devra, aussitôt que possible avant de quitter le navire, faire une inspection de l'équipage, des passagers et des Emigrants. Le dit Officier de Douane ou Pilote se servira pour cette inspection d'une copie de la liste signée par le capitaine et par le Protecteur des Emigrants, en vertu de la Section 53, qui lui sera fournie par le capitaine, et après avoir fait l'inspection, il signera la dite liste en y indiquant les erreurs qu'il pourra y avoir remarquées.—(*Section* 53 : *voir le No.* 76.)

79.—Tout Officier de Douane et tout Pilote qui fera l'inspec- Idem, Art 56.
tion requise par l'Article précédent devra aussi déclarer qu'autant qu'il peut le savoir aucun autre émigrant n'a été reçu à bord depuis la signature de la liste par le Protecteur, et qu'il n'a été commis à

Protector, and that nothing else has been done or omitted to be done in the vessel, contrary to the provisions of this Act. Every such Muster-Roll and declaration shall be transmitted without delay to the Protector of Emigrants at the port of embarkation.

Idem, Art. 57. 80.—It shall be the duty of the Protector of Emigrants on the receipt of the Muster-Roll furnished by the Officer of Customs or Pilot under the last preceding Section, carefully to compare the same with the list, signed by the Master, filed in the Office of the Protector, and to report any discrepancy to the Local Government.

Idem, Art. 58. 81.—The Protector of Emigrants shall, by every vessel which carries Emigrants, send to the Protector of Emigrants or other, the proper Government authority at the place for which the Emigrants embark, a correct and detailed list of all Emigrants embarked in such vessel, compiled from the passes of the Emigrants, and from the list signed by the Master as aforesaid.

Idem, Art. 59. 82.—The Master of every vessel carrying Emigrants from the port of Calcutta shall proceed on his voyage and depart with his vessel from Garden Reach, within twenty-four hours after the embarkation of such of the Emigrants, as shall have first embarked.

Idem, Art. 60. 83.—Every vessel sailing from the port of Calcutta with Emigrants shall proceed from Garden Reach to sea, under tow of a competent Steamer.

Idem, Art. 61. 84.—Two copies of this Act and of all Rules made by the Governor-General of India in Council under Section LXIII, and two copies of a translation of this Act, and of such Rules, in such language or languages as the Local Government may direct, shall be delivered to the Master of every vessel carrying Emigrants, by the Emigration Agent at the time of clearance, and shall be kept on board of every such vessel during the whole voyage, and one of such copies or translations shall, upon request made at all reasonable times to the Master of the vessel, be produced to any Emigrant or passenger for his perusal.—(*Sect* : 63. *See No.* 86.)

bord du navire aucune contravention aux dispositions du présent Acte. Chaque liste et chaque déclaration seront immédiatement transmises au Protecteur des Emigrants du Port d'embarquement.

80.—Il sera du devoir du Protecteur des Emigrants, en recevant la liste fournie par l'Officier de Douane ou par le Pilote d'après l'Article précédent, de la comparer soigneusement avec la liste signée par le Capitaine et déposée dans le bureau du Protecteur, et de porter les erreurs qu'il pourrait remarquer en faisant cet examen, à la connaissance du Gouvernement Local. Idem, Art. 57.

81.—Le Protecteur des Emigrants devra, par chaque navire transportant des émigrants, expédier au Protecteur des Emigrants ou à tout autre fonctionnaire autorisé à cet effet par le Gouvernement, à l'endroit où les émigrants doivent se rendre, une liste exacte et détaillée de tous les émigrants embarqués à bord du dit navire, préparée d'après les permis délivrés aux émigrants et d'après la liste signée par le Capitaine comme il est dit ci-dessus. Idem, Art. 58.

82.—Le Capitaine de tout navire transportant des émigrants du Port de Calcutta quittera Garden Reach pour prendre la mer vingt quatre heures après l'embarquement des premiers émigrants embarqués. Idem, Art. 59.

83.—Tout navire à voiles quittant le Port de Calcutta avec des émigrants devra quitter Garden Reach remorqué par un Steamer d'une force suffisante. Idem, Art. 60.

84.—Il sera délivré au Capitaine de tout navire transportant des émigrants, lorsqu'il sera expédié, par l'Agent d'Emigration, deux copies de cet Acte et de tous les réglements passés par le Gouverneur Général de l'Inde en Conseil en vertu de la Section 63, ainsi que deux copies d'une traduction de cet Acte dans toute langue ou dans toutes les langues que le Gouvernement Local déterminera, et ces copies devront être gardées à bord du dit navire pendant tout le voyage, et une de ces copies ou traductions devra, lorsqu'elle sera demandée au Capitaine à un moment convenable, être remise à l'Emigrant ou au passager qui la demandera, afin qu'il puisse en prendre connaissance.—(*Section* 63 *: voir le No.* 86.) Idem, Art. 61.

Idem, Art. 62. 85.—In case of sickness breaking out on board of any vessel conveying Emigrants to the British Dependency of Seychelles, such Emigrants may be taken to the Quarantine Station of the Island of Mauritius, and in such case such Emigrants may, at their option, contract for service at the said Island of Mauritius, or may proceed to the said Dependency of Seychelles; and if they shall elect to contract for service in the Island of Mauritius, such Emigrants shall then be regarded and treated, in all respects, as if they had emigrated to the said Island under the provisions of this Act.

Idem, Art. 63. 86.—It shall be lawful for the Governor-General of India in Council from time to time to make rules, and to repeal, alter and amend the same, not inconsistent with the provisions of this Act.

1o. To regulate the proportion of women to be taken with Emigrants, and the age below and above which, children shall not be taken.

2o. To prescribe the description, quantity and quality of provisions to be taken by vessels carrying Emigrants, the daily allowance of food and water to be issued to each Emigrant during the voyage, and the nature and the amount of clothing which shall be supplied to the Emigrants.

3o. To provide for the medical care of Emigrants during their residence at the depots and on the voyages.

4o. To prescribe the nature, quality and quantity of medical drugs, and other stores to be carried on board such vessel.

5o. To provide for the ventilation and cleanliness of vessels during their voyages and for their being furnished with a sufficient number of suitable boats for use in case of shipwreck or fire.

6o. To provide for a Journal being kept by the Surgeon of every such vessel, of the health of the Emigrants, and of his treatment

85.—Dans le cas où une maladie éclaterait à bord d'un navire transportant des Emigrants à la Dépendance Anglaise des Seychelles, les dits Emigrants pourront être conduits à la Station de Quarantaine de l'Ile Maurice, et dans ce cas, les dits Emigrants pourront à leur option passer des contrats de service pour la dite Ile Maurice, ou se rendre à la dite Dépendance des Seychelles; et s'ils préfèrent passer des contrats de service pour l'Ile Maurice, les dits Emigrants seront alors considérés et traités, sous tous les rapports, comme s'ils avaient émigré dans la dite Ile en vertu des dispositions de cet Acte. Idem, Art. 62.

86.—Le Gouverneur Général de l'Inde en Conseil pourra de temps à autre faire des Réglements qui ne soient pas contraires aux dispositions de cet Acte, et pourra de même rapporter et modifier les dits Réglements. Idem, Art. 63.

1o. Pour fixer la proportion des femmes qui doivent être embarquées avec les Emigrants, et l'âge au-dessous ou au-dessus duquel les enfants ne pourront être embarqués.

2o. Pour déterminer le genre, la quantité et la qualité des provisions qui doivent être embarquées à bord des navires transportant des Emigrants, la ration journalière de nourriture et d'eau qui doit être distribuée à chaque Emigrant pendant le voyage, et la nature et la quantité des vêtements qui doivent être fournis aux Emigrants.

3o. Pour pourvoir aux soins médicaux qui doivent être donnés aux Emigrants pendant leur séjour dans les Dépôts, et pendant les voyages.

4o. Pour déterminer la nature, la quantité et la qualité des médicaments et autres articles pharmaceutiques qui doivent être embarqués à bord des dits navires.

5o. Pour pourvoir à la ventilation et à la propreté des dits navires pendant leurs voyages, et à ce qu'il se trouve à leur bord un nombre suffisant de bateaux convenables dont on puisse se servir en cas de naufrage ou d'incendie.

6o. Pour pourvoir à ce qu'il soit tenu par le Docteur de chacun des dits navires un Journal de l'état de santé des Emigrants, et du

of the sick, together with full explanations of the causes of every death.

| 7o. And generally to provide for the security, well being, and protection of Emigrants. All such rules shall be published in the Gazette of India, and shall have the same force and effect as if they were contained in this Act.

Idem, Art. 64. 87.—Whenever the Governor-General of India in Council shall have reason to believe, that in any place to which emigration is lawful under this Act, proper measures have not been taken for the protection of Emigrants immediately upon their arrival in such place or during their residence therein, or for their safe return to India, or to provide a return passage to India for any such Emigrants at or about the time at which they are entitled to such return passage, it shall be lawful for the said Governor-General of India in Council, by notification published in the Gazette of India, to declare that Emigration to such place shall cease and be prohibited from a certain day to be specified in the notification.

Idem, Art. 65. 88.—After any notification shall have been published under the last preceding Section, Emigration to such place as is specified in such notification, shall be suspended from the day specified in the notification ; but such suspension shall not affect any act done, offence committed or proceedings commenced before such suspension.

Idem, Art. 66. 89.—During the time of such suspension, any provisions of this or of any other Act in force for the time being, prohibiting Emigration, or the aiding or abetting of Emigration, or the making of any contract for labor to be performed by any Native of India out of the British Territories in India, shall take effect and be in force so far as relates to the place specified in the notification, in the same manner and to the same extent as if Emigration to such place had never been declared to be lawful.

Idem, Art. 67. 90.—Whenever the Governor-General of India in Council shall be satisfied that, in the place specified in any notification under Section LXIV, proper measures have been taken and will

traitement des maladies, ainsi que des explications détaillées des causes de chaque mort.

7o. Et en général pour pourvoir à la sécurité, au bien-être et à la protection des Emigrants. Tous ces Réglements devront être publiés dans la Gazette de l'Inde, et auront le même effet que s'ils avaient été contenus dans le présent Acte.

87.—Toutes les fois que le Gouverneur-Général de l'Inde en Conseil aura raison de croire que dans un endroit quelconque auquel l'Emigration est permise, il n'a pas été pris des mesures convenables pour la protection des Emigrants aussitôt après leur arrivée dans le dit endroit, ou pendant leur séjour dans le dit endroit, ou pour leur retour dans l'Inde, ou pour procurer un passage de retour dans l'Inde aux dits Emigrants à l'époque ou vers l'époque à laquelle ils ont droit au dit passage de retour, le Gouverneur-Général de l'Inde en Conseil pourra, par des avis publiés dans la Gazette de l'Inde, déclarer la cessation et l'interdiction de l'émigration au dit endroit à partir d'une date qui devra être spécifiée dans les avis. Idem, Art. 64.

88.—Lorsqu'un avis aura été publié en vertu de l'Article précédent, l'émigration à l'endroit qui aura été spécifié dans le dit avis sera suspendue à partir du jour qui aura été spécifié dans le dit avis, mais la dite suspension ne pourra affecter aucun acte et aucun délit qui auront été commis, ou les poursuites qui auront été commencées avant la dite suspension. Idem, Art. 65.

89.—Pendant la durée de la dite suspension, toutes les dispositions du présent Acte ou de tout autre Acte en vigueur à cette époque qui pourraient prohiber l'émigration, ou défendre qu'on facilite l'émigration ou qu'on y participe, ou qu'il soit passé aucun contract de service qui doive être exécuté par un natif de l'Inde hors des territoires de l'Angleterre dans l'Inde, seront mis en vigueur et auront force de loi, en autant qu'elles se rapporteront à l'endroit spécifié dans l'avis, de même et tout autant que si l'émigration à cet endroit n'eût jamais été permise. Idem, Art. 66.

90.—Toutes les fois que le Gouverneur-Général de l'Inde en Conseil sera satisfait qu'il a été ou qu'il sera pris, dans l'endroit spécifié dans l'avis publié en vertu de la Section 64, des Idem, Art. 67.

be adopted for the protection of Emigrants immediately upon their arrival thereat and during their residence therein, and for their safe return to India and for providing return passages to India for such Emigrants at or about the time at which they are entitled to such return passages, it shall be lawful for the said Governor-General of India in Council to notify in the Gazette of India that Emigration to such place shall again be allowed from a day to be specified in such notification; and, thereupon, all the provisions of this or any other Act in force for the time being, authorizing Emigration to such place, shall, from the day so specified, be revived and have the same force and effect as if such Emigration had not been suspended, except as to acts done, offences committed, and proceedings commenced during the time of such suspension.—(*Sect* : 64. *See No.* 87.)

Idem, Art. 68. 91.—All fees received by any Magistrate, Protector of Emigrants, or other Officer under this Act, shall be accounted for to Government in such manner as the Governor-General of India in Council may direct.

Idem, Art. 69. 92 —Whoever shall, except under and in conformity with the provisions of this Act, make any contract with any Native of India for labor to be performed in any place beyond British India to which Emigration is not authorized under this Act, or under the said Acts XLVI of 1860, and VII of 1862, shall be deemed to have committed the offence specified in Section 363 of the Indian Penal Code: and whoever shall knowingly enable or assist any Native of India to emigrate to any such place, or aid in or abet the Emigration of any Native of India to any such place, shall be deemed to have abetted the commission of that offence. (*The Acts* 46 *of* 1860 *and* 7 *of* 1862 *refer to Emigration to French Colonies.*)

Idem, Art. 70. 93.—Whoever not being a Recruiter duly licensed under this Act, shall act or be employed as a Recruiter of laborers, or shall, contrary to the provisions of this Act, enter into any contract with a Native of India for labor to be performed by such Native of India in any place beyond British India, (whether Emigration to such place is or is not authorized under this Act or under the said Acts XLVI of 1860 and VII of 1862), shall be liable to a fine not exceeding five hundred Rupees.

mesures convenables pour la protection des Emigrants aussitôt après leur arrivée dans le dit endroit et pendant le temps qu'ils y séjourneront, ainsi que pour leur retour dans l'Inde, et pour pourvoir à ce que les dits Emigrants obtiennent des passages de retour dans l'Inde à ou vers l'époque à laquelle ils ont droit aux dits passages de retour, le Gouverneur-Général de l'Inde en Conseil pourra donner avis dans la Gazette de l'Inde que l'Emigration à cet endroit est de nouveau permise, à partir de la date qui sera spécifiée dans le dit avis ; et, à partir de cette date, toutes les dispositions du présent Acte ou de tout autre Acte ayant force de loi à cette époque, autorisant l'Emigration à cet endroit, seront remis en vigueur et auront le même effet que si l'Emigration n'avait pas été suspendue, excepté en tant qu'elles concerneront les actes et les délits commis ainsi que les poursuites commencées pendant le cours de la dite suspension.—(*Section* 64 : *voir le No.* 87.)

91.—Il sera rendu compte de tous droits perçus par un Magistrat, un Protecteur des Emigrants, ou tout autre fonctionnaire, en vertu de cet acte, de telle manière que le Gouverneur-Général de l'Inde en Conseil l'ordonnera. Idem, Art. 68.

92.—Quiconque passera avec un natif de l'Inde un contrat de service pour être exécuté dans un endroit situé hors de l'Inde Anglaise auquel l'Emigration n'est pas permise par le présent acte ou par les actes 46 de 1860 et 7 de 1862, et ne se conformera pas aux dispositions du présent acte sera considéré avoir commis le délit spécifié dans la Section 363 du Çode Pénal de l'Inde ; et quiconque fournira sciemment à un natif de l'Inde les moyens d'émigrer, ou participera à l'émigration d'un natif de l'Inde au dit endroit, sera considéré avoir participé à la commission de ce délit. (*Les Actes 46 de* 1860 *et 7 de* 1862 *se rapportent à l'Emigration aux Colonies françaises.*) Idem, Art. 69.

93.—Quiconque n'étant pas un Recruteur dûment autorisé en vertu de cet acte, agira ou s'emploiera comme Recruteur de laboureurs, ou passera, contrairement aux dispositions de cet acte, un contrat de service avec un natif de l'Inde pour être exécuté dans un endroit hors de l'Inde Anglaise (que l'Emigration au dit endroit soit ou ne soit pas permise par cet acte ou par les dits actes 46 de 1860 et 7 de 1862) sera passible d'une amende n'excédant pas cinq cents roupies. Idem, Art. 70.

Idem, Art. 71. 94.—Whoever being a duly licensed Recruiter shall remove any Emigrant whom he may engage in any district or place other than the Towns of Calcutta, Madras or Bombay, from such district or place without such Emigrant having appeared along with the Recruiter before the Magistrate of the District, in order that such person might be examined and registered; and whoever shall remove any Emigrant whom he may engage in any one of the Towns of Calcutta, Madras or Bombay, from such Town or to an Emigration depot without such Emigrant having appeared with the Recruiter before the Protector of Emigrants, in order that such person might be examined and registered; and whoever shall by means of intoxication, violence, fraud, or false pretences induce any Native of India to enter into a contract for labor to be performed by him in any place to which Emigration shall be lawful under this Act, or to proceed to any such place without having entered into any contract; and whoever shall fail to supply any Emigrant whom he shall have engaged, and who shall be registered, with suitable food, or shall otherwise ill-treat such Emigrant on his journey to the depot; and whoever shall forward, send, or convey any such Emigrant otherwise than is provided in Section XXXVI, or to any house or place in or near the Towns of Calcutta, Madras, or Bombay, respectively, other than the depot for the Emigrants for the place at which such Emigrant shall have contracted to labor,—shall be liable to a fine not exceeding five hundred Rupees.—(*Sect*: 36. *See No.* 59.)

Idem, Art. 72. 95.—Whoever being a duly licensed Recruiter, shall forward or send any Emigrant from the District or Town in which he has entered into an engagement, to any Emigration depot without such Emigrant having been duly registered in accordance with the provisions of Sections XXX and XXXIII; and whoever being a duly licensed Recruiter shall induce or knowingly permit any such Emigrant to leave such District or Town or to proceed to any Emigration depot, for the purpose of emigrating to any place without the Emigrant being duly registered as aforesaid,—shall be liable to a fine not exceeding five hundred Rupees.—(*Sect*: 30. *See No.* 53.—*Sect*: 33. *See No.* 56.)

Idem, Art. 73. 96.—Whoever without lawful authority, shall issue any written

94.—Quiconque étant un Recruteur dûment autorisé emménera un Emigrant, qu'il aura engagé dans un District ou un endroit autre que les villes de Calcutta, de Madras et de Bombay, du dit District ou du dit endroit, sans que le dit Emigrant ait comparu avec le Recruteur devant le Magistrat du District afin que le dit Emigrant soit examiné et enregistré; et quiconque emménera un Emigrant, qu'il aura engagé dans une des villes de Calcutta, de Madras et de Bombay, de la dite ville ou d'un Depôt d'Emigration sans que le dit Emigrant ait comparu avec le Recruteur devant le Protecteur des Emigrants afin que le dit Emigrant soit examiné et enregistré; et quiconque, au moyen de boissons enivrantes, par la violence, la fraude ou de fausses représentations, induira un natif de l'Inde à passer un contrat de service pour être exécuté dans un lieu auquel l'Emigration est permise par cet Acte, ou à se rendre dans le dit lieu, sans avoir passé de contrat de service; et quiconque ne fournira pas à un Emigrant qu'il aura engagé, et qui aura été enregistré, une nourriture convenable et suffisante, ou qui de toute autre manière maltraitera le dit Emigrant pendant le voyage au Dépôt; et quiconque expédiera, enverra, ou transportera un Emigrant autrement que ne l'ordonne la Section 36, ou l'expédiera, l'enverra ou le transportera dans une maison ou dans un endroit quelconque dans les villes de Calcutta, de Madras et de Bombay ou dans leurs environs, autre que le Dépôt des Emigrants de l'endroit où le dit Emigrant se sera engagé à travailler,—sera passible d'une amende n'excédant pas cinq cent roupies.—(*Section* 36 : *voir le No.* 59.) Idem, Art. 71.

95.—Quiconque étant un Recruteur dûment autorisé expédiera, ou enverra un Emigrant du District ou de la ville, où il a passé son engagement, à un Dépôt d'Emigration, sans que le dit Emigrant ait été enregistré d'après les dispositions des Sections 30 et 33; et quiconque étant un Recruteur dûment autorisé, poussera le dit Emigrant à quitter le dit District ou la dite ville ou à se rendre à un Dépôt d'Emigration, ou lui permettra sciemment de le faire, dans le but d'émigrer à un endroit quelconque, sans que l'Emigrant ait été enregistré comme il est dit ci-dessus—sera passible d'une amende n'excédant pas cinq cents roupies.—(*Section* 30 : *voir le No.* 53.—*Section* 33 : *voir le No.* 56.) Idem, Art. 72.

96.—Quiconque, sans autorisation légale, délivrera un perwan- Idem, Art. 73.

perwannah or order to the Police to assist himself, or any other person, to procure laborers, to proceed to any place beyond British India, or shall falsely represent that such laborers are required by the Government, or are to be engaged on behalf of Government, shall be liable to a fine not exceediug five hundred Rupees.

Idem, Art. 74. 97.—If the Master of any vessel which shall not have been licensed as provided in Section XLVI, shall knowingly receive any Emigrant on board in order to convey such Emigrant to any place contrary to the provisions of this Act, such Master of such vessel shall be liable to simple or rigorous imprisonment for a period not exceeding one year, and also to a fine not exceeding one thousand Rupees for every such Emigrant received on board, and the vessel shall be liable to be forfeited.—(*Sect*: 46. *See No.* 69.)

Idem, Art. 75. 98.—If the Master of any vessel shall at the Port of Calcutta, the Port of Madras, or the Port of Bombay, clear such vessel for any place to which Emigration shall be lawful under this Act, and take on board any Emigrant without having fully complied with every particular required in Sections XLVIII and L, he shall be liable to a fine not exceeding two hundred Rupees for every Emigrant so taken on board.—(*Sect*: 48. *See No.* 71.—*Sect*: 50. *See No.* 73.)

Idem, Art. 76. 99.—If the Master of any vessel shall, after having cleared such vessel for any place, to which Emigration shall be lawful under this Act, take on board any Emigrant without such Emigrant having been duly entered in the lists mentioned in Sections LIII and LIV, and in the manner in those Sections prescribed, he shall be liable to a fine not exceeding two hundred Rupees for every Emigrant so taken on board his vessel.—(*Sect*: 53. *See No.* 76.—*Sect*: 54. *See No.* 77.)

Idem, Art. 77. 100.—If the Master of any vessel cleared for any place to which Emigration shall be lawful under this Act, shall after having obtained a certificate in accordance with the provisions of Section XLVI, fraudulently do, or suffer to be done, any act or thing whereby such certificate shall become inapplicable to the altered state of the vessel, or other matter to which such certificate relates, such Master shall be liable to a fine not exceeding five

nah ou ordre par écrit à la Police de l'aider lui-même ou d'aider toute autre personne à recruter des laboureurs pour un endroit quelconque hors de l'Inde Anglaise, ou qui représentera faussement que les dits laboureurs sont requis par le Gouvernement, ou qu'ils doivent être engagés pour le Gouvernement,—sera passible d'une amende qui n'excédera pas cinq cents roupies.

97.—Tout capitaine de navire qui n'aura pas obtenu l'autorisation prescrite par la Section 46, et qui recevra sciemment un Emigrant à bord de son bâtiment dans le but de le transporter dans un lieu quelconque contrairement aux dispositions de cet Acte, pourra être condamné à l'emprisonnement simple ou rigoureux pour un terme n'excédant pas un an, ainsi qu'à une amende n'excédant pas mille roupies pour chaque Emigrant qu'il aura reçu à son bord, et le navire pourra être confisqué.—(*Section* 46 : *voir le No.* 69.) **Idem, Art. 74.**

98.—Tout capitaine de navire qui fera expédier son bâtiment à Calcutta, à Madras, ou à Bombay pour un endroit auquel l'Emigration sera permise, et qui recevra un Emigrant à son bord avant d'avoir rempli toutes les formalités requises par les Sections 48 et 50, pourra être condamné à une amende n'excédant pas deux cents roupies pour chaque Emigrant qu'il aura ainsi embarqué.—(*Section* 48 : *voir le No.* 71.—*Section* 50 : *voir le No.* 73.) **Idem, Art. 75.**

99.—Tout capitaine qui, après avoir expédié son navire pour un endroit auquel l'émigration sera permise d'après cet Acte, recevra à son bord un Emigrant qui n'ait pas été porté sur les listes mentionnées dans les Sections 53 et 54 de la manière prescrite dans ces sections, pourra être condamné à une amende n'excédant pas deux cents roupies pour chaque émigrant qui aura été ainsi embarqué à bord de son navire.—(*Section* 53 : *voir le No.* 76.—*Section* 54 : *voir le No.* 77.) **Idem, Art. 76.**

100.—Tout Capitaine d'un navire expédié pour un Port auquel l'émigration sera permise d'après cet Acte, qui, après avoir obtenu un certificat selon les dispositions de la Section XLVI, commettra, ou laissera commettre quelque acte frauduleux, ou quoi que ce soit qui puisse rendre le dit certificat inapplicable au navire par suite des modifications qui y auront été apportées, ou toute autre chose concernant le certificat, sera passible d'une amende n'ex- **Idem, Art. 77.**

5

thousand Rupees, besides incurring a forfeiture of any bond executed in consideration of any license obtained for the vessel as originally described.—(*Sect* : 46. *See No.* 69.)

Idem, Art. 78. 101.—If the Master of a vessel sailing from the Port of Calcutta, licensed under Section XLVI, and sailing with Emigrants on board, shall without reasonable excuse, cause or allow his vessel to proceed from Garden Reach to Sea, or to proceed any part of the distance between Garden Reach and Sea, without his vessel being under tow of a competent Steamer, or if such vessel shall not have left Garden Reach and proceed on her voyage within the time prescribed in Section LIX, the Master of such vessel shall be liable to a fine not exceeding one thousand Rupees. (*Sect* : 46 *and* 59. *See Nos.* 69 *and* 82.)

Idem, Art. 79. 102.—All the powers vested by law in the Officers of Customs in regard to the searching and detention of vessels, or otherwise for the prevention of smuggling on board thereof, may be exercised by such Officers for the prevention of the illegal embarkation of Emigrants on board vessels bound for any place to which Emigration shall be lawful under this Act, and of other offences against this Act ; and all Pilots in the service of, or licensed by Government are hereby vested with the same powers, and charged with the same duties as Officers of Customs in this behalf.

Idem, Art. 80. 103.—Any Officer of Customs or Pilot who shall wilfully make a false, erroneous, or incomplete report of the Emigrants on board of any vessel, or who shall connive at the unauthorized embarkation of any Emigrants shall be liable, besides dismissal, to a fine of five hundred Rupees.

Idem, Art. 81. 104.—All prosecutions under this Act shall be instituted on information laid at the instance of an Emigration Agent, or of a Protector of Emigrants, or of an Officer appointed for the purpose by the local Government, before a Magistrate of Police, or before the Magistrate of the District, according as they shall be instituted for offences committed within or for offences committed beyond the limits of the Town of Calcutta, Madras and Bombay.

cédant pas cinq mille Roupies, en outre de la confiscation de la caution fournie pour obtenir une autorisation pour le navire ainsi qu'il est dit ci-dessus.—(*Section* 46 : *voir le No.* 69.)

101.—Tout Capitaine qui, muni d'une autorisation en vertu de l'Article XLVI, fera voile du Port de Calcutta avec des Emigrants à son bord, et qui, sans une excusé raisonable, fera parcourir, ou laissera faire parcourir à son navire la distance qui sépare Garden Reach de la mer, ou une partie quelconque de cette distance, sans que son navire soit remorqué par un steamer d'une force suffisante, ou qui n'aura pas quitté Garden Reach et pris la mer pendant le délai prescrit par la Section LIX, sera passible d'une amende qui n'excédera pas mille Roupies.—(*Sections* 46 *et* 59 : *voir les Nos.* 69 *et* 82.) **Idem, Art. 78.**

102.—Tous les pouvoirs que la loi accorde aux Officiers de Douane afin qu'ils puissent détenir et visiter les navires dans le but d'empêcher la contrebande, pourront être exercés par les dits Officiers dans le but d'empêcher l'embarquement illégal d'émigrants sur des navires destinés pour un Port auquel l'émigration sera permise en vertu de cet Acte, ou toute autre contravention au présent Acte ; et tous les Pilotes au service du Gouvernement, ou autorisés par le Gouvernement, sont par ces présentes revêtus des mêmes pouvoirs et chargés des mêmes fonctions qui, sous ce rapport, incombent aux Officiers de Douane. **Idem, Art. 79.**

103.—Tout Officier de Douane ou tout Pilote qui fera volontairement un rapport faux, erroné ou incomplet sur les Emigrants embarqués sur un navire quelconque, ou qui se prêtera à l'embarquement illégal d'émigrants, sera passible d'une amende de cinq cents Roupies et sera renvoyé du service. **Idem, Art. 80.**

104.—Toutes les poursuites en vertu du présent Acte seront instituées sur une plainte portée par un agent d'Emigration, par un Protecteur des Émigrants ou par le fonctionaire nommé à cet effet par le Gouvernment Local, devant un Magistrat de Police ou devant le Magistrat du District, selon qu'elles seront instituées pour des délits commis dans les limites des villes de Calcutta, de Madras et de Bombay, ou pour des délits commis hors des limites de ces villes. **Idem, Art. 81.**

All fines imposed under the authority of this Act, may, in case of non-payment thereof, be levied by distress and sale of the goods and chattels of the Offender, by warrant of the officer imposing the fine. When a warrant of distress is issued, the said Officer may order the Offender to be detained and kept in safe custody, until return can be conveniently made to such warrant, unless the Offender enter into a recognizance, with or without sureties, conditional for his appearance before him on the day appointed for such return, such day not being more than eight days from the time of taking such recognizance; but, if before issuing such warrant of distress, it shall appear to the Officer imposing the fine by the admission of the Offender or otherwise, that no sufficient distress can be had within the jurisdiction of such Officer whereon to levy such fine or penalty, he may, if he thinks fit, refrain from issuing such warrant of distress, and in such case, or if such warrant shall have been issued, and upon the return thereof such insufficiency as aforesaid shall be made to appear to the Officer imposing the fine, he shall, by warrant, commit the Offender to jail, there to be imprisoned, with or without labor, for any term not exceeding two months where the amount of the fine shall not exceed fifty Rupees, and for any term not exceeding four months where the amount shall not exceed one hundred Rupees, and for any term not exceeding six months in any other case; the commitment to be terminable in each of the cases aforesaid on payment of the amount. The fine, or any part thereof which remains unpaid, may be levied at any time within six years after the passing of the order imposing it; and the death of the Offender does not discharge from the liability any property which would, after his death, be legally liable for his debts.

Idem, Art. 82. 105.—It shall be lawful for the local Government, from time to time, to authorize any person invested with the powers of a Magistrate, as defined in the Code of Criminal Procedure, to perform the duties, and exercise the powers by this Act assigned to, and conferred on, the Magistrate of the District; and every person so authorized, shall, in all respects for the purposes of this Act, be deemed to be included in the words "the Magistrate of the District."

Toutes les amendes infligées en vertu de cet Acte pourront, en cas de non-paiement, être recouvrées par la saisie et la vente des biens, meubles et effets mobiliers du délinquant, sur l'ordre du fonctionnaire qui aura infligé l'amende. Lorsqu'il aura délivré un ordre de saisie, le dit Fonctionnaire pourra ordonner la détention et l'emprisonnement du délinquant jusqu'à ce que l'huissier ait eu un temps convenable pour faire son rapport, à moins que le délinquant ne fournisse un cautionnement, avec ou sans cautions, pour comparaître devant lui le jour fixé pour l'audience, pourvu qu'il n'y ait pas un intervalle de plus de huit jours entre la date du cautionnement et le dit jour d'audience ; mais si, avant de délivrer le dit ordre de saisie, il paraît au fonctionnaire qui aura imposé l'amende, sur la déclaration du délinquant ou autrement, qu'il ne pourra saisir dans sa juridiction suffisamment de biens pour en recouvrer la dite amende ou pénalité, il pourra, s'il le juge convenable, s'abstenir de délivrer le dit ordre de saisie ; et dans le cas ci-dessus, ou bien, dans le cas ou après la délivrance du dit ordre de saisie, le fonctionnaire qui aura imposé l'amende jugerait, d'après le rapport de l'huissier, qu'il y a insuffisance, il devra ordonner l'emprisonnement du délinquant, avec ou sans travaux forcés, pour un temps qui n'excédera pas deux mois lorsque l'amende ne dépassera pas cinquante Roupies, et pour un temps qui n'excédera pas quatre mois lorsque l'amende ne dépassera pas cent Roupies, et pour un temps qui n'excédera pas six mois dans tous les autres cas ; le dit emprisonnement devant cesser sur le paiement de l'amende. L'amende, ou toute fraction d'icelle qui n'aura pas été payée, pourra être recouvrée de la même manière dans les six ans qui suivront la condamnation, et, après la mort du délinquant, on pourra poursuivre le recouvrement de la dite amende sur tous les biens qui resteront le gage de ses dettes.

105.—Le Gouvernement local pourra de temps à autre autoriser toute personne revêtue des pouvoirs d'un Magistrat, tels que ces pouvoirs sont définis dans le Code de Procédure Criminelle, à remplir les fonctions et à exercer les pouvoirs que le présent Acte assigne et confère au Magistrat de District, et toute personne ainsi autorisée, devra, sous tous les rapports, pour les fins du présent Acte, être considérée comme étant désignée par ces mots : " Magistrat du District." **Idem, Art. 82**

Idem, Art. 83. 106.—So much of Section VIII of Act XLVI of 1860, as enacts that a fee not exceeding one Rupee per Emigrant, as may be regulated from time to time by the local Government, shall be demandable in respect of every license in the said Section mentioned, is hereby repealed. Save as aforesaid, nothing in this Act shall be held to repeal the said Act XLVI of 1860, or Act VII of 1862: but Section XIX to Section XLI, both included, being provisions for regulating the recruitment of Native laborers, which will have effect on the recruitment of laborers for British Colonies, shall, as provided in Section IV of the said Act XLVI of 1860, apply to Emigration under the said Acts XLVI of 1860, and VII of 1862.*—(*Sect*: 19. *See No.* 42.—*Sect*: 41. *See No.* 64.)

Idem, Art. 84. 107.—This Act shall come into operation on the first day of July 1864.

Idem, Art. 85. 108.—Nothing in this Act or in any Rule to be made by the Governor-General of India in Council under Section LXIII, shall apply to any vessel in the service of the Lords Commissioners of the Admiralty, or to any of Her Majesty's Vessels.—(*Sect*: 63. *See No.* 86.)

Ord. No. 16 of 1862, Art. 1. 109.—Requisitions by persons in Mauritius wishing to introduce or engage Immigrants from India, shall, in future, be framed in terms of Schedule A, hereto annexed; and shall be made alternatively for male Immigrants to be engaged in India to serve the Requisitionists, or for male Immigrants to be allotted to Requisitionists in Mauritius.

SCHEDULE A.

Requisition.

I, the undersigned Requisitionist, request the Protector of Immigrants to take the steps required by law for obtaining for me from the Presidency of Male Immigrants (*specially engaged in India*

* Act XLVI of 1860 and Act VII of 1862 authorize Emigration of Natives of India to the French Colonies.

106.—La portion de la Section VIII de l'Acte XLVI de 1860, qui décrète qu'un droit qui n'excèdera pas une Roupie par Emigrant, et qui pourra être fixé de temps à autre par le Gouvernement local, pourra être perçu pour chaque autorisation dont mention est faite dans la dite Section, est, par ces présentes, abrogée. Excepté comme il est dit ci-dessus, aucune des dispositions du présent Acte ne sera considérée comme abrogeant le dit Acte XLVI de 1860, ou l'Acte VII de 1862; mais les dispositions comprises entre les Sections XIX et XLI inclusivement, étant des dispositions promulguées dans le but de régler le recrutement des Laboureurs indigènes et qui affecteront le recrutement des Laboureurs pour les Colonies Anglaises, s'appliqueront, ainsi qu'il est prévu dans la Section IV du dit Acte XLVI de 1860, à l'Emigration qui aura lieu en vertu des dits Actes XLVI de 1860 et VII de 1862.*—(*Section* 19 : *voir le No.* 42.—*Section* 41 : *voir le No.* 64.) Idem, Art. 83.

107.—Le présent Acte aura force de loi à partir du 1er Juillet 1864. Idem, Art. 84.

108.—Rien de ce qui est contenu dans le présent Acte, ni aucun réglement qui pourra être fait par le Gouverneur-Général de l'Inde en Conseil en vertu de la Section LXIII, ne s'appliquera à un navire au service des Lords Commissaires de l'Amirauté, ou à aucun des vaisseaux de Sa Majesté.—(*Section* 63 : *voir le No.* 86.) Idem, Art. 85.

109.—Les demandes par les personnes à Maurice qui désireront introduire ou engager des Immigrants de l'Inde, seront à l'avenir faites conformément à la Cédule A ci-annexée, et seront faites alternativement pour des Immigrants à engager dans l'Inde, au service des requérants, ou pour des Immigrants à répartir entre les requérants à Maurice. Ord. No. 16 de 1862, Art. 1.

CÉDULE A.

Réquisition.

. Je soussigné Requérant, prie le Protecteur des Immigrants de prendre les mesures requises par la loi, pour obtenir pour moi de la Présidence de Immigrants (*engagés spécialement dans l'Inde pour*

* Les Actes XLVI de 1860 et VII de 1862 se rapportent à l'émigration des Laboureurs indigènes aux Colonies Françaises.

to be employed by me, or,—to be allotted to me on their arrival at Mauritius for employment—as the case may be), as on the Estate, in the District of

I undertake to give to each Immigrant who shall engage with me in virtue of this requisition, the wages and allowances following: (*or the wages and allowances fixed by the Government Scale in force at the time of engagement,—as the case may be*).

(*This scale is liable to be modified from time to time* (*see No.* 113) *and is therefore not inserted here.—See Appendix.*)

Proper lodging and medical care shall also be furnished by me to the said Immigrants.

I appoint A. B. my Special Agent, (*or—I appoint no Special Agent,—as the case may be.*)

C. D.,
Requisitionist.

The above requisition has been received by me this day of 186 .

E. F.,
Protector of Immigrants.

Govt. Notice No. 166 of 11th Nov. 1868 Art. 1.

110.—Every requisition under Article 1 of Ordinance No. 16 of 1862 shall be made in triplicate. One copy thereof shall be retained by the Protector of Immigrants; another, signed or initialed by him, and bearing the date of its registration, shall be returned by him to the Requisitionist; and the third shall be forwarded by the Protector of Immigrants to the Emigration Agent for Mauritius at the port of India whence the Immigrants are required.—(*Art.* 1 *of Ord.* 16 *of* 1862. *See No.* 109.)

Idem, Art. 3.

111.—When any requisition shall specify the Wages and Allowances which the Requisitionist undertakes to give, the said Wages shall not be less than eight shillings sterling per calendar month for each male Immigrant above 18 years of age; and the said Allowances shall not be less than the following:—

Rice, one pound and a half, or two pounds of pounded maize, or two pounds and a half of cooked manioc, or five pounds of raw manioc	per diem.
Dholl, half a pound	„ week.
Salt fish, half a pound	„ „
Ghee or Oil, four ounces	„ „
Salt, four ounces	„ „

être employés par moi, ou pour m'être délivrés à leur arrivée à Maurice pour me servir selon le cas) comme sur la Propriété dans le District de

Je m'engage à donner à chaque Immigrant qui s'engagera avec moi en vertu de cette Réquisition (les gages et rations suivants :—*ou les gages et rations fixés par l'échelle du Gouvernement en vigueur à l'époque de l'engagement—selon le cas*) :

(*Cette échelle pouvant être modifiée de temps à autre* (*voir le No.* 113) *n'est pas pour cette raison donnée ici.—Voir l'Appendice.*)

Un logement convenable et les soins médicaux seront aussi par moi donnés aux dits Immigrants.

(Je nomme A. B. mon agent spécial, (*ou—Je ne nomme aucun agent spécial,—selon le cas*).

C. D.,
Requérant.

La réquisition ci-dessus a été reçue par moi, ce jour de 186 .

E. F.
Protecteur des Immigrants.

110.—Chaque réquisition en vertu de l'Article 1er de l'Ordonnance No. 16 de 1862 sera faite en triplicata. Un des originaux sera gardé par le Protecteur des Immigrants, un autre signé par lui ou portant ses initiales ainsi que la date de son enregistrement, sera rendu par lui au Requérant, et le troisième sera envoyé par le Protecteur des Immigrants à l'Agent de l'Emigration pour Maurice au port de l'Inde d'où les Immigrants sont demandés.—(*Art.* 1 *de l'Ord.* 16 *de* 1862 : *voir le No.* 109.) **Avis du Gouv. No. 166 du 11 Nov. 1868, Art. 1.**

111.—Lorsqu'une réquisition spécifiera les gages et rations que le requérant s'engage à donner, les dits gages ne seront pas au-dessous de huit shellings par mois, pour chaque Immigrant au-dessus de 18 ans ; et les dites rations ne seront pas au-dessous des suivantes : **Idem, Art. 3.**

Riz, une livre et demie, ou deux livres de maïs concassé, ou deux livres et demi de manioc cuit, ou cinq livres de manioc cru	par jour.
Dholl, une demi-livre	par semaine.
Poisson salé, une demi-livre	„
Mantègue ou huile, quatre onces	„
Sel, quatre onces	„

When any requisition shall be made for male Immigrants under 18 years of age, or for female Immigrants, the minimum rates of the wages and allowances to be proposed to them shall be fixed by the Protector of Immigrants.

Idem, Art. 4. 112.—For all cases in which no wages and allowances shall be stipulated in the Requisition, or in which Requisitionists will leave it to Government to stipulate on their behalf the wages and allowances to be proposed to intending Emigrants in India, a Government *Scale of Wages* and Allowances shall be framed and published and shall be communicated to the Emigration Agents of the Colony for their guidance.—(*Scale of wages, &c.—See No.* 109).

Idem, Art. 5. 113.—Such Government Scale shall be liable to be altered from time to time as the Governor may deem proper as regards any future contracts.

Ord. No. 16 of 1862, Art. 2. 114.—Every such requisition shall be accompanied by a Bond in the form and terms of Schedule B, hereto annexed,—which shall be signed by the Requisitionist and two Sureties, on whose sufficiency the Protector of Immigrants for the time being shall determine.

SCHEDULE B.

Requisitionist's Bond.

A. B., of (*dwelling-place, and profession or calling.*)
C. D., of (*do.* *do.*)
and E. F, of (*do.* *do.*) hereby jointly and severally promise and bind themselves towards the Protector of Immigrants on behalf of the Government of Mauritius, as follows :

The said A. B. having this day made requisition under the provisions of Ordinance No. for Indian Immigrants (*to be specially engaged in India, or to be allotted to him on their arrival at Mauritius,—as the case may be*), hereby undertakes to accept that number or any lesser number of Immigrants that may be introduced, pursuant to his requisition. The said Requisitionist, and the said C. D. and E. F. acting as Sureties for the said Requisitionist, bind themselves jointly and severally to pay all expenses attendant upon the introduction of such Immigrants and of the females by regulation required to accompany them, including in such expenses the cost of the maintenance of such Immigrants at the Port Louis Depôt, at the rate of six pence per diem for each Immigrant, from the date of his landing until the date of his leaving the Depôt to enter on the service of the said Requisitionist. The said Requisitionist and the said Sureties promise to pay to the Protector of Immigrants all such expenses of introduction upon

Lorsqu'une réquisition sera faite pour des Immigrants au-dessous de 18 ans, ou pour des Immigrantes, le minimum des gages et des rations qu'on pourra leur offrir, sera fixé par le Protecteur des Immigrants.

112.—Dans tous les cas où il n'aura été stipulé ni gages ni rations dans la Réquisition, ou dans ceux où les Requérants laisseront au Gouvernement de stipuler pour eux les gages et rations à proposer aux Emigrants ayant l'intention de quitter l'Inde, une *Echelle du Gouvernement pour les gages* et les rations sera préparée et publiée, et sera communiquée aux Agents de l'Emigration de la Colonie pour leur servir de guide.—(*Echelle de gages, &c.—Voir le No.* 109.) Idem, Art. 4.

113.—Cette Echelle du Gouvernement pourra être modifiée de temps à autre selon que le Gouverneur le jugera convenable, relativement aux contrats à venir. Idem, Art. 5.

114.—Chaque demande sera accompagnée d'une obligation dans la forme et teneur de la Cédule B ci-annexée,—qui sera signée du Requérant et de deux cautions dont la solvabilité sera laissée à l'appréciation du Protecteur des Immigrants alors en fonctions. Ord. No. 16 de 1862, Art. 2.

CÉDULE B.

Obligation du Requérant.

A. B. de (*demeure et profession ou état*).
C. D. de (*do.* *do.*)
et E. F. de (*do.* *do.*)
par ces présentes conjointement et individuellement promettent et s'obligent envers le Protecteur des Immigrants agissant pour le Gouvernement de Maurice, comme suit :

Le dit A. B. ayant ce jour fait une réquisition d'après les dispositions de l'Ordonnance No. pour Immigrants Indiens (*à être spécialement engagés dans l'Inde, ou à lui être délivrés à leur arrivée à Maurice,—selon le cas*), s'engage à accepter ce nombre ou tout nombre moindre d'Immigrants qui auront été introduits en vertu de cette réquisition. Le dit Requérant et les dits C. D. et E. F. agissant comme cautions du dit Requérant, s'obligent conjointement et individuellement à payer toutes les dépenses encourues pour l'introduction de ces Immigrants et des femmes qui, d'après les réglements, devront les accompagner, en comprenant dans ces dépenses les frais d'entretien de ces Immigrants au Dépôt du Port Louis, au taux de six pence par jour pour chaque Immigrant, à partir du jour de son débarquement jusqu'à la date de son départ du Dépôt pour entrer au service du dit Requérant. Le dit Requérant et les dites cautions promettent de payer

the said Immigrants being delivered to the said Requisitionist; such payment to be exigible previous to their leaving the Depôt.

In default of the said Requisitionist's claiming such Immigrants within seven clear days after they shall have been received at the Port Louis Depôt, the said Requisitionist and the said Sureties bind themselves to pay to the Protector of Immigrants one shilling per day for each Immigrant as his cost of maintenance during the interval between his arrival at the Depôt and his entering on service; and in case of such default and of any of the said Immigrants electing to be free from their engagement, the said Requisitionist and the said Sureties do further bind themselves to pay to the Protector the whole expense attending the introduction of the Immigrants so electing and of the females accompanying them.

The said Requisitionist and the said Sureties hereby consent that the Certificate of the Protector of Immigrants shall be conclusive evidence against them, in all Courts and places, of the amount chargeable against them, in respect of the said expenses of introduction, or of the said cost of maintenance, as the case may be.

Approved : A. B., Requisitionist.
Approved : C. D., Surety.
Approved : E. F., Surety.

The above Bond has been signed in my presence and deposited with me this day of 186 .

G. H.,
Protector of Immigrants.

Idem, Art. 3 **115.**—Every such requisition shall remain in force for the period of twelve months, and no longer, from its date to the date of any Contract passed in India in execution thereof.

Provided, that any Requisitionist may stipulate that his requisition shall remain in force for any shorter period to be specified by him.

Govt. Notice No. 166 of 11th Nov. 1868 Art. 2. **116.**—Any requisition may be cancelled, by the Requisitionist's subscribing in the Immigration office a withdrawal in the form of the Schedule A hereunto annexed; but such withdrawal shall only take effect one month after it shall have reached the Emigration Agent to whom the Requisition has been forwarded.

SCHEDULE A.

Withdrawal of Requisition.

I request that steps be taken by the Protector of Immigrants to cancel the Requisition No. of 186 signed by on the

au Protecteur des Immigrants tous ces frais d'introduction lorsque les dits Immigrants seront livrés au dit Requérant ; ce paiement sera exigible avant qu'ils ne quittent le Dépôt.

Faute par le dit Requérant de réclamer ces Immigrants dans le délai de sept jours pleins après qu'ils auront été reçus au Dépôt du Port Louis, le dit Requérant et les dites cautions s'engagent à payer au Protecteur des Immigrants un schelling par jour pour chaque Immigrant pour les frais de son entretien pendant l'intervalle entre son arrivée au Dépôt et son entrée en Service ; et dans le cas de pareil défaut, et si quelques uns des Immigrants désiraient être affranchis de leur engagement, le dit Requérant et ses dites cautions s'engagent en outre à payer au Protecteur toutes dépenses faites pour l'introduction des Immigrants dont le désir sera tel, et des femmes les accompagnant.

Le dit Requérant et les dites cautions consentent par ces présentes, à ce que le certificat du Protecteur des Immigrants soit preuve concluante contre eux, dans toutes les cours et places, de la somme due par eux relativement aux dites dépenses d'introduction ou des frais d'entretien, selon le cas.

Approuvé : A. B., Requérant.
Approuvé : C. D., Caution.
Approuvé : E. F., Caution.

L'obligation ci-dessus a été signée en ma présence et déposée entre mes mains ce jour de 186 .

G. H.,
Protecteur des Immigrants.

115.—Chaque demande de ce genre sera en vigueur pendant douze mois, et pas davantage, à compter de sa date à la date de tout Contrat passé dans l'Inde, en exécution de la dite demande. Idem, Art. 3

Cependant tout requérant pourra stipuler que sa demande ne sera en vigueur que pendant un temps plus court qu'il aura à indiquer.

116.—Toute réquisition pourra être annulée si le Requérant signe au Bureau de l'Immigration un acte, par lequel il la retire, dans la forme de la Cédule A, annexée à ces présentes ; mais cet acte de retrait, n'aura son effet qu'un mois seulement après qu'il aura été reçu par l'Agent de l'Emigration auquel la Réquisition a été envoyée. Avis du Gouv. No. 166 du 11 Nov. 1868, Art. 2.

CÉDULE A.

Annulation de la Réquisition.

Je requiers que le Protecteur des Immigrants prenne des mesures pour annuller la Réquisition No. de 186 signée

day of last for Immigrants to be engaged for at

Immigration Office, 186 .

Forwarded for the information and guidance of the Mauritius Emigration Agent at

H. B.,
Protector of Immigrants, Mauritius.

Ord. No. 16 of 1862, Art. 5. **117.**—Every Male Immigrant leaving India to come to Mauritius for hire, shall, before leaving India, either be engaged to an employer named in his Contract, or shall be taken bound to serve an employer to whom he shall be allotted by the Protector of Immigrants, on his arrival at Mauritius.

Idem, Art. 6. **118.**—Every such Immigrant shall, in India, sign a Contract either in the terms and form of Schedule C, or in the form of Schedule D, hereto annexed, according as it may be necessary for him to enter into a Special Contract to serve an individual employer therein named, or a Contract with the Government of Mauritius to serve any employer to whom he may be allotted by this Government; and, in either case, the Contract to be so signed, shall, *inter alia,* bind him to a service for five years.

SCHEDULE C.

SPECIAL CONTRACT FOR MAURITIUS.

Entered into under Requisition No. dated 186 .

We, the undersigned Immigrants from hereby engage to serve as on the Estate called in the District of in the Island of Mauritius, for the period of five years from the date of the registration of this Contract by the Protector of Immigrants at Mauritius; provided that we shall receive the Wages stated hereunder opposite to our respective names, and the Allowances following:

Rice, one pound and a half, or two pounds of pounded maize, or two pounds and a half of cooked manioc, or five pounds of raw manioc	per diem.	Half of these rations to be given to those of us who are under 10 years of age.
Dholl, two pounds	per mensem.	
Salt Fish, two pounds ...	do.	
Ghee or Oil, one pound ...	do.	
Salt, one pound...	do.	

Provided also that proper lodging and medical care shall be supplied to us.

par le dernier pour Immigrants à être engagés pour à

Bureau de l'Emigration, 186 .

Transmise pour l'information et la gouverne de l'Agent de l'Emigration pour Maurice à

H. B.,

Protecteur des Immigrants à Maurice.

117.—Tout Immigrant partant de l'Inde pour venir travailler à gages à Maurice, sera, avant de quitter l'Inde, engagé à un employeur qui sera désigné dans son contrat, ou engagé à un employeur auquel il devra être alloué par le Protecteur des Immigrants à son arrivée à Maurice. Ord. No. 16 de 1862, Art. 5.

118.—Chacun de ces Immigrants signera dans l'Inde un contrat soit dans les termes et la forme de la Cédule C, soit dans la forme de la Cédule D, ci-annexées, selon qu'il lui faudra passer un Contrat spécial pour servir un employeur particulier y dénommé, ou un Contrat avec le Gouvernement de Maurice pour servir tout employeur auquel il pourra être alloué par le Gouvernement ; et ce contrat *inter alia* l'obligera à un service de cinq ans. Idem, Art. 6.

CÉDULE C.

CONTRAT SPÉCIAL POUR MAURICE.

Passé en vertu de la Réquisition No. datée 186 .

Nous soussignés, Emigrants de nous engageons par ces présentes à servir comme sur la propriété appelée dans le district de à l'Ile Maurice, pendant une période de cinq années à compter de la date de l'enregistrement de ce Contrat par le Protecteur des Immigrants à Maurice ; à la condition que nous recevions les gages indiqués en regard de nos noms respectifs et les rations suivantes :

Riz, une livre et demie, ou deux livres de maïs moulu, ou deux livres et demie de manioc cuit, ou cinq livres de manioc cru	par jour.	La moitié seulement de ces rations sera donnée à ceux d'entre nous qui auront moins de 10 ans.
Dholl, deux livres	par mois.	
Poisson salé, deux livres... ...	do.	
Mantègue ou huile, une livre...	do.	
Sel, une livre	do.	

A la condition aussi qu'un logement convenable et des soins médicaux nous seront donnés.

And we further agree that if the above-mentioned Estate be sold, alienated, or transferred to another person, or succeeded to by another person, before the expiration of our service, we shall serve such other person according to the terms of this Contract; such new Employer being held bound towards us in all the stipulations and obligations incumbent upon the Employer so replaced by him.

No.	Name of Emigrants.	Father's Name.	Age.	Married or Single.	WAGES PER MONTH.					Emigrant's Signature.	Remarks.
					1st Year.	2nd Year.	3rd Year.	4th Year.	5th Year.		

On behalf of   of Mauritius, I accept the services of the above-mentioned Emigrants on the terms and conditions hereabove stipulated.

A. B.,
Special Agent.

The above Contract was fully explained to the above-mentioned Emigrants (*and when there is a Special Agent*) to A. B. the Special Agent) in my presence this   and signed by them before me.

C. D.
Mauritius Emigration Agent.

SCHEDULE D.

CONTRACT WITH THE GOVERNMENT OF MAURITIUS.

Entered into under Requisition from the Protector of Immigrants at Mauritius, dated   186 .

We, the undersigned Emigrants from   to Mauritius, hereby engage to serve the Employers whom we may respectively be allotted to by the Government of Mauritius during the period of five years from the date of our allotment in Mauritius; provided that we shall receive the Wages stated hereunder opposite our respective names, and the Allowances following:

Et en outre nous consentons, si la propriété ci-dessus mentionnée venait à être vendue, aliénée ou transférée à une autre personne, ou venait à échoir par héritage à une autre personne avant l'expiration de notre engagement, à servir la dite autre personne suivant les termes de notre Contrat, ce nouvel Employeur s'engageant envers nous à remplir toutes les stipulations et obligations à la charge de l'Employeur ainsi remplacé par lui.

No.	Noms.	Noms de leur Père.	Age.	Mariés ou non mariés.	GAGES MENSUELS.					Signature des Emigrants.	Remarques.
					1re Année.	2me Année.	3me Année.	4me Année.	5me Année.		

Au nom de de Maurice j'accepte les services des Emigrants ci-dessus dénommés aux conditions ci-dessus stipulées.

A. B.,
Agent Spécial.

Le Contrat ci-dessus a été parfaitement expliqué aux Emigrants ci-dessus dénommés (*et quand il y a un Agent Spécial*, à A. B., Agent Spécial) en ma présence, ce et signé par eux devant moi.

C. D.,
Agent de l'Emigration pour Maurice.

SCHEDULE D.

CONTRAT AVEC LE GOUVERNEMENT DE MAURICE.

Passé en vertu de la Réquisition reçue du Protecteur des Immigrants à Maurice, datée 186 .

Nous soussignés, Emigrants de pour Maurice nous engageons à servir les Employeurs auxquels nous pourrons être respectivement répartis par le Gouvernement de Maurice pendant une période de cinq années à compter de la date de cette répartition, à la condition que nous recevrons les gages mentionnés en regard de nos noms respectifs, et les rations suivantes :

Rice, one pound and a half,—or two pounds of pounded maize, or two pounds and a half of cooked manioc, or five pounds of raw manioc	per diem.	Half of these rations only to be given to those of us who are under ten years of age.
Dholl, two pounds	per mensem.	
Salt Fish two pounds ...	do.	
Ghee, or Oil, one pound...	do.	
Salt, one pound...	do.	

Provided also that proper lodging and medical care shall be supplied to us during the time of our service.

And we further agree that if the Estates on which we shall become bound to serve under the aforesaid allotment, be sold, alienated, or transferred to other persons, or succeeded to by other persons, before the expiration of our service, we shall serve such other persons according to the conditions of our respective Contracts and until their expiration, our said new Employers being held bound towards us in all the stipulations and obligations incumbent upon the Employers to whom we shall previously have been allotted.

No.	Name of Emigrant.	Father's Name.	Age.	Married or Single.	WAGES PER MONTH. 1st Year.	2nd Year.	3rd Year.	4th Year.	5th Year	Emigrant's Signature.	Remarks.

The above Contract was explained in my presence to the said Emigrants and signed by them before me, this day of 186 .

A. B.,

Mauritius Emigration Agent.

Govt. Notice No. 166 of 11th Nov. 1868 Art. 7.

119.—In all cases in which advances of wages shall be demanded in India by Emigrants before their embarkation, such advances shall not exceed the amount of one month's wages, and shall only be made to them on their consenting to the insertion of the following clause into their contract of service :—

" We acknowledge having received the advances of wages borne opposite to our respective names, and agree to deductions being made from our wages in Mauritius, to the extent of one fourth of the rates at which we respectively engage to serve, until the full

Riz, une livre et demie,—ou deux livres de maïs moulu, ou deux livres et demie de manioc cuit, ou cinq livres de manioc cru .. .. par jour.		La moitié seulement de ces rations sera donnée à ceux d'entre nous qui auront moins de dix ans.
Dholl, deux livres ... ... par mois.		
Poisson salé, deux livres... ... do.		
Mantègue, ou huile, une livre ... do.		
Sel, une livre ... ... do.		

A la condition aussi qu'un logement convenable et des soins médicaux nous seront donnés pendant la durée de notre service.

Et nous consentons en outre, si les propriétés sur lesquelles nous serons obligés de servir, en vertu de la dite répartition, venaient à être vendues, aliénées, ou transférées à d'autres personnes, ou venaient à échoir par héritage à d'autres personnes, avant l'expiration de notre service, à servir ces autres personnes d'après les conditions de nos contrats respectifs et jusqu'à leur expiration, nos dits nouveaux employeurs étant tenus de remplir toutes les stipulations et obligations à la charge des employeurs auxquels nousa vions d'abord été répartis.

No.	Nom de l'Immigrant.	Nom du Père.	Age.	Marié ou non marié.	GAGES MENSUELS'					Signature de l'Emigrant.	Remarques.
					1re Année.	2me Année.	3me Année.	4me Année.	5me Année.		

Le Contrat ci-dessus a été expliqué en ma présence aux dits Emigrants, et signé par eux devant moi ce jour de 186

A. B.,

Agent de l'Emigration pour Maurice.

119.—Dans tous les cas où des avances de gages seront demandées dans l'Inde par des Emigrants avant leur embarquement, ces avances n'excéderont pas le montant des gages d'un mois, et ne leur seront faites que s'ils consentent à l'insertion de la clause suivante dans leur contrat de service :— Avis du Gouv. No. 166 du 11 Nov. 1868, Art. 7.

" Nous reconnaissons avoir reçu les avances de gages portées en
" regard de nos noms respectifs, et nous consentons à ce que des
" déductions mensuelles soient faites de nos gages à Maurice, jus-
" qu'à concurrence d'un quart des sommes pour lesquelles nous

amount of such advances shall have been recovered by our Employers."

Idem, Art. 6. 120.—The Emigration Agent shall carefully explain to each intending Emigrant the terms and conditions of the engagement proposed to him, and shall not allow any contract to be executed by intending Emigrants unless he be satisfied that the conditions thereof are fully understood by each of them.

Idem, Art. 8. 121.—The Emigration Agent shall, as soon as practicable after the execution of each contract, despatch the Emigrants engaged therein to the Protector of Immigrants in Mauritius, forwarding with them their contract in duplicate, their passes, and the other papers and documents required by law to be despatched with them.

Idem, Art. 9. 122.—He shall also despatch with every gang of male Emigrants the number of females required by the rules in force at the time.*

Ord. No. 31 of 1867, Art. 9. 123.—If any New Immigrant, on first introduction, be under the age of 10 years, he shall, on attaining that age, be liable to work for his introducer or substituted employer at the Government Scale for the time being of Wages and Allowances, until the expiry of the term of industrial residence of the relative or friend under whose charge such Immigrant shall have been introduced, or for so much of such term as such relative or friend shall continue in the service of such employer.

Govt. Notice No. 166 of 11th Nov. 1868 Art. 10. 124.—The arrival at Port Louis of any Immigrants engaged in India under requisitions forwarded as hereabove mentioned, and the day on which such Immigrants may leave the Immigration Depot, shall be announced by the Protector of Immigrants, as soon as possible after their arrival, in one or more of the colonial newspapers.

Ord. No. 16 of 1862, Art. 4. 125.—Any Immigrant who shall be engaged or allotted to any person in terms of any such requisition, shall be held to have been introduced into the Colony at the expense of the Requisitionist,

---

* Under the present arrangements, 40 women are despatched with each gang of 100 men.

" nous sommes respectivement engagés à servir, jusqu'à ce que le " montant total de ces avances aient été recouvré par notre em- " ployeur."

120.—L'Agent de l'Emigration expliquera avec soin à chaque Emigrant ayant l'intention de partir, les termes et les conditions de l'engagement qui lui sera proposé ; et il ne permettra pas aux Emigrants ayant l'intention de partir de s'engager par contrat, à moins qu'il ne soit satisfait que les conditions de ce contrat ont été entièrement comprises par chacun d'eux. Idem, Art. 6.

121.—L'Agent de l'Emigration devra, aussitôt que cela sera possible après que le contrat aura été passé, expédier les Emigrants qui se seront engagés par ce contrat, au Protecteur des Immigrants à Maurice, et envoyer en même temps qu'eux leur contrat en duplicata, leurs passes, et les autres papiers et documents requis par la loi et qui doivent être envoyés avec eux. Idem, Art. 8.

122.—Il expédiera aussi avec chaque bande d'Emigrants du sexe masculin le nombre de femmes requis par les réglements en vigueur à ce moment.* Idem, Art 9

123.—Si un nouvel Immigrant, lors de sa première introduction, a moins de 10 ans, il pourra, lorsqu'il atteindra cet âge, être obligé de travailler pour celui qui l'aura introduit ou pour celui qui aura été substitué à ce dernier aux gages et rations fixés par l'échelle du Gouvernement alors en vigueur, jusqu'à l'expiration de la résidence industrielle du parent ou de l'ami sous la garde duquel cet Immigrant aura été introduit, ou pour tout le temps que ce parent ou cet ami passera au service de cet Employeur. Ord. No. 31 de 1867, Art. 9.

124.—L'arrivée au Port Louis d'Immigrants engagés dans l'Inde en vertu des réquisitions envoyées ainsi qu'il est expliqué plus haut, et le jour que les Immigrants pourront quitter le Dépôt de l'Immigration, seront annoncés par le Protecteur des Immigrants, aussitôt après leur arrivée, dans un ou plusieurs des journaux de la Colonie. Avis du Gouv. No. 166 du 11 Nov. 1868, Art. 10.

125.—Tout Immigrant qui sera engagé à une personne ou qui lui sera réparti en vertu d'une demande de cette nature, sera considéré comme ayant été introduit dans la Colonie aux frais du re- Ord. No. 16 de 1862, Art. 4.

* D'après les réglements actuellement en vigueur, 40 femmes doivent être expédiées avec chaque bande de 100 hommes.

who shall be bound, in the first instance, to repay to the Government the whole expense of introduction of such Immigrant, and other incidental expenses, including the proportional expense of introducing Females. Any sums on these accounts which may be recovered from any substituted, or other employer of the Immigrant, shall be applied towards extinction or diminution of such obligation to repay.

Idem, Art. 22. 126.—All sums due to Government under any Bonds which shall have been executed in virtue of the provisions of *Ordinance No.* 5 *of* 1849, and all sums due to Government for the introduction, engagement, or allotment of any new Immigrant whatever, shall be recoverable in any District Court in which the party liable to the same shall have his domicil at the time;—notwithstanding that the amount of any such debt aforesaid may be beyond the ordinary jurisdiction of District Courts. (*Ord.* 5 *of* 1849 *was repealed by Ord.* 31 *of* 1867.)

In case of such debt being due upon any Bond, the District Magistrate shall entertain, and proceed in the cause, and shall give judgment in the same respectively, upon receiving a written application from the Protector of Immigrants for the time being, without its being necessary for any person or officer to attend the District Court in such cause.

Govt. Notice No. 166 of 11th Nov. 1868 Art. 11. 127.—An acquittance in the form of the Schedule B hereto annexed, shall be delivered by the Protector on his receiving from any Requisitionist the cost of the introduction of any Immigrants imported for him. In such case, the Immigrants introduced for the Requisitionist shall also be immediately delivered to him, with a duplicate or copy of their contract, and the tickets belonging to them.

SCHEDULE B.

Acquittance for costs of introduction.

I hereby acknowledge having received from the sum of pounds shillings and pence sterling, being the full amount of the costs attending the introduction of Immigrants who have been this day delivered over to

Immigration Office, 186 .

H. B.,

Protector of Immigrants.

quérant qui sera dans l'obligation tout d'abord de rembourser au Gouvernement tous les frais d'introduction de cet Immigrant, et tous autres frais incidents y compris les frais proportionnels pour l'introduction des femmes.—Toutes sommes qui pourront être recouvrées en remboursement des frais ci-dessus, d'une personne subrogée aux droits de l'employeur ou de tout autre employeur de l'Immigrant, seront affectées à l'extinction ou à la réduction de la dite obligation.

126.—Toutes sommes dues au Gouvernement en vertu des obligations qui auront été souscrites en exécution des dispositions de *l'Ordonnance No.* 5 *de* 1849, et toutes sommes dues au Gouvernement pour l'introduction, l'engagement ou la répartition d'un nouvel Immigrant, seront recouvrables devant la Cour du District dans la juridiction de laquelle la partie qui les devra aura alors son domicile ; quoique le chiffre de la dette ci-dessus mentionnée puisse dépasser la limite de la juridiction ordinaire des Cours de District.—(*L'Ord.* 5 *de* 1849 *a été abrogée par l'Ord.* 31 *de* 1867.) Idem, Art. 22.

Dans le cas où ces sommes seraient dues en vertu d'une obligation écrite, le Magistrat de District connaîtra de l'affaire et rendra son jugement sur la demande qui lui en sera faite par écrit par le Protecteur des Immigrants en fonctions, sans qu'il soit nécessaire qu'aucune personne ou qu'aucun officier public se présente pour le Gouvernement devant la Cour de District.

127.—Une quittance dans la forme de la Cédule B annexée à ces présentes, sera remise par le Protecteur lorsqu'il recevra d'un requérant les frais de l'introduction des Immigrants importés pour lui. Dans ce cas, les Immigrants introduits pour le requérant lui seront aussi immédiatement remis avec un duplicata ou une copie de leur contrat, et les tickets leur appartenant. Avis du Gouv. No. 166 du 11 Nov. 1868, Art. 11.

CÉDULE B.

Quittance pour les frais d'introduction.

Je reconnais par ces présentes avoir reçu de la somme de livres schellings et pence sterling, représentant la totalité des frais d'introduction de Immigrants qui ont été délivrés ce jour à

Bureau de l'Immigration, 186 .

H. B.,

Protecteur des Immigrants.

Idem, Art. 12. 128.—Before such Immigrants leave the Immigration Depot, a Certificate of Engagement in the form of the Schedule C, shall be delivered to each of them by the Protector of Immigrants.

SCHEDULE C.

*Certificate of Engagement.**

I hereby certify that the undermentioned newly-arrived Immigrant has entered into a contract of service with Mr. of Estate, in the District of for five years from this day of one thousand eight hundred and sixty- :—

Name... ... ...
Father's Name... ... ...
Number ... ...
Age ... ...

H. B.,
Protector of Immigrants.

Ord. No. 31 of 1867, Art. 2. 129.—In case any Requisitionist shall not claim the Immigrants introduced under his requisition, whether specially engaged to him in India or otherwise, within seven days after their arrival at the Depot in Mauritius, (*such arrival* having been duly published or notified in terms of the Regulations to be made under the provisions of this Ordinance) the Protector of Immigrants shall be at liberty to allot such Immigrants to any other persons who may be willing to engage them. Such allotment may be made, if the Protector deem it necessary, upon payment of a less amount than the cost of introduction chargeable against the Requisitionist; and the amount received shall be applied in reduction of the amount due to Government by such Requisitionist in respect of the actual costs of introduction of the Immigrants so unclaimed by him.—(*Notification of arrival.—See No.* 124.)

Govt. Notice No. 166 of 11th Nov. 1868 Art. 13. 130.—A certificate of allotment in the terms of the Schedule D, hereto annexed, shall be delivered by the Protector of Immigrants to each Employer to whom an allotment of Immigrants shall be made in conformity with *Article* 2 *of Ordinance No.* 31 *of* 1867. Such certificate shall operate as a binding obligation on the Employers and Immigrants therein mentioned to enter into a Contract of Service in the terms therein specified.—(*Art.* 2 *of Ord.* 31 *of* 1867.—*See No.* 129.)

* For this document, a fee of one shilling is paid by the Employer to the Protector of Immigrants.

128.—Avant que ces Immigrants ne quittent le Dépôt de l'Immigration, un certificat d'engagement dans la forme de la Cédule C, sera délivré à chacun d'eux par le Protecteur des Immigrants. Idem, Art. 12.

CÉDULE C.

*Certificat d'Engagement.**

Je certifie par ces présentes que l'Immigrant ci-dessous dénommé, nouvellement arrivé en cette Colonie, a passé un contrat de service avec M de l'établissement dans le District de pour cinq ans à partir du mil huit cent soixante :—

Nom de l'Immigrant... ... ...
Nom de son père ... ...
Numéro ... ...
Age ... ...

H. B.,
Protecteur des Immigrants.

129.—Dans le cas où un Requérant ne réclamerait pas les Immigrants introduits en vertu de sa réquisition, qu'ils aient été spécialement engagés avec lui dans l'Inde ou autrement, dans les sept jours qui suivront leur arrivée au Dépôt à Maurice, (*cette arrivée* ayant été dûment publiée ou notifiée conformément aux Réglements qui seront faits en vertu des dispositions de la présente Ordonnance) le Protecteur des Immigrants sera libre de répartir ces Immigrants à toute autre personne qui serait disposée à les engager. Cette répartition pourra être faite, si le Protecteur le croit nécessaire, sur le paiement d'une somme moindre que les frais d'introduction dus par le Requérant ; et le montant reçu sera déduit de la somme due au Gouvernement par le Requérant pour les frais d'introduction des Immigrants qu'il n'aura pas réclamés ainsi qu'il vient d'être expliqué.—(*Notification de l'arrivée.—Voir le No.* 124.) Ord. No. 31 de 1867, Art. 2.

130.—Un certificat de répartition dans les termes de la Cédule D annexée à ces présentes, sera délivré par le Protecteur des Immigrants à chaque Employeur auquel une répartition d'Immigrants sera faite conformément à *l'Article* 2 *de l'Ordonnance No.* 31 *de* 1867. Ce certificat vaudra obligation, de la part des Employeurs et des Immigrants qui y seront mentionnés, de passer un contrat de service selon les conditions qui y seront spécifiées.—(*Art.* 2 *de l'Ordonnance* 31 *de* 1867.—*Voir le No.* 129.) Avis du Gouv. No. 166 du 11 Nov. 1868, Art. 13.

* L'Employeur paie pour ce document un droit d'un schelling au Protecteur des Immigrants.

SCHEDULE D.

Certificate of Allotment.

I certify that I have this day allotted to the Immigrants hereunder mentioned, to enter into a contract with for years, to be employed on the Estate in the District of as on the wages mentioned opposite to their respective names, and on the allowances of the Government Scale now in force.

Immigration Office, 186 ,

H. B.,
Protector of Immigrants.

LIST OF IMMIGRANTS ALLOTTED.

Name of Immigrant.	No.	Wages.			Name of Immigrants.	No.	Wages.		
		£	S.	D.			£	S.	D.

Idem, Art. 14. 131.—Every such certificate shall be full authority to the Stipendiary Magistrate having jurisdiction in the premises, to make out and execute a formal written contract of service in the terms of the Schedule E hereunto appended ; and in so doing, he shall not enquire whether the Immigrant and Employer consent to such contract, nor shall it be necessary for these parties to attend before him for the purpose of executing the same.

SCHEDULE E.

Contract of Service passed with allotted Immigrants.

For the Estate of in the District of

Be it remembered that on this day of in the year of Our Lord one thousand eight hundred and , , of , Employer under their Contract of Service having deposited in my hands a certificate of allotment of the Immigrants undermentioned, dated day of one thousand eight hundred and , and signed by Esquire, Protector of Immigrants, in terms of Ordinance No. 31 of 1867 and relative regulations, I, Esquire, a Stipendiary Magistrate of this Colony of Mauritius, do hereby declare that the said Immigrants are engaged to the said Employer in the capacity of for five years commencing on this date, and terminating on the day of one thousand eight hundred and .

CÉDULE D.

Certificat de Répartition.

Je certifie par ces présentes que les Immigrants ci-dessous mentionnés ont été répartis par moi à afin qu'ils passent un contrat avec pour ans, pour travailler sur l'établissement dans le District de aux gages mentionnés en regard de leurs noms avec les rations stipulées dans l'Echelle établie par le Gouvernement et actuellement en vigueur.

Bureau de l'Immigration, 186 .

H. B.,
Protecteur des Immigrants.

LISTE DES IMMIGRANTS RÉPARTIS.

Nom de l'Immigrant.	No.	Gages.			Nom de l'Immigrant.	No.	Gages.		
		£	s.	D.			£	s.	D.

131.—Chacun de ces certificats sera une autorisation suffisante pour que le Magistrat Stipendiaire ayant juridiction à cet effet, prépare et sanctionne un contrat de service écrit en bonne et due forme selon les termes de la Cédule E annexée à ces présentes, et en le faisant, il ne demandera pas si l'Immigrant et l'Employeur consentent à ce contrat, et il ne sera pas non plus nécessaire que ces parties se présentent devant lui dans le but de rendre ce contrat parfait. Idem, Art. 14.

CÉDULE E.

Contrat de Service passé avec des Immigrants répartis.

Pour l'Etablissement District de

Qu'il soit notoire que ce jour de en l'an de Notre-Seigneur mil huit cent , , de , Employeur en vertu d'un contrat de service, passé avec les Immigrants ci-dessus dénommés, ayant déposé entre mes mains un certificat de répartition des dits Immigrants, daté le de mil huit cent , et signé par , Protecteur des Immigrants, aux termes de l'Ordonnance No. 31 de 1867 et des réglements qui en dépendent, je soussigné, , Magistrat Stipendiaire de cette Colonie de Maurice, déclare par ces présentes que les dits Immigrants sont engagés au dit Employeur comme pour cinq ans à partir de cette date et à finir le jour de mil huit cent .

The conditions of the said engagement are that the said Immigrants shall be employed as

And it is further agreed that the said shall pay to the said Immigrants, the wages mentioned opposite to their respective names in the list hereto subjoined, and that such wages shall be paid monthly.

And it is also agreed that the services of the said Immigrants shall be further remunerated by the delivery to them of the various articles hereunder specified, vizt. :—

Rice	pounds	per diem.
Dholl	„	per week.
Salt Fish	„	„
Oil	„	„
Salt	„	„

Proper lodging and medical care shall be provided by the said to the said Immigrants.

And it is further agreed, that if the said shall, at any time, employ the said Immigrants on any other Estate than that which is known by the name of and situate in the District of except with the consent of the said Immigrants given in the presence of the Stipendiary Magistrate of the said District, then this present contract of service shall *ipso facto* become null and void.

And it is further agreed, that if the above mentioned Estate be sold, alienated or transferred to another person, or succeeded to by another person before the expiration of this present contract, the said Immigrants shall serve such other person according to the terms of this contract, such new Employer being held bound towards the said Immigrants in all the stipulations and obligations incumbent upon the Employer so replaced by him.

District of this day of one thousand eight hundred and sixty

H. D.,
Stipendiary Magistrate.

Name of Immigrant.	No.	Wages.			Name of Immigrant.	No.	Wages.		
		£	S.	D.			£	S.	D.

Idem, Art. 18. 132.—If a new Immigrant on his arrival, consent to have his contract transferred by his Introducer to another Employer, the Protector of Immigrants, on all parties to the transfer expressing

Les conditions du dit engagement sont que les dits Immigrants seront employés comme

Et il est en outre convenu que le dit paiera aux dits Immigrants les gages mentionnés en regard de leurs noms sur la liste ci-jointe et que ces gages seront payés mensuellement.

Et il est en outre convenu que les dits Immigrants recevront en sus les rations ci-dessous mentionnées, à savoir :

Riz	livres par jour.
Dholl	„ par semaine.
Poisson salé	„
Huile	„
Sel	„

Un logement convenable et des soins médicaux seront donnés par le dit aux dits Immigrants.

Et il est en outre convenu que si le dit faisait à une époque quelconque travailler les dits Immigrants sur tout autre établissement que celui qui est connu sous le nom de dans le District de excepté avec le consentement des dits Immigrants donné en présence du Magistrat Stipendiaire du dit District, le présent contrat de service deviendrait par ce fait nul et sans effet.

Et il est en outre convenu que si le dit Etablissement venait à être vendu, aliéné ou transféré à une autre personne, ou venait à échoir par héritage à une autre personne avant l'expiration du présent contrat, les dits Immigrants devront servir la dite personne selon les termes du dit contrat, le nouvel Employeur se mettant au lieu et place de l'Employeur ainsi remplacé par lui quant aux stipulations et obligations qui lui incombaient.

District de ce jour de mil huit cent soixante

H. D.,
Magistrat Stipendiaire.

Nom de l'Immigrant.	No.	Gages.			Nom de l'Immigrant.	No.	Gages.		
		£	S.	D.			£	S.	D.

132.—Si un nouvel Immigrant, à son arrivée, consent à ce que son contrat soit transféré par celui qui l'a introduit à un autre Employeur, le Protecteur des Immigrants, si toutes les parties au Idem, Art. 18.

their consent thereto in his presence, shall make them sign a transfer in the form of the Schedule I, hereto appended, and his confirmation thereof shall be inscribed upon the contract and shall be briefly endorsed upon the ticket of the Immigrant.

If the transfer do not include all the Immigrants who are parties to the contract, a copy of the contract, bearing only the names of the Immigrants who consent to the transfer, shall be drawn up and delivered to the substituted Employer, with the Protector's confirmation of its transfer inscribed upon it.

SCHEDULE I.

*Transfer of a Special Contract.**

I, and the undernamed Immigrants, being respectively the intended Master and Servants under a contract of service made before the Government Emigration Agent at on the day of 186 , do hereby agree that the whole rights and obligations of the said first party under the said contract shall be, and the same are, hereby transferred, as at the date hereof, to who hereby agree to accept the said transfer and all rights and obligations accruing therefrom.

Name of Immigrant.	No.	Wages.			Name of Immigrant.	No.	Wages.		
		£	S.	D.			£	S.	D.

Employer mentioned in Contract.

Substituted Employer.

(*Confirmation by Protector of Immigrants.*)

CHAPTER II.

Illegal introduction of Labor from British India.

Ord. No. 26 of 1857, Art. 1. 133.—From and after the date when this Ordinance shall come into operation, every person who shall knowingly aid or abet

* On the transfer of a Contract, a fee of 2 shillings is paid by the Substituted Employer to the Protector of Immigrants.

transfert expriment leur consentement à cet effet en sa présence, leur fera signer un transfert dans la forme de la Cédule I annexée à ces présentes, et son approbation à ce transfert sera inscrite sur le contrat, et sera endossé brièvement sur le ticket de l'Immigrant.

Si le transfert ne comprend pas tous les Immigrants qui sont parties au contrat, une copie du contrat portant seulement les noms des Immigrants qui consentent au transfert, sera dressée et livrée à l'Employeur substitué; elle devra contenir l'approbation du Protecteur au transfert.

CÉDULE I.

*Transfert d'un Contrat Spécial.**

Je, et les Immigrants ci-dessous dénommés, le maître et les serviteurs désignés dans un contrat de service passé devant l'Agent d'Emigration du Gouvernement à le 186 , consentons à ce que tous les droits qui appartiennent et toutes les obligations qui incombent au maître en vertu du dit contrat, soient, par ces présentes, transférés, à partir de la date de ce contrat, à qui accepte le dit transfert ainsi que tous les droits et toutes les obligations qui en dépendent.

Nom de l'Immigrant.	No.	Gages.			Nom de l'Immigrant.	No.	Gages.		
		£	S.	D.			£	S.	D.

Employeur désigné dans le contrat.

Employeur Substitué.

(*Approbation du Protecteur des Immigrants.*)

CHAPITRE II.

De l'Introduction illégale de travailleurs de l'Inde Anglaise.

133.—A partir de la mise en vigueur de la présente Ordonnance, toute personne qui, sciemment, aidera ou encouragera tout Ord. No. 26 de 1857, Art. 1.

* Pour le transfert d'un contrat le Protecteur des Immigrants perçoit un droit de deux shillings de l'employeur substitué.

any native of India in emigrating from any place within the territories under the Government of the Honorable East India Company (except Calcutta, Madras and Bombay and any other port or place from which such Emigration may hereafter be allowed by the said Honorable Company), for the purpose of being employed as a laborer within this Colony, or any dependency thereof, shall be liable to a fine not exceeding £ 20 sterling for every native aforesaid who shall have so emigrated and shall have arrived in this Colony, or any dependency thereof; and in default of payment, shall be liable to imprisonment for a term not exceeding twelve months.—(*See No.* 30.)

Idem, Art. 2. **134.**—From and after the date aforesaid, the Master of any ship or vessel in which any Emigrant, being a native of India, shall have been conveyed to the Colony, or any dependency thereof, from Calcutta, Madras or Bombay, or any other port or place aforesaid, for the purpose of laboring for hire in the Colony, or any dependency thereof, without a license authorizing the conveyance of such Emigrant in such ship or vessel having been obtained from the Government of the Presidency in which the port or place is situated from which such Immigrant shall be conveyed, shall be liable in a fine not exceeding £ 20 sterling for every Immigrant so illegally conveyed, and in default of payment, shall be liable to imprisonment for a period not exceeding twelve months. —*See Nos.* 69 *and* 97.)

Idem, Art. 3. **135.**—Provided always that nothing in this Ordinance contained shall be taken to apply to any native seaman who shall, of his own free will, contract to navigate any vessel from any port or place within the territories of the Honorable East India Company to the said Colony or any Dependency thereof, or who shall embark on board any such vessel in pursuance of such contract, or to any person who shall embark under a contract as a menial servant, or to any person who shall embark on board any such vessel as a *bonâ fide* passenger paying his own passage-money and other expenses, or the wife or child of such person.—(*See No.* 26.)

Idem, Art. 4. **136.**—Whenever any native of India shall be introduced into the Colony or any dependency thereof in the manner hereinbefore

natif de l'Inde a émigrer d'un endroit situé sur les territoires de l'Honorable Compagnie des Indes Orientales (à l'exception de Calcutta, de Madras et de Bombay, et de tout autre port ou lieu d'où la dite émigration pourra, plus tard, être permise par la dite Honorable Compagnie) dans le but d'être employé comme travailleur dans cette Colonie ou dans une Dépendance d'icelle, sera passible d'une amende qui n'excédera pas £ 20 sterling pour chaque natif sus-dit qui aura ainsi émigré et sera arrivé dans cette Colonie ou dans une Dépendance d'icelle, et, à défaut de paiement, elle sera passible d'un emprisonnement dont la durée n'excédera pas douze mois.—(*Voir le No.* 30.)

134.—A partir de la sus-dite époque, le Capitaine de tout vaisseau ou navire dans lequel un Emigrant, natif de l'Inde, aura été amené dans la Colonie ou dans toute Dépendance d'icelle, de Calcutta, de Madras et de Bombay, ou de tout autre port ou lieu mentionné ci-dessus, dans le but de travailler à gages dans la Colonie ou dans une Dépendance d'icelle, sans qu'un permis autorisant le transport du dit Emigrant par le dit vaisseau ou navire, ait été obtenu du Gouvernement de la Présidence dans laquelle le port ou le lieu duquel le dit Immigrant aura été amené, est situé, sera passible d'une amende qui n'excédera pas £ 20 sterling pour chaque Immigrant ainsi amené illégalement, et à défaut de paiement, d'un emprisonnement dont la durée n'excédera pas douze mois.—(*Voir les Nos.* 69 *et* 97.) Idem, Art. 2.

135.—Pourvu toutefois que rien de ce qui est contenu dans la présente Ordonnance ne soit réputé s'appliquer aux marins indigènes qui s'engageront volontairement dans un port ou dans un lieu faisant partie des terrritoires de l'Honorable Compagnie des Indes Orientales pour manœuvrer un navire jusque dans la dite Colonie ou dans une Dépendance d'icelle, ou qui s'embarqueront sur le dit navire par suite du dit engagement ; ni aux personnes qui s'embarqueront sur le dit navire avec engagement de servir comme Domestiques, ni aux personnes qui s'embarqueront sur le dit navire en qualité de passagers réels et payant leur passage et autres frais,—pas plus qu'aux femmes ou enfants des dites personnes.—(*Voir le No.* 26.) Idem, Art. 3.

136.—Lorsqu'un natif de l'Inde aura été introduit dans cette Colonie ou dans une Dépendance d'icelle, de la manière exposée Idem, Art. 4.

set forth, it shall be in the power of the Governor to direct that he be delivered, and he shall accordingly be delivered to the Protector of Immigrants, by whom such steps shall be taken as the Governor may direct for the protection of such native of India; and in the event of the Governor directing that he shall be sent to India, the expense of so doing shall be recoverable from the Master of the vessel or any other person by whom the said Indian may have been so introduced as aforesaid.

CHAPTER III.

Introduction of Labor from elsewhere than British India.

Ord. 23 of 1857, Art. 1. 137.—From and after the date when the present Ordinance shall come into operation, the introduction of Immigrants from any place or places not within the territories under the Government of the Honorable the East India Company, shall be conducted in the manner hereinafter provided; and no Immigrant from any place or places aforesaid shall be introduced except in terms of the provisions of this Ordinance. The Immigrants so introduced shall, under the conditions and in the manner hereinafter specified, be competent to enter into contracts of service as defined in the Order in Council of 7th September 1838, for any period not exceeding 3 years.

Idem, Art. 2. 138.—Any person desirous of introducing into the Colony such Immigrants, may, previous to the departure of the vessel from the Colony, if such vessel shall be chartered in the Colony, apply to the Governor for a license authorizing such introduction; which license, the Governor shall have power to grant under such conditions as to him may seem proper.

In case the vessel in which it is desired to introduce such Immigrants, shall be chartered at any place out of the Colony, such license may be granted by any British Consul, Agent, or Emigration Agent, at or near such place, whom the Governor shall authorize to grant the same, and every such license shall be granted under such conditions as the Governor may direct.

ci- dessus, le Gouverneur pourra ordonner qu'il soit livré, et il sera, en conséquence, livré au Protecteur des Immigrants, qui prendra telles mesures que le Gouverneur ordonnera pour la protection du dit natif de l'Inde; et dans le cas où le Gouverneur ordonnera qu'il soit envoyé dans l'Inde, les frais pour ce faire seront recouvrés du Capitaine du navire, ou de toute autre personne qui aura introduit le dit indien de la manière mentionnée ci-dessus.

CHAPITRE III.

De l'introduction de travailleurs d'endroits autres que l'Inde Anglaise.

137.—A partir de la mise à exécution de la présente Ordonnance, l'introduction des Immigrants venant de lieux qui ne sont pas sous le Gouvernement de l'Honorable Compagnie des Indes Orientales, sera dirigée de la manière prévue ci-après; et il ne sera introduit d'Immigrants venant des dits lieux que d'après les dispositions de la présente Ordonnance. Les Immigrants ainsi introduits pourront, aux conditions et de la manière ci-après déterminées, passer des contrats de service ainsi que les définit l'Ordre en Conseil du 7 Septembre 1838, pour un temps n'excèdant pas trois ans. Ord. 23 de 1857, Art. 1.

138.—Quiconque désirera introduire de ces Immigrants dans la Colonie, pourra, avant le départ du navire de la Colonie, si le dit navire est affrété dans la Colonie, s'adresser au Gouverneur pour avoir un permis autorisant la dite introduction; lequel permis le Gouverneur aura le droit d'accorder aux conditions qui lui paraîtront convenables. Idem, Art. 2.

Dans le cas où le navire par lequel on se proposera d'introduire les dits Immigrants serait affrété dans un port situé hors de la Colonie, le dit permis pourra être accordé par tout Consul, Agent ou Agent d'Emigration Anglais de ce port, ou d'un port voisin, que le Gouverneur autorisera à accorder le dit permis, lequel permis sera donné aux conditions que le Gouverneur prescrira.

Every license to be granted under the provisions hereof shall be limited to the vessel and to the place or places which shall be specified therein and shall require to be renewed upon every successive voyage.

Idem, Art. 3. 139.—In the event of any Immigrants or intended Immigrants being introduced into the Colony or being brought into any Roadstead or Harbour thereof, from any place or places not within the territories aforesaid, without a previous license being obtained therefor as aforesaid, or without the conditions being fulfilled under which such license (if obtained) shall have been granted, the Master, Owner and Agent of the ship respectively, shall, for every Immigrant introduced or brought as aforesaid, be liable to a fine not exceeding £ 50, or to imprisonment for a period not exceeding three months : Provided that such imprisonment shall not, in any case, exceed the period of three years. The said penalties may be inflicted cumulatively on a repetition of the offence.

Idem, Art. 4. 140.—In the event specified in the preceding section, it shall moreover be lawful to the Governor to prevent any such Immigrants or intended Immigrants from being landed upon any part of the Colony, and in case any of them shall have been so landed, it shall be lawful to him to direct measures to be taken at the expense of the Owner, Agent, or Master of the ship for having them sent back to the place from which they were taken : Provided that if the Governor shall allow any such Immigrants to land or remain in the Colony, they shall not be competent to enter into contracts of service for a longer period than one year.

Idem, Art. 5. 141.—On the arrival of any ship or vessel at Mauritius with Immigrants or intended Immigrants brought from any port or place not within the territories aforesaid, and immediately after such ship or vessel shall have received pratique, the Protector of Immigrants shall repair on board and shall ascertain, as far as possible, by personal inspection and examination whether the provisions of this Ordinance and of any regulations to be framed in virtue hereof and the conditions of the license aforesaid for such vessel (where such license shall have been obtained) have been duly complied with ; and if he shall be satisfied that such is the case, he shall, without delay, grant a certificate to that effect. If he shall not be satisfied thereof, he shall immediately report the

Tout permis qui sera accordé en vertu du présent article, sera limité au navire et au lieu ou lieux qui y seront indiqués, et devra être renouvelé à chaque voyage successif.

139.—Dans le cas où des Immigrants seraient introduits dans la Colonie ou amenés sur ses rades ou dans ses ports, d'un lieu ou de lieux situés en dehors des territoires susdits, sans qu'il ait été préalablement obtenu de permis à cet effet, ainsi qu'il est dit ci-dessus, ou sans que l'on se soit conformé aux conditions auxquelles le dit permis (s'il a été obtenu) aura été accordé, le Capitaine, l'Armateur et l'Agent du navire, respectivement, encourront pour chaque Immigrant introduit ou amené comme il est dit ci-dessus, une amende qui n'excèdera pas £50, ou un emprisonnement qui n'excèdera pas trois mois : Pourvu que le dit emprisonnement n'excède en aucun cas le terme de trois ans ; les dites peines pourront être infligées cumulativement en cas de récidive. Idem, Art. 3.

140.—Dans le cas spécifié dans l'article précédent, le Gouverneur pourra, en outre, empêcher le débarquement des dits Immigrants dans la Colonie, et, dans le cas où il en serait ainsi débarqué, il pourra ordonner que des mesures soient prises aux frais de l'armateur, de l'agent ou du capitaine du navire pour les renvoyer à l'endroit où ils auront été pris : Pourvu que si le Gouverneur permet aux dits Immigrants de débarquer et de rester dans la Colonie, ils ne puissent passer de contrats de service pour plus d'une année. Idem, Art. 4.

141.—A l'arrivée à Maurice d'un navire ou vaisseau avec des Immigrants venant d'un port ou lieu qui ne sera pas situé dans les territoires susdits, et immédiatement après l'admission du dit navire ou vaisseau à la libre pratique, le Protecteur des Immigrants se rendra à bord et s'assurera, autant que faire se pourra, par inspection et examen personnels, si l'on s'est exactement conformé aux dispositions de la présente Ordonnance et de tous réglements qui seront faits en vertu d'icelle, et aux conditions du permis ci-dessus mentionné pour le dit navire (lorsque ce permis aura été obtenu) ; et si le Protecteur des Immigrants reconnaît qu'on s'est conformé aux dites dispositions et conditions, il donnera sans délai un certificat à cet effet. Dans le cas Idem, Art 5.

matter to the Governor, under whose directions such certificate shall be granted or withheld as to him may seem fit.

Idem, Art. 6. **142.**—As soon as practicable after the said certificate (if granted) shall have been obtained, the Master of the vessel shall land such of the Immigrants therein as are intended for introduction into the Colony, and shall deliver them to the Protector of Immigrants, together with a sufficient quantity of good and wholesome provisions for their maintenance during the space of 48 hours next after their landing.

Idem, Art. 7. **143.**—All such Immigrants shall (except as hereinafter provided) remain under the charge of the Protector of Immigrants until they shall have procured employment, and no contract of service shall be entered into with any Immigrant arriving at Mauritius until after he shall have been 48 hours on shore, or until he shall have obtained from the Protector of Immigrants a Ticket of Registration as hereinafter provided. Every contract of service made before that time shall be null and void to all intents and purposes.

Idem, Art. 8. **144.**—The Protector of Immigrants shall keep a separate Register in the form of the Schedule A hereunto annexed for the Immigrants introduced into the Colony under the provisions of this Ordinance. A ticket shall also be given to each of such Immigrants in the form of the Schedule B hereunto annexed, in which shall be specified the period for which the said Immigrant is competent to engage.

SCHEDULE A.

REGISTER OF IMMIGRANTS UNDER ORDINANCE No. 23 OF 1857.

Number.	Name of Immigrant.	Name of Father.	Name of Mother.	Sex.	Age.	Stature.	Marks.	Caste, (if any).	Native Country and Village.	Port or Place where embarked.	Name of vessel and Captain by which introduced.	Whether accompanied by children, and if so, their names, sexes and ages.	Time during which competent to engage.	REMARKS.

contraire, il fera immédiatement son rapport au Gouverneur, d'après les instructions duquel le dit certificat sera accordé ou refusé selon qu'il le jugera convenable.

142.—Aussitôt que possible, après que le dit certificat (s'il est accordé) aura été obtenu, le Capitaine du navire débarquera ceux d'entre les Immigrants qui doivent être introduits dans la Colonie, et les remettra au Protecteur des Immigrants, avec des vivres de bonne qualité en quantité suffisante pour la nourriture des dits Immigrants pendant les 48 heures qui suivront le débarquement. Idem, Art. 6.

143.—Tous les dits Immigrants (excepté ainsi qu'il est ordonné ci-après) resteront sous la garde du Protecteur des Immigrants jusqu'à ce qu'ils aient trouvé de l'emploi, et nul engagement de service ne sera fait avec un de ces Immigrants à son arrivée à Maurice, à moins qu'il n'ait passé 48 heures à terre, ou qu'il n'ait obtenu du Protecteur des Immigrants un Ticket d'enregistrement ainsi qu'il est dit ci-après. Tout contrat de service fait et passé avant ce temps sera nul et de nul effet à tous égards. Idem, Art. 7.

144.—Le Protecteur des Immigrants tiendra un registre séparé, en la forme indiquée dans la Cédule A ci-après annexée, pour les Immigrants introduits dans la Colonie en vertu des dispositions de la présente Ordonnance. Un ticket sera aussi donné à chacun des dits Immigrants en la forme de la Cédule B ci-après annexée et mentionnant le temps pour lequel le dit Immigrant pourra s'engager. Idem, Art. 8.

CÉDULE A.

REGISTRE D'IMMIGRANTS AUX TERMES DE L'ORDONNANCE No. 23 DE 1857.

Numéro.	Nom de l'Immigrant.	Nom de — Son père.	Nom de — Sa mère.	Sexe.	Age.	Taille.	Marques.	Caste (s'il y en a).	Pays natal et Village.	Port ou lieu de l'embarquement.	Nom du navire et du Capitaine sur et par lequel il a été introduit.	Si des enfants l'accompagnent, leurs noms, sexe et âge.	Temps pour lequel il peut passer un engagement de service.	OBSERVATIONS.

SCHEDULE B.

Ticket of Immigrant under Ordinance No. 23 *of* 1857.

1 Name of Immigrant,
2 Number,
3 { Name of Father,
  Name of Mother,
4 Sex,
5 Age,
6 Stature,
7 Marks,
8 Caste,
9 Native Country and Village,
10 Name of Vessel and Captain by which introduced,
11 Whether accompanied by children, and, if so, their names, sexes and ages,
12 Time during which competent to engage,
13 Remarks.

Protector of Immigrants.

Idem, Art. 9. 145.—It shall not be lawful for the said Protector to issue any ticket to any such Immigrant, unless proof shall have previously been given to him that the person desiring to engage such Immigrant has paid or satisfied the Master, Owner or Agent of the vessel in which the said Immigrant was brought, for the passage-money, and all other expenses due in respect of such Immigrant, as the same shall be fixed in the manner hereinafter provided, or unless the said Master, Owner or Agent shall consent to such ticket being issued. But provided that the said Protector shall be entitled, and on application therefor shall be bound to issue a ticket authorizing an engagement for any period not exceeding one year to any Immigrant who shall have been allowed to land or to remain in the Colony in terms of Art. 4th hereof, or who shall have been under charge of the said Protector, as aforesaid, for any longer period than 14 days without having been engaged in terms of the preceding articles hereof.—(*Art.* 4.—*See No.* 140.)

Idem, Art. 10. 146.—In case any person shall have made arrangements with the Master, Owner or Agent of any Vessel for the introduction of Immigrants with a view to their engagement with himself in terms of this Ordinance, and in case any of the Immigrants introduced in consequence of such arrangements shall be induced to engage with another person, such other person shall, in addition

CÉDULE B.

Ticket d'Immigrant d'après l'Ordonnance No. 23 *de* 1857.

1 Nom de l'Immigrant,
2 Numéro,
3 { Nom du Père,
  Nom de la Mère,
4 Sexe,
5 Age,
6 Taille,
7 Marques,
8 Caste,
9 Pays natal et village,
10 Nom du navire et capitaine par lesquels introduits,
11 S'il est accompagné par des enfants ; en ce cas, leurs noms sexe et âge,
12 Temps pour lequel il peut passer des engagements de service,
13 Observations.

Protecteur des Immigrants.

145.—Le dit Protecteur ne pourra pas délivrer de Tickets aux dits Immigrants tant qu'il ne lui aura pas été prouvé que la personne qui désire engager les dits Immigrants a payé ou satisfait le Capitaine, l'Armateur ou l'Agent du navire sur lequel les dits Immigrants seront arrivés, quant au passage et à toutes les autres dépenses faites pour les dits Immigrants, ainsi que le tout sera fixé de la manière qui sera indiquée ci-après, ou à moins que le dit Capitaine, Armateur ou Agent ne consente à la remise des dits Tickets. Mais pourvu que le dit Protecteur ait le droit, et, sur la demande qui lui en sera faite, soit tenu de délivrer des Tickets autorisant l'engagement pour un terme n'excédant pas une année, de tous les Immigrants auxquels il aura été permis de débarquer ou de rester dans la Colonie aux termes de l'Article 4 de la présente Ordonnance, ou qui auront été sous la garde du dit Protecteur, comme il est dit ci-dessus, pendant plus de 14 jours sans avoir été engagés aux termes des précédents articles de la présente Ordonnance.—(*Art.* 4.—*Voir le No.* 140.) Idem, Art. 9.

146.—Dans le cas où une personne aurait pris des arrangements avec le Capitaine, l'Armateur ou l'Agent d'un navire pour l'introduction d'Immigrants dans le but de les engager à son service aux termes de la présente Ordonnance, et dans le cas où les Immigrants introduits par suite de ces arrangements s'engageraient avec une autre personne, la dite autre personne devra payer Idem, Art. 10.

to the passage money and all other expenses payable as aforesaid on account of the Immigrants so to be engaged by him, and previous to the issuing of a ticket as hereinaforesaid, pay to the Protector 25 per cent on the amount thereof; which 25 per cent shall be paid by the Protector to the person by whom the aforesaid arrangement for the introduction of the said Immigrants shall have been made: Provided that, previous to the departure of the Vessel from the Colony for the purpose of bringing such Immigrants, if the vessel shall be chartered there, or from any other place where she shall be chartered for the said purpose, such person shall have transmitted to the Protector of Immigrants a certificate signed by himself and by the Master, Owner, or Agent of the Vessel, as nearly as may be in the form of Schedule C hereunto annexed, and also Provided that the said Protector shall be satisfied from entries in the Ship's books or any other evidence that the Immigrants in respect of whom the said 25 per cent shall be claimed were embarked under the said arrangement on account of the person claiming the same.

SCHEDULE C.

Port Louis, Mauritius,
day of 186 .

We A. B. (*designation*) and C. D., master (*or* owner *or* agent) of the (*name of vessel*) of (*Port of Registry*), certify that an arrangement was on the day of entered into between (*mention by whom arrangement made*) for the introduction into this Colony in the said vessel of (*mention number*) male and (*mention number*) female Immigrants on account of the said A. B.

The above certificate deposited in my office this day (*date*) } A. B.
C. D.

E. F.,
Protector of Immigrants.

Idem, Art. 11. **147.**—The maximum sum which the Master, Owner, or Agent of any Vessel that shall have brought Immigrants to Mauritius under the provisions of this Ordinance may demand on account of passage-money and all other expenses due for such Immigrants, shall be determined according to a scale that shall be fixed by a Committee composed of the Collector of Customs, the Protector of Immigrants and the Harbour-Master, and a Member of the Chamber of Commerce and of the Chamber of Agriculture res-

au Protecteur, en outre du passage et des autres avances remboursables comme il est dit ci-dessus, pour les Immigrants qu'elle engagera ainsi, et avant la délivrance des Tickets comme il est dit ci-dessus, 25 pour cent sur le total de toutes ces avances; lesquels 25 pour cent seront comptés par le Protecteur à la personne par laquelle les sus-dits arrangements pour l'introduction des dits Immigrants auront été pris : Pourvu qu'avant que le navire quitte la colonie pour aller chercher les dits Immigrants, si le navire est affrêté dans la colonie, ou tout autre lieu où il sera affrêté dans ce but, la dite personne ait transmis au Protecteur des Immigrants un certificat signé par elle et par le Capitaine, l'Armateur ou l'Agent du navire, aussi exactement que possible dans la forme de la Cédule C annexée à la présente Ordonnance, et pourvu aussi qu'il soit démontré au dit Protecteur, par les livres du navire, ou par toute autre preuve, que les Immigrants pour lesquels les dits 25 pour cent sont réclamés, ont été embarqués par suite des dits arrangements pour le compte de la personne qui réclame cette indemnité.

CÉDULE C.

Port Louis, Maurice,
le 185 .

Nous A. B. (*désignation*) et C. D. Capitaine (*ou* Armateur *ou* Agent) du (*nom du navire*) de (*Port d'enregistrement*), certifions qu'un accord a été passé ce entre (*mentionner les noms des parties contractantes*), pour l'introduction en cette Colonie par le dit navire de (*mentionner le nombre*) Immigrants du sexe masculin et (*mentionner le nombre*) Immigrants du sexe féminin, pour le compte du dit A. B.

Le certificat ci-dessus a été déposé à mon bureau ce jour (*date*) } A. B. C. D.

E. F.
Protecteur des Immigrants.

147.—La somme la plus élevée que le Capitaine, l'Armateur ou l'Agent d'un navire qui aura transporté à Maurice des Immigrants en vertu des dispositions de la présente Ordonnance, aura droit de réclamer pour le passage et toutes autres dépenses faites pour les dits Immigrants, sera déterminée d'après une échelle qui sera établie par un Comité composé du Collecteur des Douanes, du Protecteur des Immigrants, du Capitaine de Port, et d'un membre de la Chambre de Commerce et de la Chambre d'Agriculture res- Idem, Art. 11.

pectively, to be named by the Governor, three members of which Committee shall form a quorum; and which scale may by them be altered from time to time as occasion may require. Such scale shall, after having been approved by the Governor, be posted up in the Custom-House, the Immigration Depot, and the Port-Office, and be published in the Government Gazette for general information.

Idem, Art. 12. 148.—In the event of any Immigrants being brought to this Colony from any Port or Place, the rate of passage-money from which and other expenses which may be demanded on account of such Immigrants shall not appear in the said scale, the said Committee shall, as soon as may be after the arrival of the Vessel in which such Immigrants shall have come, fix and determine the amount of passage-money and other expenses aforesaid, and the amount so fixed shall not be subject to alteration or review by any Court or Tribunal whatever.

Idem, Art. 13. 149.—The passage-money and expenses aforesaid shall in no case be a debt recoverable from the Immigrant, but shall be paid by the Master, with whom any such Immigrant may first enter into a written contract of service.

Idem, Art. 14. 150.—The Master of any Ship or Vessel by which Immigrants shall have been brought to Mauritius from any Port or Place not within the territories aforesaid, who shall not have furnished to such Immigrants, during the voyage, a sufficient quantity of good and wholesome provisions and water, or who shall have in any way ill-treated any such Immigrant while on board his Vessel, shall incur a penalty not exceeding £ 50; and, in default of payment, shall be imprisoned for a period not exceeding twelve months; which punishments may be inflicted cumulatively, and may be doubled in aggravated cases, as well as on a repetition of the offence.

Idem, Art. 15. 151.—Any person who shall unlawfully detain any Immigrants, one or more, against their will in any place within the Colony or Dependencies, shall incur a penalty not exceeding £ 50 for every such Immigrant and another penalty of £ 5 for each month beyond the first month during which such detention may have been continued, and, in default of payment, shall be imprisoned for a period not exceeding two years.

pectivement, qui seront nommés par le Gouverneur. Ce Comité pourra délibérer avec trois membres, et il pourra changer de temps à autre la dite échelle ainsi que les circonstances l'exigeront. La dite échelle, après avoir été approuvée par le Gouverneur, sera affichée à la Douane, au Dépôt de l'Immigration et au Bureau du Port, et publiée dans la Gazette du Gouvernement, pour l'information générale.

148.—Dans le cas où des Immigrants seraient introduits dans cette Colonie d'un port ou d'un lieu quelconque, et que le prix du passage de ce port et les autres avances qui pourront être réclamées pour les dits Immigrants, ne se trouveraient pas mentionnés dans la dite échelle, le dit Comité, aussitôt que possible, après l'arrivée du navire sur lequel seront venus les dits Immigrants, fixera et déterminera le montant du prix du passage et autres avances susdites, et le montant ainsi fixé ne pourra être changé ou révisé par aucune Cour ou Tribunal quelconque. Idem, Art. 12.

149.—Le prix du passage et autres avances susdites ne seront en aucun cas recouvrables de l'Immigrant ; ils seront payés par le premier Maître avec lequel le dit Immigrant voudra passer un engagement de service. Idem, Art. 13.

150.—Le Capitaine du navire ou vaisseau qui transportera des Immigrants à Maurice, d'un port ou lieu qui n'est pas pas situé dans les territoires sus-dits, et qui n'aura pas fourni aux dits Immigrants pendant le voyage, une quantité suffisante de provisions et d'eau de bonne qualité, ou qui aura maltraité les dits Immigrants de quelque manière que ce soit pendant leur séjour à bord de son navire, encourra une pénalité qui n'excèdera pas £ 50, et à défaut de paiement d'icelle, sera emprisonné pendant un temps qui n'excèdera pas douze mois ; ces peines pourront être prononcées cumulativement et pourront être doublées dans les cas graves ainsi qu'en cas de récidive. Idem, Art. 14.

151.—Toute personne qui détiendra illégalement un ou plusieurs Immigrants contre leur volonté, dans un endroit quelconque dans la Colonie ou ses Dépendances, encourra une amende qui n'excèdera pas £ 50 pour chaque dit Immigrant, et, de plus, une amende de £ 5 pour chaque mois qui suivra le premier mois de cette détention, et à défaut de paiement, la dite personne subira un emprisonnement qui n'excèdera pas deux années. Idem, Art. 15.

Idem. Art. 16. 152.—The provisions of any subsisting law relating to forfeitures of wages, rations and penalties incurred for unlicensed absences from work, and any law relating to the recovery of wages and arrears of wages, the providing of rations and medical treatment, and the annulling or cancelling of contracts of service, are hereby extended to Immigrants engaged under the powers conferred by this Ordinance.

Idem, Art. 17. 153.—Any person intending to come to this Colony as an Immigrant in terms of this Ordinance and having been legally married according to the forms and ceremonies of his Religion or of the Law of his domicile at the time of marriage, may go before any one of the persons hereinafter empowered to receive declarations of marriage, accompanied by his wife and children (if any) the issue of such marriage; and such intending Immigrant and his wife may in the presence of two witnesses make a declaration before such person (in the form of the Schedule D hereunto annexed) that they have been lawfully married according to the forms and ceremonies aforesaid, and that the children (if any) accompanying them are the lawful issue of such marriage; and such declaration shall be signed by the parties making the same and by two witnesses thereto respectively, if able to write. If any of the said parties or witnesses are unable to write, they shall affix their marks to the said declaration, which shall in every case be attested by the person before whom it shall be made.

SCHEDULE D.

Descriptive Roll of *the* *day of* 186 *, proceeding to Mauritius per*

Mauritius Registered No.	Name.	Names of Fathers and Mothers.	Sex.	Caste (if any).	Ages.	Place or Places of Nativity.	Remarks.
	Husband Wife (Children)						

Certified that the above described whose signatures are hereunto attached, have this day come before me and each of them separately and also in the presence of one another, has declared to me before the two witnesses who have also signed this certificate that they

152.—Les dispositions en vigueur relatives à la retenue des gages et rations, et aux pénalités encourues pour absences du travail sans autorisation, et les lois relatives au recouvrement des gages et arriérés de gages, aux rations et soins médicaux, et à l'annulation ou résiliation des contrats de service, sont par le présent rendues applicables aux Immigrants engagés en vertu des pouvoirs conférés par la présente Ordonnance. Idem, Art. 16.

153.—Tout individu qui se proposera de venir dans cette Colonie comme Immigrant aux termes de la présente Ordonnance, et qui sera marié légitimement d'après les formes et cérémonies de sa religion ou de la loi de son domicile à l'époque de son mariage, pourra se présenter devant l'une des personnes ci-après autorisées à recevoir les déclarations de mariage, accompagné de de sa femme et des enfants (s'il y en a) qui sont issus de ce mariage, et le dit futur Immigrant et sa femme pourront en présence de deux témoins, déclarer devant la dite personne (dans la forme de la cédule D ci-après annexée) qu'ils ont été mariés légitimement selon les formes et cérémonies sus-dites, et que les enfans (s'il y en a) qui les accompagnent, sont issus du dit mariage ; et la dite déclaration sera signée par les parties déclarantes et par deux témoins, respectivement, s'ils savent signer. Les parties ou témoins qui ne sauront pas signer feront leur marque sur la dite déclaration, laquelle sera dans tous les cas attestée par la personne devant laquelle elle aura été faite. Idem, Art. 17.

CÉDULE D.

Etat descriptif de le jour de 186 se rendant à Maurice par

Enregistré pour Maurice No.	Nom.	Noms des Pères et Mères.	Sexe.	Caste..	Ages.	Lieu ou Lieux de Naissance.	Remarq.
	Mari. Femme. (Enfants.)						

Certifié que ci-dessus dénommés dont les signatures sont apposées ci-après, ont ce jour, comparu devant moi et que chacun d'eux séparément et aussi en présence l'un de l'autre a déclaré devant les deux témoins qui ont également signé ce certificat, qu'ils sont légale-

are legally married to each other according to the forms and ceremonies of their religion or of the law of being their domicile at the time of marriage (*as the case may be*) and that the children above named are the lawful issue of such marriage.

Witness' signature or mark.

Witness' signature or mark.

(Signed) X.,
Consul at
(*or otherwise, as the case may be*).

We, the above described (or I, being the survivor of the above described) hereby declare that we have been married to each other according to the forms and ceremonies above mentioned (and that the children above named are the lawful issue of such marriage.)

Witness to the above declaration :

A.
B.

Confirmed before me this day of 186 .

E. H.,
Protector of Immigrants.

Idem, Art. 18. 154.—A similar declaration (according to the form in the Schedule E hereunto annexed) may be made in the country from which such Immigrant is embarked for introduction into this Colony, by one of the parties to any such marriage intending to proceed to the Colony to join the other party there.

SCHEDULE E.

Descriptive Roll of proceeding to Mauritius per to join (her husband) there.

Mauritius Registered No.	Name.	Names of Father and Mother.		Sex.	Caste (if any.)	Ages.	Place or Places of Nativity.	Remarks.
	Crustangee, the wife of Sigham (children.)	Eravandree	Esoba	Female	Muratta	32	Singera	
				Male.	Muratta	36	Singera	

ment mariés l'un à l'autre selon les formes et cérémonies de leur religion, ou selon la loi du lieu où ils avaient leur domicile lors de leur mariage, (*suivant le cas*) et que les enfants ci-dessus dénommés sont nés légitimement du dit mariage.

Signature ou croix du Témoin.

Signature ou croix du Témoin.

(Signé) X.,

Consul à

(*ou tout autre, selon le cas*)

Nous, les sus-dénommés, déclarons, (ou je déclare étant le seul survivant des sus-dénommés), par ces présentes, avoir été mariés l'un à l'autre selon les formes et cérémonies ci-dessus mentionnées (et que les enfants ci-dessus-dénommés sont nés légitimement du dit mariage.)

Témoins de la déclaration ci-dessus :

A.
B.

Confirmé devant moi ce jour de 186 .

E. H.,

Protecteur des Immigrants.

154 —Une déclaration semblable (selon la forme de la Cédule E ci-après annexée) pourra être faite dans le pays où le dit Immigrant sera embarqué pour être introduit en cette Colonie, par l'une des parties ayant contracté mariage et qui se proposera de venir dans la Colonie pour y rejoindre l'autre conjoint. Idem, Art. 18.

CÉDULE E.

Etat descriptif de se rendant à Maurice par pour y rejoindre (son mari.)

Enregistré pour Maurice No.	Nom.	Noms des Père et Mère.		Sexe.	Caste.	Age.	Lieu ou Lieux de Naissance.	Remarques.
	Crustangee, femme de Sigham (enfants.)	Eravandree	Esoba	Féminin	Muratta	32	Singera	
				Masculin	Muratta	36	Singera	

Certified that the above named woman Crustangee whose signature is hereunto attached has this day voluntarily come before me and has declared to me before two witnesses who have also signed this certificate that she has been lawfully married to the above-named Sigham according to the forms and ceremonies of their religion, or of the laws of being their domicile at the time of marriage, *(as the case may be)* ; that the children above named are the lawful issue of such marriage, and that she is about to proceed to Mauritius to join her said husband who is there resident.

Witness to the above declaration :

A.
B. } *signature or mark.* Crustangee's signature or mark.

(Signed) X.,
Consul at
(or otherwise as the case may be.)

We, the above named Sigham and Crustangee, or I, being the survivor of the above described, hereby, in the presence of the Protector of Immigrants at Mauritius confirm the declaration made by Crustangee, and acknowledge that we have been married to each other in accordance to the forms and ceremonies above mentioned, and that the children above named are the lawful issue of such marriage.

X. Sigham
X. Crustangee } *marks or signatures.*

Confirmed before me this day of 186 .

E. H.,
Protector of Immigrants.

Idem, Art. 19. **155.**—Such declarations of marriage may be taken and made in the country aforesaid by or before any British consular officer therein when such country is not a dependency of the British Crown ; or by or before any Judge, Magistrate, or Justice of the Peace when such country is a dependency aforesaid ; and in either case by or before any Immigration Agent appointed by the Government for the place where such declaration shall be made.

Idem, Art. 20. **156.**—When any such declaration of marriage shall have been made as aforesaid, the parties therein declaring themselves to have been lawfully married, or the survivor of them in case the other shall have died in the interval, may appear before the Protector of Immigrants in this Island and may in his presence confirm the said Declaration. And the Protector, if satisfied of the

Je certifie que la femme Crustangee sus-dénommée dont la signature est apposée ci-après, a ce jour, volontairement comparu devant moi et m'a déclaré devant deux témoins qui ont également signé le présent certificat, qu'elle a été légalement mariée au sus-dénommé Sigham selon les formes et cérémonies de leur religion, ou selon les lois de leur domicile à l'époque de leur mariage (*selon le cas*), que les enfants sus-dénommés sont nés légitimement de leur mariage et qu'elle est au moment de partir pour Maurice pour y rejoindre son sus-dit mari qui y réside.

Témoins de la déclaration sus-dite :

A.
B. } *Signatures ou croix.* Signature ou croix de Crustangee.

(Signé) X.,
Consul à
(*ou autre, suivant le cas.*)

Nous les sus-dénommés Sigham et Crustangee (ou, moi le survivant des sus-mentionnés) confirmons par le présent, devant le Protecteur des Immigrants à Maurice, la déclaration faite par Crustangee, et reconnaissons que nous avons été mariés l'un à l'autre selon les formes et cérémonies ci-dessus mentionnées, et que les enfants sus-dénommés sont nés légitimement de ce mariage.

X. Sigham
X. Crustangee } *Croix ou signatures.*

Confirmé devant moi, ce jour de 186 .

E. H.,
Protecteur des Immigrants.

155.—Ces déclarations de marriage pourront être faites dans le pays sus-dit devant un Officier Consulaire Anglais y résidant, lorsque ce pays ne sera pas une des dépendances de la Couronne Britannique ; ou devant un Juge, un Magistrat, ou un Juge de Paix, lorsque le dit pays fera partie des Dépendances sus-dites ; et dans l'un ou l'autre cas, devant tout Agent d'Immigration nommé par le Gouvernement pour le lieu où la dite déclaration sera faite. Idem, Art. 19.

156.—Lorsqu'une déclaration de mariage aura été faite, ainsi qu'il est dit ci-dessus, les parties déclarant en icelle avoir été mariées légitimement, (ou la partie survivante, dans le cas où l'autre serait décédée dans l'intervalle), pourront se présenter devant le Protecteur des Immigrants en cette île, et pourront confirmer la dite déclaration en sa présence. Et si le Protecteur Idem, Art. 20.

identity of the parties, and of the death of one of the parties in case the declaration shall be made by the other as survivor, shall certify the fact of such confirmation upon the face of the declaration.

Idem, Art. 21. **157.**—A certified copy* of every declaration of marriage so made and confirmed shall be deemed for all purposes sufficient *primâ facie* evidence of the marriage of the parties and of the legitimacy of the children (if any) named therein.

Idem, Art. 22. **158.**—The originals of all Declarations of marriage made and confirmed as hereinbefore mentioned shall be deposited at the Office of the Protector of Immigrants, who shall, in the month of January in each year, deliver over to the Officer of the Civil Status of Port Louis, all the said Declarations of marriage which shall have been deposited in his office during the preceding year, such declarations having been first properly bound up together in a book. The said book shall be filed and kept as record in the Office of the said Officer of the Civil Status.

Idem, Art. 23. **159.**—The provisions of any existing Law as to the trial and punishment of persons who shall entice or harbour the wives of Indian Immigrants are hereby extended to persons who shall entice or harbour the wives of Immigrants introduced in terms of this Ordinance.—(*See Nos.* 533 *and* 534.)

Idem, Art. 24. **160.**—The Governor in Executive Council shall have power to pass and publish in the Government Gazette regulations for carrying out the objects of this Ordinance, which regulations shall have the same force and effect as if *verbatim* embodied in this Ordinance and in any licence to be granted as hereinaforesaid.

Idem, Art. 25. **161.**—All contraventions of the provisions in this Ordinance contained, for which there is imposed a penalty not exceeding that which may be inflicted by a District Magistrate, shall, if committed within the limits of any District in the Colony, be prosecuted and tried before the Magistrate of such District.

---

* For this document a fee of two shillings is paid by the applicant to the Protector of Immigrants.—*See No.* 525, § 5.

acquiert la preuve de l'identité des parties, et du décès de l'une d'elles lorsque la déclaration sera faite par l'autre comme partie survivante, il certifiera le fait de la dite confirmation sur la déclaration elle-même.

157.—Une copie certifiée* de toute déclaration de mariage ainsi faite et confirmée, sera considérée à tous égards comme preuve suffisante, sauf la preuve contraire, du mariage des parties et de la légitimité des enfants (s'il y en a) dénommés en icelle. Idem, Art. 21.

158.—Les originaux de toutes les déclarations de mariage faites et confirmées comme il est dit ci-dessus, seront déposés au Bureau du Protecteur des Immigrants qui remettra, dans le mois de Janvier de chaque année, à l'Officier de l'Etat Civil du Port Louis, toutes les déclarations de mariage qui auront été déposées à son bureau pendant l'année précédente, après qu'elles auront été reliées convenablement en un volume. Le dit volume sera reçu et conservé comme faisant partie des registres du bureau du dit Officier de l'Etat Civil. Idem, Art. 22.

159.—Les dispositions de toutes les lois en vigueur concernant les poursuites et peines encourues par les personnes qui embauchent ou recèlent les femmes des Immigrants Indiens, sont par le présent, rendues applicables aux personnes qui embaucheront ou recèleront les femmes introduites aux termes de la présente Ordonnance.—(*Voir les Nos.* 533 *et* 534.) Idem, Art. 23.

160.—Le Gouverneur en Conseil Exécutif aura le pouvoir de faire et de publier dans la Gazette du Gouvernement des règlements pour l'exécution de la présente Ordonnance ;— lesquels règlements auront la même force et valeur que s'ils faisaient littéralement partie de la présente Ordonnance, ou de tout permis qui sera accordé ainsi qu'il est dit ci-dessus. Idem, Art. 24.

161.—Toutes les contraventions aux dispositions de la présente Ordonnance pour lesquelles il a été décrété une pénalité que puisse infliger un Magistrat de District, seront, si elles sont commises dans les limites de l'un des Districts de la Colonie, poursuivies devant le Magistrat du dit District et jugées par lui. Idem, Art. 25.

---

* Le requérant paie pour ce document un droit de deux schellings au Protecteur des Immigrants.—*Voir le No.* 525, § 5.

And all contraventions thereof for which there is imposed a penalty as aforesaid, if committed any where beyond the limits of any District in the Colony, shall be prosecuted and tried before one of the District Magistrates of Port Louis.

All contraventions of the said provisions, wherever they shall have been committed, for which the penalty exceeds that which may be inflicted by a District Magistrate shall be prosecuted and tried before the Supreme Court of this Colony.

Idem, Art. 26. 162.—So much of the Order in Council of 7th September 1838 as is repugnant to the provisions in this Ordinance contained, and all Proclamations and Regulations respecting Immigration from Madagascar, the Comoro Islands, Zanzibar and other Ports and places not within the Jurisdiction of the East India Company, are hereby repealed.

CHAPTER IV.

Liberated African Slaves.

Ord. No. 18 of 1865, Art. 1. 163.—All persons of African origin who shall be found in vessels captured by any of Her Majesty's Cruisers engaged in the suppression of the Slave Trade, and shall be landed in Mauritius or Seychelles as liberated slaves may be engaged in Contracts of Service, in accordance with the provisions of this Ordinance.

Idem, Art. 2. 164.—Such Contracts of Service may be for any period not exceeding five years. They shall be in writing, and shall be entered into before, and authenticated by, a Stipendiary Magistrate of the place in which they are made.—(*See No.* 221 *et seq.*)

Idem, Art. 3. 165.—Every such Contract shall be for an allowance of *Wages and Rations* in accordance with the Regulations to be framed under the provisions of this Ordinance. The employer shall further be obliged to give his servant proper *lodging and medical care.*—

Et toutes les contraventions pour lesquelles il a été décrété une peine de la nature de celle dont il est fait mention ci-dessus, si elles sont commises en dehors des limites d'un District de la Colonie, seront poursuivies devant l'un des Magistrats du Port Louis, et jugées par lui.

Toutes les contraventions aux dites dispositions, quel que soit le lieu où elles auront été commises, pour lesquelles il a été décrété une peine qui excède celle qui peut être prononcée par un Magistrat de District, seront poursuivies devant la Cour Suprême de la Colonie, et jugées par cette Cour.

162.—Toutes les dispositions de l'Ordre en Conseil du 7 Septembre 1838 qui sont contraires à la présente Ordonnance, et toutes les Proclamations et Règlements concernant l'Immigration de Madagascar, des Iles Comores, de Zanzibar et d'autres ports et lieux en dehors de la juridiction de la Compagnie des Indes Orientales, sont rapportés par le présent. Idem, Art. 26.

CHAPITRE IV.

Des Esclaves Africains Libérés.

163.—Toutes les personnes d'origine africaine qui seront trouvées sur des navires capturés par un des croiseurs de Sa Majesté employés à la suppression de la Traite, et qui seront débarquées soit à Maurice, soit aux Seychelles, comme esclaves libérés, pourront être engagées par des Contrats de Service conformément aux dispositions de la présente Ordonnance. Ord. No. 18 de 1865, Art. 1.

164.—Ces Contrats de Service pourront être pour un temps qui n'excèdera pas cinq ans. Ils seront faits par écrit et seront passés par-devant le Magistrat Stipendiaire du lieu où ils seront faits, qui leur donnera toute authenticité.—(*Voir le No.* 221 *et suiv.*) Idem, Art. 2.

165.—Chacun de ces contrats stipulera *les gages et les rations* qui seront donnés conformément aux Réglements qui seront faits en vertu des dispositions de la présente Ordonnance. L'employeur sera, de plus, obligé de donner à son serviteur un *logement* con- Idem, Art. 3.

(*Wages and Rations,—See No.* 176. — *Lodging and Medical care,* —*See Nos.* 353, 354 *et seq.*)

Idem, Art. 4. **166.**—In the event of any Liberated Slaves being landed at any of the Seychelles Dependencies, and of there not being, within these Dependencies, persons whom the Civil Commissioner thereof shall consider fit, and who shall be willing, to enter into contracts of service with them, in accordance with this Ordinance and relative Regulations, it shall be lawful to the Civil Commissioner of Seychelles to cause them to be forwarded to Mauritius, to be there engaged in contracts of service aforesaid. In such case the said Liberated Slaves shall be forwarded by the first convenient opportunity.

Idem, Art. 5. **167.**—During the interval between their arrival at Seychelles and their being forwarded to Mauritius, such Liberated Slaves shall receive food, clothing, lodging, and medical care, at the expense of the Government, and under the superintendence of the Civil Commissioner of Seychelles, and may be employed in any Government works either without wages, or at such rate of wages as shall be fixed by Regulations.

Idem, Art. 6. **168.**—Liberated Slaves landed at Mauritius by any of Her Majesty's cruisers, or arriving in Mauritius from Seychelles under the aforesaid provision, shall be received in the Immigration Depot, and, until they shall be engaged as herein aforesaid, shall receive food and others aforesaid, at the expense of the Government, under the superintendence of the Protector of Immigrants.

Idem, Art. 7. **169.**—The person with whom any Liberated Slave shall enter into a contract of service, shall pay to the Government such sum as shall be fixed by Regulations to be passed under this Ordinance from time to time, in order to defray a due proportion of the expense incurred by the Government in relation to such Liberated Slaves.

Govt. Notice of 9th August 1867. **170.**—The sums to be paid to Government under *Article 7 of Ordinance No,* 18 *of* 1865, shall be as follows, viz. :

venable et des *soins médicaux*.—(*Les gages et rations*,—*Voir le No.* 176.—*Logement et soins médicaux*—*Voir les Nos.* 353, 354 *et suiv.*)

166.—Dans le cas où des esclaves libérés, seraient débarqués sur l'une des Iles Seychelles, dépendances de Maurice, et qu'il ne se trouvât personne dans ces dépendances que le Civil Commissioner des Seychelles jugeat apte, ou qui fut disposé, à passer un contrat de service avec eux conformément à la présente Ordonnance et aux Réglements qui en dépendent, le Civil Commissioner des Seychelles pourra les expédier à Maurice pour y être engagés par des contrats de service comme il est dit ci-dessus. Dans ce cas, les dits esclaves libérés seront envoyés par la première occasion convenable. Idem, Art. 4.

167.—Pendant le temps qui s'écoulera entre leur arrivée aux Seychelles et leur expédition pour Maurice, ces esclaves libérés seront nourris, habillés, logés et soignés aux frais du Gouvernement et sous le contrôle du Civil Commissioner, et pourront être employés aux travaux du Gouvernement, soit sans gages, soit aux gages qui seront fixés par des Réglements. Idem, Art. 5.

168.—Les esclaves libérés débarqués à Maurice par un des croiseurs de Sa Majesté, ou arrivés des Seychelles à Maurice, comme il est prévu ci-dessus, seront reçus au Dépôt de l'Immigration, et jusqu'à ce qu'ils soient engagés, ainsi qu'il est dit ci-dessus, seront nourris, habillés, logés et soignés aux frais du Gouvernement, sous le contrôle du Protecteur des Immigrants. Idem, Art. 6.

169.—La personne avec laquelle un esclave libéré passera un contrat de service, paiera au Gouvernement la somme qui sera fixée par les Réglements qui seront faits, de temps à autre, en vertu de la présente Ordonnance, afin de contribuer dans une proportion raisonnable aux dépenses encourues par le Gouvernement pour ces esclaves libérés. Idem. Art. 7.

170.—Les sommes à payer au Gouvernement, conformément à l'*Article* 7 *de l'Ordonnance No.* 18 *de* 1865, seront comme suit : Avis du Gouv. du 9 Août 1867.

Liberated Slaves landed in Mauritius.

For every Male above 14 years of age............	£ 6.	0.	0
„ „ under 14 „	4.	0.	0
„ Female above 14 years of age.........	5.	0.	0
„ „ under 14 „	4.	0.	0

Liberated Slaves landed at Seychelles.

For men, women, and children, a uniform rate of.. £ 1. 10. 0
(*Art.* 7 *of Ord. No.* 18 *of* 1865.—*See No.* 169).

Ord. No. 18 of 1865, Art. 8. **171.**—The Liberated Slaves aforesaid shall be engaged to the persons to whom they shall be allotted by the Protector of Immigrants, if in Mauritius, and if in Seychelles, by the Civil Commissioner thereof in accordance with the Regulations to be framed under this Ordinance.

Idem, Art. 9. **172.**—The undermentioned sections of the following Ordinances are hereby extended, and made applicable to liberated slaves entering into contracts of service in Mauritius or Seychelles, viz :

Ordinance No. 13 of 1857,	§	29 —	See No.	545
Ordinance No. 16 of 1862,	§§	7	„	246
„	„	8	„	247
„	„	9	„	248
„	„	10	„	236
„	„	18	„	400
„	„	19	„	401
„	„	20	„	402
„	„	23	„	254.

Idem, Art. 10. **173.**—The Protector of Immigrants and Civil Commissioner of Seychelles are hereby appointed *ex-officio* guardians, respectively, to every orphan liberated slave, whether legitimate or illegitimate, in Mauritius and Seychelles respectively.

Idem, Art. 11. **174.**—It shall be lawful to the Governor in Executive Council from time to time to make Regulations for carrying out the purposes of this Ordinance, and from time to time to alter the same;

Pour les Esclaves Libérés débarqués à Maurice.

Pour chaque esclave libéré au-dessus de 14 ans..	£6.	0.	0
„ „ „ au-dessous de 14 „ ..	4.	0.	0
„ „ libérée au-dessus de 14 „ ..	5.	0.	0
„ „ „ audessous de 14 „ ..	4.	0.	0

Pour les Esclaves Libérés débarqués aux Seychelles.

Pour les hommes, les femmes et les enfants un taux uniforme de £1. 10. 0
(*Art.* 7 *de l'Ord. No.* 18 *de* 1865.—*Voir le No.* 169.)

171.—Les dits esclaves libérés seront engagés avec les personnes auxquelles ils seront répartis par le Protecteur des Immigrants s'ils sont à Maurice, et, s'ils sont aux Seychelles, par le Civil Commissioner de ces îles, conformément aux Réglements qui seront faits en vertu de la présente Ordonnance. Ord. No. 18 de 1865, Art. 8.

172.—Les dispositions des Ordonnances suivantes sont par ces présentes étendues et rendues applicables aux esclaves libérés qui passeront des Contrats de Service à Maurice ou aux Seychelles, à savoir : Idem, Art. 9.

L'Ordonnance No. 13 de 1857,	§ 29	—Voir le No.	545.
L'Ordonnance No. 16 de 1862,	§§ 7	„	„	246.
„	„ 8	„	„	247.
„	„ 9	„	„	248.
„	„ 10	„	„	236.
„	„ 18	„	„	400.
„	„ 19	„	„	401.
„	„ 20	„	„	402.
„	„ 23	„	„	254.

173.—Le Protecteur des Immigrants et le Civil Commissioner des Seychelles sont, par ces présentes, nommés chacun en ce qui le concerne, tuteurs d'office de tout esclave libéré orphelin, qu'il soit enfant légitime ou illégitime, à Maurice et aux Seychelles. Idem, Art. 10.

174.—Le Gouverneur en Conseil Exécutif pourra de temps à autre faire des Réglements pour mettre en vigueur les dispositions de la présente Ordonnance, et pourra aussi de temps à autre Idem. Art. 11.

and all such Regulations, on being published in the Government Gazette, shall have the same effect as if they had been contained *verbatim* herein, provided that they are not inconsistent with the spirit and meaning of any of the provisions hereof.

Govt. Notice No. 111 of 4th Nov. 1865, Art. 1.

175.—A Certificate of Allotment, in the form of the Schedule A, hereto annexed, shall be issued by the Protector of Immigrants, under his signature, to every person about to engage Liberated Slaves under Ordinance No. 18 of 1865.—(*Ord.* 18 *of* 1865.—*See No.* 163 *et seq.*)

Idem, Art. 2.

176.—The Certificate of Allotment shall mention the Wages and Rations to be given to the said Liberated Slaves during the period for which they are about to be engaged.

SCHEDULE A.

Certificate of Allotment.

The Liberated Slaves mentioned in the margin, are hereby allotted to , of , to be employed on the Estate, in the District of , as field-laborers (or domestic servants, *as the case may be*), for a period of years from the date of the Contract of service to be passed with them before the Depôt Stipendiary Magistrate.

The Wages and Rations of the said Liberated Slaves during the said period, shall be as follows :—

WAGES.

AGE.	PER MONTH.				
	1st Year.	2nd Year.	3rd Year.	4th Year.	5th Year.
	s.	s.	s.	s.	s.
From 7 to 9 years inclusive......	2	4	6	7	8
,, 10 to 12 ,, ...	4	6	8	9	10
,, 13 to 16 ,, ...	6	8	10	11	12
,, 17 to 20 ,, ...	8	10	11	12	13
,, 21 and upwards	10	11	12	13	14

modifier ces Réglements ; et les dits Réglements, lorsqu'ils auront été publiés dans la Gazette du Gouvernement, auront le même effet que s'ils avaient été contenus mot pour mot dans la présente Ordonnance, pourvu qu'ils ne soient pas incompatibles avec l'esprit et le sens d'aucune des dispositions de cette Ordonnance.

175.—Un Certificat de répartition, dans la forme de l'Annexe A, sera remis par le Protecteur des Immigrants, revêtu de sa signature, à toute personne disposée à engager des Esclaves Libérés en vertu de l'Ordonnance No. 18 de 1865.—(*Ord* : 18 *de* 1865.—*Voir le No.* 163 *et suiv.*) Avis du Gouv. No. 111 du 4 Nov. 1865, Art. 1.

176.—Le Certificat de répartition mentionnera les Gages et les Rations à donner aux dits Esclaves Libérés pendant la durée de leur engagement. Idem, Art. 2.

ANNEXE A.

Certificat de Répartition.

Les Esclaves Libérés mentionnés en marge sont par le présent répartis à de pour être employés sur l'établissement, , dans le District de , comme laboureurs (ou domestiques, *selon le cas*) pour années à partir de la date du Contrat de Service qui sera passé avec eux devant le Magistrat Stipendiaire du Dépôt.

Les Gages et Rations des dits Esclaves Libérés pendant la durée de ce contrat seront comme suit :

GAGES.

AGE.	PAR MOIS.				
	1re Année.	2me Année.	3me Année.	4me Année.	5me Année.
	s.	s.	s.	s.	s.
De 7 à 9 ans inclusivement	2	4	6	7	8
„ 10 à 12 „ „	4	6	8	9	10
„ 13 à 16 „ „	6	8	10	11	12
„ 17 à 20 „ „	8	10	11	12	13
„ 21 et au-dessus	10	11	12	13	14

ALLOWANCES.

Liberated Slaves of 10 years of age, and upwards, shall receive the following rations :

Rice,—one pound and a half, or two pounds of pounded Maize, or two pounds and a half of cooked Manioc, or five pounds of raw Manioc.	Per diem.
Dholl,—two pounds. Salt Fish,—two pounds. Ghee or Oil,—one pound. Salt,—one pound.	Per mensem.

N. B.—Liberated Slaves under 10 years of age, shall receive half of the above mentioned rations.

This day of 186 .

H. B.,
Protector of Immigrants.

Idem, Art. 4. 177.—To every Liberated Slave allotted by the Protector of Immigrants, a Ticket shall be delivered in the form of the Schedule B hereto annexed,—upon which Ticket the Engagement of the said Liberated Slave, shall be endorsed by the Depot Stipendiary Magistrate.

SCHEDULE B.

Liberated Slave arrived at the Depot on the 186 .

Number	(*Portrait.*)
Name	
Mother's Name	
Sex	
Age	
Stature	
Marks	
To whom allotted	
Date of allotment	
Term of allotment	

H, B.,
Protector of Immigrants.

This Chapter contains the whole of the legislation specially applicable to liberated African slaves. In all matters for which no provision is made here those servants fall within the common law of the Colony affecting laborers in general, and in such matters their rights and obligations may be ascertained on reference to the section of this work treating of the subject on which information is required.

RATIONS.

Les Esclaves Libérés âgés de 10 ans et plus, recevront les rations suivantes :

Riz,—une livre et demie, ou deux livres de maïs concassé, ou deux livres et demie de manioc cuit, ou cinq livres de manioc cru....	Par jour.
Dholl,—deux livres. Poisson salé,—deux livres. Ghee ou Huile,—une livre. Sel,—une livre.	Par mois.

N. B.—Les Esclaves Libérés âgés de moins de dix ans, recevront la moitié des rations sus-mentionnées.

Ce jour de 186 .

H. B.

Protecteur des Immigrants.

177.—Un Ticket dans la forme de l'Annexe B sera remis à chaque Esclave Libéré réparti par le Protecteur des Immigrants, et sur ce Ticket le Magistrat Stipendiaire du Dépôt inscrira l'engagement du dit Esclave Libéré. Idem, Art. 4.

CÉDULE B.

Esclave libéré arrivé au Dépôt le 186 .

Numéro ... ...
Nom .. ..
Nom de la Mère ... ...
Sexe... ... ...
Age ... ...
Taille.. ... ...
Marques ... ...
A qui réparti ... .
Date de la répartition ... ...
Durée de l'engagement... ... ...

(*Portrait.*)

H. B.,

Protecteur des Immigrants.

Ce Chapitre contient toute la législation qui se rapporte d'une manière spéciale aux Esclaves Africains Libérés. Dans tous les cas qui ne sont pas prévus ici, ces serviteurs sont régis par la loi ordinaire de la Colonie sur les travailleurs en général, et dans chacun de ces cas on pourra s'assurer de leurs droits et obligations en consultant la section de cet ouvrage qui traite du sujet sur lequel on désire se renseigner.

INDUSTRIAL RESIDENCE AND STAMP DUTY.

I.—*Definition, Release and Exemption.*
II.—*Redemption Money and Stamp Duty.*

CHAPTER I.

Definition, Release and Exemption.

Ord. No. 31 of 1867, Art. 1, Sect. 3.

178.—The term "Industrial Residence" * means a residence of five years in this Colony, or its Dependencies, under written contract of service for hire and performance of such Contract.

Idem, Art. 1, Sect. 4.

179.—The "Industrial Residence" shall be deemed to have been completed:

1st.—By service under such contract, one or more, for the term of five years, testified by a discharge therefrom under the hand of a Stipendiary Magistrate.

2nd.—By redemption, as hereinafter provided.— (*See Nos.* 186 *et seq.*)

3rd.—By release, as hereinafter provided.—(*See Nos.* 180 *et seq.*)

4th.—By exemption by the Governor, as hereinafter provided.— *See No.* 183.)

As to the effect of Industrial Residence on Immigrants who, on their arrival in the Colony, are under the age of 10 years,—See No. 123.

Idem, Art. 17.

180.—The following Employers are hereby empowered to release any new Immigrant from the whole or any unexpired residue of the term of Industrial Residence :

---

* All male Indian laborers who are introduced into Mauritius from British India at the expense of Government or of individual employers, are bound to complete an Industrial Residence of five years; after which, they may return to India at their own expense, or may remain in the Colony; in the latter case they enjoy the same rights as the rest of the population.

DE LA RÉSIDENCE INDUSTRIELLE ET DU DROIT DE TIMBRE.

I.—*De la Définition, de la Remise, et de l'Exemption.*
II.—*Du Rachat de la Résidence Industrielle et du Droit de Timbre.*

CHAPITRE I.

De la Définition, de la Remise, et de l'Exemption.

178.—L'expression " Résidence Industrielle * " signifie une résidence, en cette Colonie ou ses Dépendances de cinq années passées sous engagement par contrats de service écrits et dûment exécutés. Ord. No. 31 of 1867, Art. 1, Sect. 3.

179.—La " Résidence Industrielle " sera considérée comme étant achevée : Idem, Art. 1, Sect. 4.

1o.—Par le service en vertu d'un ou de plusieurs des dits contrats, pendant cinq années, certifié par la décharge du dit service signée par un Magistrat Stipendiaire.

2o.—Par le rachat ainsi qu'il est expliqué ci-après.—(*Voir les Nos.* 186 *et suiv.*)

3o.—Par la remise ainsi qu'il est expliqué ci-après.—(*Voir les Nos.* 180 *et suiv.*)

4o.—Par l'exemption émanant du Gouverneur, ainsi qu'il est expliqué ci-après.—*Voir le No.* 183.)

Quant à la Résidence Industrielle en ce qui concerne les Immigrants qui, à leur arrivée dans la colonie, ont moins de dix ans, voir le No. 123.

180.—Les Employeurs suivants sont autorisés par ces présentes à décharger tout nouvel Immigrant de la totalité ou de partie du temps requis pour leur résidence industrielle. Idem, Art. 17.

* Tous les laboureurs Indiens qui sont introduits à Maurice de l'Inde Anglaise aux frais du Gouvernement ou de simples particuliers, sont tenus d'achever une Résidence Industrielle de cinq ans. Ils peuvent ensuite soit retourner dans l'Inde ou se fixer dans la colonie ; dans ce dernier cas, ils jouissent des mêmes droits que le reste de la population.

1st. Any one of the Employers mentioned in *Article* 10.—(*Art* 10.—*See No.* 190.)

2nd. Any other Employer who shall have entered into a contract of service with such Immigrant for the unexpired residue of his Industrial Residence.

Provided that such release can only be effected during the currency of the contract of service with the Employer desirous of effecting the release, or upon the expiration or other determination of such contract, and before the Immigrant shall have engaged with any other Employer.

Govt. Notice No. 166 of 11th Nov. 1868, Art. 16.

181.—If any Requisitionist desire to release any New Immigrant on his arrival, from the contract passed between them, such Requisitionist shall either personally, or by his written authority given to another person, appear before the Protector of Immigrants, who shall thereupon explain to the Immigrant the effect of such release; and if the Immigrant agree thereto, the Protector shall cause both parties to sign in his presence a memorandum in the form of the Schedule G hereto annexed;—and the Immigrant so released shall thereupon be entitled to receive an Old Immigrant's *ticket* before leaving the Depot.—(*Ticket.—See No.* 275.)

SCHEDULE G.

*Release of a New Immigrant from Industrial Residence on his arrival.**

We being respectively the Employer and the Servant under a Contrat of Service made at in India, and dated the day of do hereby consent that the said second party shall from this day and henceforth be released from the said Contract and all obligations under the same.

The nature and effect of the above release have been explained by me to the said Immigrant who, having expressed his full consent hereto, both parties signed the same in my presence this day of one thousand eight hundred and sixty

H. B.

Protector of Immigrants.

---

* For this document a fee of two shillings is paid by the applicant to the Protector of Immigrants.—*See No.* 525.

1o. Tous les Employeurs mentionnés en l'*Article* 10.—(*Art.* 10.—*Voir le No.* 190).

2o. Tout autre Employeur qui aura passé un contrat de service avec cet Immigrant pour le temps restant à courir sur sa résidence industrielle.

Pourvu que cette remise ne puisse être effectuée que pendant le cours du contrat de service passé avec l'Employeur désirant faire cette remise, ou à l'expiration ou extinction pour toute autre cause de ce contrat, et avant que l'Immigrant ne se soit engagé avec un autre Employeur.

181.—Si un requérant désire dégager un nouvel Immigrant lors de son arrivée, du contrat passé entre eux, ce requérant devra, soit personnellement, soit par un agent dûment autorisé par lui par écrit, comparaître devant le Protecteur des Immigrants qui expliquera alors à l'Immigrant l'effet de ce dégagement ; et si l'Immigrant y consent, le Protecteur fera signer aux deux parties en sa présence un procès-verbal dans la forme de l'Annexe G ; et l'Immigrant ainsi dégagé aura le droit de recevoir un *ticket* d'ancien Immigrant avant de quitter le Dépôt.—(*Ticket.*—*Voir le No.* 275.) Avis du Gouv. No. 166 du 11 Nov. 1868, Art. 16.

CÉDULE G.

Remise à un Nouvel Immigrant de sa Résidence Industrielle lors de son arrivée. *

Nous, , étant respectivement l'Employeur et le Serviteur en vertu d'un contrat de service fait à dans l'Inde, et en date du jour de consentons par ces présentes que le dit serviteur soit à partir de ce jour déchargé du dit contrat et de toutes les obligations y contenues.

La nature et les effets de la dite décharge ont été expliqués par moi au dit Immigrant qui y a donné sa complète adhésion, et les deux parties l'ont signée en ma présence ce jour de mil huit cent soixante

H. B.
Protecteur des Immigrants.

---

* Un droit de deux schellings doit être payé pour ce document au Protecteur des Immigrants par celui qui lui en fera la demande.—*Voir le No.* 525.

Idem, Art. 17. **182.**—If an Employer desire to release any New Immigrant from any residue of Industrial Residence, under the provisions of *Article* 17 of Ordinance No. 31 of 1867, such release shall be confirmed by the Stipendiary Magistrate of their District on both parties expressing their consent thereto in his presence, and a memorandum of such release in form of the Schedule H hereto annexed, signed by both parties and certified by the Magistrate, shall be delivered to the Immigrant, who, on production thereof to the Protector of Immigrants, shall be entitled to receive an Old Immigrant's ticket.—(*Art.* 17.—*See No.* 180).

SCHEDULE H.

*Release of a New Immigrant from a residue of Industrial Residence.**

We being respectively the Employer and the Servant under a Contract of Service made in the District of on the day of do hereby consent that the said second party shall from this day and henceforth be released from the said Contract and all further obligations in respect of his Industrial Residence.

The nature and effect of the above release explained by me to the said Immigrant who, having expressed his full consent thereto, both parties signed the same in my presence this day of one thousand eight hundred and sixty

C. D.

Stipendiary Magistrate for the District of

Ord. No. 31 of 1867, Art. 18. **183.**—The Governor may, upon the certificate of the Protector of Immigrants or of a Stipendiary Magistrate, exempt, wholly or in part, from the obligation of Industrial Residence, any New Immigrant incapacitated from labor by infirmity, accident, sickness, or other cause, and not being, at the time of such exemption, under contract of service with any Employer.

The Governor may further grant to any such Immigrant, a free passage back to India.

Every such exemption shall be registered in the Protector's Office.

---

* This document bears a stamp of one shilling, to be paid by the applicant.—See No. 487.

182.—Si un Employeur désire remettre à un nouvel Immigrant le reste de sa résidence industrielle, en vertu des dispositions de l'*Article* 17 de l'Ordonnance No. 31 de 1867, cette remise sera confirmée par le Magistrat Stipendiaire de leur District, si les deux parties expriment leur consentement en sa présence, et un procès-verbal de cette remise dans la forme de l'Annexe H, signé par les deux parties et certifié par le Magistrat, sera remis à l'Immigrant qui, en le produisant au Protecteur des Immigrants, aura le droit de recevoirun ticket d'ancien Immigrant. —(*Art.* 17.—*Voir le No.* 180.) Idem, Art. 17.

CÉDULE H.

*Remise à un Nouvel Immigrant du reste de sa Résidence Industrielle.**

Nous étant respectivement l'Employeur et le Serviteur en vertu d'un contrat de service fait dans le District de le consentons par ces présentes que le dit serviteur soit à partir de ce jour déchargé du dit contrat et de toutes autres obligations relatives à sa Résidence Industrielle.

La nature et les effets de la dite décharge ont été expliqués par moi au dit Immigrant qui y a donné sa complète adhésion, et les deux parties l'ont signée en ma présence ce de mil huit cent soixante

C. D.
Magistrat Stipendiaire du District de

183.—Le Gouverneur pourra, sur le certificat du Protecteur des Immigrants ou d'un Magistrat Stipendiaire, exempter, totalement ou en partie, de l'obligation de la résidence industrielle, tout nouvel Immigrant incapable de travailler pour cause d'infirmités, d'accident, de maladie ou d'autre motifs, et ne se trouvant pas, au moment de cette exemption, engagé par contrat de service avec son Employeur. Ord. No. 31 de 1867, Art. 18.

Le Gouverneur pourra de plus accorder à cét Immigrant un passage gratuit pour retourner dans l'Inde.

Chacune de ces exemptions sera enregistrée au Bureau du Protecteur.

---

* Ce document est frappé d'un timbre d'un schelling qui est payé par celui qui en fait la demande.—Voir le No. 487.

Within eight days after completion of his Industrial Residence, the Immigrant must either obtain a Police Pass or re-engage under written contract.—*See No.* 280.

Immigrants who, on account of desertion or otherwise are not in possession of regular papers and are unable to prove that they are not bound in Industrial Residence, may be re-registered as new Immigrants by the Protector of Immigrants under *Art.* 15 *of Ord.* 16 *of* 1862, a special form of Ticket being thereupon issued to them.—(*Art.* 15 *of Ord.* 16 *of* 1862.—See No. 274.)

Ord. No. 16 of 1862, Art. 16. 184.—All persons receiving such Tickets, shall be dealt with on the same footing as new Immigrants subject to allotment as at the date of their several Tickets ;—but without prejudice to their being entitled to relief from any burden consequent thereon, upon shewing that they had previously completed the whole or part of their industrial residence in the Colony.

The rules existing at the time as to allotments, may be applied to all Immigrants receiving such Tickets, and also to all New Immigrants whose contracts of service shall be broken on account of any misconduct on their part.

Govt. Notice No. 166 of 11th Nov. 1868, Art. 31. 185.—If after his re-registration as aforesaid an Immigrant shews proof of his having previously gone through the whole or a part of his Industrial Residence, his Ticket shall be altered accordingly by the Protector of Immigrants, and mention of such alteration shall be made against the Immigrant's registration in the Immigration Office.

Any Immigrant intending to leave the Colony is bound to prove that he has completed his Industrial Residence.—(*See No.* 540.)

Subject to certain conditions New Immigrants are entitled to free themselves, by purchase, from the obligation of Industrial Residence.—(*See Nos.* 186 *et seq.*)

CHAPTER II.

Redemption-Money and Stamp-Duty.

In former times, the passage-money and other expenses connected with the introduction of Immigrants from British India were paid by the Colonial Government, which recovered a portion of its

Dans les huit jours qui suivront l'achèvement de sa Résidence Industrielle, l'Immigrant devra obtenir une Passe de la Police ou se réengager par contrat écrit.—(*Voir le No.* 280).

Les Immigrants qui, par suite de désertion ou pour toute autre cause n'ont pas des papiers réguliers, et qui ne peuvent pas prouver qu'ils ont achevé leur Résidence Industrielle ; peuvent être enregistrés une seconde fois comme de nouveaux Immigrants, conformément à l'*Article* 15 *de* l'*Ordonnance No.* 16 *de* 1862, par le Protecteur des Immigrants qui leur délivre alors un Ticket spécial.—(*Art.* 15 *de l'Ordonnance No.* 16 *de* 1862.—*Voir le No.* 274).

184.—Tous ceux qui recevront de pareils Tickets, seront traités sur le même pied que les nouveaux Immigrants et pourront être répartis à partir de la date de leurs Tickets ;—mais sans préjudice de leur droit de s'affranchir de toute obligation qui dépendra de leur ré-enregistrement s'ils peuvent prouver qu'ils se sont déjà libéré en totalité ou en partie de leur Résidence Industrielle dans la Colonie. Ord. No. 16 de 1862, Art. 16.

Les réglements relatifs à la répartition qui seront alors en vigueur s'appliqueront à tous Immigrants recevant de pareils Tickets ainsi qu'à tous les nouveaux Immigrants dont les Contrats de Service auront été rompus pour cause de mauvaise conduite de leur part.

185.—Si après son ré-enrégistrement comme il est dit plus haut, un Immigrant fournit la preuve qu'il s'est libéré de sa Résidence Industrielle en totalité ou en partie, son Ticket sera modifié en conséquence par le Protecteur des Immigrants, et mention de cette modification sera faite en regard de l'enregistrement de l'Immigrant au bureau de l'Immigration. Avis du Gouv. No. 166 du 11 Nov. 1868, Art. 31.

Tout Immigrant ayant l'intention de quitter la Colonie est tenu de prouver qu'il a achevé sa Résidence Industrielle.—(*Voir le No.* 540.)

Les nouveaux Immigrants, peuvent, sous certaines conditions, se libérer de l'obligation de la Résidence Industrielle.—(*Voir les Nos.* 186 *et suiv.*)

CHAPITRE II.

Du Rachat de la Résidence Industrielle et du Droit de Timbre.

Le prix du passage et les autres frais d'introduction d'Immigrants de l'Inde Anglaise étaient autrefois payés par le Gouvernement Colonial, qui se remboursait de cette avance en percevant, des

expenditure on this head by levying, on employers of New Immigrants, a tax or duty the amount of which was in proportion to the period for which the laborers were engaged: this duty was collected by means of Stamps. Under the present system of Immigration, the expenses of introduction are borne directly by the person at whose instance the men are brought to the Colony, and the Immigrants are bound to remain in the service of their introducer for the whole term of their industrial residence, *i. e.* five years: if the Contract be prematurely terminated, the New Immigrant must complete his industrial residence under written engagement with some other employer, who thereupon pays, on behalf of the introducer, the Stamp Duty above mentioned.

By an extension of the principle of securing to the introducer either the labor of the New Immigrant, or a proportional refund of the introduction-expenses, any New Immigrant, free from engagement, is entitled to rid himself of the obligation of working out the remainder of his industrial residence, by the payment of a certain sum on behalf of his introducer; and the sum so paid is called "Redemption-Money."

Ord. No. 31 of 1867, Art. 12.

186.—Any New Immigrant who, upon the expiration or other determination of any contract of service under which he has been engaged, shall be desirous of redeeming the remainder of his industrial residence, may do so by payment to the Protector of Immigrants, or to any other Officer duly appointed to receive the same, of a sum calculated at the rate of £1.12 per annum for the whole time required to complete his industrial residence; and thereupon he shall be entitled to receive a *ticket* of Old Immigrant. (*Ticket.—See No.* 275.)

Provided that for every fraction of a shilling calculated as payable in respect of redemption-money, one shilling shall be charged.

(For the disposal of redemption-money, see Nos. 196 *et seq*).

Idem, Art. 13.

187.—No redemption money shall be received from any New Immigrant under the provisions of the preceding Article, except upon production by him of his Ticket and other documentary proof shewing that he is free from engagement.

Idem, Art. 14.

188.—Any New Immigrant having good and sufficient reason, of a special and exceptional nature, for desiring to obtain his discharge from any Contract of Service under which he is engaged,

personnes qui employaient de nouveaux Immigrants, une taxe ou un droit dont le montant était en proportion du temps pour lequel les laboureurs étaient engagés ; ce droit était recouvré au moyen de timbres. D'après le système d'Immigration actuellement en vigueur, les frais d'introduction sont directement à la charge de la personne sur la demande de laquelle les Immigrants ont été introduits dans la Colonie, et ces Immigrants sont tenus de servir cette même personne pendant toute la durée de leur résidence industrielle, *i. e.* cinq ans. Dans le cas de la résolution prématurée du contrat, les nouveaux Immigrants sont tenus d'achever leur résidence industrielle sous engagement par contrat écrit avec une autre personne qui, lors de la passation du contrat, paie le droit de timbre ci-dessus mentionné, et cet argent est ensuite versé à la personne aux frais de laquelle les Immigrants ont été introduits.

Par une extension de ce principe d'assurer à la personne qui introduit des Immigrants dans la Colonie, soit le travail de ces Immigrants soit le remboursement proportionnel des frais encourus pour leur introduction, tout nouvel Immigrant qui n'est pas lié par un contrat de service, peut se libérer de l'obligation de telle portion de sa résidence industrielle qu'il lui reste à achever, en payant une certaine somme pour le compte de celui qui l'a introduit ; et la somme qu'il paie de cette façon s'appelle " Argent de Rachat de la Résidence Industrielle."

186.—Tout nouvel Immigrant qui, à l'expiration ou lors de la résolution pour toute autre cause d'un Contrat de Service par lequel il aura été engagé, voudra racheter le temps à courir sur sa résidence industrielle, pourra le faire en payant au Protecteur des Immigrants ou à tout autre officier dûment autorisé à cet effet, une somme calculée au taux de £ 1.12 par année pour tout le temps nécessaire pour achever sa résidence industrielle ; et sur ce paiement il aura le droit de recevoir un *ticket* d'Ancien Immigrant.—(*Ticket.—Voir le No.* 275.) Ord. No. 31 de 1867, Art. 12.

Pourvu que, pour chaque fraction d'un schelling payable pour ce rachat, il soit réclamé un schelling.

(Pour le remboursement, etc., de l'Argent de Rachat, voir les Nos. 196 et suivant.)

187.—Aucune somme pour rachat ne sera reçue d'un nouvel Immigrant, en vertu des dispositions de l'Article précédent, s'il ne produit pas son ticket et d'autres preuves écrites démontrant qu'il est libre de tout engagement. Idem, Art. 13.

188.—Tout nouvel Immigrant ayant des raisons bonnes et suffisantes, d'une nature spéciale et exceptionnelle, pour désirer obtenir sa décharge d'un Contrat de Service par lequel il est Idem, Art. 14.

may apply to the Stipendiary Magistrate of the District in which he is performing such Contract, stating the reasons for which he is desirous of obtaining such discharge, and the Magistrate shall thereupon give notice to the employer, and shall appoint a day for enquiring into the matter, and for hearing any evidence which the Immigrant or his employer may respectively adduce.

The Magistrate shall transmit to the Procureur General the proceedings upon such enquiry; and, in case the Procureur General shall be satisfied that good and sufficient reasons have as aforesaid been shewn for granting such discharge, he may authorize the Magistrate to grant the same upon previous payment of an indemnity by the Immigrant to Government for the benefit of the employer.

Such indemnity shall be calculated upon the sum paid by the employer for costs of introduction, as certified by the Protector, or for the stamp duty upon engagement, of such Immigrant, as the case may be, and shall be proportionate to the unexpired term of Service relatively with the whole term as stipulated in the Contract.

Govt. Notice No. 166 of 11th Nov. 1868, Art. 20.

189.—When any New Immigrant shall be entitled under Ordinance No. 31 of 1867 to redeem the remainder of his industrial residence, the redemption-money which he shall have to pay shall be received by the Chief Clerk of the Senior Stipendiary Magistrate's Office if it be in Port Louis, or by the District Cashier if it be in a Rural District; and an acquittance in the form of the Schedule K hereto annexed, shall thereupon be delivered to such Immigrant; upon presentation of which in the Immigration Office he shall be entitled to receive an old Immigrant's ticket.

SCHEDULE K.

Received from No. the sum of pounds shillings and pence sterling being the full amount due by him as redemption-money for the residue of his Industrial Residence.

District of this day of 186 .

Ord. No. 31 of 1867, Art. 10.

190.—No stamp duty or other impost is chargeable by or on behalf of Government in respect of passing any contract of service entered into between any new Immigrant, and :—

engagé, pourra s'adresser au Magistrat Stipendiaire du District dans lequel il remplit son engagement, et lui déclarer les raisons pour lesquelles il désire obtenir cette décharge, et le Magistrat en donnera alors avis à l'employeur, et fixera un jour pour instruire l'affaire et entendre tous témoignages que l'Immigrant ou son Employeur pourrait invoquer.

Le Magistrat transmettra au Procureur Général le résultat de l'enquête; et dans le cas où le Procureur Général sera satisfait que l'Immigrant a fait valoir des raisons bonnes et suffisantes comme il est dit plus haut pour que sa décharge lui soit accordée, il pourra autoriser le Magistrat à l'accorder après le paiement préalable par l'Immigrant au Gouvernement d'une indemnité au profit de l'employeur.

Cette indemnité sera calculée sur la somme payée par l'employeur comme frais d'introduction, dont le certificat du Protecteur fera foi, ou comme droit de timbre sur l'engagement de cet Immigrant, selon le cas, et sera proportionnée au temps de service non expiré par rapport à tout le temps stipulé au Contrat.

189.—Lorsqu'un nouvel Immigrant aura le droit, en vertu de l'Ordonnance No. 31 de 1867, de racheter le reste de sa Résidence Industrielle, la somme pour rachat qu'il aura à payer sera reçue par le premier commis du Senior Magistrat Stipendiaire si c'est au Port-Louis, ou par le caissier de district si c'est dans un District Rural; et un reçu dans la forme de l'Annexe K sera alors remis à cet Immigrant; sur la présentation de ce reçu au bureau de l'Immigration il aura le droit de recevoir un Ticket d'Ancien Immigrant. Avis du Gouv. No. 166 du 11 Nov. 1868, Art. 20.

CÉDULE K.

Reçu de No. la somme de livres shillings et pence sterling montant total dû par lui pour le rachat du reste de sa Résidence Industrielle.

District de ce jour de 186 ;

190.—Aucun droit de timbre ou autre impôt ne sera réclamé par ou pour le Gouvernement en raison d'un Contrat de Service passé entre un nouvel Immigrant et :— Ord. No. 31 de 1867, Art. 10.

1st.—The *Requisitionist* at whose expense such Immigrant shall have been introduced into the Colony, or those in his rights;

2nd.—The *Substituted Employer* of such Immigrant, or those in his rights.

(*Requisitionist,—Substituted Employer.*—For the legal meaning of these terms, see No. 550.)

Idem. Art. 11. 191.—Saving in the above cases, all contracts of service entered into with new Immigrants before a Stipendiary Magistrate, shall be subject to a stamp duty at the rate of £1. 12 per annum, payable by the Employer for the term of the engagement, or for so much thereof as may be requisite for the completion of the Immigrant's industrial residence.

It shall, however, be lawful for the Protector of Immigrants to authorize the engagement of any new Immigrant without payment of the above stamp duty, in any case where it shall appear to him necessary, in consequence of the bodily weakness or infirmity of such Immigrant, so to do, in order to enable such Immigrant to find employment.

Ord. No. 7 of 1858, Art. 1. 192.—When any New Immigrant engaged under a Contract of Service for which the proper duty has been paid shall, before the expiry of the time specified in the said Contract, agree to annul such Contract and to enter into a New Engagement with the same Employer, for a period comprehending any portion of the time embraced by such previous contract, no Stamp Duty shall be paid upon such New Engagement in so far as it relates to the aforesaid portion of time, but the New Engagement shall nevertheless be charged with the duty applicable to the additional or extended period of employment.

Idem, Art. 3. 193.—Provided that nothing in this Ordinance contained shall be held to extend to cases in which the first Engagement was broken by the Stipendiary Magistrate having jurisdiction therein on account of any act of misconduct or breach of contract by either of the parties thereto.

Govt. Notice No. 166 of 11th Nov. 1868 Art. 22. 194.—In all cases in which stamp-duty or redemption-money shall be chargeable on the Engagement of a New Immigrant, dis-

1o.—Le *Requérant* aux frais duquel cet Immigrant aura été introduit dans la Colonie, ou ceux à ses droits ;

2o.—*L'Employeur substitué* de cet Immigrant ou ceux à ses droits.

(*Le Requérant,—l'Employeur substitué.*—Pour l'explication légale de ces termes, voir le No. 550.)

191.—Excepté dans les cas prévus ci-dessus, tous les Contrats de Service passés avec de nouveaux Immigrants devant un Magistrat Stipendiaire, seront soumis à un droit de timbre au taux de £1.12 par année, payable par l'Employeur pour le temps de l'engagement, ou pour le temps qui pourra être nécessaire pour l'achèvement de la résidence industrielle de l'Immigrant. Idem, Art. 11.

Néanmoins, le Protecteur des Immigrants pourra autoriser l'engagement d'un nouvel Immigrant sans exiger le paiement du dit droit de timbre toutes les fois qu'il lui paraîtra nécessaire de le faire en raison de la faiblesse physique ou des infirmités de cet Immigrant, afin de permettre à ce dernier de trouver de l'emploi.

192.—Lorsqu'un nouvel Immigrant engagé par un contrat de service pour lequel le droit prescrit aura été payé, conviendra avant l'expiration de ce contrat, d'annuler le dit contrat et de passer un nouvel engagement avec le même employeur pour un temps comprenant une portion quelconque du temps stipulé dans le contrat précédent, aucun droit de timbre ne sera payé sur ce nouvel engagement en tant qu'il aura rapport à la dite portion de temps ; mais le dit nouvel engagement sera néanmoins soumis au droit payable pour tout le reste de sa durée. Ord. No. 7 de 1858, Art. 1.

193.—Pourvu que rien en la présente Ordonnance ne puisse être considéré comme devant s'étendre aux cas où le premier engagement aura été annulé par un Magistrat Stipendiaire compétent, pour cause de mauvaise conduite ou d'inexécution du contrat par l'une ou l'autre des parties. Idem, Art. 3.

194.—Dans tous les cas où un droit de timbre ou une somme de rachat sera dû lors de l'engagement d'un nouvel Immigrant Avis du Gouv. No. 166 du 11 Nov. 1868, Art. 22.

charged from a previous contract, the Stipendiary Magistrate before whom he shall be discharged shall distinctly endorse upon the Immigrant's ticket the amount chargeable on the said Immigrant's subsequent engagement, and the name and residence of the party to whom such stamp-duty or redemption-money shall be due.—(*See also No.* 198).

Idem, Art. 21. 195.—The Stamp-Duty chargeable on contracts of New Immigrants shall be received by the Chief Clerk of the Senior Stipendiary Magistrate in Port Louis, and by the District Cashier in each of the Rural Districts.

Ord. No. 31 of 1867, Art. 16. 196.—Saving in the case provided for by *Art.* 15, whenever any New Immigrant shall have entered into a Contract of Service with any of the Employers mentioned in *Article* 10, and such Contract shall for any cause whatever be determined prior to the completion of the term of Industrial residence of such Immigrant, such Employer shall be entitled to demand and receive from the Government any sum which may have been received by the Government by way of Stamp Duty upon any subsequent engagement of such Immigrant with a New Employer, or in respect of any Redemption of Industrial Residence by such Immigrant.—(*Arts.* 10 *and* 15,— *See Nos.* 190 *and* 197.)

Idem, Art. 15. 197.—In case any Contract of Service between a New Immigrant and any of the Employers mentioned in *Article* 10, or any Employer who shall have engaged such Immigrant for the unexpired residue of his industrial residence, shall have been cancelled by a Stipendiary Magistrate, upon the complaint of the Immigrant, under the provisions of any law in force at the time being, such employer shall have no right to any sum which may be received by the Government by way of Stamp Duty upon any subsequent Contract of Service entered into between such Immigrant and another employer, nor to any sum which may be received by the Government in respect of any Redemption of Industrial Residence by such Immigrant.—(*Art.* 10,—*See No.* 190.)

Govt. Notice No. 166 of 11th Nov. 1868, Art. 23. 198.—In every case in which the right to Stamp-Duty or Redemption-Money shall be forfeited under *Art.* 15 of Ordinance No. 31 of 1867, the Magistrate shall enter upon the Ticket of the Immigrant the following endorsement :

libéré d'un contrat précédent, le Magistrat Stipendiaire devant lequel il sera dégagé endossera distinctement sur le ticket de l'Immigrant la somme qui sera dûe lors de l'engagement subséquent du dit Immigrant, et le nom et la résidence de la personne à laquelle le montant de ce droit de timbre ou de cette somme de rachat sera du.—(*Voir aussi le No.* 198.)

195.—Le droit de timbre dû sur les contrats des nouveaux Immigrants sera reçu par le premier commis du Senior Magistrat Stipendiaire au Port Louis et par le Caissier de District dans chacun des Districts Ruraux. Idem, Art. 21.

196.—Excepté dans le cas prévu par l'*Article* 15, toutes les fois qu'un nouvel Immigrant aura passé un contrat de service avec un des employeurs mentionnés en l'*Article* 10 et que ce contrat sera éteint pour une raison quelconque, avant l'achèvement de la Résidence Industrielle de cet Immigrant, cet employeur aura le droit de demander et de recevoir du Gouvernement toute somme qui pourra avoir été reçue par le Gouvernement sous forme de droit de timbre sur l'engagement subséquent de cet Immigrant avec un nouvel employeur, ou pour rachat de Résidence Industrielle par le dit Immigrant.—(*Arts.* 10 *et* 15.—*Voir les Nos.* 190 *et* 197.) Ord. No. 31 de 1867, Art. 16.

197.—Dans le cas où un contrat de service entre un nouvel Immigrant et l'un des employeurs mentionnés dans l'*Article* 10 ou tout employeur qui aura engagé cet Immigrant pour le temps restant à courir sur sa Résidence Industrielle, aura été annulé par un Magistrat Stipendiaire, sur la plainte de l'Immigrant, en vertu des dispositions de toute loi alors en vigueur, cet employeur n'aura aucun droit aux sommes qui pourraient être reçues par le Gouvernement sous forme de droit de timbre pour tout contrat de service subséquent passé entre cet Immigrant et un autre employeur, ni aux sommes qui pourraient être reçues par le Gouvernement pour tout rachat de Résidence Industrielle par le dit Immigrant.—(*Art.* 10.—*Voir le No.* 190.) Idem, Art. 15.

198.—Toutes les fois qu'il y aura lieu à confiscation du droit de timbre ou de l'argent de rachat en vertu de l'*Article* 15 de l'Ordonnance No. 31 de 1867 le Magistrat endossera le ticket de l'Immigrant de la manière suivante : Avis du Gouv. No. 166 du 11 Nov. 1868, Art. 23.

"The Stamp-Duty or Redemption-Money chargeable on the future engagements of this Immigrant shall be due to Government."—(*Art.* 15,—*See No.* 197.)

Idem, Art. 24. 199.—The Stamp Duty or Redemption Money received by the Chief Clerk of the Senior Stipendiary Magistrate, or by any District Cashier, shall in each case be paid out by him on demand to the party entitled to claim and receive it, or to any other party in his right, if the claim be preferred within three months after the reception of the money by such Clerk or Cashier, and if proof be shewn, to the Stipendiary Magistrate of the District, of the claimant's right to receive such money.—(*See also No.* 203.)

Idem, Art. 25. 200.—The Chief Clerk of the Senior Stipendiary Magistrate's Office, and the District Cashiers in the Rural Districts, shall within the first week of each month, publish in the Government Gazette a return of all sums so received by them and still remaining unclaimed in their hands, stating the names and residences of the parties on whose behalf such sums have been recovered;—and a printed copy of every such return shall be conspicuously posted up in each of the Stipendiary Magistrates' Offices, and in the Immigration Office.

Idem, Art. 26. 201.—All such sums, if they remain unclaimed during three months, shall be paid into the Public Treasury.

Idem, Art. 27. 202.—The Treasurer shall have power to refund every sum so transferred to the Public Treasury; but not otherwise than on a certificate signed by the Stipendiary Magistrate of the District whence the amount shall have been transferred, setting forth that the claimant is entitled to receive the said money.

Idem, Art. 28. 203.—Accounts shall be kept by the Chief Clerk of the Senior Stipendiary Magistrate's Office and by the District Cashiers in the Rural Districts, of all such sums received, whether as Stamp-duty or as Redemption-money; of all reimbursements thereof made by them; and of all remittances thereof made to the Public Treasury; and, in case of each reimbursement, the signature of the Recipient of the money refunded, and that of the Stipendiary Magistrate, shall be taken on the Registers of such accounts.

" Le droit de timbre ou l'argent de rachat à percevoir lors de l'engagement futur de cet Immigrant sera dû au Gouvernement."—(*Art.* 15.—*Voir le No.* 197.)

199.—Le droit de timbre ou l'argent reçu par le premier commis du Senior Magistrat Stipendiaire ou par un Caissier de District sera payé par lui sur la demande de la partie ayant le droit de le réclamer et de le recevoir, ou à tout autre à ses droits, si la demande est faite dans les trois mois qui suivront l'encaissement de l'argent par le dit commis ou Caissier, et si preuve du droit du réclamant est fournie au Magistrat Stipendiaire du District.—(*Voir aussi le No.* 203.) Idem, Art. 24.

200.—Le premier commis du Senior Magistrat Stipendiaire et les Caissiers de District dans les Districts Ruraux feront dans la première semaine de chaque mois publier dans la Gazette du Gouvernement un état de toutes les sommes ainsi reçues par eux et restant entre leurs mains sans réclamation, et contenant les noms et résidences des personnes au profit desquelles ces sommes ont été recouvrées ; et une copie imprimée de chacun de ces états sera affichée dans les bureaux de tous les Magistrats Stipendiaires et dans celui de l'Immigration. Idem, Art. 25.

201.—Toutes les dites sommes seront versées au Trésor public si elles ne sont pas réclamées dans les trois mois qui suivront leur encaissement. Idem, Art. 26.

202.—Le Trésorier pourra rembourser toutes sommes ainsi versées au Trésor public ; mais seulement sur un certificat signé par le Magistrat Stipendiaire du District d'où la somme aura été envoyée, déclarant que la demande du réclamant est bien fondée. Idem, Art. 27.

203.—Le premier Commis du Senior Magistrat Stipendiaire et les Caissiers de District dans les Districts Ruraux tiendront des comptes de toutes les sommes ainsi reçues soit comme droit de timbre ou comme argent de rachat, de tous les remboursements faits par eux, et de toutes les remises faites au Trésor public ; et en cas de remboursement la signature de celui auquel l'argent aura été remboursé, et celle du Magistrat Stipendiaire seront prises sur les registres desdits comptes. Idem, Art. 28.

Immigrants who, on account of desertion or otherwise, are not in possession of regular papers and are unable to prove that they are Old Immigrants may be re-registered as New Immigrants, and re-allotted by the Protector under Articles 15 and 16 of Ordinance No. 16 of 1862,—for which see Nos. 274 and 184.

Idem. Art. 30. 204.—If an Immigrant re-registered under *Articles* 15 *and* 16 of Ordinance No. 16 of 1862 and thereafter engaged, be discovered to be under a previous Contract and such Contract be enforced, the whole or a part (as the case may be) of the Stamp-Duty received from the last Employer shall be refunded to him on his applying to the Protector of Immigrants :—the amount of every such repayment shall be proportional to the time of Service remaining to be performed under the Immigrant's last Contract. —(*Articles* 15 *and* 16,—*See Nos.* 274 *and* 184).

CONTRACTS OF SERVICE.

I.—*Engagements and Discharges.*
II.—*Duration, &c., of labor.—Effect on Contract of Imprisonment,—and of Sale &c., of estate.*
III.—*Ill-usage.*
IV.—*Breach of Contract by the Master.*
V.—*Breach of Contract by the Servant.*
VI.—*Causes of premature termination of the Contract.*
VII.—*Illegal employment, Harbouring, &c., of Laborers.*
VIII.—*Apprenticeship.*

CHAPTER I.

Engagements and Discharges.

Order in Council, 7th Sept. 1838, Cap. 2, Sect. 1. 205.—No Contract of Service shall be of any force or effect within any of the *Colonies aforesaid,* unless the same shall be made within the limits and upon the land of the Colony in which the same is to be performed.—(*Colonies aforesaid.* i. e. *British Guiana, Trinidad, St-Lucia and Mauritius.*)

Les Immigrants qui, par suite de désertion ou pour toute autre cause, ne possèdent pas des papiers réguliers ou ne peuvent pas prouver qu'ils sont d'anciens Immigrants, peuvent être enregistrés et répartis une seconde fois comme de nouveaux Immigrants par le Protecteur, conformément aux Articles 15 et 16 de l'Ordonnance No. 16 de 1862.—Voir pour ces Articles les Nos. 274 et 184.

204.—Si l'on découvre qu'un Immigrant ré-enregistré en vertu des *Articles* 15 *et* 16 de l'Ordonnance No. 16 de 1862 et qui se sera ensuite engagé, est lié par un contrat précédent, et si l'on cherche à se prévaloir de ce contrat, la totalité ou partie (selon le cas) du droit de timbre reçu du dernier employeur sera remboursé, s'il le réclame du Protecteur des Immigrants ; le montant de ce remboursement sera en proportion du temps de service que l'Immigrant restera devoir en vertu de son dernier contrat.—(*Arts.* 15 *et* 16.—Voir les Nos. 274 et 184. Idem, Art. 30.

DES CONTRATS DE SERVICE.

I.—*Des Engagements et des Décharges.*
II.—*De la durée, etc., du travail.—Effet sur le Contrat de l'Emprisonnement,—et de la vente &c., de l'établissement.*
III.—*Des mauvais traitements.*
IV.—*De la violation du Contrat par le Maître.*
V.—*De la violation du Contrat par le Serviteur.*
VI.—*Des causes de la résolution prématurée du Contrat.*
VII.—*De l'Emploi illégal, etc., des laboureurs.*
VIII.—*De l'Apprentissage.*

CHAPITRE I.

Des Engagements et des Décharges.

205.—Aucun contrat de service n'aura aucune force ou effet dans aucune des dites *colonies,* à moins qu'il ne soit fait dans les limites et sur le territoire de la colonie dans laquelle il doit être exécuté.—(*Colonies,* i. e. *la Guiane Anglaise, Trinidad, Ste-Lucie et Maurice.*) Ordre en Conseil du 7 Sept. 1838, Ch. 2, Sect. 1.

Under the present law there are two exceptions to this rule: 1st. as to Contracts passed within the limits of the United Kingdom, (*See No.* 206); and 2nd. as to laborers engaged in India under Contracts of Service to be performed in Mauritius.—(*See No.* 109.)

Order in Council 23rd June 1841.

206.—Whereas an order was made by Her Majesty by the advice of Her Privy Council on the 7th of September 1838 for the regulation of the relative rights and duties of Masters and Servants within the Colonies of British Guiana, Trinidad, St.-Lucia and Mauritius.—And whereas it is by the 1*st. Section of the 2nd Chapter* of the aforesaid order provided that no Contract of Service shall be of any force or effect within any of the Colonies aforesaid unless the same shall be made within the limits and upon the land of the Colony in which the same is to be performed.—And whereas it is expedient that an exception should be made in the provision aforesaid as to any Contracts of Service made within the limits of the United Kingdom. It is therefore hereby ordered by the Queen's Most Excellent Majesty by and with the advice of Her Privy Council that the said recited provision shall not extend to any Contracts of Service made within the limits of the United Kingdom.—(*Sect.* 1, *Chap.* 2,—*See No.* 205.)

Order in Council 7th Sept. 1838, Cap. 2, Sect 2.

207.—No Contract of Service shall be in force within any of the said Colonies for more than four weeks from the date thereof, unless the same shall be reduced into writing, with all the formalities subsequently mentioned.—(*See No.* 221.)

Ord. No. 15 of 1852, Art. 2.

208.—Every oral engagement with any other *Servant* than a *New Immigrant*, unless it be otherwise stipulated, shall be held to have been made and to be binding for the period of one calendar month: and if a notice of an intention to terminate the engagement be not given by either party, at least 14 days before the expiration of any such month, the engagement shall be considered to have been renewed for another month, and to be binding upon both; and in the case of a *Master* dismissing a Servant without such notice, he shall be bound to pay one month's wages to the Servant, and in case of a Servant quitting a Master without such notice, he shall forfeit to the Master the like sum, or be subject, in default of immediate payment, to imprisonment for a period not exceeding ten days.—(*Servant, New Immigrant, Master.—For the legal meaning of these words see Nos.* 549 *and* 550.)

D'après la loi actuelle il y a deux exceptions à cette règle: 1o. Quant aux contrats passés dans le Royaume Uni, (*Voir le No.* 206); et 2o. quant aux engagements dans l'Inde d'Immigrants pour Maurice.—(*Voir le No.* 109.)

206.—Attendu que le 7 Septembre 1838, il a été fait par Sa Majesté de l'avis de son Conseil Privé, un ordre à l'effet de régler les droits et les devoirs respectifs des maîtres et des serviteurs dans les colonies de la Guiane Anglaise, Trinidad, Ste-Lucie et Maurice.—Et attendu que par *la première Section du second Chapitre* du sus-dit ordre, il est ordonné qu'aucun contrat de service ne sera valable dans l'une des colonies mentionnées ci-dessus, qu'autant qu'il aura été passé dans les limites et sur le territoire de la colonie, où le dit contrat doit recevoir son exécution. Et attendu qu'il est convenable qu'une exception soit faite à cette disposition de la section première du second chapitre de l'ordre dont s'agit, relativement aux contrats de service passés dans les limites du Royaume Uni. Il est en conséquence ordonné par ces présentes par Sa Très Excellente Majesté la Reine, de l'avis de son Conseil privé, que la disposition ci-dessus relatée ne s'appliquera pas aux contrats de service passés dans les limites du Royaume-Uni.—(*Section* 1, *Chap.* 2,—*Voir le No.* 205.) Ordre en Conseil du 23 Juin 1841.

207.—Aucun Contrat de Service ne sera valable dans aucune des dites colonies pour plus de quatre semaines à partir de sa date, à moins qu'il ne soit rédigé par écrit, avec toutes les formalités ci-dessous mentionnées.—(*Voir le No.* 221.) Ordre en Conseil du 7 Sept. 1838, Ch. 2, Sect. 2.

208.—Tout engagement verbal contracté avec tout autre *Serviteur* qu'un *nouvel Immigrant*, sera, à moins qu'il n'ait été stipulé autrement, réputé avoir été fait et être obligatoire pour la durée d'un mois ; et si avis de l'intention de terminer l'engagement n'est pas donné de part ou d'autre, au moins 14 jours avant l'expiration du-dit mois, l'engagement sera considéré comme ayant été renouvelé pour un autre mois, et, comme liant les deux parties ; et lorsqu'un *Maître* congédiera un serviteur sans lui donner le dit avis, il devra payer un mois de gages à ce serviteur, et lorsqu'un serviteur quittera le service de son maître sans lui donner le dit avis, il indemnisera son maître de la même somme ou sera soumis, à défaut de paiement immédiat, à l'emprisonnement, pendant un temps qui n'excèdera pas dix jours.—(*Serviteur, Nouvel Immigrant, Maître.—Pour la définition légale de ces termes.—Voir les Nos.* 549 *et* 550.) Ord. No. 15 de 1852, Art. 2.

Govt. Notice No. 166 of 11th Nov. 1868, Art. 45.

209.—Any person convicted of having passed a fictitious verbal engagement with a laborer, and having thus assisted such laborer in procuring a *Police-Pass* under false pretences, shall be liable to a fine not exceeding Ten Pounds.—(*Police Pass.—See Nos.* 280 *et seq.*)

A similar penalty may be inflicted in cases of fictitious written contracts with Immigrants.—*See No.* 258.

Ord. No. 31 of 1867, Art. 4.

210.—No Contract of Service entered into in this Colony or its Dependencies with a new Immigrant, is valid unless made in writing before a Stipendiary Magistrate.

Order in Council, 7th Sept. 1838, Cap. 2, Sect. 4.

211.—No such written Contract for service shall be valid for more than one year from its date.

Until lately there were only three exceptions to this rule: 1o. As to contracts for three years made with Immigrants from elsewhere than British India,—(*See No.* 137); 2o. As to Five years Engagements entered into with Immigrants in India,—(*See No.* 118); and 3o. As to Liberated African Slaves landed in Mauritius and contracting for Five years,—(*See No.* 164): but the following provision (No. 212), authorising any servant, except a Female Immigrant, to engage for any term not exceeding Five years, seems to have virtually and wholly repealed that Section.

Ord. No. 31 of 1867, Art. 3.

212.—Contracts of Service, whether made in India under the provisions of any law in force at the time being, or made in this Colony or its Dependencies before a Stipendiary Magistrate, are valid and binding for such term, not exceeding five years, as shall be stipulated in the contract.

The present article does not apply to contracts of service made with female Immigrants: special provision having been made for the same by *Art.* 11 *of Ord.* 16 *of* 1862.—(*Art.* 11 *of Ord.* 16 *of* 1862.—*See No.* 219.)

Order in Council 7th Sept. 1838, Cap. 2, Sect. 5.

213.—Every such written Contract shall expire at the close of the stipulated time of service without any notice on either side for that purpose.

Idem, Cap. 2, Sect. 6.

214.—Every such written Contract shall specify as accurately as may be, the general nature of the employment in which the servant is to be engaged.

209.—Toute personne trouvée coupable d'avoir passé un engagement verbal fictif avec un travailleur, et d'avoir ainsi aidé ce travailleur à se procurer une *Passe de Police* sous de faux prétextes, sera passible d'une amende n'excédant pas Dix Livres Sterling.—(*Passe de Police.—Voir les Nos.* 280 *et suiv :*) Avis du Gouv. No. 166 du 11 Nov. 1868, Art. 45.

Une pénalité semblable peut être infligée dans les cas où des contrats écrits fictifs sont passés avec des Immigrants.—(*Voir le No.* 258.)

210.—Aucun Contrat de Service passé en cette Colonie ou ses Dépendances avec un nouvel Immigrant, n'est valable à moins qu'il ne soit fait par écrit devant un Magistrat Stipendiaire. Ord. No. 31 de 1867, Art. 4.

211.—Aucun Contrat de Service fait par écrit ne sera valable pour plus d'un an à partir de sa date. Ordre en Conseil du 7 Sept. 1838, Ch. 2, Sect. 4.

Tout récemment il n'y avait que trois exceptions à cette règle : 1o. Quant aux contrats pour trois ans passés avec des Immigrants d'ailleurs que de l'Inde Anglaise,—(*Voir le No.* 137) ; 2o. Quant aux engagements de cinq ans passés avec des Immigrants dans l'Inde,—(*Voir le No.* 118) ; et 3o. Quant aux Esclaves Africains Libérés qui à leur débarquement à Maurice contractaient des engagements de cinq ans,—(*Voir le No.* 164) : mais la disposition suivante (No. 212) qui permet à tout serviteur, excepté les Immigrants du sexe féminin, de s'engager pour tout laps de temps n'excédant pas cinq ans, semble avoir virtuellement et entièrement abrogé cet Article.

212.—Les Contrats de Service, qu'ils soient faits dans l'Inde en vertu des dispositions d'une loi actuellement en vigueur, ou dans cette Colonie ou ses Dépendances devant un Magistrat Stipendiaire, sont valables et lient les parties pour tout laps de temps, n'excédant pas cinq ans, qui sera stipulé dans le contrat. Ord. No. 31 de 1867, Art. 3.

Le présent Article ne s'applique pas aux Contrats de Service faits avec les Immigrants du sexe féminin ; une disposition spéciale à cet effet existant dans l'*Art.* 11 *de l'Ordonnance No.* 16 *de* 1862.— (*Art.* 11 *de l'Ordonnance No.* 16 *de* 1862.—*Voir le No.* 219.)

213.—Chaque Contrat de Service par écrit cessera à l'expiration du tems de service stipulé, sans qu'il soit besoin d'avertissement de part ou d'autre à cet effet. Ordre en Conseil du 7 Sept. 1838, Ch. 2, Sect. 8.

214.—Chaque Contrat de Service par écrit devra spécifier, aussi exactement que possible, la nature générale de l'emploi pour lequel le serviteur est engagé. Idem, Ch. 2, Sect. 6.

Idem, Cap. 2, Sect. 8.

215.—In cases in which the remuneration or any part of it is to be made not in money but in kind, the Contract must specify, with all practicable precision, the nature and amount and quality of the articles to be supplied to the servant, and the time when, and the places or place at which such articles are to be delivered.

Idem, Cap. 2, Sect. 7.

216.—When the Contract is for work to be performed not by the piece, but by the time, it shall specify, as precisely as may be, the number of hours of daily labour, and the hours of the day at which such labour is to commence and to be suspended, and to recommence and to terminate.—(*See also Nos.* 241 *et seq.*)

Idem, Cap. 2, Sect. 10.

217.—All Contracts of Service shall be drawn up as nearly as possible in the following terms *:—

"Be it remembered, that on this day of , in the year of our Lord , A. B. of and C. D. of appeared before me, E. F., a Stipendiary Magistrate of the Colony of , and in my presence signed their names or marks (as the case may be) to the following Contract of Service.

"The said A. B. agrees to hire the services of the said C. D., and the said C. D. agrees to render to the said A. B. his services in the capacity of a for calendar months, commencing on the day of inst., and terminating on the day of in the year . And it is further agreed between the said parties, that the said C. D. shall be employed in [field labour], or as [a household servant], or [as a boatman] (as the case may be), and that the hours of labour of the said C. D. shall not be more than daily, commencing at the hour of and terminating at the hour of with [one hour] (or as the case may be) for breakfast at of the clock, and [one hour] (as as the case may be) for dinner at of the clock, daily. And it is further agreed, that the said A. B. shall pay to the said C., D. as such servant as aforesaid, wages at and after the rate of by the [day, week, month, or year], (as the case may be), and that such wages shall be paid on the day of each [week or month] (as the case may be). And it is further agreed, that the services of the said C. D. shall be partly or wholly (as the case may be) remunerated by the delivery to the said C. D. of the various articles and allowances specified in the list hereunto subjoined, which shall be of such amounts and qualities as are specified in the said list, so far as such specification is possible.

[Here add any special engagement compatible with the law and not adverted to in this form.]

(Signed) A. B.
C. D.

---

* The forms of engagements may be altered from time to time.—*See No.* 301.—For Contracts of Service made in India, or passed with allotted Immigrants in Mauritius, or with Female Immigrants,—*See Nos.* 118, 131 *and* 219.

215.—Dans les cas où toute ou partie de la rétribution doit être donnée non en argent mais en nature, le contrat devra spécifier avec toute la précision possible, la nature, le montant et la qualité des articles qui doivent être donnés aux serviteurs, et l'époque ainsi que les lieux ou le lieu où ils devront être livrés. Idem. Ch. 2, Sect. 8.

216.—Lorsque le contrat a pour objet un ouvrage à faire non à la pièce, mais à la journée, il spécifiera, aussi précisément que possible, le nombre d'heures de travail journalier, et les heures du jour auxquelles le dit ouvrage devra commencer, être suspendu, recommencer et finir.—(*Voir aussi les Nos.* 241 *et suiv*). Idem, Ch. 2, Sect. 7.

217.—Tous les Contrats de Service seront rédigés autant que possible dans les termes suivants * :— Idem, Ch. 2, Sect. 10.

" Qu'il soit notoire que ce jour de de l'année de Notre Seigneur , A. B. de et C. D. de ont comparu devant moi E. F., Magistrat salarié de la Colonie de , et ont en ma présence signé leurs noms ou apposé leur marque (selon le cas) au Contrat de Service suivant.

" Le dit A. B. s'engage à louer les services du dit C. D., et le dit C. D. s'engage à donner au dit A. B. ses services en qualité de pour mois, à partir du jour de de l'année finissant le jour de de l'année .

" Et il est de plus convenu entre les dites parties que le dit C. D. sera employé [au travail des champs] ou comme [domestique] ou comme [batelier] (suivant le cas) et que les heures de travail du dit C. D. n'excèderont pas par jour, commençant à l'heure de et finissant à l'heure de , avec [une heure] (ou comme le cas l'exigera) pour déjeûner à heures, et [une heure] (ou comme le cas l'exigera) pour le diner à heures, chaque jour.

" Et il est de plus convenu que le dit A. B. paiera au dit C. D. son serviteur comme ci-dessus désigné, des gages à raison de par [jour, semaine, mois ou an] (suivant le cas) et que les dits gages seront payés le jour de chaque [semaine ou mois] (suivant le cas.)

" Et il est de plus convenu que les services du dit C. D. seront en partie, ou entièrement (suivant le cas) rétribués par la remise au dit C. D. des divers articles et fournitures spécifiés dans la liste ci-jointe, lesquels seront de la valeur et de la qualité spécifiées dans la dite liste, autant qu'une telle spécification est possible.

(Ajoutez ici toute stipulation d'engagement compatible avec la loi, et qui ne serait pas prévue par la présente forme.)

(Signé :) A. B.
C. D.

---

* La forme des engagements peut être modifiée de temps à autre.—*Voir le No.* 301. —Pour les Contrats passés dans l'Inde, ou à Maurice avec des Immigrants répartis, ou avec des Immigrantes,—.*Voir les Nos*. 118, 131 *et* 219.

"The preceding agreement was signed by the above-named parties in my presence on the day and year above written, voluntarily, the same being as far as I am able to judge fully understood by them respectively.

(Signed) E. F.,
Stipendiary Magistrate.

Govt. Notice No. 166 of 11th Nov. 1868, Art. 15.

218.—All Contracts of Service passed before any Stipendiary Magistrate with laborers who are *allotted Immigrants,** shall be in the form of the Schedule F hereto annexed.—(*Allotted Immigrants,—See Nos.* 129 *et seq.*)

SCHEDULE F.

General form of Contract of Service.

Be it remembered that on this day of in the year of Our Lord one thousand eight hundred and sixty of and the Immigrants named on the list hereto subjoined, appeared before me, Stipendiary Magistrate, and in my presence signed their names or marks to the following Contract of Service.

The said agree to hire the services of the said Immigrants and the said Immigrants agree to render to the said their services in the capacity of for calendar months, commencing on the day of in the year one thousand eight hundred and sixty .

And it is further agreed that the said shall pay to the said Immigrants, the wages mentioned opposite to their respective names in the list hereto subjoined and that such wages shall be paid monthly.

And it is also agreed that the services of the said Immigrants shall be further remunerated by the delivery to them of the various articles hereunder specified, viz :—

Rice...	pounds, per diem.
Dholl.	pounds, per week.
Salt Fish...	do.
Oil	do.
Salt	do.

Proper lodging and medical care shall be provided by the said to the said Immigrants.

And it is further agreed, that if the said shall at any time employ the said Immigrants on any other Estate than that which

* If the Contract be made with one or more Old Immigrants, it must bear a stamp of two shillings to be paid by the Employer.—*See No,* 487.

" L'engagement précédent a été signé, en ma présence et volontairement, par les sus-nommés, les jours et an indiqués ci-dessus, et autant que j'en puis juger, il a été bien compris par les parties respectivement.

(Signé :) E. F.,
Magistrat salarié.

218.—Tous les Contrats de Service passés devant le Magistrat Stipendiaire avec des travailleurs qui ne seront pas des *Immigrants répartis,** seront faits dans la Forme de la Cédule F annexée à ces présentes.—(*Immigrants répartis.—Voir les Nos.* 129 *et suiv.*) Avis du Gouv. No. 166 du 11 Nov. 1868, Art. 15.

CÉDULE F.

Forme générale d'un contrat de Service.

Ce jour de mil huit cent soixante , de et les Immigrants nommés dans la liste ci-jointe ont comparu devant moi Magistrat Stipendiaire, et en ma présence ont signé leurs noms ou apposé leurs marques au contrat de service suivant.

Le dit consent à louer les services des dits Immigrants et les dits Immigrants consentent à rendre au dit leurs services en qualité de pour mois, commençant le jour de mil huit cent soixante .

Et il est de plus convenu que le dit paiera aux dits Immigrants les gages mentionnés en regard de leurs noms respectifs dans la liste ci-jointe et que les dits gages seront payés mensuellement.

Et il est de plus convenu que les services des dits Immigrants seront en outre rémunérés par la distribution des divers articles ci-dessous spécifiés, savoir :

Riz...	livres par jour.
Dholl	livres par semaine.
Poisson salé...	do.
Huile	do.
Sel...	do.

Des logements convenables et des soins médicaux seront fournis par le dit aux dits Immigrants

Et il est de plus convenu, que si le dit emploie jamais les dits Immigrants sur une autre propriété que celle connue sous le nom

---

* Si le Contrat est passé avec un ou plusieurs anciens Immigrants, il doit être frappé d'un timbre de deux schellings qui sont payés par l'Employeur.—*Voir le No.* 487.

is known by the name of   and situate in the District of   except with the consent of the said Immigrants given in the presence of the Stipendiary Magistrate of the said District, then this present contract of service shall *ipso facto* become null and void.

And it is further agreed that if the above-mentioned Estate be sold, alienated or transferred to another person, or succeeded to by another person before the expiration of this present contract, the said Immigrants shall serve such other person according to the terms of this contract, such new employer being held bound towards the said Immigrants in all the stipulations and obligations incumbent upon the Employer so replaced by him.

The preceding agreement was signed by the abovenamed parties in my presence the day and year above written, voluntarily, the same being, as far as I am able to judge, fully understood by them respectively.

District of   , this   day of   one thousand eight hundred and sixty   .

Stipendiary Magistrate.

Name of Immigrant.	No.	Wages.			Name of Immigrant.	No.	Wages.		
		£	S.	D.			£	S.	D.

Ord. No. 16 of 1862, Art. 11. **219.**—Female Immigrants from India may be engaged either in India or in Mauritius, upon Contracts in the terms of Schedule F ;—provided that they shall only be employed in such lighter kind of labour as they may be fitted for, and also provided that no such Contract be for a longer period than one year.

SCHEDULE F.

Form of contract for Female Emigrants.

We, the undersigned Indian Women, emigrating from   to Mauritius, hereby engage to serve the Employers to whom we may be allotted by the Government of Mauritius, as   , for a period of one year from the date of such allotment, provided that we shall only have to perform such work as shall be fixed and determined by the Protector of Immigrants, in our respective certificates of allotment ; that the Special Contracts we shall enter into at Mauritius shall be liable to be modified or suspended either by the Protector or

de et située dans le district de si ce n'est du consentement des dits Immigrants donné en présence du Magistrat Stipendiaire du dit District, le présent contrat de service deviendra nul de plein droit.

Et il est de plus convenu que si la dite propriété est vendue, aliénée ou transférée à une autre personne, ou échoit par succession à une autre personne avant l'expiration du présent contrat, les dits Immigrants serviront cette autre personne aux conditions de ce contrat, le nouvel employeur se trouvant lié envers les dits Immigrants par toutes les stipulations et obligations contractées par l'employeur remplacé par lui.

Les conventions qui précèdent ont été signées par les parties susdites en ma présence les jours et an sus-dits, volontairement, les dites parties les ayant bien comprises, autant que j'aie été capable d'en juger.

District de , ce jour de mil huit cent soixante .

Magistrat Stipendiaire.

Nom de l'Immigrant.	No.	Gages.			Nom de l'Immigrant.	No.	Gages.		
		£	s.	D.			£	s.	D.

219.—Les Immigrantes Indiennes pourront être engagées soit dans l'Inde soit à Maurice par Contrats dans les termes de la Cédule F; pourvu qu'elles soient employées à tel genre de travail plus doux qui pourra mieux leur convenir, et pourvu aussi que tout Contrat sus-dit ne soit pas pour plus d'un an. Ord. No. 16 de 1862, Art. 11.

CÉDULE F.

Forme de Contrat pour les Emigrantes.

Nous, femmes Indiennes, soussignées, émigrant de à Maurice, nous engageons à servir les employeurs auxquels nous serons réparties par le Gouvernement de Maurice comme pour une année à compter de la date de cette répartition à la condition que nous n'aurons à faire d'autre ouvrage que celui qui sera fixé et déterminé par le Protecteur des Immigrants dans nos certificats respectifs de répartition ; que les contrats spéciaux que nous passerons à Maurice pourront être modifiés ou suspendus par le Protecteur, ou

by the Stipendiary Magistrates, in cases provided for by law; and that we shall receive the Wages mentioned hereunder opposite to our respective names, and the Allowances following:

Rice, one pound and a half, or two pounds of pounded Maize, or two pounds and a half of cooked Manioc, or five pounds of raw Manioc	per diem	Half of these Rations to be given to those of us who are under 10 years of age.
Dholl, two pounds	per mensem	
Salt Fish, two pounds... ...	do.	
Ghee or Oil, one pound ...	do.	
Salt, one pound	do.	

Provided also that proper lodging and medical care be supplied to us.

And we further agree that if the Estate on which we shall be bound to serve, be sold, alienated, or transferred to another person, or succeeded to by another person, before the expiration of our service, we shall serve such other person according to the terms of this Contract, such new Employer being held bound towards us in all the stipulations and obligations incumbent upon the Employer so replaced by him.

No.	Name of Emigrant.	Father's Name.	Age	Married or Single.	Wages per Month.	Emigrant's Signature.	Remarks.

The above Contract was fully explained to the above mentioned Female Emigrants in my presence, this and signed by them before me.

A. B.

Mauritius Emigration Agent.

Idem, Art. 12. **220.**—It shall be lawful to the Protector of Immigrants, or the Stipendiary Magistrate of the District, to modify, and,—if necessary,—to suspend the Contract of any female who shall be unable to perform the conditions thereof, on account of family or domestic duties, or of advanced pregnancy.

Every such modification or suspension shall be made on terms equitable for both parties, and shall be endorsed, by the Protector or the Stipendiary Magistrate, on the Contract.

les Magistrats Stipendiaires, dans les cas prévus par la loi, et que nous recevions les gages mentionnés devant nos noms respectifs, et les rations suivantes :

Riz une livre et demie, ou deux livres de maïs moulu ou deux livres et demie de manioc cuit, ou cinq livres de manioc cru	par jour	La moitié de ces rations sera donnée à celles de nous qui sont au-dessous de l'âge de 10 ans.
Dholl, dix livres	par mois	
Poisson salé deux livres	do.	
Mantègue ou huile, une livre ...	do.	
Sel, une livre	do.	

A la condition aussi qu'il nous soit donné un logement convenable et les soins médicaux.

Et nous consentons de plus, que si le dit Etablissement venait à être vendu, aliéné ou transféré à une autre personne ou venait à échoir par héritage à une autre personne, avant l'expiration de notre Contrat à servir cette autre personne aux conditions de ce Contrat, notre nouvel Employeur étant lié envers nous par toutes les stipulations et obligations à la charge de l'Employeur qu'il aura ainsi remplacé.

No.	Nom de L'Emigrante.	Nom du père.	Age.	Mariée ou non mariée.	Gages par mois.	Signature de l'Emigrante.	Remarques.

Le dit Contrat a été bien expliqué aux Emigrantes sus-mentionnées en ma présence, ce et signé par elles devant moi.

A. B.

Agent d'Emigration pour Maurice.

220.—Le Protecteur des Immigrants ou le Magistrat Stipendiaire du District aura le droit de modifier, et, si cela est nécessaire, de suspendre le Contrat de toute femme qui sera incapable d'en remplir les conditions en raison de devoirs de famille ou de devoirs domestiques, ou d'une grossesse avancée. Idem, Art. 12.

Toute modification ou suspension sera faite dans des termes équitables pour les deux parties, et sera par le Protecteur ou le Magistrat Stipendiaire, écrite sur le dos du Contrat.

Order in Council 7th Sept. 1838, Cap. 2, Sect. 3.

221.—No written Contract of Service shall be in force within any of the said Colonies, unless it shall be signed with the name, or in case of illiterate persons, with the mark of each of the contracting parties in the presence of a Stipendiary Magistrate, nor unless such Stipendiary Magistrate shall subscribe the written Contract in attestation of the fact that it was entered into by the parties voluntarily, and with a clear understanding of its meaning and effect.

The Stipendiary Magistrate does not intervene in Contracts passed in India for service in the Colony.

Ord. No. 31 of 1867, Art. 74.

222.—It shall be lawful for the Governor to authorize any Clerk or Officer attached to the Stipendiary Court to perform all acts necessary for the passing of contracts of engagement and discharges of laborers, in lieu and stead of the Stipendiary Magistrate of such Court, subject to such Regulations as may be from time to time in that behalf made by the Governor in Executive Council, and published in the Government Gazette.

All contracts of engagement and discharges, passed or issued by any Clerk or Officer so authorized as above, shall be as valid and effectual, to all intents and purposes, as if passed or issued by the Stipendiary Magistrate.

Govt. Notice No. 166 of 11th Nov. 1868, Art. 87.

223.—No person shall be allowed to sign a Contract of Service or a Security-bond in the name and on behalf of any Employer unless he produce a power-of-attorney in due form signed by such Employer.

Ord. No. 31 of 1867, Art. 8.

224.—No written Contract of Service shall be passed with any minor under the age of 10 years.

No written Contract of Service shall be passed with any minor above the age of 10 years, and under the age of 15 years, unless with the consent of the Parent or Guardian of such minor *.

* The Protector of Immigrants is the Guardian of all Orphans of Indian extraction who have no relatives in the Colony.—*See No.* 509.

221.—Aucun Contrat de Service par écrit ne sera valable dans aucune des dites Colonies, à moins qu'il n'ait été signé du nom, ou si les personnes ne savent écrire, de la marque de chacune des parties contractantes en présence d'un Magistrat Salarié, et à moins que ce Magistrat n'y appose aussi sa signature pour attester le fait qu'il a été contracté volontairement par les parties, avec une connaissance claire de son objet et de ses effets. Ordre en Conseil du 7 Sept. 1838, Ch. 2, Sect. 3.

Le Magistrat Stipendiaire n'intervient pas dans les contrats passés dans l'Inde pour être exécutés dans la Colonie.

222.—Le Gouverneur pourra autoriser tout Commis ou Officier attaché à un Tribunal Stipendiaire à faire tous les actes nécessaires pour passer les Contrats d'Engagement et régulariser les décharges de travailleurs, au lieu et place du Magistrat Stipendiaire de ce Tribunal, en se conformant aux Réglements qui seront faits de temps à autre à cet effet par le Gouverneur en Conseil Exécutif, et publiés dans la Gazette du Gouvernement. Ord. No. 31 de 1867, Art. 74.

Tous Contrats d'Engagements qui auront été faits, et toutes décharges qui auront été régularisées par tout Commis ou Officier autorisé comme dessus, seront aussi valables et auront autant d'effet à tous égards que s'ils avaient été faits ou que si elles avaient été régularisées par le Magistrat Stipendiaire.

223.—Personne ne pourra signer un Contrat de Service ou un cautionnement au nom d'un employeur, s'il ne produit pas une procuration en bonne forme signée par cet employeur. Avis du Gouv. No. 166 du 11 Nov. 1868, Art. 87.

224.—Aucun Contrat de Service ne sera passé avec un mineur au-dessous de l'âge de 10 ans. Ord. No. 31 de 1867, Art. 8.

Aucun Contrat de Service ne sera passé avec un mineur au-dessus de l'âge de 10 ans mais au-dessous de l'âge de 15 ans, sans le consentement du Père ou de la Mère ou du tuteur de ce mineur *.

* Le Protecteur des Immigrants est le Tuteur de tous les Orphelins d'origine Indienne qui n'ont pas de parents dans la Colonie.—*Voir le No. 509.*

Any minor of the full age of 15 years or upwards, shall be free to engage under written contract of service, if the Parent or Guardian of such minor do not appear and object thereto at the time of passing such contract.

In case any minor above the age of 15 years shall have engaged under contract of service without the consent of his or her Parent or Guardian, such contract may, upon the application of the Parent or Guardian, and upon good and sufficient cause shewn to the satisfaction of the Stipendiary Magistrate, after hearing the employer and such further evidence as the Magistrate shall think fit, be cancelled.

Nothing in the present article contained shall be construed as invalidating any Contract of Service made in India.—(*See also No.* 123.)

Govt. Notice No. 166 of 11th Nov. 1868, Art. 35.

225.—Whenever any party shall appear before a Stipendiary Magistrate for the purpose of passing a Contract of Service with a laborer, if the status of such party and his capability of fulfilling the conditions of the proposed contract be not well known to the Magistrate, the contract shall not be passed until inquiries respecting such party shall have been made by the Magistrate through the Chief Police Officer of the District;—and, if the Magistrate be not satisfied that the person proposing to engage the laborer is in a position to pay his wages, the passing of the contract shall not be allowed.

Ord. No. 31 of 1867, Art. 20.

226.—Whenever any party shall appear before a Stipendiary Magistrate for the purpose of passing a contract of service with a laborer, and the said Magistrate shall have good grounds for believing that the said proposed contract is a fictitious contract, and that the parties thereto have no *bonâ fide* intention of executing the conditions thereof, or that the intended employer has not the means of paying the wages of the laborer, if engaged to him, it shall be in the discretion of the Magistrate either to refuse to pass the contract, or to postpone passing the same until the intended employer shall have proved to his satisfaction the *bonâ fides* of the proposed contract, or that he shall be able to pay the laborer's wages as they become due, as the case may be. — (*See also Nos.* 257 *and* 258).

Tout mineur qui aura atteint l'âge de 15 ans révolus sera libre de s'engager par Contrat de Service, si le Père ou la Mère ou le tuteur de ce mineur ne vient pas s'y opposer au moment de l'engagement.

Dans le cas où un mineur au-dessus de l'âge de 15 ans se serait engagé par Contrat de Service sans le consentement de son Père ou de sa Mère ou de son tuteur, le contrat pourra être annulé sur la demande du Père ou de la Mère ou du tuteur, pour des raisons bonnes et valables laissées à l'appréciation du Magistrat Stipendiaire, après qu'il aura entendu l'Employeur et toutes autres preuves qu'il jugera convenable.

Rien de ce qui est contenu dans le présent article ne sera considéré comme infirmant des Contrats de Service passés dans l'Inde.—(*Voir aussi le No.* 123.)

225.—Toutes les fois qu'une personne se présentera devant un Magistrat Stipendiaire dans le but de passer un Contrat de Service avec un travailleur, si la position de cette personne et les moyens de remplir les conditions du contrat proposé ne sont pas bien connus du Magistrat, le contrat ne sera pas passé jusqu'à ce que des recherches concernant cette personne aient été faites par le Magistrat par l'entremise de l'Officier en Chef de Police du District; et, si le Magistrat n'est pas convaincu que la personne proposant d'engager le travailleur a les moyens de lui payer ses gages, le contrat ne sera pas passé. **Avis du Gouv. No. 166 du 11 Nov. 1868, Art. 35.**

226.—Toutes les fois qu'une personne se présentera devant un Magistrat Stipendiaire dans le but de passer un Contrat de Service avec un travailleur, et que le dit Magistrat aura de bonnes raisons pour supposer que le dit contrat sera fictif, et que les parties n'ont pas l'intention d'en exécuter de bonne foi les conditions, ou que l'employeur proposé n'aurait pas les moyens de payer les gages du travailleur s'il était engagé avec lui, le Magistrat aura le pouvoir discrétionnaire soit de refuser de passer le contrat ou d'en ajourner la passation jusqu'à ce que l'employeur proposé ait prouvé à sa satisfaction la bonne foi du contrat proposé, ou qu'il aura les moyens de payer les gages du travailleur à mesure qu'ils seront dûs, selon le cas.—(*Voir aussi les Nos.* 257 *et* 258.) **Ord. No. 31 de 1867, Art. 20.**

Idem, Art. 6. 227.—No engagement of any Immigrant shall be passed before a Stipendiary Magistrate except upon production by such Immigrant of his *Ticket* and either a *Certificate of Discharge* as prescribed in Ordinance No. 15 of 1852, or a *Certificate of the Protector of Immigrants* to the effect that such Immigrant is free to contract an engagement. — (*For the Ticket of Old Immigrant,— See No.*275 ;—*Certificate of Discharge,—No.*238 ;—*and Certificate of the Protector,—Nos.* 273 *and* 408.)

The Stipendiary Magistrate, on passing any such engagement, shall deliver to the employer the Ticket of the Immigrant, with the engagement noted thereon : which Ticket the employer shall be bound to hand over to the Stipendiary Magistrate, with a Certificate of Discharge, at the termination of the engagement, or, in default thereof, to pay to the Government, on behalf of the Immigrant, the price of a Duplicate Ticket as fixed by the Tariff in force at the time being.

The employer is bound to produce the Ticket on demand of any Magistrate, or Officer of Police.—*See No* 299.

Govt. Notice No. 166 of 11th Nov. 1868, Art. 68. 228.— The price of a Duplicate Ticket under *Article* 6 of Ordinance No. 31 of 1867 shall be held to mean the fee for a new ticket and the charge for a portrait. The amount thereof shall in each case be delivered to the Immigrant whose ticket has been lost by his employer*.—(*Art.* 6.— *See No.* 227.)

Ord. No. 31 of 1867, Art. 41. 229.—At and after the expiration of three calendar months from the date when this Ordinance shall come into operation, no Contract of Service shall be passed before any Stipendiary Magistrate between any Employer and an Old Immigrant, excepting upon production by such Immigrant of a Ticket in the form prescribed in *Article* 39.—(*Art.* 39,—*See No.* 275.)

The Ordinance No. 31 of 1867 came into operation on 2nd May 1868 ; the delay above mentioned has therefore expired.

Idem, Art. 45. 230.—At and after the expiration of three calendar months from the date when this Ordinance shall come into operation, no Con-

---

* The Fee for a New Ticket and Portrait is £ 1-4s.—(*See No.* 525.)

227.—Aucun engagement d'un Immigrant quelconque ne sera passé devant un Magistrat Stipendiaire si cet Immigrant ne produit pas son *Ticket* et soit un *Certificat de Décharge* conformément à l'Ordonnance No. 15 de 1852, soit un *Certificat du Protecteur des Immigrants* constatant que cet Immigrant est libre de contracter un engagement.—(*Pour le Ticket d'Ancien Immigrant.—Voir le 275,—le Certificat de Décharge,—le No. 238,— et le Certificat du Protecteur,—les Nos. 273 et 408.*) Idem, Art. 6.

Le Magistrat Stipendiaire en passant le dit engagement, remettra à l'Employeur le Ticket de l'Immigrant sur lequel sera inscrit l'engagement : l'Employeur sera tenu de remettre ce Ticket au Magistrat Stipendiaire, avec un Certificat de Décharge, à la fin de l'engagement ; à défaut de quoi il paiera au Magistrat Stipendiaire, en faveur de l'Immigrant, le prix d'un Duplicata de Ticket, selon le montant qui sera fixé par le Tarif qui sera en vigueur à ce moment.

L'Employeur est tenu de produire le Ticket sur la demande d'un Magistrat ou d'un Officier de Police.—(*Voir le No.* 299.)

228.—Le prix d'un Duplicata de Ticket en vertu de l'*Article* 6 de l'Ordonnance No. 31 de 1867, sera considéré comme signifiant le droit pour un nouveau ticket et pour un portrait. Le montant du dit prix sera remis dans chaque cas à l'Immigrant dont le ticket aura été perdu par son employeur.*—(*Art.* 6. *Voir le No.* 227.) Avis du Gouv. No. 166 du 11 Nov. 1868, Art. 68.

229.—Après l'expiration de trois mois à partir de la date de la mise en vigueur de la présente Ordonnance, aucun Contrat de service ne sera passé devant un Magistrat Stipendiaire entre un employeur et un Ancien Immigrant si cet Immigrant ne produit pas un Ticket en la forme prescrite par l'*Article* 39.—(*Art.* 39. —(*Voir le No.* 275.) Ord. No. 31 de 1867, Art. 41.

L'Ordonnance No. 31 de 1867 ayant été mise en vigueur le 2 Mai 1868, le délai ci-dessus mentionné est expiré.

230.—Après l'expiration de trois mois à partir de la mise en vigueur de la présente Ordonnance, aucun Contrat de Service ne Idem, Art. 45.

---

* Le prix d'un nouveau Ticket avec Portrait est de £1 4s.—(*Voir le No.* 525.)

tract of Service shall be passed before any Stipendiary Magistrate between any Old Immigrant and an Employer, except upon production by such Immigrant of a Pass duly issued to him under the provisions of the two last preceding *Articles.*—(*Articles* 43 *and* 44,—*See Nos.* 280 *and* 286.)

Nevertheless such Pass shall not be necessary if such engagement be entered into within eight days following the completion of any previous written Contract of Service, or of industrial residence.

Duplicate Police Passes may be obtained by Immigrants who have lost the originals issued to them.—(*See Nos.* 290 *and* 290 *bis.*)

Govt. Notice No. 166 of 11th Nov. 1868, Art. 34.

231.—If any Immigrant be bound by law to have a Police pass, he shall not be allowed to enter into any written engagement unless he produce such pass; and the pass, if it has not been issued in the District in which the engagement is proposed to be entered into, shall not be accepted by the Magistrate unless it bear the acknowledgment of notice mentioned in *Regulation* 44. —(*Reg.* 44,—*See No.* 288.)

If there be no such reason not to admit the pass it shall be received from the Immigrant and forwarded to the Inspector of Police of the District in which it was issued, with a brief endorsement explaining the engagement entered into by the Immigrant from whom it has been withdrawn.

Ord. No. 15 of 1852, Art. 5.

232.—Every Stipendiary Magistrate, on passing any Contract of Service, shall require the above prescribed *Certificate of Discharge* to be produced, or accounted for to his satisfaction, unless the Servant re-engage at the time of his discharge and before the same Stipendiary Magistrate, in which case a certificate of discharge shall be unnecessary, the Stipendiary Magistrate shall retain the certificate of discharge produced to him, and shall furnish the Servant with a certificate of his new engagement in the form No. 1 or No. 2 in the annexed Schedule B, according as the Servant is an Immigrant or otherwise.—(*Certificate of Discharge.*—*See No.* 238.)

sera passé devant un Magistrat Stipendiaire entre un Ancien Immigrant et un Employeur, si ce n'est sur la production par cet Immigrant d'une passe qui lui aura été dûment délivrée en vertu des dispositions des deux *Articles* qui précèdent immédiatement celui-ci.—(*Articles* 43 *et* 44,—*Voir les Nos.* 280 *et* 286.)

Toutefois cette passe ne sera pas nécessaire si cet engagement est passé dans les huit jours qui suivront l'achèvement d'un Contrat de Service écrit ou de la résidence industrielle.

Des duplicatas de Passes de Police peuvent être délivrés aux Immigrants qui ont perdu les originaux qu'ils avaient reçus.—(*Voir les Nos.* 290 *et* 290 *bis.*)

231.—Si un Immigrant est tenu par la loi d'avoir une Passe de Police, il ne lui sera pas permis de passer un engagement écrit à moins qu'il ne produise cette passe ; et si la passe n'a pas été donnée dans le District où il se propose de passer l'engagement, elle ne sera pas acceptée par le Magistrat à moins qu'elle ne porte la reconnaissance de l'avis mentionnée dans le *Réglement* 44.—(*Réglement* 44,—*Voir le No.* 288.)

Avis du Gouv. No. 166 du 11 Nov. 1868, Art. 34.

Si cette raison pour la non-admission de la passe n'existe pas, elle sera reçue de l'Immigrant et envoyée à l'Inspecteur de Police du District dans lequel elle a été donnée, avec un endossement expliquant brièvement l'engagement passé par l'Immigrant des mains duquel elle a été retirée.

232.—Tout Magistrat Stipendiaire, en passant un Contrat de Service, devra exiger que le *certificat de décharge* ci-dessus prescrit lui soit produit, ou qu'il lui en soit rendu compte à sa satisfaction, à moins que le serviteur ne se réengage au moment de sa décharge, et devant le même Magistrat Stipendiaire, dans lequel cas un certificat de décharge ne sera pas nécessaire ; le Magistrat Stipendiaire retiendra le certificat de décharge qui lui aura été produit, et fournira au serviteur un certificat de son nouvel engagement selon la forme No. 1 ou No. 2, indiquée dans la Cédule B ci-annexée, selon que le serviteur est un Immigrant ou tout autre.—(*Certificat de décharge.*—*Voir le No.* 238.)

Ord. No. 15 de 1852, Art. 5.

SCHEDULE B.

FORM No. 1.

*Certificate of Engagement.**

I hereby certify that (here insert the names and country of the servant) has entered into a contract of service with M of in the district of for months from this day of 18 as (here state the capacity in which he is to be employed.)

C. D.
Stipendiary Magistrate.

FORM No. 2.

*Certificate of Engagement.**

I hereby certify that the undermentioned Immigrant has entered into a contract of service with M of estate, in the District of for months from this day of 18

Immigrant (old or new, as the case may be.)
Name ... ...
Number... ... ...
Age . ...
Marks ... ...

C. D.
Stipendiary Magistrate.

For certificate of engagement issued to newly arrived Immigrants on leaving the Depot,—see No. 128.

Govt. Notice No. 166 of 11th Nov. 1868, Art. 33.

233.—On re-engaging any laborer discharged from a previous contract, the Stipendiary Magistrate shall withdraw from him his certificate of discharge, and cancel it; except in cases where the certificate mentions that the wages of the laborer have not been wholly paid to him,—in which cases the new engagement shall be inscribed upon the certificate of discharge, and the certificate returned to the laborer, but such certificate shall not operate as a certificate of engagement.—(*See also No.* 330.)

Ord. No. 31 of 1867, Art. 7.

234.—Upon the passing of a Contract of Service before a Stipendiary Magistrate between any Immigrant and his Employer,

* This document bears a stamp of one shilling to be paid by the Employer.—*See* No. 487.

CÉDULE B.

FORME No. 1.

*Certificat d'Engagement.**

Je certifie par le présent que (désigner les noms et le pays du serviteur) a passé un Contrat de Service avec M. de dans le District de pour mois à compter de ce 18 , en qualité de (désigner ici pour quel emploi.)

C. D.
Magistrat Stipendiaire.

FORME No. 2.

*Certificat d'Engagement.**

Je certifie par le présent que l'Immigrant mentionné ci-dessus a passé un Contrat de Service avec M de dans le District de pour mois à compter de ce 18

Immigrant (ancien ou nouveau selon le cas.)
Nom ... ...
Numéro... ... ...
Age ... ...
Marques.. ... ...

C. D.
Magistrat Stipendiaire.

Pour le certificat d'engagement délivré aux Immigrants nouvellement arrivés dans la Colonie, lorsqu'ils quittent le Dépôt,—voir le No. 128.

233.—En ré-engageant un travailleur déchargé d'un contrat précédent, le Magistrat Stipendiaire lui retirera son certificat de décharge et l'annulera : excepté dans le cas où le certificat mentionnera que les gages du travailleur ne lui ont pas été payés entièrement, dans ce cas, le nouvel engagement sera inscrit sur le certificat de décharge, et le certificat rendu au travailleur, mais ce certificat ne vaudra pas un certificat d'engagement.—(*Voir aussi le No.* 330.) Avis du Gouv. No. 166 du 11 Nov. 1868, Art. 33.

234.—Lorsqu'il sera passé un Contrat de Service devant un Magistrat Stipendiaire entre un Immigrant et son Employeur, le Ord. No. 31 de 1867, Art. 7.

---

* Ce document est frappé d'un timbre d'un schelling qui est payé par l'employeur. —*Voir le No.* 487.

the Magistrate shall deliver into the hands of the Immigrant his Certificate of Engagement, which the latter shall have the right to retain in his possession during the whole term of his engagement, and shall deliver up to the Stipendiary Magistrate upon his discharge therefrom.

Any employer or the agent of any employer, who shall take or retain possession of the certificate of engagement of any Immigrant so engaged to the employer as aforesaid, shall be liable to a penalty not exceeding £5.—(*See also No.* 300.)

Govt. Notice No. 166 of 11th Nov. 1868, Art. 32.

235.—Any Immigrant presenting himself to be re-engaged before the expiration of his contract, or before his discharge from such contract, and not producing his certificate of engagement, shall be bound to procure a duplicate of such certificate of engagement before entering into a new contract.

Job-Contractors, on engaging laborers before the Stipendiary Magistrate, must provide a guarantee for wages.—*See Nos.* 305 *et seq.* and produce their license.—*See No.* 303.

Ord. No. 16 of 1862, Art. 10.

236.—Any Immigrant under written Contract, may have his Contract transferred to any other employer for the residue of its term;—provided the transfer be made by the Stipendiary Magistrate, with the consent of the Immigrant and the then present and future employers.

For transfer of the Contract on the arrival of the Immigrant.—*See No.* 132.

Govt. Notice No. 166 of 11th Nov. 1868, Art. 19.

237.—If any Contract be transferred under the provisions of *Article* 10 of Ordinance No. 16 of 1862, a certificate in the form of the Schedule J, in the appendix hereto annexed shall be endorsed upon it.—(*Art.* 10.—*See No.* 236.)

SCHEDULE J.*

Transfer of contract for the residue of its term.

I,   and the undernamed Immigrants, being respectively the intended Master and Servants under a Contract of Service

---

* This document bears a stamp of two shillings, to be paid by the new employer. —*See No.* 487.

Magistrat remettra entre les mains de l'Immigrant son Certificat d'Engagement, que ce dernier aura le droit de retenir en sa possession pendant tout le temps de son engagement, et qu'il rendra au Magistrat Stipendiaire après sa décharge.

Tout Employeur ou agent d'Employeur qui prendra ou retiendra le Certificat d'Engagement d'un Immigrant ainsi engagé avec le dit Employeur, sera passible d'une amende n'excédant pas £5. —(*Voir aussi le No.* 300.)

235.—Tout Immigrant se présentant pour être ré-engagé avant l'expiration de son Contrat, ou avant d'avoir obtenu la décharge de ce contrat, et ne produisant pas son certificat d'engagement, sera tenu de se procurer un duplicata de ce certificat d'engagement avant de passer un nouveau contrat. Avis du Gouv. No. 166 du 11 Nov. 1868, Art. 32.

Les Entrepreneurs lorsqu'ils engagent des laboureurs devant un Magistrat Stipendiaire doivent fournir une garantie pour le paiement des gages.—*Voir les Nos.* 305 *et suiv.*—et produire leur patente.—*Voir le No.* 303.

236.—Tout Immigrant engagé par Contrat écrit pourra obtenir le transfert de ce Contrat à tout autre employeur pour le temps qu'il reste devoir d'après ce Contrat, pourvu que le transfert soit fait devant un Magistrat Stipendiaire du consentement de l'Immigrant et de l'employeur actuel et du futur employeur. Ord. No. 16 de 1862, Art. 10.

Pour le transfert du Contrat à l'arrivée de l'Immigrant.—*Voir le No.* 132.

237.—Si un Contrat est transféré en vertu des dispositions de l'*Article* 10 de l'Ordonnance No. 16 de 1862, un certificat dans la forme de la Cédule J, dans l'appendice annexé à ces présentes, sera endossé sur ce contrat.—(*Art.* 10.—*Voir le No.* 236.) Avis du Gouv. No. 166 du 11 Nov. 1868, Art. 19.

CÉDULE J.*

Transfert de Contrat pour le reste de son temps.

Je,   et les Immigrants ci-dessous nommés, étant respectivement le maître et les serviteurs mentionnés dans le Contrat de

---

* Ce document est frappé d'un timbre de deux schellings qui est payé par le nouvel employeur.—*Voir le No.* 487.

made before in the District of on the day of 186 do hereby agree that the whole rights and obligations of the said first party under the said Contract from the date hereof shall be, and the same are hereby transferred to who hereby agree to accept the said transfer and all the rights and obligations accruing therefrom.

Name of Immigrant.	No.	Wages.			Name of Immigrant.	No.	Wages.		
		£	S.	D.			£	S.	D.

A. B.
Employer mentioned in Contract.

C. D.
Substituted Employer.

This transfer has been signed by all the parties thereto, in my presence, its nature and effect having been fully explained to them.

District of this day of 186 .

E. F.
Stipendiary Magistrate.

As to the cancellation of new Immigrant's Contracts with the mutual consent of the parties and the release of the laborer from Industrial Residence.—*See Nos.* 180 *et seq.*

Ord. No. 15 of 1852, Art. 4.

238.—Every Master shall, within 24 hours after the discharge of any Servant who has been in his employment, either by the termination of the Contract of Service or otherwise, send or produce to the Stipendiary Magistrate of the District a certificate of discharge in the form of the Schedule A hereunto annexed, in which shall be inserted whether any and what amount of wages is due under a penalty not exceeding one pound, which certificate the said Magistrate shall sign or stamp ; and the said Servant shall, within 48 hours of such discharge, be bound to apply to the Stipendiary Magistrate for such certificate, in default whereof his engagement shall be deemed to be unfinished and he shall be liable to the penalty of the *7th Section* of the 4th Chapter of the Royal Order in Council of 7th September 1838, provided always that

Service fait devant dans le District de le jour de 186 , consentons par ces présentes que tous les droits et obligations du dit maître en vertu du dit Contrat à partir de ce jour soient et ils sont par ces présentes transférés à qui consent par ces présentes à accepter le dit transfert et tous les droits et obligations qui en résultent.

Nom de l'Immigrant.	No.	Gages.			Nom de l'Immigrant.	No.	Gages.		
		£	s.	d.			£	s.	d.

A. B.
Employeur mentionné au Contrat.

C. D.
Employeur substitué.

Ce transfert a été signé par toutes les parties en ma présence, sa nature et ses effets leur ayant été pleinement expliqués.

District de ce jour de 186 .

E. F.
Magistrat Stipendiaire.

Pour l'annulation, par consentement mutuel des parties, des Contrats passés avec de nouveaux Immigrants et la libération du laboureur de sa résidence industrielle.—*Voir les Nos.* 180 *et suiv.*

238.—Tout maître, dans les 24 heures qui suivront la décharge Ord. No. 15 de rt. 4.

238.

Pour la décharge d'un Contrat Verbal aucun Certificat n'est nécessaire; mais lorsqu'il s'agit d'un Ancien Immigrant, cette décharge doit être endossée sur sa Passe.—Voir le No. 573.

tenu, dans les 24 heures de la dite décharge, de s'adresser au Magistrat Stipendiaire pour avoir le dit certificat, à défaut de quoi son engagement sera réputé non-achevé, et il sera passible de la peine prévue par la *Section* 7 du Chapitre 4 de l'Ordre Royal en Conseil du 7 Septembre 1838 ; pourvu toutefois que le dit servi-

the said Servant shall not have illegally absented himself from his work, in which case he shall complete the deficient time of service before he can claim a certificate of discharge.—(*7th. Section.—See No.* 252.)

SCHEDULE A.

Certificate of Discharge. *

I hereby certify that A. B. (insert the names and country of the servant and, if an Immigrant, state whether "Old" or "New" and his number) has this day completed his engagement with me, that his wages have been paid to him (or that the sum of is still due to him for his wages) and that I have explained to him that he is required by law to apply to the Stipendiary Magistrate of the District for his certificate within 48 hours.

C. D.

This day of 18

Seen and certified on the day of 186

E. F.

Stipendiary Magistrate.

The Stipendiary Magistrate's duties under the above provision, may now be performed by any officer duly authorized by the Governor.—*See No*, 222.

Duplicate Certificate of Discharge may be obtained by Immigrants who have lost the originals issued to them.—*See No.* 273.

Govt. Notice No. 166 of 11th Nov. 1868, Art. 83.

239.—Any Stipendiary Magistrate shall have power to issue a certificate of discharge, free of cost, to any laborer who may be infirm and unfit for labor. In every such case the Magistrate shall make mention of the exemption from payment in the Register of Discharges, and shall affix his initials to the entry made to that effect.

On the discharge of a New Immigrant the Stamp duty or Redemption money recoverable on account of the Industrial Residence still due by him must be endorsed on his Ticket.—*See Nos.* 194 *and* 198.

Idem, Art. 29.

240.—If any New Immigrant discharged from a Contract of Service does not redeem the remainder of his industrial residence, or re-engage himself, within eight days from the date of his certi-

* This document bears a stamp of six pence, to be paid by the Employer.—*See No.* 487.

teur ne se soit pas absenté illégalement de son travail, car dans ce cas il devra compléter le temps de service qu'il restera devoir avant de pouvoir exiger un certificat de décharge.—(*Sect.* 7.—*Voir le No.* 252.)

CÉDULE A.

*Certificat de Décharge.**

Je certifie par le présent que A. B. (désigner les noms et le pays du serviteur, et si c'est un Immigrant, déclarer si c'est un Ancien ou un Nouvel Immigrant, et indiquer son numéro) a, ce jour, achevé son engagement avec moi, que ses gages lui ont été payés (ou que la somme de lui est encore due sur ses gages) et que je lui ai expliqué qu'il est requis par la loi de s'adresser dans les 48 heures au Magistrat Stipendiaire du District pour avoir son certificat.

C. D.

Ce jour de 18

Vu et certifié le 186

E. F.
Magistrat Stipendiaire.

Les fonctions du Magistrat Stipendiaire d'après l'Article ci-dessus peuvent être remplies par tout fonctionnaire dûment autorisé à cet effet par le Gouverneur.—*Voir le No.* 222.

Des duplicatas de Certificats de Décharge peuvent être délivrés aux Immigrants qui ont perdu les originaux qu'ils avaient reçus.—*Voir le No.* 273.

239.—Tout Magistrat Stipendiaire aura le pouvoir de donner un certificat de décharge, sans frais, à tout travailleur infirme ou incapable de travailler. Dans ce cas, le Magistrat mentionnera l'exemption de paiement sur le Registre des Décharges, et apposera ses initiales à l'entrée faite à cet effet. Avis du Gouv. No. 166 du 11 Nov. 1868, Art. 83.

Lorsqu'un Nouvel Immigrant est déchargé d'un contrat, le droit de timbre ou l'argent de rachat payable pour la résidence industrielle qu'il reste devoir sera endossé sur son ticket.—*Voir les Nos.* 194 *et* 198.

240.—Si un nouvel Immigrant dégagé d'un Contrat de Service ne rachète pas le reste de sa résidence industrielle ou ne s'engage pas de nouveau, dans les huit jours qui suivront la date de son Idem, Art. 29.

* Ce document est frappé d'un timbre de six pence qui est payé par l'Employeur.—*Voir le No.* 487.

ficate of discharge, he shall be sent to the Protector of Immigrants, who shall endeavour to procure employment for him. If any such Immigrant refuse to take any employment which may be offered to him on terms approved by the Protector of Immigrants, such Immigrant shall become liable to be sent by the Protector to any work-house legally established, to be there detained till he consent to take such employment ; and during such detention, he shall be subject to the regulations in force in such work-house.

Any Old Immigrant who on being discharged from a written contract is not in possession of a Portrait-Ticket, is bound forthwith to obtain one from the Protector (*See No.* 278) ; and must either enter into a new written contract within eight days from the date of his discharge, or apply to the Police for a Pass.—(*See No.* 280.)

CHAPTER II.

Duration, &c., of Labor.— Effect on Contract, of imprisonment,— and of transfer &c., of Estate.

Ord. No. 31 of 1867, Art. 22. **241.**—No laborer engaged for field labor shall be bound to work more than nine hours per day, exclusive of the hour for breakfast. Whether he be employed at day-work or task-work, he shall be entitled to have one full hour for breakfast, before 10 a. m.

Ord. No. 17 of 1841, Art. 1. **242.**—The ordinary works of cultivation or manufacture shall not on a Sunday be exacted from labourers employed on rural estates, and such labourers on that particular day shall only be subjected to works of immediate necessity having for object the care and feeding of animals, the cleanliness of yards, styes and folds, stables, manufactories and buildings and other works indispensable for the preservation of the estate, which works moreover shall not be of more than two hours duration nor be continued after the hour of eight in the morning.

Idem, Art. 2. **243.**—Any contravention to the provisions of the preceding Article shall be reputed a violation of the Contracts of Service and the offender shall be liable to the penalties mentioned in the *7th, and 8th, Sections* Chapter 4, of the Order in Council of the 7th September 1838.—(*Sections 7 and* 8.—*See Nos.* 252 *and* 251.)

certificat de décharge, il sera envoyé au Protecteur des Immigrants qui tâchera de lui procurer de l'emploi. Si cet Immigrant refuse l'emploi qui lui sera offert aux conditions approuvées par le Protecteur des Immigrants, cet Immigrant pourra être envoyé par le Protecteur à toute maison de force légalement établie, et y sera retenu jusqu'à ce qu'il consente à prendre le dit emploi ; et pendant son séjour dans la dite maison de force il sera soumis à tous les réglements qui y seront en vigueur.

Tout Ancien Immigrant qui, lors de sa décharge d'un Contrat de Service écrit, ne possède pas un ticket contenant son portrait, est tenu d'en obtenir un sur le champ du Protecteur des Immigrants, (*voir le No* 278)—et doit ensuite, soit se ré-engager par contrat écrit ou s'adresser à la Police pour obtenir une passe.—(*Voir le No.* 280.)

CHAPITRE II.

Durée, &c., du travail.—Effet sur le Contrat, de l'emprisonnement,—et du transfert, &c., de l'Etablissement.

241.—Aucun travailleur engagé pour le travail des champs ne sera tenu de travailler plus de neuf heures par jour, exclusivement de l'heure pour le déjeûner. Qu'il soit employé à la journée ou à la tache, il aura droit à une heure entière pour déjeûner, avant 10 heures du matin. Ord. No. 31 of 1867, Art. 22.

242.—Il ne sera pas exigé le dimanche des laboureurs employés sur les habitations, aucun des travaux ordinaires de culture ou de manufacture, mais seulement les travaux de première nécessité, ayant pour objet le soin et la nourriture des animaux, la propreté des cours, parcs, écuries, usines et bâtimens et autres ouvrages indispensables pour la conservation de la propriété. Ces travaux ne pourront d'ailleurs durer plus de deux heures ni être prolongés au-delà de huit heures du matin. Ord. No. 17 of 1841, Art. 1.

243.—Toute contravention aux dispositions de l'Article précédent sera considérée comme une violation du Contrat de Service, et passible des peines prevues par les Sections 7 et 8 du Chapitre 4, de l'Ordre en Conseil du 7 Septembre 1838.—(*Sections 7 et 8.—Voir les Nos.* 252 *et* 251.) Idem, Art. 2.

Ord. No. 31 of 1867, Art. 23. **244.**—It shall be optional with the employer of any laborer engaged for field labor, to require the latter to work by task-work, giving him such daily tasks as can reasonably be required of him. If any question arise as to the reasonableness of any task, the same shall be decided by the Stipendiary Magistrate, who may, if he think fit, take the advice of one or two competent Appraisers, who shall, in such case, take an oath before him to execute such duty truly and faithfully.

The cost of appraisement, which shall not exceed £ 1. per appraiser, shall be borne by the losing party.

Idem, Art. 54. **245.**—No imprisonment undergone by a laborer for any offence committed by him before the expiration of his Contract of Service, shall release him from such Contract; nor shall the time of his imprisonment be reckoned as part of the term of Service under his Contract except in case of imprisonment for unlawful absence under the provisions of *Article* 18 *of Ordinance No.* 16 *of* 1862.—(*Article* 18.—*See No.* 400.)

As to the right of an employer to obtain the release from prison of any Immigrant in his Service,—*See No.* 254.

Ord. No. 16 of 1862, Art. 7. **246.**—If, after the date when this Ordinance shall come into operation, the Estate on which any Immigrant shall be engaged to work, shall be sold, alienated, succeeded to, or transferred to another person, during the currency of the Contract,—the Immigrant shall be bound to perform all the conditions of the Contract to the new proprietor of the Estate, who, in like manner, shall be held bound to perform the stipulations thereof incumbent upon the employer.

The provisions in this Article shall only apply to such Contracts in which they shall be embodied.*

---

* On the descent of an estate by inheritance, right to the services of Indian laborers is transmissible — (*Thamun and others* versus *Widow D'Emmeres.*—Piston's Reports 1861.) In a previous case (*Pandoo and others* versus *Reid, Irving & Co.* 1859) the Supreme Court decided that such right was not transmissible upon purchase.—It is not probable, however, that questions such as these will again arise, inasmuch as the forms of Contracts, now used in Stipendiary Courts, contain a clause which brings the employer and the Immigrant within the provisions of Par. I of Art. 7, of Ord. 16 of 1862.

244.—L'employeur d'un travailleur engagé pour le travail des champs aura l'option d'exiger de ce dernier de travailler à la tache, en lui donnant une tache raisonnable pour chaque jour. Si la question de savoir si cette tache est ou non raisonnable s'élève, elle sera décidée par le Magistrat Stipendiaire qui pourra, s'il le juge convenable, prendre l'avis d'un ou de plusieurs experts qui, dans ce cas, prêteront serment devant lui de remplir leur devoir avec conscience et selon la vérité. Ord. No. 31 de 1867, Art. 23.

Les frais de l'expertise qui n'excèderont pas £ 1 par expert seront supportés par la partie qui succombera.

245.—Aucun emprisonnement subi par un travailleur pour un délit quelconque commis par lui avant l'expiration de son Contrat de Service ne le dégagera de ce Contrat ; et le temps qu'il aura passé en prison ne sera pas compté comme partie du temps de service en vertu de son Contrat, excepté en cas d'emprisonnement pour absence illégale en vertu des dispositions de l'*Article* 18 *de l'Ordonnance No.* 16 *de* 1862.—(*Article* 18.—*Voir le No.* 400.) Idem, Art. 54.

Quant au droit de l'employeur de demander la mise en liberté d'un Immigrant à son Service qu'il aurait fait mettre en prison.—*Voir le No.* 254.

246.—Si après l'époque où cette Ordonnance sera mise en vigueur, l'Établissement sur lequel un Immigrant se sera engagé à travailler, venait à être vendu, aliéné, transféré ou à échoir en héritage, à une autre personne pendant la durée du Contrat, l'Immigrant sera tenu de remplir toutes les conditions de son Contrat avec le nouveau propriétaire de l'Établissement qui, également, sera considéré comme tenu d'en exécuter les clauses à la charge de l'employeur. Ord. No. 16 de 1862, Art. 7.

Les dispositions de cet article ne s'appliqueront qu'aux Contrats dans lesquels elles seront insérées.*

---

* En cas de succession les héritiers ont droit aux services des laboureurs Indiens. (*Thamun et 'autres, v. veuve D'Emmerez.*—Piston's Reports 1861.) Dans une affaire précédente (*Pandoo et autres, v. Reid Irving & Cie.* 1859) la Cour Suprême a décidé que ce droit n'était pas transmissible en cas de vente. Il n'est pas probable cependant que des questions de cette nature soient de nouveau soulevées devant la Cour, les formes des Contrats de Service qui sont employées actuellement par les Cours Stipendiaires contenant une clause qui soumet l'Employeur et l'Immigrant aux dispositions de l'Ordonnance 16 de 1862, Art. 7, Par. I,

Idem, Art. 8. 247.—Upon any new proprietor being substituted under a Contract, in terms of the foregoing provisions,—the former employer will be entitled to be freed from the obligations incumbent on him by the Contract;—provided that he shall satisfy the Stipendiary Magistrate of the District that the Immigrant will not suffer thereby, and provided that all arrears of Wages be paid before the former proprietor shall be so liberated. In every such case, a docket in the terms of Schedule E. shall be endorsed on the Contract by the Stipendiary Magistrate.

SCHEDULE E.

I hereby declare that A. B., the Employer mentioned in this Contract, who has been lawfully replaced as such, is henceforth freed from the obligations incumbent on him under this Contract.

This day of 186 .

C. D.

Stipendiary Magistrate in and for the District of

Idem, Art. 9. 248.—The provisions in the last preceding Articles are without prejudice to any obligation incumbent on any Immigrant by the law now existing; and more especially without prejudice to the obligation under which it is hereby declared every Immigrant laborer lies to perform his Contract of Service, notwithstanding any transfers or sales, one or more, of the Estate upon which he agreed to work,—provided always that in such case the original employer, or any employer substituted to him in terms of any law existing at the time, shall remain bound to perform the stipulations of such Contract incumbent upon him.

CHAPTER III.

Ill-Usage.

Ord. No. 15 of 1852, Art. 14. 249.—Every Manager, Overseer, Sirdar, or other person placed by a Master in authority over the laborers in his employ, shall for all offences committed in the exercise of his functions, be held and considered to be liable to the same penalties as a Master, within the meaning of the above cited *Order in Council*, and in like manner a Master shall be liable for any offence committed

247.—Lorsqu'un nouveau propriétaire se trouvera aux droits de l'employeur mentionné dans le Contrat, suivant les dispositions qui précèdent, l'employeur ainsi remplacé pourra se faire affranchir des obligations à sa charge d'après le Contrat, s'il prouve au Magistrat Stipendiaire du District que l'Immigrant n'en souffrira pas, et pourvu que tous arriérés de gages soient payés avant qu'il soit ainsi affranchi. Dans chacun de ces cas un certificat dans les termes de la Cédule E sera endossé sur le Contrat par le Magistrat Stipendiaire. Idem, Art. 8.

CÉDULE E.

Je déclare par ces présentes que l'Employeur mentionné dans ce Contrat, qui a été légalement remplacé comme tel, est dorénavant libéré des obligations qui lui sont imposées par ce Contrat.

Ce de 186 .

C. D.

Magistrat Stipendiaire pour le District de

248.—Les dispositions du dernier article ne pourront infirmer aucune obligation à la charge de tout Immigrant en vertu de la loi actuellement en vigueur ; et plus particulièrement l'obligation qui, ainsi qu'il est décrété par ces présentes, incombe à tout Immigrant laboureur d'exécuter son Contrat de Service malgré tous transfers, ventes, une ou plusieurs, de l'établissement sur lequel il a consenti à travailler,—pourvu cependant que dans chaque cas l'employeur originaire, ou tout employeur le remplaçant en vertu de la loi alors en vigueur, reste tenu de remplir les obligations du Contrat à sa charge. Idem, Art. 9.

CHAPITRE III.

Des Mauvais Traitements.

249.—Tout administrateur, régisseur, commandeur, sirdar, ou autre personne investie par le maître d'une autorité sur les travailleurs qui sont à son service, sera, pour tout délit commis dans l'exercice de ses fonctions, considéré comme passible des mêmes peines que le maître, dans le sens de l'*Ordre en Conseil* ci-dessus cité ; et de la même manière, un maître sera responsable Ord. No. 15 de 1852, Art. 14.

by any of the aforesaid persons, under or by virtue of such Master's order or instruction.—(*Order in Council. i. e. of 7th Sept.* 1838.—*See No.* 549.)

For ill-usage of the Servant by the Master, the Magistrate may, if he shall see fit, order the Contract of Service to be cancelled in addition to, or in substitution for, any compensation awarded to the Servant.—*See No.* 251.

In lieu of the compensation referred to, the Magistrate may inflict a fine not exceeding £ 10.—*See No.* 328.

Order in Council 7th Sept. 1838, Cap. 4, Sect. 9.

250.—Nothing herein contained shall prevent, or be construed to prevent, any proceeding before the ordinary Tribunals of the Colony for any ill-usage * of a Servant by his Master, or of a Master by his Servant, if the Stipendiary Magistrate shall decline to entertain any such case, and shall see fit to refer the same to the ordinary course of law.

Notwithstanding the terms of the foregoing Section, cases of ill-usage of a Master by his Servant are in practise tried before the ordinary Tribunals of the Colony and not before the Stipendiary Courts.—This want of uniformity in jurisdiction is owing to the fact that, though the law on labor (*See No.* 251) provides a remedy for the ill-usage of a Servant by his Master, it contains no penalty (*See No.* 252) applicable in cases of ill-usage of a Master by his Servant.

CHAPTER IV.

Breach of Contract by the Master.

Idem, Cap. 4, Sect. 8.

251.—On complaint preferred and proof made by a servant before any Stipendiary Magistrate that his Master has not paid the Servant's Wages, or delivered to him the Articles stipulated for, or that the Articles so delivered were not of the prescribed amount and quality, or that by the negligence, or other improper conduct of the Master, the Contract of Service has not been faith-

* *Unlawful detention of laborers by their Employers.*—In the appeal case of Montille *versus* the Queen (Piston's Reports 1865,) the Supreme Court supported the conviction pronounced by the District Court of Grand Port against the appellants inflicting on them both imprisonment and fine, for having unlawfully sequestered some of their indian laborers in a building, used as a prison, on the Beaufond estate.

de tout délit commis par l'une des dites personnes, d'après et en vertu des ordres et des instructions du dit maître.—(*Ordre en Conseil, i. e. du 7 Sept.* 1838.—*Voir le No.* 549.)

Pour mauvais traitements d'un maître envers son serviteur, le Magistrat peut, s'il le juge convenable, ordonner l'annullation du contrat, soit en outre ou au lieu de la compensation accordée au serviteur.—*Voir le No.* 251.

Au lieu de la compensation ci-dessus mentionnée, le Magistrat pourra infliger une amende n'excédant pas £ 10.—*Voir le No.* 328.

250.—Rien de ce qui est contenu au présent n'empêchera, ou ne sera entendu empêcher la poursuite devant les tribunaux ordinaires de la colonie, pour mauvais traitements * d'un serviteur envers son maître, ou d'un maître envers son serviteur, si le Magistrat salarié refuse de connaître d'un tel cas, et juge convenable de le renvoyer aux cours ordinaires de la loi. Ordre en Conseil du 7 Sept. 1838, Ch. 4, Sect. 9.

Nonobstant les termes de la Section précédente les cas de mauvais traitements d'un serviteur envers son maître, sont, en pratique, jugées par les Tribunaux ordinaires de la Colonie et non par les Cours Stipendiaires. Ce manque d'uniformité en matière de juridiction s'explique par le fait que bien que la loi sur les travailleurs (*Voir le No.* 251) décrète une pénalité dans les cas de mauvais traitements d'un maître envers son serviteur elle n'a prévue aucune peine (*Voir le No.* 252) qu'on puisse appliquer dans les cas de mauvais traitements d'un serviteur envers son maître.

CHAPITRE IV.

Violation du Contrat de la part du Maître.

251.—Sur la plainte portée et la preuve fournie par un serviteur devant un Magistrat Salarié, que son maître ne lui a pas payé ses gages, ou ne lui a pas fourni les objets stipulés, ou que les objets fournis n'étaient pas conformes au montant et à la qualité prescrits, ou que, par la négligence ou toute autre conduite inconvenable du maître, le Contrat de Service n'a pas été fidèlement Idem, Ch. 4, Sect. 8.

* *Emprisonnement illégal de laboureurs par leurs Employeurs.*—Sur l'appel formé par Montille *contre* la Reine. (Piston's Reports 1865), la Cour Suprême maintint le jugement prononcé par la Cour de District du Grand Port contre les Appelants et leur infligeant l'emprisonnement et une amende pour avoir illégalement détenu quelques uns de leurs laboureurs Indiens dans un batiment qui servait de prison sur l'Etablissement "Beau Fond."

fully performed, or that the Master has ill used the Servant, the Stipendiary Magistrate may make order for the payment of the Wages in arrear, or for the delivery of the stipulated Articles, or for compensation to be made to the Servant for any injury by him sustained by such negligence or improper conduct of the Master, or by his non-fulfilment of the Contract, or by his ill-usage of the Servant; and if such order be not complied with according to the exigency and tenor thereof, the Magistrate shall and may issue a Warrant for the seizure and sale of the Goods of the Master, or so much thereof as may be requisite for making such compensation; and failing any sufficient distress, the Magistrate shall and may make Order for the commitment of the Master to prison, for any time not exceeding one month, unless compensation be sooner made. The Magistrate may also in any of the cases aforesaid, if he shall see fit, order the Contract of Service to be cancelled either in addition to, or in substitution for, any such order as aforesaid.

In lieu of the compensation referred to in the foregoing Section, the Magistrate may, according to the circumstances of the case, inflict a fine not exceeding £10.—*See No* 328.

The penalties mentioned in No. 251 may be inflicted on a Master, for infraction of the law on Sunday labor.—*See No.* 243.

If the Servant's Wages are three months in arrear, he is entitled to claim the dissolution of the Contract.—*See No.* 329.

Failure to provide Hospital accommodation for the Servant within a certain delay is a breach of the Contract.—*See No.* 361.

CHAPTER V.

Breach of Contract by the Servant.

Order in Council 7th Sept. 1838, Cap. 4, Sect. 7.

252.— On complaint preferred, and proof made, before any Stipendiary Magistrate, that any servant has neglected to perform his stipulated work, or that he has performed it negligently * or

---

* *Responsibility of the Master for injuries caused by the Servant.*— In the case of Salsse *versus* Sérendat (Piston's Reports 1863) damages of £1000 were awarded against the Defendant, whose laborers, in carelessly burning some weeds and other rubbish cleared by them from off their employer's land, had set fire to, and destroyed the Plaintiff's house and furniture. On appeal to the Privy Council, this judgment was maintained.—(*See Piston's Reports*, 1866.)

exécuté, ou que le maître a maltraité le serviteur, le Magistrat Salarié peut décerner un ordre pour le paiement des gages arriérés, ou la remise des objets stipulés, ou pour une compensation à donner au serviteur pour le tort qu'il a éprouvé par la négligence ou la conduite inconvenable de son maître, ou à la non-exécution du contrat de la part de celui-ci, ou par ses mauvais traitements envers le serviteur; et si cet ordre n'est pas pleinement exécuté selon sa teneur, le Magistrat pourra rendre une ordonnance pour la saisie et vente des biens du maître, ou de telle portion de ses biens qu'il sera nécessaire pour effectuer cette compensation; et, en cas d'insuffisance, le Magistrat décernera contre le maître un mandat d'emprisonnement pour un temps qui n'excèdera pas un mois, à moins que l'indemnité ne soit payée plus tôt. Le Magistrat pourra aussi dans les cas ci-dessus, s'il le juge convenable, ordonner l'annullation du Contrat de Service, soit en addition, ou au lieu d'aucune des dispositions susdites.

Au lieu de la compensation mentionnée dans l'Article précédent, le Magistrat peut, selon les circonstances du cas, infliger une amende n'excédant pas £ 10,—*Voir le No.* 328.

Les pénalités mentionnées au No. 251 peuvent être infligées à un maître qui contreviendra à la loi sur la corvée du Dimanche.—*Voir le No.* 243.

Si les gages du serviteur sont arriérés de trois mois, il a le droit de réclamer la dissolution du Contrat.—*Voir le No.* 329.

Tout employeur qui, dans un certain délai, n'aura pas pour ses serviteurs un hôpital convenablement installé, s'exposera à la dissolution du Contrat.—*Voir le No.* 361.

CHAPITRE V.

Violation du Contrat de la part du Serviteur.

252.—Sur la plainte portée, et la preuve fournie devant tout Magistrat salarié, qu'un serviteur a négligé de faire le travail stipulé, ou qu'il l'a fait négligemment,* ou d'une manière inconve- Ordre en Conseil du 7 Sept. 1838, Ch. 4, Sect. 7.

---

* *Le Maître est responsable des dommages causés par son serviteur.*—Dans l'affaire *Saisse v. Sérendat* (Piston's Reports, 1863), la Cour a condamné le défendeur à payer des dommages s'élevant à £1000, ses laboureurs ayant par négligence, en brûlant des herbes et d'autres débris enlevés du terrain de leur employeur, incendié la maison et les meubles du plaignant. Sur l'appel formé devant le Conseil Privé, ce jugement fut maintenu.—(*Voir Piston's Reports* 1866.)

improperly, or that by negligence or other improper conduct he has injured the property of his Master entrusted to his care, the Magistrate may, in his discretion, adjudge the servant to any one or more of the following penalties; that is to say, a pecuniary penalty for the benefit of the master not exceeding one month's wages, or the commitment of the servant to prison with or without hard labour, for any term not exceeding fourteen days, or the dissolution of the Contract of Service.

In lieu of the pecuniary penalty referred to in the foregoing Section, the Magistrate may, according to the circumstances of the case, inflict a fine not exceeding £ 10.—*See No.* 328.

The penalties mentioned in No. 252 may be inflicted on a servant who refuses to perform the Sunday labor lawfully required from him.—*See No.* 243.

As to violation of the Contract by the servant by unlawful absence or desertion.—*See Nos.* 399 *et seq.*

Absence from work with refusal to enter hospital is held to be a breach of the Contract.—*See No.* 362.

Ord. No. 4 of 1864, Art. 17.

253.—All persons who shall undergo punishment under sentences of Stipendiary Magistrates, on account of non performance of any obligations of their Contracts of Service, may be dealt with in the same manner as Vagrants under the provisions of this Ordinance.—(*See also No.* 429.)

Ord. No. 16 of 1862, Art. 23.

254.—Any employer shall be entitled, on application to the Stipendiary Magistrate of the District, to obtain the release of any Immigrant in his service, who shall have been imprisoned on his complaint for any act or non-feasance not involving a breach of the peace, or of the public Law of the Colony.

CHAPTER VI.

Causes of premature termination of the Contract.

If within seven days after his arrival at the Depot, the Immigrant be not claimed by the person upon whose requisition he has been introduced, the Protector of Immigrants may allot him to any other person.—*See No.* 129.

nable, ou que, par négligence ou autre conduite inconvenable, il a préjudicié à la propriété de son maître, confiée à ses soins, le Magistrat peut, à sa discrétion, condamner le serviteur aux peines suivantes, cumulativement ou séparément, savoir : une indemnité au profit du maître qui ne pourra excéder un mois de gages, un emprisonnement avec ou sans travail forcé, pour un temps n'excédant pas quatorze jours, ou l'annulation du Contrat de Service.

Au lieu de l'indemnité mentionnée dans l'article précédent, le Magistrat peut, selon les circonstances du cas, infliger une amende n'excédant pas £10.—*Voir le No.* 328.

Les pénalités mentionnées au No. 252 peuvent être infligées à un serviteur qui refuse de faire la corvée du Dimanche qui peut légalement être exigée de lui.—*Voir le No.* 243.

Quant à la violation du contrat, résultant de l'absence illégale ou de la désertion, voir les Nos. 399 et suiv.

Absence du travail avec refus d'entrer à l'hôpital est considérée comme une violation du contrat.—*Voir le No.* 362.

253.—Toutes les personnes qui seront punies par sentence d'un Magistrat Stipendiaire pour n'avoir pas rempli une obligation quelconque de leur Contrat de Service, pourront être traitées de la même manière que les vagabonds conformément aux dispositions de cette Ordonnance.—(*Voir aussi le No.* 429.) Ord. No. 4 de 1864, Art. 17.

254.—Tout employeur aura le droit, en en faisant la demande au Magistrat Stipendiaire du District, d'obtenir la libération de tout Immigrant à son service, qui aura été emprisonné sur sa plainte, pour tout acte ou omission, qui ne portera pas atteinte à la tranquillité publique, ni aux lois générales de la Colonie. Ord. No. 16 de 1862, Art. 23.

CHAPITRE VI.

Causes de la résolution prématurée du Contrat.

Si dans les sept jours qui suivront son arrivée au Dépôt, l'Immigrant n'est pas réclamé par la personne sur la réquisition de laquelle il a été introduit, le Protecteur des Immigrants pourra le répartir à toute autre personne.—*Voir le No.* 129.

Any New Immigrant may be released by his employer from the obligation of Industrial Residence and from the Contract passed between them.—*See Nos.* 180 *et seq.*

Ord. No. 31 of 1867, Art. 14. 255.—Any New Immigrant having good and sufficient reason, of a special and exceptional nature, for desiring to obtain his discharge from any Contract of Service under which he is engaged, may apply to the Stipendiary Magistrate of the District in which he is performing such Contract, stating the reasons for which he is desirous of obtaining such discharge, and the Magistrate shall thereupon give notice to the employer, and shall appoint a day for enquiring into the matter, and for hearing any evidence which the Immigrant or his employer may respectively adduce.

The Magistrate shall transmit to the Procureur-General the proceedings upon such enquiry; and, in case the Procureur General shall be satisfied that good and sufficient reasons have as aforesaid been shewn for granting such discharge, he may authorize the Magistrate to grant the same upon previous payment of indemnity by the Immigrant to Government for the benefit of the employer.

Such indemnity shall be calculated upon the sum paid by the employer for costs of introduction, as certified by the Protector, or for the stamp duty upon engagement, of such Immigrant, as the case may be, and shall be proportionate to the unexpired term of service relatively with the whole term as stipulated in the Contract.

The laborer is entitled to demand the cancellation of his Contract on failure by the Master to provide him with proper lodging.—*See No.* 353.

Failure to provide Hospital accommodation within a certain delay exposes the Master to dissolution of the Contract.—*See No.* 361.

Idem, Art. 19. 256.—In case any Immigrant engaged under written Contract of Service shall, through infirmity, accident, sickness, or other cause, become permanently incapacitated from the performance of his Contract, it shall be lawful for his Employer, upon a certificate to that effect being given by a duly qualified Medical Practitioner, to send such Immigrant to the Protector of Immigrants;

Tout Nouvel Immigrant peut être libéré par son employeur de l'obligation de la Résidence Industrielle ainsi que du Contrat passé entre eux.—*Voir les Nos.* 180 *et suiv.*

255.—Tout nouvel Immigrant ayant des raisons bonnes et suffisantes, d'une nature spéciale et exceptionnelle, pour désirer obtenir sa décharge d'un Contrat de Service en vertu duquel il est engagé, pourra s'adresser au Magistrat Stipendiaire du District dans lequel il remplit son engagement, et lui déclarer les raisons pour lesquelles il désire obtenir cette décharge ; le Magistrat en donnera alors avis à l'employeur, et fixera un jour pour instruire l'affaire et entendre tous témoignages que l'Immigrant ou son Employeur pourrait invoquer. Ord. No. 31 de 1867, Art. 14.

Le Magistrat transmettra au Procureur-Général le résultat de l'enquête ; et dans le cas où le Procureur-Général sera satisfait que l'Immigraut a fait valoir des raisons bonnes et suffisantes comme il,est dit plus haut pour que sa décharge lui soit accordée, il pourra autoriser le Magistrat à l'accorder après le paiement préalable par l'Immigrant au Gouvernement d'une indemnité au profit de l'employeur.

Cette indemnité sera calculée sur la somme payée par l'employeur pour frais d'introduction, ainsi qu'en fera foi le certificat du Protecteur, ou pour le droit de timbre sur l'engagement de cet Immigrant, selon le cas, et sera proportionnée au temps de service non expiré par rapport à tout le temps stipulé au Contrat.

Le laboureur peut demander l'annulation de son Contrat si l'employeur ne lui donne pas un logement convenable.—*Voir le No.* 353.

Si l'employeur n'a pas dans un certain délai un hôpital convenable où il puisse envoyer ses serviteurs, le Contrat pourra être annulé.—*Voir le No.* 361.

256.—Dans le cas où un Immigrant engagé par Contrat de Service écrit deviendra, par suite d'infirmités, d'accident, de maladie ou d'autres causes, incapable de remplir les conditions de son contrat, son employeur pourra, sur un certificat à cet effet donné par un médecin exerçant dûment qualifié, envoyer cet Immigrant au Protecteur des Immigrants ; et le contrat de cet Im- Idem, Art. 19.

and the Contract of such Immigrant shall thereupon be deemed and taken as cancelled.—(*The Certificate of Discharge may in such case be issued to the laborer free of cost.—See No.* 239.)

The expenses attending the care and maintenance of such Immigrant up to the time of his being so sent, together with the cost of sending him to the Immigration Depot, shall be defrayed by the Employer.

The Contracts of Female Immigrants may in certain cases be suspended.—*See No.* 220.

For non-payment of wages due, non-delivery of rations, or for ill-usage, &c., the Magistrate may, if he shall see fit, order the dissolution of the Contract.—*See No.* 251.

If the Servant's wages are three months in arrear he is entitled to claim his release from the engagement.—*See No.* 329.

In connection with the guarantee to be provided by Job-Contractors the Magistrate is required in certain cases to cancel the engagement.—*See Nos.* 305 *and* 309.

Contracts entered into with minors above the age of fifteen years without the consent of the Parents or Guardians may be cancelled.—*See No.* 224.

Ord. No. 31 of 1867, Art. 21.

257.—Whenever any Stipendiary Magistrate shall have reason to suspect that any written Contract of Service between an Old Immigrant and an alleged employer is a fictitious Contract, and that the same is not being *bonâ fide* carried out, he shall have power to summon the parties before him, and if, after due enquiry, it shall appear to him that the Employer and Immigrant named in the said Contract had at the time of passing the same no *bonâ fide* intention of carrying out the same, and that the relationship of Master and Servant does not *de facto* exist between the parties,—in any such case, the Magistrate shall have power to cancel and annul such Contract.

Govt. Notice No. 166 of 11th Nov. 1868, Art. 36.

258.—Any person who shall be convicted by a Stipendiary Magistrate of having entered into a fictitious Contract of Service with any Immigrant, shall incur a fine not exceeding Ten Pounds.—(*See also No.* 209.)

For negligence, &c., on the part of the Servant, the Magistrate may, in his discretion, order the dissolution of the Contract.—*See No.* 252.

migrant sera alors considéré et tenu comme étant annulé.—*(Dans ce cas le travailleur pourra obtenir son Certificat de Décharge sans frais.—Voir le No.* 239.)

Les dépenses résultant des soins à donner à cet Immigrant jusqu'au moment de son envoi au Protecteur, ainsi que les frais de l'envoi au Dépôt de l'Immigration, seront supportés par l'employeur.

Les Contrats passés avec des Immigrantes peuvent dans certains cas être suspendus.—*Voir le No.* 220.

Pour le non-paiement de gages dûs, pour la non-distribution des rations, ou pour mauvais traitements, le Magistrat peut, s'il le juge convenable, ordonner l'annullation du Contrat.—*Voir le No.* 251.

Si les gages dûs au Serviteur ne sont pas payés pendant 3 mois, le serviteur a le droit de demander d'être libéré de son Contrat.—*Voir le No.* 329.

Relativement à la garantie que doivent fournir les Entrepreneurs, le Magistrat est obligé dans certain cas d'annuler l'engagement.—*Voir les Nos.* 305 *et* 309.

Les contrats passés avec des mineurs au-dessus de quinze ans sans le consentement de leur parents ou de leurs tuteurs peuvent être annulés.—*Voir le No.* 224.

257.—Toutes les fois qu'un Magistrat Stipendiaire aura quelque raison de soupçonner qu'un Contrat de Service écrit entre un ancien Immigrant et un soi-disant employeur est un Contrat fictif, ou qu'il n'est pas exécuté de bonne foi, il aura le pouvoir de sommer les parties à comparaître devant lui, et si, après une enquête, il lui paraît que l'Employeur et l'Immigrant désignés dans le dit Contrat n'avaient pas, au moment de passer ce Contrat, l'intention de l'exécuter de bonne foi, et que les rapports de maître à serviteur n'existent pas en fait entre les parties,—dans ces cas le Magistrat aura le pouvoir d'annuler le dit Contrat. Ord. No. 31 de 1867, Art. 21.

258.—Toute personne qui sera trouvée coupable par un Ma- Avis du Gouv. ...6 du ...1868, ...36.

258.

La pénalité prévue par cet Article s'applique aussi au Serviteur.—Voir le No. 563.

The Contract may be cancelled for refusal on the part of the Servant to perform lawful Sunday labor,—or for unlawful employment of the Servant on Sunday by the Master.—*See Nos.* 242 *and* 243.

In certain cases where an Immigrant being under written Contract absconds from his Master and engages with another Employer, and is thereafter discovered, the latter Contract ceases if the former be enforced.—*See Nos.* 274, 184, 204 *and* 436.

Ord. No. 15 of 1852, Art. 3. 259.—Any Stipendiary Magistrate, on the application of a Master, may annul the engagement of any Servant in his employment who has been convicted of misdemeanor or felony.

For confirmed vagrancy or criminal conduct the Governor may send Immigrants back to India (*see No.* 544); apparently notwithstanding any Contract of Service they may then be under.

CHAPTER VII.

Illegal Employment, Harbouring &c. of Laborers.

Ord. No. 6 of 1838, Art. 328. (Penal Code.) 260.—Whosoever shall be convicted of having enticed away, concealed, secreted, or employed any servant or apprentice duly engaged, or of having persuaded or endeavoured to persuade such servant or apprentice to leave the service of his master, or to absent himself therefrom, shall be condemned to imprisonment not exceeding six months, and to a fine not exceeding twenty five pounds sterling, and, in every case, to eight shillings per day as damages to the master.

One moiety of such fine shall go to the *Caisse de Bienfaisance* and the other moiety to the informer.

Ord. No. 15 of 1852, Art. 7. 261.—Any person illegally harbouring, lodging or employing a servant engaged in the service of another person, shall be liable to a penalty not exceeding £ 10, and to damages in favor of the person to whom such servant is engaged, not exceeding eight shillings for each day of such illegal harbouring, lodging or employing, to be recovered before a Stipendiary Magistrate.

Pour cause de refus de la part du serviteur de se soumettre à la corvée qui peut être légalement exigée de lui le Dimanche ou pour emploi illégal du serviteur par le maître le Dimanche, le Contrat peut être annulé.—*Voir les Nos.* 242 *et* 243.

Dans certains cas où un Immigrant engagé par Contrat écrit déserte le service de son Maître et s'engage avec un autre Employeur, le dernier Contrat passé par lui devient nul si l'on découvre ensuite qu'il était déjà lié par un autre Contrat et que l'on désire se prévaloir de ce premier Contrat.—*Voir les Nos.* 274, 184, 204 *et* 436.

259.—Tout Magistrat Stipendiaire, sur la demande d'un Maître, pourra annuler l'engagement de tout serviteur employé chez lui qui aura été convaincu de délit ou de crime. Ord. No. 15 de 1852, Art. 3.

Les Immigrants qui sont des vagabonds incorrigibles ou qui ont commis des actes criminels peuvent être renvoyés dans l'Inde par le Gouverneur (*voir le No.* 544) ; et apparemment même lorsqu'ils sont liés par des Contrats de Service.

CHAPITRE VII.

De l'emploi illégal, du Recèlement, etc., des laboureurs.

260.—Quiconque sera convaincu d'avoir embauché, caché, recélé, ou employé des serviteurs ou apprentis dûment engagés, ou de leur avoir persuadé ou cherché à persuader de quitter le service de leurs maîtres, ou de s'en absenter, sera condamné à un emprisonnement qui n'excèdera pas six mois, et à une amende qui n'excèdera pas vingt-cinq livres sterling, et dans tous les cas, à huit shillings par jour de dommages-intérêts au profit du maître. Ord. No. 6 de 1838, Art. 328. (Penal Code.)

L'amende sera appliquée moitié à la Caisse de Bienfaisance et moitié au dénonciateur.

261.—Toute personne qui recèlera, logera ou emploiera illégalement un serviteur engagé au service d'une autre personne, sera passible d'une peine qui n'excèdera pas £10, et de dommages-intérêts au profit de la personne avec laquelle le dit serviteur est engagé, lesquels n'excèderont pas huit shillings par chaque jour du dit recèlement, logement ou emploi illégal, recouvrables devant un Magistrat Stipendiaire. Ord. No. 15 de 1852, Art. 7.

Govt. Notice No. 166 of 11th Nov. 1868, Art. 74.

262.—Any person who shall be convicted of having knowingly harboured a Vagrant shall be liable to a fine not exceeding Five Pounds.

Ord. No. 31 of 1867, Art. 5.

263.—Any person illegally employing, lodging, or harbouring a new Immigrant not engaged under written Contract, shall, over and above any other penalty to which he may become subject, be liable to a penalty not less than £ 2 and not exceeding £ 5, one half of which penalty may be awarded to the informer of the contravention of the law.

The present Article shall not apply to persons employing new Immigrants in pursuance of any Contract of Service made in India, under the provisions of any law in force at the time being.

Job-Contractors who have no License or have not furnished the guarantee required by law for the payment of their servants' wages &c., are liable to a fine for each laborer so employed by them.—*See Nos.* 311, 312 *and* 313.

If a Stipendiary Magistrate is satisfied that a Contract of Service with an Old Immigrant is fictitious he may cancel it, (*See No.* 257), and fine the parties, (*See No.* 258.) A penalty may also be inflicted where a Police Pass has been obtained through a fictitious verbal engagement.—*See No.* 209.

In order to avoid committing an infraction of the law by illegal employment (*See Nos.* 260 *et seq.*,) it is prudent, previous to employing a servant, to ascertain as far as possible that he is not already bound by contract to another person, and that he is otherwise free to engage himself. This information must, according to the class of the laborer, be gathered sometimes from his verbal statement and at others from the papers which he should have in his possession. The indications contained in this note are given more particularly for the guidance of persons about to employ servants under a *verbal* engagement than with reference to *written* contracts, for on passing these latter the Stipendiary Magistrate takes care that the necessary papers are produced to him. The papers of the several classes of laborers, which are different for each class, are as follows :—

New Immigrants.—The definition of this class will be found at No. 550; they are the only laborers whom it is unlawful to employ under verbal engagement (*See No.* 263). They should hold a Ticket in the form shewn at page 208 or at No. 274, and either the Certificate of Discharge mentioned at Nos. 238 and 232, or a Certificate from the Protector of Immigrants as provided by Nos. 273 and 408.

262.—Toute personne qui sera trouvée coupable d'avoir sciemment donné asile à un vagabond sera passible d'une amende n'excédant pas cinq livres sterling. Avis du Gouv. No. 166 du 11 Nov. 1868, Art. 74.

263.—Toute personne employant autrement qu'en vertu d'un Ord. No. 31 de ... t. 5.

263.

Les Entrepreneurs ne peuvent plus aujourd'hui employer des hommes sous Contrat Verbal ni hors de leur District.—Voir le No. 567.

Les personnes qui emploient des Immigrants dont les Permis sont expirés sont passibles d'une amende.—Voir le No. 571.

Les Entrepreneurs qui n'ont pas de patente, ou qui n'ont pas fourni la garantie requise par la loi pour le paiement des gages des laboureurs etc., sont passibles d'une amende pour chaque laboureur qu'ils emploient dans ces conditions.—*Voir les Nos.* 311, 312 *et* 313.

Si un Magistrat Stipendiaire est satisfait qu'un Contrat passé avec un Ancien Immigrant est fictif il peut l'annuler (*Voir le No.* 257), et condamner les parties à l'amende (*Voir le No.* 258). Une amende peut aussi être infligée lorsqu'une Passe de Police a été obtenue au moyen d'un engagement verbal fictif.—*Voir le No.* 209.

Afin d'éviter toute infraction à la loi pour emploi illégal de travailleurs (*Voir les Nos.* 260 *et suiv* :), il est prudent, avant d'employer un serviteur, de s'assurer, autant que possible, qu'il n'est pas déjà lié envers une autre personne par un Contrat de Service,—et qu'il est de toute autre manière libre de s'engager. On obtient ces renseignements, selon la classe de travailleurs que l'on veut employer, tantôt de la bouche du serviteur lui-même, et tantôt des papiers qu'il doit avoir en sa possession. Les indications données dans cette note ont plus particulièrement pour but de guider les personnes qui sont sur le point d'employer des serviteurs par des Contrats Verbaux ; car, dans le cas d'un engagement par Contrat écrit, le Magistrat Stipendiaire s'assure que tous les papiers nécessaires lui sont produits. Les papiers des diverses classes de travailleurs, qui diffèrent selon la classe à laquelle ils se rapportent, sont comme suit :

Nouveaux Immigrants.—On trouvera la définition de cette classe de travailleurs au No. 550 ; ce sont les seuls qu'on ne puisse employer en vertu d'un engagement verbal (*Voir le No.* 263). Ils doivent être munis d'un Ticket dans la forme indiquée à la page 209 ou au No. 274 , et soit du Certificat de Décharge mentionné au Nos. 238 et 232, ou d'un Certificat du Protecteur des Immigrants d'après les Nos. 273 et 408.

Old Immigrants.—Written Contracts.—The papers which should be produced to the Stipendiary Magistrate by these men at the time of the engagement, are set forth in Nos. 227, 229 et seq.

Old Immigrants.—Verbal Contracts.—Before employing a laborer of this class it should be seen that he is in possession of a Portrait-Ticket as provided by No. 275, and, if any engagement has been noted on the back thereof, that he holds a regular Certificate of Discharge (No. 238). If the delay fixed by Nos. 280 and 281 has expired since the date of such discharge, the laborer should also have a Police Pass for the district in which he offers his services.

The Tickets of Immigrants, under written contract, are handed by the Stipendiary Magistrate to the employer, with whom they remain until the completion of the contract (No. 227); and in verbal engagements it is customary for the Master to retain the laborer's papers as evidence shewing that he was entitled to employ the man verbally, and as a guarantee against desertion: thus the production by the Servant of all his papers *en règle* shews that he is not bound by any written contract, and it may be taken as fair proof that he is also free from verbal engagement.

As regards the employment of Old Immigrants by the day or by the job, the laborer should be in possession of his Ticket and Police Pass as above mentioned, of the License referred to in No, 283, and should wear on his right arm the badge indicated by No. 285.

Immigrants of uncertain status.—In case application is made to the Protector by an Immigrant for a Duplicate Ticket, the original of which is supposed to have been lost by that laborer, the course indicated by No. 279 is followed; and any person may lawfully employ a laborer holding the *Permit to work*, until it expires.

Indian Passengers.—These servants arrive at Mauritius at their own expense; they come chiefly from Pondicherry and Bourbon. On landing here they are furnished by the Police Department with a certificate as shewn in page 208 and they should be required to produce that paper before being employed.

Laborers of Indian Extraction, Born in Mauritius.—There is no law requiring servants of this class to hold any papers whatever; but, as they cannot always be distinguished from Immigrants long resident in the Colony, it is prudent not to employ them unless they produce their Act of Birth.

Liberated African Slaves.—On the arrival in the Colony of these laborers (*See Nos.* 163 *et seq.*) they are usually engaged for five

Anciens Immigrants.—Contrats Ecrits.—Les papiers que ces travailleurs doivent produire au Magistrat Stipendiaire, lors de leur engagement, sont énumérés aux Nos. 227, 229 et suiv.

Anciens Immigrants.—Contrats Verbaux.—Avant d'employer un travailleur de cette classe, il est nécessaire de s'assurer qu'il est muni d'un Ticket avec son portrait y attaché, conformément au No. 275 ; et, si un engagement est endossé sur ce Ticket, qu'il possède aussi un Certificat de Décharge régulier.—(*Voir le No.* 238.)

Si le délai fixé par les Nos. 280 et 281 est expiré depuis la date de la dite décharge, le travailleur doit aussi avoir une Passe de Police pour le District dans lequel il désire s'employer.

Les Tickets des Immigrants engagés par Contrats Ecrits, sont

PAGE 199.

Par : 4.

Depuis que cette note a été imprimé, une pénalité a été décrétée contre l'Ancien Immigrant ne travaillant pas sous Contrat écrit qui ne produit pas son Ticket.—Voir le No. 574.

l'entreprise, on doit exiger la production par le Ticket et de sa Passe comme il est dit ci-dessus, et de plus de la Patente dont il est fait mention au No. 283 ; et le travailleur doit aussi porter sur le bras droit la plaque indiquée au No. 285.

Immigrants dont la condition est incertaine.—Lorsqu'un Immigrant s'adresse au Protecteur pour obtenir le Duplicata d'un Ticket, dont l'original est supposé avoir été perdu par ce travailleur, les formalités prescrites par le No. 279 sont observées,—et toute personne peut légalement employer un travailleur muni d'un *Permis de Travailler*, pendant toute la durée de ce Permis.

Passagers Indiens.—Ces serviteurs arrivent à Maurice, à leurs propres frais, principalement de Pondichéry et de Bourbon. A leur débarquement dans la Colonie, le Département de la Police leur fournit le certificat dont il est fait mention à la page 209, et l'on doit, avant de les employer, exiger qu'ils produisent ce document.

Travailleurs d'Origine Indienne, nés dans la Colonie.—Il n'y a pas de loi qui oblige les serviteurs de cette classe à avoir aucuns papiers, mais, comme on ne peut pas toujours les distinguer des Immigrants qui sont depuis longtemps dans la Colonie, il est prudent de ne pas les employer à moins qu'ils ne produisent leur acte de naissance.

Esclaves Africains Libérés.—A l'arrivée de ces travailleurs dans la Colonie (*Voir les Nos.* 163 *et suiv.*), ils sont généralement engagés

years and receive a Portrait-Ticket in the form provided by No. 177; on the termination of their engagement they receive a Certificate of Discharge (No. 238,) and should produce both those documents when about to be engaged either verbally or by written contract.

Creole Laborers.—The men of this class are not required to be in possession of papers. They seldom, if ever, enter into written Contracts of Service.

CHAPTER VIII.

Apprenticeship of Children.

Order in Council 7th Sept. 1838, Cap. 3, Sect. 1.

264.—Children above the age of ten, and under the age of sixteen years, may be apprenticed by their fathers, or, in the case of fatherless children, by their mothers, or, in the case of orphans, by their guardians, to any trade in the practice of which any peculiar art or skill is requisite.—(*See also No.* 224.)

Idem, Cap. 3, Sect. 2.

265.—No child may be apprenticed as a labourer in husbandry, or in the manufacture of colonial produce.

Idem, Cap. 3, Sect. 3.

266.—The apprenticeship of such children may be for any time not exceeding five years.

Idem, Cap. 3, Sect. 4.

267.—Any person of the full age of sixteen years or upwards may, by his or her consent, be apprenticed to any trade, in the practice of which any peculiar art or skill is required, for any term not exceeding five years.—(*See also No.* 224.)

Idem, Cap. 3, Sect. 5.

268.—The law respecting apprentices in England shall, as far as may be practicable, be applied to the case of such apprenticeships as aforesaid; but there shall be no apprenticeship of any kind, or under any circumstances, of persons as labourers in husbandry, or in the manufacture of colonial produce. All engagements for those purposes must be made in pursuance of the rules contained in the second Chapter of these Regulations.

Idem, Cap. 3, Sect. 6

269.—Provided that the powers which in England are vested in the Justices of the Peace for enforcing or dissolving Contracts of Apprenticeship, and for authorizing the making of such Contracts,

pour cinq ans, et reçoivent un Ticket avec leur Portrait y attaché, dans la forme prévue par le No. 177; à l'expiration de leur engagement ils reçoivent un Certificat de Décharge (No. 238,) et doivent ensuite produire ces deux documents lorsqu'ils veulent s'engager soit verbalement soit par contrat écrit.

Travailleurs Créoles.—Les travailleurs de cette classe ne sont pas tenus d'avoir aucuns papiers. Ils passent rarement, si ce n'est jamais, des Contrats de Service écrits.

CHAPITRE VIII.

De l'Apprentissage des Enfants.

264.—Les enfants au-dessus de l'âge de dix ans et au-dessous de seize, peuvent être mis en apprentissage par leur père, ou, s'ils n'ont pas leur père, par leur mère, ou s'ils sont orphelins, par leur tuteur, pour tout métier dont l'exercice exige un art ou une habileté particulière.—(*Voir aussi le No.* 224.) Ordre en Conseil du 7 Sept. 1838, Ch. 3, Sect. 1.

265.—Aucun enfant ne peut être mis en apprentissage pour travailler à la culture, ou à la manufacture des produits coloniaux. Idem, Ch. 3, Sect. 2.

266.—L'apprentissage de tous enfants ci-dessus désignés, peut être stipulé pour un temps quelconque, n'excédant pas cinq années. Idem, Ch. 3, Sect. 3.

267.—Toute personne de l'âge de seize ans ou au-dessus, peut, de son consentement, entrer en apprentissage d'un métier quelconque exigeant un art ou une habileté particulière, pour un temps n'excédant pas cinq années.—(*Voir aussi le No.* 224.) Idem, Ch. 3, Sect. 4.

268.—La loi concernant les apprentis en Angleterre sera, autant que possible, appliquée aux apprentissages ci-dessus mentionnés; mais il ne peut y avoir d'apprentissage d'aucun genre, et dans aucune circonstance, pour les travailleurs employés à la culture, ou à la manufacture de produits coloniaux. Tous engagements à cet effet doivent être passés conformément aux dispositions du Chapitre 2 des présents réglements. Idem, Ch. 3, Sect. 5.

269.—Il est entendu que les pouvoirs qui appartiennent aux Juges de Paix en Angleterre pour forcer l'exécution ou prononcer la dissolution des Contrats d'Apprentissage, et pour autoriser Idem, Ch. 3, Sect. 6.

shall, in the said Colonies, be vested in the Stipendiary Magistrates thereof respectively.

Govt. Notice of 16th Jan. 1840.

270.—Whereas by Chap. 3, Sect. 5, of an Order of the Queen's Most Excellent Majesty in Council, dated September 7th, 1838, made for regulating the relative duties of masters and servants, it is enacted and ordered : " That the law respecting apprentices in " England shall, as far as may be practicable, be applied in the " Colony of Mauritius, to the case of such apprentices as are in " the said Order in Council mentioned."

His Excellency the Governor directs the following extracts from the statute law of England applicable to apprentices to be published for general information :—

STATUTES.
5 Eliz. Chap. 4.
43 Eliz. Chap. 2.
1 James 1st. Chap. 25.
7 James 1st. Chap. 3
8 & 9 Wm. & Mary Chap. 30.
2 & 3 Anne Chap. 6.
4 Anne Chap. 19.
17 George 2 Chap. 5.
18 George 3 Chap. 47.

All bindings of apprentices must be by indenture under seal, the original remaining with the parents or guardians of the infant apprentice,—in case of parish apprentices, with the overseers of the poor of the parish,—and the counter-part, of course, with the master to whom the apprentice is bound.

"

Children of poor persons may be apprenticed out by the overseers, with consent of two Justices of the Peace, till 21 years of age, to such persons as are thought fitting, who are also compellable to take them, and it is held that Gentlemen of fortune and clergymen are equally liable with others to such compulsion.

"

The Justices should attest their approbation of the apprenticeship indentures by signing their consent in writing at the foot of the same, or by indorsement.

STATUTE.
5 Eliz. Chap. 4.

Apprentices may be discharged on reasonable cause, either at the request of themselves or masters, at the Quarter Sessions (here the Petty Ses-

la passation des dits contrats, seront dévolus aux Magistrats Salariés des dites colonies respectivement.

270.—Attendu que par le Chap. 3 de la Section 5 d'un Ordre de Sa Très Grâcieuse Majesté la Reine en Conseil, en date du 7 Septembre 1838, ayant pour objet de régler les devoirs respectifs des maîtres et des serviteurs, il est dit et ordonné : " Que la loi " concernant les apprentis en Angleterre sera, autant que possible " appliquée dans la Colonie de Maurice, aux cas de tels apprentis " qui sont mentionnés dans le dit Ordre en Conseil." Avis du Gouv. du 16 Janv. 1840.

Son Excellence le Gouverneur ordonne que les extraits suivants de la loi d'Angleterre applicable aux apprentis soient publiés pour l'information générale :—

STATUTS. 5 Eliz. Chap. 4. 43 Eliz. Chap. 2. 1 James I Chap. 25. 7 James I Chap. 3. 8 & 9 Wm. & Marie Chap. 30. 2 & 3 Anne Chap. 6. 4 Anne Chap. 19. 17 George 2 Chap. 5. 18 George 3 Chap. 47.

Tout engagement d'apprentis doit être fait par acte scellé dont l'original restera entre les mains des parens ou tuteurs de l'enfant mis en apprentissage, (si c'est un apprenti de paroisse, entre les mains des commissaires des pauvres de la paroisse) et la copie entre celles du maître envers qui l'enfant est engagé.

"

Les enfans de personnes indigentes peuvent être mis en apprentissage par les commissaires des pauvres (à Maurice les administrateurs de la Caisse de Bienfaisance), avec le consentement de deux Juges de Paix, jusqu'à l'âge de 21 ans, sous la direction de personnes jugées convenables, qui pourront être forcées de prendre les dits apprentis ; et il est entendu que les particuliers les plus aisés et les ecclésiastiques seront soumis à cette obligation comme toutes autres personnes.

"

Les Juges de Paix devront, pour attester leur approbation, écrire et signer le consentement qu'ils auront donné au Contrat d'Apprentissage au bas ou au dos de cet acte.

STATUT. 5 Eliz. Chap. 4.

Les apprentis peuvent être dégagés pour une cause raisonnable, soit à leur demande, soit à celle des maîtres par les quarter sessions (à Mau-

sions) or by one Justice, subject to an appeal to the Sessions, who may, by the equity of the statute, if they think it reasonable, direct restitution of a rateable share of the money which may have been given with the apprentice.

STATUTE.
20 Geo. 2. Chap. 19.

Parish apprentices (or poor apprentices) may be discharged in the same manner by two Justices out of sessions.

STATUTE.
6 Geo. 3. Chap. 28.

If an apprentice with whom less than £ 10 has been given, runs away from his Master, he is compellable to serve out his time of absence, or to make compensation to his master for the same, at any time within seven years after the expiration of his original Contract of Apprenticeship.

STATUTE.
32 Geo. 3. Chap. 57.

When a parish apprentice (or poor apprentice) is discharged from a master, on account of the misconduct of the master, the Justices may order the master to deliver up his clothes and to pay a sum not exceeding ten pounds to place him with another master.

Every Juvenile offender at the expiration of his period of detention in a Reformatory School is bound to enter into an engagement as servant or apprentice for a time not exceeding three years, but the consent of the youth's parent or guardian to the Contract is not essential to its validity.—*Ord. No.* 1 *of* 1867.

Ord. No. 21 of 1853, Art. 12.

271.—The powers and authority formerly vested in the President of the Court of First Instance, by Ordinance No. 8 of 1839, for the purpose of appointing a guardian to every illegitimate orphan child, and all other powers given to the same by the said Ordinance, are hereby transferred to and shall be exercised by the District Magistrate in their districts respectively.

The Protector of Immigrants is the guardian *ex-officio* of all orphan Immigrants whether natural or legitimate, and to all orphans of Indian extraction, who have no relatives in the Colony.—*See Nos.* 588 *and* 589.

rice par les petites sessions), ou par un Juge de Paix, sauf l'appel aux sessions qui pourront, selon l'équité du statut, s'il leur paraît raisonnable, ordonner la restitution d'une partie proportionnée de la somme d'argent qui aura été remise avec l'apprenti.

STATUT. 20 Geo. 2. Chap. 19.

Les apprentis de paroisses (ou les apprentis de parens indigens) peuvent être dégagés de la même manière, par deux Juges de Paix hors des sessions.

STATUT. 6 Geo. 3. Chap. 28.

Si un apprenti avec lequel il a été remis moins de £ 10, s'enfuit de chez son maître, il peut être contraint de remplacer ce temps d'absence ou de donner à son maître une compensation équivalente, à aucune époque durant les sept années qui suivront son contrat d'apprentissage originaire.

STATUT. 32 Geo. 3. Chap. 57.

Si un apprenti de paroisse (ou de parens indigens) est dégagé vis-à-vis de son maître, pour raison de conduite inconvenable de celui-ci, les Juges pourront condamner le maître à remettre à l'apprenti ses effets et à payer une somme n'excédant pas £ 10 pour placer l'apprenti sous un nouveau maître.

Tout jeune détenu à l'expiration du temps qu'il a été condamné à passer dans une Ecole Pénitentiaire est tenu de s'engager comme domestique ou comme apprenti pour un temps n'excédant pas trois ans, mais le consentement de ses parents ou de son tuteur à ce contrat n'est pas nécessaire pour le rendre valable.—*Ord. No.* 1 *de* 1867.

271.—Les pouvoirs et l'autorité donnés anciennement au Président du Tribunal de Première Instance, par l'Ordonnance No. 8 de 1839, à l'effet de nommer des tuteurs aux enfants illégitimes orphelins, et tous autres pouvoirs donnés à ce Tribunal par la dite Ordonnance, sont par ces présentes transmis aux Magistrats de Districts et seront par eux respectivement exercés dans leurs districts. Ord. No. 21 de 1853, Art. 12.

Le Protecteur des Immigrants est d'office le tuteur de tous les Immigrants orphelins, qu'ils soient enfants naturels ou légitimes, ainsi que tous les orphelins d'origine indienne qui n'ont pas de parents dans la Colonie.—*Voir les Nos.* 538 *et* 539.

Ord. No. 18 of 1865, Art. 10. 272.—The Protector of Immigrants and Civil Commissioner of Seychelles are hereby appointed *ex-officio* guardians, respectively, to every orphan liberated slave, whether legitimate or illegitimate, in Mauritius and Seychelles respectively.

Ord. No. 33 of 1853, Art. 109. 272 (*bis*).—Where any person shall have been an apprentice to a Bankrupt at the time of the filing of a petition for adjudication of Bankruptcy, the filing of such petition, or the issuing of such fiat, shall be and enure as a complete discharge of the indenture whereby such apprentice was bound: and if any sum have been really and *bonâ fide* paid, by or on the behalf of such apprentice, to the Bankrupt, as an Apprentice fee, it shall be lawful for the Court, upon proof thereof, to order any sum to be paid out of the estate of the said Bankrupt, to or for the use of such apprentice, which such Court shall think reasonable, regard being had in estimating such sum, to the amount of the sum so paid by or on behalf of such apprentice, and to the time during which such apprentice shall have resided with the Bankrupt previous to the filing of such petition or to the issuing of such fiat.

TICKETS, POLICE PASSES AND OTHER PAPERS.

The introduction into Mauritius, from other countries, of laborers bound to remain and work in the Colony for a fixed period, has made it necessary to have always at hand some mode of distinguishing these men from others who are under no such obligation, of identifying them, of ascertaining how far they have completed their industrial residence, and of thereafter knowing what are their means of existence. With this object they are furnished with papers shewing their status. and they are liable to much personal inconvenience and even punishment if they are unable to produce them when law fully required to do so.

The Emigration Agents, in British India, forward to the Protector of Immigrants in Mauritius, by the vessel which conveys the laborers, a Ticket in the following form for each Immigrant. This document is handed to the Employer when the newly arrived Immigrant is delivered to him.—*See No.* 127.

272.—Le Protecteur des Immigrants et le Civil Commissioner des Seychelles sont, par ces présentes, nommés d'office, chacun en ce qui le concerne, tuteurs de tout esclave libéré orphelin, qu'il soit enfant légitime ou illégitime, à Maurice et aux Seychelles. Ord. No. 18 de 1865, Art. 10.

272 (*bis*).—Lorsqu'une personne aura été en apprentissage avec un failli au moment du dépôt d'une requête en déclaration de faillite ou de la délivrance d'un permis de poursuivre en matière de faillite, le dépôt de la dite pétition ou la délivrance du dit permis vaudra et sortira effet comme décharge complète de l'engagement par lequel le dit apprenti était lié; et si une somme a été réellement et de bonne foi payée par ou pour le dit apprenti, au failli, comme honoraires pour l'apprentissage, la Cour pourra, sur la preuve qui en sera fournie, ordonner de payer, sur les biens du dit failli, au dit apprenti ou à son profit, telle somme que la Cour jugera convenable, eu égard, pour l'évaluation de la dite somme, au montant de la somme ainsi payée par ou pour le dit apprenti, et au temps pendant lequel le dit apprenti aura résidé avec le failli avant le dépôt de la dite requête ou la délivrance du dit permis. Ord. No. 33 de 1853, Art. 109.

DES TICKETS, PASSES DE POLICE ET AUTRES PAPIERS.

L'Introduction à Maurice de laboureurs emigrant d'autres Pays et s'obligeant à demeurer et à travailler dans la Colonie pendant un laps de temps déterminé, a rendu nécessaire d'avoir continuellement sous la main un moyen de distinguer ces hommes de ceux qui ne sont liés par aucune obligation de ce genre, de les identifier, de s'assurer s'ils ont achevé leur Résidence Industrielle et de se rendre compte, par la suite, de leurs moyens d'existence.—Dans ce but on leur fournit des papiers qui établissent leur position, et ils sont exposés à bien des embarras, et même à certaines pénalités, s'ils ne peuvent produire ces papiers toutes les fois qu'on peut légalement l'exiger deux.

Les Agents d'Emigration dans l'Inde Anglaise transmettent au Protecteur des Immigrants à Maurice par le navire qui transporte les laboureurs, un Ticket dans la forme suivante pour chaque Immigrant. Ce document est remis au Maître lorsque l'Immigrant nouvellement arrivé lui est délivré.—(*Voir le No.* 127.)

NEW IMMIGRANT'S TICKET.

Embarked at *on the* 186 .

Name ....
Father's Name ....
Emigration No. in India { Depot ...... Ship ....
Age ....
Sex ....
Stature ....
If married, to whom.......................
Village ....
Marks ....

I hereby certify that the above described whom I have engaged as a Laborer on the part of has appeared before me and declared willingness and desire to proceed to work for Hire in the Colony of Mauritius.

J. F. *Protector of Emigrants.*

C. E. *Mauritius Immigration Agent.*

Arrived per Ship No. . Left Depôt 186 .
Immigrant's No. in Mauritius

H. B.
Protector of Immigrants.

On the arrival in the Colony of Immigrants from elsewhere than British India, a Ticket is issued to each of them by the Protector of Immigrants.—*See No.* 144.

Indians arriving at Mauritius at their own expense as Passengers, are furnished by the Police Department with a certificate in the following form:

PASSENGER'S CERTIFICATE.

[FREE.] ORIGINAL CERTIFICATE No.

I certify that the Indian named arrived in this Colony as Passenger from per on the 18 .

DESCRIPTION:

Examined. { Native of.......................
Father's Name.. ....
Age ....
Complexion..................
Height.........................
Marks .... }

General Police Office, 186.

J. S.
Pro Inspector General of Police.

TICKET DE NOUVEL IMMIGRANT.

Emigrant embarqué à *le* 186 .

Nom ....
Nom du Père ....
No. d'Émigration dans l'Inde { Dans le Dépot.... A bord du navire.
Age ....
Sexe ....
Taille..
S'il est marié, le nom de sa femme ....
Village ....
Marques ....

Je certifie par le présent que ci-dessus dénommé que j'ai engagé comme Laboureur pour a comparu devant moi et exprimé le désir de se rendre dans la Colonie de Maurice pour y travailler.

J. F.
Protecteur des Emigrants.

C. E.
Agent d'Immigration pour Maurice.

Arrivé par le Navire No.
No. de l'Immigrant à Maurice

Quitté le Dépôt le 186 .

H. B.
Protecteur des Immigrants.

A l'arrivée dans la Colonie d'Immigrants d'endroits autres que l'Inde Anglaise un Ticket est délivré à chacun d'eux par le Protecteur des Immigrants.—*Voir le No.* 144.

Les Indiens arrivant à Maurice à leurs propres frais, reçoivent du Département de la Police un certificat dans la forme suivante :

CERTIFICAT DE PASSAGER.

[Sans Frais.] Certificat original No.

Je certifie que l'Indien nommé est arrivé en cette Colonie comme passager de par le le 18 .

SIGNALEMENT :

Examiné. {
Natif de..........................
Nom du père..............
Age ....
Teint ....
Taille ....
Marques ....

Bureau de la Police Générale, 186.

J. S.
Pour l'Inspecteur Général de Police.

For the form of Ticket issued by the Protector of Immigrants on the allotment of Liberated African Slaves.—*See No.* 177.

Before leaving the Immigration Depôt, each newly arrived Immigrant receives a Certificate of Engagement from the Protector.—*See No.* 128.

On the passing of any written Contract of Service in the Colony, the Stipendiary Magistrate furnishes the servant with a certificate of his engagement.—*See Nos.* 234 *and* 238,—and, if the servant is an Immigrant, such engagement is endorsed on his Ticket.—*See No.* 227.—At the termination of a Contract of Service the servant receives a Certificate of Discharge from the Stipendiary Magistrate.—*See Nos.* 238 *et seq.*

Govt. Notice No. 166 of 11th Nov. 1868, Art. 37.

273.—Any Immigrant who has lost his Certificate of Discharge within two months from its date, may obtain a duplicate thereof, from the Clerk of the Court in which he was discharged, on payment of the fee * mentioned in the tariff; provided he produce his Ticket bearing his Portrait.

If more than two months' time has elapsed since the date of his discharge, he will have to apply to the Protector of Immigrants for a Permit to engage.*

In cases where, on account of desertion or otherwise, Immigrants were not in possession of regular papers and could not or would not shew how far they had completed their Industrial Residence, much difficulty formerly arose in exacting from them the performance of that obligation, owing to the uncertainty of their status in that respect: the following provision was introduced to remedy the evil by enabling the Protector to furnish them with regular papers as re-registered New-Immigrants.

Ord. No. 16 of 1862, Art. 15.

274.—It shall be lawful to the Protector of Immigrants to issue, to any persons who he shall be satisfied are Indian Immigrants, and who shall not be able to shew that they are not bound in Industrial Residence in the Colony, Tickets in the form of Schedule H.

* The cost of a duplicate Certificate of Discharge is two shillings,—*See No.* 487.—For every Permit issued by the Protector of Immigrants a fee of five shillings is chargeable.—*See No.* 525.

Pour la forme du Ticket délivré par le Protecteur des Immigrants aux Esclaves Africains Libérés lors de leur répartition.—*Voir le No.* 177.

Avant de quitter le Dépôt d'Immigration, chaque Immigrant nouvellement arrivé reçoit un certificat d'Engagement du Protecteur.—*Voir le No.* 128.

Lorsqu'un Contrat de Service écrit est passé dans la Colonie, le Magistrat Stipendiaire fournit au serviteur un Certificat de son Engagement,—*Voir les Nos* 234 et 238,—et si le serviteur est un Immigrant, le dit engagement est endossé sur son Ticket.—*Voir No.* 227. A l'expiration du Contrat de Service, le serviteur reçoit un Certificat de Décharge du Magistrat Stipendiaire.—*Voir les Nos.* 238 *et suiv.*

273.—Tout Immigrant qui aura perdu son Certificat de Décharge dans les deux mois qui suivront sa date, pourra en obtenir un duplicata, du commis du Tribunal où il a été dégagé, en payant le droit * mentionné au tarif, pourvu qu'il produise son Ticket avec son Portrait. Avis du Gouv. No. 166 du 11 Nov. 1868, Art. 37.

Si plus de deux mois se sont écoulés depuis la date de sa décharge, il devra s'adresser au Protecteur des Immigrants pour un Permis d'Engagement.*

Dans les cas où, pour cause de désertion ou pour tout autre motif, des Immigrants n'avaient pas de papiers réguliers, et ne voulaient pas ou ne pouvaient pas fournir de renseignements relativement à leur Résidence Industrielle, on éprouvait autrefois beaucoup de difficultés pour leur faire remplir cette obligation à cause de l'incertitude dans laquelle on se trouvait quant à la portion de Résidence Industrielle qu'ils pouvaient rester devoir ; et, afin de remédier à cet inconvénient, on promulgua la disposition suivante qui permet au Protecteur de leur délivrer des papiers réguliers comme de nouveaux Immigrants ré-enregistrés.

274.—Le Protecteur des Immigrants pourra délivrer à tous individus qui lui auront été prouvés être des Immigrants Indiens, et qui ne pourront pas justifier qu'ils ne doivent pas une Résidence Industrielle dans la Colonie, des Tickets dans la forme de la Cédule H. Ord. No. 16 de 1862, Art. 15.

---

* Le coût d'un duplicata de Certificat de Décharge est deux shillings.—*Voir le No.* 487. Chaque Permis délivré par le Protecteur des Immigrants coûte cinq shillings.—*Voir le No.* 525.

SCHEDULE H.

No.
1 Name of Immigrant.
2 Name of Father.
3 Name of Mother.
4 Whence imported.
5 Place of Nativity.
6 Age (*in letters.*)
7 Stature (*in feet and inches.*)
8 Caste.
9 Time remaining to serve as New Immigrant.
10 To whom allotted.

Delivered this 186 .

E. F.
Protector of Immigrants.

If any Immigrant receiving such Ticket shews that he has completed any portion of his Industrial Residence, a note to that effect is endorsed on this Ticket.—*See Nos.* 184 *and* 185.

Ord. No. 31 of 1867, Art. 39.

275.—The Protector of Immigrants shall, upon proof to him of any Immigrant having duly completed his Industrial Residence, register such Immigrant as an Old Immigrant, giving him a Ticket as such, with his portrait thereon, and in the form of the Schedule hereunto annexed.

No fee shall be charged for any such Ticket, but the cost of the portrait affixed thereto shall be paid by the Immigrant according to the rate fixed by the Regulations in that behalf.

SCHEDULE

Old Immigrant's Ticket. *

Name of Immigrant...	Portrait.
Number	
Name of Father...	
Name of Mother	
Age (*in letters*)	
Stature (*in feet and inches*). ...	
Caste	
Marks	
Native Country...	
Number of Vessel by which introduced ...	

This Immigrant is free to engage himself.

Delivered this 186 .

Signed: H. B.
Protector of Immigrants.

* For the Portrait affixed to this document a fee of four shillings is paid by the Applicant to the Protector of Immigrants.—*See No.* 525.

CÉDULE H.

No.
1 Nom de l'Immigrant.
2 Nom du père.
3 Nom de la mère.
4 De quel port arrivé.
5 Lieu de naissance.
6 Age (*en toutes lettres.*)
7 Taille (*en pieds et pouces.*)
8 Caste.
9 Temps qu'il lui reste à servir comme Nouvel Immigrant.
10 A qui réparti.

Délivré ce 186 .

E. F.
Protecteur des Immigrants.

Si un Immigrant qui a reçu un Ticket dans la forme ci-dessus prouve qu'il a achevé une partie quelconque de sa Résidence Industrielle, mention en est faite sur son Ticket.—*Voir les Nos.* 184 *et* 185.

275.—Le Protecteur des Immigrants devra, sur la preuve qui lui sera faite qu'un Immigrant a dûment achevé sa Résidence Industrielle, enregistrer cet Immigrant comme un Ancien Immigrant, et lui donnera un Ticket à cet effet, sur lequel se trouvera son portrait, et dans la forme de la Cédule annexée à ces présentes. Ord. No. 31 de 1867, Art. 39.

Il ne sera réclamé aucun droit pour ce Ticket, mais le coût du portrait y attaché sera payé par l'Immigrant au taux fixé par les Réglements relatifs à ce sujet.

CÉDULE.

*Ticket d'Ancien Immigrant.**

Nom de l'Immigrant... ... ...
Numéro ... ...
Nom du père ... ...
Nom de la mère... ... ...
Age (*en lettres*)... ... ...
Stature (*en pieds et pouces*) ...
Caste ... ...
Marques ... ...
Pays Natal... ... ...
No. du navire qui l'a introduit... ... ...

Portrait.

Cet Immigrant est libre de s'engager.

Délivré ce 186 .

Signé : H. B.
Protecteur des Immigrants.

* Pour le Portrait attaché à ce document un droit de quatre shillings est payé par celui qui en fait la demande au Protecteur des Immigrants.—*Voir le No.* 525.

Govt. Notice No. 166 of 11th Nov. 1868, Art. 82.

276.—The Protector shall have power to exempt any infirm or destitute Immigrant from the payment of the fee chargeable for his portrait.

Ord. No. 31 of 1867, Art. 40.

277.—All tickets which, prior to the passing of this Ordinance, shall have been issued by the Protector to Old Immigrants without portraits affixed thereto, shall be delivered up to the Protector, who, in lieu thereof, shall deliver to such Immigrants Tickets as prescribed by Article 39.—(*Art.* 39,—*See No.* 275.)

Idem, Art. 42.

278.—At and after the *last mentioned period,* no Ticket other than in the form prescribed in *Article* 39 shall be of any avail as proof of the status of Old Immigrant of the party described therein. And the holder of any ticket other than in the above form shall be liable to be detained and forwarded to the Protector of Immigrants.—

Last mentioned period, i. e. three months from the coming into force of Ord. No. 31 of 1867.—That law was put into operation, on 2nd May 1868, and the above mentioned delay has therefore expired.—(*Art.* 39.—*See No.* 275.)

The present Article shall not apply to any Immigrant engaged under written contract of service entered into prior to the said period fixed in *Article* 41, and still unexpired.—(*Art.* 41,—*See No.* 229.)

Provided always that any such Immigrant shall be bound, upon being discharged from such contract of service, to appear forthwith before the Protector of Immigrants, and to exchange his Ticket as aforesaid.

Govt. Notice No. 166 of 11th Nov. 1868, Art. 67.

279.—The issue of Duplicate Tickets to Immigrants shall be subject to the following rules :

1o.—If the applicant present his name and number and has not been *declared as a deserter* a *Permit to work* in the form of the Schedule R hereto annexed may be issued to him, authorising him to remain absent from the Depot and take employment for any period not exceeding one month ; during which time it shall be notified in the Government Gazette that he has applied for a Duplicate-Ticket ; and, at the end of such period, if he has not

276.—Le Protecteur aura le droit d'exempter tout Immigrant infirme ou indigent du paiement du droit dû pour son portrait. Avis du Gouv. No. 166 du 11 Nov. 1868, Art. 82.

277.—Tous les Tickets qui, avant la présente Ordonnance, auront été délivrés par le Protecteur à d'Anciens Immigrants, sans portraits y attachés, seront rendus au Protecteur qui, à leur place, remettra à ces Immigrants des Tickets dans la forme prescrite par l'Article 39.—(*Art.* 39,—*Voir le No.* 275.) Ord. No. 31 de 1867, Art. 40.

278.—A partir de *l'époque ci-dessus mentionnée en dernier lieu,* aucun Ticket autre que celui en la forme prescrite par l'*Article* 39, ne pourra servir de preuve pour établir la qualité d'Ancien Immigrant de la personne y décrite. Et le porteur d'un Ticket autre que celui en la forme sus-dite, pourra être arrêté et conduit au Protecteur des Immigrants.— . Idem, Art. 42.

L'époque ci-dessus mentionnée en dernier lieu, i. e. trois mois à compter de la mise en vigueur de l'Ordonnance No. 31 de 1867. Cette loi a été mise en vigueur le 2 Mai 1868, et le délai ci-dessus mentionné est par conséquent expiré.—*Art.* 39,—*Voir le No* 275.

Le présent Article ne s'appliquera pas à un Immigrant engagé par Contrat de Service écrit passé avant l'époque fixée par l'*Article* 41, et encore valable.—(*Art.* 41,—*Voir le No.* 229.)

Néanmoins cet Immigrant sera tenu, lorsqu'il sera déchargé de ce Contrat de Service, de comparaître immédiatement devant le Protecteur des Immigrants pour faire l'échange de son Ticket comme il est expliqué plus haut.

279.—L'émission des Duplicata de Tickets aux Immigrants Avis du Gouv. No. 166 du 1868, 67.

279.

Une addition a été faite à cet Article, relativement aux Permis expirés.—Voir le No. 571.

pendant ce temps il sera notifié dans la Gazette du Gouvernement qu'il a demandé un duplicata de Ticket ; et à la fin de ce temps s'il n'a pas été dénoncé au Protecteur comme déserteur, un

been denounced to the Protector as a deserter, a Duplicate-Ticket * shall be issued to him, on payment of the fees mentioned in the tariff hereto appended.—(*Declaration of Deserters.—See No.* 407.)

SCHEDULE R.

*Permit to Work.**

The Immigrant No. who is an applicant for a Duplicate Ticket, is hereby authorised to remain absent from the Depot and take employment until the 186; during which time his name shall be published in the Government Gazette, in conformity with Regulation No. 67 under Ordinance No. 31 of 1867.

Immigration Office, 186 .

H. B.

Protector of Immigrants.

2o. If the applicant do not present his name and number, he shall either be detained in the Depot till inquiries be made respecting him, or shall be sent with a Depot-Pass * for such information as may be necessary for his identification; after which, a *Permit to work* duly numbered and visaed by the Police, may be issued to him as above-mentioned; and, on the expiration of the period therein fixed, if he be not claimed as a deserter, a Duplicate-Ticket * may be given to him, on payment of the fees thereupon due under the tariff hereto appended.

3o.—Every Immigrant to whom a Duplicate-Ticket shall be delivered under this Regulation shall, within eight days from the date thereof, either enter into a Contract of Service, or apply to the Central Police Office of the District in which he elects his domicile, for a *Police-Pass.* Such delay of eight days shall be liable to the extension mentioned in *Regulation* 42.—(*Police-Pass.—See Nos.* 280 *et seq*:—*Regulation* 42.—*See No.* 281.)

In no case, except upon the special and written authorization of the Protector, shall any such Permit be renewable.

Ord. No. 31 of 1867, Art. 43.

280.—Every Old Immigrant not under engagement by written Contract of Service, shall be bound to appear at the Central Station of Police for the District in which he is resident, and then

* For each Duplicate-Ticket and the Portrait affixed thereto a fee of £ 1. 4s. is paid by the applicant to the Protector of Immigrants. For each Permit or Pass issued by the Protector a fee of 5 shillings is chargeable.—*See No.* 525.

duplicata de Ticket * lui sera remis, s'il paie les droits mentionnés au tarif ci-annexé.— (*Déclaration de Déserteurs.—Voir le No.* 407.)

ANNEXE R.

*Permis de Travailler.**

L'Immigrant No. qui a demandé un duplicata de ticket, est autorisé par ces présentes à rester absent du Dépôt et à prendre de l'emploi jusqu'au 186 ; pendant ce temps son nom sera publié dans la Gazette du Gouvernement, conformément au Réglement No. 67 en vertu de l'Ordonnance No. 31 de 1867.

Bureau de l'Immigration, 186 .

H. B.

Protecteur des Immigrants.

2o. Si le requérant ne donne pas son nom et son numéro, il sera détenu au Dépôt jusqu'à ce que l'on ait pris des renseignements sur lui, ou bien une Passe du Dépôt * lui sera donnée afin qu'il obtienne les renseignements nécessaires pour établir son identité ; après quoi, un *Permis de travailler,* dûment numéroté et visé par la Police, lui sera remis ainsi qu'il est dit ci-dessus ; et à l'expiration du temps qui y sera fixé, s'il n'est pas réclamé comme déserteur, un duplicata de Ticket * lui sera donné, s'il paie les droits mentionnés au tarif ci-annexé.

3o. Tout Immigrant à qui un duplicata de Ticket sera remis en vertu du présent Réglement devra, dans les huit jours de sa date, passer un Contrat de Service, ou s'adresser au Bureau Central de Police du district dans lequel il aura élu son domicile, pour une *Passe de Police.* Ce délai de huit jours pourra être étendu ainsi qu'il est dit au Réglement 42.—(*Passe de Police.—Voir les Nos.* 280 *et suiv.—Réglément* 42.—*Voir le No.* 281.)

En aucun cas, excepté avec l'autorisation écrite et spéciale du Protecteur, les dits Permis ne pourront être renouvelés.

280.—Tout Ancien Immigrant qui ne sera pas sous engagement par Contrat de Service écrit, sera tenu de comparaître à la Station Centrale de Police du District dans lequel il réside, et de Ord. No. 31 de 1867, Art. 43.

* Pour chaque Duplicata de Ticket et le Portrait y attaché un droit de £1. 4. est dû par celui qui en fait la demande au Protecteur des Immigrants. Chaque Permis ou Passe délivré par le Protecteur se paie 5 shillings.—*Voir le No.* 525.

and there to justify to the Inspector of Police, or *such other Officer* as shall be designated in that behalf by Regulation to be made as hereinafter provided, his Status of Old Immigrant by production of his Ticket, and further to declare to the said Officer his place of abode, and occupation, employment, or other means of subsistence. The said Officer shall thereupon deliver to such Immigrant, *a Pass in the form* provided by Regulations to be made under this Ordinance; the counterpart whereof shall be filled up and kept on record at the said Central Station.—(*Such other Officer,—See No.* 289.—*Form of Pass,—See No.* 289.)

Every Immigrant on completing his industrial residence and receiving an Old Immigrant's Ticket, and every Old Immigrant on the expiry of his written Contract, shall, within eight days, (unless before the expiry of that time he shall re-engage under written Contract of Service), appear before the said Officer of Police of the District in which he resides or has taken up his abode, and shall make declaration as above: whereupon the said Officer shall issue his Pass as hereinbefore provided.

Govt. Notice No. 166 of 11th Nov. 1868, Art. 42.

281.—It shall be lawful for the Protector of Immigrants or for any Stipendiary Magistrate, or any Superintendent, Adjutant, or Inspector of Police, upon good cause being shewn to him for his so doing, to extend the delay of eight days allowed by *Article* 43 *of Ordinance No.* 31 *of* 1867 and by *Regulation* 67 *infra* for the declaration of abode and occupation to be made by Old Immigrants. Such extension of delay shall not exceed fifteen days, and shall be borne by the Officer who grants it, on the certificate of discharge of the Immigrant to whom it is granted; and on the expiration of such new delay, no further delay shall be granted.—(*Article* 43,—*See No.* 280.—*Regulation* 67,—*See No.* 279.)

Idem, Art, 49.

282.—No Police-Pass shall be issued to any Old Immigrant declaring that he is, or is about to be, verbally engaged by a *Job-Contractor*, unless the latter personally appear before the Officer of Police entrusted with the delivery of Passes and satisfy him that the alleged verbal engagement is a *bonâ fide* one, and that under such engagement the Immigrant will not be without domicile, employment, or means of subsistence.—(*Job-Contractor,—See Nos.* 303 *et seq.*)

justifier à l'Inspecteur de Police, ou à *tel autre officier* qui sera désigné par des Réglements ultérieurs, sa qualité d'Ancien Immigrant par la production de son Ticket, et de plus d'indiquer au dit Officier le lieu de sa demeure, et son genre d'occupation, d'emploi ou ses autres moyens d'existence. Le dit Officier remettra alors à cet Immigrant une *Passe dans la forme* prévue par les Réglement qui seront faits en vertu de la présente Ordonnance ; la contre partie de cette Passe sera remplie et gardée au Bureau de la dite Station Centrale.—(*Tel autre Officier.—Voir le No.* 289 : *Forme de Passe.—Voir le No.* 289.)

Tout Immigrant après avoir achevé sa Résidence Industrielle et reçu un Ticket d'Ancien Immigrant, et tout Ancien Immigrant à l'expiration de son Contrat écrit, devra, dans les huit jours, (à moins qu'avant l'expiration de ce temps il ne se réengage par Contrat de Service écrit), comparaître devant l'Officier de Police du District dans lequel il réside ou dans lequel il a fixé sa demeure, et fera la même déclaration que ci-dessus ; et le dit Officier lui remettra alors sa Passe ainsi qu'il a été dit plus haut.

281.—Il sera permis au Protecteur des Immigrants, ou à tout Avis du Gouv. No. 166 du 11 Nov. 1868, Art. 42.

281.

Cet Article a été modifiée, et une clause pénale y a été ajoutée.—Voir le No. 564.

282.

Cette disposition a été abrogée.—Voir le No. 567, qui lui a été substitué.

Idem, Art. 49.

282.—Aucune Passe de Police ne sera remise à un Ancien Immigrant déclarant qu'il est, ou qu'il est au moment d'être, engagé verbalement avec un *Entrepreneur*, à moins que ce dernier ne comparaisse en personne devant l'Officier de Police chargé de la distribution des Passes et ne lui prouve que le prétendu engagement verbal est fait de bonne foi, et qu'en vertu de cet engagement l'Immigrant ne sera pas sans domicile, et sans emploi ou moyens d'existence.—(*Entrepreneur.—Voir les Nos.* 303 *et suiv.*)

Idem, Art. 54. 283.—No Police-Pass shall be given to any Old Immigrant who shall declare that he lives on daily labor or on the proceeds of job-work, unless such Immigrant first procure from the Chief Clerk of the Senior Stipendiary Magistrate's office if it be in Port Louis, or from the District Cashier if it be in a country District, a license in the form of the Schedule O hereto annexed.

SCHEDULE O.*

License.

This is to authorize to exercise the trade and calling of a Job-man or Day-laborer within the district of for the period of one year from this date.

(*Date*) 186 .

(*Signature.*)

Idem, Art. 55. 284.—Every day-laborer or job-man who shall not exhibit his license on demand to any Officer or Constable of Police or to any Inspector of Licenses, or shall not renew his license at its expiration, shall be liable to a fine not exceeding Two Pounds.

Idem, Act. 56. 285.—Every Immigrant licensed to work by the day, or to perform job-work, shall be bound to wear conspicuously on his right arm a badge bearing upon it the word "Job-man" and the number of his license.

Ord. No. 31 of 1867, Art. 44. 286.—Every Old Immigrant having obtained such Pass as aforesaid, shall be bound, on change of residence, to appear before the Inspector or *other Officer* of Police as aforesaid, of the District in which he resides or is about to reside, as the case may be, and shall obtain from the said Officer a new Pass in similar form to his former Pass, which he shall deliver up to the said Officer. On the new Pass shall be endorsed the number and date of any former Pass, and the District from which the same shall have been issued.—(*Other Officer.—See No.* 289.)

Govt. Notice No. 166 of 11th Nov. 1868, Art. 43. 287.—Every Immigrant, on changing his abode or occupation within the District of his domicile, shall report the same at the

* This document bears a stamp of 4 shillings to be paid by the Applicant.—*See No.* 487.

283.—Aucune Passe de Police ne sera donnée à un Ancien Idem, Art. 54.

283.—285.

Pour les additions à ces clauses.—Voir les Nos. 569. 570.

ANNEXE O.*

Patente.

Autorisation est donnée par ces présentes à d'exercer le métier ou l'industrie de journalier ou de travailleur à la tâche dans le District de pendant un an à partir de ce jour.

(*Date*) 186 .

(*Signature.*)

284.—Tout journalier ou travailleur à la tâche qui n'exhibera pas sa patente sur la réquisition d'un Officier ou d'un Constable de Police ou d'un Inspecteur de Patentes, ou qui ne renouvellera pas sa patente à son expiration, sera passible d'une amende n'excédant pas deux livres. Idem, Art. 55.

285.—Tout Immigrant patenté pour travailler à la journée ou à la tâche sera tenu de porter sur son bras droit, à un endroit visible, une plaque portant ce mot " Journalier " (Job-man) et le numéro de sa patente. Idem, Art. 56.

286.—Tout Ancien Immigrant ayant obtenu la dite Passe, sera tenu, lorsqu'il changera de demeure, de comparaître devant l'Inspecteur ou *autre Officier* de Police sus-dit du District dans lequel il réside ou est au moment de résider, selon le cas, et obtiendra du dit Officier une nouvelle Passe en la même forme que la première qu'il rendra au dit Officier. Sur le dos de la nouvelle Passe seront inscrits le numéro et la date de toute Passe antérieure et le District où elle aura été émise.—(*Autre Officier.—Voir le No.* 289.) Ord. No. 31 de 1867, Art. 44.

287.—Tout Immigrant, en changeant de résidence ou d'occupation dans le District où il est domicilié, en donnera avis au Bureau Avis du Gouv. No. 166 du 11 Nov. 1868, Art. 43.

---

* Ce document est frappé d'un timbre de 4 shillings payable par celui qui en fait la demande.—*Voir le No.* 487.

Central Police Office of his District, so that his Pass and and the counterpart of his Pass may be rectified accordingly. In default thereof, he shall be liable to a fine not exceeding Two Pounds.

Idem, Art. 44. 288.—If any Immigrant, to whom a Police Pass shall have been issued under the provisions of the last preceding regulation, wish to reside in another District, he shall first give notice of such intended change of abode to the Inspector of Police of the District which he intends to leave ; and such Police Inspector, or *other Officer* duly authorized to act in his stead, shall forthwith enter an acknowledgment of such notice on the Immigrant's Pass and on the counterpart of such Pass. No new Pass shall be issued to any Immigrant who has removed from one District to another unless such notice has been previously given by him.—(*Other Officer.—See No.* 289.)

Idem, Art. 40. 289.—Every Old Immigrant who declares his abode and occupation at a Central Police Station under *Article* 43 *of Ordinance* 31 *of* 1867, and every Old Immigrant who makes a new declaration under *Article* 44 of the said Ordinance shall receive a Police Pass in the form of the Schedule L hereto annexed, free of charge. Such Pass shall be signed by the Inspector of Police, or by the District Sergeant-Major of Police, or by any non-commissioned Officer of Police, or Clerk duly authorised so to do :—and its issue, in the case of a removal from one District to another, shall be subject to the provisions of *Regulation* 44.—(*Articles* 43 *and* 44,—*See Nos.* 280 *and* 286.—*Regulation* 44,—*See No.* 288.)

SCHEDULE L.

Counterpart of Pass.	LAST PASS. District No. Date.	*Pass.*	LAST PASS. District No. Date.
District of		District of	
District No.________		District No. __	
Name______________		Name______________	
Immigration No.______		Immigration No. ______	
Ordinary Residence___		Ordinary Residence ___	
Trade______________		Trade______________	
Date		Date	
M. N.		M. N.	
Inspector of Police.		*Inspector of Police.*	

Central de Police de son District, afin que sa Passe et le talon de sa Passe soient rectifiés en conséquence, à défaut de quoi il sera passible d'une amende n'excédant pas deux livres.

~~288.—Si un Immigrant~~ [illegible] ... 44.

287.—288.

Pour les additions à ces clauses.—Voir les Nos. 565. 506.

[illegible] Immigrant et sur le talon de cette Passe qu'il a reçu le dit avis.

Il ne sera pas donné de nouvelle Passe à un Immigrant qui a changé de District, à moins que le dit avis n'ait préalablement été donné par lui.—(*Autre Officier.—Voir le No.* 289.)

289.—Tout Ancien Immigrant qui déclare sa résidence et son industrie à un Bureau Central de Police en vertu de l'*Article* 43 *de l'Ord. No.* 31 *de* 1867, et tout Ancien Immigrant qui fait une nouvelle déclaration en vertu de l'*Article* 44 de la dite Ordonnance, recevra une Passe de Police dans la forme de l'Annexe L, sans frais. Cette Passe sera signée par l'Inspecteur de Police ou par le Sergent-Major de Police du District, ou par tout Sous-Officier de Police ou Commis dûment autorisé à cet effet,—et son émission, en cas de changement de district sera soumise aux dispositions du *Réglement* 44.—(*Articles* 43 *et* 44.—*Voir les Nos.* 280 *et* 286.—*Réglement* 44.—*Voir le No.* 288.) Idem, Art. 40.

ANNEXE L.

Talon de la Passe.

District de
No. de District______
Nom______________
No. d'Immigration____
Résidence ordinaire___
Industrie____________
Date
| |

M. N.
Inspecteur de Police,

DERNIÈRE PASSE.
District
No.
Date

Passe.

District de
No. de District______
Nom______________
No. d'Immigration____
Résidence ordinaire___
Industrie____________
Date
| |

M. N.
Inspecteur de Police.

DERNIÈRE PASSE.
District
No.
Date

Idem, Art. 46. **290.**—If any Old Immigrant allege that he has lost a Pass issued to him at a Central Police Station as hereabove mentioned, and there be no reason to presume that his statement is untrue, a duplicate of such Pass shall be issued to him, on his paying the fee * mentioned in the tariff hereto annexed;—and the issue of such duplicate shall be recorded on the counterpart of such Pass. Further issues of Passes to the same Immigrant in the same district shall be subject to similar conditions *; but every Immigrant convicted of having claimed a renewal of his Pass on false pretences shall be liable to a fine not exceeding Ten Pounds or to imprisonment not exceeding Three months.

Idem, Art. 48. **290** (*bis.*)—Any Stipendiary Magistrate to whom the loss of a Police-Pass shall be satisfactorily explained, shall have power to direct a second or any subsequent issue of such Pass, free of charge. In every such case an Exemption-Order in the form of the Schedule N shall be given to the Immigrant claiming a renewal of his Pass; which Exemption-Order shall be filed at the Police Station whence the renewed Pass shall be issued.

SCHEDULE N.

Counterpart of Exemption-Order.	*Exemption-Order.*
No.	No.
1. Immigrant's Name............ 2. ,, No.............. 3. Document ordered to be issued	The Immigrant No. is hereby exempted from the payment of the fee chargeable under the tariff now in force for a
Signature or Initials.	(*Date*)
Date	(*Signature.*)

Ord. No. 31 of 1867, Art. 46. **291.**—At and after the period fixed in *Article* 45, any Old Immigrant not being engaged under written Contract of Service passed prior to the above period, who shall fail, on demand of any Magistrate, or of the Police, to produce his Pass issued under the provisions of the said *Articles* 43 *or* 44, or a Certificate of En-

* The cost of a Duplicate Pass is 2 shillings.—For a third or any following issue of a Pass, the charge is 4 shillings.—*See No.* 487.

290.—Si un Ancien Immigrant allègue avoir perdu une Passe à lui donnée à un Bureau Central de Police ainsi qu'il est dit ci-dessus, et qu'il n'y ait pas de raison de présumer que sa déclaration soit fausse, un duplicata de cette Passe lui sera remis, s'il paie le droit * mentionné au tarif ci-annexé, et l'émission de ce duplicata sera mentionnée au talon de cette Passe. De nouvelles émissions de Passes au même Immigrant dans le même district seront soumises à des conditions * semblables ; mais tout Immigrant trouvé coupable d'avoir reclamé le renouvellement de sa Passe sous de faux prétextes, sera passible d'une amende n'excédant pas Dix Livres, où d'un emprisonnement n'excédant pas trois mois. Idem, Art. 46.

290 (*bis.*)—Tout Magistrat Stipendiaire à qui la perte d'une Passe de Police sera expliquée d'une manière suffisante, aura le pouvoir d'ordonner la remise d'une ou de plusieurs autres Passes, sans frais. Dans chacun de ces cas, un ordre d'exemption dans la forme de l'Annexe N sera donné à l'Immigrant qui réclamera un renouvellement de sa Passe ; cet ordre d'exemption sera déposé à a Station de Police d'où la Passe renouvelée sera émise. Idem, Art. 48.

ANNEXE N.

Talon de l'Ordre d'Exemption.	*Ordre d'Exemption.*
No.	No.
1. Nom de l'Immigrant ...... 2. No. do. ...... 3. Document livré par ordre ..	L'Immigrant No. est exempté par ces présentes du paiement du droit dû en vertu du tarif actuellement en vigueur, pour un
Signature ou Initiales.	(*Date*)
Date	(*Signature.*)

291.—Après le temps fixé par l'*Article* 45, tout Ancien Ord. No. 31 de 1867, Art. 46.

291.

Tout Ancien Immigrant ne travaillant pas sous Contrat écrit est tenu de produire son Ticket lorsqu'il en est requis.—Voir le No. 574.

gagement duly signed by a Stipendiary Magistrate, shall be liable to be detained and forwarded to the Immigration Depot, and be there further detained until enquiries shall have been made about him; and if, upon the result of such enquiries, it shall appear that he is not following any *bonâ fide* employment, whether on his own account or in the Service of a third party, and that he has no visible means of subsistence, he shall be deemed and taken to be a Vagrant; and may be dealt with as such. If, upon the result of such enquiries, it shall appear that he is not a Vagrant, he may be sent back to the District in which he resides, to obtain a Pass under the provisions of *Articles* 43 *or* 44.—(*Arts.* 43, 44, 45.—*See Nos.* 280, 286, *and* 230.)

Govt. Notice No. 166 of 11th Nov. 1868, Art. 41.

292.—If it appear to the Inspector of Police, or other Officer duly authorised to deliver Police-Passes to Immigrants, that the statement of any applicant for a Pass as to his abode or occupation is untrue, or that his occupation is not such as to justify the issue of a Pass to him, the case shall immediately be reported to the Stipendiary Magistrate, and fully inquired into without delay; and, if the applicant be convicted by the Magistrate of having no fixed residence or *bonâ fide* occupation, employment or means of subsistence, he shall immediately be dealt with as a Vagrant.

If the statement of the applicant as to his abode and occupation prove to be true, a Pass shall forthwith be delivered to him.

Ord. No. 31 de 1867, Art. 47.

293.—Whenever any Stipendiary Magistrate shall have reasonable grounds for thinking that any Old Immigrant to whom shall have been issued a Pass under the provisions of *Articles* 43 *or* 44, is not *bonâ fide* resident, occupied, or employed in the manner declared by such Immigrant on obtaining his said Pass, or that such Immigrant is without any fixed place of residence, or without any *bonâ fide* occupation, employment, or means of subsistence, it shall be lawful for such Magistrate to issue a summons; and, in default of compliance therewith, to issue a warrant for the appearance before him of such Immigrant; and if, after due investigation, the said Magistrate shall be satisfied that the said Immigrant has falsely declared any of the above particulars, or that he is without fixed residence, occupation,

signé par un Magistrat Stipendiaire, pourra être détenu et envoyé au Dépôt de l'Immigration jusqu'à ce qu'on ait pris des renseignements sur lui ; et s'il résulte de ces renseignements, qu'il n'a aucun emploi véritable et consciencieux, soit pour son propre compte, soit au service d'un tiers, et qu'il n'a pas de moyens apparents d'existence, il sera considéré comme un vagabond, et traité comme tel. S'il résulte de ces renseignements qu'il n'est pas un vagabond, il pourra être envoyé devant le Magistrat Stipendiaire du District dans lequel il réside pour obtenir une Passe en vertu des dispositions des *Articles* 43 *ou* 44.—(*Articles* 43, 44 *et* 45.—*Voir les Nos.* 280, 286 *et* 230.)

292.—S'il paraît à l'Inspecteur de Police ou à tout autre officier dûment autorisé à délivrer des Passes de Police à des Immigrants que la déclaration de celui qui demande une Passe est fausse quant à sa résidence ou à son genre d'occupation, ou que celles-ci ne soient pas de nature à justifier l'émission de la Passe qu'il réclame, il en sera immédiatement référé au Magistrat Stipendiaire qui examinera de suite la question ; et si le requérant est trouvé coupable par le Magistrat de n'avoir pas de résidence fixe, ni d'emploi ou de moyens d'existence connus, il sera immédiatement traité comme vagabond. Avis du Gouv. No. 166 du 11 Nov. 1868, Art. 41.

Si la déclaration du requérant relativement à sa résidence et à ses moyens d'existence est trouvée exacte, il lui sera de suite donnée une Passe.

293.—Toutes les fois qu'un Magistrat Stipendiaire aura des motifs raisonnables de supposer qu'un Ancien Immigrant, à qui il aura été accordé une Passe en vertu des dispositions des *Articles* 43 *ou* 44, n'est pas réellement résident, occupé ou employé de la manière déclarée par cet Immigrant lorsqu'il a obtenu sa Passe, ou que cet Immigrant n'a pas de demeure fixe, ou d'occupation ou d'emploi réel, ou des moyens d'existence, il sera permis au dit Magistrat de lui envoyer une sommation de comparaître devant lui ; et s'il n'obéit pas à cette sommation, de décerner un mandat d'arrêt pour la comparution de cet Immigrant devant lui ; et si, après une enquête convenable, le Magistrat est satisfait que le dit Immigrant lui a fait une fausse déclaration relativement à l'une des indications ci-dessus, ou qu'il est sans demeure fixe, sans Ord. No. 31 de 1867, Art. 47.

employment, or means of subsistence, thereupon the said Magistrate may condemn him as a Vagrant.—(*Articles* 43 *and* 44.—*See Nos.* 280 *and* 286.

Any person who by means of a fictitious verbal engagement assists a laborer in procuring a Police Pass is liable to a fine.—*See No.* 209.

Govt. Notice No. 166 of 11th Nov.1868, Art. 47.

294.—Any Immigrant convicted of using a Police-Pass which is not his own shall be liable to a fine not exceeding Five pounds.

Ord. No. 16 of 1862, Art. 21.

295.—The penalty of imprisonment, for a period not exceeding three months, shall be incurred by any one:

Who shall obtain or attempt to obtain an Old Immigrant's Ticket, or a duplicate Old or New Immigrant's Ticket, by means of false pretences;

Who, being in possession of an Old or New Immigrant's Ticket not intended for himself, shall, for any purpose whatever, personify the Immigrant therein designed;

Who shall use as his own, and for any purpose whatever, an Immigrant's Ticket designed for another person;

Who shall give up, either temporarily or permanently, to any one, any Immigrant's Ticket in his possession, in order that the same may be used for any fraudulent purpose;

Who shall aid or abet, counsel or assist any person in committing any of the foregoing offences.

The Stipendiary Magistrate within whose jurisdiction any of these offences shall have been committed, shall have jurisdiction to try the same, and to adjudge and impose the punishment therefor.

Ord. No. 31 of 1867, Art. 58.

296.—Any person falsifying or altering an Immigrant's Ticket, Pass, or Certificate, or any endorsement thereon, and any Immigrant using a falsified or altered Immigrant's Ticket, Pass, or Certificate, or any genuine Immigrant's Ticket, Pass, or Certificate bearing a falsified or altered endorsement, shall be liable to imprisonment with hard labor for a period not exceeding three months, to be awarded by the Stipendiary Magistrate, without

occupation ou emploi, ou sans moyens d'existence, il pourra le condamner comme vagabond.—(*Articles* 43 *et* 44.—*Voir les Nos.* 280 *et* 286.)

Toute personne qui, au moyen d'un engagement verbal fictif, aide un laboureur à se procurer une Passe de Police est passible d'une amende.—*Voir le No.* 209.

294.—Tout Immigrant trouvé coupable d'avoir fait usage d'une Passe de Police qui ne lui appartient pas, sera passible d'une amende n'excédant pas cinq livres. Avis du Gouv. No. 166 du 11 Nov. 1868, Art. 47.

295.—La peine d'emprisonnement pour un temps qui n'excèdera pas trois mois sera encourue par toute personne : Ord. No. 16 de 1862, Art. 21.

Qui obtiendra ou cherchera à obtenir un Ticket d'Ancien Immigrant, ou un double de Ticket d'Ancien ou de Nouvel Immigrant, sous de faux prétextes ;

Qui, ayant en sa possession un Ticket d'Ancien ou de Nouvel Immigrant, qui ne lui est pas destiné, se fera, pour quelque raison que ce soit, passer pour l'Immigrant y désigné ;

Qui se servira comme du sien propre, pour quelque raison que ce soit, d'un Ticket d'Immigrant destiné à une autre personne ;

Qui donnera, soit momentanément, soit pour toujours, à quelqu'un, un Ticket d'Immigrant en sa possession afin qu'on puisse faire usage de ce Ticket dans un but frauduleux ;

Qui aidera, conseillera ou assistera tout individu dans la commission des offences ci-dessus.

Le Magistrat Stipendiaire dans la juridiction duquel une de ces offences aura été commise, pourra en connaître et prononcer et appliquer la peine prévue par la loi.

296.—Toute personne contrefaisant ou altérant un Ticket, une Passe ou un Certificat d'Immigrant, ou toute écriture sur le dos de ces pièces, et tout Immigrant se servant d'un Ticket, Passe ou Certificat contrefait ou altéré, ou d'un Ticket, Passe, ou Certificat non contrefait ni altéré, mais portant un endossement contrefait ou altéré, sera passible d'un emprisonnement avec travail forcé, pour un temps n'excédant pas 3 mois, qui sera infligé par le Ma- Ord. No. 31 de 1867, Art. 58.

prejudice to an action for forgery, if cause exist. In which latter case, the Stipendiary Magistrate may commit the offender to prison, in order that the Procureur General, to whom he shall forthwith report the circumstances of the case, may, if he think fit, enter proceedings against the said offender for such forgery.

Ord. No. 15 of 1852, Art. 6.

297.—Any person writing, fabricating or delivering a false Certificate of Discharge or any other false Certificate or Permission in his own name or in that of any other person, or in a suppositious name, and any servant making use of any such Certificate or Permission given to another person, shall be liable to imprisonment with hard labour for a period not exceeding one month to be awarded by the Stipendiary Magistrate, without prejudice to an action for forgery if any cause for such action should exist. In which latter case the Stipendiary Magistrate may commit the offender to prison in order that the Procureur General, to whom he shall forthwith report the circumstances of the case, may enter proceedings against the said offender for forgery.

Ord. No. 31 of 1867, Art. 57.

298.—Any person not vested with any legal authority to issue Passes or Permits, who shall give a Pass or Permit to any laborer not lawfully in his service, shall be liable to a fine not exceeding £5, or to imprisonment with hard labour not exceeding one month, without prejudice to the penalties prescribed by law against unlawfully harbouring or employing deserters.— (*See No.* 260.)

Any laborer using any such unlawful Pass or Permit as aforesaid, shall be liable to imprisonment not exceeding one month.

Idem, Art. 56.

299.—Any Magistrate or Officer of Police shall be entitled to demand production of the Ticket and Contract of Service of any Immigrant who may be working for any Employer, and any person who, having such Contract or Ticket in his possession, shall refuse to produce the same when so required as aforesaid, shall be liable to a fine not exceeding £ 10.

gistrat Stipendiaire, sans préjudice des poursuites pour faux s'il y y a lieu. Dans ce dernier cas, le Magistrat Stipendiaire pourra envoyer le délinquant en prison, afin que le Procureur Général, à qui il fera immédiatement un rapport des circonstances de l'affaire, puisse, s'il le juge convenable, commencer des poursuites pour crime de faux contre ce délinquant.

297.—Toute personne qui écrira, fabriquera, ou délivrera un faux Certificat de Décharge, ou tout autre faux Certificat ou fausse Permission, en son propre nom, ou au nom de toute autre personne, ou sous un nom supposé, et tout serviteur qui fera usage d'un Certificat ou d'une Permission de cette nature, donné à une autre personne, sera passible d'un emprisonnement avec travail forcé pour un temps qui n'excèdera pas un mois, laquelle peine sera prononcée par le Magistrat Stipendiaire sans préjudice des poursuites qui pourraient être exercées contre le délinquant pour faux s'il y a lieu de le faire. Et dans ce dernier cas, le Magistrat Stipendiaire pourra faire mettre le délinquant en prison, afin que le Procureur-Général, auquel il fera connaître immédiatement les circonstances du cas, puisse commencer des poursuites contre le dit délinquant, pour le dit faux. Ord. No. 15 de 1852, Art. 6.

298.—Toute personne qui ne sera pas investie par la loi de l'autorisation d'émettre des Passes ou Permis, et qui donnera une Passe ou un Permis à un travailleur qui n'est pas légalement à son service, sera passible d'une amende n'excédant pas £ 5, ou d'un emprisonnement avec travail forcé n'excédant pas un mois, sans préjudice des peines prescrites par la loi contre ceux qui recèlent ou emploient illégalement des déserteurs.—(*Voir le No.* 260.) Ord. No. 31 de 1867, Art. 57.

Tout travailleur se servant d'une Passe ou d'un Permis illégal comme il est dit plus haut, sera passible d'un emprisonnement n'excédant pas un mois.

299.—Tout Magistrat ou Officier de Police aura le droit de demander la production du Ticket et du Contrat de Service d'un Immigrant travaillant pour un employeur, et toute personne, qui, ayant ce Ticket ou ce Contrat en sa possession, refusera de le produire lorsqu'elle en sera requise comme il vient d'être dit, sera passible d'une amende n'excédant pas £ 10. Idem, Art. 56.

Govt. Notice No. 166 of 11th Nov. 1868, Art. 73.

300.—Any person convicted by a Stipendiary Magistrate of having unlawfully detained an Immigrant's Ticket, Certificate, or Pass, shall be liable to a fine not exceeding Five Pounds,—without prejudice to any action for damages which the said Immigrant may be entitled to institute against such person in any competent Court.

Ord. No. 31 of 1867, Art. 73.

301.— Any forms of Bonds, Engagements, Tickets, or Passes, prescribed by any law relating to Immigrants or Laborers, may from time to time be altered by Regulations to be passed as hereinafter mentioned.—(*See No.* 486.)

Govt. Notice No. 166 of 11th Nov. 1868, Art. 89.

302.—Whenever any document requiring to have any official signature of any Magistrate or Public Officer under these regulations, or under any other law relative to Immigration or to Masters and Servants, shall purport *ex facie* to have such signature, it shall be received in all Courts of Justice as genuine, without such signature requiring to be proved; and it shall continue to be so received until the said signature shall have been proved to be a forgery.

JOB-CONTRACTORS.

The mode of cultivation adopted on many sugar estates in Mauritius, renders it profitable to the planter not to have permanently in his employ a large number of laborers, but to engage temporarily the services of additional men according as he requires them. Under this system, there has sprung up a class of men called Job-Contractors, who engage to themselves bands of indians and hire out their services for piece or job-work to the planters.—The number of these Job-Contractors having much increased of late years, it has been found expedient to introduce special legislation concerning them.

Idem, Art. 50.

303.—No person shall be allowed to engage laborers as a Job-Contractor* unless he produce a License taken under *Ordinance*

---

* In the case of *Pillay v. Eroolapen* (Piston's Reports, 1865), it was held that a Job-Contractor is not a Trader: the Bankruptcy Ordinance No. 33 of 1853, Art. 20 providing that " no sugar or other planter, farmer, ...shall be deemed, as such, a trader liable to become Bankrupt."

Suits arising from failure on the part of Job-Contractors to execute the work they have agreed to perform, seem to lie within the jurisdiction of the Stipendiary Courts.—See note to No. 456.

300.—Toute personne trouvée coupable par un Magistrat Stipendiaire d'avoir illégalement retenu le Ticket, le Certificat ou la Passe d'un Immigrant, sera passible d'une amende n'excédant pas cinq livres, sans préjudice de toute action en dommages intérêts que le dit Immigrant pourra intenter contre cette personne devant un Tribunal compétent. Avis du Gouv. No. 166 du 11 Nov. 1868, Art. 73.

301.— Toutes formes d'Obligations, d'Engagements, de Tickets, ou de Passes, prescrites par les lois relatives aux Immigrants ou aux Travailleurs, pourront de temps à autre être modifiées par des Réglements qui seront faits ainsi qu'il sera dit ci-après.—(*Voir le No.* 486). Ord. No. 31 de 1867, Art. 73.

302.—Toutes les fois qu'un document qui devra porter la signature officielle d'un Magistrat ou d'un Officier Public en vertu des présents Réglements, ou en vertu de toute autre loi relative à l'Immigration ou aux Maîtres et Serviteurs, portera cette signature, la dite signature sera reçue dans tous les Tribunaux comme vraie, et il ne sera pas nécessaire de prouver qu'elle est vraie, et elle continuera à être tenue pour vraie jusqu'à ce qu'il ait été prouvé qu'elle est fausse. Avis du Gouv. No. 166 du 11 Nov. 1868, Art. 89.

DES ENTREPRENEURS.

Le mode de culture adopté sur beaucoup d'Établissements rend plus avantageux au Planteur de ne pas avoir d'une manière permanente à son service un grand nombre de travailleurs, mais d'engager provisoirement les services d'un nombre additionnel d'hommes au fur et à mesure qu'il en a besoin. Ce système a donné naissance à une classe d'industriels appelés Entrepreneurs (Job-Contractors) qui engagent des bandes d'Indiens et louent leurs services aux planteurs pour des travaux d'entreprise.—Le nombre de ces Entrepreneurs ayant beaucoup augmenté depuis ces dernières années a rendu nécessaire la promulgation de lois se rapportant spécialement à eux.

303.—Personne ne pourra engager des travailleurs comme entrepreneur* à moins qu'il ne produise une Patente prise en vertu Idem, Art. 50.

---

* Dans l'affaire *Pillay, v. Eroolapen* (Piston's Reports, 1865), la Cour a décidé que l'Entrepreneur (job-contractor) n'est pas un commerçant, l'Ordonnance concernant les Faillites No. 38 of 1853, Art. 20 décrétant "qu'aucun planteur, sucrier ou autre........ne sera comme tel, réputé commerçant pouvant être mis en faillite."

Les procès provenant de la non-exécution par des entrepreneurs des travaux qu'ils se sont engagés à faire, semblent être du ressort des Cours Stipendiaires.— Voir la note au No. 456.

No. 31 *of* 1865; nor shall any Job-Contractor be allowed to engage laborers for any period extending beyond the term of his license.—(*Ord. No.* 31 *of* 1865.—*See No.* 304.)

Any such license may be renewed at any time of the year and for whatever period the Job-Contractor may wish to renew it.

Ord. No. 31 of 1865, Art. 1.

304.—Every Company or Society, and every individual in Mauritius, being within any of the descriptions in this Ordinance, shall be bound to take out a License, and to pay License Duty therefor, as hereinafter set forth :—

....

(4) Every Job-Contractor, or Company, or Firm of Job-Contractors.................................. £5

Every Member of any Company or Firm of Job-Contractors shall pay an additional duty of.......... £1

The laws of the Colony affecting Licenses in general, are applicable to Job-Contractors' Licenses.—*See also No.* 312.

As to verbal engagements between Job-Contractors and Old Immigrants,—*see No.* 282.

Govt. Notice No. 166 of 11th Nov. 1868, Art. 51.

305.—No Job-Contractor shall be allowed to engage laborers for any Estate by written contract unless the owner or lessee of such Estate, or the lawful representative of such owner or lessee, subscribe a guarantee for the whole term of the contract in conformity with the provisions of *Ordinance No.* 7 *of* 1865.—(*Ord. No.* 7 *of* 1865.—*See Nos.* 307 *et seq.*)

If such guarantee expire, or otherwise determine, before the expiration of the Contract of Service, a fresh guarantee shall be furnished to the satisfaction of the Stipendiary Magistrate; otherwise the contract shall be held as cancelled, and the laborers engaged thereunder shall be discharged by the Stipendiary Magistrate ex-officio.—(*See also No.* 309.)

Ord. No. 31 of 1867, Art. 64.

306.—The provisions of *Ordinance No.* 7 *of* 1865, entituled "An Ordinance to secure the rights of New Immigrants under "contracts of service with Job-Contractors, and to extend the

de l'*Ordonnance No.* 31 *de* 1865 ; et un Entrepreneur ne pourra pas engager des travailleurs pour un temps s'étendant au-delà du terme de sa patente.—(*Ord : No.* 31 *de* 1865.—*Voir le No.* 304.)

Toute patente de ce genre pourra être renouvelée à n'importe quel moment de l'année et pour le temps que l'entrepreneur le désirera.

304.—Toute Compagnie ou Société, et toute personne à Maurice qui se trouve dans un des cas prévus par cette Ordonnance, seront tenues de prendre une Patente, et de payer pour cette Patente les droits qui seront fixés ci-après :— Ord. No. 31 de 1865, Art. 1.

....

(4) Tout Entrepreneur, ou toute Compagnie ou Société d'Entrepreneurs.............................. £5

Tout Membre d'une Compagnie ou Société d'Entrepreneurs paiera un droit additionnel de £1

Les lois de la Colonie sur les Patentes en général s'appliquent aux Entrepreneurs.—*Voir aussi le No.* 312.

Quant aux engagements verbaux entre les Entrepreneurs et les Anciens Immigrants,—*voir le No.* 282.

305.—Aucun Entrepreneur ne pourra engager des travailleurs Avis du Gouv. No. 166 du 1868.

305.

Pour les additions à cette clause.—Voir le No. 568.

Si cette garantie expire, ou vient à cesser d'une autre manière, avant la fin du contrat de service, une nouvelle garantie sera fournie à la satisfaction du Magistrat Stipendiaire ; autrement le contrat sera considéré comme annulé, et les travailleurs engagés par ce contrat seront déchargés d'office par le Magistrat Stipendiaire. —(*Voir aussi le No.* 309.)

306.—Les dispositions de *l'Ordonnance No. 7 de* 1865, intitulée « Ordonnance pour garantir les droits des Nouveaux Immi- « grants engagés par contrat de service avec des Entrepreneurs, Ord. No. 31 de 1867, Art. 64.

"jurisdiction of Stipendiary Magistrates to claims for wages "founded on guarantee," shall henceforth apply to contracts of service between any Job-Contractor and any Indian Immigrant.—(*Ord. No. 7 of* 1865.—*See No.* 307 *et seq.*)

Ord. No. 7 of 1865, Art. 1.

307.—Every Stipendiary Magistrate before passing a Contract of Service between any Job-contractor and any laborer, being a New Immigrant from India, for employment in agricultural labour, may and shall require the wages, rations, lodging, and medical care, of such labourer to be guaranteed in manner prescribed in this Ordinance, and such Magistrate shall refuse to pass such Contract of Service without such guarantee.

In like manner a guarantee shall be given for the wages and others aforesaid of every Immigrant who shall be engaged in India to a Job-Contractor for employment as aforesaid. Such guarantee shall be given before the said Immigrant shall be handed over by the Protector of Immigrants to the Job-Contractor to whom he shall be engaged.

As to the obligation of Job-Contractors to provide Hospital accommodation for their laborers.—*See Nos.* 355 *et seq.*

Idem, Art. 2.

308.—The guarantee to be required as hereinaforesaid shall be by writing duly signed before and authenticated by the Stipendiary Magistrate at the Immigration Depot in Port Louis, when the guarantee is given in regard to Immigrants engaged to Job-Contractors in India, and for whom the guarantee is given on their arrival; in other cases where the guarantee is given at the commencement of the engagement it shall be by writing signed before and authenticated by the Stipendiary Magistrate before whom the Contract of Service is passed.

It shall be granted by the proprietor of the estate on which the labourer shall be intended to work, or by the lessee thereof in case of its being let: and it shall be by way of a joint and several obligation on the part of such owner or lessee along with the Job-Contractor for payment of the wages, rations, lodging, and medical care, of the said labourer during such time (not being longer than that mentioned in the Contract of Service) as he shall be employed in working for the said owner or lessee.

" et pour étendre la compétence des Magistrats Stipendiaires à " des réclamations pour gages fondés sur des cautions," s'appliqueront dorénavant à tous contrats de service entre un Entrepreneur et tout Immigrant Indien.—(*Ord. No. 7 de* 1865.—*Voir les Nos.* 307 *et suiv.*)

307.—Avant de passer un Contrat de Service entre un Entrepreneur et un laboureur, qui est un nouvel Immigrant Indien, pour des travaux agricoles, tout Magistrat Stipendiaire pourra exiger, et exigera que les gages, les rations, le logement et les soins médicaux, dûs au laboureur, soient garantis de la manière prescrite par cette Ordonnance ; et le Magistrat refusera de passer le Contrat de Service à moins que cette garantie n'ait été donnée. Ord. No. 7 de 1865, Art. 1.

De la même manière il sera donné une garantie pour les gages etc. mentionnés ci-dessus de tout Immigrant engagé dans l'Inde à un Entrepreneur pour travailler comme il est dit ci-dessus. Cette garantie sera donnée avant que le dit Immigrant ne soit livré par le Protecteur des Immigrants à l'Entrepreneur auquel il aura été engagé.

Quant à l'obligation des Entrepreneurs d'avoir un Hôpital pour leurs laboureurs.—*Voir les Nos.* 355 *et suiv.*

308.—La garantie qu'il exigera comme il est dit ci-dessus, sera par acte écrit dûment signé devant le Magistrat Stipendiaire au Dépôt de l'Immigration au Port Louis, qui lui donnera toute authenticité, lorsque la garantie sera donnée pour des Immigrants engagés à des Entrepreneurs dans l'Inde, et pour lesquels la garantie est donnée à leur arrivée. Dans les autres cas, lorsque la garantie sera donnée au commencement de l'engagement, elle sera donnée par acte écrit signé devant le Magistrat Stipendiaire devant lequel le Contrat sera passé, qui lui donnera toute authenticité. Idem, Art. 2.

Cette garantie sera donnée par le propriétaire de l'établissement sur lequel le laboureur doit travailler, ou par le locataire de l'établissement dans le cas où l'établissement est loué ; et le dit propriétaire ou locataire s'obligera solidairement avec l'Entrepreneur au paiement des gages, à la fourniture des rations, logement et soins médicaux, dûs au dit laboureur, pendant tout le temps (qui n'excédera pas le terme mentionné dans le Contrat) que le laboureur sera employé à travailler pour le dit propriétaire ou locataire.

The amount of the guarantee shall be limited to the sum payable by the owner or lessee to the Job-Contractor under the Contract between them : and for this purpose the monthly value of the rations, lodging, and medical care, shall be estimated at twelve shillings sterling.

The guarantee shall, as nearly may be, be in the form of Schedule A.

SCHEDULE A.

Whereas certain New Immigrants from India, whose names are appended hereto, have entered into a Contract of Service as agricultural laborers for the period of months with Job-Contractor, residing at which said contract is dated the day of 18 .

And whereas it has been agreed between the said Job-Contractor and me proprietor (or lessee, or administrator), of the estate of in the district of that the said laborers shall be employed in agricultural labour on the said estate :

Now this is to witness that I do hereby oblige myself jointly and severally with the said Job-Contractor for the wages, rations, lodging and medical care of such of the said laborers, as shall be employed as aforesaid, and during the whole period of such employment ; but provided that the amount payable by me under this guarantee shall not exceed which I hereby declare to be the sum payable by me to the said Contractor under the contract between us, for the work to be performed by the said laborers.

(Proprietor's or lessee's signature.)

Signed before me this day of 18 .

C. D.

Stipendiary Magistrate of the District of

If this Security-Bond be not signed by the guarantee in person, his proxy must produce a power of attorney.—*See No.* 223.

Idem, Art. 3. 309.—In case the person granting such guarantee shall, during the currency of the Contract of Service, die, or shall become bankrupt or insolvent, or shall from any cause cease to be owner or lessee, as the case may be, of the estate to which his guarantee applied, the Stipendiary Magistrate, on such fact coming to his knowledge, may and shall require the new owner or lessee of the estate, or in case of bankruptcy or insolvency the person adminis-

Le montant de la garantie sera limitée à la somme payable par le propriétaire ou le locataire à l'Entrepreneur, en vertu du Contrat subsistant entre eux ; et à cet effet, la valeur mensuelle des rations, du logement et des soins médicaux est estimée à douze shillings sterling.

Autant que faire se peut, cette garantie sera dans la forme de la Cédule A.

CÉDULE A.

Attendu que certains nouveaux Immigrants Indiens dont les noms sont ci-joints, ont passé un Contrat de Service comme laboureurs agricoles pour mois avec , Entrepreneur, demeurant à , lequel contrat est daté du 18 .

Et attendu qu'il a été convenu entre le dit Entrepreneur et moi propriétaire (ou locataire) de l'établissement connu sous le nom de , dans le district de , que les dits laboureurs seront employés aux travaux d'habitation sur le dit établissement.

C'est pourquoi par le présent acte je me rends responsable solidairement avec le dit Entrepreneur des gages, des rations, du logement et des soins médicaux dûs à ceux de ces laboureurs qui seront employés comme il est dit ci-dessus, et ce pendant tout le temps qu'ils seront ainsi employés, mais pourvu que la somme payable par moi en vertu de cette garantie, n'excède pas que je déclare par les présentes être la somme payable par moi au dit Entrepreneur, en vertu du contrat passé entre nous, pour l'ouvrage qui doit être fait par les dits laboureurs.

(*Signature du propriétaire ou locataire.*)

Signé devant moi, ce de 18 .

C. D.
Magistrat Stipendiaire du District de

Si cette garantie n'est pas signée par la personne qui la donne, la personne qui se présente pour la signer en son nom, doit produire une procuration.—*Voir le No.* 223.

309.—Dans le cas où la personne qui donne cette garantie viendrait à mourir pendant la durée du Contrat, ou deviendrait failli ou insolvable, ou, pour une cause quelconque, cesserait d'être propriétaire ou locataire, selon le cas, de l'Etablissement auquel la garantie s'étend, le Magistrat Stipendiaire exigera, aussitôt qu'il en aura connaissance, que le nouveau propriétaire ou locataire, ou, en cas de faillite ou d'insolvabilité, que l'ad- Idem, Art. 3.

tering the estate, to subscribe a fresh guarantee for the wages and others aforesaid of the laborers being New Immigrants engaged to any Job-Contractor and employed on the estate as aforesaid, and in the event of such guarantee not being found, the Magistrate may and shall cancel the Contract of Service of the Immigrant unless the Job-Contractor shall secure his employment on another estate under the conditions provided in the next Article of this Ordinance.—(*See also No.* 305.)

Idem, Art, 4. **310.**—In case any Job-Contractor shall wish to have any laborers being New Immigrants engaged to him employed on an estate to which the guarantee aforesaid shall not apply, a fresh guarantee to the effect and in the form as hereinaforesaid shall require to be granted by the owner or lessee of such estate, for the wages of the laborers aforesaid who may be employed thereon.

Such guarantee shall be by writing signed before and authenticated by the Magistrate of the District within which the men are to be employed as aforesaid.

Idem, Art. 5. **311.**—Every Job-Contractor by whom any laborer being a New Immigrant, under a written Contract of Service shall be employed on any estate without a guarantee as herein-before specified shall incur a penalty of two shillings sterling for each day or part of a day during which every such laborer shall have been employed by him without such guarantee.

Govt Notice No. 166 of 11th Nov. 1868, Art. 52. **312.**—Any Job-Contractor who shall employ laborers without a license, or without having furnished or renewed a guarantee as aforesaid, shall be liable to a fine not exceeding Two Pounds for each laborer so employed without prejudice to the penalties provided in *Ordinance No. 7 of* 1865.—(*Ord. No. 7 of* 1865.—*See No.* 311.)

Ord. No. 7 of 1865, Art. 6. **313.**—The said penalty shall be recoverable before the Stipendiary Magistrate of the district in which such employment shall have taken place ; whose judgment inflicting the same shall be final in all cases where the amount of the fine shall not exceed £10 sterling for every laborer so unlawfully employed, but shall be subject to review by the Supreme Court when the amount is above the said sum.—(*See No.* 502 *et seq.*)

ministrateur de l'Etablissement souscrive une nouvelle garantie pour les gages, etc., mentionnés ci-dessus des laboureurs qui sont de nouveaux Immigrants Indiens engagés à des Entrepreneurs et employés sur le dit bien comme il est dit ci-dessus ; et dans le cas où cette garantie ne serait pas fournie, le Magistrat pourra et devra annuler le Contrat de Service de l'Immigrant, à moins que l'Entrepreneur ne trouve de l'ouvrage sur une autre propriété aux conditions énoncées dans l'article suivant de cette Ordonnance.—(*Voir aussi le No.* 305.)

310.—Dans le cas où un Entrepreneur désirerait employer des laboureurs qui lui sont engagés sur un Etablissement autre que celui auquel la garantie s'étend, il devra fournir une nouvelle garantie du propriétaire ou du locataire de cet Etablissement pour les gages des laboureurs qui y seront employés. Idem, Art. 4.

Cette garantie sera par écrit et sera signée devant le Magistrat du District dans lequel les laboureurs doivent être employés comme il est dit ci-dessus, qui lui donnera toute authenticité.

311.—Tout Entrepreneur qui emploiera sur un Etablissement, sans avoir fourni la garantie mentionnée ci-dessus, un laboureur, qui est nouvel Immigrant, par un Contrat de Service écrit, sera passible d'une amende de deux shillings sterling pour chaque journée, ou portion de journée, pendant laquelle le dit laboureur aura été employé par lui sans cette garantie. Idem, Art. 5.

312.—Tout Entrepreneur qui emploiera des travailleurs sans patente, ou sans avoir fourni ou renouvelé la garantie sus-dite, sera passible d'une amende n'excédant pas dix livres par chaque travailleur ainsi employé sans préjudice des peines mentionnées dans l'*Ordonnance No.* 7 *de* 1865.—(*Ord. No.* 7 *de* 1865.—*Voir le No.* 311.) Avis du Gouv. No. 166 du 11 Nov. 1868, Art. 52.

313.—Cette amende pourra être recouvrée devant le Magistrat Stipendiaire du District dans lequel la contravention aura eu lieu ; et le jugement du Magistrat prononçant l'amende, sera définitif dans tous les cas où l'amende n'excèdera pas £ 10 sterling pour chaque laboureur illégalement employé comme il est dit ci-dessus ; si l'amende excède cette somme, on pourra faire appel du jugement devant la Cour Suprême.—(*Voir le No.* 502 *et seq.*) Ord. No. 7 de 1865, Art. 6.

Payment of the said fine may be enforced in the mode provided in the *8th Section of the 4th Chapter of the Royal Order in Council of 7th September* 1838.—(*Section* 8.—*See No.* 251.)

Idem, Art. 7. 314.—The provisions of the **1st, 2nd, 3rd and 5th Articles** hereof, shall not apply to such Contracts of Service as have already been entered into between Job-Contractors and laborers aforesaid. But in regard to such Contracts, it shall be lawful to the Stipendiary Magistrate to require the guarantee of the proprietor or lessee of the estate on which the laborers being New Immigrants shall be employed, whenever he shall deem such guarantee necessary for securing payment of their wages. (*1st, 2nd, 3rd, and 5th Articles.— See Nos.* 307, 308, 309 *and* 311.)

It shall moreover be lawful to the Magistrate to prohibit the employment of any New Immigrant in such case, until the said guarantee should be duly found as aforesaid; and any Job-Contractor, who shall employ any such New Immigrant after notice of such prohibition shall have been served on him, shall incur the penalty specified in the *5th Article of this Ordinance* to be recovered as herein aforesaid.—(*5th Article.—See No.* 311.)

Govt. Notice No. 166 of 11th Nov. 1868, Art. 53. 315.—All wages guaranteed to Immigrants under *Article* 64 *of Ordinance No.* 31 *of* 1867 shall be paid to such Immigrants in presence of the proprietor or lessee by whom such wages shall have been guaranteed, or in presence of some person authorised to represent the said proprietor or lessee; and such proprietor or lessee, or his representative, shall sign the Pay-Book on which such wages shall be borne, in attestation of his having witnessed the payment thereof; in default of which the payment of such wages shall not be recognised by the Stipendiary Magistrate, and the proprietor or lessee shall not be held discharged from his guarantee in respect of such wages.—(*Article* 64.—*See No.* 306.—*See also No.* 326.)

Ord. No. 7 of 1865, Art. 8. 316.—When any laborer aforesaid shall seek to recover payment of his wages from any person in virtue of the guarantee aforesaid, it shall not be a lawful answer to such claim that the owner or lessee has already paid to the Job-Contractor, all or any sums due under his contract with such Job-Contractor.

Le paiement de l'amende pourra être exigé de la manière indiquée dans la 8me. *Section du* 4me. *Chapitre de l'Ordre Royal en Conseil du* 7 *Septembre* 1838.—(*Section* 8.—*Voir le No.* 251.)

314.—Les dispositions des *Articles* 1, 2, 3 *et* 5 de cette Ordonnance ne s'appliqueront pas aux Contrats de Service déjà passés entre des Entrepreneurs et des laboureurs mentionnés ci-dessus. Mais à l'égard de ces Contrats, le Magistrat Stipendiaire pourra exiger la garantie du propriétaire ou du locataire de l'établissement sur lequel les laboureurs ci-dessus mentionnés, s'ils sont de nouveaux Immigrants, travaillent, toutes les fois qu'il jugera la garantie nécessaire pour assurer le paiement de leurs gages.—(*Articles* 1, 2, 3 *et* 5.—*Voir les Nos.* 307, 308, 309 *et* 311.) Idem, Art. 7.

Le Magistrat pourra en outre défendre que tout Nouvel Immigrant soit employé dans ce cas jusqu'à ce que la garantie ci-dessus mentionnée soit donnée; et tout Entrepreneur employant un Nouvel Immigrant après que cette défense lui aura été signifiée, sera passible de l'amende fixée par le 5me. *Article de cette Ordonnance*, qui pourra être recouvrée de la manière y indiquée. (5me. *Article.*—*Voir le No.* 311.)

315.—Tous les gages garantis aux Immigrants en vertu de l'*Art.* 64 *de l'Ordonnance. No.* 31 *de* 1867 seront payés aux dits Immigrants en présence du propriétaire ou locataire par lequel ces gages auront été garantis, ou en présence de quelque personne autorisée à représenter le dit propriétaire ou locataire; et ce propriétaire ou locataire ou son représentant signera le Livre de Paie sur lequel ces gages seront portés, pour attester qu'il a été présent au paiement; à défaut de quoi le paiement des dits gages ne sera pas reconnu par le Magistrat Stipendiaire, et le propriétaire ou locataire ne sera pas déchargé de sa garantie relativement aux dits gages. (*Article* 64.—*Voir le No.* 306.—*Voir aussi le No.* 326.) Avis du Gouv. No. 166 du 11 Nov. 1868, Art. 53.

316.—Lorsqu'un laboureur cherchera à recouvrer le paiement de ses gages d'une personne quelconque en vertu de la garantie ci-dessus mentionnée, il ne pourra pas être opposé à sa demande que le propriétaire ou le locataire a déjà payé à l'Entrepreneur les sommes qu'il lui devait en vertu de son Contrat avec le dit Entrepreneur. Ord. No. 7 de 1865, Art. 8.

Idem, Art. 9. 317.—Whenever any *servant*, as the said term is defined in the Royal Order in Council of the 7th September 1838, shall seek to recover wages or rations, or other allowances, under his Contract of Service, from any person not being his master, in virtue of any guarantee of such wages or other aforesaid, the Stipendiary Magistrate having jurisdiction to adjudicate on the claim by the servant against the master, shall also have jurisdiction to try, decide and give judgment upon the claim made against the persons so guaranteeing the wages, and others aforesaid. —(*Servant.—See No.* 549.)

The law and regulations as to the procedure for adjudicating on and recovering such wages and others aforesaid, when claimed from the master of the said servant, shall apply to proceedings for recovery thereof from the person so guaranteeing the same.

Idem, Art. 10. 318.—Every labourer being a New Immigrant, who shall have worked on any estate under Contract of Service with a Job-Contractor, shall have the same privilege over the said estate as if he had been engaged to the owner thereof,—to the effect of securing payment of his wages for all the time during which he shall have laboured on such estate, but provided that the amount recoverable under such privilege, shall not exceed the amount payable by the owner of the estate to the Job-Contractor as provided in *Article* 2 hereof.—(*Article* 2.—*See No.* 308.)

The provisions of the 17*th Article of Ordinance No.* 15 *of* 1852, shall apply to the wages aforesaid due to any such labourer.—(*Article* 17.—*See No.* 343.)

Idem, Art. 11. 319.—This Ordinance shall apply to Mauritius and all its Dependencies.

WAGES, RATIONS, AND LODGING.

I. — *Wages and Rations.*
II. — *Lodging.*

CHAPTER I.

Wages and Rations.

Requisitions for the introduction into the Colony of Indian Immigrants, above 18 years of age, may specify the Wages and Rations

317.—Lorsqu'un *Serviteur,* ainsi que ce terme est défini dans l'Ordre Royal en Conseil du 7 Septembre 1838, cherchera à recouvrer ses gages ou ses rations ou autres allocations auxquelles il a droit par son Contrat de Service, d'une personne qui n'est pas son maître, en vertu d'une garantie pour ses gages etc., le Magistrat Stipendiaire qui pourra connaître de la réclamation du serviteur contre le maître, pourra l'entendre et rendre jugement dans l'affaire contre les personnes qui ont garanti le paiement des gages, etc., mentionnés ci-dessus.—(*Serviteur.—Voir le No.* 549.) Idem, Art. 9.

Les lois et réglements quant à la procédure en matière de jugements pour les gages, etc., mentionnés ci-dessus, et leur recouvrement lorsqu'on les réclame du maître du laboureur, seront applicables aux réclamations contre les personnes qui en auront garanti le paiement.

318.—Tout laboureur nouvel Immigrant, qui aura travaillé sur un établissement sous Engagement de Service avec un Entrepreneur, aura le même privilège sur cet établissement, que s'il avait été engagé au propriétaire,—à l'effet d'assurer le paiement de ses gages pendant tout le temps qu'il aura travaillé sur le dit établissement ; mais pourvu que la somme qui pourra être recouvrée en vertu de ce privilège, n'excède pas la somme payable par le propriétaire de l'établissement à l'Entrepreneur, comme il est dit ci-dessus à l'*Article* 2.—(*Article* 2.—*Voir le No.* 308.) Idem, Art. 10.

Les dispositions du 17*me Article de l'Ordonnance No.* 15 *de* 1852, seront applicables aux gages dûs au dit laboureur.—(*Article* 17.—*Voir le No.* 343.)

319.—Cette Ordonnance s'étendra à l'Ile Maurice et à toutes ses Dépendances. Idem, Art. 11.

GAGES, RATIONS, ET LOGEMENT.

I. — *Gages et Rations.*
II. — *Logement.*

CHAPITRE I.

Gages et Rations.

Les réquisitions pour l'introduction dans la Colonie d'Immigrants Indiens, au-dessus de 18 ans, peuvent spécifier les Gages et

the Requisitionist undertakes to give, which cannot however be less than the minimum scale provided by law.—See No. 111. If no Wages or Rations be so stipulated, the remuneration in the Contract is fixed according to the Government Scale.—See No. 112. and also Appendix No. 26. As regards male Immigrants, under 18 years of age, and female Immigrants, the law empowers the Protector to determine the minimum rates of Wages and Rations to be proposed to them.—See No. 111. Advances of Wages are sometimes made in India; in which case, a clause is inserted in the Contract enabling the Master to repay himself from the laborer's wages.—See No. 119.

Order in Council of 7th Sept. 1838, Cap.2, Sect. 9.

320.—No servant's wages, if contracted for in money, may be paid in kind, or if contracted for in kind may be paid in money, or in any other than the stipulated kind, except by the express consent of the servant.

Ord. No. 16 of 1862, Art. 13.

321.— Any Indian Immigrant who shall be incapacitated by sickness from labour during his Contract, shall be entitled to lodging, food, as well as medical care, at the expense of his employer, during such incapacity.

The foregoing provision is understood to mean, *inter alia*, that during sickness the laborer is not entitled to Wages.

For illegal absence from work on the part of a Servant no wages or allowances are due to him during such absence, and the Master is moreover entitled, subject to certain conditions, to indemnify himself by a proportional deduction from the Servant's Wages.—*See Nos.* 399 *and seq.*

Ord. No. 15 of 1852, Art. 13.

322.—No debts which a laborer may have incurred at a shop belonging to his employer, or kept on his estate, or in which he may have an interest, shall be admitted or deducted as a part payment of his wages or as a set off against the same.

Order in Council of 7th Sept. 1838, Cap.4. Sect. 8.

323.— On complaint preferred and proof made by a servant before any Stipendiary Magistrate that his Master has not paid the Servant's Wages,* or delivered to him the Articles stipulated for, or that the Articles so delivered were not of the prescribed

---

* Arrears of Wages cannot be recovered by proceedings against the Sequestrator of an estate if he was *functus officio* when the suit was instituted. (*Boullé v. Arbuthnot*,—Piston's Reports, 1866.)

Rations que le Requérant s'engage à donner, mais ces Gages et Rations ne peuvent cependant être au-dessous du minimum établi par la loi.—Voir le No. 111.—Si les Gages et Rations ne sont pas stipulés dans la réquisition, ils sont fixés d'après l'échelle du Gouvernement.—Voir le No. 112.—et l'Appendice No. 26. Quant aux Immigrants au-dessous de 18 ans, et aux Immigrantes, la loi autorise le Protecteur à déterminer le minimum des Gages et Rations, qu'on peut leur offrir.—Voir le No. 111. Des avances de Gages sont quelquefois faites dans l'Inde, et dans ce cas une clause est insérée au Contrat, qui permet au Maître de se rembourser de ces avances des Gages du laboureur.—Voir le No. 119.

320.—Les gages d'un serviteur, s'ils sont stipulés payables en argent, ne peuvent être payés en nature, ou s'ils sont stipulés payables en nature, ne peuvent être payés en argent, ou en aucuns autres objets que ceux stipulés, si ce n'est du consentement exprès du serviteur. Ordre en Conseil du 7 Sept. 1838, Ch. 2, Sect. 9.

321.—Tout Immigrant Indien qui pendant son contrat sera hors d'état de travailler pour cause de maladie, aura droit à son logement et à sa nourriture ainsi qu'aux soins médicaux, aux frais de son employeur, pendant cette maladie. Ord. No. 16 de 1862, Art. 13.

L'interprétation qui est donnée à l'article précédent est, *inter alia*, que pendant la maladie du travailleur, celui-ci n'a pas droit à ses gages.

Pour absence illégale de son travail, le serviteur perd tous ses droits à ses gages et rations pour le temps pendant lequel il s'est ainsi absenté; et dans certains cas, le maître peut de plus s'indemniser des cette absence au moyen d'une déduction proportionnelle des gages du serviteur.—*Voir les Nos.* 399 *et suiv.*

322.—Aucune dette que pourra avoir contractée un travailleur dans une boutique appartenant à son employeur, ou tenue sur sa propriété, ou dans laquelle il peut avoir un intérêt, ne sera admise ou déduite en partie de paiement de ses gages, ou comme compensation des dits gages. Ord. No. 15 de 1852, Art. 13.

323.—Sur la plainte portée et la preuve fournie par un Serviteur devant un Magistrat Salarié, que son Maître ne lui a pas payé ses Gages, * ou ne lui a pas fourni les objets stipulés, ou que les objets fournis n'étaient pas conformes au montant et à la qua- Ordre en Conseil du 7 Sept. 1838, Ch. 4, Sect. 8.

* Des arriérés de Gages ou de Salaires ne peuvent être recouvrés du Gardien Séquestre d'un Établissement s'il était *functus officio* lorsque la réclamation a été formulée. (*Boullé v. Arbuthnot*,—Piston's Reports, 1866.)

amount and quality, or that by the negligence, or other improper conduct of the Master, the Contract of Service has not been faithfully performed, or that the Master has ill used the Servant, the Stipendiary Magistrate may make order for the payment of the Wages in arrear, or for the delivery of the stipulated Articles, or for compensation to be made to the Servant for any injury by him sustained by such negligence or improper conduct of the Master, or by his non-fulfilment of the Contract, or by his ill-usage of the Servant; and if such order be not complied with according to the exigency and tenor thereof, the Magistrate shall and may issue a Warrant for the seizure and sale of the Goods of the Master, or so much thereof as may be requisite for making such compensation; and failing any sufficient distress, the Magistrate shall and may make order for the commitment of the Master to prison, for any time not exceeding one month, unless compensation be sooner made. The Magistrate may also in any of the cases aforesaid, if he shall see fit, order the Contract of Service to be cancelled either in addition to, or in substitution for, any such order as aforesaid.

Claims for Wages &c., against persons furnishing a guarantee on behalf of Job-Contractors, are within the jurisdiction of the Stipendiary Courts,—*See No.* 317.

Ord. No. 31 of 1867, Art. 31.

324.—The *said claims* for salary are cognizable by the Stipendiary Magistrate in the same manner, to all intents and purposes, as claims for wages due to laborers. — (*Said claims, i. e., claims for wages by the manager and employés upon an estate other than gens de service.*)

Ord. No. 15 of 1852, Art. 12.

325.—Every bond, note, or recognizance for money subscribed by any employer, or the manager of the estate of such employer in favor of a servant employed on the same, shall be recoverable by such servant as Wages due to him in the *manner prescribed for the recovery of Wages by the Order in Council of 7th September* 1838, unless it be proved to the satisfaction of the Stipendiary Magistrate, that the Wages due to such servant during the whole period of his service with the said employer have been actually paid to him; and every claim arising from any bond, note, or recognizance for money so subscribed in favor of a servant by his employer, or by the manager of the estate on which he is employed, shall

lité prescrits, ou que, par la négligence ou toute autre conduite inconvenable du Maître, le Contrat de Service n'a pas été fidèlement exécuté, ou que le Maître a maltraité le Serviteur, le Magistrat Salarié peut décerner un ordre pour le paiement des Gages arriérés, ou la remise des objets stipulés, ou pour une compensation à donner au serviteur pour le tort qu'il a éprouvé par la négligence ou la conduite inconvenable de son Maître, ou par la non-exécution du Contrat de la part de celui-ci, ou par ses mauvais traitements envers le Serviteur ; et si cet ordre n'est pas pleinement exécuté selon sa teneur, le Magistrat pourra rendre une ordonnance pour la saisie et la vente des biens du Maître, ou de telle portion de ses biens qu'il sera nécessaire pour effectuer cette compensation ; et, en cas d'insuffisance, le Magistrat décernera contre le maître un mandat d'emprisonnement pour un temps qui n'excèdera pas un mois, à moins que l'indemnité ne soit payée plus tôt. Le Magistrat pourra aussi dans les cas ci-dessus, s'il le juge convenable, ordonner l'annulation du Contrat de Service, soit en addition, ou au lieu d'aucune des dispositions sus-dites.

Les réclamations pour Gages, etc., contre des personnes qui en ont garanti le paiement pour des Entrepreneurs, sont de la compétence des Cours Stipendiaires.—*Voir le No.* 317.

324.—Les *dites réclamations* pour Salaires sont de la compétence du Magistrat Stipendiaire de la même manière à tous égards que les réclamations pour gages dûs aux travailleurs.—(*Dites réclamations, i. e., les réclamations pour Gages dûs aux administrateurs et autres employés de l'établissement autres que les gens de service.*) Ord. No. 31 de 1867, Art. 31.

325.—Tout bon, billet, ou reconnaissance d'argent, souscrit par un employeur ou par l'administrateur de la propriété du dit employeur, au profit d'un serviteur employé sur la dite propriété, sera recouvrable par le dit serviteur comme Gages à lui dûs, *de la manière prescrite pour le recouvrement des Gages par l'Ordre en Conseil du 7 Septembre* 1838, à moins qu'il ne soit prouvé à la satisfaction du Magistrat Stipendiaire que les Gages dûs au dit serviteur, pendant tout le temps de son service avec le dit employeur, lui ont été réellement payés, et toute réclamation résultant de tout bon, billet, ou reconnaissance d'argent, ainsi souscrit en faveur d'un serviteur par son employeur, ou par l'administrateur Ord. No. 15 de 1852, Art. 12.

be cognizable in like summary manner by the Stipendiary Magistrate of the District or by a *Court of Pelty Sessions.*— (*Manner prescribed for recovery of Wages,— See No.* 323.— *Court of Petty Sessions,—See No.* 484.)

Govt. Notice No. 166 of 11th Nov. 1868, Art. 88. 326.— No Wages-book shall be admitted in evidence by a Stipendiary Magistrate unless it be kept in English or French, or be produced with a literal translation made and signed by a Sworn Translator.

Ord. No. 31 of 1867, Art. 32. 327.—The provisions of Article 1781* of the Civil Code are not applicable to any proceedings before a Stipendiary Magistrate for the recovery of any arrears of Wages or Salary claimed by any person from his Employer.

Ord. No. 15 of 1852, Art. 10. 328.—In every case in which a complaint has been proved against a Master or Servant, under the provisions of the *7th and 8th Sections* of the 4th Chapter of the above cited Order in Council, and in every case of ill-usage of a Servant by his Master, whether by assault or otherwise, the Stipendiary Magistrate may, according to the circumstances, award a fine not exceeding £ 10 in place of compensation to the complaint as provided for in the said Sections.—(*7th and 8th Sections.—See Nos.* 252 *and* 251.)

Idem, Art. 11. 329.—The non-payment of Wages for three months beyond the term at which such Wages become due, shall be held to be a breach of Contract by the Master, and on a Stipendiary Magistrate awarding payment of such Wages, the servant shall be at liberty to claim the dissolution of his Contract.

Ord. No. 31 of 1867, Art. 36. 330.—When a certificate of discharge sent or produced to a Magistrate under *Article* 4 *of Ordinance No.* 15 *of* 1852, shall state that any amount of Wages remains unpaid to the laborer discharged, the Magistrate shall, upon the production of the cer-

---

* Article 1781 of the Civil Code is as follows :—" The Master shall be believed " on his affirmation, as to the rate of wages, as to the payment of the wages for the " year last expired, and as to payments on account for the current year." On the matter of personal interrogatories, see also the decision of the Supreme Court, in the case of *Montille v. Goburdhun and ors.* (Piston's Reports, 1867.)

de la propriété sur laquelle il est employé, sera jugée de la même manière sommaire par le Magistrat Stipendiaire du district ou par une Cour de "Petty Sessions".—(*Manière prescrite pour le recouvrement des Gages.—Voir le No.* 323.—*Cour de "Petty Sessions.—Voir le No.* 484.)

326.—Aucun livre de Gages ne sera admis comme preuve par un Magistrat Stipendiaire s'il n'est tenu en anglais ou en français, ou si l'on n'en produit pas en même temps une traduction littérale dans une de ces deux langues faite et signée par un traducteur juré. Avis du Gouv. No. 166 du 11 Nov. 1868, Art. 88.

327.—Les dispositions de l'Art. 1781 * du Code Civil ne sont pas applicables aux poursuites devant un Magistrat Stipendiaire ayant pour but le recouvrement d'arriérés de Gages ou de Salaires réclamés par un employé de son employeur. Ord. No. 31 de 1867, Art. 32.

328.—Dans tous les cas où une plainte aura été prouvée contre un maître ou un serviteur conformément aux dispositions des *Sections 7 et* 8 du Chapitre 4 de l'Ordre en Conseil précité; et dans tous les cas de mauvais traitements de la part d'un maître envers son serviteur, soit par voies de fait ou autrement, le Magistrat Stipendiaire pourra, selon les circonstances, prononcer une amende qui n'excédera pas £ 10, au lieu de l'indemnité à donner au plaignant comme le portent les dites Sections.—(*Sections* 7 *et* 8.—*Voir les Nos.* 252 *et* 251.) Ord. No. 15 de 1852, Art. 10.

329.—Le défaut de paiement de Gages, pendant trois mois après l'échéance des dits Gages, sera considéré comme une violation du Contrat de la part du maître, et lorsqu'un Magistrat Stipendiaire condamnera au paiement des dits Gages, le serviteur sera libre de réclamer la dissolution de son Contrat. Idem, Art. 11.

330.—Lorsqu'un certificat de décharge envoyé ou produit à un Magistrat en vertu de *l'Article* 4 *de l'Ordonnance No.* 15 *de* 1852, déclarera qu'il reste dûe au travailleur déchargé une somme quelconque pour Gages, le Magistrat, avant de signer le certificat, assi- Ord. No. 31 de 1867, Art. 36.

---

* L'article 1781 du Code Civil est comme suit :—" Le maître est cru sur son affirmation, pour la quotité des gages, pour le paiement du salaire de l'année échue, et pour les à-comptes donnés pour l'année courante."—En matière d'interrogatoire sur faits et articles, voir aussi l'arrêt de la Cour Suprême dans l'affaire *Montille v. Goburdhun et autres.* (Piston's Reports, 1867.)

tificate, condemn the Employer to pay to the laborer the Wages which appear to be due to him, granting a reasonable delay for the payment into Court of the amount so due.—(*Article* 4.—*See No.* 238.)

Govt. Notice No. 166 of 11th Nov. 1868, Art. 38.

331.—In every case in which a judgment shall be given in favor of a laborer under *Article* 36 *of Ordinance No.* 31 *of* 1867, on account of wages stated to be due to him on his certificate of discharge, a summary mention of such judgment stating the day on which the delay granted for its execution shall expire shall be inscribed upon the certificate and shall be authenticated by the signature of the Magistrate. The delay so granted shall be well explained to the laborer, and notice thereof, in the form of the Schedule M in the Appendix, shall be served upon the Employer, at his expense, if he be not present.—(*Article* 36.—*See No.* 330.)

SCHEDULE M.

To Proprietor (or Lessee) of Estate in the District of

Take notice that Judgment has this day been given by me, in favor of the Immigrants mentioned in margin for the amounts of wages due by you to them and which are stated opposite to their respective names; and that a delay of months has been granted to you for the payment of the said wages into this Court.

If, at the expiration of the said delay, the aforesaid judgment be not satisfied, proceedings shall be taken for the execution thereof, unless a fresh delay be acceded to by the said Immigrants.

Stipendiary Court of this day of 186 .

C. D.
Stipendiary Magistrate.

Idem, Art. 39.

332.—At the expiration of such delay, if the judgment be not satisfied, proceedings shall be taken for the execution thereof, unless at the instance of the laborer a fresh delay be granted; in which case execution shall be deferred till the expiration of such new delay.

On the re-engagement of a laborer whose Certificate of Discharge shews that wages are due to him, he is allowed to retain that Certificate after the Stipendiary Magistrate has noted thereon the new engagement.—*See No.* 233.

gnera l'employeur devant lui, et le condamnera à payer au travailleur les Gages qui paraîtront lui être dûs, et lui accordera un délai raisonnable pour le paiement en Cour du montant ainsi dû.—(*Article* 4.—*Voir le No.* 238.)

331.—Dans tous les cas où un jugement sera rendu en faveur d'un travailleur en vertu de l'*Article 36 de l'Ordonnance No.* 31 *de* 1867 pour gages à lui dûs d'après son Certificat de Décharge, mention sommaire de ce jugement, énonçant le jour de l'expiration du délai accordé pour son exécution, sera faite sur le certificat et signée par le Magistrat, le délai ainsi accordé sera expliqué au travailleur, et avis de ce délai, dans la forme de l'Annexe M, sera signifié à l'employeur, a ses frais, s'il n'est pas présent.—(*Article* 36.—*Voir le No.* 330.) Avis du Gouv. No. 166 du 11 Nov. 1868, Art. 38.

ANNEXE M.

A   propriétaire (ou locataire) de la propriété
dans le District de

Avis vous est donné que jugement a ce jour été rendu par moi en faveur des Immigrants mentionnés en marge pour le montant des gages à eux dûs par vous et qui sont énoncés en regard de leurs noms respectifs, et qu'un délai de   mois vous a été accordé pour le paiement des dits gages à ce Tribunal.

Si, à l'expiration du dit délai, il n'a pas été satisfait au dit jugement, il sera exécuté à moins qu'un nouveau délai ne soit consenti par les dits Immigrants.

Tribunal Stipendiaire de   ce   jour de   186 .

C. D.
Magistrat Stipendiaire.

332.—A l'expiration du dit délai, si les gages n'ont pas été payés, le jugement sera exécuté, à moins qu'un nouveau délai ne soit accordé à la requête du travailleur ; dans ce cas l'exécution sera différée jusqu'à l'expiration de ce nouveau délai. Idem, Art. 39.

Si, lors du ré-engagement d'un travailleur, son Certificat de Décharge fait mention de gages à lui dûs, on lui permet de conserver ce certificat après que le Magistrat Stipendiaire a inscrit le nouvel engagement sur ce document.—*Voir le No.* 233.

Ord. No. 31 of 1867, Art. 25. **333.**—Whenever any employer shall have been summoned before a Stipendiary Magistrate upon the complaint of any Manager, Employé, or laborer in his service, the plea of infancy, if set up and established by such Employer, shall be no valid or sufficient defence to such complaint. If it be proved to the satisfaction of the Magistrate that the complainant has been actually employed in the service of the minor, he shall deal with the complaint in the same manner as if the Employer were of full age.

Idem, Art. 33. **334.**—Any judgment of a Stipendiary Magistrate condemning an Employer to the payment of wages or salary, may, at any time before such judgment shall have been satisfied, be attacked by *tierce opposition* on the ground that such judgment has been obtained by fraud or collusion. The said Stipendiary Magistrate shall have jurisdiction, and shall be bound to hear and determine such *tierce opposition.* The party forming the same, if he fail therein, shall be condemned to pay all costs of suit.

Tierce opposition. — Tierce opposition is an exceptional mode of attacking a judgment. The right of employing it accrues to any person aggrieved by the judgment and not having been a party to the suit either personally or as the representative of others.

Idem, Art. 35. **335.**— In case any domestic servant shall have obtained judgment against his Employer for arrears of wages, no seizure of moveables made in the house or premises of the Employer shall be set aside or invalidated on the ground that such moveables are the property of the wife of the Employer, unless she be living apart from her husband under judicial authority.

Code of Civil Procedure, Art. 626. **336.**—The seizure of crop (*saisie brandon*) shall only be lawful during the six weeks immediately preceding the usual period of the ripening of the crop; the seizure shall be preceded by a notice, an interval of one day shall elapse between the notice and the seizure.

Idem, Art. 627. **337.**—The memorandum of seizure shall set forth the description of each portion of ground, its area and situation, and at least two of its boundaries, as also the description of the crop.

Ord. No. 15 of 1852, Art. 15. **338.**—No sale of property or of goods seized in virtue of a Stipendiary Magistrate's Order, shall be effected in any other place than that appointed by him, nor until ten days after the publication of a notice in the Government Gazette, and the posting

333.—Toutes les fois qu'un employeur aura été sommé de comparaître devant un Magistrat Stipendiaire sur la plainte d'un travailleur à son service, la défense basée sur la minorité, présentée et établie par cet employeur, ne sera pas une défense valable et suffisante pour repousser cette plainte. S'il est prouvé à la satisfaction du Magistrat que le travailleur a été réellement employé au service du mineur, il prendra connaissance de la plainte de la même manière que si l'employeur était majeur. Ord. No. 31 de 1867, Art. 25.

334.—Tout jugement d'un Magistrat Stipendiaire condamnant un employeur au paiement de gages ou salaires, pourra, à à quelque moment que ce soit, avant que ce jugement n'ait été exécuté par le paiement, être attaqué par voie de *tierce opposition*, sur le motif qu'il a été obtenu par fraude ou collusion. Le dit Magistrat Stipendiaire sera compétent pour recevoir et juger cette *tierce opposition*, et sera tenu de le faire. La partie qui l'aura formée sera condamnée à tous les frais si elle succombe. Idem, Art. 33.

Tierce opposition.—La tierce opposition est une voie extraordinaire ouverte contre tout jugement à une tierce personne qui n'y a point été partie par elle-même, ou par ceux qu'elle représente, et aux droits de laquelle ce jugement préjudicie.

335.—Dans le cas où un domestique aura obtenu jugement contre son employeur pour gages arriérés, aucune saisie de meubles faite dans la maison ou sur les lieux occupés par l'employeur, ne sera annulée sur le motif que ces meubles sont la propriété de la femme de l'employeur, à moins qu'elle ne vive séparée de son mari avec l'autorisation de la justice. Idem, Art. 35.

336.—La Saisie-Brandon ne pourra être faite que dans les six semaines qui précèderont l'époque ordinaire de la maturité des fruits ; elle sera précédée d'un commandement, avec un jour d'intervalle. Code de Procédure Civile Art. 626.

337.—Le procès-verbal de saisie contiendra l'indication de chaque pièce, sa contenance et sa situation, et deux au moins de ses tenans et aboutissans, et la nature des fruits. Idem, Art. 627.

338.—Aucune vente de propriétés mobilières ou effets saisis en vertu de l'ordre d'un Magistrat Stipendiaire n'aura lieu dans aucun autre endroit que celui désigné par lui, ni moins de dix jours après l'insertion d'un avis dans la Gazette du Gouvernement et Ord. No. 15 de 1852, Art. 15.

up of a similar notice at the office of the Stipendiary Magistrate of the district, and in the other usual public places within the same.

Idem, Art. 16. **339.**—No opposition, seizure, or detainer exercised upon goods previously seized by order of the Stipendiary Magistrate, or upon any proceeds of the sale of such goods, shall operate so as to interfere with the effect of such order.

Ord. No. 31 of 1867, Art. 34. **340.**—No opposition or attachment lodged in the hands of any Stipendiary Magistrate or District Cashier against any monies payable to laborers for arrears of Wages, shall be valid or effectual. The sums so payable shall be paid to the laborers entitled to receive the same, any such opposition or attachment notwithstanding.

Idem, Art. 37. **341.**—Whenever a Stipendiary Magistrate shall have given a judgment condemning an Employer to the payment of any sum for arrears of Wages or Salaries,* any third party may obtain subrogation into the rights and privilege of the laborers or *employés* under such judgment, by paying into the hands of the Stipendiary Magistrate the amount due under such judgment, and by thereupon obtaining from the Magistrate a subrogative receipt, under the hand and seal of the Magistrate, for the amount paid, which receipt the Magistrate shall be bound, if required, to give at the time of the money being paid.

SUBROGATIVE RECEIPT.

(*Schedule V of Government Notice No.* 166 *of* 11*th November* 1868.)

This is to acknowledge that the several sums mentioned in the margin hereof were due under a judgment given in this Court on the as arrears of Wages or Salaries to the laborers or *employés* opposite to whose names they are respectively set forth ;—that the said sums have been paid into this Court by who is hereby subrogated under Article 37 of Ordinance No. 31 of 1867 to all the rights and privileges of the said laborers or *employés* under the said judgment.

Stipendiary Court of 186 .

C. D.

Stipendiary Magistrate.

---

* In the case of *Piat, Allandy and ors. v. Creditors of F. Tonnet and H. Nina and ors.* (Piston's Reports, 1866), the appellants, purchasers of "Belle Vue" estate, having paid, under their deed of sale, arrears of Wages due to *employés* and laborers of that estate, were not allowed to rank in the "Ordre" as privileged creditors occupying the place of the *employés* and laborers, inasmuch as the latter had not had their claims established by a judgment.

après l'affiche d'un avis semblable au bureau du Magistrat Stipendiaire du district et aux autres lieux publics usités du dit district.

339.—Aucune opposition, saisie ou séquestre exercé sur des meubles ou effets précédemment saisis par ordre du Magistrat Stipendiaire, ou sur le produit de la vente des dits meubles ou effets ne pourra contrarier l'effet du dit ordre. Idem, Art.

340.—Aucune opposition ou saisie-arrêt mise aux mains d'un Magistrat Stipendiaire ou d'un Caissier de District, pour des sommes dûes aux travailleurs pour Gages arriérés, ne seront valables et n'auront d'effet. Les sommes ainsi dûes seront payées aux travailleurs ayant le droit de les recevoir, nonobstant la dite opposition ou saisie-arrêt. Ord. No. 31 1867, Art. 34.

341.—Toutes les fois qu'un Magistrat Stipendiaire aura rendu un jugement condamnant un employeur au paiement d'une somme pour Gages ou Salaires arriérés,* un tiers pourra obtenir subrogation dans les droits et privilège appartenant aux travailleurs ou employés en vertu de ce jugement, en payant entre les mains du Magistrat Stipendiaire le montant dû en vertu de ce jugement, et en obtenant du Magistrat un reçu avec subrogation, signé et scellé par le dit Magistrat, pour le montant payé, lequel reçu le Magistrat sera tenu de remettre, s'il en est requis, au moment même du paiement. Idem, Art. 37.

QUITTANCE SUBROGATIVE.

(*Cédule V de l'Avis du Gouvernement No.* 166 *du* 11 *Novembre* 1868.)

Ceci est pour reconnaître que les différentes sommes mentionnées en marge étaient dûes en vertu d'un jugement rendu en ce tribunal le pour Gages ou Salaires arriérés dûs aux travailleurs ou employés dont les noms sont en regard des dites sommes ;—que les dites sommes ont été payées en ce tribunal par qui est par ces présentes subrogé en vertu de l'Article 37 de l'Ordonnance No. 31 de 1867 dans tous les droits et privilèges des dits travailleurs ou employés en vertu du dit jugement.

Tribunal Stipendiaire de 186 .

Magistrat Stipendiaire.

---

* Dans l'affaire *Piat, Allandy et autres v. les créanciers de F. Tonnet et H. Nina et autres* (Piston's Reports, 1866), les Appelants, acquéreurs de l'établissement "Belle Vue," qui avaient payé, en vertu d'une clause de l'acte de vente, des arriérés de Gages dûs aux employés et travailleurs de cet établissement, ne purent figurer à l'Ordre comme créanciers privilégiés au lieu et place de ces employés et travailleurs, parceque ces derniers n'avaient pas déjà établi leur droit par un jugement.

Idem, Art 38. 342.—Whenever, in execution of any Judgment for Compensation or Wages, there shall not have been found sufficient goods and chattels to satisfy the said Judgment, the Stipendiary Magistrate may issue a Writ of execution against any real estate belonging to the debtor, in whatever District the same may be situated; but no such Writ of execution shall be acted upon without the authority of one of the Judges of the Supreme Court, and the return of such Writ shall be made to the Registrar of the said Court.

Upon such authority being obtained, the Writ shall be notified to the Employer in the form of a " Commandement " ; and the seizure shall thereupon be made subject to the delays prescribed by law between the " Commandement " and the Seizure.

The proceedings of the sale of such estate shall be made and taken under the authority of the Supreme Court, in the form and manner prescribed by the law existing at the time being.

If such estate be already under seizure, the creditor under any such judgment as aforesaid may ask of the Master of the Supreme Court subrogation in the seizure, upon the simple production of the said Writ of execution issued by the Stipendiary Magistrate as aforesaid.

Ord. No. 15 of 1852, Art. 17. 343.— In every case of a forced or judicial sale of a landed Estate, upon which laborers are or have been employed,* and to whom arrears of Wages are due, the amount of such Wages with any costs incurred, shall be paid by the purchaser out of the purchase money of such Estate, into the hands of the Stipendiary Magistrate of the District in which such Estate is situate, in preference to all other creditors, and upon no other formalities than the Order † to that effect of one of the Judges of the Supreme

* The Judgment of a Stipendiary Magistrate for Wages, under the Ordinance No. 15 of 1852, Article 17, ought to specify minutely the time during which the labor was performed.—(*Dioré* v. *Beeharry and others*.—(Piston's Reports 1863.)

If this be not done the servants may lose their claim to the privilege under that Article;—but, on the distribution by way of an " Ordre " of the sale price of the estate, they may still vindicate their preference under Articles 2101 and 2104 of the Civil Code.

† The non-compliance with a Judge's Order issued under this provision was held by the Supreme Court, in the case of *The Ceylon Company Limited* v. *Hardy* (Piston's Reports, 1867), not to entitle the prosecution of the re-sale of the property by " Folle Enchère" where no breach of the conditions of sale existed.

342.—Toutes les fois qu'en exécution d'un jugement pour Compensation ou pour Gages, on n'aura pas trouvé une quantité suffisante de biens mobiliers pour éteindre la dette résultant du dit jugement, le Magistrat Stipendiaire pourra décerner un Writ d'exécution contre tous biens immobiliers appartenant au débiteur, dans quelque district qu'ils soient situés ; mais on ne pourra agir en vertu de ce Writ d'exécution qu'avec l'autorisation d'un des Juges de la Cour Suprême, et le rapport ou procès-verbal de l'huissier chargé de l'exécution de ce Writ, sera fait au Greffier de la dite Cour. Idem, Art. 38.

Sur cette autorisation le Writ sera notifié à l'employeur dans la forme d'un commandement et la saisie sera faite après les délais prescrits par la loi entre le commandement et la saisie.

La procédure de la vente de cet immeuble sera faite sous le contrôle de la Cour Suprême, en la forme et de la manière prescrites par la loi alors en vigueur.

Si cet immeuble est déjà sous saisie, le créancier, en vertu du jugement susdit, pourra demander au Master de la Cour Suprême la subrogation dans la saisie, sur la simple production du dit Writ d'exécution décerné par le Magistrat Stipendiaire comme il est expliqué plus haut.

343.—Dans tous les cas de vente forcée ou judiciaire d'une propriété immobilière sur laquelle ont été ou sont employés * des travailleurs auxquels il sera dû des Gages arriérés, le montant de ces Gages et de tous frais encourus sera payé par l'acquéreur sur le prix d'adjudication de l'immeuble, entre les mains du Magistrat Stipendiaire du district dans lequel sera situé le dit immeuble, par préférence à tous autres créanciers, et sans autres formalités que l'ordre † délivré à cet effet par l'un des Juges de la Cour Ord. No. 15 de 1852, Art. 17.

* Le jugement d'un Magistrat Stipendiaire pour salaires de gens de service, en vertu de l'Article 17 de l'Ordonnance No. 15 de 1852, doit spécifier d'une manière précise l'époque à laquelle le travail a eu lieu.— (*Dioré* v. *Beeharry & autres*,— Piston's Reports, 1863.) Dans le cas où cette formalité ne serait pas remplie, les serviteurs pourraient perdre leurs droits au privilège accordé par l'article ci-dessus ; ils pourront cependant, à la distribution par voie " d'Ordre " du prix de vente de l'établissement, revendiquer leur privilège en vertu des articles 2101 et 2104 du Code Civil.

† La Cour Suprême a décidé dans l'affaire " *The Ceylon Company Limited* " v. *Hardy*, (Piston's Reports, 1867,) que le fait qu'il n'avait pas été satisfait à l'ordre d'un Juge, délivré en vertu de la disposition ci-dessus, ne donnait pas le droit de poursuivre la vente de la propriété par voie de " Folle Enchère," lorsqu'il n'y avait eu aucune violation des conditions de la vente.

Court, to be given upon application made in the name of the said laborers, within three months after the said sale, and on the production of the judgment * of the Stipendiary Magistrate condemning the former proprietor of the estate to the payment of such Wages, which order shall be final and without appeal. The aforesaid privilege of laborers for the payment of arrears of Wages shall be and is hereby, for the purpose of this Ordinance, limited to the period of *one year* without prejudice to any other of their existing legal rights.—(*One year.—See also No.* 349.)

Ord. No. 31 of 1867, Art. 26. 344.—The word "laborer" in *Article* 17 *of Ordinance No.* 15 *of* 1852, extends to all persons working for any Employer as domestic servants, field laborers, handicraftsmen, or overseers of labour, whether of Indian or other extraction, whose wages, irrespective of allowances, shall not exceed £ 4 per month.—(*See also No.* 348 *and the foot-note thereto.*)

As to the privilege of Immigrants, engaged to Job-Contractors, over the estate on which they are employed, for Wages due to them,—*See No.* 318.

The remuneration due to Medical Practitioners on estates may be recovered from the sale price of the property in the same way as is provided with regard to Laborers Wages.—*See No.* 375.

Civil Code, Art. 2101. 345.—The privileged claims which affect personal property in general are those hereinafter mentioned; they rank as follows:

1o. Judicial costs;

2o. Funeral expenses;

3o. Expenses of every description incurred in the last illness equally and "*pari passu*" among those to whom the same are due.

4o. Wages of *gens de service* for the year expired, and what may be due for the current year.‡—(*Gens de service.—See Nos.* 344 *and* 348.)

---

* The occasional employment of laborers elsewhere than on the estate against which they claim need not materially affect their position as laborers of the property. —(*Mohabut and ors.* v. *De Courson and Kivern.*—Piston's Reports, 1866.)

‡ Under the present law (See No. 349) this privilege is limited to wages for one year next preceding the jugdment of the Stipendiary Magistrate.—As to the mode of reckoning the privilege under the former law, see the decision of the Supreme Court in the case of *Lamarre* v. *Joly and others*,—(Piston's Reports, 1867.)

Suprême, sur la demande faite au nom des dits travailleurs, dans les trois mois qui suivront la dite vente, et sur la production du jugement * du Magistrat Stipendiaire qui aura condamné le précédent propriétaire du bien au paiement des dits Gages ; lequel ordre sera définitif et sans appel. Le sus-dit privilège des travailleurs pour le paiement de leurs Gages arriérés, sera et est par le présent, pour les effets de cette Ordonnance, limité à une année, sans préjudice à aucun autre de leurs droits légaux.— (*Une année.—Voir aussi le No.* 349.)

344.—Le mot " Travailleur " dans l'*Article* 17 *de l'Ordonnance No.* 15 *de* 1852 s'étend à toutes personnes travaillant pour un employeur comme domestiques, travailleurs des champs, artisans, ou surveillants des travaux, qu'ils soient d'origine Indienne ou autre, et dont les gages, indépendamment des rations, n'excèderont pas £ 4 par mois.—(*Article* 17.—*Voir le No.* 343.—*Voir aussi le No.* 348 *et la note qui y est jointe.*) Ord. No. 31 de 1867, Art. 26.

Pour le privilège des Immigrants engagés à des Entrepreneurs, sur l'établissement sur lequel ils travaillent, pour gages à eux dûs.—*Voir le No.* 318.

La rémunération dûe aux Médecins attachés aux établissements peut être recouvrée du prix de vente de la propriété de la même manière que les Gages des laboureurs.—*Voir le No.* 375.

345.—Les créances privilégiées sur la généralité des meubles sont celles ci-après exprimées, et s'exercent dans l'ordre suivant : Code Civil, Art. 2101.

1o. Les frais de justice ;

2o. Les frais funéraires ;

3o. Les frais quelconques de la dernière maladie, concurremment entre ceux à qui ils sont dûs ;

4o. Les salaires des *gens de service* pour l'année échue et ce qui est dû sur l'année courante.‡—(*Voir les Nos.* 344 *et* 348.)

---

* Les travailleurs d'une propriété ne perdent pas leur privilège, sur cette propriété pour Gages arriérés, parcequ'ils ont été de temps à autre employés ailleurs que sur cette propriété. (*Mohabut & autres* v. *De Courson & K1 Vern.*—Piston's Reports 1866.)

‡ D'après la loi actuelle (voir le No. 349) ce privilège est limité aux gages dûs pour l'année précédant immédiatement le jugement du Magistrat Stipendiaire. Pour la manière dont le privilège était établie d'après l'ancienne loi, voir l'Arrêt de la Cour Suprême dans l'affaire *Lamaire* v. *Joly et autres*,—Piston's Reports, 1867.)

5o. The house-keeping supplies furnished to the debtor and his family: namely, during the last six months, by retail shopkeepers, such as Bakers, Butchers and the like, and during the last year by eating-house keepers and wholesale dealers.

Idem, Art. 2104. 346.—The privileged claims which affect both personal and real property are those indicated in *Article* 2101.—(*Article* 2101. —*See No.* 345.)

Idem, Art. 2105. 347.—When through insufficiency of personal property payment of the privileged debts mentioned in the preceding article is claimed from the sale price of a real estate in competition with the mortgaged creditors thereof, payment shall be made in the following order:

1o. Judicial costs and the other claims set forth *in Article* 2101.

2o. The claims indicated in *Article* 2103.—(*Article* 2101.—*See No.* 345.—(*The Article* 2103 *is not inserted here as it does not bear upon the subject of this work.*)

Ord. No. 31 of 1867, Art. 27. 348.—The term "gens de service," as used in *Article* 2101 of the Civil Code, extends and applies to the several classes * of persons mentioned in the *preceding article.* —(*Article* 2101. —*See No.* 345.—*Preceding Article, i. e. Article* 26.—*See No.* 344.)

Idem, Art. 28. 349.—The privilege for arrears of wages conferred upon the several above mentioned classes of persons as "*gens de service*" under the said *Article* 2101 of the Civil Code, is hereby limited to arrears of wages due for any period not exceeding one year next preceding the judgment of the Stipendiary Magistrate condemning the Employer to the payment of such arrears.—(*Article* 2101. —*See No.* 345.—*See also No.* 343.)

Idem, Art. 29. 350.— The said privilege shall be admitted in its proper rank as established by the Civil Code, in any distribution by way of contribution of monies belonging to the employer, or in any dis-

* As to the classes of persons who, under the former law, were considered not to be "gens de service," on account of the rate of Wages received by them,—see the decisions of the Supreme Court in the cases of *Montille* v. *Goburdhun and ors.*, and of *The Credit Foncier of Mauritius Limited* v. *Géraufié and anor.*— (Piston's Report, 1868.)

5o. Les fournitures de subsistence faités au débiteur et à sa famille, savoir : pendant les six derniers mois, par les marchands en détail, tels que boulangers, bouchers et autres ; et pendant la dernière année, par les maîtres de pension et marchands en gros.

346.—Les privilèges qui s'étendent sur les meubles et les immeubles sont ceux énoncés en l'*Article* 2101.—(*Article* 2101.—*Voir le No.* 345.) Idem, Art. 2104.

347.—Lorsqu'à défaut de mobiliers, les privilégiés énoncés en l'article précédent se présentent pour être payés sur le prix d'un immeuble en concurrence avec les créanciers privilégiés sur l'immeuble, les paiements se font dans l'ordre qui suit : Idem, Art, 2105.

1o. Les frais de justice et autres énoncés en l'*Article* 2101.

2o. Les créances désignées en l'*Article* 2103.—(*Article* 2101.—*Voir le No.* 345.— *L'Article* 2103 *n'est pas inséré ici parce qu'il ne se rapporte pas au sujet de cet ouvrage.*)

348.—L'expression "*gens de service*" employée par l'*article* 2101 du Code Civil * s'étend et s'applique aux différentes classes de personnes mentionnées dans *l'article précédent.*— (*Article* 2101. —*Voir* le *No.* 345.—*Article précédent, i. e. Article* 26.—*Voir le No.* 344.) Ord. No. 31 de 1867, Art. 27.

349.—Le privilège pour gages arriérés conféré aux différentes classes de personnes sus-mentionnées comme "*gens de service*" en vertu du dit *article* 2101 du Code Civil, est limité par ces présentes aux arriérés de gages dûs pour un temps n'excédant pas une année précédant immédiatement le jugement du Magistrat Stipendiaire condamnant l'employeur au paiement des dits arriérés.—(*Article* 2101.—*Voir le No.* 345.—*Voir aussi le No.* 344.) Idem, Art. 28.

350.—Le dit privilège sera admis au rang qui lui est propre ainsi qu'il est établi par le Code Civil, dans toutes distributions par contribution de sommes appartenant à l'employeur, ou dans Idem, Art. 29.

* Pour les classes de personnes qui, d'après l'ancienne loi, étaient considérées comme n'étant pas des "*gens de service*" à cause du taux de leurs salaires,—voir les Arrêts de la Cour Suprême dans les affaires *Montille* v. *Goburdhun et autres* et le *Crédit Foncier of Mauritius Limited* v. *Géraudflé et autres.*—(Piston's Report 1868.)

tribution by way of order of the sale price of the immoveable property of the employer, at whatever date subsequent to the judgment such distribution of either kind shall take place : provided the parties producing such privileged claim justify that they have used due diligence to enforce payment of their claim, and that they have been unavoidably prevented from obtaining payment at an earlier period. Provided also that several judgments, in favor of the same party, shall in no case entitle him to claim payment of Wages by way of privilege for more than the period to which such privilege is limited as above, which period shall be computed backwards from the date of the last of such judgments.

Idem, Art. 30. 351.— The manager and *employés* upon an estate other than the *gens de service* as hereinbefore defined, have a privilege for arrears of salary taking rank immediately after the privilege of the said *gens de service,* and limited to six months next preceding the judgment condemning the employer to the payment of such salaries. The privilege of the several parties above mentioned shall be admitted in its rank, as hereby established, in the same manner and subject to the same conditions as is hereinbefore provided for the privilege of the *gens de service.*

Ord. No. 33 of 1853, Art. 107. 352.— When any Bankrupt shall have been indebted at the time of issuing the fiat or filing the petition for adjudication of Bankruptcy to any clerk or servant of such Bankrupt in respect of the wages or salary of such clerk, or servant, it shall be lawful for the Court upon proof thereof to order so much as shall be so due, not exceeding three months wages or salary, and not exceeding thirty pounds, to be paid to such clerk, or servant, out of the estate of such Bankrupt; and such clerk or servant shall be at liberty to prove for any sum exceeding such amount.

Idem, Art. 108. 352 (*bis.*)— When any Bankrupt shall have been indebted, at the time of issuing the fiat or filing the petition for adjudication of Bankruptcy, to any agricultural laborer or workman, in respect of the wages or labor of such laborer or workman, it shall be lawful for the Court, upon proof thereof, to order so much as shall be so due, not exceeding one year's wages to be paid to such laborer

toutes distributions par voie d'Ordre du prix de vente des biens immobiliers de l'employeur, à quelque date postérieure au jugement que les dites distributions aient lieu ; pourvu que les personnes produisant cette créance privilégiée prouvent qu'elles ont fait toute diligence pour obtenir le paiement de leur créance, et qu'elles ont été empêchées par des circonstances indépendantes de leur volonté d'en obtenir le paiement plus tôt. Pourvu aussi que plusieurs jugements en faveur de la même partie ne lui donnent en aucun cas le droit de réclamer le paiement de Gages par privilège pour un temps plus long que celui auquel ce privilège est limité ci-dessus, et ce temps sera calculé en partant du dernier de ces jugements.

351.—L'administrateur d'une propriété et les employés autres que les *gens de service* tels qu'ils sont définis plus haut, ont un privilège pour salaires arriérés prenant rang immédiatement après le privilège des gens de service sus-dits, limité aux six mois qui précéderont immédiatement le jugement condamnant l'employeur au paiement des dits salaires. Le privilège des différentes personnes sus-mentionnées sera admis à son rang, ainsi qu'il est établi par ces présentes, de la même manière et aux mêmes conditions que celles déjà prévues pour le privilège des gens de service. Idem, Art. 30.

352.—Lorsqu'un failli devra, au moment de la délivrance du permis de poursuivre ou du dépôt de la requête en déclaration de faillite, à un commis ou serviteur du dit failli pour les Gages ou Salaires de ce commis ou serviteur, la Cour pourra, sur preuve de ce fait, ordonner que portion du montant de la dette, n'excédant pas trois mois de Gages ou Salaires et n'excédant pas trente livres sterling, soit payée au dit commis ou serviteur, sur les biens du dit failli, et le dit commis ou serviteur pourra prouver le surplus de sa créance. Ord. No. 33 de 1853, Art. 107.

352 (*bis*).—Lorsqu'un failli devra, au moment de la délivrance du permis de poursuivre ou du dépôt de la requête en déclaration de faillite, à un travailleur agricole ou à un ouvrier, etc., pour Gages ou travail du dit travailleur ou ouvrier, la Cour pourra, sur preuve de ce fait, ordonner que portion du montant de la dette, n'excédant pas une année de Gages, soit payée au dit travailleur Idem, Art. 108.

out of the estate of such Bankrupt; and such laborer or workman shall be at liberty to prove for any sum exceeding such amount.

For the disposal of Wages due to deceased Indian Immigrants or Liberated African Slaves.—*See Nos.* 546 *et seq.*

CHAPTER II.

Lodging.

Ord. No. 31 of 1867, Art. 24.

353.—Every person employing laborers upon a country estate, shall provide them with sufficient and wholesome lodging, according to the usage of the Colony; and whenever it shall be proved to the satisfaction of the Stipendiary Magistrate of the District that the lodging of any laborer is insufficient, unhealthy, or otherwise unfit to be inhabited by such laborer, the said Magistrate shall order that, within a certain period to be by him fixed, the employer shall cause such dwelling to be altered or repaired, so as to render it wholesome and sufficient, or another dwelling to be supplied to the laborer; and he may require the employer to make the laborer an allowance or indemnity of three pence for each day from the date of his order until the laborer be properly lodged, to the satisfaction of the said Magistrate; and any Master failing to comply with any such order of the Magistrate, shall be liable to a fine not exceeding £5, and the laborer shall be entitled to demand cancellation of his contract.—(*See also Nos.* 378 *and* 510.)

MEDICAL CARE AND BURIAL.

I.—*Medical Care.*
II.—*Burial.*

CHAPTER I.

Medical Care.

Ord. No. 29 of 1865, Art. 2.

354.—Every person who shall have in his employment and residing on his premises, under written or verbal Contract of

sur les biens du dit failli ; et le dit travailleur ou ouvrier pourra prouver le surplus de sa créance.

Pour la manière de disposer des Gages dûs à des Immigrants Indiens ou à des Esclaves Africains Libérés qui meurent dans la Colonie,— *Voir les Nos.* 546 *et suiv.*

CHAPITRE II.

Logement.

353.—Toute personne qui emploiera des travailleurs sur un établissement rural, leur préparera des logements suffisants et sains, conformément aux usages de la Colonie ; et toutes les fois qu'il sera prouvé à la satisfaction du Magistrat Stipendiaire du District, que le logement d'un travailleur est insuffisant, malsain, ou autrement impropre à être habité par ce travailleur, le dit Magistrat ordonnera que dans un certain délai qui sera par lui fixé, l'employeur fasse modifier ou réparer le logement dont on se sera plaint, de manière à le rendre sain et suffisant, ou qu'un autre logement soit fourni au travailleur ; et il exigera que l'employeur paie au travailleur une compensation ou indemnité de trois pence par jour à partir de la date de la plainte jusqu'à ce que le travailleur soit logé convenablement, à la satisfaction du dit Magistrat ; et tout maître qui ne se conformera pas au dit ordre du Magistrat, sera passible d'une amende n'excédant pas £ 5, et le travailleur aura le droit de demander l'annulation de son contrat.—(*Voir aussi les Nos.* 378 *et* 510.) Ord. No. 31 de 1867, Art. 24.

DES SOINS MÉDICAUX ET DE L'INHUMATION.

I. — *Soins Médicaux.*
II. — *Inhumation.*

CHAPITRE I.

Soins Médicaux.

354.—Toute personne qui aura à son service et résidant sur son établissement, en vertu d'un contrat de service écrit ou Ord. No. 29 de 1865, Art. 2.

Service, thirty or more *Servants* as the term is defined in the Royal Order in Council of 7th September 1838, shall require to have, for the accommodation and treatment of such servants in case of sickness, an Hospital in accordance with the provisions of this Ordinance. The provisions of this Article shall apply whether the Master is proprietor or only occupant of the said premises, and although the same are only used by him for the lodging of his servants. The said provisions shall also apply whether the said servants be engaged in agricultural or other kind of labor. Provided always that persons having establishments of servants aforesaid within the district of Port Louis, shall be held to comply with the said provisions in regard to such servants by sending those of them who require Hospital treatment to the Civil Hospital of Port Louis, and retaining them therein until they shall be discharged from the said Hospital.—(*Servant.—For the definition of this term—,see No.* 549.)

Idem, Art. 3. 355.—Every Job-Contractor having in his employment thirty or more servants aforesaid, whether the said servants do or do not reside on the premises of the Job-Contractor, shall be bound either to have an Hospital in terms of this Ordinance upon premises belonging to or hired by him, or to have, by arrangements with the owner or lessee of the estate on which his laborers work, sufficient accommodation, in the Hospital of the said estate, for his servants working thereupon, according to the scale hereinafter provided. In the latter case the Job-Contractor shall be bound to notify to the Stipendiary Magistrate the said arrangement; and, on failure to do so, shall be held not to have complied with the provisions of this article.

Idem, Art. 4. 356.— The provisions of the two preceding articles shall apply in all cases where servants, to the number of 30 or more, are, in the opinion of the Stipendiary Magistrate, really engaged for one and the same undertaking, notwithstanding that in their contracts of service different persons appear as their masters.

Idem, Art. 5. 357.—The following rules shall be observed, regarding all

verbal, trente ou un plus grand nombre de *serviteurs*, tels qu'ils sont définis par l'Ordre Royal en Conseil du 7 Septembre 1838, devra avoir, pour loger et soigner les dits serviteurs en cas de maladie, un Hôpital établi conformément aux dispositions de la présente Ordonnance.—(*Serviteur.—Pour la définition de ce terme—voir le No.* 549.)

Les dispositions de cet article s'appliqueront également, que le maître soit propriétaire, ou qu'il soit simple locataire de l'établissement, et quoiqu'il ne s'en serve que pour loger ses serviteurs. Les dites dispositions s'appliqueront également, que les dits serviteurs soient employés à des travaux agricoles, ou à tous autres travaux. Néanmoins les personnes qui auront, dans les limites du District de Port Louis, des établissements où seront logés des serviteurs au nombre ci-dessus fixé, seront considérées comme ayant satisfait aux dites dispositions à l'égard des dits serviteurs, si elles envoient ceux d'entre eux qui auront besoin de se faire soigner dans un Hôpital, à l'Hôpital Civil du Port Louis, et les y laissent jusqu'à ce qu'ils soient déchargés du dit Hôpital.

355.—Tout Entrepreneur (*job-contractor*) ayant à son service trente ou un plus grand nombre de serviteurs comme il est dit plus haut, que les dits serviteurs résident ou ne résident pas sur l'établissement de l'Entrepreneur, sera tenu d'avoir, soit un Hôpital conformément aux dispositions de cette Ordonnance, sur un établissement à lui appartenant, ou loué par lui, soit, par convention avec le propriétaire ou locataire du domaine sur lequel ses serviteurs travailleront, des places suffisantes dans l'Hôpital du dit domaine, à la disposition de ceux de ses serviteurs qui y travailleront, dans la proportion qui sera ci-après établie. Dans ce dernier cas, l'Entrepreneur sera tenu de notifier la dite convention au Magistrat Stipendiaire ; à défaut de quoi, il sera considéré comme n'ayant pas satisfait aux dispositions de cet article. Idem, Art. 3.

356.—Les dispositions des deux articles précédents seront applicables dans tous les cas où des serviteurs, au nombre de 30 ou plus, seront, dans l'opinion du Magistrat Stipendiaire, réellement engagés pour une seule et même entreprise, quoique dans leurs contrats de service différentes personnes paraissent comme leurs maîtres. Idem, Art. 4.

357.—Les règles suivantes seront observées relativement à Idem, Art. 5.

Hospitals which shall be established under the provisions of this Ordinance, vizt :—

1stly. The Hospital shall require to be situated on a convenient site, and to be of sufficient construction, as the same shall respectively be certified by one of the Inspecting Medical Officers hereinafter mentioned.

2ndly. It may be built of stone, planking, or palissades, and may be roofed with tiles, bardeaux, slates, thatch, or metal : provided that in the last mentioned case there be a ceiling underneath the roofing, with proper means of ventilation, certified as aforesaid.

3rdly. The size of the Hospital shall require to be on the footing of at least sixty square feet Imperial Standard measure, and five hundred cubic feet aforesaid, respectively, for each bed.

4thly. It shall be separated from any camp of laborers, and be completely enclosed, by means of a fence, to the satisfaction of such Inspecting Officer, as certified by him.

5thly. It shall contain, at all times, sufficient accommodation and beds, or other sleeping places, for at least the following proportion of the servants,—the number and sufficiency to be certified as aforesaid, vizt : Three per centum on the number of the servants engaged at the time : but provided that in no case shall the Hospital contain beds or sleeping places for fewer than four servants.

6thly. It shall be suitably provided with medecines of the kinds, quantities, and qualities, respectively, to the satisfaction of the Stipendiary Magistrate, after receiving the report of the Medical Attendant of the servants for whom the Hospital is intended, and making such further enquiries as he may consider necessary.

7thly. It shall be provided with Hospital Attendants, qualified for the duty of attending to the sick as such Attendants, certified by the Medical Attendant aforesaid.

8thly. It may consist of either one building, or of two or more separate buildings.

tous les Hôpitaux qui seront établis conformément aux dispositions de la présente Ordonnance, savoir :

1o. L'Hôpital devra être situé dans un endroit convenable, et de dimension suffisante, ainsi que devra respectivement en faire foi le certificat de l'un des Médecins Inspecteurs ci-après mentionnées.

2o. Il pourra être construit en pierres, en planches ou en palissades, et pourra être couvert en tuiles, bardeaux, ardoises, paille ou métal, pourvu que dans ce dernier cas il y ait un plafond sous le toit, et les moyens d'une ventilation convenable, le tout certifié ainsi qu'il est dit plus haut.

3o. La dimension de l'hôpital devra être dans la proportion d'au moins soixante pieds carrés (mesure impériale) et de cinq cents pieds cubes, respectivement, pour chaque lit.

4o. Il devra être séparé des camps de travailleurs et entièrement enclos au moyen d'une haie, à la satisfaction du dit Inspecteur, ainsi qu'il sera certifié par lui.

5o. Il devra contenir en tous temps une installation suffisante et des lits ou couchettes au moins dans la proportion suivante des serviteurs, les dits nombre et suffisance devront être certifiés ainsi qu'il est dit plus haut : Trois pour cent du nombre des serviteurs engagés à ce moment : mais pourvu que, en aucun cas, l'Hôpital ne contienne pas moins de quatre lits ou couchettes pour les dits serviteurs.

6o. Il sera convenablement approvisionné de médecines de tous genres, en quantité et de qualité à la satisfaction du Magistrat Stipendiaire, après qu'il aura reçu le rapport du Médecin des serviteurs auxquels l'Hôpital sera destiné, et après avoir pris tous autres renseignements qu'il jugera convenable de prendre.

7o. Il sera pourvu d'infirmiers capables de remplir les fonctions d'infirmiers ainsi qu'il sera certifié par le dit Médecin de l'Hôpital.

8o. Il pourra se composer d'un seul corps de logis ou de deux ou plusieurs bâtiments séparés.

9thly. It shall be reserved exclusively for the purposes of an Hospital.

10thly. In case the Inspecting Medical Officer shall refuse to grant a certificate in any of the cases in this article provided, he shall be bound without delay, on application of any party concerned, to put such refusal in writing, and to deliver to the said party a copy thereof certified by him to be correct; upon which the said party shall be entitled to appeal against such refusal to the General Board of Health, who, after hearing parties and making such inquiry as they shall deem proper, shall determine whether or not such certificate ought to be granted, and, in the event of their deciding that it ought to be granted, their decision and resolution to that effect shall be equivalent in all respects to the certificate of the Inspecting Medical Officer in the matter or matters to which the same shall relate.

Idem, Art. 6. 358.— The requirements of the preceding article shall be applicable to all Hospitals already existing upon estates, but provided that any Hospital which shall have been approved under the provisions of Article 1st of *Ordinance No.* 6 *of* 1845, shall be held sufficient under the provisions of this Ordinance, so far as relates to its construction, site, and enclosures. Every such Hospital, however, shall require to contain accommodation and beds, or other sleeping places, on the scale hereinbefore provided. — (*Ordinance No.* 6 *of* 1845 *was the former law on Estate-Hospitals; it was repealed by Ord. No.* 29 *of* 1865.—*See No.* 28 *of the Appendix.*)

Idem, Art. 7. 359.—Moreover, every person as described in *Articles 2nd and 3rd*, respectively, shall be bound, in case of epidemic or infectious disease breaking out among his servants, to build or procure additional Hospital accommodation, of a temporary nature, for such of his servants as cannot be duly accommodated in the Hospital existing on his premises at the time. Such temporary Hospitals shall be built or procured on the order of the Stipendiary Magistrate, and shall require to be to his satisfaction, after due enquiry. —(*Articles 2nd and 3rd.*—*See Nos.* 354 *and* 355.)

9o. Il sera consacré exclusivement aux besoins d'un Hôpital.

10o. Dans le cas où le Médecin Inspecteur refuserait d'accorder un certificat dans l'un des cas prévus par cet article, il sera tenu, sur la demande d'une partie intéressée, de mettre sans retard ce refus par écrit, et d'en délivrer à cette partie une copie certifiée conforme par lui; sur ce, la dite partie aura le droit d'appeler de ce refus à la Commission Générale de Santé qui, après avoir entendu les parties et pris les renseignements qu'elle jugera nécessaires, décidera si ce certificat doit ou non être accordé, et dans le cas où elle déciderait qu'il doit être accordé, sa décision sera équivalente à tous égards au certificat du Médecin Inspecteur pour les matières auxquelles elle aura rapport.

358.—Les conditions exigées par l'article précédent seront applicables à tous les Hôpitaux existant déjà sur les propriétés, néanmoins tout Hôpital qui aura été approuvé conformément aux dispositions de *l'Article* 1*er de l'Ordonnance No.* 6 *de* 1845, sera considéré comme suffisant d'après les dispositions de la présente Ordonnance, mais seulement en ce qui concernera sa construction, sa situation et ses clôtures. Cet Hôpital devra cependant contenir une installation convenable et des lits ou couchettes dans la proportion déjà établie plus haut.—(*L'Ordonnance No.* 6 *de* 1845 *était l'ancienne loi sur les Hôpitaux ; elle a été abrogée par l'Ordonnance No.* 29 *de* 1865—*Voir le No.* 23 *de l'Appendice.*) Idem, Art. 6.

359.—De plus, toute personne mentionnée dans les *Articles* 2 *et* 3, respectivement, sera tenue, dans le cas où une épidémie ou une maladie contagieuse éclaterait parmi ses serviteurs, de construire ou de se procurer une installation additionnelle, d'une nature temporaire, pour les soins à donner à ceux de ses serviteurs qui ne pourront pas être convenablement logés dans l'Hôpital existant à ce moment sur l'établissement. Ces Hôpitaux temporaires devront être construits ou acquis sur l'ordre du Magistrat Stipendiaire, et devront être à sa satisfaction après qu'il aura pris tous les renseignements nécessaires.—(*Articles* 2 *et* 3.—*Voir les Nos.* 354 *et* 355.) Idem, Art. 7.

Idem, Art. 8. 360.—Any person who shall be required by this Ordinance to have an Hospital, under the provisions of the preceding *Articles 2nd, 3rd, 4th, 5th, and 6th,* and who shall fail to have such Hospital completed, furnished, and equipped, in terms of this Ordinance, within six. calendar months from the date when this Ordinance shall come into operation (or, in case the servants for whom such Hospital is required shall not be in his service till after this Ordinance shall come into operation, then within four calendar months after they shall be so in his service), shall incur a penalty of not less than £ 5 or more than £ 20 Sterling; and the Stipendiary Magistrate shall appoint a period,not exceeding three calendar months, within which such Hospital shall be provided. Every such person failing to have such Hospital as aforesaid within such period, shall incur a penalty of not less than £ 20 or more than £ 50 sterling; which penalty shall be repeated as often as he shall fail to comply with the order of the Stipendiary Magistrate to have an Hospital as aforesaid within any subsequent period to be fixed as aforesaid. The same penalties shall be incurred by any person aforesaid who shall fail to keep up an Hospital in terms of *Articles 2nd, 3rd, 4th, 5th and 6th.*— (*Articles 2 et seq*: — *See No.* 354 *et seq.*)

The same penalties shall also be incurred in case any person aforesaid shall fail to build or procure temporary Hospital accommodation as required by *Article 7th* hereof: but, in this case, the periods to be fixed by the Magistrate for the same, shall not exceed three weeks.—(*Article 7th.—See No.* 359.)

Idem, Art. 9. 361.—With regard to any servant aforesaid, being one for whom Hospital accommodation is required under the provisions of this Ordinance, it shall be a sufficient ground for breaking his contract of service, that his master shall have failed to have an Hospital completed, furnished, and provided, in terms of *Articles 2nd, 3rd, 4th, 5th, and 6th of this Ordinance*: provided such failure shall have continued during three calendar months after the master shall have been called upon so to do by notice from the Stipendiary Magistrate, in terms of Schedule A.—(*Articles 2 et seq.—See Nos.* 354 *et seq.*)

360.—Toute personne qui sera requise par cette Ordonnance d'avoir un Hôpital, en vertu des *Articles* 2, 3, 4, 5 *et* 6 qui précèdent et qui n'aura pas achevé, meublé et installé cet Hôpital conformément aux dispositions de cette Ordonnance, dans les six mois à partir de la date de la mise en vigueur de cette Ordonnance (ou, dans le cas où les serviteurs, pour lesquels cet Hôpital sera requis, n'entreront à son service qu'après la mise en vigueur de cette Ordonnance, dans les quatre mois après qu'ils seront entrés à son service) sera passible d'une amende qui ne sera pas de moins de £ 5 ni de plus de £ 20 sterling ; et le Magistrat Stipendiaire fixera un délai qui n'excédera pas trois mois, pendant lequel cet Hôpital devra être installé. Et si cette personne ne fait pas installer cet Hôpital pendant le dit délai, elle sera passible d'une amende qui ne sera pas moins de £ 20 ni de plus de £ 50 sterling ; et cette amende, lui sera infligée à chaque fois qu'elle négligera de se conformer à l'ordre du Magistrat Stipendiaire d'installer un Hôpital comme il est dit ci-dessus, pendant tout autre délai qu'il pourra lui accorder de la manière indiquée ci-dessus. Les mêmes peines seront encourues par toute personne sus-dite qui n'entretiendra pas un Hôpital conformément aux dispositions des *Articles* 2, 3, 4, 5 *et* 6.—(*Articles* 2 *et suiv* :—*Voir les Nos*. 354 *et suiv*.) Idem, Art. 8.

Les mêmes peines seront aussi encourues dans le cas où l'une des personnes sus-dites manquerait de construire ou de se procurer un Hôpital temporaire tel qu'il est requis par *l'article* 7 ; mais en ce cas, les délais qui seront accordés par le Magistrat pour l'installation de cet Hôpital, n'excéderont pas trois semaines.—(*Article* 7.—*Voir le No*. 359.)

361.—A l'égard des serviteurs sus-mentionnés, s'ils sont de la catégorie de ceux pour lesquels l'installation d'un Hôpital est requise en vertu des dispositions de cette Ordonnance, il y aura cause suffisante pour rompre leur contrat de service, si leur maître n'a pas achevé, meublé et pourvu un Hôpital conformément aux dispositions des *Articles* 2, 3, 4, 5 *et* 6 *de cette Ordonnance* : pourvu que le dit maître soit resté trois mois sans se conformer à l'avis qui lui aura été donné à cet effet par le Magistrat Stipendiaire, aux termes de l'Annexe A.—(*Articles* 2 *et suiv* :—*Voir les Nos*. 354 *et suiv*.) Idem. Art. 9.

SCHEDULE A.

Take notice that it has been brought to my knowledge that you, although bound to provide for your servants at , in this District, an Hospital completed, furnished, and provided, in terms of the Ordinance above mentioned, yet you have failed so to do, and more especially (*The particulars of the failure to be mentioned here.*) You are accordingly hereby required to comply with the provisions of the said Ordinance, and more particularly in the respects above mentioned. And you will take notice, that, if you shall fail so to do, for the period of three calendar months from the date of this notice, the said servants will be entitled to have their contracts of service with you broken, in terms of the aforesaid Ordinance.

Stipendiary Court House of	Signed: C. D.,
this day of 186 .	*Stipendiary Magistrate for the District of* .

Idem, Art. 10. **362.**—Any person who shall have an Hospital as hereinbefore provided, shall be entitled to insist that any one of the laborers for whom such Hospital shall be intended, shall proceed to such Hospital when he shall be sick, and shall remain therein until his recovery. Any laborer who shall refuse so to do, and who shall absent himself from his work, shall, during the whole time of such refusal and absence, be regarded in law and fact as *unlawfully absent*, and shall be liable to *punishment* accordingly.—(*Punishment for unlawful absence.—See No.* 399 *et seq.*)

Moreover, in case any laborer aforesaid who shall be insane or suffering under infectious or epidemic disease, shall refuse to proceed to or remain in any Hospital aforesaid, or in any temporary Hospital accommodation which shall be provided in terms of *Article* 7 hereof, it shall be lawful for the employer of such laborer, on the written requisition of the Medical Attendant of his laborers, to force the said laborer to proceed to and remain in such Hospital or Hospital accommodation, until duly discharged therefrom.—(*Article 7.—See No.* 359.)

The provisions of this Article shall apply to the servants, although fewer in number than 30, on any premises upon which there shall be an Hospital certified to be properly built, furnished, and provided, as aforesaid.

Idem, Art. 11. **363.**—When any person or persons shall have laborers aforesaid in their service, but residing at different places, it shall be

ANNEXE A.

Avis vous est donné qu'il a été porté à ma connaissance que, quoique vous soyez tenu d'avoir pour vos Serviteurs à , dans ce District, un Hôpital achevé, meublé et pourvu selon les termes de l'Ordonnance sus-mentionnée, vous avez omis de le faire, et plus particulièrement (*Les détails de l'omission seront mentionnés ici.*) Vous êtes en conséquence requis par ces présentes de vous conformer aux dispositions de la dite Ordonnance, et plus particulièrement en ce qui concerne les détails sus-mentionnés. Et avis vous est donné que si vous omettez de le faire pendant trois mois à partir de la date de cet avis, les dits Serviteurs auront le droit de faire rompre leurs contrats de service avec vous, aux termes de la dite Ordonnance.

Tribunal du Magistrat Stipendiaire de

ce jour de 186 .

Signé : C. D.,

Magistrat Stipendiaire du District de

362.—Toute personne qui aura un Hôpital ainsi qu'il est prévu ci-dessus, aura le droit d'insister pour que les travailleurs, pour lesquels cet Hôpital aura été bâti, s'y rendent toutes les fois qu'ils seront malades, et y restent jusqu'à leur guérison. Tout travailleur qui refusera de le faire, et qui s'absentera de son travail, sera, pendant tout le temps de ce refus et de cette absence, considéré en droit et en fait comme *illégalement absent,* et sera en conséquence passible d'une peine.—(*Peines infligées en cas d'absence illégale.*—(*Voir le No.* 399 *et suiv.*) Idem, Art. 1

De plus, dans le cas où un des dits serviteurs serait atteint d'aliénation mentale, ou souffrirait d'une maladie contagieuse ou épidémique, et refuseroit d'aller et de rester dans les dits Hôpitaux ou dans les Hôpitaux temporaires qui seront préparés conformément aux dispositions de *l'Article* 7 de cette Ordonnance, l'employeur du dit serviteur pourra, sur la réquisition écrite du Médecin de ses serviteurs, forcer le dit serviteur à se rendre et à rester dans le dit Hôpital, fixe ou temporaire, jusqu'à ce qu'il soit guéri.— (*Article 7.*—*Voir le No.* 359.)

Les dispositions de cet Article sont applicables aux serviteurs quoique en nombre inférieur à 30, sur tout Établissement où il y aura un Hôpital qui sera certifié être convenablement bâti, meublé et pourvu, comme il est dit ci-dessus.

363.—Lorsque une ou plusieurs personnes auront des travailleurs à leur service, mais résidant en différents endroits, elles Idem, Art. 11.

lawful for him or them to provided a "Union" Hospital for such laborers: provided that the said Hospital be not situated at a greater distance than three British statute miles from the places where the said laborers reside. The foregoing provisions of this Ordinance shall apply to all such Hospitals.

Idem, Art. 12. 364.—Every person having in his service 30 or more servants aforesaid, for whom, by terms of his Contract or by any law he shall be bound to provide medical attendance, is required within one month from the *date of this Ordinance coming into operation*, to engage a duly qualified Medical Practitioner, for professional attendance on his said servants, and to notify to the Stipendiary Magistrate of the District the name of such Medical Attendant, the number, as nearly as may be, of laborers he is engaged to attend, and also the acceptance by the Medical Attendant of the said employment.—(*The Ordinance came into operation on the 1st January* 1866.)

The said notification shall be made in duplicate in terms of Schedule B to this Ordinance; one of which duplicates shall be retained by the said Magistrate, and the other of which shall be marked with his *visa* and be returned to the person who sent the same Any person aforesaid failing to make such notification, shall incur a penalty of Forty shillings sterling, to be imposed by the Stipendiary Magistrate.

SCHEDULE B.

To the Stipendiary Magistrate of the District of (*Date*)

Sir,

I hereby notify to you that I have engaged , residing at , being a duly qualified Medical Practitioner, to attend professionally the servants in my employment and residing at , in the District of , and that the number, as nearly as may be, of laborers whom he is engaged to attend, is

I have, &c.

* (*Signature.*)

I, the above named Medical Practitioner, do hereby certify that I have agreed to attend the servants above mentioned from the day of till the day of 18 .

(*Signature.*)

Dated this day of 186 .

* If the party cannot write, he will mark with a cross in the presence of the Stipendiary Magistrate, who will certify to the said mark.

pourront avoir un Hôpital commun pour ces travailleurs ; pourvu que le dit Hôpital ne soit pas situé à plus de trois milles anglais des endroits où résideront ces travailleurs.—Les dispositions ci-dessus de cette Ordonnance seront applicables à tous ces Hôpitaux.

364.—Toute personne ayant à son service 30 ou un plus grand nombre de serviteurs sus-dits, auxquels, aux termes de son contrat ou en vertu d'une loi, elle sera tenue de donner des soins médicaux, devra, dans le mois qui suivra *la date de la mise en vigueur de cette Ordonnance,* s'entendre avec un Médecin dûment diplômé, pour soigner ses dits serviteurs, et devra notifier au Magistrat Stipendiaire du District le nom de ce Médecin, et le nombre aussi exact que possible de travailleurs qu'il se sera engagé à visiter, et aussi l'acceptation du dit service médical par le dit Médecin.—(*Cette Ordonnance a été mise en vigueur le* 1*er Janvier* 1866.) Idem, Art. 12.

La dite notification sera faite en duplicata, conformément à l'Annexe B de cette Ordonnance ; l'un des duplicatas sera gardé par le dit Magistrat, l'autre sera visé par lui et rendu à la personne qui l'aura envoyé.—Toute personne sus-dite qui omettra de donner cet avis, encourra une amende de quarante shillings sterling qui sera prononcée par le Magistrat Stipendiaire.

ANNEXE B.

Au Magistrat Stipendiaire du District de } (*Date*)

Monsieur,

Je vous donne avis par ces présentes que je suis convenu avec demeurant à , Médecin pratiquant, dûment qualifié qu'il visitera professionnellement les travailleurs à mon service, et demeurant à dans le District de , et que le nombre, aussi exact que possible, de travailleurs qu'il s'est engagé à visiter, est de

J'ai l'honneur d'être, etc.

* (*Signature.*)

Je soussigné, le Médecin, sus-mentionné, certifie par ces présentes, que je me suis engagé à visiter les serviteurs sus-mentionnés depuis le jour de jusqu'au jour de 186 .

(*Signature.*)

Daté ce jour de 186 .

* Si la personne ne peut écrire, elle fera sa croix en présence du Magistrat Stipendiaire qui la certifiera comme vraie.

Ord. No. 31 of 1867, Art. 65. **365.—A penalty not exceeding £ 20 and not less than £ 5, shall be incurred by :—**

1st. Any person who, in any notification as provided in *Article* 12 *of Ordinance No.* 29 *of* 1865, shall knowingly state the number of servants for whom he has engaged a Medical Practitioner, at a smaller number than that of all the servants employed and residing at the place referred to in the said notification.

2nd. Any Medical Practitioner who shall grant any Certificate as in Schedule B to the said Ordinance, knowing that the number of laborers stated in the notification preceding, and referred to in such certificate, is smaller than the whole number of laborers employed and residing at the place specified in the said notification. – (*Article* 12.—*See No.* 364.)

Ord. No. 29 of 1865, Art. 13. **366.—All persons who, after this Ordinance shall have come into operation, shall have in their service 30 or more laborers, as described in the immediately *preceding Article,* shall be bound to make a similar notification to the Stipendiary Magistrate, without delay. Any such person who shall fail, for six days after receiving a written requisition from the Stipendiary Magistrate of his District, to give such notification, shall be liable to the penalty provided in the last *preceding Article.* Provided that nothing in this Ordinance contained shall be held to affect the obligation of any employer having fewer than 30 laborers in his service, to provide Medical Attendance for them in terms of law.– (*Preceding Article.—See No.* 364.—*See also No.* 321.)**

Idem, Art 14. **367.—When any person having the number of Servants mentioned in the *two last preceding Articles,* shall, from any cause whatever, cease to have for his Servants the Medical Attendant whom he shall have notified in terms of either of the *preceding Articles,* or when the Attendance of such Medical Attendant on his Servants shall be interrupted for any period of fourteen days or upwards, such person shall be bound, within one week from such cessation or interruption, to procure another Medical Attendant duly qualified as aforesaid, in his place, and to notify the name of such Medical Attendant to the Stipendiary Magistrate,**

365.—Une amende n'excédant pas £ 20 mais qui ne sera pas au-dessous de £ 5, sera encourue par :— Ord. No. 31 de 1867, Art. 65.

1o. Toute personne qui, dans un des avis prévus par *l'Article 12 de l'Ordonnance No. 29 de* 1865, donnera sciemment comme étant le nombre des serviteurs pour lesquels il s'est assuré les soins d'un Médecin, un nombre inférieur à celui de tous les serviteurs employés et demeurant à l'endroit mentionné dans le dit avis.

2o. Tout Médecin qui accordera un Certificat selon la Cédule B annexée à la dite Ordonnance, sachant que le nombre des travailleurs indiqué dans l'avis mentionné dans ce Certificat, est moindre que le total des travailleurs employés et demeurant à l'endroit spécifié dans le dit avis.—(*Article* 12.—*Voir le No.* 364.)

366.—Toute personne qui, après que cette Ordonnance aura été mise en vigueur, aura à son service 30 ou un plus grand nombre de travailleurs, ainsi qu'il est expliqué dans *l'Article précédent*, sera tenue de donner un avis semblable au Magistrat Stipendiaire, sans délai. Toute personne qui omettra dans les six jours qui suivront la réception d'une demande écrite du Magistrat Stipendiaire de son District, de donner cet avis, encourra la peine prévue en *l'Article précédent*. Pourvu que rien de ce qui est contenu en cette Ordonnance ne puisse être considéré comme affectant l'obligation de tout employeur ayant moins de 30 travailleurs à son service, de leur assurer de soins Médicaux, conformément aux termes de la loi.—(*Article précédent.—Voir le No.* 364.—*Voir aussi le No.* 321.) Ord. No. 29 de 1865, Art. 13.

367.—Lorsqu'une personne ayant à son service le nombre de Serviteurs mentionnés dans les *deux derniers articles qui précèdent*, cessera, pour une cause quelconque, d'avoir pour ses serviteurs l'assistance du Médecin dont il aura donné avis aux termes de l'un ou de l'autre des *articles précédents*, ou lorsque les visites de ce Médecin à ses serviteurs seront interrompues pendant 14 jours ou plus, cette personne sera tenue dans la semaine qui suivra la cessation ou l'interruption de ces visites, de se procurer un autre Médecin dûment qualifié comme il est dit ci-dessus, et de notifier le nom de ce nouveau Médecin au Magistrat Stipendiaire, et en Idem, Art. 14.

and, in case of failure, shall be liable to a penalty of Forty shillings.—(*Preceding Articles.—See Nos.* 364 *et* 366.)

Notwithstanding, it shall be lawful to any Medical Attendant, aforesaid, when unable from any cause to perform his professional duties personally, to perform the same by a substitute, being a duly qualified Medical Practitioner in the Colony; and, where such substitute shall perform the said duties, the Attendance of the said Medical Attendant shall not be considered as interrupted.

Idem. Art, 15. 368.—Every Medical Practitioner who shall have agreed to attend upon any Servants under the provisions of this Ordinance, shall be bound, under a penalty not less than £ 2 or more than £ 10 sterling, to make not fewer than the following number of visits, periodically, to such Servants, such periodical visits being in addition to any occasional visits which shall be requisite under special circumstances, vizt.:—

Where the servants are not fewer than 50 or more than 200, one visit per week.

Where they are 200 or more, two visits per week.

The provisions of this Article shall be held to have been observed, if the said Medical Practitioner shall have obtained the attendance as aforesaid of any qualified Medical Practitioner as his substitute.

Idem, Art. 16. 369.—There shall be kept, on all premises to be visited by any Medical Practitioner in terms of this Ordinance, a Register in the form hereunto appended, Schedule C, in which Register shall be entered, regularly, by the said Medical Practitioner, at the time of his visits, a note of the several items in the said Schedule mentioned; and such Register, the said Medical Practitioner shall be bound, on the requirement of the Stipendiary Magistrate or Inspecting Medical Officer of the District, to verify by a Certificate appended to the said form. When the entries aforesaid are not made in the handwriting of the Medical Attendant, he shall be bound to sign the same at the time of his visit.

cas d'omission, encourra une amende de quarante shillings.—(*Articles précédents.—Voir les Nos. 364 et 366.*)

Néanmoins, tout Médecin sus-dit pourra, lorsqu'il ne pourra remplir ses devoirs professionnels en personne, se faire remplacer par un substitut qui devra être un Médecin dûment qualifié pour exercer en cette Colonie ; et lorsque ce substitut remplira les dits devoirs, les visites du dit Médecin ordinaire ne seront pas considérées comme étant interrompues.

368.—Tout Médecin qui sera engagé à donner des soins à des serviteurs en vertu des dispositions de cette Ordonnance. sera tenu, sous peine d'être condamné à une amende qui ne sera pas moins de £ 2 ou de plus de £ 10 sterling, de faire au moins le nombre suivant de visites périodiques à ces serviteurs, ces visites devant être faites en outre des visites qui pourront de temps à autre être nécessaires dans des circonstances spéciales, à savoir : Idem, Art. 15.

Lorsque le nombre des serviteurs n'est pas moins de 50 ou pas plus de 200, une visite par semaine.

Lorsqu'il est de 200 ou plus, deux visites par semaine.

Les dispositions de cet Article seront considérées comme ayant été observées, si le dit Médecin s'est fait remplacer dans ses visites, comme il est dit plus haut, par un Médecin ayant qualité d'exercer comme son substitut.

369.—Il sera tenu sur tous les établissements visités par un Médecin aux termes de cette Ordonnance, un Registre dans la forme de l'Annexe C, dans lequel le dit Médecin devra faire régulièrement, au moment de ses visites, toutes les entrées qui sont détaillées dans la dite annexe ; et le dit Médecin sera tenu, sur la réquisition du Magistrat Stipendiaire ou du Médecin Inspecteur du District d'attester la fidélité de ce registre par un Certificat dans la forme de l'annexe C. Lorsque les dites entrées ne seront pas de l'écriture du Médecin, il sera tenu de les signer au moment de sa visite. Idem, Art. 16.

SCHEDULE C.

Medical Register for the Servants in the employment of , and residing at , in the District of

Date.	Hour of visit.	Names of		Age.	Sex.	Country.	Diseases.	Treatment.	Prescribed Diet, Wine, &c.	Result.	Remarks.
		Persons attended in Hospital.	Persons attended out of Hospital.								

I, *A. B.*, Medical Attendant of the Servants in the employment of , at , in the District of , do hereby certify that the entries in the above Register are true and correct, to the best of my knowledge and belief.

Signed :

A. B.

Doctor of Medicine.

Idem, Art. 17. 370.—A fine not less than £2 or more than £10 sterling, to be imposed by the Stipendiary Magistrate of the District, shall be incurred by :

1st. Every person having in his employment 30 servants, or more, for whom he is bound to provide medical attendance, who shall fail to provide and keep on his premises a Register as hereinbefore provided.

2nd. Every such person who shall fail to produce such Register to the Stipendiary Magistrate or to the Inspecting Medical Officer of the District, on being required by them, respectively, in writing, so to do.

3rd. Every Medical Practitioner who shall knowingly make or sign any false entry in any such Register.

4th. Every Medical Practitioner who, after receiving a written requisition from the Stipendiary Magistrate or Inspecting

ANNEXE C.

Registre d'Hôpital pour les Serviteurs employés par et demeurant à dans le District de

Date.	Heure de la visite.	Noms des		Age.	Sexe.	Pays	Maladies.	Traitement.	Régime prescrit, Vins, &a.	Résultat.	Remarques.
		Personnes visitées à l'Hôpital.	Personnes visitées hors de l'Hôpital.								

Je soussigné, *A. B.*, Médecin des Serviteurs employés par à , dans le District de , certifie par ces présentes que les entrées faites dans le Registre ci-dessus sont fidèles et correctes, autant que je puisse me le rappeler ;

Signé :

A B,
Docteur en Médecine.

370.—Une amende qui ne sera pas moins de £ 2 sterling ni plus de £ 10 sterling et qui sera imposée par le Magistrat Stipendiaire du District, sera encourue par : Idem, Art. 17.

1o. Toute personne ayant à son service trente serviteurs ou plus, auxquels il est tenu d'assurer des soins médicaux, et qui omettra de tenir sur son établissement un registre comme il est expliqué ci-dessus.

2o. Toute personne qui omettra de produire ce Registre au Magistrat Stipendiaire ou au Médecin Inspecteur du District, sur la demande écrite qui lui en sera faite par eux.

3o. Tout Médecin qui sciemment fera ou signera une entrée fausse sur ce Registre.

4o. Tout Médecin qui, après avoir reçu une réquisition écrite du Magistrat Stipendiaire ou du Médecin Inspecteur sus-dit,

Medical Officer aforesaid, shall fail to make and subscribe a certificate as hereinbefore provided, or who shall knowingly make any false statement in any such certificate.

Idem, Art. 18. 371.—In case any Medical Practitioner attending any Estate shall refuse or neglect, for any period of a fortnight or more at a time, to make his entries in the said "Register" as required by the foregoing provisions, it shall be lawful to the Stipendiary Magistrate, with the concurrence of the Protector of Immigrants, to prohibit the attendance of such Medical Practitioner at the premises to which such failure shall apply: such prohibition to continue for such time, not exceeding three calendar months, as the Protector of Immigrants and Stipendiary Magistrate shall jointly determine. The person whose Servants shall have been attended by such Medical Practitioner previous to the prohibition, shall be bound, on receiving written notice thereof from the Stipendiary Magistrate, to employ another Medical Attendant, (if any such can be procured within a reasonable distance), and to notify such employment to the Stipendiary Magistrate in terms of *Article* 12. In case of failure, he shall be liable to the penalties provided in the said Article.—(*Article* 12.—*See No.* 364)

Idem, Art. 19. 372.—Every Medical Practitioner who shall be engaged to attend professionally any Servants under the provisions of this Ordinance, shall be entitled, in any proceedings which shall be taken for recovering payment of his professional remuneration, to claim and obtain judgment therefor at the rate of four shillings sterling per annum for each Servant whom he shall be so engaged to attend. The said rate shall not be subject to modification or increase, in respect of any alleged contract between the Medical Practitioner and the Master of the said Servants.

Idem, Art. 20. 373.—The said rate shall be held to include an allowance for the Medical Attendance on the wives and children of the Servants for whom it is made, and which attendance shall be furnished accordingly: the term "wives" being held to include those married according to the customs of their country, although not regularly married according to the laws of the Colony.

Idem, Art. 21. 374.—Payment of the said remuneration may be recovered by summary process before the Stipendiary Magistrate, and may be

omettra de donner et de signer un certificat tel qu'il est requis plus haut, ou qui, sciemment, fera une fausse déclaration dans ce certificat.

371.—Dans le cas où le Médecin visitant une propriété, refuserait ou négligerait de faire ses entrées, dans le dit registre ainsi qu'il en est requis par les dispositions qui précèdent, pendant quatorze jours ou plus, le Magistrat Stipendiaire aura le droit, avec l'approbation du Protecteur des Immigrants, de défendre au Médecin de continuer ses visites sur l'établissement où cette omission aura eu lieu : cette défense continuera pendant tout le temps n'excédant pas trois mois, que le Protecteur des Immigrants et le Magistrat Stipendiaire fixeront conjointement. La personne dont les serviteurs auraient été visités par ce Médecin, avant cette défense, sera tenue, à la réception d'un avis écrit de cette défense, donné par le Magistrat Stipendiaire, d'employer un autre Médecin (si l'on peut s'en procurer un autre à une distance raisonnable) et de donner avis de son choix au Magistrat Stipendaire aux termes de l'*Article* 12. En cas d'omission, elle encourra les peines prévues par le dit Article.—(*Article* 12.—*Voir le No.* 364.) Idem, Art, 18.

372.—Tout Médecin qui se sera engagé à visiter professionnellement des serviteurs en vertu des dispositions de cette Ordonnance, aura le droit, lorsqu'il réclamera judiciairement le paiement de sa rémunération professionnelle, de demander et d'obtenir jugement à raison de quatre shillings sterling par an pour chaque serviteur qu'il se sera ainsi engagé à visiter. Ce dit taux ne pourra être ni diminué ni augmenté, en raison d'une prétendue convention entre le Médecin et le Maître de ces serviteurs. Idem, Art. 19.

373.—Le dit taux sera considéré comme comprenant une allocation pour les soins médicaux aux femmes et aux enfants des serviteurs pour lesquels il est établi, lesquels soins leur seront en conséquence donnés : le mot “femmes” comprend celles qui sont mariées suivant les coutumes de leur pays, quoiqu'elles ne soient pas régulièrement mariées suivant les lois de la Colonie. Idem, Art. 20.

374.—Le paiement de la dite rémunération peut être recouvré d'une manière sommaire devant le Magistrat Stipendiaire qui Idem, Art. 21.

enforced by imprisonment of the person liable therefor, in the same way and under the same conditions as are provided, regarding the Wages of Servants, by the Royal Order in Council of 7th September 1838.—(*See No.* 323.)

Every Medical Attendant who shall be engaged to attend any laborers under the provisions of this Ordinance, shall be bound to make, within one month after the expiry of each quarter of the year, a Return to the Stipendiary Magistrates of the several Districts in which he attends such laborers; in which Return he shall state the names of all persons in every such District who shall then be in arrear to him of his professional remuneration for such attendance, and the amount of such arrear.—And the Stipendiary Magistrate shall be bound without delay to institute proceedings *ex officio* for the recovery of such arrears, in the same manner as if complaint for the same had been laid before him by the said Medical Attendant.

Idem, Art. 22. 375.—There shall be a privilege upon the property on which the Servants work, and upon the goods and chattels belonging to their Master, for the remuneration hereinaforesaid, during a period of one year only; but such privilege shall not take priority of that of the laborers on the same Estate, for the recovery of their wages. Upon the sale of the said property, the Medical Attendant shall be entitled to payment of his said remuneration, on the Order of any Judge of the Supreme Court in Chambers, in the same way as is provided, with regard to Laborers' Wages, by *Ordinance No.* 15 *of* 1852, *Article* 17.—(*Article* 17.—*See No.* 343.)

Idem, Art. 23. 376.—It shall be lawful to the Governor to appoint two or more persons qualified as Medical Practitioners in the Colony, to be Inspecting Medical Officers for the purpose of carrying out the provisions of this Ordinance, and to assign to them such *Districts* as he shall think fit for the performance of their duties. Every such Medical Practitioner shall be remunerated in such a way as shall be fixed by the Governor with the advice of the Council of Government.—(*Districts.*—*See Nos.* 382 *and* 383.)

Idem, Art. 24. 377.—The General Sanitary Inspector shall be such Medical Inspecting Officer, within the District of Port Louis and such other District or Districts as shall be assigned to him.

pourra, en cas de non-paiement, ordonner l'emprisonnement de la personne qui en est responsable, de la même manière et aux mêmes conditions que celles qui sont prévues en ce qui concerne les gages des serviteurs, par l'Ordre Royal en Conseil du 7 Septembre 1838.—(*Voir le No* 323.)

Tout Médecin qui se sera engagé à visiter des travailleurs aux termes de cette Ordonnance, sera tenu de faire dans le mois qui suivra l'expiration de chaque trimestre de l'année, un Rapport aux Magistrats Stipendiaires des différents Districts dans lesquels il visitera ces travailleurs ; et de donner dans ce Rapport les noms de toutes les personnes qui resteront ses débiteurs pour la rémunération professionnelle à laquelle il a droit pour ses visites, et le montant de cet arriéré.—Et le Magistrat Stipendiaire sera tenu de commencer, d'office et sans délai, des poursuites pour le recouvrement de ces arriérés, comme si une plainte lui avait été portée dans ce but par le dit Médecin.

375.—Il y aura un privilège sur chaque propriété où les serviteurs travaillent, et sur les biens appartenant à leur maître, pour la rémunération mentionnée plus haut, pendant une année seulement ; mais ce privilège n'aura pas priorité sur celui des travailleurs de la même propriété pour le recouvrement de leurs gages. A la vente de la dite propriété, le Médecin aura le droit de se faire payer de sa dite rémunération, sur l'ordre d'un Juge de la Cour Suprême en Chambre, de la même manière qu'il est prévu par *l'Ordonnance No.* 15 *de* 1852 *Article* 17, à l'égard des gages des travailleurs.—(*Article* 17.—*Voir le No.* 343.) Idem, Art. 22.

376.—Le Gouverneur aura le droit de nommer une ou plusieurs personnes, exerçant comme Médecins dans la Colonie, Médecins-Inspecteurs dans le but de faire exécuter les dispositions de cette Ordonnance, et de leur assigner un ou plusieurs *Districts*, ainsi qu'il le jugera convenable, pour y remplir leurs fonctions. Chacun de ces Médecins sera rétribué de la manière qui sera déterminée par le Gouverneur de l'avis du Conseil du Gouvernement.—(*Districts.*—*Voir les Nos.* 382 *et* 383.) Idem, Art. 23.

377.—L'Inspecteur Sanitaire Général sera le Médecin-Inspecteur du District du Port Louis et de tels autres Districts qui lui seront assignés. Idem, Art. 24.

Every other such Medical Inspecting Officer shall, within the District or Districts to which he shall be appointed, perform the duties of an Inspecting Sanitary Officer under the provisions of Article 34 of Ordinance No. 18 of 1860 ; and, with reference to such duties, shall be termed Assistant General Sanitary Inspector within his said Districts ; provided that he shall not be, *ex-officio*, a Member of the General Board of Health. Provided also that nothing herein contained shall be held to interfere with the right of the General Board of Health to require the General Sanitary Inspector to act along with the said Board or under its direction, or to carry out and superintend the execution of any resolution or order of the said Board, respectively, in any part of the Colony.

Idem, Art. 25. 378.—Every person who shall be so appointed, shall have a right, at all times, and without any Warrant from a Magistrate, to visit any place within any District to which he shall be appointed, in which any servants. whatever be their number, shall be lodged, excepting only the Master's dwelling-house, when they shall be lodged therein, and also to enter and inspect all Hospitals for the accommodation of servants within his District, and all dependencies of such Hospitals, and to call for, and inspect, all Registers herein aforesaid. But provided that it shall not be lawful for any such Medical Inspector to interfere with the treatment, in a medical point of view, of any laborer by the Medical Attendant engaged by such laborer's employer. Any one who shall obstruct or impede any Medical Inspector aforesaid in any visit or inspection in terms of this Article, shall incur a penalty, not exceeding £ 20 sterling, to be imposed by the District Magistrate of the District.—(*See also No.* 353.)

Ord. No. 31 of 1867, Art. 76. 379.—All complaints for contraventions of *Ordinance No.* 29 *of* 1865 and of *this Ordinance*, may be made to and adjudicated on by the Stipendiary Magistrate of the district in which the Servants reside to which the said complaints refer.—(*Ordinance No.* 29 *of* 1865.—*See Nos.* 354 *et seq.*— *This Ordinance.*—*See No.* 365.)

Ord. No. 29 of 1865, Art. 27. 380.—Every judgment of a District or Stipendiary Magistrate under the provisions of this Ordinance, shall be subject to appeal to the Supreme Court, in questions both of law and of fact, when the same shall be for any amount exceeding £ 10 sterling.

Tout autre Médecin-Inspecteur devra remplir, dans les Districts pour lesquels il sera nommé, les fonctions d'un Inspecteur Sanitaire aux termes de l'Article 34 de l'Ordonnance No. 18 de 1860; et à l'égard de ces fonctions il sera appelé Assistant Inspecteur Sanitaire Général dans les limites de ses Districts; néanmoins il ne pourra pas être d'office un membre de la Commission Générale de Santé. Pourvu, toutefois, que rien de ce qui est ici contenu ne soit considéré comme touchant au droit de la Commission Générale de Santé de requérir l'Inspecteur Sanitaire Général d'agir avec la dite Commission et sous ses ordres, ou de veiller à l'exécution d'une résolution ou d'un ordre de la dite Commission en une partie quelconque de la Colonie.

378.—Toute personne ainsi nommée, aura le droit, en tout temps, et sans warrant d'un Magistrat, de visiter tout endroit, dans les limites du District pour lequel il sera nommé, dans lequel des serviteurs, quel que soit leur nombre, seront logés, excepté seulement la maison d'habitation du maître lorsqu'ils y seront logés, et aussi d'entrer dans tous Hôpitaux destinés aux serviteurs dans son District et toutes dépendances de ces Hôpitaux et de les inspecter, et de demander à voir et vérifier tous les Régistres ci-dessus mentionnés. Néanmoins le dit Médecin-Inspecteur ne pourra pas s'immiscer, au point de vue médical, dans la manière dont le Médecin ordinaire soignera les travailleurs qu'il se sera engagé à visiter. Quiconque empêchera le dit Médecin-Inspecteur de faire ses visites et inspections aux termes de cet Article, ou s'y opposera d'une manière quelconque, encourra une amende qui n'excédera pas £20 sterling et qui sera imposée par le Magistrat Stipendiaire du District.—(*Voir aussi le No.* 353.) Idem, Art. 25.

379.—Toutes plaintes pour contraventions à l'*Ordonnance No.* 29 *de* 1865 et à la *présente Ordonnance* pourront être faites au Magistrat Stipendiaire du District dans lequel résident les serviteurs auxquels les dites plaintes auront rapport, et jugées par lui.—(*Ordonnance No.* 29 *de* 1865—. *Voir les Nos.* 354 *et suiv.—Présente Ordonnance.—Voir le No.* 365.) Ord. No. 31 de 1867, Art. 76.

380.—Tout jugement d'un Magistrat de District ou Stipendiaire rendu en vertu des dispositions de cette Ordonnance, sera sujet à appel devant la Cour Suprême, sur des questions de droit et de fait, lorsque l'amende excédera £ 10 sterling. Ord. No. 29 de 1865, Art. 27.

Idem, Art. 28. 381.—The General Board of Health shall have power to frame Regulations for carrying out the objects of this Ordinance within the whole or any part of the Colony. All such Regulations, on being approved by the Governor in Executive Council and published in the Government Gazette, shall, in so far as they shall not be inconsistent with any provisions of this Ordinance, be equally valid and effectual as if they had been contained *verbatim* herein.

Proclamation 5th Jan. 1866, Art. 1. 382.—The General Sanitary Inspector shall be Medical Inspector, under Ordinance No. 29 of 1865, for the Districts of Port Louis, Moka, and Black River.—(*See also No.* 377.)

Idem, Art. 2. 383.—There shall be two Assistant General Sanitary Inspectors, each being also a Medical-Inspector, under the said Ordinance respectively. One of them shall perform the duties of these offices for the Districts of Pamplemousses, Rivière du Rempart, and Flacq, and the other for the Districts of Plaines Wilhems, Savanne, and Grand Port.—(*See also No.* 376.)

Idem, Art. 3. 384.—None of these three Officers shall be allowed to take private practice as a Physician, or Surgeon.

Idem, Art. 4. 385.—They shall reside, respectively, in one or other of the Districts over which their duties shall extend.

dem, Art. 5. 386.—The visits made by the Medical-Inspectors under the Ordinance above mentioned, shall be not fewer in number than one in each Quarter of the year to each Hospital.—(*See also No.* 378.)

These visits shall be made at irregular intervals, and without previous notice to the Employer.

Idem, Art. 6. 387.—Each Medical Inspector shall, as soon as may be after each Quarter, transmit to the Colonial Secretary, for the information of the Governor, a Report of his Inspections; and as soon as may be after the end of each year, he shall make, in the same manner, an Annual Report thereupon.

381.—La Commission Générale de Santé aura le pouvoir de faire des réglements pour l'exécution des dispositions de cette Ordonnance dans toute la Colonie ou dans l'un de ses Districts. Tous ces réglements, après avoir été approuvés par le Gouverneur en Conseil Exécutif, et publiés dans la Gazette du Gouvernement, seront, en tant qu'ils ne seront pas incompatibles avec les dispositions de cette Ordonnance, aussi valables que s'ils y étaient contenus mot pour mot. Idem, Art. 28.

382.—L'Inspecteur Sanitaire Général sera le Médecin Inspecteur, conformément à l'Ordonnance No. 29 de 1865, dans les Districts du Port Louis, de Moka, et de la Rivière Noire.—(*Voir aussi le No.* 377.) Proclamation, 5 Janv. 1866, Art. 1.

383.—Il y aura deux Sous-Inspecteurs Sanitaires, qui seront aussi Médecins-Inspecteurs conformément à la dite Ordonnance. L'un deux remplira ces fonctions dans les Districts des Pamplemousses, de la Rivière du Rempart, et de Flacq, et l'autre dans les Districts des Plaines Wilhems, de la Savanne, et du Grand Port.—(*Voir aussi le No.* 376.) Idem, Art. 2.

384.—Aucun de ces trois Officiers ne pourra avoir une clientèle privée comme Médecin ou Chirurgien. Idem, Art. 3.

385.—Ils résideront dans l'un ou dans l'autre des Districts où ils auront à remplir leurs fonctions. Idem, Art. 4.

386.—Les visites à faire par les Médecins Inspecteurs conformément à l'Ordonnance sus-mentionnée ne seront pas moins d'une par trimestre à chaque Hôpital.—(*Voir aussi le No.* 378.) Idem, Art. 5.

Ces visites seront faites à des intervalles irréguliers et sans avis préalable au propriétaire.

387.—Chacun des Médecins Inspecteurs devra, aussitôt que possible après chaque trimestre, transmettre au Secrétaire Colonial, pour l'information du Gouverneur, un Rapport de ses Inspections ; et aussitôt que possible après la fin de chaque année il devra faire, de la même manière, un Rapport Annuel de ses Inspections. Idem, Art. 6.

These Reports shall contain, in a Tabulated Form, (hereto appended), the information therein mentioned.

DISTRICT N°

MEDICAL INSPECTOR'S RETURN FOR THE QUARTER ENDING 186 .

No. of Hospital.	District.	Estate.	Name of Employer.	No. of Servants, &c.			No. treated in Hospital.			No. treated out of Hospital.			No. of Deaths in Hospital.			No. of Deaths out of Hospital.			Condition of Hospital.	Date of Inspection.
				M.	W.	C.	M.	W.	C.	M.	W.	C.	M.	W.	C.	M.	W.	C.		

Date 186 .

C. E.

Medical Inspector.

A Duplicate of each of these Reports shall be filed in the Office of the General Board of Health: for which purpose the Medical Inspectors mentioned in *Article 2nd* shall forward regularly to the General Sanitary Inspector duplicates of their Reports.—(*Article* 2.—*See No.* 383.)

Idem, Art. 7. 388.—The Medical Inspectors shall endeavour to observe as much similarity as possible in the mode in which they perform their duties. Any differences among them which they are unable to settle by mutual conference, shall be referred by them to the General Board of Health, for consideration and decision.

Idem, Art. 8. 389.—Each Medical Inspector shall be provided with, and shall keep in his hands, a sufficient number of Forms as in the Schedule to the Ordinance No. 29 of 1865; and also of Certificates that Hospitals are sufficient under the said Ordinance: copies of which Forms shall be furnished by them, gratuitously, to all persons having need thereof.

Ces Rapports devront contenir, sous la forme du Tableau ci-joint, les renseignements qui y sont indiqués.

DISTRICT N°

RAPPORT DU MÉDECIN INSPECTEUR POUR LE TRIMESTRE FINISSANT LE 186.

No. de l'Hôpital.	District.	Propriété.	Nom de l'employeur.	Nombre de Serviteurs &c.			Nombre traité à l'Hôpital			Nombre traité hors de l'Hôpital			Nombre de morts à l'Hôpital			Nombre de morts hors de l'Hôpital			Condition de l'Hôpital.	Date de l'inspection.
				H.	F.	E.	H.	F.	E.	H.	F.	E.	H.	F.	E.	H.	F.	E.		

Date 186 .

C. E.

Inspecteur Médical.

Un Duplicata de chacun de ces Rapports sera déposé au Bureau de la Commission Générale de Santé; dans ce but les Médecins Inspecteurs mentionnés en l'*Article* 2 enverront régulièrement à l'Inspecteur Sanitaire Général des duplicatas de leurs Rapports.—(*Article* 2.—*Voir le No.* 383.)

388.—Les Médecins Inspecteurs devront tâcher de procéder dans l'accomplissement de leurs fonctions autant que possible de la même manière. Les divergences d'opinion sur lesquelles ils ne pourraient pas s'entendre, devront être portées par eux devant la Commission Générale de Santé qui en prendra connaissance et décidera. Idem, Art. 7.

389.—Chacun des Médecins Inspecteurs sera tenu d'avoir entre les mains une quantité suffisante de Formes selon l'Annexe de l'Ordonnance No. 29 de 1865; et aussi de Certificats constatant que les Hôpitaux sont suffisants conformément à la dite Ordonnance; des copies de ces Formes seront fournies par eux gratuitement à toutes les personnes qui en auront besoin. Idem, Art. 8.

Number of Hospital.	Recommendations made during the period of this Return.	How far recommendations have been complied with.	REMARKS.

C. E.
Medical Inspector.

Idem, Art. 9. **390.**—Upon any Certificate of the nature last mentioned being given, a duplicate thereof shall, without delay, be forwarded to the General Board of Health Office,—where all such Duplicates shall be registered and filled.

Idem, Art. 10. **391.**—The Medical Inspector of Port Louis shall, as soon as may be, call on all Employers within Port Louis, who by law are required to have Hospital accommodation for their laborers, to inform him, in writing, whether they intend to have Hospitals on their premises, or to send their sick servants to the Civil Hospital. This shall also he done in regard to all persons who shall become Employers, as aforesaid, in future.

The Returns shall be registered and filed by the Medical Inspector.

Idem, Art. 11. **392.**—Every Employer who shall avail himself of the Civil Hospital for his servants, shall keep on his premises a Register in which he shall enter the name of any servant sent to the Hospital, and the date of his admission, and discharge or death. A Receipt shall be given by the Officer in Charge of the Civil Hospital at the time, on the arrival of any such servant; and all such Receipts shall be regularly filed and preserved by the Employer for at least one year.

The Register and File of Receipts, shall always be open to the Inspection of the Medical Inspector of the District.

Numéro de l'Hôpital.	Recommandations faites pendant le trimestre précédant ce Rapport.	Comment les recommandations ont été suivies.	REMARQUES.

C. E.
Inspecteur Médical.

390.—Lorsqu'un Certificat de la nature ci-dessus mentionnée en dernier lieu, aura été donné, un duplicata de ce certificat sera, sans délai, envoyé au Bureau de la Commission Générale de Santé, où tous les Duplicatas de cette nature seront enregistrés et conservés dans les archives de ce bureau. Idem, Art. 9.

391.—Le Médecin Inspecteur du Port-Louis devra, aussitôt que possible, inviter tous les Employeurs dans le District du Port-Louis, qui sont tenus par la loi d'avoir des Hôpitaux pour leurs travailleurs, à l'informer par écrit s'ils ont l'intention d'avoir des Hôpitaux sur leurs Établissements ou d'envoyer leurs serviteurs malades à l'Hôpital Civil. Cette mesure sera aussi prise à l'égard de toutes les personnes qui deviendront par la suite Employeurs ainsi qu'il est expliqué plus haut. Idem, Art. 10.

Ces Réponses seront enregistrées et conservées par le Médecin Inspecteur.

392.—Tout Employeur qui profitera de l'Hôpital Civil pour ses serviteurs, tiendra sur son Etablissement un Registre dans lequel il inscrira le nom du serviteur envoyé à l'Hôpital, la date de son admission et celle de son renvoi ou de sa mort. L'Officier en charge de l'Hôpital Civil à ce moment donnera un reçu à l'arrivée de ce serviteur ; et tous ces Reçus seront régulièrement conservés par l'Employeur pendant une année au moins. Idem, Art. 11.

Le Registre et la liasse des Reçus pourront être examinés par le Médecin Inspecteur du District toutes les fois qu'il le jugera convenable.

Idem, Art. 12. 393.—The provisions of the last preceding article shall apply, *mutatis mutandis*, to Employers who avail themselves of the provisions of the Ordinance No. 29 of 1865 as to *Union Hospitals*.—(*Union Hospitals.—See No.* 363.)

Idem, Art. 13. 394.—The Stipendiary Magistrates shall furnish to the Medical-Inspectors for the several Districts, all information the latter may apply for, and the Magistrates can give, in regard to the number of men engaged by the different Employers in each District.

Idem, Art. 14. 395.—As soon as may be after the commencement of each year, each Stipendiary Magistrate shall forward to the Medical Inspector of his District a Statement, in duplicate, in the following form, of the laborers known to him to be so employed at the time.—

Date.	Name of Employer.	No. of men employed.	Places where employed.

C. D.
Stipendiary Magistrate.

One duplicate shall be preserved and filed, by the Medical-Inspector. The other shall be *visaed* by him, and returned to the Stipendiary Magistrate, by whom it shall be preserved and filed.

Ord. No. 28 of 1868, Art. 4, Sect. 3. 396.—Persons who are not required to provide Hospital Accommodation for their servants under the provisions of Ordinance *No.* 29 *of* 1865, shall be allowed to have such of their servants, as require Hospital treatment, received and treated in *Hospital*, on payment therefor at a *rate* to be fixed as aforesaid, when such servants and laborers can be received therein.—(*Ordinance No.* 29 *of* 1865,—*See Nos.* 354 *et seq.—Hospital i. e. the Hospital established by the Poor Law Commission.—Rate i. e. the tariff fixed by that Commission with the approval of the Governor.*)

393.—Les dispositions du dernier Article qui précède seront applicables, *mutatis mutandis*, aux Employeurs qui voudront profiter des dispositions de l'Ordonnance No. 29 de 1865 relatives aux *Hôpitaux Communs*.—(*Hôpitaux Communs.—Voir le No.* 363.) Idem, Art. 12.

394.—Les Magistrats Stipendiaires des différents Districts fourniront aux Médecins Inspecteurs tous les renseignements que ceux-ci leur demanderont, et que les Magistrats pourront donner concernant le nombre d'hommes engagés par les différents Employeurs dans chaque District. Idem, Art. 13.

395.—Aussitôt que possible après le commencement de chaque année, chaque Magistrat Stipendiaire enverra au Médecin Inspecteur de son District un Etat en duplicata, dans la forme suivante, des travailleurs qu'il saura être employés à ce moment : Idem. Art. 14.

Date.	Nom de l'Employeur.	Nombre des hommes employés.	Lieux où ils sont employés.

C. D.
Magistrat Stipendiaire.

Un Duplicata sera conservé par le Médecin-Inspecteur. L'autre sera visé par lui, et renvoyé au Magistrat Stipendiaire qui devra le conserver dans les archives de son bureau.

396.—Les personnes qui ne sont pas obligées d'avoir un Hôpital pour leurs serviteurs en vertu des dispositions de *l'Ordonnance No. 29 de* 1865 pourront envoyer ceux de leurs serviteurs qui auront besoin d'être soignés, *à l'Hôpital,* en payant le *prix* qui sera fixé comme il est dit plus haut, et ces domestiques seront admis s'il y a de la place pour les recevoir. —(*Ordonnance No.* 29 *de* 1865.—*Voir les Nos.* 354 *et suiv.— Hôpital, i. e. l'Hôpital établi par la Commission des Pauvres.— Prix i. e. le tarif fixé par cette Commission et approuvé par le Gouverneur.*) Ord. No. 28 de 1868, Art. 4, Sect. 3.

Idem, Art. 4, Sect. 4. 397.—The Public Hospital shall further be available for the members of the Police Force, for the Officers of the Prisons Department, for laborers in the Government Service, and for all other persons who are entitled to Medical treatment at the expense of Government, on payment therefor by the Government according to the aforesaid Tariff.

CHAPTER II.

Burial.

Ord. No. 18 of 1860, Art. 90. 398.—Each *Local Board* may, at such times, and in such situation, as it may deem proper, provide, and fit up, rooms or premises, in which corpses may be received, and decently and carefully kept, previously to interment. And they may make all necessary arrangements for the decent and economical interment of any corpses which may be received into such premises, and of any dead bodies, for the burial of which proper arrangements shall not be made. The expense incurred thereby respectively shall be recovered from the relations of the deceased if any there be liable therefor in law, or from his Employer if he was in service. If the deceased shall have no such relations, or employer, and shall not have left funds to defray the said expense, it shall be payable by the *Poor Relief Committee of the District* upon whom the deceased was chargeable at the time of his death, and by the *Corporation of Port Louis,* if the deceased was at such time chargeable on the said Corporation as administering the relief of the Poor within the said Town.—(*Local Board, i. e. Local Board of Health. When applying this Article as regards any Rural District, the words "General Board of Health" must be read in lieu of "Local Board," the duties and powers of the Local Boards of Health of the Rural Districts having been transferred to the General Board of Health by Ordinance No.* 27 *of* 1866.

Moreover there is no longer a Poor Relief Committee for each District, and the Corporation of Port Louis is not now charged with the relief of the poor in Town. The duties of those bodies in this respect were transferred by Ordinance No. 11 *of* 1868 *to "The Poor Law Commission" in which is centred the Poor Law Administration for the whole Colony.*)

397.—Les Hôpitaux Publics de chaque district pourront aussi servir aux membres de la Police et aux Officiers des Prisons aux travailleurs au service du Gouvernement, ainsi qu'aux autres personnes qui ont droit aux Soins Médicaux aux frais du Gouvernement, pourvu que le Gouvernement paie pour leur traitement suivant le tarif sus-dit. Idem, Art. 4, Sect. 4.

CHAPITRE II.

De l'Inhumation.

398.—Chaque *Commission Locale* pourra aux époques et dans les localités qu'elle jugera convenables, établir et installer des appartements ou bâtiments dans lesquels les corps seront reçus et gardés décemment et avec soin avant leur enterrement. Et elle pourra prendre toutes les dispositions nécessaires pour l'inhumation décente et économique des corps qui seront reçus dans les dits bâtiments, et de tous autres corps pour l'enterrement desquels des dispositions convenables n'auraient pas été prises. Les dépenses encourues à cet effet seront payés par les parents du décédé s'il en existe que la loi y oblige, ou par son maître si le décédé était employé lors de sa mort. Dans le cas où le décédé n'aurait pas de parents à ce degré, ni de maître, et qu'il n'aurait pas laissé assez de fonds pour payer la dite dépense, elle sera remboursée par le *Comité de Secours du District* à la charge duquel il se trouvait à l'époque de sa mort, et par la *Municipalité du Port-Louis* si le décédé était à cette époque à la charge de la dite Municipalité comme chargée de distribuer des Secours aux Pauvres de la dite ville.—(*Commission Locale, i. e. Commission Locale de Santé.—En appliquant cet article, lorsqu'il s'agit d'un District Rural, les mots " Commission Générale de Santé " doivent être substitués aux mots " Commission Locale ",—les fonctions et les pouvoirs des Commissions Locales de Santé dans les Districts Ruraux ayant été transférés à la Commission Générale de Santé par l'Ordonnance No.* 27 *de* 1866. Ord. No. 18 de 1860, Art. 90.

De plus il n'y a plus aujourd'hui un Comité de Secours pour chaque District, et la Municipalité du Port-Louis n'est plus chargée d'administrer des Secours aux Pauvres de la Ville. Les devoirs qui incombaient à ces Comités et à la Corporation sous ce rapport ont été transférés par l'Ordonnance No. 11 *de* 1868 *à la " Commission de la loi sur les Pauvres " qui est seule chargée d'administrer des Secours aux Pauvres dans toute la Colonie.*

DESERTION AND VAGRANCY.

I.—*Unlawful Absence and Desertion.*
II.—*Vagrancy.*

CHAPTER I.

Unlawful Absence and Desertion.

Ord. No. 31 of 1867, Art. 49.

399.—Any laborer who shall absent himself from his work without the leave of his employer, or any justifiable cause, shall be considered guilty of an unlawful absence, and liable to the punishments enacted against unlawful absences in *Article* 18 *of Ordinance No.* 16 *of* 1862.—(*Article* 18.—*See No.* 400.)

Absence from work on the plea of sickness with refusal to go to Hospital, is held to be unlawful absence.—*See No.* 362.

Ord. No. 16 of 1862, Art. 18.

400.—Any Immigrant who shall unlawfully absent himself from work, shall (besides losing his claim to wages and allowances during such absence) forfeit to his employer one halfpenny for each shilling of his monthly wages, for each day of absence. This forfeiture may be applied by the employer in the first instance, but subject to his justifying the same to the Stipendiary Magistrate, in the event of the Immigrant complaining that his wages have not been fully paid. Instead of the forfeiture hereinbefore mentioned, the Immigrant shall be liable, on complaint by his employer, to be sentenced by the Stipendiary Magistrate of his District to imprisonment for a period not exceeding fourteen days, or (at the option of the employer) to a prolongation of the Contract equivalent to the time of absence.*

---

* Repeated refusals to work may be met by a sentence of imprisonment on each refusal. In the case of *Itoo and others*, v. *Barron*, *Moon and others*, (Piston's Reports, 1862.) the laborers of the "Mony Musk" Estate refused at the expiration of their Contract, to make good their unlicensed absences, and were sent to prison for that refusal. On their release they again refused to work and were sentenced to a second term of imprisonment. An appeal was made against the latter judgment on the ground that the Stipendiary Magistrate had punished them a second time for the same offence,—" autrefois convict." The Supreme Court however dismissed the appeal.

DE LA DÉSERTION ET DU VAGABONDAGE.

I.—*De l'Absence illégale et de la Désertion.*
II.—*Du Vagabondage.*

CHAPITRE I.

De l'Absence Illégale et de la Désertion.

399.—Tout travailleur qui s'absentera de son travail sans la permission de son employeur ou sans cause légitime, sera considéré comme étant coupable d'une absence illégale, et passible des peines décrétées contre les absences illégales par *l'Article* 18 *de l'Ordonnance No.* 16 *de* 1862.—(*Article* 18.—*Voir le No.* 400.) Ord. No. 31 de 1867, Art. 49.

L'absence du travail sous prétexte de maladie, jointe au refus de se rendre à l'hôpital, est considérée comme une absence illégale.—*Voir le No.* 362.

400.—Tout Immigrant qui s'absentera illégalement de son travail s'exposera (en sus de la perte de tout droit à ses gages et à ses rations pendant cette absence) au paiement au profit de son employeur d'une indemnité à raison d'un demi penny par schelling de ses gages mensuels pour chaque jour d'absence. Cette indemnité pourra être recouvrée en premier lieu par l'employeur, mais pourvu qu'il en justifie au Magistrat Stipendiaire dans le cas où l'Immigrant se plaindrait que ses gages n'ont pas été intégralement payés. Au lieu de l'indemnité susdite, l'Immigrant pourra, sur la plainte de l'employeur, être condamné par le Magistrat Stipendiaire de son District à un emprisonnementpour un temps qui n'excédera pas quatorze jours, ou (au choix de l'employeur) à une prolongation du Contrat égale au temps de son absence.* Tout Ord. No. 16 de 1862, Art. 18.

* Des refus réitérés de travailler peuvent être punis par l'emprisonnement pour chaque refus. Dans l'affaire *Itoo et autres v. Barron, Moon et autres.*—(Piston's Reports, 1862.) les laboureurs de l'Etablissement "Mony Musk" refusèrent à l'expiration de leur engagement de remplacer leurs absences illégales et furent condamnés à la prison pour ce refus. A leur sortie de prison, ils refusèrent encore de travailler et furent condamnés à un second emprisonnement. Un appel fut formé contre ce dernier jugement sur le motif que le Magistrat Stipendiaire n'avait pas le droit de les punir une seconde fois pour le même délit—"autrefois convict." La Cour Suprême rejeta néanmoins l'appel.

Every Immigrant sentenced to prolongation of his service, shal. be entitled to redeem such prolongation by paying to his employer at the rate of six shillings sterling for every calendar month thereof.

The foregoing article (No. 400) originally applied to Immigrant-laborers alone, it now extends to laborers of all classes —*See No.* 399.

Imprisonment under that article (No. 400) reckons as part of the term of service under the Contract, in all other cases the laborer is bound to make good any period passed by him in prison.—*See No.* 245.

Any Immigrant imprisoned for non-performance of his Contract of Service may be released at the instance of his Master.—*See No.* 254.

Idem, Art. 19. 401.—No such forfeiture, imprisonment, or prolongation, respectively, as in the *last preceding Article* provided, shall be incurred if the wages of the Immigrant shall have been unpaid for any period longer than two calendar months before his absences, or if more than two calendar months shall have elapsed between the Immigrant's return from such absence and the application of the forfeiture, or lodging of the complaint against him, as the case may be.—(*Last preceding Article,* i. e. *Article* 18.—*See No.* 400.)

Further, no such forfeiture, imprisonment, or prolongation, shall apply if the employer shall have refused an application for payment of the wages lawfully due to the Immigrant, before the time of such absence.— (*See also No.* 403.)

Idem, Art. 20. 402.—In the case of any service being prolonged, *as herein aforesaid,* the extent of prolongation shall be endorsed on the Immigrant's contract and ticket; and, during such prolongation, he shall be subject to all the conditions of his contract, and to the punishment by this Ordinance provided, in case of unlawful absence.—(*As herein aforesaid.—See No.* 400.)

Ord. No. 31 of 1867, Art. 50. 403.—Any laborer under written engagement who shall absent himself from his work without the leave of his employer, or any justifiable cause, and shall moreover abscond from his dwelling place, for a space of more than three consecutive days, shall be considered a Deserter, and shall be liable to be apprehended and punished as such by imprisonment not exceeding three months.

Immigrant condamné à une prolongation de son service, aura le droit de se libérer de la dite prolongation à raison de six schellings sterling pour chaque mois d'absence.

L'Article ci-dessus (No. 400) ne s'appliquait dans le principe qu'aux travailleurs Immigrants, il s'étend aujourd'hui à tous les travailleurs quels qu'ils soient.—*Voir le No.* 399.

L'emprisonnement infligé en vertu de cet article (No. 400) compte comme partie du temps de service mentionné dans le contrat : dans tous les autres cas, le travailleur est obligé de remplacer le temps qu'il a passé en prison.—*Voir le No.* 245.

Tout Immigrant emprisonné pour n'avoir pas rempli les conditions de son Contrat de Service, peut être mis en liberté à la requête de son Maître.—*Voir le No.* 254.

401.—Aucune indemnité, aucun emprisonnement ou aucune prolongation, respectivement, comme il est decrété dans l'*Article précédent*, ne sera encouru, si les gages de l'Immigrant étaient dûs pour un temps quelconque excédant deux mois avant ses absences ou si un temps excédant deux mois s'est écoulé entre le retour de l'Immigrant de l'absence sus-dite et le recouvrement de l'indemnité, ou la déposition de la plainte contre lui, selon le cas.— (*Article précédent*, i. e. l'*Article* 18.—*Voir le No.* 400.) Idem, Art. 19.

De même, cette indemnité, cet emprisonnement ou cette prolongation, ne pourra être exigé, si l'employeur a refusé de payer des gages légalement dûs à l'Immigrant avant le temps de la dite absence.—(*Voir aussi le No.* 403.)

402.—Dans le cas où le contrat de service serait prolongé *comme il est dit ci-dessus*, la durée de cette prolongation sera endossée sur le contrat de l'Immigrant, et pendant cette prolongation, il sera soumis à toutes les conditions de son contrat, et aux peines prévues par cette Ordonnance en cas d'absence illégale.—(*Comme il est dit ci-dessus.*—*Voir le No.* 400.) Idem, Art. 20.

403.—Tout travailleur sous engagement écrit qui s'absentera de son travail sans la permission de son employeur ou sans cause légitime, et qui de plus s'absentera de son logement pendant plus de trois jours consécutifs, sera considéré comme Déserteur, et pourra être arrêté et puni comme tel d'un emprisonnement n'excédant pas trois mois. Néanmoins on considérera que l'employeur a Ord. No. 31 de 1867, Art. 50.

Provided always that any such desertion shall be deemed to have been condoned by the employer, if the latter shall have allowed the laborer to resume work without previous prosecution for such offence.—(*See also No.* 401.)

The punishment imposed in and by *Article* 13 *of Ordinance No.* 4 *of* 1864, upon persons convicted of vagrancy, shall not be applied to any Deserter as defined in the present article, who shall be condemned as such upon the complaint of his employer.—(*Article* 13.—*See No.* 416.—*See also No.* 253.)

Idem, Art. 51. 404.—If any laborer desert from his employer's service, it shall be lawful for such employer, or any servant of such employer, acting with his authority and on his behalf, without a warrant and without the assistance of the Police, to apprehend such laborer in any public place where he may be found; provided that if the party making the arrest in so doing use any unnecessary violence, or do not forthwith, after such arrest, hand over the laborer to a Police Officer or Constable, together with a statement in writing, or to be taken down in writing by the Police, mentioning the name and residence of the party making the arrest, and the charge upon which the laborer has been arrested, or do not appear and support the charge before the Stipendiary Magistrate having jurisdiction to entertain the same, such party shall be liable to a fine not exceeding £10, or to imprisonment not exceeding one month.

Idem. Art. 52. 405.—Any Officer or Constable of Police may, at the instance of any Employer, or of any person acting with the authority or on behalf of the employer, and upon being furnished with a statement containing the particulars specified in the preceding article, arrest any laborer charged under such statement with Desertion, without warrant, in any public place where such laborer may be found; provided that such laborer, upon being so arrested, be forthwith taken before the nearest Stipendiary Magistrate to be dealt with according to law. If the party at whose instance such laborer shall have been arrested do not after due notice of the arrest and of the time and place of hearing, appear and support the charge before the Stipendiary Magistrate having jurisdiction to entertain the same, such party shall be liable to the penalties enacted in the preceding article.

pardonné cette désertion, s'il a permis au travailleur de reprendre son travail sans qu'il l'ait préalablement poursuivi pour ce délit.—(*Voir aussi le No.* 401.)

La peine infligée par l'*Article* 13 *de l'Ordonnance No.* 4 *de* 1864 aux personnes condamnées pour vagabondage, ne sera pas applicable à un Déserteur, tel qu'il est défini par le présent article, qui sera condamné comme tel sur la plainte de son employeur.—(*Article* 13.—*Voir le No.* 416.—*Voir aussi le No.* 253.)

404.—Si un travailleur déserte le service de son employeur, Idem, Art. 51. il sera permis à celui-ci, ou à un serviteur de cet employeur agissant avec son autorisation et en son nom, sans warrant et sans l'assistance de la Police, d'arrêter ce travailleur dans tout lieu public où il sera trouvé; néanmoins, si la personne opérant l'arrestation use de violence inutile en la faisant, ou ne livre pas immédiatement après cette arrestation, le travailleur à un Officier ou à un Constable de Police, avec une déclaration par écrit, ou si elle est faite verbalement, qui sera mise par écrit par la Police, mentionnant les noms et demeure de la personne qui aura opéré l'arrestation, et le motif pour lequel le travailleur a été arrêté, ou ne paraît pas pour soutenir l'accusation devant le Magistrat Stipendiaire compétent pour en connaître, cette personne sera passible d'une amende n'excédant pas £ 10, ou d'un emprisonnement n'excédant pas un mois.

405.—Tout Officier ou Constable de Police pourra, à la requête Idem, Art, 52. d'un employeur, ou d'une personne agissant avec l'autorisation et au nom de l'employeur, et après avoir reçu une déclaration contenant les détails spécifiés dans l'article précédent, arrêter tout travailleur accusé de désertion par cette déclaration, sans warrant, dans tout lieu public où ce travailleur pourra être rencontré; toutefois ce travailleur devra, immédiatement après avoir été ainsi arrêté, ou aussitôt que possible, être conduit devant le Magistrat Stipendiaire le plus voisin afin d'être traité conformément à la loi. Si la personne à la requête de laquelle ce travailleur aura été arrêté ne paraît pas pour soutenir l'accusation devant le Magistrat Stipendiaire compétent pour en connaître, après qu'elle aura été avertie de cette arrestation ainsi que du jour et du lieu où l'affaire doit être jugée, cette personne sera passible des peines prévues par l'article précédent.

Idem, Art. 53. 406.—If any laborer be wrongfully apprehended, the person apprehending him, or on whose charge or by whose order he shall have been so apprehended, and all persons who shall have aided or abetted the apprehender in effecting the apprehension, shall be liable to a fine not exceeding £ 10, a part of which may be paid to the laborer so apprehended, as damages, or to an imprisonment not exceeding one month. But any Officer or Constable of Police shall be deemed to have been justified in arresting or detaining a laborer upon a charge of desertion, if he shall have acted *bonâ fide* in conformity with the provisions of either of the two *preceding Articles.—(Preceding Articles i. e. Arts.* 51 *and* 52,*—See Nos.* 404 *and* 405.)

Govt. Notice No. 166 of 11th Nov.1868, Art. 61. 407.—A Deserters' Book shall be opened in the Immigration Office, and all desertions declared to the Protector shall be inserted therein. Such declaration shall be made in the form of the Schedule P hereto annexed.

SCHEDULE P.

Declaration of Deserters.

I, the undersigned Proprietor (or Lessee, or Manager) of Estate, in the District of declare that the undermentioned Immigrants have deserted from the said Estate.

Name of Deserters.	New or Old Immigrant.	No.	Date of Engagement.		Period for which engaged.		Date of Desertion.		Remarks.
					Yrs.	Mths.			

Forwarded to the Protector of Immigrants this day of 186 .

(*Signature.*)

Idem, Art. 62. 408.—If any Immigrant admitted into the Immigration Depot be declared as a Deserter, he shall be detained in the Depot, and his detention, as soon as may be, shall be notified to his employer

406.—Si un travailleur a été arrêté injustement, la personne qui l'aura arrêté ou sur l'autorisation ou l'ordre de laquelle il aura été ainsi arrêté, et toutes les personnes qui auront aidé à opérer l'arrestation, seront passibles d'une amende n'excédant pas £ 10, dont partie pourra être payée au travailleur ainsi arrêté, comme dommages-intérêts, ou d'un emprisonnement qui n'excédera pas un mois. Mais tout Officier ou Constable de Police sera considéré comme ayant agi légalement en arrêtant ou en détenant un travailleur sous une accusation de Désertion, s'il a agi de bonne foi et conformément aux dispositions de l'un ou l'autre des deux articles précédents.—(*Articles précédents, i. e. les articles* 51 *et* 52.—*Voir les Nos.* 404 *et* 405.) Idem, Art. 53.

407.—Un Régistre de Déserteurs sera tenu au Bureau de l'Immigration, et tous les Déserteurs déclarés au Protecteur y seront inscrits. Cette déclaration sera faite dans la forme de l'Annexe P. Avis du Gouv. No. 166 du 11 Nov. 1868, Art. 61.

ANNEXE P.

Déclaration de Déserteurs.

Je, le propriétaire soussigné (ou locataire, ou administrateur de la propriété , dans le District de , déclare que les Immigrants ci-dessous mentionnés ont déserté la dite propriété.

Noms des Déserteurs.	Nouveaux ou Anciens Immigrants.	No.	Date de l'engagement.	Temps pour lequel ils sont engagés.		Date de la désertion.	Remarques.
				Années.	Mois.		

Envoyé au Protecteur des Immigrants ce jour de 186 .

(*Signature.*)

408.—Si un Immigrant admis au Dépôt de l'Immigration est déclaré comme Déserteur, il sera détenu à ce dépôt, et cette détention sera, aussitôt que possible, notifiée à son employeur si sa Idem, Art. 62.

if his residence be known to the Protector. The names and numbers of all Deserters so detained and the names of their employers, if they be known to the Protector, shall besides be published in the Government Gazette; and if, within one week from the date of any such publication, any Immigrant mentioned in such notice be not claimed by his employer, the former shall be free to enter into another contract of service,—on presentation of a certificate in the form of the Schedule Q to any Stipendiary Magistrate. It shall however be in the power of the Protector to transfer such Immigrant to the Central Police Office of Port Louis, to be handed over to his employer.

SCHEDULE Q.

This is to certify that the Immigrant mentioned in margin has been detained in the Immigration Depot under Regulation 62, since the ; that his detention as a Deserter from Estate was notified in the Government Gazette of (*date*); and that he has not hitherto been claimed by his employer; in consequence of which the said Immigrant is free, under the above-mentioned regulation, to enter into another contract of service.

Immigration Office, 186 .

H. B.

Protector of Immigrants.

CHAPTER II.

Vagrancy.

Idem, Art. 41. 409.—If it appear to the Inspector of Police or *other Officer* duly authorized to deliver Police-Passes to Immigrants that the statement of any applicant for a pass as to his abode or occupation is untrue, or that his occupation is not such as to justify the issue of a pass to him, the case shall immediately be reported to the Stipendiary Magistrate, and fully inquired into without delay; and, if the applicant be convicted by the Magistrate of having no fixed residence or *bonâ fide* occupation, employment or means of subsistence, he shall immediately be dealt with as a Vagrant.—If the statement of the applicant as to his abode and occupation prove to be true, a pass shall forthwith be delivered to him.—(*Other Officer.—See No.* 289.)

résidence est connue du Protecteur. Les noms et numéros de tous les Déserteurs ainsi détenus, et les noms de leurs employeurs, s'ils sont connus du Protecteur, seront de plus publiés dans la Gazette du Gouvernement ; et si, dans la semaine qui suivra la date de cette publication, tout Immigrant mentionné dans le dit avis n'est pas réclamé par son employeur, le premier sera libre de s'engager par un autre contrat de service, en présentant un certificat dans la forme de l'Annexe Q à tout Magistrat Stipendiaire. Néanmoins le Protecteur pourra envoyer le dit Immigrant au bureau Central de Police du Port Louis, pour être remis à son employeur.

ANNEXE Q.

Ceci est pour certifier que l'Immigrant mentionné en marge a été détenu au Dépôt de l'Immigration en vertu du Réglement 62 depuis le ; que sa détention comme déserteur de la propriété a été notifiée dans la Gazette du Gouvernement *(date)* ; et qu'il n'a pas été jusqu'ici réclamé par son employeur : en conséquence de quoi le dit Immigrant est libre, en vertu du dit Réglement, de passer un autre contrat de service.

Bureau de l'Immigration 186 .

H. B.

Protecteur des Immigrants.

CHAPITRE II.

Du Vagabondage.

409.—S'il parait à l'Inspecteur de Police ou à tout *autre Officier* dûment autorisé à délivrer des Passes de Police à des Immigrants que la déclaration de celui qui demande une passe est fausse quant à sa résidence ou à son genre d'occupation, ou que celle-ci ne soit pas de nature à justifier l'émission de la passe qu'il réclame, il en sera immédiatement référé au Magistrat Stipendiaire qui examinera de suite la question ; et, si le requérant est trouvé coupable par le Magistrat de n'avoir pas de résidence fixe, ni d'emploi ou de moyens d'existence reconnus, il sera immédiatement traité comme vagabond.—Si la déclaration du requérant relativement à sa résidence et à ses moyens d'existence est trouvé exacte, il lui sera de suite donné une passe. (*Autre Officier.—Voir le No.* 289.) Idem. Art. 41.

Ord. No. 31 of 1867, Art. 46. 410.—At and after the period fixed in *Article* 45, any Old Immigrant not being engaged under written contract of service passed prior to the above period, who shall fail, on demand of any Magistrate, or of the Police, to produce his pass issued under the provisions of the said *Articles* 43 *or* 44, or a certificate of engagement duly signed by a Stipendiary Magistrate, shall be liable to be detained and forwarded to the Immigration Depot, and be there further detained until enquiries shall have been made about him ; and if, upon the result of such enquiries, it shall appear that he is not following any *bonâ fide* employment, whether on his own account or in the service of a party, and that he has no visible means of subsistence, he shall be deemed and taken to be a Vagrant ; and may be dealt with as such. If, upon the result of such enquiries, it shall appear that he is not a Vagrant, he may be sent back to the District in which he resides, to obtain a pass under the provisions of *Articles* 43 *or* 44.—(*Articles* 43, 44 *and* 45.—*See Nos.* 280, 286 *and* 230.)

Idem, Art. 47. 411.—Whenever any Stipendiary Magistrate shall have reasonable grounds for thinking that any Old Immigrant to whom shall have been issued a pass under the provisions of *Articles* 43 *or* 44, is not *bonâ fide* resident, occupied, or employed in the manner declared by such Immigrant on obtaining his said pass, or that such Immigrant is without any fixed place of residence, or without any *bonâ fide* occupation, or employment, or means of subsistence, it shall be lawful for such Magistrate to issue a summons ; and, in default of compliance therewith, to issue a warrant for the appearance before him of such Immigrant ; and if, after due investigation, the said Magistrate shall be satisfied that the said Immigrant has falsely declared any of the above particulars, or that he is without fixed residence, occupation, employment, or means of subsistence, thereupon the said Magistrate may condemn him as a Vagrant.—(*Articles* 43 *and* 44.—*See Nos.* 280 *and* 286.)

Idem, Art. 55. 412.—Any Officer or Constable of Police, or any other person authorised by the Governor, may, at any time of the day, or at any time of the night, under warrant of a Stipendiary or District Magistrate, enter any premises wherein any Immigrant is employed or resides, and may ascertain whether such Immigrant is a new Immigrant under contract of service, or an old Immigrant

410.—Après le délai fixé par l'*Article* 45, tout Ancien Immigrant non engagé par contrat de service écrit passé avant la dite époque, qui ne pourra pas, sur la demande d'un Magistrat, ou de la Police, produire sa passe émise en vertu des dispositions des dits *Articles* 43 *ou* 44, ou un certificat d'engagement dûment signé par un Magistrat Stipendiaire, pourra être détenu et envoyé au Dépôt de l'Immigration jusqu'à ce qu'on ait pris des renseignements sur lui ; et s'il résulte de ces renseignements, qu'il n'a aucun emploi véritable et consciencieux, soit pour son propre compte, soit au service d'un tiers, et qu'il n'a pas de moyens apparents d'existence, il sera considéré comme un vagabond, et traité comme tel. S'il résulte de ces renseignements qu'il n'est pas un vagabond, il pourra être envoyé devant le Magistrat Stipendiaire du District dans lequel il réside pour obtenir une passe en vertu des dispositions des *Articles* 43 *ou* 44.—(*Articles* 43, 44 *et* 45.—*Voir les Nos.* 280, 286 *et* 230.) Ord. No. 31 de 1867, Art. 46.

411.—Toutes les fois qu'un Magistrat Stipendiaire aura des motifs raisonnables de supposer qu'un Ancien Immigrant à qui il aura été accordé une passe en vertu des dispositions des *Articles* 43 *ou* 44 n'est pas réellement résident, occupé ou employé de la manière déclarée par cet Immigrant lorsqu'il a obtenu sa passe ou que cet Immigrant n'a pas de demeure fixe, ou d'occupation ou d'emploi réel, ou des moyens d'existence, il sera permis au dit Magistrat de lui envoyer une sommation de comparaître ; et, s'il n'obéit pas à cette sommation, de décerner un mandat d'arrêt pour la comparution de cet Immigrant devant lui ; et si, après une enquête convenable, le Magistrat est satisfait que le dit Immigrant lui a fait une fausse déclaration relativement à l'une des indications ci-dessus, ou qu'il est sans demeure fixe, sans occupation ou emploi, ou sans moyens d'existence, il pourra le condamner comme vagabond.—(*Articles* 43 *et* 44.—*Voir les Nos.* 280 *et* 286.) Idem, Art. 47.

412.—Tout Officier ou Constable de Police, ou toute autre personne autorisée par le Gouverneur, pourra, pendant le jour ou pendant la nuit, en vertu d'un warrant d'un Magistrat de District ou Stipendiaire, pénétrer en tous lieux où des Immigrants travaillent et résident, et pourra vérifier si un Immigrant est un nouvel Immigrant sans contrat de service, ou un ancien Immigrant Idem, Art. 55.

having a ticket and pass in due form as prescribed under the provisions of this Ordinance ; and, in case of such person not being satisfied with regard to the status of such Immigrant, he may apprehend him and take him before the Stipendiary Magistrate of the District, to be dealt with according to law.

Idem, Art. 48. 413.—Any Immigrant found in a District where he has no residence, or in any house or premises, and being unable to give a satisfactory reason for his being in such District, house, or premises, as the case may be, may be arrested by any Officer or Constable of Police, without warrant, and brought before the Stipendiary Magistrate of the District in which he shall have been found, who shall have power to forward him to the Immigration Depot to be there detained until enquiries shall have been made about him, and, according to the result of such enquiries, such Immigrant shall either be discharged from the Depot, or be otherwise dealt with, according to law.

Govt. Notice No. 166 of 11th Nov. 1868, Art. 74. 414.—Any person who shall be convicted of having knowingly harboured a Vagrant shall be liable to a fine not exceeding five pounds.

Idem, Art. 60. 415.—If it appear that any *such Immigrant* is a Vagrant, according to the definition of that term in *Article* 46 of the abovementioned Ordinance, and if he refuse to take such employment as may be offered to him by the Protector, he shall be sent to the Stipendiary Magistrate to be dealt with as a Vagrant.—(*Such Immigrant*, i. e., *any Immigrant detained in the Immigration Depot.—See Nos.* 517 *et seq.—Article* 46.—*See No.* 410.)

Ord. No. 4 of 1864, Art. 13. 416.—Any person, who shall be convicted of Vagrancy, except as after mentioned, shall be liable to imprisonment for any period not exceeding 28 days :—Every person who shall be convicted of Vagrancy after two or more previous convictions therefor within the preceding two years shall be liable to imprisonment for any period not less than six or more than nine calendar months.

In convictions for Vagrancy, the Stipendiary Magistrate may include several persons in the same warrant.—*See No.* 476.

ayant un ticket et une passe en bonne forme ainsi qu'il est prescrit par les dispositions de la présente Ordonnance ; et dans le cas où cette personne ne sera pas satisfaite de la qualité prise par cet Immigrant, elle pourra l'arrêter et le conduire devant le Magistrat Stipendiaire du District pour être traité conformément à la loi.

413.—Tout Immigrant trouvé dans un District où il n'a pas de résidence ou dans une maison ou sur un emplacement, et qui ne pourra pas donner une raison satisfaisante de sa présence dans ce District, cette maison ou cet emplacement, selon le cas, pourra être arrêté par tout Officier ou Constable de Police, sans warrant, et conduit devant le Magistrat Stipendiaire du District dans lequel il aura été trouvé, qui aura le pouvoir de l'envoyer au Dépôt de l'Immigration afin qu'il y soit détenu jusqu'à ce qu'on ait pris des renseignements sur lui, et, suivant le résultat de ces renseignements, il sera libéré ou autrement traité conformément à la loi. Idem, Art. 48.

414.—Toute personne qui sera trouvée coupable d'avoir sciemment donné asile à un vagabond sera passible d'une amende n'excédant pas cinq livres sterling. Avis du Gouv. No. 166 du 11 Nov. 1868, Art. 74.

415.—S'il paraît que *le dit Immigrant* est un vagabond, selon la définition de cette expression dans l'*Article* 46 de l'Ordonnance ci-dessus mentionnée, et s'il refuse de prendre l'emploi qui lui sera offert par le Protecteur, il sera envoyé au Magistrat Stipendiaire pour être traité comme vagabond.—(*Le dit Immigrant* i. e. *tout Immigrant détenu au Dépôt de l'Immigration.—Voir les Nos.* 517 *et suiv.—Article* 46.—*Voir le No.* 410.) Idem, Art. 60.

416.—Toute personne qui sera condamnée pour vagabondage excepté comme il est dit ci-après, sera passible d'emprisonnement pour un terme qui n'excédera pas 28 jours ; et toute personne condamnée pour vagabondage après avoir subi deux ou plus de deux condamnations pour cette cause dans les deux années précédentes sera condamnée à l'emprisonnement pour un terme qui ne sera pas moins de six mois et pas plus de neuf mois ordinaires. Ord. No. 4 de 1864, Art. 13.

En condamnant pour vagabondage le Magistrat Stipendiaire peut inclure plusieurs personnes dans le même warrant.—Voir le No. 476.

Ord. No. 42 of 1844, Art. 1. 417.—Every person being able wholly or in part to maintain himself or herself, or his wife, or his or her children or child, by work or other lawful means, and who shall wilfully refuse or neglect so to do, and thereby become burthensome, or render his wife, or his or her children or child burthensome, upon any public funds set apart for the relief of the poor, every common prostitute wandering in the public streets or highways or any place of public resort, and behaving in a riotous or indecent manner, and every person who is able to labour or who is receiving aid from any public funds and who shall be found wandering abroad, or placing himself or herself in a public place, street, warf, highway, lane, court, piazza or passage to beg or gather alms, or causing or procuring or encouraging any child or children so to do, shall be deemed an idle and disorderly person within the true intent and meaning of this Ordinance; and it shall be lawful for any Stipendiary Magistrate to commit such offender, being thereof convicted before him by his own view or by the confession of such offender, or by the evidence on oath of one or more credible witness or witnesses, to the house of correction, there, or on the public streets and highways to be kept to hard labour, for any time not exceeding one calendar month. Provided nevertheless, that no person shall be deemed to be an offender under this Ordinance, by reason of any such begging or gathering alms as aforesaid, or by reason of his or her causing or procuring or encouraging any child or children so to do, unless it shall be made to appear to the satisfaction of the Stipendiary Magistrate before whom he or she shall be charged with such offence, that the offender could by his or her own labour or other lawful means, or by any public funds appropriated for that purpose, have been provided with the necessaries of life.

Idem, Art. 2. 418.—Every person committing any of the offences in the first article of the present Ordinance, after having been convicted as an idle and disorderly person;

2o. Every person pretending to deal in witchcraft, every person pretending or professing to tell fortunes or using or pretending to use any subtle craft or device by palmistery or any such like superstitious means, to deceive or impose on any of Her Majesty's subjects;

417.—Toute personne qui, étant en état, par son travail on tous autres moyens légitimes, de suffire, entièrement ou en partie, à son entretien et à celui de sa femme et de ses enfants, refusera ou négligera volontairement de le faire et qui, par suite, se rendra lui-même ou sa femme ou ses enfants une charge pour des fonds publics quelconques destinés au soulagement des pauvres ; toute prostituée errant dans les rues ou chemins publics, ou dans aucun lieu ouvert au public, et s'y conduisant d'une manière indécente et dissolue ; et toute personne qui, étant en état de travailler ou recevant quelque assistance de fonds publics sera trouvée errant de côté et d'autre, ou se tenant dans aucun lieu, rue, quai et chemin public, ou dans aucune ruelle, cour, varangue, ou passage public, pour demander ou recevoir l'aumône, ou qui emploierait et encouragerait un enfant à cet effet, sera considérée comme une personne oisive et déréglée dans le véritable sens et esprit de la présente Ordonnance ; et tout Magistrat Salarié pourra, soit sur la conviction qu'il aura acquise par ses propres yeux ou de l'aveu du délinquant, soit par le témoignage sous serment d'un ou de plusieurs témoins digne de foi, ordonner l'emprisonnement du dit délinquant dans une maison de correction, afin qu'il soit employé dans la dite maison ou sur les rues et chemins publics aux travaux forcés, pendant un tems qui n'excèdera pas un mois. Aucune personne néanmoins ne pourra être condamnée en vertu de cette Ordonnance, pour avoir demandé ou reçu l'aumône ainsi qu'il est dit ci-dessus ou pour avoir employé, ou encouragé un enfant ou des enfants à le faire à moins qu'il ne soit prouvé à la satisfaction du Magistrat devant lequel cette personne aura été accusée d'un tel délit, qu'elle aurait pu par son propre travail ou autres moyens légitimes ou par des secours publics destinés à cet usage se procurer sa subsistence. Ord. No. 42 de 1844, Art. 1.

418.—Toute personne qui commettra quelqu'un des actes mentionnés dans l'article précédent, après avoir été condamnée une première fois comme une personne oisive et déréglée ; Idem, Art. 2.

2o. Toute personne prétendant dire la bonne aventure, ou en faisant profession, ou employant aucune ruse ou stratagême, ou tous autres semblables moyens superstitieux, pour tromper ou abuser aucun des sujets de Sa Majesté ;

3o. Every person wandering abroad and lodging in any out-house or shed, or in any deserted or unoccupied building, or in any mill, sugar or coffee works, watch-house, trash-house, or other buildings, or within any cane, coffee, provision piece, pasture or inclosure, not having any visible means of subsistence, and not giving an account of himself or herself;

4o. Every person wilfully exposing to view in any street, road highway or public place, any obscene print, picture or other indecent exhibition;

5o. Every person wilfully, openly, lewdly and obscenely exposing his or her person in any street, public place or high way or in the view thereof, or any place of public resort;

6o. Every person wandering abroad and endeavouring by the exposure of wounds or deformities to obtain or gather alms;

7o. Every person endeavouring to procure charitable contributions of any nature or kind whatsoever under any false or fraudulent pretence;

8o. Every person running away and leaving his wife or his children or her children or child chargeable or whereby she or they or any of them shall become chargeable to any public fund set apart for the use of the poor;

9o. Every person playing or betting in any street, road, high way or other open and public place at, or with any table or instrument of gambling, any game or pretended game of chance;

10o. Every person having in his or her custody or possession any pick lock, key, crow, jack, bit, or other implement, with intent feloniously to break into any dwelling-house, warehouse, store, shop, coach-house, stable, or out building, or being armed with any gun, pistol, hanger, cutlass, bludgeon, or other offensive weapon, or having upon him or her any instrument with intent to commit any felonious act;

3o. Tout personne errant de côté et d'autre, et se logeant sous quelque appentis, hangar, ou dépendance, ou dans quelque bâtiment abandonné ou inoccupé, ou dans un moulin à cannes ou autre, case de gardien, hangar à bagasse, ou autres bâtimens, dans quelque champ de cannes, de café ou des plantes vivrières, dans des pâturages ou enclos, et qui n'aurait aucuns moyens apparents de subsistance, et ne pourrait rendre aucun compte d'elle-même ;

4o. Toute personne qui volontairement et à dessein, exposera à la vue du public, dans quelque rue, route, grand chemin ou lieu public, aucune peinture ou gravure obscène ou tout autre représentation indécente ;

5o. Toute personne qui volontairement et à dessein, et ouvertement, se montrera dans une posture obscène sur quelque chemin, rue, ou lieu public, ou en vue d'iceux, ou dans aucun lieu ouvert au public ;

6o. Toute personne errant ça et là et cherchant, par l'exposition de blessures ou difformités, à obtenir et recevoir l'aumône ;

7o. Toute personne qui cherchera à obtenir des contributions charitables de quelque nature que ce soit sous des prétextes faux ou frauduleux ;

8o. Toute personne qui abandonnera sa femme ou ses enfans et les laissera à la charge de fonds publics destinés au soulagement du pauvre ou qui sera cause que par ce fait ils se trouvent à la charge des dits fonds ;

9o. Toute personne qui jouera ou pariera, dans quelque rue, route, grand chemin, ou autres lieux ouverts au public, ou au moyen de quelque table ou instrument de jeu, à aucun jeu de hasard ou prétendu tel ;

10o. Toute personne ayant en sa garde ou en sa possession quelque crochet, clé, pince, jack ou bit ou autre instrument, dans l'intention de s'introduire à l'aide d'effraction, dans quelque habitation, entrepôt, magasin, boutique, remise, étable, écurie, ou dépendances, ou qui serait armé d'un fusil, pistolet, couteau, coutelas, bâton plombé, ou toute autre arme offensive, ou qui aurait sur elle un instrument quelconque dans l'intention de commetttre quelque action coupable ;

11o. Every person being found in, or upon any dwelling-house, warehouse, store, shop, coach-house, stable, out house, or lock up place in which goods are kept, or in any enclosed yard, pen, garden, or crane, for any unlawful purpose;

12o. Every suspected person or reputed thief frequenting any wharf or warehouse, near or adjoining thereto, or any street, highway, or avenue leading thereto, or any place of public resort, or any avenue leading thereto, or any street, highway or place adjacent thereto, with intent to commit felony;

And every person apprehended as an idle and disorderly person, and violently resisting any Police or Peace Officer, constable or Police guard, so apprehending him or her, and being subsequently convicted of the offence for which he or she shall be so apprehended;

Shall be deemed a rogue and vagabond within the true intent and meaning of this Ordinance; and it shall be lawful for any Stipendiary Magistrate to commit such offender, being thereof convicted before him on his own view, or by the confession of such offender or by the evidence on oath of one or more credible witness or witnesses, to the house of correction, there or on the public streets and high ways to be kept to hard labour for any time not exceeding 60 days;* and every such pick-lock, key, crow, jack, bit, and other implement; every such gun, pistol, hanger, cutlass, blungeon, or other offensive weapon; and every such instrument as aforesaid, shall by the conviction of the offender become forfeited to Her Majesty, and the same shall be destroyed or sold by order of the Stipendiary Magistrate, and if sold the proceeds applied to the use of the Colony."—(*See also No.* 416.)

Idem, Art. 3. **419.**—Every person breaking or escaping out of any place of legal confinement before the expiration of the term for which he or she shall have been committed or ordered to be confined, by virtue of this Ordinance, every person committing any offence

* On approving of this Ordinance Her Majesty reduced the maximum imprisonment to 28 days.—Proclamation of 5th March 1845.

11o. Toute personne qui sera trouvée dans ou près de quelque demeure, entrepôt, magasin, boutique, remise, écurie ou étable, dépendance, ou tous endroits fermés dans lesquels sont placées des marchandises, ou dans quelque cour, poulailler, jardin ou parc pour quelque objet illicite ;

12o. Tout individu suspect ou réputé pour voleur fréquentant les quais ou magasins, ou leur voisinage, ou les rues, grands chemins ou avenues y conduisant, ou tous lieux publics et les rues ou routes y conduisant, ou des rues, grands chemins ou places adjacentes, dans l'intention de commettre quelque délit ;

Et toute personne arrêtée comme étant une personne oisive et déréglée, qui résistera avec violence à aucun officier de Paix ou de Police, constable, ou garde de Police, et sera subséquemment convaincue du délit pour lequel elle aura été arrêteé ;

Sera considérée comme un vagabond et une personne sans aveu dans le véritable sens et esprit de la présente Ordonnance ; et tout Magistrat Salarié sur la conviction qu'il aura acquise, soit par ses propres yeux ou par l'aveu du délinquant, soit par le témoignage sous serment d'un ou de plusieurs témoins dignes de foi, pourra condamner le dit délinquant à l'emprisonnement dans une maison de correction pour être employé dans la dite maison, ou dans les rues ou sur les chemins publics, aux travaux forcés, pour un temps qui n'excédera pas 60 jours * ; et tout crochet, clé, pince ou tout autre instrument, et tout fusil, pistolet, couteau, casse-tête ou toute autre arme offensive, trouvés en la garde et possession ou sur la personne du délinquant, seront, par le fait de la condamnation du délinquant, confisqués au profit de Sa Majesté, pour être vendus ou détruits, et, en cas de vente, le produit en sera appliqué aux besoins de la Colonie.—(*Voir aussi le No.* 416.)

419.—Toute personne qui s'évadera au moyen d'effraction ou de toute autre manière d'aucun lieu légal de détention avant l'expiration du temps pour lequel elle aura été condamnée à être emprisonnée en vertu de la présente ordonnance ; toute personne qui Idem, Art. 3.

---

* En confirmant cette Ordonnance, Sa Majesté a réduit le maximum de l'emprisonnement à 28 jours.—Proclamation du 5 Mars 1845.

against this Ordinance, which shall subject him or her to be dealt with as a rogue and vagabond, such person having been at some former time, adjudged so to be, and duly convicted thereof, and every person apprehended as a rogue and vagabond, and violently resisting any Police or Peace Officer, Constable or Police Guard so apprehending him or her, shall be deemed an incorrigible rogue within the true intent and meaning of this Ordinance, and it shall be lawful for any Stipendiary Magistrate to commit such offender to any lawful place of confinement, there to remain until the next sitting of the Court of First Instance* in correctional matters, then and there to be dealt with as hereinafter directed.—(*See also No.* 416.)

Idem, Art. 4. 420.—It shall be lawful for any Police or Peace Officer, Constable or Police Guard whatsoever to apprehend any person who shall be found offending against this Ordinance and forthwith to take and convey him or her before some Stipendiary Magistrate to be dealt with in such manner as is hereinbefore directed, provided always that in case no such Police or Peace Officer, Constable or Police Guard, shall be within a reasonable distance of the place where such offender shall be so found, it shall be lawful for any person whomsoever to apprehend such offender, and forthwith thereafter to carry him or her before some Stipendiary Magistrate or to deliver him or her to any Police or Peace Officer, Constable or Police Guard of the place where he or she shall have been apprehended, to be so taken and conveyed as aforesaid, and in case any Police or Peace Officer, Constable or Police Guard, shall refuse or wilfully neglect to take such offender into his custody and to take and convey him or her before any Stipendiary Magistrate, or shall not use his best endeavours to apprehend and convey before some Stipendiary Magistrate any person that he shall find offending against this Ordinance, it shall be deemed a neglect of duty in such Police or Peace Officer, Constable or Police Guard, and he shall, on conviction, be punished in such manner as is hereinafter directed.—(*See No.* 424.)

Idem, Art. 5. 421.—It shall be lawful for any Stipendiary Magistrate upon oath being made before him that any person has committed or is

---

* The Court of First Instance was abolished by Article 5 of Ordinance No. 2 of 1850,—by which law the "Supreme Court of the Colony of Mauritius" was established.

commettra quelqu'un des délits prévus par les dispositions ci-dessus, la mettant dans le cas d'être traitée comme vagabond et personne sans aveu, et qui aura été condamnée comme tel; et toute personne arrêtée comme vagabond et personne sans aveu qui résistera avec violence à tout officier de Paix ou de Police, constable ou garde de Police, sera considérée comme vagabond incorrigible dans le véritable sens et esprit de la présente Ordonnance, et tout Magistrat Salarié pourra faire détenir un tel délinquant dans tout lieu légal de détention pour y rester jusqu'à la première séance du tribunal de première instance * pour les matières correctionnelles, et pour y être traité de la manière qui sera ordonnée par le dit tribunal.—(*Voir aussi le No.* 416.)

420.—Tout officier de Paix ou de Police, tout constable ou garde de Police pourra, (et il leur est donné par la présente Ordonnance tout pouvoir et autorité à cet effet) arrêter toute personne qui sera trouvée commettant quelque infraction à la présente Ordonnance, à la charge de conduire ou envoyer immédiatement cette personne devant un Magistrat Salarié pour être procédé à son égard, ainsi qu'il a été dit ci-dessus; et, dans le cas où il n'y aurait aucun officier de Paix ou de Police, ni constable ou garde de Police à une distance raisonnable du lieu où le dit délinquant serait ainsi trouvé, toute personne est autorisée à se saisir de lui, et à le conduire de suite devant un Magistrat Salarié, ou le remettre et délivrer à tout officier de Paix ou de Police ou à tout constable ou garde de Police du lieu où le dit délinquant aura été arrêté, pour être conduit devant le Magistrat ainsi qu'il est dit ci-dessus. Tout officier de Paix ou de Police ou tout constable ou agent de Police, qui refuserait ou négligerait à dessein, de prendre un tel délinquant sous sa garde et de le conduire devant le Magistrat ou qui ne ferait pas tous ses efforts pour saisir et conduire devant un Magistrat Stipendiaire toute personne qui sera trouvée commettant une infraction à la présente Ordonnance, sera considéré comme coupable de négligence dans l'accomplissement de ses devoirs, et pourra être puni de la manière qui sera prescrite ci-après.—(*Voir le No.* 424.) Idem, Art. 4.

421.—Tout Magistrat Salarié, sur le serment qui sera fait devant lui, qu'une personne a commis un délit ou est soupçonnée Idem, Art. 5.

---

* Le Tribunal de Première Instance a été aboli par l'Article 5 de l'Ord. No. 2 de 1850.—C'est par cette loi que la "Cour Suprême de la Colonie de Maurice" a été établie.

suspected to have committed any offence against this Ordinance to issue his warrant and bring before him, or some other Stipendiary Magistrate, the person so charged, to be dealt with, as it is directed by this Ordinance.

Idem, Art. 6. 422.—When any such idle and disorderly person, rogue and vagabond shall give notice of his or her intention to appeal against the conviction of him or her, and shall enter into recognizance as hereinafter directed to prosecute such appeal, such Stipendiary Magistrate shall require the person by whom such offender shall be apprehended, and the person or persons whose evidence shall appear to him to prove the offence and to support such conviction, to become bound in recognizance to Her Majesty, her heirs and successors, to appear at the next sitting of the Court of First Instance, in correctional matters, to give evidence against such offender touching such offence; and in case any such person or persons aforesaid shall refuse to enter into such recognizance, it shall be lawful for such Stipendiary Magistrate to commit such person or persons so refusing to any lawful place of confinement, there to remain until he, she, or they shall enter into such recognizance or shall be otherwise discharged by due course of law.

Idem, Art. 7. 423.— When any person shall be committed for trial before the said Court of First Instance, charged with being an incorrigible rogue, it shall be lawful for the Court to examine into the circumstances of the case, and on conviction to order, if the Judge think fit, that such offender be imprisoned in some lawful place of confinement, and there, or on the public streets or highways, to be kept to hard labour for any time not exceeding six calendar months from the time of the date of the sentence.

Idem, Art. 8. 424.— In case any Police or Peace Officer, Constable, of Police Guard, shall neglect his duty in any thing required of him by this Ordinance, or in case any person shall disturb or hinder any Police or Peace Officer, Constable or Police Guard, in the execution of the present Ordinance, or shall be aiding, abetting or assisting therein and shall be thereof convicted upon the oath of one or more witness or witnesses before the Court of First Instance, every such offender shall for every such offence forfeit any sum not exceeding 20 pounds sterling. And in case such offender

d'avoir commis une infraction à la présente Ordonnance, pourra décerner un mandat pour l'arrêter et la faire conduire devant lui ou devant quelqu'autre Magistrat Salarié pour qu'il soit procédé à son égard de la manière prescrite par cette Ordonnance.

422.—Dans le cas où toute personne condamnée comme oisive et déréglée, vagabond ou personne sans aveu, donnerait avis de son intention d'appeler du jugement et souscrirait un engagement, comme il est dit ci-après, de suivre sur son appel, le Magistrat Salarié devra requérir la personne qui aura arrêté le délinquant et la personne ou les personnes dont le témoignage lui paraîtra nécessaire pour prouver le délit et soutenir sa décision, de souscrire un engagement envers Sa Majesté, ses héritiers et successeurs de comparaître à la première séance du Tribunal de Première Instance en matière de Police Correctionnelle, pour donner leur témoignage contre le délinquant, et dans le cas où quelqu'une des personnes ci-dessus mentionnées refuserait de souscrire un tel engagement, tout Magistrat Salarié pourra sur son refus, la faire détenir dans un lieu légal de détention pour y rester jusqu'à ce qu'elle ait souscrit l'engagement exigé ou qu'elle en ait été légalement dispensée. Idem, Art. 6.

423.—Lorsqu'une personne sera détenue pour être traduite devant le Tribunal de Première Instance sous la prévention d'être un vagabond incorrigible, le tribunal pourra examiner les circonstances du cas ; et si le délit est prouvé, ordonner, s'il le juge convenable, que le délinquant soit enfermé dans un lieu légal de détention pour être employé dans cette prison, ou dans les rues ou sur les chemins publics aux travaux forcés pendant un temps qui n'excèdera pas six mois à partir de la date du jugement. Idem, Art. 7.

424.—Dans tous les cas où quelque officier de Police ou de Paix, constable ou agent de la Police, négligerait son devoir dans aucune chose requise de lui par la présente ordonnance ou dans le cas où quelque personne troublerait un officier de Paix ou de Police, un constable agent de la Police dans l'exécution de cette Ordonnance, ou prêterait aide et assistance pour y résister, et serait convaincue du fait par le témoignage sous serment d'un ou de plusieurs témoins devant le Tribunal de Première Instance, le Idem, Art. 8.

shall not forthwith pay such sum so forfeited, the same shall be levied by distress and sale of the offender's goods by warrant from such Court, and if sufficient distress cannot be found, it shall be lawful to commit the person so offending to any lawful place of confinement, there to be kept for any time not exceeding thirty days, or until such fine be paid, which shall be paid over to the Colonial Treasury for the use of the Colony.

Idem, Art. 9. **425.**—It shall be lawful for any Stipendiary Magistrate upon information on oath before him made, that any person hereinbefore described to be an idle and disorderly person or a rogue and vagabond, or an incorrigible rogue is, or is reasonably suspected to be harboured or concealed in any house or place, by warrant under his hand and seal to authorize any Police or Peace Officer, Constable or other person or persons to enter at any time into such house or place and to apprehend and bring before him or any other Stipendiary Magistrate every such idle and disorderly person, rogue and vagabond and incorrigible rogue, as shall be then and there found, to be dealt with in the manner hereinbefore directed.

Idem, Art. 10. **426.**—Every conviction of any offender as an idle and disorderly person, or as a rogue and vagabond, or as an incorrigible rogue under this Ordinance shall be in the form following, or as near thereto as circumstances will permit, that is to say :

Mauritius. In the District (or Town) of

Be it remembered that on the day of in the year of our Lord, at in the Colony of Mauritius, is convicted before me. for that the said did (specify the offence, time and place when and where the same was committed as the case may be) and the said adjudge the said for the said offence, to be imprisoned in the house of correction, and there, or on the streets and highways, kept to hard labour for the space of days ensuing from the date hereof, this day to be accounted one.

Given under my hand and seal the day and year first above mentioned.

A. B.

Stipendiary Magistrate.

délinquant encourra une amende, qui n'excédera pas 20 livres sterling, et dans le cas ou le délinquant ne paierait pas immédiatement l'amende, elle sera prélevée au moyen de la saisie et de la vente de ses meubles, effectuée en vertu d'un Ordre de cette Cour; et s'il n'est pas trouvé de meubles suffisans, le tribunal pourra faire enfermer le délinquant dans un lieu légal de détention, pour y être détenu pendant un temps qui n'excèdera pas trente jours, ou jusqu'à ce que l'amende soit payée, laquelle sera versée au Trésor Colonial au profit de la Colonie.

425.—Tout Magistrat Salarié pourra sur l'information sous serment donnée devant lui, que toute personne ci-dessus désignée comme une personne oisive et déréglée, un vagabond ou un vagabond incorrigible, est, ou est soupçonnée avec quelque raison, d'être logée ou recelée dans aucune maison ou endroit quelconque, décerner un mandat de sa main et sous son sceau pour autoriser tout Officier de Paix ou de Police ou tout autre personne à entrer à n'importe quel moment dans la dite maison ou le dit lieu, et à arrêter et conduire devant lui ou tout autre Magistrat Salarié toute personne oisive et déréglée, vagabond ou vagabond incorrigible qui y sera trouvé, pour qu'il soit procédé à son égard de la manière et ainsi qu'il est dit ci-dessus. Idem, Art. 9.

426.—Tout jugement rendu contre aucun délinquant comme personne oisive et déréglée, vagabond ou vagabond incorrigible, en vertu de la présente Ordonnance sera redigé de la manière mentionnée dans la forme ci-après, ou à peu près, selon que les circonstances le permettront, savoir : Idem, Art. 10.

Maurice. Dans le quartier (ou la ville) de

Qu'il soit notoire que le jour de de l'an de Notre Seigneur, dans la Colonie de Maurice ; est convaincu devant moi d'avoir (spécifier le délit, le temps, le lieu où il a été commis) et moi condamne le dit pour le dit délit à l'emprisonnement dans et à y être employé aux travaux forcés, pendant jours, à compter de la date du présent jugement, ce jour compris.

Ecrit de ma main et sous mon sceau, les jour, mois et an ci-dessus.

A. B.

Magistrat Stipendiaire.

The Stipendiary Magistrates before whom any such conviction shall take place, shall, and he and they is and are hereby required to transmit the said conviction to the Court of First Instance, there to be filed and kept on record; and a copy of the conviction so filed, duly certified by the Registrar of that Court, shall and may be read as evidence in any Court of record or before any Stipendiary Magistrate acting under the powers and provisions of this Ordinance.

Idem, Art. 11. 427.—Any persons aggrieved by any act or determination of any Stipendiary Magistrate in or concerning the execution of this Ordinance may appeal to the said Court of First Instance, giving to the Stipendiary Magistrate whose act and determination shall be appealed against, notice in writing of such appeal and of the ground thereof, and entering within seven days into a recognizance with such sufficient surety before a Stipendiary Magistrate of the said Colony, personally to appear and prosecute such appeal, and upon such notice being given and such recognizance being entered into, such Stipendiary Magistrate is hereby empowered to discharge such person out of custody, and the said Court shall hear and determine the matter of such appeal, and shall make such order therein as shall to the said Court seem meet, and in case of the dismissal of the appeal, or the affirmance of the conviction, shall issue the necessary process for the apprehension and punishment of the offender, according to the conviction, provided always, that such appellant shall be bound to prosecute his said appeal before the next sitting of the said Court of First Instance in correctional matters.

Idem, Art. 12. 428.—All Laws and Ordinances now in force in the Colony for the prevention or punishment of Vagrancy shall be and the same are repealed.

Ord. No. 4 of 1864, Art. 10. 429.—All warrants of imprisonment for Vagrancy in any part of the Colony may be executed, either in whole or in part, by confinement in any Vagrant Depot under the provisions of this Ordinance.

Idem, Art. 14. 430.—The names and descriptions of all persons who shall be undergoing punishment for Vagrancy in any Prison or Depot, or

Le Magistrat Salarié qui aura prononcé le jugement, sera tenu de le transmettre au greffe du Tribunal de Première Instance, pour y être déposé et enregistré ; et une copie du dit jugement ainsi enregistré, dûment certifiée par le greffier du dit Tribunal, fera foi et pourra être reçue comme preuve devant toute Cour de Record ou devant tout Magistrat Salarié, agissant en vertu des pouvoirs et des dispositions de la présente Ordonnance.

427.—Toute personne qui se prétendra lésée par aucun acte ou décision de tout Magistrat Salarié donné en exécution ou concernant l'exécution de la présente Ordonnance, pourra en appeler devant le Tribunal de Première Instance, en donnant au Magistrat Salarié dont l'acte ou la décision sera attaquée, avis par écrit de l'appel et des motifs sur lesquels il est fondé, et souscrira dans le délai de sept jours, devant un Magistrat Salarié de la dite Colonie, un engagement avec caution suffisante de comparaître en personne et de suivre sur son appel ; sur l'avis donné et le cautionnement fourni, le Magistrat Salarié est autorisé à mettre la dite personne en liberté, et le dit Tribunal prendra connaissance de l'objet du dit appel et rendra telle décision qu'il jugera convenable ; en cas de rejet de l'appel ou de la confirmation de la décision le juge du dit Tribunal delivrera les ordres et mandats nécessaires pour l'arrestation et la punition du délinquant, conformément au jugement, pourvu toutefois que l'appelant soit tenu de suivre sur son appel à la prochaine séance du Tribunal de Première Instance en matières correctionnelles. Idem, Art. 11.

428.—Toutes les lois et Ordonnances actuellement en vigueur dans la Colonie pour la répression et la punition du Vagabondage seront et sont par les présentes rapportées. Idem, Art. 12.

429.—Tous warrants d'emprisonnement pour vagabondage dans toute partie de la Colonie pourront être exécutés soit en totalité ou en partie par un emprisonnement dans un Dépôt quelconque conformément aux dispositions de cette Ordonnance. Ord. No. 4 de 1864, Art. 10.

430.—Les noms et le signalement de toutes les personnes subissant l'emprisonnement pour Vagabondage dans une prison ou Idem, Art. 14.

who shall be employed at public works as herein aforesaid, shall be advertized, from time to time, in such manner as shall be provided by regulation.

Proclamation 24th March 1864, Art. 40. 431.—Whenever a Vagrant arrives at the Depot, the Depot Sergeant Major shall endeavour to ascertain the name and residence of his employer, and whenever he shall obtain such information, he shall, within 48 hours thereafter, despatch by messenger or through the Post Office, written notice to such employer, of the detention of his Vagrant servant at the Depot, in order that such employer may claim and receive his servant at the expiration of his term of imprisonment at the Depot. The names of all Vagrants, with the dates of their release from prison, and where obtainable, the names of their employers, shall be published weekly in the Government Gazette, and the Depot Sergeant Major shall furnish a return weekly for that purpose.

Idem, Art. 41. 432.—Any Vagrant who may not be claimed by his employer after notice has been sent to such employer, shall be taken before the Stipendiary Magistrate of Port Louis, who shall order whether he shall be set at liberty for the purpose of proceeding to his employer, or be conducted under escort thereto.

Idem, Art. 37. 433.—No person shall be admitted to the Depot to visit a prisoner without a written authority from the Inspector General of Police, but Masters or their Agents, seeking for their servants, may be permitted to do so between 5 and 6 o'clock a. m., and 5 and 6 o'clock p. m. daily.

Ord. No. 4 of 1864, Art. 12, § 1, 2, 3. 434.—Any person, who shall undergo punishment for Vagrancy either in any Prison, or in any Vagrant Depot in the Colony, shall upon the termination of the period of such punishment, be dealt with in one or other of the following ways as the case may be :

1o. If such Vagrant be under engagement and be claimed by his employer, he shall be delivered to such employer or to any person having his authority. It shall be lawful in such case for the Chief Officer in charge of the Depot at the time to deliver the Vagrant to any constable to be conducted to his employer by such constable or by any other constable to whose custody he shall

un dépôt, ou qui seront employées aux travaux publics comme il est dit ci-dessus, seront de temps à autre publiés de la manière qui sera ultérieurement fixée par des Réglements.

431.—Lorsqu'un Vagabond arrivera au Dépôt, le Sergent Major du Dépôt tâchera de s'assurer du nom et de la demeure de son employeur, et lorsqu'il aura obtenu cette information il donnera avis par écrit dans les quarante huit heures, par courrier ou par la poste, à l'employeur, de l'emprisonnement dans le Dépôt de son employé Vagabond, afin que l'employeur puisse réclamer et recevoir son employé Vagabond à l'expiration de son emprisonnement dans le Dépôt. Les noms de tous les Vagabonds et la date de leur mise en liberté de la prison, et (lorsque l'on peut se procurer le renseignement) le nom de leurs employeurs, seront publiés toutes les semaines dans la Gazette du Gouvernement, et le Sergent Major du Dépôt fournira à cet effet un état hebdomadaire. Proclamation du 24 Mars 1864, Art. 40.

432.—Tout Vagabond qui ne sera pas réclamé par son employeur après qu'on lui aura donné l'avis ci-dessus, sera conduit devant le Magistrat Stipendiaire du Port Louis, qui ordonnera sa mise en liberté pour qu'il retourne à son employeur ou qu'il lui soit conduit sous escorte. Idem, Art. 41.

433.—On n'admettra personne au Dépôt pour visiter un prisonnier sans un permis par écrit de l'Inspecteur Général de Police, mais les employeurs ou leurs agents cherchant leurs employés pourront le faire de cinq à six heures du matin et de cinq à six heures du soir tous les jours. Idem, Art. 37.

434.—Toute personne qui subira une peine prononcée contre elle pour Vagabondage, soit dans une prison, soit dans un dépôt de Vagabonds dans la Colonie, sera à l'expiration de sa condamnation traitée d'une des maniéres suivantes : Ord. No. 4 de 1864, Art. 12, § 1, 2, 3.

1o. Si le dit Vagabond est lié par un engagement et que son employeur le réclame il sera livré à son employeur ou à une personne quelconque autorisée par lui.—Dans ce cas le Chef Officier chargé du dépôt pourra livrer le Vagabond à un constable pour être conduit à son employeur par le dit constable ou par tout autre constable à qui il aura été transféré à cet effet, et tout

be transferred for the said purpose ; and every Vagrant shall be held to be under lawful custody while being so conducted to such employer.—For the purpose of the last foregoing provision it shall be lawful to every Stipendiary Magistrate to swear in as special constables one or more persons in employment on any estate in his District who shall be presented to him for such purpose by their employers, provided that the Magistrate be satisfied that such persons are fit for such duty. Every special constable aforesaid shall have the powers of an ordinary constable of police in conducting to his employer's property any Vagrant under the provisions of this Ordinance.—Such special constables shall not have constabulary powers of any kind beyond those hereinbefore described.

2o. If the Vagrant, being under engagement, shall not be claimed by his employer, notice shall be sent to the employer, if known, by the Chief Officer in charge of the Depot, in order that the employer may claim and receive such Vagrant.

3o. If the Vagrant, being under engagement to a known employer, shall not be claimed by such employer, after notice as aforesaid, he shall either be permitted to leave the Depot in order to go to his employer's property, or he shall be conducted to such property in manner herein-aforesaid according as shall be determined by the Stipendiary Magistrate of the District.

Govt. Notice No. 86 of 4th Aug. 1864, Sect. 5.

435.—Should the Depot Sergeant Major not be able to ascertain the employer of any unclaimed Vagrant at the termination of the term of imprisonment of such vagrant, such Vagrant shall be employed at public works for a period not less than three months, at the expiration of such period of three months such Vagrant shall be forwarded to the Protector of Immigrants for allotment to a new master, unless it should be proved that he is under an unexpired contract.

Ord. No. 4 of 1864, Art. 12, § 4, 5.

436.—4o. If the Vagrant shall not be found to be under engagement to any known employer he shall be employed at public works on such wages and allowances as shall be fixed by regulation for such period not being less than three months, as shall be fixed by regulation, and, as soon as may be thereafter, he shall be allotted to an employer to be named for him by the Protector of Immigrants, with which employer he shall be bound to enter into

Vagabond sera considéré être en état d'arrestation légale pendant qu'il sera ainsi conduit à son employeur.—Pour donner effet à la dernière disposition, tout Magistrat Stipendiaire pourra assermenter comme constables spéciaux une ou plusieurs personnes employées sur un établissement dans son district qui lui seront présentées par leurs employeurs, pourvu que le Magistrat soit satisfait que ces personnes sont capables de remplir ces fonctions. Tout constable spécial sus-dit aura les pouvoirs d'un constable ordinaire de la Police lorsqu'il conduira un Vagabond à la propriété de son employeur conformément aux dispositions de cette Ordonnance.—Ces constables spéciaux n'auront pas les pouvoirs de constables ordinaires au-delà de ceux déjà mentionnés.

2o. Si le Vagabond quoique lié par un engagement n'est pas réclamé par son employeur, avis en sera donné à l'employeur, s'il est connu, par l'Officier en Chef chargé du Dépôt, afin que l'employeur puisse réclamer et recevoir le dit Vagabond.

3o. Si le Vagabond est lié par engagement à un employeur connu, et n'est pas réclamé par cet employeur après que l'avis ci-dessus mentionné lui aura été donné, il sera permis au Vagabond de quitter le dépôt afin de se rendre à la propriété de son employeur ou il y sera conduit de la manière ci-dessus mentionnée selon que le Magistrat Stipendiaire du District en déterminera.

435.—Si le Sergent Major du Dépôt ne peut pas trouver le nom de l'employeur d'un Vagabond non réclamé à l'expiration du terme de son emprisonnement, il sera employé aux travaux publics pour un terme qui ne sera pas moins de trois mois. A l'expiration de ce terme de trois mois il sera envoyé au Protecteur des Immigrants pour être engagé à un nouveau maître à moins qu'il ne soit prouvé qu'il est encore lié par un engagement non expiré. Avis du Gouv. No. 86 du 4 Août 1864, Sect. 5.

436.—4o. S'il n'est pas reconnu que le Vagabond est lié par un engagement à un employeur connu, il sera employé aux travaux publics, aux gages et rations fixés par les Réglements, pour tout terme n'étant pas moins de trois mois qui sera fixé par les Réglements ; et sera ensuite aussitôt que possible réparti à un employeur qui lui sera désigné par le Protecteur des Immigrants, et avec lequel il sera dans l'obligation de passer un contrat de service, aux gages Ord. No. 4 de 1864, Art. 12, § 4, 5.

a contract of service at such rate of wages and allowances as shall be provided by regulations under this or any other Ordinance, and for such period as shall be determined by the said Protector of Immigrants to be requisite for the completion of his original obligation of five years industrial residence in the Colony.—Provided that the entering into any such contract of service shall not be held to free the Vagrant from any lawful engagement to which he was subject at the time ; or to impair the right of his employer under any previous contract of service to enforce such contract against him.—Until the Vagrant shall enter into a contract of service as herein-before provided (Par. 4o.) he shall continue to be employed at public works as hereinaforesaid.

5o. During the time the Vagrant shall be employed at public works as herein-before provided (paragraph 4o.) he shall remain liable to detention in any Vagrant Depôt; and while detained therein shall be subject to all the rules for the discipline thereof in the same manner as if he were at the time undergoing punishment as a Vagrant therein.

Proc. of 24th March 1864, Art. 38.

437.—Any prisoner claimed by his employer shall, at the expiration of his term of imprisonment, be delivered up to his employer, or to any special constable employed by him, and legally sworn in as such before the Stipendiary Magistrate of the District in which he resides.

Idem, Art. 48.

438.—The appointment of a special constable under *Article 12 of the Ordinance* shall be only for 12 calendar months, but any such constable may be re-appointed. The oath to be taken by special constables under the said article, shall be in the terms of Schedule A.—(*Article* 12,—*See No.* 434.)

SCHEDULE A.

I do solemnly swear (or affirm and declare as the case may be), that I shall faithfully perform the duties of Special Constable, appointed for 12 months, from this date for Mr. of in the District of for the purpose of conveying Vagrants from the Vagrant Depot to the said Estate.

Constable's Signature or Mark.

Sworn (or solemnly affirmed) before me, Stipendiary Magistrate for the District of this day of 186 .

C. D.

Stipendiary Magistrate.

et rations qui seront fixés par les Réglements faits en vertu de cette Ordonnance ou de toute autre Ordonnance, pour tout le temps que le dit Protecteur des Immigrants jugera nécessaire pour l'achèvement de son obligation d'une résidence industrielle de cinq ans dans la colonie. Pourvu que ce contrat de service ne soit pas considéré comme libérant le Vagabond d'un engagement légal par lequel il était lié lors de la passation de ce contrat, ni comme portant atteinte au droit que peut avoir son employenr en vertu de tout autre contrat de service antérieur de le forcer à exécuter ce contrat. Jusqu'à ce que le Vagabond consènte à s'engager par contrat de service comme il est dit ci-dessus (par : 4o.) il continuera à être employé aux travaux publics comme il est dit ci-dessus.

5o. Pendant le temps que le Vagabond sera employé aux travaux publics conformément aux dispositions précédentes (par : 4o.) il pourra être détenu dans un dépôt de Vagabonds quelconque ; et pendant qu'il y sera détenu il sera soumis aux réglements pour la discipline du dépôt de la même manière que s'il y subissait à cette époque une punition comme Vagabond.

437.—Tout prisonnier réclamé par son employeur, sera, à l'expiration de son terme d'emprisonnement, livré à son employeur ou à tout constable spécial employé par lui et légalement assermenté comme tel devant le Magistrat Stipendiaire du District ou il demeure. Proc. du 21 Mars 1864, Art. 38.

438.—La nomination d'un constable spécial conformément à *l'Article* 12 *de l'Ordonnance* ne sera valable que pour un an, mais ce constable spécial pourra être nommé de nouveau. Le serment que prêteront les constables spéciaux sera dans les termes de la Cédule A.—(*Article* 12.—*Voir le No.* 434.) Idem, Art. 48.

CÉDULE A.

Je jure solennellement (ou affirme et déclare selon le cas) que je remplirai fidèlement les devoirs de Constable Spécial, nommé pour un an, à compter de ce jour pour M. de dans le district de afin de conduire des Vagabonds du Dépôt des Vagabonds à la dite habitation.

Signature ou marque du Constable.

Assermenté ou (solennellement affirmé) devant moi, Magistrat Stipendiaire du District de ce 186 .

C. D.

Magistrat Stipendiaire.

Every Stipendiary Magistrate on swearing in any special constable, shall deliver to such constable a certificate in terms of Schedule B, signed by such Magistrate, and shall, as soon as may be, forward a duplicate thereof to the Chief Officer of the Depot.

SCHEDULE B.

I do hereby certify that I have this day sworn in (Constable's name and nationality), as Special Constable under Ordinance No. 4 of 1864 for 12 months from this date for M of in the District of

A. B.

Stipendiary Magistrate for the District of

A list in the Form of Schedule C, of all special constables duly appointed with the items specified in the said Schedule, shall be affixed at a conspicuous place at the Depot, and shall be renewed, or corrected on the first day of each month.

SCHEDULE C.

List of Special Constables appointed and sworn under Ordinance No. 4 of 1864.

Constable's Name.	Date of appointment.	For whom appointed.	For what property appointed.	For what District appointed.

A similar list of all the special constables of the District shall be affixed at the Stipendiary Magistrate's Court House in each District. Any special constable may have his authority to act as such withdrawn by the Stipendiary Magistrate of his District, on the application of his employer, or without such application in case of misconduct of any kind on the part of the constable; notice of such withdrawal shall be forthwith sent to the Chief Officer of the Depot, and the list at the Depot and the Stipendiary Court shall be corrected accordingly.

Idem, Art. 39. 439.—Every such special constable shall, before receiving any Vagrant into his custody, produce a certificate from the Stipen-

Tout Magistrat Stipendiaire en assermentant un constable spécial, lui donnera un certificat dans les termes de la Cédule B, signé par lui, et aussitôt que faire se pourra, il en enverra un duplicata à l'Officier en Chef du Dépôt.

CÉDULE B.

Je certifie que j'ai ce jour assermenté (nom du Constable et sa nationalité) comme Constable Spécial, conformément à l'Ordonnance No. 4 de 1864 pour un an à compter de ce jour pour M de dans le District de

A. B.
Magistrat Stipendiaire du District de

Une liste dans la forme de la Cédule C, de tous les constables spéciaux dûment nommés, avec les détails mentionnés dans la dite Cédule, sera affichée dans un endroit apparent au Dépôt, et sera renouvelée ou corrigée le 1er de chaque mois.

CÉDULE C.

Liste des Constables Spéciaux nommés et assermentés conformément à l'Ordonnance No. 4 de 1864.

Nom du Constable.	Date de nomination.	Pour qui nommé.	Pour quelle propriété nommé.	Pour quel District nommé.

Une liste pareille de tous les constables spéciaux du district sera affichée à la Cour du Magistrat Stipendiaire dans chaque District. Tout Magistrat Stipendiaire pourra, à la demande de l'employeur, révoquer la nomination d'un constable spécial de son district, et, en cas d'inconduite de la part du constable, il pourra le faire sans la demande de l'employeur. Avis de la révocation sera envoyé à l'Officier en Chef du Dépôt et les listes affichées au Dépôt et à la Cour Stipendiaire, seront corrigées en conséquence.

439.—Avant de recevoir en sa garde un Vagabond, tout constable spécial, produira un certificat du Magistrat Stipendiaire de Idem. Art. 39.

diary Magistrate of his district, setting forth that he has been lawfully sworn in as a special constable under Ordinance No. 4 of 1864, and the name of his employer.

COALITION.

Ord. No. 6 of 1838, Art. 340, (Penal Code.) **440.**—Any coalition among persons employing workmen, servants, labourers, or others, either in town or in the country, having for object unjustly and abusively to force the lowering of wages, shall be punished by imprisonment not exceeding three months, and by a fine not exceeding two hundred pounds sterling.

Idem, Art. 341. **441.**—Any coalition among workmen, servants, labourers, or others, either in town or in the country, to cease from working at the same time, or to forbid work, or to prevent others from proceeding to or remaining at their work, before or after certain hours, or generally to suspend or prevent any work, or to raise the price thereof, shall be punished by imprisonment not exceeding three months. The principals or ringleaders shall be punished by the maximum of this punishment.

Idem, Art. 342. **442.**—The punishment set forth in the preceding article shall be applied, under the like distinctions, to any workmen, servants, labourers or others, as well as to masters who shall have imposed any fine, prohibition, interdiction or any other proscription, under whatever denomination, whether against one another or against managers of working establishments, or undertakers of works.

Order in Council 7th Sept. 1838, Cap. 6, Sect. 1. § 1. **443.**—The Act of the British Parliament passed in the Sixth year of the Reign of George the Fourth, intituled "An Act to repeal the Laws relative to the combination of Workmen, and for other purposes therein mentioned," shall be in force in the said Colonies, and applied in the administration of the law therein, so far as it may be practicable to apply the same; but the powers thereby vested in the Justices of the Peace in England shall in

son District, constatant qu'il a été légalement assermenté comme constable spécial, conformément à l'Ordonnance No. 4 de 1864, et donnant le nom de son employeur.

COALITION.

440.—Toute coalition entre ceux qui font travailler des ouvriers, domestiques, laboureurs et employés, à la ville ou à la campagne, tendant à forcer injustement et abusivement l'abaissement des salaires, sera puni d'un emprisonnement qui n'excèdera pas trois mois et d'une amende qui ne pourra excéder deux cents livres sterling. Ord. No. 6 de 1838, Art. 340. (Code Pénal)

441.—Toute coalition de la part des ouvriers, domestiques, laboureurs et employés, à la ville ou à la campagne, pour faire cesser en même temps de travailler, interdire le travail, empêcher de s'y rendre et d'y rester avant ou après de certaines heures, et en général, pour suspendre, empêcher, enchérir les travaux, sera puni d'un emprisonnement de trois mois au plus. Les chefs ou moteurs seront punis du maximum de cette peine. Idem, Art. 341.

442.—Seront aussi punis de la peine portée au précédent article, et d'après les mêmes distinctions, les ouvriers, domestiques, laboureurs ou employés, comme aussi les maîtres de ceux-ci, qui auront prononcé des amendes, des défenses, des interdictions, ou toutes autres proscriptions, sous quelque qualification que ce puisse être, soit contre les directeurs d'ateliers et entrepreneurs d'ouvrages, soit les uns contre les autres. Idem, Art. 342.

443.—L'Acte du Parlement Britannique, passé dans la sixième année du règne de George IV, intitulé : " Acte pour rapporter les lois relatives à la coalition des ouvriers et pour d'autres objets y mentionnés ", sera mis en vigueur dans lesdits colonies, et y sera appliqué dans l'administration de la justice, autant qu'il sera praticable ; mais les pouvoirs qui sont donnés aux Juges de Paix en Angleterre appartiendront, dans les dites colonies, aux Ordre en Conseil du 7 Sept. 1838, Ch. 6, Sect. 1, § 1.

the said Colonies be vested in the said Stipendiary Magistrates, and the power thereby vested in any Court of General or Quarter Sessions shall in the said Colonies be vested in the said beforementioned Court of Petty Sessions, and the power thereby vested in Her Majesty's Superior Courts of Westminster shall in the said Colonies respectively be vested in the Superior Courts of Civil and Criminal Justice thereof; and for the better adaptation of the said Act of Parliament, to the circumstances of the said respective Colonies, such analogous forms of proceeding shall be prescribed, in manner aforesaid, by the Governor of each such Colony respectively, with the sanction of the Chief Judge of the same.

Satute. 6, Geo. 4. Cap. 129, Sect. 3.

444.—And be it further enacted, that from and after the passing of this Act, if any person shall by violence to the person or property, or by threats or intimidation, or by molesting or in any way obstructing another, force or endeavour to force any journeyman, manufacturer, workman or other person not being hired or employed in any manufacture, trade, or business, to depart from his hiring, employment or work, or to return his work before the same shall be finished, or prevent or endeavour to prevent any journeyman, manufacturer, workman or other person not being hired or employed from hiring himself to, or from accepting work or employment from any person or persons; or if any person shall use or employ violence to the person, or property of another, or threats or intimidation, or shall molest or in any way obstruct another for the purpose of forcing or inducing such person to belong to any club or association, or to contribute to any common fund; or to pay any fine or penalty, or on account of his not belonging to any particular club or association, or not having contributed or having refused to contribute to any common fund, or to pay any fine or penalty, or on account of his not having complied or of his refusing to comply with any rules, orders, resolutions or regulations made to obtain an advance or to reduce the rate of wages, or to lessen or alter the hours of working or to decrease or alter the quantity of work, or to regulate the mode of carrying on any manufacture, trade, or business or the management thereof; or if any person shall by violence to the person or property of another, or by threats or intimidation, or by molesting or in any way obstructing another, force or endeavour to force any manufacturer or person carrying on any trade

Magistrats Salariés, et les pouvoirs des Cours de " General " ou " Quarter Sessions " seront dévolus, dans lesdites colonies, aux Cours de " Petty Sessions " ci-dessus mentionnées, et les pouvoirs attribués aux Cours Supérieures de Sa Majesté dans Westminster seront, dans les dites colonies respectivement, dévolus aux Cours Supérieures de Justice civile et criminelle, et pour mieux adapter le dit Acte du Parlement aux localités desdites colonies respectivement, des formes analogues de procédure seront prescrites, de la manière ci-dessus indiquée, par le Gouverneur de chaque colonie respectivement, avec la sanction du Chef-Juge. "

444.—Et il est en outre ordonné qu'à partir du jour où le dit acte sera passé, toute personne qui usera de violence envers la personne ou la propriété d'autrui ou qui se servira de menaces ou qui intimidera ou molestera ou contrariera en aucune manière une personne quelconque, et par ces moyens forcera ou cherchera à forcer un ouvrier, un manufacturier, ou tout autre individu loué ou employé dans une manufacture ou à un commerce ou à une occupation quelconque à quitter son service, son emploi ou son ouvrage, ou à rendre son travail avant qu'il ne soit achevé, ou qui empêchera ou cherchera à empêcher un ouvrier, un manufacturier, ou une autre personne quelconque qui ne serait pas louée ou employée, de se louer ou d'accepter de l'ouvrage ou de l'emploi de tout individu quelconque, ou toute personne qui usera de violence envers la personne ou la propriété d'autrui, ou qui se servira de menaces, ou qui intimidera ou molestera ou contrariera en aucune manière une autre personne dans le but de forcer ou d'engager cette personne à appartenir à un club ou à une association quelconque, ou à contribuer à un fond commun, ou à payer une amende quelconque, ou par le motif qu'il n'appartient à aucun club ni à aucune association particulière, ou qu'il n'a pas contribué ou qu'il a refusé de contribuer à un fond commun quelconque ou de payer une amende, ou par le motif qu'il ne s'est pas conformé ou qu'il a refusé de se conformer à aucuns réglements, ordres ou résolutions adoptés dans le but d'obtenir une avance de gages ou d'en réduire le taux, ou de diminuer ou de changer les heures de travail, ou de diminuer ou de changer la quantité de travail, ou de régler le mode d'administration d'une manufacture, d'un commerce ou d'une occupation quelconque, ou

Acte du Parlement. 6, Geo. 4, C. 129, Sect. 3.

or business, to make any alteration in his mode of regulating, managing, conducting or carrying on such manufacture, trade or business or to limit the number of his apprentices, or the number or description of his journeymen, workmen, or servants; every person so offending, or aiding, abetting or assisting therein, being convicted thereof in manner hereinafter mentioned, shall be imprisoned only, or shall and may be imprisoned and kept to hard labour, for any time not exceeding three calendar months.

Idem, Sect. 4. 445.—Provided always and be it enacted, that this Act shall not extend to subject any persons to punishment, who shall meet together for the sole purpose of consulting upon and determining the rate of wages or prices, which the persons present, at such meeting or any of them shall require or demand for his or their work, or the hours or time for which he or they shall work in any manufacture, trade, or business, or who shall enter into any agreement, verbal or written, among themselves, for the purpose of fixing the rate of wages or prices which the parties entering into such agreement, or any of them shall require or demand for his or their work, or the hours or time for which he or they will work in any manufacture, trade or business; and that persons so meeting for the purposes aforesaid or entering into any such agreement as aforesaid, shall not be liable to any prosecution or penalty for so doing; any law or statute to the contrary notwithstanding.

Idem. Sect. 5. 446.—Provided also, and be it further enacted that this act shall not extend to subject any person, to punishment, who shall meet together for the sole purpose of consulting upon and determining the rate of wages or prices, which the persons present at such meeting, or any of them, shall pay to his or their journeymen, workmen or servants, for their work or the hours or time of working in any manufacture, trade or business or who shall enter into any agrement, verbal or written, among themselves, for the

toute personne qui usera de violence envers la personne ou la propriété d'autrui, ou qui se servira de menaces ou qui intimidera ou molestera ou contrariera d'une manière quelconque une autre personne, et qui par ces moyens forcera ou cherchera à forcer un manufacturier ou un individu exerçant un commerce ou un métier quelconque à changer sa manière d'administrer la dite manufacture ou d'exercer le dit commerce ou métier, ou de limiter le nombre de ses apprentis ou le nombre ou l'espèce de ses ouvriers ou domestiques ; toute personne qui sera convaincue de la manière indiquée ci-dessus, d'avoir commis les actes sus-mentionnés ou d'avoir aidé ou concouru à les commettre sera emprisonnée seulement ou sera et pourra être emprisonnée et tenue aux travaux forcés pendant un temps qui n'excèdera pas trois mois.

445.—Pourvu néanmoins et il est ordonné que le présent Acte n'aura pas pour effet d'assujetir à une punition quelconque toutes personnes qui se réuniront dans le seul but de se consulter et de prendre une détermination sur le taux des gages ou des prix que demanderont pour travailler les individus qui seront présens aux dites réunions ou qu'ils exigeront pour les heures ou le temps de travail qu'ils passeront dans une manufacture ou dans un commerce ou à une occupation quelconque, ou qui contracteront ou passeront un engagement quelconque, verbal ou écrit, dans l'intention de fixer le taux des gages ou des prix que demanderont les parties contractantes pour le travail ou les heures de travail qu'elles feront ou qu'elles passeront dans une manufacture ou dans un commerce ou une occupation quelconques et que toutes personnes qui se réuniront dans le but sus-mentionné ou qui passeront des engagements pour les fins sus-énoncées ne seront exposées à aucune poursuite ni à aucune amende pour avoir agi ainsi, nonobstant toute loi ou tout statut à ce contraire. Idem, Sect. 4.

446.—Pourvu néanmoins et il est de plus ordonné que cet acte n'aura pas pour effet d'exposer à une punition quelconque toutes personne qui se réuniront dans le seul but de se consulter et de prendre une détermination sur le taux des gages ou des prix que les personnes présentes aux dites réunions devront payer à leurs ouvriers ou domestiques pour leur travail ou pour les heures ou le temps qu'ils passeront dans une manufacture ou à travailler à un commerce, ou à une occupation quelconques ou qui feront ou pas- Idem, Sect. 5.

purpose of fixing the rate of wages or prices, which the parties entering into such agreement, or any of them, shall pay to his or their journeymen, workmen or servants for their work, or the hours or time of working in any manufacture, trade or business; and that persons so meeting for the purposes aforesaid, or entering into any such agreement as aforesaid, shall not be liable to any prosecution or penalty for so doing, any law or statute to the contrary notwithstanding.

Idem, Sect. 6. 447.—And be it further enacted that all and every persons or person who shall and may offend against this act, shall and may, equally with all other persons, be called upon and compelled to give his or her testimony and evidence as a witness or witnesses on behalf of His Majesty, or of the Prosecutor or Informer, upon any information to be made or exhibited under this act against any other person or persons not being such witness or witnesses as aforesaid; and that in all such cases every person having given his or her testimony or evidence as aforesaid, shall be and is hereby indemnified of, from, and against any information to be laid or prosecution to be commenced against him or her for having offended in the matter wherein or relative to which he, she or they shall have given testimony or evidence as aforesaid.

Idem, Sect. 7. 448.—And for the more effectually enforcing and carrying into execution the provisions of this Act, be it further enacted that on complaint and information on oath before any one or more Justice or Justices of the Peace, of any offence having been committed against this Act, within his or their respective jurisdiction, and within six calendar months before such complaint or information shall be made, such Justice or Justices are hereby authorized and required to summon the person or persons charged with being an offender or offenders against this Act, to appear before any two such Justices, at a certain time or place to be specified; and if any person or persons so summoned shall not appear according to such summons, then such Justices, (proof on oath having been first made before them of the due service of such summons upon such person or persons, by delivering the same to him or them, personally, or leaving the same at his or their usual place of abode, provided the same shall be so left twenty four

seront un contrat ou engagement verbal ou écrit entre elles, afin de fixer le taux des gages ou les prix que chacune des parties contractantes devra payer à ses ouvriers ou à ses domestiques pour leur travail ou pour les heures de travail passées dans une manufacture ou dans un commerce ou à une occupation quelconques. Et que les personnes qui se réuniront dans le but sus-mentionné ou qui feront ou passeront un engagement comme sus-énoncé ne seront assujetties à aucune poursuite ni à aucune amende pour avoir agi de cette manière nonobstant toute loi ou tout statut à ce contraire.

447.—Et il est en outre ordonné que toute personne qui transgressera le présent acte pourra, de même que tous autres individus, être appelée et forcée à déposer comme témoin en faveur de Sa Majesté ou du poursuivant ou du dénonciateur, dans toute instruction qui serait faite en vertu de cet acte, contre toutes personnes autres que le témoin ou les témoins sus-mentionnés et que dans tous ces cas la personne qui aura déposé comme susdit est et sera par le présent à l'abri de toute poursuite quelconque qui pourrait être intentée contre elle pour avoir contrevenu à la loi dans l'affaire pour laquelle elle aura déposé comme sus-mentionné. Idem, Sect. 6.

448.—Et afin de mettre en vigueur d'une manière plus efficace les dispositions de cet Acte, il est en outre ordonné que sur la plainte ou la dénonciation sous serment qui sera faite devant un ou plusieurs Juges de Paix qu'un délit aura été commis relativement au présent Acte dans leur juridiction respective et dans les six mois révolus qui auront précédé la dite plainte ou dénonciation, les dits Juges de Paix sont autorisés et requis par le présent, d'assigner la personne qui sera accusée d'avoir transgressé le présent Acte à comparaître devant deux des dits Juges de Paix aux lieu et heure qui seront indiqués et si la personne qui aura été ainsi assignée ne comparaît pas conformément à la dite assignation, les dits Juges de Paix (sur la preuve sous serment qui aura été fournie devant eux que la dite assignation a été duement notifiée à personne ou domicile vingt-quatre heures au moins avant l'heure indiquée pour comparaître devant les dits Juges de Paix), délivreront un mandat d'arrêt contre les personnes assignées Idem, Sect. 7.

hours at the least before the time which shall be appointed to attend the said Justices upon such summons) shall make or issue their warrant or warrants for apprehending the person or persons so summoned, and not appearing as aforesaid, and bringing him or them before such Justices; or it shall be lawful for such Justices, if they shall think fit, without issuing any previous summons, and instead of issuing the same, upon such complaint and information as aforesaid, to make and issue their warrant or warrants for apprehending the person or persons by such information charged to have offended against this Act, and bringing him or them before such Justices; and upon the person or persons complained against appearing upon such summons, or being brought by virtue of such warrant or warrants before such Justices, or upon proof on oath of such person or persons absconding, so that such warrant or warrants cannot be executed, then such Justices shall and they are hereby authorized and required forthwith to make inquiry touching the matters complained of, and to examine into the same by the oath or oaths of any one or more credible person or persons as shall be requisite, and to hear and determine the matter of every such complaint; and upon confession by the party, or proof by one or more credible witness or witnesses upon oath, to convict or acquit the party or parties against whom complaint shall have been made as aforesaid.

Idem, Sect. 8. 449.—And be it further enacted, that it shall be lawful for the Justices of the Peace before whom any such complaint and information shall be made as aforesaid, and they are hereby authorized and required, at the request in writing of any of the parties, to issue his or their summons to any witness or witnesses to appear and give evidence before such Justices, at the time and place appointed for hearing and determining such complaint, and which time and place shall be specified in such summons; and if any person or persons so summoned to appear as a witness or witnesses as aforesaid, shall not appear before such Justices at the time and place specified in such summons; or offer some reasonable excuse for the default, or appearing according to such summons, shall not submit to be examined as a witness or witnesses, and give his or her evidence before such Justices, touching the matter of such complaint, then and in every such case, it shall be lawful for such Justices, and they are hereby authorized (proof on

comme sus-dit et ne comparaîssant pas ou les dits Juges de Paix pourront s'ils le jugent convenable, et sans assignation préalable délivrer sur la plainte ou la dénonciation sus-mentionnée un mandat d'arrêt contre la personne accusée d'avoir transgressé le présent Acte et lorsque la personne contre laquelle plainte aura été portée, comparaîtra en vertu de la dite assignation, ou sera amenée conformément au sus-dit mandat devant les dits Juges ou lorsque preuve sous serment aura été fournie que la dite personne s'est sauvée et que conséquemment le dit mandat ne peut être exécuté, les dits Juges sont requis et autorisés dans ce cas à s'informer des faits pour lesquels on a porté plainte et à interroger sur iceux et sous serment une ou plusieurs personnes dignes de foi, ainsi qu'il sera nécessaire, et à prononcer sur la dite plainte et sur l'aveu de la partie ou sur la preuve fournie par un ou plusieurs témoins dignes de foi, à condamner et à acquitter la partie contre laquelle plainte aura été portée comme sus-dit.

449.—Et il est en outre ordonné que les Juges de Paix devant qui une plainte aura été portée ou une dénonciation faite comme susdit pourront et ils sont par ces présentes requis et autorisés sur la demande par écrit de l'une des parties à assigner un ou plusieurs témoins pour déposer devant eux au lieu et à l'heure spécifiés dans la dite assignation et indiqués à l'effet de statuer sur la dite plainte. Et si la personne ainsi citée comme témoin ne comparait pas devant les dits Juges au lieu et à l'heure mentionnés dans l'assignation ou si elle ne donne aucune excuse raisonnable pour son absence ou si comparaissant conformément à l'assignation elle ne se soumet pas à l'interrogatoire qu'elle doit subir comme témoin et ne dépose pas devant les dits Juges sur la dite plainte, les dits Juges de Paix pourront, dans ce cas et ils sont par ces présentes requis et autorisés (la preuve sous serment dans le cas où la personne ne comparait pas conformément à la dite assignation ayant d'abord été fournie devant les dits Juges de Paix à Idem, Sect. 8.

oath, in the case of any person not appearing according to such summons, having been first made before such Justices of the Peace, of the due service of such summons on every such person, by delivering the same to him or her; or by leaving the same twenty four hours before the time appointed for such person to appear before such Justices at the usual place of abode of such person), by warrant under the hands of such Justices, to commit such person or persons so making default in appearing or appearing and refusing to give evidence, to some prison within the jurisdiction of such Justices, there to remain without bail or mainprize for three calendar months, or until such person or persons shall submit to be examined and give evidence before such Justices as aforesaid.

Idem, Sect. 9. 450.—And be it further enacted, that the Justices before whom any person or persons shall be convicted of any offence against this Act, or by whom any person shall be committed to prison for not appearing as a witness, or not submitting to be examined, shall cause all such convictions and the warrants or orders for such commitments, to be drawn up in the form or to the effect set forth in the Schedule to this Act annexed.

SCHEDULE.

Form of Conviction and Commitment.

Form of conviction. Be it remembered, that on the day of in the year of His Majesty's Reign, and in the year of Our Lord A. B is convicted before us (*naming the Justices*) two of His Majesty's Justices of the Peace for the County (*or Riding, Division, City, Liberty, Town or Place*) of having (*stating the offence*) contrary to the Act made in the sixth year of the Reign of King GEORGE the Fourth, intituled " An Act (*here set forth the title of this Act*) : And we, the said Justices do hereby order and adjudge the said A. B. for the said offence to be committed to and confined in the common Gaol for the said County (*or Riding, Division, City, Liberty, Town or Place*) for the space of or to be committed to the house of correction at within the said County (*or Riding, Division, City, Liberty, Town or Place*) there to be kept to hard labour for the space of

Given under our hands, the day and year above written.

(*Signatures.*)

Form of Commitment of a person summoned as a witness.

Commitment. Whereas E. D. hath been duly summoned to appear and give evidence before us (*naming the Justices who issued the*

l'effet d'établir que la dite assignation a duement été notifiée à la dite personne ou laissée à son domicile vingt-quatre heures avant l'heure fixée pour comparaître) à faire incarcérer par mandat signé des dits Juges la personne qui n'aura pas comparu comme sus-dit ou qui comparaissant aura refusé de déposer, dans l'une des prisons situées dans la juridiction des dits Juges et à y détenir la dite personne sans caution pendant trois mois révolus ou jusqu'à ce que la dite personne consente à être interrogée et à déposer devant les dits Juges de Paix comme sus-dit.

450.—Et il est en outre ordonné que les juges devant lesquels une personne quelconque aura été convaincue d'avoir transgressé le présent acte, ou par qui une personne quelconque aura été emprisonnée pour n'avoir pas comparu comme témoin, ou pour n'avoir pas voulu se laisser interroger, feront rédiger les dites condamnations, mandats ou ordres dans la forme indiquée par la cédule annexée au présent acte. Idem. Sect. 9.

CÉDULE.

Forme de Condamnation et de Mandat d'Emprisonnement.

Forme de condamnation. Qu'il soit notoire que ce jour de dans la année du Règne de Sa Majesté, et dans l'année de notre Seigneur A. B. a été convaincu devant nous (*noms des juges*) deux juges de paix de Sa Majesté pour le Comté, (*ou la division, la ville ou l'endroit*) de d'avoir (*spécifier le délit*) contrairement à l'Acte passé dans la sixième année du règne du roi George IV, intitulée : " Acte (*indiquer le titre du présent Acte.*) Et nous, les dits juges, ordonnons par le présent que le dit A. B. soit incarcéré pour avoir commis le susdit délit, dans la prison du dit Comté, (*ou division, ville ou endroit*) pendant ou que le dit A. B. soit détenu dans la maison de correction de dans le dit Comté (*ou division, ville ou endroit*) pour y être employé aux travaux forcés pendant

Donné sous notre seing, les jour et an ci-dessus.

(*Signatures.*)

Forme de Mandat d'Emprisonnement contre une personne assignée comme témoin.

Emprisonnement. Attendu que E. D. a été dûment assigné à comparaître et à déposer devant nous (*noms des juges qui ont délivré l'assigna-*

summons) two of His Majesty's Justices of the Peace for the County (*or Riding, Division, City, Liberty, Town or Place*) of on this day of at being the time and place appointed for hearing and determining the complaint made by (*the informer or prosecutor*) before us, against A. B. of having (*stating the offence as laid in the information*) contrary to the Act made in the year of the Reign of King GEORGE the Fourth, intituled " An Act (*here insert the title of this Act*). And whereas the said E. D. hath not appeared before us at the time and place aforesaid specified for that purpose, or offered any reasonable excuse for his (*or her*) default, (or and whereas the said E. D. having appeared before us, at the time and place aforesaid, specified for that purpose, hath not submitted to be examined as a witness and give his (*or her*) evidence before us touching the matter of the said complaint, but hath refused so to do) ; therefore we, the said Justices, do hereby, in pursuance of the said statute, commit the said E. D. to the (*describing the prison*), there to remain without bail or mainprize, for his (*or her*) contempt aforesaid, for three calendar months, or until he (*or she*) shall submit himself (*or herself*) to be examined, and give his (*or her*) evidence before us, touching the matter of the said complaint, or shall otherwise be discharged by due course of law. And you (*the Constable or other Peace Officers or Officers to whom the warrant is directed*) are hereby authorized and required to take into your custody the body of the said E. D. and him (*or her*) safely to convey to the said prison, and him (*or her*) there to deliver to the Gaoler or Keeper thereof, who is hereby authorized and required to receive into his custody the body of the said E. D. and him (*or her*) safely to detain and keep, pursuant to this commitment.

Given under our hands, this day of in the year of Our Lord

(*Signatures.*)

(This commitment to be directed to the proper Peace Officer, and the Gaoler or Keeper of the Prison.)

Idem, Sect. 10. 451.—And be it further enacted, that the Justices before whom any such conviction shall be had, shall cause the same (drawn up to the form or to the effect hereinbefore directed) to be fairly written on parchment and transmitted to the next General Sessions or General Quarter Sessions of the Peace, to be holden for the county, riding, division, city, liberty, town or place wherein such conviction was had, to be filed amongst the records of the said General Sessions or General Quarter Sessions ; and in case any person or persons shall appeal, in manner hereinafter mentioned, from the judgment of the said Justices, to the said General Sessions or General Quarter Sessions, the Justices in such General Sessions or General Quarter Sessions are hereby required upon receiving such conviction to proceed to the hearing and determining of the matter of the said appeal according to the directions of this Act.

tion) deux des juges de paix de Sa Majesté dans le Comté (ou la division, la ville ou l'endroit) de ce jour de à jour et heure fixés, pour procéder à l'instruction et à la décision de la plainte faite par (*nommez le poursuivant ou le dénonciateur*) devant nous contre A. B. pour avoir, (*faites connaître le délit tel qu'il est mentionné dans la dénonciation*) contrairement à l'Acte passé dans la sixième année du règne du roi George IV, intitulé : " Acte (*ici indiquez le titre de l'Acte.*) Et attendu que le dit E. D. n'a pas comparu pardevant nous, à l'heure et au lieu indiqués, et n'a présenté aucune excuse valable pour son absence (ou et attendu que le dit E. D. ayant comparu par devant nous à l'heure et au lieu indiqués ne s'est point laissé interroger comme témoin et n'a pas déposé sur les faits de la dite plainte mais a refusé de le faire.) En conséquence nous les dits Juges, conformément au statut sus-mentionné, ordonnons que le dit E. D., à cause du mépris qu'il nous a témoigné comme susdit, soit incarcéré (*désignez la prison*) sans caution, pendant trois mois révolus ou jusqu'à ce qu'il se laisse interroger et qu'il dépose sur les faits de la dite plainte, ou qu'il soit autrement élargi conformément à la loi. Et vous (*le constable ou tout autre officier de paix à qui le mandat est adressé*) êtes autorisé et requis par le présent de prendre sous votre garde la personne du dit E. D., de le conduire en sûreté à la dite prison et de le remettre entre les mains du geôlier d'icelle qui est requis par le présent de recevoir sous sa garde la personne du dit E. D. et de le détenir sûrement, conformément au présent ordre d'emprisonnement.

Donné sous notre seing, ce jour de dans l'année de Notre Seigneur

(*Signatures.*)

(Ce mandat d'emprisonnement doit être adressé à l'Officier de paix et au geolier compétents.)

451.—Et il est de plus ordonné que les juges qui auront prononcé une condamnation quelconque, la feront transcrire au net sur parchemin et dans la forme indiquée ci-dessus, et la transmettront aux prochaines sessions générales, ou aux sessions générales trimestrielles des Juges de Paix qui seront tenues dans le comté, l'arrondissement, le quartier, la ville, la cité, la franchise ou le lieu où la dite condamnation aura été prononcée afin qu'elle soit déposée au nombre des archives des dites sessions générales ou Sessions Générales Trimestrielles et dans le cas où une personne quelconque ferait appel, de la manière ci-après indiquée, du jugement des dits Juges de Paix, aux dites Sessions Générales ou Sessions Générales Trimestrielles, les dites Sessions sont requises et autorisées par le présent aussitôt qu'elles auront reçu la condamnation susdite, à procéder à l'instruction et à la décision du dit Appel, ainsi qu'il est prescrit par le présent Acte. Idem, Sect. 10.

Idem, Sect. 12. 452.—Provided always and be it further enacted, that if any person convicted of any offence or offences punishable by this Act, shall think himself or herself aggrieved by the judgment of such Justices, before whom he or she shall have been convicted, such person shall have liberty to appeal from every such conviction to the next Court of General Sessions or General Quarter Sessions of the Peace, which shall be held in the County, Riding, Division, City, Liberty, Town or Place wherein such offence was committed; and that the execution of every judgment so appealed from shall be suspended, in case the person so convicted shall immediately enter into recognizances before such Justices, (which they are hereby authorized and required to take) himself in the penal sum of ten pounds, with two sufficient Sureties in the penal sum of ten pounds of lawful money of Great Britain, upon condition to prosecute such appeal with effect, and to be forthcoming to abide the judgment and determination of the said next General Sessions or General Quarter Sessions, and to pay such costs as the Court shall award on such occasion; and the Justices in the said next Court of General Sessions or General Quarter Sessions are hereby authorized and required to hear and determine the matter of the said appeal, and to award such costs as to them shall appear just and reasonable, to be paid by either party, which decision shall be final; and if upon hearing the said Appeal, the judgment of the Justices before whom the appellant shall have been convicted shall be affirmed, such appellant shall immediately be committed by the said Court to the common Gaol or House of Correction without bail or mainprize, according to such conviction, and for the space of time therein mentioned.

Idem, Sect. 13. 453.—Provided also and be it further enacted, that no Justice of the Peace, being also a master in the particular trade or manufacture, in or concerning which any offence is charged to have been committed under this Act, shall act as such Justice under this Act.

452.—Pourvu toutefois et il est de plus décrété que quiconque aura été condamné pour avoir contrevenu à cet Acte et se croira lésé par la décision des Juges par lesquels il aura été condamné, pourra en appeler aux prochaines Sessions Générales ou Sessions Générales Trimestrielles des Tribunaux de Paix qui seront tenus dans le Comté, le Canton, la Province, la Cité, le District, la Ville ou l'endroit où la contravention a eu lieu, et que l'exécution du jugement dont on aura ainsi appelé sera suspendue si la personne qui aura été condamnée fournit sur le champ devant les dits Juges (qui sont par ces présentes autorisés et requis de la recevoir) une caution personnelle de dix livres avec deux bonnes garanties collatérales pour la somme de dix livres d'argent ayant cours dans la Grande Bretagne, s'engageant à poursuivre le dit appel et à se présenter pour se soumettre au jugement et à la décision rendus par les dites Sessions Générales ou Sessions Générales Trimestrielles, ainsi qu'à payer tels frais que la Cour accordera en cette circonstance; et les Juges de la dite Cour des Sessions Générales ou Sessions Générales Trimestrielles sont par ces présentes autorisés et requis d'entendre et décider sur le dit appel, et d'accorder tels frais qu'ils croiront justes et raisonnables et qui seront à la charge d'une des parties. La décision des dits Juges sera décisive et sans appel. Dans le cas où la décision rendue par les Juges par lesquels l'appelant a été condamné serait confirmée en appel, le dit appelant devra être immédiatement incarcéré par la dite Cour dans la Prison Commune ou dans une Maison de Correction sans qu'il puisse être accepté aucune caution, aux termes du jugement, et pour le temps qui y sera mentionné. Idem, Sect. 12.

453.—Pourvu toutefois et il est de plus décrété qu'aucun Juge de Paix qui sera en même temps propriétaire d'un établissement ou d'une manufacture dans laquelle ou au sujet de laquelle il sera présumé qu'une contravention à cet Acte a été commise, ne pourra remplir des fonctions de Juge d'après cet Acte. Idem, Sect. 13.

STIPENDIARY COURTS.

I.—*Jurisdiction, Procedure, &c.*
II.—*Tariff of Costs.*
III.—*Prise à partie.*
IV.—*Appeal.*

CHAPTER I.

Jurisdiction, Procedure, &c.

Order in Council 7th Sept. 1838, Cap. 5, Sect. 1.

454.—Every Stipendiary Magistrate shall hold his office, during Her Majesty's pleasure, and shall be liable to be suspended therefrom by the Governor of the Colony, until Her Majesty's pleasure shall be known.

Idem, Cap. 5, Art. 2.

455.—Every such Magistrate shall act for such District or Districts as shall from time to time be assigned for that purpose by the Governor. Every such Magistrate shall be obedient to the lawful commands of the Governor in all things relating to the duties of the office of such Magistrate.* Every such Stipendiary Magistrate shall be bound to make to the Governor such general or special reports of his proceedings in the discharge of his duty as the Governor shall from time to time require of him.

Idem, Cap. 4, Art. 1.

456.—The Stipendiary Magistrates shall have an exclusive jurisdiction for the enforcement of all contracts of service, and for imposing all penalties for the breach, neglect, or non-performance thereof.†

Idem, Cap. 4, Art. 2.

457.—This jurisdiction shall be exercised in a summary manner.

---

* In the case of *Dupont* v. *Pellereau* (Piston's Reports, 1864), where a Stipendiary Magistrate, in obedience to the order of the Governor of the Colony, had refused to allow a Job-Contractor to engage Indian laborers, except on his finding security for their wages,—the Supreme Court declined to issue a Writ of Mandamus to require the Magistrate to accept the Contract without security, as *primâ facie*, the Magistrate had a warrant for his refusal, in the directions of his superior, whom by the Order in Council of 7th September 1838, he was bound to obey in all things lawful.

† In the case of *Renne and ors,* v. *Rondeaux* (Piston's Reports, 1863), the Supreme Court decided that proceedings, instituted by the manager of an estate against persons who had contracted to cut all the canes thereon at so much per acre, but who had abandoned their work before completion, should be taken before a Stipendiary Court, and that the District Court had no jurisdiction in the matter.

DES COURS STIPENDIAIRES.

I.—*De la Juridiction, Procédure, &c.*
II.—*Du Tarif des frais.*
III.—*De la Prise à partie.*
IV.—*De l'Appel.*

CHAPITRE I.

De la Juridiction. Procédure, &c.

454.—Tout Magistrat Salarié tiendra son office pendant le bon plaisir de Sa Majesté, et pourra en être suspendu par le Gouverneur de la Colonie, jusqu'à ce que le bon plaisir de Sa Majesté soit connu. Ordre en Conseil du 7 Sept. 1838. Ch. 5, Sect. 1.

455.—Tout Magistrat Salarié exercera dans le district pour lequel, de temps à autre, il sera désigné par le Gouverneur. Tout Magistrat Salarié obéira aux ordres légaux du Gouverneur en tout ce qui concerne les devoirs de son office comme Magistrat Salarié.* Chaque Magistrat Salarié sera tenu de faire au Gouverneur tels rapports généraux ou particuliers de ses actes dans l'accomplissement de son devoir, que le Gouverneur requèrera. Idem, Chap. 5, Art. 2.

456.—Les Magistrats Salariés auront une juridiction exclusive pour l'exécution de tous contrats de service et pour l'application des peines en cas de violation, négligence ou non-exécution des dits contrats.† Idem, Chap. 4, Art. 1.

457.—Cette juridiction s'exercera d'une manière sommaire. Idem, Chap. 4, Art. 2.

---

* Dans l'affaire *Dupont* v. *Pellereau* (Piston's Reports 1864) où un Magistrat Stipendiaire avait, par ordre du Gouverneur de la Colonie, refusé de passer un contrat d'engagement entre un Entrepreneur (Job-Contractor) et des laboureurs Indiens à moins que le dit Entrepreneur ne fournisse une caution pour le paiement des gages, la Cour Suprême a refusé d'accorder un *Writ of Mandamus* obligeant le Magistrat à passer le Contrat sans caution,—le Magistrat étant de prime abord autorisé dans son refus de passer le Contrat par l'ordre de son supérieur, auquel, d'après l'Ordre en Conseil du 7 Septembre 1838, il est tenu d'obéir en toute chose légale.

† Dans l'affaire *Renne et autres* v. *Rondeaux* (Piston's Reports, 1863) la Cour Suprême a décidé que les poursuites, exercées par l'Administrateur d'un Établissement contre des personnes qui s'étaient engagées à couper toutes les cannes de cette propriété à tant par arpent, mais qui avaient abandonné leur travail avant qu'il fût achevé, étaient du ressort des Cours Stipendiaires, et que les Cours de District n'avaient aucune juridiction dans l'espèce.

Idem, Cap. 4, Sect. 9. **458.**—Nothing herein contained shall prevent, or be construed to prevent, any proceeding before the ordinary tribunals of the colony for any ill-usage of a servant by his master, or of a master by his servant, if the Stipendiary Magistrate shall decline to entertain any such case, and shall see fit to refer the same to the ordinary course of law.—(*See notes to No.* 250.)

Idem, Cap. 4, Sect. 10. **459.**—If any question shall arise between a master and a servant respecting the meaning of their contract, or the rights of either party under the same, or the obligation imposed on either party thereby, it shall be lawful for the Stipendiary Magistrate, on the application of either party, to arbitrate between them; and his award, on all such questions so brought before him, shall be conclusive and without appeal.

Ord. No. 15 of 1852, Art. 8. **460.**—Every complaint of a master against a servant or of a servant against a master, shall be tried before the Stipendiary Magistrate of the district in which the complainant resides, and all proceedings had upon the same complaint before another Magistrate shall be considered null and void, provided that it shall be lawful for the Governor to appoint any other Stipendiary Magistrate for the trial in the same district of any complaint by a master or a servant.

Ord. No. 31 of 1867, Art. 76. **461.**—All complaints for contraventions of *Ordinance No.* 29 *of* 1865 and of this Ordinance, may be made to and adjudicated on by the Stipendiary Magistrate of the district in which the servants reside to which the said complaints refer.—(*Ordinance No.* 29 *of* 1869, *i. e. the law on Estate-Hospitals.—See Nos.* 354 *et seq.*)

Idem, Art. 77. **462.**—All penalties provided by this Ordinance or by any Regulations which shall be made in virtue thereof, shall be sued for and be recoverable before a Stipendiary Magistrate.

Idem, Art. 75, § 4 and 5. **463.**—The fees on every proceeding shall (unless otherwise provided by the regulations aforesaid) be paid in the first instance by the complainant or party instituting the proceedings. Provided that in any case of a complaint made by a laborer against his employer, it shall be in the discretion of the Stipendiary Magistrate before whom such complaint is made, to dispense the laborer from payment of such fees.

458.—Rien de ce qui est contenu au présent n'empêchera, ou ne sera entendu empêcher la poursuite devant les tribunaux ordinaires de la colonie, pour mauvais traitements d'un serviteur envers son maître, ou d'un maître envers son serviteur, si le Magistrat Salarié refuse de connaître d'un tel cas, et juge convenable de le renvoyer aux Tribunaux ordinaires.—(*Voir les notes au No.* 250.) Idem, Chap. 4, Sect. 9.

459.—S'il s'élève quelque contestation entre un maître et un serviteur sur l'interprétation du contrat, les droits qu'il donne ou les obligations qu'il impose à chacune des parties, respectivement, le Magistrat Salarié pourra, sur la demande de l'une des parties, arbitrer le différend ; et son jugement sur toutes questions de ce genre ainsi portées devant lui, sera définitif et sans appel. Idem, Chap. 4, Sect. 10.

460.—Toute plainte d'un maître contre un serviteur, ou d'un serviteur contre un maître, sera jugée devant le Magistrat Stipendiaire du district dans lequel le plaignant réside, et toute poursuite faite sur la même plainte devant un autre Magistrat sera considérée comme nulle et non avenue, le Gouverneur pourra, néanmoins, nommer tout autre Magistrat Stipendiaire pour le jugement, dans le même district, de toute plainte portée par un maître ou un serviteur. Ord. No. 15 de 1852, Art. 8.

461.—Toutes plaintes pour des contraventions à l'*Ordonnance No.* 29 *de* 1865 et à cette Ordonnance peuvent être entendues et jugées par le Magistrat Stipendiaire du District dans lequel résident les serviteurs que les plaintes concernent.—(*Ordonnance No.* 29 *de* 1865 *i. e. la Loi sur les Hôpitaux.— Voir les Nos.* 354 *et suiv.*) Ord. No. 31 de 1867, Art. 76.

462.—Toutes les pénalités prévues par cette Ordonnance ou par tous réglements qui pourront être faits en vertu d'icelle, seront recouvrées devant un Magistrat Stipendiaire. Idem, Art. 77.

463.—Les droits sur chaque procédure seront (à moins que les dits réglements n'en ordonnent autrement) payés d'abord par le plaignant ou la personne commençant ces procédures. Néanmoins dans le cas des plaintes portées par un travailleur contre son employeur, il sera à la discrétion du Magistrat Stipendiaire devant lequel la plainte sera portée, de dispenser le travailleur du paiement de ces droits. Idem, Art. 75, § 4 et 5.

Govt. Notice No. 166 of 11th Nov. 1868, Art. 76.

464.—On the institution of a complaint by a laborer no fees shall be charged for the issue of the consequent summonses or warrants, if, in the opinion of the Stipendiary Magistrate, the laborer is unable to prepay such fees and yet appears to have a reasonable ground of complaint.

Idem, Art. 77.

465.—The Stipendiary Magistrate shall have power to order ex-officio the issue of any summonses, warrants, or other process without prepayment of fees. In every such case an order, in the form of the Schedule U hereto annexed, shall be a sufficient authority for the Clerk or Cashier issuing the process. The recovery of the fees due upon such process shall be effected in accordance with the subsequent order or decision of the Magistrate.

SCHEDULE U.

Issue of Process without prepayment.	*Issue of Process without prepayment.*
Cause No. Summons to party charged Do. witness Warrant	This is to authorise the issue of the undermentioned process in Cause No. Summons to party charged Do. witness Warrant
(Date)	Stipendiary Court of 186 .
C. D. *Stipendiary Magistrate.*	C. D. *Stipendiary Magistrate.*

Order in Council 7th Sept. 1838, Cap. 5, Sect. 4.

466.—All Constables and other Officers of Police in the said Colonies, respectively, shall obey and carry into execution all lawful orders and warrants of the respective Stipendiary Magistrates or of any such *Petty Sessions* as aforesaid.—(*Petty Sessions.—See Nos.* 484 *et seq.*)

Ord. No. 31 of 1867, Art. 70.

467.—Any process issuing out of a Stipendiary Court, may, when the Stipendiary Magistrate shall so specially order, be served or executed by the District Court Usher of the District, who shall thereupon receive fees to be taxed by the Stipendiary Magistrate in accordance with the tariff of the District Court in such matters.

Govt. Notice No. 166 of 11th Nov. 1868, Art. 78.

468.—In every case in which the party against whom a complaint shall be made shall appear in Court for trial, before the

464.—Lorsqu'un travailleur portera une plainte il ne sera pas perçu de droits pour la signification des assignations ou warrants qui en seront la conséquence, si dans l'opinion du Magistrat Stipendiaire le travailleur n'est pas capable de payer d'avance les dits droits, et paraît avoir de bonnes raisons pour se plaindre. (Avis du Gouv. No. 166 du 11 Nov. 1868, Art. 76.)

465.—Le Magistrat Stipendiaire aura le pouvoir d'ordonner d'office la signification de tous warrants, assignations ou autres actes de procédure sans le paiement préalable des droits. Dans chacun des dits cas un ordre, dans la forme de l'Annexe U sera une autorisation suffisante pour le commis ou caissier chargé de la procédure. Le recouvrement des droits dûs sur cette procédure sera effectué conformément à l'ordre ou au jugement subséquent du Magistrat. (Idem, Art. 77.)

ANNEXE U.

Signification de la procédure sans paiement préalable.	*Signification de la procédure sans paiement préalable.*
Cause No. Sommation à la partie accusée. Do. témoin. Warrant (Date) C. D. *Magistrat Stipendiaire.*	Ceci est pour autoriser la signification de la procédure ci-dessous dans la cause No. Sommation à la partie accusée. Do. témoin. Warrant. Tribunal Stipendiaire de 186 . C. D. *Magistrat Stipendiaire.*

466.—Tous les constables ou autres officiers de Police dans les dites colonies, respectivement, recevront et exécuteront tous ordres et mandats légaux des Magistrats Salariés respectivement, ou de toutes cours de *Petty Sessions* ci-dessus mentionnées.—(*Cours de Petty Sessions.—Voir les Nos.* 484 *et suiv.*) (Ordre en Conseil du 7 Sept. 1838, Ch. 5, Sect. 4.)

467.—Toute procédure émanant d'un Tribunal Stipendiaire pourra, lorsque le Magistrat Stipendiaire l'ordonnera spécialement, être signifiée ou exécutée par l'huissier du Tribunal de District de ce District qui recevra alors des frais taxés par le Magistrat Stipendiaire conformément au tarif du Tribunal de District en matières semblables. (Ord. No. 31 de 1867, Art. 70.)

468.—Dans tous les cas dans lesquels la partie contre laquelle une plainte sera portée paraîtra au Tribunal pour être entendue, (Avis du Gouv. No. 166 du 11 Nov. 1868, Art. 78.)

issue of a summons or a warrant,—the Clerk of the Court shall take down the complaint in writing, stating therein the voluntary appearance of the defendant, or his arrest without a warrant as the case may be. Every such complaint shall be subject to the fee * mentioned in the tariff hereto annexed.

Ord. No. 31 of 1867, Art. 67. 469.—Any person who, having been duly served with any summons issued by a Stipendiary Magistrate, shall refuse or neglect, without sufficient cause, to appear or to produce any books, papers, or writings required by such summons to be produced, and also every person present in Court who, on being required to give evidence, shall refuse to be sworn or to give evidence, shall forfeit and pay a fine not exceeding £ 10 sterling.

Ord. No. 15 of 1852, Art. 9. 470.—Any person giving a false evidence before a Stipendiary Magistrate, shall, on conviction, be punished by imprisonment not exceeding three months, to be awarded by the Stipendiary Magistrate, who may refer the case to the ordinary course of law.

Idem, Art. 1. 471.—Every Stipendiary Magistrate dismissing a complaint made before him by either a master or a servant, as being frivolous or unfounded, shall condemn the plaintiff, if a servant, to a penalty not exceeding ten shillings, and if a Master to a penalty not exceeding five pounds (£ 5). If the complaint be so dismissed as vexatious or malicious, the plaintiff, if a servant, shall be condemned to a fine not exceeding £ 2, or to imprisonment with or without hard labour for a period not exceeding one calendar month, and if a master, to a fine not exceeding £ 20.

Govt. Notice No. 166 of 11th Nov. 1868, Art. 79. 472.—In every case tried in a Stipendiary Court, the party against whom judgment shall be given shall have to pay the costs of the trial.

Idem, Art. 80. 473.—If judgment in any case be given in favor of a complainant, the fees prepaid by him shall immediately be refunded to him on the order of the Stipendiary Magistrate, by the District

---

* For the complaint made under this provision (No. 468) a fee of two shillings is paid by the complainant.—*See No. 487, § 23.*

avant la signification de l'assignation ou du warrant, le Greffier du Tribunal prendra la plainte par écrit, y énoncera la comparution volontaire du défendeur ou son arrestation sans warrant, selon le cas; chacune des dites plaintes sera soumise au droit* mentionné au tarif ci-annexé.

469.—Toute personne qui, après avoir été dûment assignée par un Magistrat Stipendiaire, refusera ou négligera, sans cause suffisante, de comparaître ou de produire tous livres, papiers, ou documents qu'elle est requise par cette sommation de produire, et de même toute personne qui, étant en Cour et étant requise de donner son témoignage, refusera de prêter serment et de déposer, sera condamnée à payer une amende qui n'excédera pas £10. Ord. No. 31 de 1867, Art. 67.

470.—Toute personne qui portera un faux témoignage devant un Magistrat Stipendiaire, sera, après conviction, punie d'un emprisonnement qui n'excèdera pas trois mois, lequel sera prononcé par le dit Magistrat, qui pourra référer le cas aux Tribunaux ordinaires. Ord. No. 15 de 1852, Art. 9.

471.—Tout Magistrat Stipendiaire qui rejettera comme frivole ou mal fondée une plainte portée devant lui, soit par un maître, soit par un serviteur, condamnera le plaignant, si c'est un serviteur, à une peine qui n'excèdera pas dix schellings, et si c'est un maître, à une peine qui n'excèdera pas cinq livres sterling. Si la plainte est ainsi renvoyée comme étant vexatoire ou malicieuse, le plaignant, si c'est un serviteur, sera condamné à une amende n'excédant pas £ 2 ou à un emprisonnement, avec ou sans travail forcé, pour un temps qui n'excèdera pas un mois, et si c'est un maître à une amende qui n'excèdera pas £ 20. Idem, Art. 1.

472.—Dans toutes les affaires jugées par un Magistrat Stipendiaire, la partie qui perdra aura à payer les frais du procès. Avis du Gouv. No. 166 du 11 Nov. 1868, Art. 79.

473.—Si le jugement est en faveur du plaignant, les droits payés préalablement par lui, lui seront immédiatement remboursés sur l'ordre du Magistrat Stipendiaire, par le Caissier de District Idem, Art. 80.

---

* Pour chaque plainte portée en vertu de cette disposition (No. 468) un droit de deux schellings est payé par le plaignant.—Voir le No. 487, § 23.

Cashier if it be in a Rural District, or by the Clerk of the Stipendiary Magistrate's Court if it be in Port Louis. If any portion of the costs be awarded against the complainant such portion shall be deducted from the amount to be refunded to him.

Ord. No. 31 of 1867, Art. 71. 474.—All penalties which shall be imposed, and all costs and damages which shall be awarded, by any Stipendiary Magistrate, may be recovered by seizure and sale of the goods of the person against whom they shall be imposed or awarded, or of so much of the said goods as may be requisite for such recovery; and, failing sufficient distress, the party may be condemned to imprisonment at the following rate, viz :

When the fine or costs, or both, amount to £ 5, or less, for a number of days equal to the number of shillings due by him. Such imprisonment, however, shall never exceed 30 days.—(*Exception,—see No.* 478.)

Where more than £ 5, to any time not exceeding 60 days.

Govt. Notice No. 166 of 11th Nov. 1868, Art. 86. 475.—If any person committed under a warrant from a Stipendiary Magistrate for the non-payment of a fine or of costs, tender payment of a part of such fine or costs to the keeper of the prison in which he is confined, the keeper shall receive such payment and immediately obtain a written authority from the Magistrate to relieve such person from an equivalent portion of the time of his imprisonment.

Idem, Art. 84. 476.—When several persons shall be convicted of vagrancy on the same day, the Magistrate convicting them may commit them to prison through a single warrant, although the terms of imprisonment to which they have been sentenced be different.

Idem, Art. 85. 477.—In every case where several persons shall be sentenced to imprisonment under the same judgment their committals may be ordered by the Magistrate through a single warrant,—although the grounds of their committals and the terms of their sentences be different.

si c'est dans un District rural, ou par le commis du Magistrat Stipendiaire, si c'est au Port Louis. Si une partie des frais a été mise à la charge du plaignant, cette partie sera déduite du montant devant lui être remboursé.

474.—Toutes les amendes qui seront imposées, et tous les frais qui seront alloués, par un Magistrat Stipendiaire, pourront être recouvrés par la saisie et la vente des biens de la personne contre laquelle ils seront alloués ou imposés, ou de la portion de ces biens qui sera nécessaire à ce recouvrement ; et dans le cas où la saisie faite ne suffirait pas au paiement intégral, la personne pourra être condamnée à l'emprisonnement dans la proportion suivante, savoir : Ord. No. 31 de 1867, Art. 71.

Lorsque l'amende ou les frais, ou tous les deux, s'élèveront à £ 5, au moins, pour un nombre de jours égal au nombre de schellings dûs par elle. Néanmoins, cet emprisonnement n'excèdera jamais 30 jours.—(*Exception,—voir le No.* 478.)

Lorsqu'ils s'élèveront à plus de £5, pour un temps n'excédant pas 60 jours.

475.—Si une personne mise en prison en vertu d'un warrant d'un Magistrat Stipendiaire pour le non-paiement d'une amende ou de frais, offre partie de cette amende ou des frais au Geolier de la prison dans laquelle elle est détenue, le Geolier acceptera ce paiement, et obtiendra immédiatement une autorisation écrite du Magistrat pour remettre à cette personne une portion équivalente du temps de son emprisonnement. Avis du Gouv. No. 166 du 11 Nov. 1868, Art. 86.

476.—Lorsque plusieurs personnes seront trouvées coupables de vagabondage le même jour, le Magistrat qui les condamnera pourra les envoyer en prison par un seul warrant, quoique le temps de l'emprisonnement ne soit pas le même pour chacune d'elles. Idem. Art. 84.

477.—Dans le cas où plusieurs personnes seront condamnées à la prison en vertu du même jugement, leur emprisonnement pourra être ordonné par le Magistrat par un seul warrant, quoique les causes de leurs condamnations et le temps de l'emprisonnement soient différents. Idem, Art. 85.

Ord. No. 31 of 1867, Art. 68. 478.—If any person shall wilfully insult a Stipendiary Magistrate, or any Clerk, or Officer of the Court during his sitting or attendance in Court, or in going to or returning from the Court, or shall wilfully interrupt the proceedings of the Court or otherwise misbehave in Court, it shall be lawful for any Officer of the Court with or without the assistance of any other person, by the order of the Magistrate, to take such offender into custody, and detain him till the rising of the Court, and the Magistrate shall be empowered, if he shall think fit, by a warrant under his hand, to commit any such offender for a time not exceeding seven days, or to impose upon such offender a fine not exceeding £5, for any such offence, and in default of payment thereof, to commit the offender for any time not exceeding seven days, unless the said fine be sooner paid.

Idem, Art. 69. 479.—If any Officer of a Stipendiary Court shall be assaulted while in the execution of his duty, or if any rescue shall be made or attempted to be made, of any goods levied under process of the Court, the person so offending shall be liable to a fine not exceeding £ 20, to be recovered by the order of the Court, and it shall be lawful for any Peace Officer, in any such case, to take the offender into custody, (with or without warrant) and bring him before such Court accordingly.

Order in Council 7th Sept. 1838, Cap. 4, Sect. 6. 480.—For all acts done by any Stipendiary Magistrate in the exercise of the jurisdiction hereby vested in him, such Magistrate shall have, and be entitled to, the same protection and indemnity as by any law in force in the Colony any Magistrate is entitled to claim, or to have, in respect of any act by him done in execution of the powers vested by law in him.

Ord. No. 18 of 1857, Art. 1. 481.—In all Rural Districts in which the functions of District and Stipendiary Magistrates are exercised by different persons, in the event of one of such officers dying or being prevented by illness or absence from performing the duties of his office, such duties shall be performed by the other of such officers until the appointment of an acting or permanent successor to the officer whose duties are so performed, or until he shall be able to resume the performance of the said duties, as the case may be. And

478.—Si une personne insulte volontairement un Magistrat Stipendiaire, ou un Clerc, ou un Officier du Tribunal, pendant sa présence à l'audience, ou pendant qu'il se rend au Tribunal ou qu'il en sort, ou interrompt volontairement l'audience ou se conduit mal d'une autre manière dans l'enceinte du Tribunal, il sera permis à tout Officier du Tribunal, avec ou sans l'assistance de toute autre personne, et sur l'ordre du Magistrat, d'arrêter le délinquant et de le détenir pendant la durée de l'audience, et le Magistrat pourra, s'il le juge convenable, par un warrant signé par lui, faire emprisonner ce délinquant pendant un temps qui n'excèdera pas sept jours, ou lui imposer une amende n'excédant pas £ 5, pour ce délit, et à défaut de paiement de cette amende, faire emprisonner le délinquant pendant un temps qui n'excèdera pas sept jours, à moins que la dite amende ne soit payée avant l'expiration des sept jours. Ord. No. 31 de 1867, Art. 68.

479.—Si un Officier d'un Tribunal Stipendiaire est attaqué pendant l'exécution de son mandat, ou si des objets saisis en vertu d'un jugement du Tribunal sont enlevés ou s'il y a tentative de violation de saisie, le délinquant sera passible d'une amende qui n'excèdera pas £ 20, et qui sera prononcée par le Tribunal Stipendiaire, et il sera permis à tout Officier de Paix, dans un pareil cas, d'arrêter le délinquant, (avec ou sans warrant) et de le conduire devant le dit Tribunal. Idem, Art. 69.

480.—Pour tous les actes faits par un Magistrat Salarié dans l'exercice de la juridiction dont il est investi, ce Magistrat aura droit à la même protection et indemnité que, par toute loi en vigueur dans la colonie, tout Magistrat a droit de réclamer ou d'obtenir à l'égard d'aucun acte par lui fait en exécution des pouvoirs dont il est revêtu par la loi. Ordre en Conseil du 7 Sept. 1838, Ch. 4, Sect. 6.

481.—Dans tous les Districts Ruraux où les fonctions de Magistrats de District et de Magistrats Stipendiaires sont remplies par des personnes différentes, s'il arrive que l'un des dits Officiers vienne à mourir ou soit empêché pour cause de maladie ou d'absence, de remplir les devoirs de sa charge, les dits devoirs seront remplis par l'autre des dits Officiers jusqu'à la nomination d'un successeur intérimaire ou permanent à l'Officier dont les devoirs seront ainsi remplis, ou jusqu'à ce que ce dernier puisse reprendre Ord. No. 18 de 1857, Art. 1.

every act, judgment, order or warrant made or issued, or other magisterial duty performed, in terms of this provision, shall have the same effect and validity as if the Magistrate making, issuing, or performing the same had been formally appointed to the office whose duties he so performs.

Idem, Art. 4.

482.—The provisions of *Article* 129 *of Ordinance No.* 35 *of* 1852 as to actions of damages for acts done by District Magistrates in execution of their office are hereby extended to all acts done by District and Stipendiary Magistrates and District Clerks in virtue of the powers *hereinbefore* conferred on them respectively.—(*Article* 129.—*See No.* 483.—*Hereinbefore.*—*See No.* 481.)

Ord. No. 35 of 1852, Art. 129.

483.—Any District Magistrate or Peace Officer mentioned in this Ordinance, shall be liable to an action of damages for any act done in the execution of his office under this Ordinance; provided that whenever such action is about to be brought against any such Magistrate or Peace Officer, notice of the said action shall be served upon him thirty days before bringing such action; and if previously to the commencement of such action, sufficient amends be tendered, such action shall be stopped; and if on or after action brought, a sum sufficient to satisfy all damages and costs be paid into Court at any time previous to final judgment, such action shall be stayed. Every such action shall be brought within two calendar months next after the alleged grievance, and in case of judgment in his favor, the defendant shall receive three times the amount of his taxed costs.

Order in Council 7th Sept. 1838, Cap. 5, Sect. 3.

484.—The Stipendiary Magistrates shall, from time to time, as occasion may appear to them to require, or where they shall be so directed by the Governor, meet together in Petty Sessions at which Sessions not less than two such Stipendiary Magistrates shall ever be present; and it shall be lawful for such Stipendiary Magistrates, in Petty Session assembled, to associate with themselves one ordinary Justice of the Peace, and no more; and such Stipendiary Magistrates and Justice, or the majority of them may, in such Petty Sessions assembled, exercise any of the powers

l'exercice des dits devoirs, suivant le cas; et tout acte, jugement, ordre, mandat, fait ou délivré, ou autre devoir de Magistrat, rempli aux termes de la présente Ordonnance, aura le même effet et la même validité que si le Magistrat qui les aura faits. délivrés ou remplis, avait été formellement nommé à la charge dont les fonctions auront été ainsi remplies.

482.—Les dispositions de l'*Article* 129 *de l'Ordonnance No.* 35 *de* 1852, quant aux demandes en dommages-intérêts pour actes faits par les Magistrats de District agissant dans l'exercice de leur charge, sont par le présent, étendues à tous actes faits par les Magistrats de District et les Magistrats Stipendiaires et par les Clercs de District en vertu des pouvoirs à eux conférés respectivement, par les *dispositions précédentes*.—(*Article* 129.—*Voir le No.* 483.—*Dispositions précédentes.*—*Voir le No.* 481.) Idem, Art. 4.

483.—Tout Magistrat de District ou Officier de Paix mentionné dans la présente Ordonnance, sera soumis à l'action en dommages et intérêts pour raison de tout acte fait dans l'exercice de ses fonctions et en vertu de la présente Ordonnance; à la condition, toutefois, qu'il sera donné avis de la dite action à l'Officier ou au Magistrat, trente jours avant qu'elle ne soit intentée. Si, avant qu'elle soit commencée, des dommages suffisants sont offerts, la dite action sera suspendue. Si déjà elle a été intentée, et que, avant le jugement définitif, il est payé en Cour une somme suffisante pour faire face aux dommages et aux frais, il n'y sera donné aucune suite. Toute action de cette nature devra être intentée dans les deux mois qui suivront le grief allégué. En cas de jugement en sa faveur, la partie poursuivie recevra le triple du montant de ses dépens fixés. Ord. No. 35 de 1852, Art. 129.

484.—Les Magistrats Salariés pourront, quand les circonstances leur paraîtront l'exiger, ou lorsqu'ils en recevront l'ordre du Gouverneur, se réunir en Cours de *Petty Sessions* auxquelles il ne pourra siéger moins de deux Magistrats Salariés; et les dits Magistrats Salariés, ainsi réunis en Cours de *Petty Sessions*, pourront s'adjoindre un Juge de Paix ordinaire et pas davantage; et les dits Magistrats Salariés et Juges de Paix, ou la majorité d'entre eux pourront, lorsqu'ils seront ainsi réunis en Cours de *Petty Sessions* exercer tout pouvoir donné par le présent aux Magistrats Ordre en Conseil du 7 Sept. 1838, Ch. 5, Sect. 3.

hereby vested in the Stipendiary Magistrate separately, provided that no such Petty Sessions be convened except by the previous sanction of the Governor of the Colony, which sanction may be given either for holding such Sessions periodically, at some times and places to be appointed by him, or for holding the same for any special occasion at any particular time and place.

Ord. No. 15 of 1852, Art. 18. 485.—The Petty Sessions mentioned in the *3rd Section* of the *5th Chapter* of the said Order in Council shall be legally formed and constituted, in the sense and for the object of the said Order in Council, by the meeting together of three Stipendiary Magistrates or of two Stipendiary Magistrates and one of the District Magistrates of Port Louis, who may be named and appointed for that purpose by the Governor.—(*3rd. Section.— See No*. 484.)

CHAPTER II.

Tariff of Costs.

Ord. No. 31 of 1867, Art. 75, § 1, 2 and 3. 486.—The Governor in Executive Council shall have power to make Regulations, and from time to time to add to, alter, or revoke the same, for the purpose of carrying out the provisions of this Ordinance and of any other laws in force at the time being relative to Immigration, or to Masters and Servants, and for establishing a tariff of fees leviable on proceedings to be had before the Stipendiary Courts, and on the delivery of tickets or other documents by the Protector of Immigrants and by Stipendiary Magistrates: which regulations may provide that any person contravening any article thereof shall be liable in such penalty, not exceeding £ 10 sterling, as in such regulations shall be provided for such contravention. All such regulations, on being published in the Government Gazette, shall be as valid and effectual as if they had been contained *verbatim* herein.—A table of such Fees shall be put up in some conspicuous place in the Court House, and in the Clerk's office.

Govt. Notice No. 166 of 11th Nov. 1868, Art. 75. 487.—From the day on which these regulations shall take effect, the fees mentioned in the tariff hereunto annexed (Schedule T)

Salariés, respectivement, pourvu qu'aucune Cour de *Petty Sessions* ne soit convoquée sans l'autorisation du Gouverneur de la Colonie, laquelle autorisation peut être donnée soit pour tenir les Sessions périodiquement à des époques et en des lieux désignés par lui, ou pour un cas spécial, à une époque et dans un lieu particulier.

485.—Les Cours de *Petty Sessions* mentionnées dans la *Section* 3 du *Chapitre* 5 du sus-dit Ordre en Conseil, seront légalement formées et constituées, dans le sens et pour l'objet du dit Ordre en Conseil, par la réunion de trois Magistrats Stipendiaires ou de deux Magistrats Stipendiaires et d'un des Magistrats de District du Port-Louis, nommé et désigné à cet effet par le Gouverneur.—(*Section* 3.—*Voir le No.* 484.) Ord. No. 15 de 1852, Art. 18.

CHAPITRE II.

Du Tarif des Frais.

486.—Le Gouverneur en Conseil Exécutif aura le pouvoir de faire des réglements, et de temps à autre d'y ajouter, de les modifier, ou de les abroger, dans le but de faciliter l'exécution des dispositions de la présente Ordonnance et de toutes autres lois actuellement en vigueur relatives à l'Immigration, ou aux Maîtres et Serviteurs, et pour établir un tarif des droits à percevoir sur les procédures qui seront faites devant les Tribunaux Stipendiaires, et sur la livraison des Tickets ou autres documents par le Protecteur des Immigrants et par les Magistrats Stipendiaires, et ces réglements pourront décréter que toute personne qui les violera sera passible de telle amende n'excédant pas £10 sterling, qui sera prévue dans les dits réglements pour cette contravention.—Tous ces réglements, après leur publication dans la Gazette du Gouvernement, seront aussi valables et auront autant d'effet que s'ils étaient contenus mot pour mot dans ces présentes.—Un tableau de ces droits sera affiché dans un endroit apparent du Tribunal, et dans le bureau du Commis. Ord. No. 31 de 1867, Art. 75, § 1, 2 et 3.

487.—A partir du jour de la mise en vigueur des présents réglements, les droits mentionnés au tarif ci-annexé (Annexe T) Avis du Gouv. No. 166 du 11 Nov. 1868, Art. 75.

shall be charged and received by the Officers therein designated, on the various documents and proceedings therein specified;—which tariff shall be liable to be altered as the Governor in Executive Council may deem fit to direct.

SCHEDULE T.

Fees to be paid to the Chief Clerk of the Senior Stipendiary Magistrate's Court in Port Louis, and to the District Cashiers in the Country Districts.

	£	S.	D.	
10.—For every release from industrial residence	0	1	0	By Applicant.
11.—For every written order of any description	0	1	0	
12.—For every security-bond for Job-Contractor	1	0	0	
13.—For every license under Regulation 54 (No. 283) per annum	0	4	0	
14.—For every contract with one or more Old Immigrants	0	2	0	By Employer.
15.—For every Certificate of Engagement	0	1	0	
16.—For every Certificate of Discharge	0	0	6	
17.—For every notice under Regulation 38. (No. 331.)	0	2	0	
18.—For every transfer of Contract	0	2	0	By New Employer.
19.—Summons to a party charged	0	2	0	By Complainant.
20.—For every summons to witness	0	1	0	
21.—For every warrant of any description.	0	2	0	
22.—For every copy of a summons	0	1	0	
23.—For every complaint under Regulation 78. (No 468)	0	2	0	
24.—For every recognizance by party appealing	0	2	0	By Appellant.
25.—For every duplicate of Certificate of Engagement	0	1	0	By Master or Servant as ordered by the Magistrate.
26.—For every duplicate Certificate of Discharge	0	2	0	
27.—For every writ of execution under Art. 38 of Ordinance 31 of 1867 (No. 342.)	0	4	0	By Judgment Debtor.
28.—For every judgment under Art. 36 of Ord. 31 of 1867 (No. 330.)	0	4	0	
29.—For every subrogative receipt under Art. 37 of Ord. 31 of 1867 (No. 341.)	0	4	0	By party subrogated.
30.—For every "tierce opposition" under Art. 33 of Ord. 31 of 1867 (No. 334.)	0	4	0	By opposing party.
31.—For every duplicate or second issue of a Police pass	0	2	0	By Applicant.
32.—For every third or any following issue of a Police pass	0	4	0	
33.—For every search in book or record	0	0	6	By party at whose request the search is made.

seront perçus par les officiers y désignés, sur les divers documents

Page. 371.

Cédule T.

Pour une modification du paragraphe 13 de ce Tarif.—Voir le No. 572.

dustrielle....................	0	1	0	Par le Requérant.
11.—Pour chaque ordre écrit, de toute nature....................	0	1	0	
12.—Pour chaque caution d'entrepreneur..	1	0	0	
13.—Pour chaque patente en vertu du Réglement 54 (No. 283.) par an	0	4	0	
14.—Pour chaque contrat avec un ou plusieurs Immigrants................	0	2	0	Par l'Employeur.
15.—Pour chaque certificat d'engagement.	0	1	0	
16.—Pour chaque certificat de décharge ..	0	0	6	
17.—Pour chaque avis en vertu du Réglement 38 (No. 331.)	0	2	0	
18.—Pour chaque transfert de contrat	0	2	0	Par le nouvel Employeur
19.—Sommation à une partie accusée	0	2	0	Par le Plaignant.
20.—Pour chaque sommation à un témoin..	0	1	0	
21.—Pour chaque warrant	0	2	0	
22.—Pour chaque copie de la sommation..	0	1	0	
23.—Pour chaque plainte en vertu du Réglement 78 (No. 468.)	0	2	0	
24.—Pour chaque caution par l'appelant ..	0	2	0	Par l'Appelant.
25.—Pour chaque duplicata de certificat d'engagement....................	0	1	0	Par le Maître ou le Serviteur selon l'ordre du Magistrat.
26.—Pour chaque duplicata de certificat de décharge....................	0	2	0	
27.—Pour chaque writ d'exécution en vertu de l'Art. 38 de l'Ord. 31 de 1867 (No. 342.)	0	4	0	Par le débiteur condamné.
28.—Pour chaque jugement en vertu de l'Art. 36 de l'Ord. 31 de 1867 (No. 330.)	0	4	0	
29.—Pour toute quittance subrogative en vertu de l'Art. 37 de l'Ord. 31 de 1867 (No. 341.)	0	4	0	Par la partie subrogée.
30.—Pour chaque tierce opposition en vertu de l'Art. 33 de l'Ord. 31 de 1867 (No. 344.)	0	4	0	Par l'opposant.
31.—Pour chaque duplicata ou seconde émission d'une passe de Police	0	2	0	Par le Requérant.
32.—Pour une troisième ou autre émission d'une passe de Police	0	4	0	
33.—Pour toute recherche dans un registre ou un dossier	0	0	6	Par la personne qui fera faire la recherche.

34.—For every guardianship of goods seized, the same fee as under Ord. 34 of 1852	By party at whose instance the seizure has been made.
35.—For every witness, the same fees and allowances as under Ord. 34 of 1852.	By party against whom the costs shall be awarded by the Magistrate.

(*See also No.* 467.)

The fees numbered 10 to 30 inclusive shall be recovered through stamps.

Ord. No. 2 of 1869, Art. 9. 488.—None of the Instruments or Writings mentioned and specified in the Schedule D, annexed to and forming part of this Ordinance, shall be subject to any Stamp-Duty.

SCHEDULE D.

....

7o. All Proceedings, Orders, or Judgments of Stipendiary Magistrates, except the Fees which are now collected or which may afterwards be collected by means of *stamps under Ordinance No.* 31 *of* 1867, and all Registers of Employers of Labor.—(*Stamps under Ordinance No.* 31 *of* 1867, *see No.* 487.)

CHAPTER III.

Prise à Partie.

Ord. No. 15 of 1852, Art. 23. 489.—Every Stipendiary Magistrate shall be liable to the "prise à partie" in the cases and the same manner and form as prescribed by *Articles* 505 *and following* of the Code of Civil Procedure, as if the said Stipendiary Magistrate had been included in the said articles.—(*Articles* 505 *and following.—See Nos.* 490 *et seq.*)

Code of Civil Procedure, Art. 505. 490.—Judges may be cited in the following cases: 1o. In cases where deceit, fraud or extortion is alleged to have taken place, either during the enquiry or at the time judgment is given; 2o. If the right of citing is expressly provided for by law; 3o. If the law declares that the Judges are responsible on pain of being sued in damages; 4o. If there is a refusal to give justice.

Idem, Art. 506. 491.—There is refusal to give justice when the Judges refuse to answer petitions or neglect to try causes in their proper turn and when the same are ready for hearing.

34.—Pour le gardiennage de biens saisis, le même droit qu'en vertu de l'Ord. 34 de 1852......................	Par la partie qui fait faire la saisie.
35.—Pour chaque témoin, les mêmes droits et allocations qu'en vertu de l'Ord. 34 de 1852......	Par la partie condamnée aux frais par le Magistrat.

(*Voir aussi le No.* 467.)

Les droits sur les Nos. 10 à 30 inclusivement seront perçus au moyen de timbres.

488.—Aucun des actes ou écrits mentionnés dans l'Annexe D qui fait partie de la présente Ordonnance ne sera soumis à un droit de timbre. Ord. No. 2 de 1869, Art. 9.

ANNEXE D.

....

7o. Tous actes, ordres ou jugements des Magistrats Stipendiaires, excepté pour les droits qui sont actuellement perçus ou qui pourront plus tard être perçus au moyen de *timbres en vertu de l'Ordonnance No.* 31 *de* 1867,—ainsi que les livres tenus par les personnes qui emploient des laboureurs.—(*Timbres en vertu de l'Ordonnance No.* 31 *de* 1867.—*Voir le No.* 487.)

CHAPITRE III.

De la Prise à Partie.

489.—Les Magistrats Stipendiaires pourront être pris à partie dans les cas et de la même manière et dans la même forme qu'il est prescrit par les *Articles* 505 *et suivants* du Code de Procédure Civile, comme si les dits Magistrats Stipendiaires avaient été compris dans les dits articles.—(*Articles* 505 *et suivants.*—*Voir les Nos.* 490 *et suiv.*) Ord. No. 15 de 1852, Art. 23.

490.—Les juges peuvent être pris à partie dans les cas suivans : 1o. S'il y a dol, fraude ou concussion, qu'on prétendrait avoir été commis, soit dans le cours de l'instruction, soit lors des jugemens ; 2o. Si la prise à partie est expressément prononcée par la loi ; 3o. Si la loi déclare les juges responsables, à peine de dommages et intérêts ; 4o. S'il y a déni de justice. Code de Procédure Civile, Art. 505.

491.—Il y a déni de justice, lorsque les juges refusent de répondre aux requêtes, ou négligent de juger les affaires en état et en tour d'être jugées. Idem, Art. 506.

Idem, Art. 507. **492.**—The refusal to give justice shall be proved by two requisitions addressed to the Judges in the person of their Registrars and served on them at an interval of at least three days as regards Justices of the Peace or Judges of Tribunals of Commerce, and at an interval of at least eight days as regards other Judges; any Usher, when called upon, shall, on pain of being suspended from office, be bound to serve these requisitions.

Idem, Art. 508. **493.**—After the two requisitions the Judge may be cited.

Idem, Art. 509. **494.**—The suits against Justices of the Peace, Judges of Tribunals of Commerce or of Courts of First Instance or any one of their members, and the suits against a Councillor at a Court of Appeal or at a Court of Assizes shall be brought before the Court of Appeal within the jurisdiction of which such suit is instituted. The suits against Courts of Assize and Appeal or one of their sections shall be brought before the High Court conformably to Art. 101 of the Act dated 18th May 1804.

Idem, Art. 510. **495.**—Nevertheless no Judge shall be cited without the previous consent of the Tribunal before which the suit is brought.

Idem, Art. 511. **496.**—For this purpose there shall be presented a petition signed by the party or by the person holding his authentic and special power of attorney; and the said power of attorney shall, on pain of nullity, be annexed to the petition, together with documentary evidence, if there be any.

Idem, Art. 512. **497.**—No abusive expression shall be made use of against the Judges, on pain, against the party of such fine,—and against his attorney of such injunction or suspension,—as may be deemed fit.

Idem, Art. 513. **498.**—If the petition is rejected, the petitioner shall be fined in a sum which shall not be less than 300 francs, without prejudice to any damages to which the parties aggrieved may be entitled.

Idem, Art. 514. **499.**—If the petition is granted, notice thereof shall be given to the Judge cited who shall be bound to file his plea within eight days. He shall abstain from enquiring into the matter in dispute, he

492.—Le déni de justice sera constaté par deux réquisitions faites aux Juges en la personne des Greffiers et signifiées de trois en trois jours au moins pour les Juges de Paix et de Commerce, et de huitaine en huitaine au moins pour les autres Juges ; tout huissier requis sera tenu de faire ces réquisitions, à peine d'interdiction. Idem,Art. 507.

493.—Après les deux réquisitions, le Juge pourra être pris à partie. Idem,Art. 508.

494.—La prise à partie contre les Juges de Paix, contre les Tribunaux de Commerce ou de Première Instance, ou contre quelqu'un de leurs membres, et la prise à partie contre un Conseiller à une Cour Royale ou à une Cour d'Assises, seront portées à la Cour Royale du ressort. La prise à partie contre les Cours d'Assises, contre les Cours Royales ou l'une de leurs sections, sera portée à la Haute Cour, conformément à l'Article 101 de l'Acte du 18 Mai 1804. Idem,Art. 509.

495.—Néanmoins aucun Juge ne pourra être pris à partie sans permission préalable du Tribunal devant lequel la prise à partie sera portée. Idem,Art. 510.

496.—Il sera présenté, à cet effet, une requête signée de la partie ou de son fondé de procuration authentique et spéciale, laquelle procuration sera annexée à la requête, ainsi que les pièces justificatives, s'il y en a, à peine de nullité. Idem,Art. 511.

497.—Il ne pourra être employé aucun terme injurieux contre les Juges, à peine, contre la partie, de telle amende, et contre son avoué, de telle injonction ou suspension qu'il appartiendra. Idem,Art. 512.

498.—Si la requête est rejetée, la partie sera condamnée à une amende qui ne pourra être moindre de trois cents francs, sans préjudice des dommages et intérêts envers les parties, s'il y a lieu. Idem,Art. 513.

499.—Si la requête est admise, elle sera signifiée dans trois jours au Juge pris à partie, qui sera tenu de fournir ses défenses dans la huitaine.—Il s'abstiendra de la connaissance du différend ; Idem,Art. 514.

shall even abstain, until the suit has been finally decided on, from trying the causes which the party, or the relations in a direct line, or the wife or husband (as the case may be) of the party, may have before his tribunal on pain of the judgments being null.

Idem, Art. 515. 500.—The suit shall be brought before the Court by means of a simple writing and shall be judged by a section other than that by which it was entertained; if the Court of Appeal consists of one section only, the hearing of the suit shall be referred to the nearest Court of Appeal by the Court of Cassation.

Idem, Art. 516. 501.—If judgment be given against the petitioner, he shall be condemned to a fine which shall not be less than 300 francs without prejudice to any damages to which the parties aggrieved may be entitled.

CHAPTER IV.

Appeals.

Order in Council 7th Sept. 1838, Cap 4, Sect. 5. 502.—No sentence, award, or order made by any Stipendiary Magistrate in the execution of the jurisdiction so vested in him, shall be liable to be reversed, set aside, appealed from, or questioned, by any Court of Justice in any of the *said Colonies*, except on the ground * of an unlawful assumption of power, or other illegality on the part of such Stipendiary Magistrate; but the same, when consistent with law, shall, to all intents and purposes, be binding, final, and conclusive.—(*Said Colonies i. e. British Guiana, Trinidad, St. Lucia and Mauritius.*)

If the matters in dispute between a Master and Servant are brought before the Stipendiary Magistrate as an arbitrator, no appeal will lie against his award.—*See No.* 459,

* The grounds of an appeal from a Stipendiary Magistrate's judgment must be shewn in the procedure.—In the case of *Duval* v. *Gogun* (Piston's Reports, 1861), the Appellant, though stating himself to be aggrieved by the judgment of the Stipendiary Court, did not specify any grievance, except that of his having been condemned to pay as wages a larger sum than the amount he acknowledged to be due by him. The appeal was dismissed.

In order to review a Magistrate's judgment by means of *Certiorari*, the application for the Writ thereof, must be made within six months.—(*Seik-Ibrahim* v. *Lablache and de Chazal.*—Pistons' Reports, 1861.)

il s'abstiendra même, jusqu'au jugement définitif de la prise à partie, de toutes les causes que la partie, ou ses parents en ligne directe, on son conjoint, pourront avoir dans son tribunal, à peine de nullité des jugemens.

500.—La prise à partie sera portée à l'audience sur un simple acte, et sera jugée par une autre section que celle qui l'aura admise ; si la Cour Royale n'est composée que d'une section, le jugement de la prise à partie sera renvoyé à la Cour Royale la plus voisine par la Cour de Cassation. Idem, Art. 515.

501.—Si le demandeur est débouté, il sera condamné à une amende qui ne pourra être moindre de trois cents francs, sans préjudice des dommages-intérêts envers les parties, s'il y a lieu. Idem, Art. 516.

CHAPITRE IV.

Des Appels.

502.—Aucune sentence, décision ou ordre, émanant d'un Magistrat Salarié dans l'exercice de la juridiction dont il est ainsi investi, ne sera sujet à être annulé, écarté, attaqué par voie d'appel, ou discuté par-devant aucune Cour de Justice dans les *dites Colonies*, si ce n'est sur le motif * d'une illégale attribution de pouvoir, ou de toute autre illégalité de la part du Magistrat Salarié ; mais les dites sentence, décision ou ordre, lorsqu'elles s'accorderont avec la loi, seront, à tous égard, obligatoires, définitifs et en dernier ressort.—(*Dites Colonies i. e. la Guiane Anglaise, Trinidad, St. Lucie and Maurice.*) Ordre en Conseil du 7 Sept. 1838, Ch. 4. Sect. 5.

Si le Magistrat Stipendiaire est pris pour arbitre pour régler un différend entre un Maître et un Serviteur, sa décision est définitive et sans appel.—*Voir le No.* 459.

---

* Dans la procédure il doit être fait mention des moyens d'appel d'un jugement de Magistrat Stipendiaire.—Dans l'affaire *Duval* v. *Gogun* (Piston's Reports, 1861), l'Appelant, quoique se disant lésé par le jugement de la Cour Stipendiaire, n'avait spécifié aucun grief, sinon qu'il avait été condamné à payer, comme gages, une somme plus forte que celle qu'il reconnaissait devoir. L'appel fut rejeté par la Cour.

Pour faire réviser un jugement d'un Magistrat Stipendiaire au moyen d'un "Writ de Certiorari," ce Writ doit être demandé dans les six mois qui suivent le jugement. (*Seik-Ibrahim* v. *Lablache et de Chasal.*—Piston's Reports, 1861.)

Ord. No. 15 of 1852, Art. 22. 503.—No judgment or order or other proceeding of any Stipendiary Magistrate or Court of Petty Sessions, shall be quashed or annulled for want of form, or be impeached or affected by reasons of any mistake, defect, error, or omission in the same; provided such judgment, order or other proceeding be in substance and effect in conformity with, or according to, the true intent and meaning of the Order in Council of 7th September 1838, and the present Ordinance.

Idem, Art. 19. 504.—If any person shall think himself aggrieved by any judgment or order of any Stipendiary Magistrate or of a Court of Petty Sessions, such person may appeal from any such order or judgment to the Supreme Court of this Colony provided the sum or penalty adjudged to be paid shall be more than £ 2 if awarded against a master, or if awarded against a servant more than the amount of one month's wages, or by a sentence of imprisonment for a time exceeding ten days; otherwise such judgment, or order shall be final and definitive to all intents and purposes; and every Stipendiary Magistrate or Court of Petty Sessions, immediately after pronouncing any order or judgment liable to appeal, shall inform the party condemned of his right to appeal provided also that every such person shall within *ten days* after such judgment or order shall be made or pronounced, from which an appeal is allowed as above, give notice in writing of such intended appeal to the Stipendiary Magistrate who shall have made or rendered such order or judgment, or in case of a Petty Session, to the Stipendiary Magistrate of the District where the plaint originated, upon which notice such Magistrate shall immediately bind the party so giving such notice by recognizance to Her Majesty, Her Heirs and Successors, with sufficient security in a penal sum of double the amount of the penalty adjudged or sum awarded, and the condition whereof shall be that such party giving such notice of appeal shall appear and prosecute such appeal with due diligence to its conclusion before the above named Supreme Court, and pay such costs as the said Court may award on such appeal, such costs in no case to exceed the sum of five pounds. The party having been so bound by recognizance, shall lodge his appeal in the Registry of the said Supreme Court, and give to the respondent notice *

* In the case of *Teeluck* v. *Heirs Trébuchet* (Piston's Reports, 1866), the appeal was dismissed with costs because the Appellant had failed to give the requisite notice to the Respondents.—A decision to the same effect was given in the case of *Inguy* v. *Ministère Public*, (Piston's Reports, 1869.)

503.—Aucun jugement ou ordre ou autre procédure d'un Magistrat Stipendiaire ou d'une Cour de *Petty Sessions* ne sera cassé ou annulé pour défaut de forme, ni ne sera attaqué ou affecté pour cause d'aucune faute, irrégularité, erreur ou omission dans les dits documents, pourvu que le dit jugement, le dit ordre ou autre procédure soit, en substance et dans son effet, conforme ou en accord avec le sens et le but véritables de l'Ordre en Conseil du 7 Septembre 1838, et de la présente Ordonnance. Ord. No. 15 de 1852, Art. 22.

504.—Toute personne qui se croira lésée par un jugement ou un ordre d'un Magistrat Stipendiaire ou d'une Cour de *Petty Sessions* pourra appeler du dit jugement ou ordre devant la Cour Suprême de cette Colonie, pourvu que la somme ou amende à payer soit audessus de £ 2 si la condamnation est contre un Maître, ou si elle est contre un Serviteur, qu'il s'agisse de plus d'un mois de gages, ou d'un emprisonnement de plus de dix jours; dans les autres cas le jugement sera final et définitif à tous égards et effets; et tout Magistrat Stipendiaire ainsi que toute Cour de *Petty Sessions,* aussitôt après avoir prononcé un ordre ou jugement sujet à appel, informeront la partie condamnée de son droit d'appeler, pourvu aussi que la dite personne, dans les *dix jours* où le dit jugement ou ordre aura été prononcé ou donné, et dont elle pourra faire appel comme il est dit ci-dessus, donne avis par écrit de son intention d'appeler au Magistrat Stipendiaire qui aura donné ou rendu le dit ordre ou jugement, ou, s'il s'agit d'une Cour de *Petty Sessions,* au Magistrat Stipendiaire du District où la plainte aura été portée, sur lequel avis le dit Magistrat obligera immédiatement la partie qui le donnera, à souscrire une reconnaissance envers Sa Majesté, ses héritiers et successeurs, avec garantie suffisante, pour une somme pénale du double de l'amende ou condamnation prononcée, et dont la condition sera que la dite partie donnant le dit avis d'appel, paraîtra et suivra son appel, avec la diligence requise, jusqu'à sa conclusion devant la Cour Suprême ci-dessus désignée, et paiera tels frais que la dite Cour adjugera sur le dit appel; les dits frais ne devant en aucun cas excéder la somme de cinq livres sterling. La partie qui se sera ainsi obligée par une reconnaissance, déposera son appel au Greffe de la dite Cour Suprême et donnera à l'intimé avis * du dit appel dans les trois Idem, Art. 19.

* Dans l'affaire *Teeluck* v. *Les Héritiers Trébuchet* (Piston's Reports, 1866), l'appel fut rejeté et les frais mis à la charge de l'Appelant parce qu'il avait omis de donner l'avis nécessaire aux Intimés. Un arrêt analogue fut rendu dans l'affaire *Inguy* v *le Ministère Public,*—(Piston's Reports, 1869.)

of the said appeal within three days from the date of the recognizance.—(*Ten days,—now limited to five days.—See No.* 505.)

Ord. No. 31 of 1867, Art. 72. 505.—The delay of appeal from any judgment or order of a Stipendiary Magistrate or of a Court of Petty Sessions is, from henceforth, limited to 5 days from the date of the judgment or order appealed from, instead of the delay of 10 days as fixed by *Article* 19 *of Ordinance No.* 15 *of* 1852.—In any case other than between master and servant, a party condemned to the payment of any sum exceeding £ 10, or to imprisonment exceeding one month,may appeal from such condemnation.—(*Article* 19.—*See No.* 504).

For the conditions of appeal against judgments pronounced under the laws concerning Job-Contractors, Estate-Hospitals, Vagrants, or Coalition, see respectively the Nos. 313, 380, 422, 452.

Ord. No. 15 of 1852, Art. 20. 506.—Every Stipendiary Magistrate, upon receiving a notice of appeal and accepting a recognizance, shall forthwith transmit to the Registrar of the Supreme Court duly certified copies of the original of the sentence or order appealed against, and of the whole of the evidence given on the hearing of the complaint to which it refers.

Idem, Art. 21. 507.—On such appeal being entered in the Registry of the said Court, and on the aforesaid proceedings being thereto transmitted, notice thereof shall be given by the Registrar to the Procureur General and without any summons or order to that effect, the cause, if the respondent be a laborer and not appearing by Counsel, shall *ex-officio* be set down for hearing between the Ministère Public and the appellant, at the first sitting of the Supreme Court which may take place not later than three days after the Registrar's receiving the aforesaid proceeding, and such appeal shall have a continued priority of audience before all other causes until finally decided.

Ord. No. 28 of 1863, Art. 2. 508.—In any case of appeal against any judgment of any Stipendiary Magistrate, the Protector of Immigrants shall have right to intervene and appear on behalf of any Immigrant laborer having an interest in the cause.

jours de la date de la reconnaissance.—(*Dix jours.—Délai aujourd'hui limité à cinq jours.—Voir le No.* 505.)

505.—Le délai d'appel d'un jugement ou ordre d'un Magistrat Stipendiaire ou d'une Cour de *Petty Sessions* est dorénavant limité à 5 jours à partir de la date du jugement ou de l'ordre dont il est fait appel, au lieu du délai de 10 jours fixé par l'*Article* 19 *de l'Ordonnance No.* 15 *de* 1852. Dans tous autres cas que ceux entre maître et serviteur une partie condamnée au paiement d'une somme excédant £ 10 ou à un emprisonnement excédant un mois, pourra appeler de cette condamnation.—(*Article* 19 —*Voir le No.* 504). Ord. No. 31 de 1867, Art. 27.

Quant aux appels de jugements rendus en vertu des lois relatives aux Entrepreneurs, aux Hôpitaux, aux Vagabonds, ou à la Coalition,—voir respectivement les Nos. 313, 380, 422 et 452.

506.—Tout Magistrat Stipendiaire, après avoir reçu un avis d'appel, et avoir accepté une reconnaissance, transmettra immédiatement au Greffier de la Cour Suprême, des copies dûment certifiées conformes à l'original du jugement ou de l'ordre dont il est fait appel, et de toutes les preuves fournies lors de l'examen de la plainte à laquelle il se rapporte. Ord. No. 15 de 1852, Art. 20.

507.—Le Greffier de la dite Cour, lorsqu'il recevra le dit appel dans son Greffe, et lorsque les dites procédures y seront transmises, en donnera avis au Procureur Général, et sans assignation ni ordre à cet effet, la cause, si l'intimé est un travailleur et ne comparait pas par son Conseil, sera inscrite d'office pour être plaidée entre le Ministère Public et l'Appelant à la première audience de la Cour Suprême qui aura lieu dans les trois jours de la réception des pièces par le Greffier, et le dit appel continuera à avoir priorité sur toutes autres causes à l'audience jusqu'à décision définitive. Idem, Art. 21.

508.—Dans tout appel contre un jugement d'un Magistrat Stipendiaire, le Protecteur des Immigrants aura le droit d'intervenir et de comparaître pour assister l'Immigrant en cause. Ord. No. 28 de 1863, Art. 2.

———

PROTECTOR AND IMMIGRATION DEPOT.

Ord. No. 31 of 1867, Art. 66.

509.—The Protector of Immigrants is hereby appointed to act as Guardian *ex-officio* to all Orphans of Indian extraction, whether born in this Colony or elsewhere, who have no relatives in this Colony competent to form a Family Council for them, in conformity with the requirements of the Civil Code. He is also hereby empowered to act as guardian *ex-officio* to all Indian Lunatics who have no relatives in the Colony by law qualified to elect a guardian and sub-guardian for them. In all such cases, the Protector shall have full power to perform of his own authority as Guardian of the Minor or Lunatic, as the case may be, any such acts as, under the Civil Code of this Colony, can only be performed with the approval of a Family Council duly homologated.

Ord. No. 16 of 1862, Art. 17.

510.—It shall be lawful for the Protector of Immigrants, at any time, either personally, or by any person deputed by him in writing in terms of Schedule I, to enter and inspect any Asylum, Hospital, School, Camp of laborers, or other establishment of any kind, in which Indian Immigrants are received, and also to enter upon any Estate or premises (except private dwelling-houses) in which any Immigrant is employed or located,—and to investigate the condition and state of any Immigrants who may be therein respectively. He shall also be entitled to require any Immigrants in any such places, respectively, to be brought before him, or the person whom he shall depute, as aforesaid, upon any such visit. Any person who shall obstruct or molest the Protector of Immigrants, or his Deputy aforesaid, in the performance of the said duty, shall, on conviction before the Stipendiary Magistrate of the District, be condemned to a fine not exceeding £20 sterling, or to imprisonment for a period not exceeding one month.

SCHEDULE I.

I hereby depute A. B. to enter and inspect, (*the estate, camp, or such other place as may require to be inspected*) belonging to C. D. (*or managed by E. F.*) in the District of , and there to investigate the state and condition of all Immigrants who may there be located or employed, in accordance with the provisions of Ord. No. 16 of 1862.

This day of 186 . H. B.

Protector of Immigrants.

DU PROTECTEUR ET DU DÉPOT D'IMMIGRATION.

509.—Le Protecteur des Immigrants est nommé par ces présentes le tuteur d'office de tous les Orphelins Indiens qui n'ont pas de parents dans la Colonie capables de former leur conseil de famille conformément aux dispositions du Code Civil. Il est aussi autorisé par ces présentes à agir comme tuteur d'office de tous les Aliénés Indiens qui n'ont pas de parents dans la Colonie ayant qualité en vertu de la loi pour lui choisir un tuteur et un subrogé-tuteur. Dans tous ces cas, le Protecteur aura pleins pouvoirs pour faire de sa propre autorité comme tuteur du mineur ou de l'aliéné, selon le cas, tous les actes qui, d'après le Code Civil de cette Colonie, ne peuvent être faits qu'avec l'approbation d'un conseil de famille dûment homologué. Ord. No. 31 de 1867. Art. 66.

510.—Le Protecteur des Immigrants pourra à toute époque, soit personnellement, soit par une personne déléguée par lui par écrit conformément à la Cédule I, visiter et inspecter tout asile, hôpital, école, camp de laboureurs, ou autre établissement de toute sorte où sont reçus des Immigrants Indiens, comme aussi de pénétrer sur toute propriété ou dans toute cour (excepté les demeures particulières) où un Immigrant est employé ou logé, et de s'assurer de la condition et de l'état des Immigrants qui peuvent s'y trouver. Il pourra aussi ordonner lors de ces visites, que tout Immigrant dans un de ces endroits soit conduit devant lui, ou devant la personne qu'il aura déléguée comme il est dit ci-dessus. Toute personne qui contrariera ou molestera le Protecteur des Immigrants ou son dit délégué, dans l'accomplissement de son dit devoir, sera, si elle est reconnue coupable devant le Magistrat Stipendiaire du District, condamnée à une amende n'excédant pas £20 sterling, ou à un emprisonnement qui n'excédera pas un mois. Ord. No. 16 de 1862, Art. 17.

CÉDULE I.

Je, par ces présentes, députe A. B. pour se rendre à, et inspecter (*l'établissement, le camp, ou tout autre endroit qui doit être inspecté*) appartenant à C. D. (*ou administré par E. F.*), dans le District de afin d'examiner quel est l'état et la condition de tous les Immigrants y demeurant ou y employés, conformément aux dispositions de l'Ordonnance No. 16 de 1862.

Ce de 186 H. B.

Protecteur des Immigrants.

Ord. No. 4 of 1864, Art. 8. 511.—The Protector of Immigrants, for the time being, shall be entitled at all times to visit and inspect every Vagrant Depot in the Colony, and to make to the Governor such reports and recommendations as he may think proper regarding the treatment of all Vagrants, being Indian Immigrants, who shall be confined in such Depot.

Ord. No. 28 of 1863, Art. 3. 512.—When any action of damages shall lie at the instance of any Immigrant aforesaid against any persons chargeable with any official duty in relation to any complaint by or against such Immigrant, or in relation to any matter arising out of any Contract of Service of such Immigrant, such action being grounded on any neglect or misconduct in relation to such duty,—the Protector of Immigrants shall, (subject to the orders of the Governor), have right to institute and carry on such action, and to obtain, and cause to be executed, judgment therein for and on behalf of the said Immigrant. Any such action at the instance of the said Protector shall not be challengeable on the ground that it embraces the rights of action of two or more Immigrants concerned,—provided the said rights are founded on the same facts and law; but without prejudice to the Court or Judge, before whom such action may be brought, directing that such proceedings in the same be conducted in such manner, by way of division or separation of the said rights or interests, as may be deemed just by the said Court or Judge.—(*See also No.* 508.)

Ord. No. 5 of 1865, Art. 1. 513.—During the absence of the Protector of Immigrants from the Immigration Depot, the Chief Clerk for the time being in the Immigration Department, shall have power to perform all the duties, and to do all acts and things, and to execute all deeds and writings which by any law or practice in the Colony, require to be performed, done or executed by the Protector of Immigrants.

Idem, Art. 2. 514.—When any writing shall be executed by the Chief Clerk aforesaid, in virtue of the provisions of this Ordinance, there shall be added in print or in manuscript to his signature to such writing the words "Chief Clerk in absence of the Protector of Immigrants," otherwise the same shall not be held to be executed in terms of this Ordinance.

511.—Le Protecteur des Immigrants en fonctions pourra en tous temps visiter et inspecter tout Dépôt de Vagabonds dans la Colonie, et faire au Gouverneur les rapports et les suggestions qu'il jugera convenables quant à la manière dont sont traités les Vagabonds qui sont des Immigrants Indiens et qui sont détenus dans le dit Dépôt. Ord. No. 4 de 1864, Art. 8.

512.—Lorsqu'il y aura lieu à une demande en dommages-intérêts à la requête d'un Immigrant contre des personnes chargées d'un devoir officiel quant à une plainte quelconque portée par ou contre l'Immigrant sus-dit, ou quant à toute question dépendant d'un contrat de service du dit Immigrant, l'instance sus-dite étant fondée sur la négligence ou l'inconduite du Fonctionnaire en cause quant à ce devoir, le Protecteur des Immigrants aura (sujet aux ordres du Gouverneur) le droit de commencer et de poursuivre l'instance et d'obtenir et de faire exécuter le jugement qui sera rendu pour et en faveur du dit Immigrant. Nulle instance sus-dite commencée par le dit Protecteur, ne pourra être attaquée pour le motif qu'elle réunit le droit de poursuite de deux ou de plus de deux Indiens y intéressés, pourvu que les dits droits découlent des mêmes faits et de la même loi ; mais sans préjudice au droit qu'aura la Cour ou le Juge devant qui l'instance sera plaidée, d'ordonner que l'instance se poursuive de cette manière en divisant ou séparant les dits droits ou intérêts, comme la dite Cour ou le dit Juge le jugera plus avantageux dans l'intérêt de la Justice.—(*Voir aussi le No.* 508.) Ord. No. 28 de 1863, Art. 3.

513.—Pendant l'absence du Protecteur des Immigrants du Dépôt d'Immigration, le Chef Commis en fonctions du Département de l'Immigration pourra remplir tous les devoirs, et faire tous actes administratifs et autres, et signer tous documents et toutes pièces écrites qui, en vertu d'une loi ou coutume de la Colonie, doivent être faits ou signés par le Protecteur des Immigrants. Ord. No. 5 de 1865, Art. 1.

514.—Lorsqu'une pièce écrite sera signée par le Chef Commis en vertu des dispositions de cette Ordonnance il sera annexé, en imprimé, ou en manuscrit, à sa signature au bas de la pièce écrite les mots " Chef Commis en l'absence du Protecteur des Immigrants," sans quoi la pièce ne sera pas considérée comme exécutée conformément aux dispositions de cette Ordonnance. Idem, Art, 2.

Idem, Art. 3. 515.—All acts and things which shall be done, and all writings which shall be executed by the Chief Clerk aforesaid, in terms of the provisions of this Ordinance, shall be equally valid and effectual to all intents and purposes as if the same had been done and executed by the Protector : and it shall not be competent to any person to challenge the same on the ground that at the time of the doing or the execution thereof, the Protector of Immigrants was not in point of fact absent from the Immigration Depot.

Ord. No. 31 of 1867, Art. 59. 516.—The Protector of Immigrants shall make arrangements for receiving into the Depot, or such other place as the Governor may appoint in that behalf, all Immigrants who cannot find employment, and shall endeavour to provide them therewith. Their admission and stay there shall be under regulations, with a view to the prevention of abuses.

Govt. Notice No. 166 of 11th Nov. 1868, Art. 59. 517.—If any such Immigrant either on his reception in any such Depot or subsequently, be recognized to be a Pauper, according to the definition of that term in the laws which provide for the relief of the Poor, he shall be forthwith transferred to the charge of the Local Board of Guardians.

Idem, Art. 57. 518.—All Immigrants admitted under the provisions of *Ordinance No.* 31 *of* 1867, into the Immigration Depot, or any Branch Depot that may be appointed by the Governor for their reception, shall be dieted during their stay therein according to such dietary rules as may be approved by the Governor, and shall besides receive such medical care as they may require.—(*Ordinance No.* 31 *of* 1867.—*See No.* 516.)

Idem, Art. 58. 519.—All such Immigrants, pending the inquiries which shall be made about them, shall be detained in the Immigration Depot, or such other Depot as aforesaid, and they shall be bound, during their stay in such Depot, to perform such work as shall be allotted to them under the directions of the Protector of Immigrants, unless they be deemed unfit for such work by the Medical Officer appointed to attend them.

Idem, Art. 65. 520.—If wages be received for the labor of any Immigrant during his stay in any of the above-mentioned Depots, the cost of his maintenance shall be deducted therefrom, and the balance, if any, shall be paid over to him.

515.—Tous actes quelconques qui seront faits et toutes pièces écrites qui seront signées par le Chef Commis conformément aux dispositions de cette Ordonnance seront aussi valides et légaux à tous égards et effets que s'ils avaient été faits par le Protecteur des Immigrants. Et personne ne pourra en mettre leur validité en doute pour le motif qu'au moment où l'acte a été fait ou la pièce signée le Protecteur des Immigrants n'était pas, de fait, absent du Dépôt de l'Immigration. Idem, Art. 8.

516.—Le Protecteur des Immigrants prendra des dispositions pour recevoir au Dépôt tous Immigrants qui ne pourront pas trouver de l'emploi, et tâchera de leur en procurer. Leur admission et leur séjour au Dépôt seront soumis à des réglements afin de prévenir des abus. Ord. No. 31 de 1867, Art. 59.

517.—Si un des dits Immigrants, soit à son entrée au dit Dépôt, soit plus tard, est reconnu être un Pauvre selon la signification de cette expression dans les lois qui régissent l'assistance des pauvres, il sera immédiatement mis à la charge du Comité Local des Pauvres. Avis du Gouv. No. 166 du 11 Nov. 1868, Art. 59.

518.—Tous les Immigrants admis en vertu des dispositions de l'*Ordonnance No.* 31 *de* 1867, au Dépôt de l'Immigration, ou à un dépôt supplémentaire qui sera choisi par le Gouverneur pour les recevoir, y suivront, pendant le séjour qu'ils y feront, le régime qui sera fixé par des réglements approuvés par le Gouverneur, et recevront de plus tous les soins médicaux que leur état pourra exiger.—(*Ordonnance No.* 31 *de* 1867.—*Voir le No.* 516.) Idem, Art. 57.

519.—Tous les dits Immigrants, pendant l'enquête qui sera faite relativement à eux, seront détenus au Dépôt de l'Immigration, ou dans tout autre dépôt susdit, et ils seront tenus, pendant leur séjour au dit dépôt de faire tous les travaux qui leur seront attribués d'après les ordres du Protecteur des Immigrants, à moins que le Médecin du Dépôt ne les déclare incapables de faire les dits travaux. Idem, Art. 58.

520.—Si des gages sont reçus pour le travail d'un Immigrant pendant son séjour dans l'un des dits Dépôts, les frais de son entretien en seront déduits, et la balance, s'il y en a une, lui sera remise. Idem, Art. 65.

Idem, Art. 66. 521.—If the cost of the maintenance of any Immigrant in any such Depot be not repaid under the last preceding article, it shall, as far as practicable, be recovered by the Protector from the person who shall offer to employ such Immigrant.

Idem, Art. 63. 522.—Any person who may wish to employ laborers shall have free access to the inmates of any of the abovementioned Depots, provided he previously obtain a written permission from the Protector; and all Immigrants in any such depot shall, at such times as may be approved by the Protector, be allowed to proceed in search of employment, under a permit signed by any Officer authorised by the Protector to issue such permits. And such permit shall not be available for more than one month and shall, to be valid, be visaed and numbered by the Police. In no case, except upon the special and written authorization of the Protector, shall any such permit be renewable.

Idem, Art. 64. 523.—Any Immigrant in one of the abovementioned Depots who, after identification, is not recognised to be either a Vagrant or a Deserter, shall be free to leave such Depot on accepting any offer of permanent employment that may be made to him through the Protector, or on satisfying the Protector that he is going to undertake, on his own account, a *bonâ fide* employment.

Ord. No. 31 of 1867, Art. 60. 524.—Any Immigrant leaving the Depot or other place aforesaid after he has become amenable to its regulations, without the sanction of the Protector, shall, on proof thereof to the satisfaction of the Stipendiary Magistrate, be liable to imprisonment with hard labour for any period not exceeding 15 days.

Govt. Notice No. 166 of 11th Nov. 1868, Art. 75. 525.—From the day on which these regulations shall take effect, the fees mentioned in the tariff hereunto annexed (Schedule T) shall be charged and received by the Officers therein designated, on the various documents and proceedings therein specified; which tariff shall be liable to be altered as the Governor in Executive Council may deem fit to direct.

521.—Si les frais d'entretien d'un Immigrant dans un des dits Dépôts, ne sont pas remboursés de la manière prévue dans l'article qui précède, ils seront, autant que cela sera possible, réclamés par le Protecteur, de la personne qui offrira d'employer le dit Immigrant. Idem, Art. 66.

522.—Toute personne qui voudra employer des travailleurs aura libre accès auprès des hommes se trouvant dans tous les dépôts sus-dits, pourvu qu'elle obtienne au préalable une permission écrite du Protecteur ; et tous les Immigrants se trouvant dans les dits dépôts pourront, toutes les fois qu'ils obtiendrout la permission du Protecteur à cet effet, sortir pour chercher de l'emploi, en vertu d'un permis signé par l'employé qui sera autorisé par le Protecteur à donner des permis de cette nature.—Chacun des dits permis ne sera valable que pour un mois et devra être visé et numéroté par la Police.—Aucun des dits permis ne pourra en aucun cas être renouvelé sans la permission spéciale et écrite du Protecteur. Idem, Art. 63.

523.—Tout Immigrant se trouvant dans un des dépôts sus-dits qui, après vérification de son identité, est reconnu être ni un vagabond, ni un déserteur, sera libre de quitter le dit dépôt en acceptant l'offre d'un emploi permanent qui lui sera faite par l'entremise du Protecteur, ou s'il prouve à la satisfaction du Protecteur qu'il va entreprendre, pour son propre compte, un travail de bonne foi. Idem, Art. 64.

524.—Tout Immigrant qui quittera le dépôt après qu'il aura été soumis à ses réglements et sans l'autorisation du Protecteur, sera, sur preuve faite à la satisfaction du Magistrat Stipendiaire passible d'un emprisonnement avec travail forcé pour un temps n'excédant pas 15 jours. Ord. No. 31 de 1867, Art. 60.

525.—A partir du jour de la mise en vigueur des présents réglements, les droits mentionnés au tarif ci-annexé (Annexe T) seront reçus par les officiers y désignés, sur les divers documents et actes y désignés ; ce tarif pourra être modifié par le Gouverneur en Conseil Exécutif, si cela est jugé nécessaire. Avis du Gouv. No. 166 du 11 Nov. 1868, Art. 75.

SCHEDULE T.

Table of Fees to be paid in the Immigration Office.

	£	s.	D.	
1.—For every duplicate of a ticket......	1	0	0	To be paid by Applicant.
2.—For every pass, duplicate pass or permit issued by the Protector............	0	5	0	
3.—For every portrait of an Immigrant under Art. 39 of Ord. 31 of 1867 (No. 275).	0	4	0	
4.—For every passport under Art. 61 of Ord. 31 of 1867 (No. 540).............	0	2	0	
5.—For every certificate of marriage......	0	2	0	
6.—For every release from industrial residence	0	2	0	
7.—For every certificate under Reg. 62 (No. 408).........................	0	1	0	
8.—For every certificate of engagement..	0	1	0	By Employer.
9.—For every transfer of contract........	0	2	0	By Substituted Employer.

(*See also No.* 536.)

Idem, Art. 81. 525 (*bis*).—It shall be lawful for the Protector to direct the delivery of any ticket, passport, permit or pass, free of charge, to infirm and destitute Immigrants; and when the loss of any such document shall be satisfactorily explained to him, to exempt the applicant for a duplicate of such document from the payment of the fee thereupon fixed by the tariff. In every such case an Exemption Order in the form of the Schedule N hereto annexed shall be delivered to the applicant, on presentation of which the document therein mentioned shall be delivered to him. All such orders shall be numbered and filed by the officer whose duty it shall be to receive them.

SCHEDULE N.

Exemption-Order.

No.	No.
1. Immigrant's Name.... 2. „ No........ 3. Document ordered to be issued............	The Immigrant No. is hereby exempted from the payment of the fee chargeable under the tariff now in force for a
(*Date*)	(*Date.*)
(*Signature*) (*or Initials.*)	(*Signature.*)

ANNEXE T.

Tableau des Droits à payer au Bureau de l'Immigration.

	£	s.	d.	
1.—Pour chaque duplicata de ticket......	1	0	0	A payer par le Requérant.
2.—Pour chaque passe, duplicata de passe ou permis donné par le Protecteur....	0	5	0	
3.—Pour chaque portrait d'un Immigrant en vertu de l'Art. 39 de l'Ord. 31 de 1867 (No. 275.)...................	0	4	0	
4.—Pour chaque passe-port en vertu de l'Art. 61 de l'Ord. 31 de 1867 (No. 540.)	0	2	0	
5.—Pour chaque certificat de mariage....	0	2	0	
6.—Pour chaque décharge de résidence industrielle	0	2	0	
7.—Pour chaque certificat en vertu du Rég. 62 (No. 408.)	0	1	0	
8.—Pour chaque certificat d'engagement..	0	1	0	Par l'Employeur.
9.—Pour chaque transfert de contrat...... (*Voir aussi le No.* 536.)	0	2	0	Par l'Employeur substitué.

525 (*bis.*)—Le Protecteur des Immigrants pourra ordonner la remise d'un ticket, d'un passeport, d'un permis ou d'une passe, francs de droits, à des Immigrants infirmes ou indigents ; et lorsque la perte d'un de ces documents lui sera expliquée d'une manière satisfaisante, il pourra exempter celui qui demandera un duplicata de ce document, du paiement du droit fixé par le tarif. Dans chacun des dits cas un ordre d'exemption dans la forme de l'Annexe N sera donné au requérant ; sur la présentation de cet ordre le document y mentionné lui sera remis. Tous les dits ordres seront numérotés et enregistrés par l'employé dont le devoir sera de les recevoir. Idem, Art, 31.

ANNEXE N.

Ordre d'Exemption.

No.	No.
1. Nom de l'Immigrant..	L'Immigrant
2. No. ,, ...	No. est exempté par ces présentes du paiement du droit dû en vertu du tarif actuellement en vigueur, pour un
3. Document livré par ordre	
(*Date.*)	(*Date*)
(*Signature*) (*ou Initiales.*)	(*Signature.*)

MARRIAGES.

I.—*Marriages of Immigrants in India.*
II.—*Marriages of Indians in Mauritius.*

CHAPTER I.

Marriages of Immigrants in India.

Ord. No. 3 of 1856, Art. 1.

526.—Any native of India intending to come to this Island as an Immigrant, and having been legally married in India according to the forms and ceremonies of his religion may go before any one of the persons hereinafter empowered to receive declarations of marriage, accompanied by his wife, and any children the issue of such marriage, and such indian and his wife may in the presence of two witnesses make a declaration before such person (in the form in the Schedule A hereunto annexed) that they have been lawfully married according to the forms and ceremonies of their religion and that the children (if any) accompanying them are the lawful issue of such marriage; such declaration shall be signed by the parties making the same and by two witnesses thereto respectively if able to write; if unable to write, they shall affix their marks thereto and the declaration shall be attested by the person taking the same.

SCHEDULE A.

Descriptive Roll of the day of 186 proceeding to Mauritius per

Mauritius Registered No.	Agent's Registered No.	Name.	Father's Name.	Sex.	Caste.	Age	Place of nativity.	Remarks.
		Husband						
		Wife						
		(children.)						

Certified that the above described Indians whose signatures are hereunto attached have this day come before me and each of them

DES MARIAGES.

I.—*Mariages des Immigrants dans l'Inde.*
II.—*Mariages des Indiens à Maurice.*

CHAPITRE I.

Mariages des Immigrants dans l'Inde.

526.—Tout natif de l'Inde qui se proposera de se rendre en cette colonie comme Immigrant et qui se sera légalement marié dans l'Inde selon les formes et cérémonies de sa religion, pourra se présenter à l'une des personnes ci-après autorisées à recevoir les déclarations de mariage, accompagné de sa femme et des enfants nés du dit mariage, et le dit indien et sa femme pourront en présence de deux témoins faire une déclaration devant la dite personne (en la forme donnée dans la cédule A ci-annexée) qu'ils ont été mariés légalement selon les formes et cérémonies de leur religion, et que les enfants (s'il en existe) qui les accompagnent sont les enfants légitimes nés de ce mariage. Cette déclaration sera signée par les parties qui la feront et, respectivement, par deux témoins présents, s'ils savent écrire ; s'il ne savent pas écrire ils feront leur marque et la déclaration sera attestée par la personne qui l'aura reçue. Ord No. 3 de 1865, Art. 1.

CÉDULE A.

Etat Descriptif de *le* *jour de* 186 *se rendant à Maurice par*

Enregistré pour Maurice No.	Enregistré par l'Agent No.	Prénom.	Nom.	Sexe.	Caste.	Age	Lieu de Naissance.	Remarques.
		Mari						
		Femme						
		(enfants.)						

Certifié que les Indiens ci-dessus dénommés dont les signatures sont apposées ci-après, ont, ce jour, comparu devant moi et que chacun d'eux

separately and also in the presence of one another, has declared to me before the two witnesses who have also signed this certificate that they are legally married to each other according to the forms and ceremonies of their Religion (and that the children above named are the lawful issue of such mariage.)

(Signed :)
(Signed :)

(Signed :) X.
Mauritius Emigration Agent
(*as the case may be*).

We the above described Indians hereby declare that we have been married to each other according to the forms and ceremonies for our creeds (and that the children above named are the lawful issue of such marriage.)

Witnesses to the above declaration.

A. B.

Confirmed before me this day of 18 .

C. D.
Protector of Immigrants.

Idem, Art. 2. 527.—A similar declaration (according to the form in the Schedule B hereunto annexed) may be made in India by one of the parties to any such marriage intending to proceed to Mauritius to join the other party there.

SCHEDULE B.

Descriptive Roll of proceeding to Mauritius per to join (her husband) there.

Mauritius Registered No.	Agent's Registered No.	Name.	Father's Name.	Sex.	Caste.	Age	Place of Nativity.	Remarks.
		Crustangee the wife of	Esoba	Female	Muratta	32	Singera	
		Sigham (children)	Eravandree	Male	Muratta	36	Singera	

Certified that the above-named indian woman *Crustangee* whose signature is hereunto attached has this day voluntarily come before me and has declared to me before two witnesses who have also signed this certificate that *she* has been lawfully married to the above-named *Singham* according to the forms and ceremonies of their religion (that the children above-named are the lawful issue of such marriage), and that *she* is about to proceed to Mauritius to join *her* said *husband* who is there resident.

Witnesses to the above declaration.

A
B (Signed :) *Crustangee.* (Signed :) X.
Justice of the Peace,
(*as the case may be*).

séparément et aussi en présence l'un de l'autre, a déclaré devant les deux témoins qui ont également signé ce certificat, qu'ils sont légalement mariés l'un à l'autre selon les formes et cérémonies de leur religion (et que les enfants dénommés ci-dessus sont nés légitimement du dit mariage.)

(Signé :) (Signé :) X.
(Signé :) Agent d'Emigration pour Maurice
(*suivant le cas.*)

Nous, les Indiens dénommés ci-dessus, déclarons, par le présent, que nous avons été mariés l'un à l'autre selon les formes et cérémonies de notre religion (et que les enfants sus-dénommés sont nés légitimement de ce mariage.)

Témoins à la déclaration ci-dessus.

A. B.

Confirmé devant moi ce jour de 18 .

C. D.
Protecteur des Immigrants.

527.—Une déclaration semblable (selon la forme B ci-annexée) pourra être faite dans l'Inde par l'une des parties qui aura contracté le mariage et qui se proposera de partir pour Maurice à l'effet d'y rejoindre l'autre contractant. Idem, Art. 2.

CÉDULE B.

Etat descriptif de se rendant à Maurice par pour y rejoindre (son mari.)

Enregistré pour Maurice No.	Enregistré par l'Agent No.	Nom.	Nom du Père.	Sexe.	Caste.	Age	Lieu de Naissance	Observations.
		Crustangee femme de Singham (enfants)	Esoba	Féminin	Maratte	32	Singera	
			Eravandree	Masculin	Maratte	36	Singera	

Certifié que la femme indienne *Crustangee* sus-dénommée dont la signature est apposée ci-après a, ce jour, volontairement comparu devant moi et m'a déclaré devant deux témoins qui ont également signé le présent certificat, qu'elle a été légalement mariée au sus-dénommé *Singham* selon les formes et cérémonies de leur religion (que les enfants sus-dénommés sont nés légitimement de leur mariage) et qu'elle est au moment de partir pour Maurice pour y rejoindre son sus-dit mari qui y réside.

Témoins à la déclaration sus-dite :

A
B (Signé :) *Crustangee.* (Signé :) X.
Juge de Paix.
(*Suivant le cas.*)

We the above named Singham and Crustangee hereby in the presence of the Protector of Immigrants at Mauritius confirm the declaration made by Crustangee in India and acknowledge that we have been married to each other in India according to the forms and ceremonies for our creeds and that the children above-named are the lawful issue of such marriage.

(Signed :) X. *Singham.*
X. *Crustangee.*

Confirmed before me this day of 186 .

E. H.
Protector of Immigrants.

Idem, Art. 3. 528.—Such declarations of marriage may be taken and made in India by and before any Protector or assistant Protector of Emigrants, or any Emigration Agent, or any Magistrate or Justice of the Peace.

Idem, Art. 4. 529.—Where any such declaration of marriage shall have been taken and made in India, the parties therein declaring themselves to have been lawfully married may appear before the Protector of Immigrants in this Island and may in his presence confirm the said declaration. And the Protector, if satisfied with the identity of the parties, shall certify the fact of such confirmation upon the face of the declaration.—(*See No.* 527.)

Idem, Art. 5. 530.—A certified copy * of any declaration of marriage so made and confirmed as aforesaid shall be deemed for all purposes sufficient *primâ facie* evidence of the marriage of the parties and of the legitimacy of the children (if any) named therein.

Idem, Art. 6. 531.— And whereas from time to time before the passing of this Ordinance natives of India intending to proceed to Mauritius have gone before one of the persons named in *Article* 3 *of this Ordinance* and have made declaration that they have been married to each other according to the forms and ceremonies of their creed and have subsequently confirmed such declaration before the Protector of Immigrants in Mauritius and whereas it is expedient to give validity to such last mentioned declarations, be it enacted that any declaration of marriage so made and confirmed as afore-

---

* For this document a fee of two shillings is paid by the applicant to the Protector of Immigrants.—See No. 525, § 5.

Nous les sus-dénommés Singham, et Crustangee, confirmons par le présent, devant le Protecteur des Immigrants à Maurice, la déclaration faite par Crustangee dans l'Inde, et reconnaissons que nous avons été mariés l'un à l'autre dans l'Inde selon les formes et cérémonies de notre religion, et que les enfants sus-dénommés sont nés légitimement de ce mariage.

(Signé :) X. *Singham,*
X. *Crustangee.*

Confirmé devant moi ce, jour de 186 .

E. H.
Protecteur des Immigrants.

528.—Les dites declarations de mariage pourront être reçues et faites dans l'Inde par et devant tout Protecteur ou Assistant Protecteur des Emigrants, Agent d'Emigration, Magistrat ou Juge de Paix. Idem, Art. 3.

529.—Lorsqu'une telle déclaration de marriage aura été reçue et faite dans l'Inde, les parties y déclarant avoir été mariées légalement pourront se présenter devant le Protecteur des Immigrants en cette Colonie et confirmer en sa présence la dite déclaration. Et le Protecteur, s'il a preuve suffisante de l'identité des parties, certifiera le fait de la dite confirmation sur la déclaration elle-même.—(*Voir le No.* 527.) Idem, Art. 4.

530.—Toute déclaration de mariage ainsi faite et confirmée comme il est dit ci-dessus, ou une copie * certifiée d'icelle, sera réputée à tous égards preuve suffisante *primâ facie* du mariage des parties et de la légitimité des enfans (s'il en existe) y dénommés. Idem, Art. 5.

531.— Et attendu que de temps à autre avant que la présente Ordonnance n'ait été passée, des natifs de l'Inde se proposant de se rendre à Maurice se sont présentés devant l'une des personnes nommées en *l'article* 3 *de la présente Ordonnance,* et ont fait la déclaration qu'ils s'étaient mariés, selon les formes et cérémonies de leur religion, et ont confirmé ensuite la dite déclaration devant le Protecteur des Immigrants à Maurice, et attendu qu'il convient de valider ces déclarations, il est ordonné que toute déclaration de mariage ainsi faite et confirmée, comme il est dit ci-dessus, avant Idem, Art. 6.

* Le requérant paie pour ce document un droit de deux schellings au Protecteur des Immigrants.—Voir le No. 525, § 5.

said before the passing of this Ordinance may be deposited in the Office of the Protector of Immigrants, and whenever any such declaration shall have been so deposited, a certified copy of the same shall be deemed for all purposes sufficient *primâ facie* evidence of the marriage of the parties named therein.—(*Article* 3.—*See No.* 528.)

Idem, Art. 7. 532.— The originals of all declarations of marriage made in India and confirmed by the Protector of Immigrants as hereinbefore mentioned shall be deposited at the Office of the Protector of Immigrants, and in the month of January in each year the Protector of Immigrants shall deliver over to the Officer of the Civil Status of Port Louis, all the declarations of marriage which shall have been deposited in his Office during the preceding year such declarations having been first properly bound up together in a book. The said book shall be filed and kept on record in the Office of the said Officer of the Civil Status.

Idem, Art. 8. 533.—The District Magistrates shall have jurisdiction in their several Districts in all cases of complaints brought before them against persons for enticing away or harbouring the wives of Indian Immigrants, where such wives shall be natives of India.

Idem, Art. 9. 534.— Any person who shall be convicted before a District Magistrate of having enticed away or harboured the wife of any Indian Immigrant, as aforesaid, shall be liable to a fine not exceeding £ 50 or imprisonment with hard labor not exceeding six months.

Idem, Art. 10. 535.—The present Ordinance may be cited for all purposes as " The Indian marriage Ordinance, 1856 " and shall take effect on and from the 5th day of April A. D. 1856.

CHAPTER II.

Marriages of Indians in Mauritius.

Ord. No. 21 of 1853, Art. 8. 536.—Instead of the " Acte de Notoriété " required by Articles 70 and 71 of the Civil Code, the following formalities shall

que la présente Ordonnance n'ait été passée, peut être déposée au Bureau du Protecteur des Immigrants, et lorsque la dite déclaration aura été ainsi déposée une copie certifiée d'icelle sera réputée à tous égards preuve suffisante *primâ facie* du mariage des parties y dénommées.— (*Art.* 3.—*Voir le No.* 528.)

532.— Les originaux de toutes déclarations de mariage faites dans l'Inde, et confirmées par le Protecteur des Immigrants de la manière mentionnée ci-dessus, seront déposés au Bureau du Protecteur des Immigrants, et au mois de Janvier de chaque année le Protecteur des Immigrants transmettra au Commissaire Civil au Port Louis, toutes les déclarations de mariage qui auront été déposées dans son bureau pendant l'année précédente, les dites déclarations ayant auparavant été réunies dans un régistre relié convenablement ; le dit régistre sera déposé et conservé au bureau du dit Commissaire Civil. Idem, Art. 7.

533.— Les Magistrats de District auront juridiction dans leurs divers districts, dans tous les cas de plaintes portées devant eux contre toutes personnes qui auront débauché ou recelé des femmes d'Immigrants Indiens, lorsque les dites femmes seront natives de l'Inde. Idem, Art. 8.

534. – Toute personne qui sera convaincue devant un Magistrat de District d'avoir débauché oủ recelé la femme d'un Immigrant Indien sera passible d'une amende n'excédant pas £ 50 ou d'un emprisonnement avec travaux forcés n'excédant par six mois. Idem, Art. 9.

535.—La présente Ordonnance pourra être citée à tous égards comme " Ordonnance de 1856 sur les Mariages Indiens," et elle sera en vigueur à partir du 5 Avril 1856. Idem, Art. 10.

CHAPITRE II.

Des Mariages des Indiens à Maurice.

536.—Au lieu de l'Acte de Notoriété requis par les Articles 70 et 71 du Code Civil, les formalités suivantes seront remplies Ord. No. 21 de 1853, Art. 8.

be fulfilled by the persons hereinafter designated, previous to the publication of their intended Marriages.

....

Sect. 3. 3o. And Immigrants shall produce a certificate of the Protector of Immigrants in this Colony, stating their names, ages, caste, place of birth, and number of their tickets. The said certificate shall mention that, to the best of the knowledge and belief of the Protector, the person named in such certificate is not married. A fee of one shilling shall be paid for each certificate.

Idem. Art. 14. 537.—The consent and authorization required for the Marriage of any illegitimate child by Arts. 159 and 160 of the Code Civil may be given by the guardians appointed under *Art.* 12 *of this Ordinance,* and for orphan Immigrants by the Protector of Immigrants.—(*Article* 12 *does not bear on the subject of this work and is therefore not inserted here.*)

Idem, Art. 13. 538.—The Protector of Immigrants is hereby appointed and shall be *ex-officio* guardian to any orphan Immigrant, either natural or legitimate.

Ord. No. 31 of 1867, Art. 66. 539.—The Protector of Immigrants is hereby appointed to act as Guardian *ex-officio* to all Orphans of Indian extraction, whether born in this Colony or elsewhere, who have no relatives in the Colony competent to form a Family Council for them in conformity with the requirements of the Civil Code. He is also hereby empowered to act as Guardian *ex-officio* to all Indian Lunatics who have no relatives in the Colony by law qualified to elect a guardian and sub-guardian for them. In all such cases, the Protector shall have full power to perform of his own authority as Guardian of the Minor or Lunatic, as the case may be, any such acts as, under the Civil Code of this Colony, can only be performed with the approval of a Family Council duly homologated.

In all matters relating to Marriage for which no special provision is made in this Section, the laborers of Mauritius are subject to the same legislation as the rest of the community.

par les personnes ci-après désignées, avant la publication de leur Mariage projeté.

....

3o. Et les Immigrants produiront un certificat du Protecteur des Immigrants en cette Colonie contenant leurs noms, âge, caste, lieu de naissance et le numéro de leurs tickets. Le dit certificat mentionnera qu'autant que le Protecteur puisse le savoir et le croire, l'individu nommé dans le dit certificat n'est pas marié. Un droit de un schelling sera payé pour chaque certificat. Sect. 3.

537.—Le consentement et l'autorisation requis par les Arts. 159 et 160 du Code Civil pour le mariage d'un enfant illégitime pourront être donnés par les tuteurs nommés en vertu de l'*Art. 12 de la présente Ordonnance,* et, pour les *orphelins Immigrants,* par le Protecteur des Immigrants.—(*L'Article* 12 *ne se rapportant pas au sujet de cet ouvrage, n'est pas inséré ici.*) Idem, Art. 14.

538.—Le Protecteur des Immigrants est nommé par les présentes et sera tuteur d'office de tout Immigrant orphelin, qu'il soit enfant naturel ou légitime. Idem, Art. 13.

539.—Le Protecteur des Immigrants est nommé par ces présentes le tuteur d'office de tous les Orphelins Indiens qui n'ont pas de parents dans la Colonie capables de former leur conseil de famille conformément aux dispositions du Code Civil. Il est aussi autorisé par ces présentes à agir comme tuteur d'office de tous les Aliénés Indiens qui n'ont pas de parents dans la Colonie ayant qualité en vertu de la loi pour lui choisir un tuteur et un subrogé-tuteur. Dans tous ces cas le Protecteur aura pleins pouvoirs pour faire de sa propre autorité comme tuteur du mineur ou de l'aliéné, selon le cas, tous les actes qui, d'après le Code Civil de cette Colonie, ne peuvent être faits qu'avec l'approbation d'un conseil de famille dûment homologué. Ord. No. 31 de 1867, Art. 66.

Pour toutes les questions se rapportant à leur mariage pour lesquelles cette Section ne contient aucune disposition spéciale, les travailleurs à Maurice sont soumis aux mêmes lois que le reste de la population.

DEPARTURES AND DEPORTATION.

Ord. No. 31 of 1867, Art. 61, Par. 1.

540.—Every Immigrant intending to leave the Colony, shall be bound to present himself before the Protector of Immigrants, and to prove that he has completed his industrial residence. And if such Immigrant be about to depart in any Ship other than a Ship chartered by Government for the conveyance to India of Return Immigrants, such Immigrant shall be bound before embarking to obtain a Passport from the Protector.

Govt. Notice No. 166 of 25th Nov. 1868. Art. 69.

541.—The Passports deliverable under *Article* 61 *of Ordinance No.* 31 *of* 1867, shall be in the form of the Schedule S hereto annexed, and shall be liable to the fee * mentioned in the tariff appended to these regulations. On delivery of every such Passport to an Immigrant his ticket and certificate, and his police-pass, if he have any, shall be withdrawn from him; and the police-passes so withdrawn shall be returned to the Inspector General of Police.—(*Article* 61.—*See No.* 540.)

SCHEDULE S.

*Passport.**

The hereunder-mentioned Immigrant having his industrial residence and being free from engagement is hereby permitted to proceed to per ship

Name..	Portrait.
Father's Name	
Registered No....	
Age	
Zillah	

Immigration Office, Mauritius 186 .

The abovementioned Immigrant is permitted to absent himself from the Depot till the 186 .

In absence of the Protector of Immigrants.

C. A.

Chief Clerk.

* For this document a fee of 2*s*. is payable by the applicant.—See No. 525, § 4.

DU DÉPART ET DE LA DÉPORTATION.

540.—Tout Immigrant ayant l'intention de quitter la Colonie, sera tenu de se présenter devant le Protecteur des Immigrants, et de lui prouver qu'il a achevé sa résidence industrielle. Et si cet Immigrant doit partir sur un navire autre qu'un bâtiment affrété par le Gouvernement pour le transport dans l'Inde des Immigrants y retournant, cet Immigrant sera tenu avant de s'embarquer d'obtenir un Passeport du Protecteur. Ord. No. 31 de 1867, Art. 61, Par. 1.

541.—Les Passeports qui seront délivrés en vertu de l'*Article* 61 *de l'Ordonnance No.* 31 *de* 1867, seront dans la forme de l'Annexe S, et seront soumis au droit * mentionné au tarif ci-annexé. En livrant un Passeport à un Immigrant, son ticket, son certificat et sa passe de police, s'il en a une, lui seront retirés, et les passes de police ainsi retirées seront envoyées à l'Inspecteur Général de Police.—(*Article* 61.—*Voir le No.* 540.) Avis du Gouv. No. 166 du 11 Nov. 1868, Art. 69.

ANNEXE S.

*Passeport**.

L'Immigrant ci-dessous mentionné ayant sa résidence industrielle et étant libre de tout engagement est autorisé par ces présentes à se rendre à par le navire

Nom ... ...
Nom du père ... ...
Enregistré No. ... ...
Age ... ...
Zillah ... ...

Portrait.

Bureau de l'Immigration, Maurice 186 .

L'Immigrant ci-dessus mentionné peut s'absenter du Dépôt jusqu'au 186 .

En l'absence du Protecteur des Immigrants.
C. A.
Premier Commis.

* Ce document coute 2*s*. à celui qui en fait la demande.—Voir le No. 525, § 4.

Ord. No. 31 of 1867, Art. 61. Par. 2.

542.—Any Master of a Ship who shall allow any Immigrant to embark on board his ship without having obtained such Passport as aforesaid, shall be liable to a fine not exceeding £20; and the Immigrant so embarking may be taken out of the ship by any Officer of the Port Department, or by any Officer or Constable of Police, and handed over to the Protector of Immigrants.

Govt. Notice No. 166 of 11th Nov. 1868, Art. 70.

543.—Any Immigrant who, with intent to leave the Colony, shall proceed on board of any ship or vessel without having obtained the Passport mentioned hereabove, and every Immigrant who, having obtained a Passport, shall attempt to proceed in a Ship other than the one mentioned in his Passport, shall be liable to a fine not exceeding three pounds, on conviction before a Stipendiary Magistrate.

The Governor may grant a free passage back to India to any Immigrant incapacitated from labor by infirmity or other cause.—*See No.* 183.

Ord. No. 31 of 1867, Art. 62.

544.—It shall be lawful for the Governor, on sufficient presumption arising from Police reports or Judicial proceedings that any Indian Immigrant is a confirmed vagrant, or is a member of any association or combination for criminal purposes, or has been implicated in any criminal acts, to send him back to India; and, in case of his returning to this Colony, to cause him to be apprehended and detained until he be again sent out of the Colony.

Govt. Notice No. 166 of 11th Nov. 1868, Art. 71.

545.—Any Immigrant liable to be embarked under *Article* 62 of the aforesaid Ordinance shall be detained until his embarkation at the Central Police Station of Port Louis, or at such other place as the Governor may direct.—(*Article* 62.—*See No.* 545.)

VACANT ESTATES.

Ord. No. 13 of 1857, Art. 29.

546.—The rules hereinbefore specified as to the entry into possession and sale of Vacant Estates shall not extend to the Estates of Immigrant Labourers who may die in the Colony. But these shall be administered in manner following:—

542.—Tout Capitaine de navire qui permettra à un Immigrant de s'embarquer à bord de son navire sans le Passeport dont il doit être muni, ainsi qu'il est dit plus haut, sera passible d'une amende n'excédant pas £20. Et l'Immigrant ainsi embarqué pourra être débarqué du navire par tout Officier du Département du Port, ou par tout Officier ou Constable de Police et remis au Protecteur des Immigrants. Ord. No. 31 de 1867, Art. 61, Par. 2.

543.—Tout Immigrant qui, avec l'intention de quitter la Colonie, se rendra à bord d'un navire sans avoir obtenu le Passeport mentionné plus haut, et tout Immigrant qui, après avoir obtenu un Passeport, tentera de partir par un navire autre que celui mentionné au dit Passeport, sera passible d'une amende n'excédant pas trois livres, s'il est trouvé coupable par un Magistrat Stipendiaire. Avis du Gouv. No. 166 du 11 Nov. 1868, Art. 70.

Le Gouverneur peut accorder un passage gratuit pour l'Inde à tout Immigrant qui sera incapable de travailler pour cause d'infirmités ou pour toute autre motif—*Voir le No.* 183.

544.—Le Gouverneur pourra, sur des présomptions suffisantes basées sur des rapports de la Police ou des procédures judiciaires, constatant qu'un Immigrant Indien est un vagabond incorrigible, ou un membre d'une association ou combinaison pour des projets criminels, ou a été compromis dans des actes criminels, le renvoyer dans l'Inde ; et, dans le cas où il retournerait dans cette Colonie, le faire arrêter et détenir jusqu'à ce qu'il soit encore renvoyé de la Colonie. Ord. No. 31 de 1867, Art. 62.

545.—Tout Immigrant qui pourra être embarqué en vertu de l'*Article* 62 de la sus-dite Ordonnance sera détenu jusqu'à son embarquement à la Station Centrale de Police du Port-Louis, ou dans tout autre lieu choisi à cet effet par le Gouverneur.—(*Article* 62.—*Voir le No.* 545.) Avis du Gouv. No. 166 du 11 Nov. 1868, Art. 71.

DES BIENS VACANTS.

546.—Les réglements ci-dessus énumérés pour l'entrée en possession et la vente des biens vacants, ne s'appliqueront pas aux biens des travailleurs immigrants qui décèderont dans la Colonie. Ces biens seront administrés de la manière suivante :— Ord No. 13 de 1857, Art. 29.

1o. The Curator, upon the authority of the Treasurer but without any previous legal formality, shall enter into and take possession of all the Estate, Assets and Effects of Immigrant Labourers dying intestate in this Colony immediately on his receiving the information officially or otherwise of any such death; and the Officer of the Civil Status of the District in which any such Immigrant shall die, shall, without delay, notify his decease to the said Curator.

2o. Every person residing in any Country District, on whose estate, plantations or premises, or in whose service any Immigrant laborer shall die, shall, when making the declaration of decease to the Officer of the Civil Status of the District deliver to the said Officer a short note or inventory in writing, duly signed by the declarant, of all the goods, chattels, personal effects, wages and other assets, which, to the knowledge of the declarant, belonged or were due to such deceased Immigrant; which note or inventory, after having been authenticated by the *visâ* of the said Officer of the Civil Status, shall by him be forthwith transmitted to the Curator.

3o. In the town of Port Louis, the delivery of all such goods, chattels, assets, wages and effects shall be made immediately by the employer to the Curator. The Curator shall, in all cases, make diligent search and inquiry whether the deceased Immigrant possessed other effects, titles or securities of any kind or description; and, in case of any such being discovered by him, he shall prepare a short inventory, which, together with that received from the Officer of the Civil Status, he shall present to the Treasurer for his *visâ*.

4o. The Curator, with the authorization of the Treasurer, shall cause all the goods, chattels and effects of all deceased Immigrants in the Town of Port Louis to be sold by auction in a summary way, and the estates of all those deceased in the Country Districts shall be sold by such person or persons as the Treasurer General shall think fit to charge therewith, who shall be entitled to receive the sum of four shillings only for each sale.

5o. All such sales may be made either in the place where the Immigrant died or at any other place which may be deemed more suitable and convenient, and that either with or without previous

1o. Le Curateur, avec l'autorisation du Trésorier, mais sans aucune formalité judiciaire préalable, prendra possession des biens, valeurs et effets des travailleurs Immigrants qui décèderont *ab intestat* dans la Colonie, aussitôt qu'il aura reçu avis, officiellement ou autrement, du décès de l'un d'eux, et l'Officier de l'Etat Civil du District dans lequel un tel Immigrant décèdera, notifiera sans délai ce décès au dit Curateur.

2o. Toute personne habitant un District Rural, sur la propriété, les plantations ou le bien de laquelle ou au service de laquelle un travailleur Immigrant décèdera, remettra à l'Officier de l'Etat Civil du District, lorsqu'elle lui fera la déclaration du dit décès, une note ou inventaire sommaire par écrit, signé du déclarant, de tous les biens meubles et effets personnels, gages et autres propriétés appartenant ou dûs, à sa connaissance, à l'Immigrant décédé; laquelle note ou inventaire après avoir été rendu authentique par le *visâ* du dit Officier de l'Etat Civil, sera par lui transmis sans délai au Curateur.

3o. Dans la ville du Port-Louis, la remise des dits biens meubles, propriétés, gages et effets, sera faite immédiatement par l'employeur au Curateur. Le Curateur fera, en tous cas, toutes diligences et enquêtes pour connaître si l'Immigrant décédé possédait d'autres effets, titres ou valeurs quelconques, et s'il en découvre, il en fera un inventaire sommaire, qu'il présentera avec celui reçu de l'Officier de l'Etat Civil, au Trésorier Général, pour qu'ils soient visés par lui.

4o. Le Curateur avec l'autorisation du Trésorier, fera vendre à l'encan d'une manière sommaire tous les biens meubles et effets de tous les Immigrants décédés dans la ville du Port Louis, et les propriétés de ceux décédés dans les districts ruraux seront vendues par la personne ou les personnes que le Trésorier jugera convenable d'en charger, lesquelles auront le droit de recevoir la somme de quatre shillings seulement pour chaque vente.

5o. Les dites ventes pourront être faites au lieu du décès de l'Immigrant, ou dans tout autre endroit qui sera jugé plus convenable, et ce avec ou sans annonce préalable, selon la valeur des

advertisement, according to the value of the property, with the exception however of all articles of jewellery, or of gold or silver, which shall always be sold in the manner hereinbefore provided.

6o. All acts, inventories and writings, made or written in virtue of the preceding paragraphs of this article, shall be exempt from the duties and formalities of stamps and registration.

7o. Whenever there shall be found any portion of real estate appertaining to the intestate succession of any Immigrant labourer, the sale thereof shall be effected by public auction in the manner herein provided regarding other real estate administered by the Curator.

The provisions of the preceding article apply to the Vacant Estates of Liberated African Slaves.—*See No.* 172.

Ord. No. 31 of 1867, Art. 63.

547.—A penalty not exceeding £ 5 shall be incurred by any employer who shall fail, within 48 hours after the death, upon his premises, of any Immigrant laborer in his service, to comply with the requirements of the *29th Article of the Ordinance No.* 13 *of* 1857, entituled " An Ordinance for amending the Law on the Curatorship of Vacant Estates," relative to the estate and effects of such deceased laborer.—Provided that if the declaration of decease of such Immigrant be made to the Officer of the Civil Status by a person other than the employer, the latter shall be bound to comply with such requirements in like manner as if the said declaration of Decease had in fact been made by him.—(*Article* 29,—*See No.* 546.)

Govt. Notice No. 166 of 11th Nov. 1868, Art. 72.

548.—At the commencement of every month, the Curator of Vacant Estates shall forward to the Protector of Immigrants a detailed list of all the Vacant Estates taken possession of under *Article* 29 *of Ordinance No* 13 *of* 1857; the list shall set forth, as correctly as possible, the name and Immigration number of the deceased Immigrant laborer to whom the property belonged, the place of his death, his age at the time of his death, and a precise description of the property taken charge of by the Curator. Every such list shall be translated into the Indian dialects and conspicuously posted up in the Immigration Office: and the cost of the translation and publication thereof shall be paid by the Treasurer out of the funds realised from such estates.—(*Article* 29.—*See No.* 546.)

propriétés, à l'exception toutefois de tous les articles de bijouterie ou d'or et d'argent, lesquels seront toujours vendus de la manière indiquée ci-dessus.

6o. Les actes, inventaires et autres documents, faits ou rédigés en vertu des paragraphes précédents du présent article, seront exempts des droits et formalités du timbre et de l'enregistrement.

7o. Lorsqu'il sera reconnu qu'un immeuble appartient à la succession vacante d'un travailleur immigrant, la vente en sera faite publiquement de la manière indiquée en la présente Ordonnance concernant les autres immeubles administrés par le Curateur.

Les dispositions précédentes s'appliquent aux biens vacants des esclaves africains libérés.—*Voir le No.* 172.

547.—Une amende n'excédant pas £ 5 sera encourue par tout employeur qui, dans les 48 heures qui suivront la mort d'un travailleur Immigrant à son service, négligera de se conformer aux dispositions de l'*Article* 29 *de l'Ordonnance No.* 13 *de* 1857 intitulée " Ordonnance pour amender la loi sur la Curatelle aux Biens Vacants," relatives aux biens laissés par ce travailleur décédé. Néanmoins si la déclaration du décès de cet Immigrant est faite à l'Officier de l'Etat Civil par une personne autre que l'employeur, ce dernier sera tenu de se conformer aux dites dispositions de la même manière que si la dite déclaration du décès avait été en réalité faite par lui.—(*Article* 29,—*Voir le No.* 546.) Ord. No. 31 de 1867, Art. 63.

548.—Au commencement de chaque mois le Curateur aux Biens Vacans enverra au Protecteur des Immigrants une liste détaillée de toutes les successions vacantes dont il aura pris possession en vertu de l'*Article* 29 *de l'Ordonnance No.* 13 *de* 1857; cette liste énoncera, aussi exactement que possible, le nom et le numéro d'Immigration du travailleur immigrant décédé à qui les biens appartenaient, le lieu du décès, son âge au moment du décès, et la description exacte des biens dont le Curateur aura pris possession. Cette liste sera traduite dans les dialectes indiens et affichée au Bureau de l'Immigration; et les frais des dites traduction et publication seront payés par le Trésorier avec les fonds réalisés des dites successions.—(*Article* 29.—*Voir le No.* 546.) Avis du Gouv. No. 166 du 11 Nov. 1868, Art. 72.

DEFINITION OF TERMS.

Order in Council 7th Sept. 1838, Preamble, Par. 4 and 5.

549.—And it is further ordered, that for the purposes and within the meaning of this present Order, the officer lawfully administering the Government of any of the said Colonies, shall be deemed and taken to be the GOVERNOR thereof; and that for the purposes and within the meaning of this present Order, the word SERVANT * shall be construed and understood to comprize any person employed for hire, wages, or other remuneration to perform any handicraft or other bodily labour in agriculture or manufactures or in domestic service, or as a boatman, porter, or other occupation in which the Emancipated Population of the said Colonies or any of them were usually employed while in a state of slavery or as Apprenticed Labourers; and that for the purposes and within the meaning of this present Order, the word MASTERS shall be construed and understood to comprize any person, whether male or female, employing for hire, wages, or other remuneration, any person falling within the before mentioned description of a servant; and that for the purposes and within the meaning of this present Order the words CONTRACT OF SERVICE shall be construed and understood to comprize any agreement whether oral or written, whether express or implied, into which any persons falling within the before mentioned description of the word servant, shall enter with any other person or persons, for the performance of any work or labour of any kind hereinbefore particularly mentioned; and that for the purposes and within the meaning of the present Order, the words STIPENDIARY MAGISTRATE shall be construed and understood to comprize such Magistrates only as shall be included in any special commission of the peace to be from time to time addressed to them in the name and on the behalf of Her Majesty by the Governor for the time being of the Colony to which such Magistrates may belong for the execution of this present Order; and that for the purposes and within the meaning of this present Order, the words CHIEF CIVIL JUDGE shall be construed and understood to mean in the Colony of British Guiana the Chief Justice of the Court of Civil

* No common laborer or workman for hire is deemed, as such, a trader liable to become bankrupt.—Ord. No. 33 of 1853, Art. 20.

DE LA DÉFINITION DES TERMES.

549.—Et il est de plus ordonné que pour l'objet et dans le sens du présent ordre, on entend par GOUVERNEUR, l'officier administrant légalement le gouvernement de chacune des dites colonies ; et par le mot SERVITEUR,* toute personne employée à loyer, à gages, ou moyennant toute autre rétribution, pour faire un métier ou tout autre travail corporel dans l'agriculture, les manufactures, ou dans le service domestique, ou comme batelier, porteur, ou pour tout autre travail auquel la population émancipée des dites colonies ou de l'une d'elles était ordinairement employée dans l'état d'esclavage ou comme apprentis ; et que pour l'objet et dans le sens du présent Ordre, le mot MAITRE sera compris et s'entendra de toute personne, homme ou femme, employant à loyer, à gages, ou moyennant une autre rétribution, toute personne comprise dans la définition ci-dessus des serviteurs ; et que pour l'objet et dans le sens du présent Ordre, les mots CONTRAT DE SERVICE s'entendront de tout accord verbal ou par écrit, exprès ou implicite, que toute personne appartenant à la classe ci-dessus décrite sous le nom de serviteurs, fera avec toute autre personne ou personnes pour l'exécution d'aucun travail ou ouvrage ci-dessus particulièrement mentionné ; et que pour l'objet et dans le sens du présent Ordre, les mots MAGISTRATS SALARIÉS s'entendront des Magistrats seulement qui seront désignés dans une commission spéciale de paix qui leur sera adressée de temps à autre au nom de Sa Majesté la Reine par le Gouverneur, alors en exercice, de la colonie à laquelle appartiendront ces Magistrats, pour l'exécution du présent Ordre ; et que pour l'objet et dans le sens du présent Ordre, les mots CHEF JUGE CIVIL s'entendront dans la colonie de la Guiane Britannique du Chef Juge de la Cour de Justice Civile et Criminelle de Demerara, dans la colonie de la Trinité du Chef Juge de la Cour de Première Instance, dans la colonie de Sainte-Lucie

Ordre en Conseil du 7 Sept. 1838. Préamb. Par. 4 and 5.

* Aucun travailleur ordinaire ou ouvrier travaillant à gages n'est considéré, comme tel, un commerçant pouvant se mettre en faillite.—Ordonnance No. 33 de 1853, Art. 20.

and Criminal Justice of Demerara, and in the Colony of Trinidad the Chief Judge of the Court of First Instance, and in the Colony of St. Lucia, the First President of the Royal Court, and in the Colony of Mauritius, the First President of the Court of Appeal.†

And it is further ordered that all words in this Order and in the said regulations importing the singular number or the masculine gender only, shall be understood to include several persons as well as one person, and females as well as males, unless it be otherwise specially provided, or there be something in the subject or context repugnant to such construction.

Ord. No. 31 of 1867, Art. 1.

550.—The term NEW IMMIGRANT extends and applies to all male Indian laborers who have immigrated into this Colony or its Dependencies since the publication of Her Majesty's Order in Council of the 15th January 1842, or who may hereafter immigrate as above from British India, and for whose introduction passage-money has been or may hereafter be paid by the Government or by any individual employer, and who have not completed an industrial residence of five years, as hereinafter defined.

The term OLD IMMIGRANT extends and applies to all male Indian laborers who have immigrated as above previous to the promulgation of the said Order in Council, or for whose introduction no such passage-money has been paid, or who shall at any time, now or hereafter, have completed their said industrial residence.

The term INDUSTRIAL RESIDENCE means a residence of five years in this Colony, or its Dependencies, under written contract of service for hire and performance of such Contract.

The industrial residence shall be deemed to have been completed:

1o.—By service under such contract, one or more, for the term of five years, testified by a discharge therefrom under the hand of a Stipendiary Magistrate.

---

† The "Court of Appeal" in Mauritius was abolished by Ordinance No. 2 of 1850 which established the "Supreme Court of the Colony of Mauritius."

du Premier Président de la Cour Royale, et dans la colonie de Maurice du Président de la Cour d'Appel.†

Et il est de plus ordonné, que tous les mots employés dans le présent Ordre et dans les dits réglemens, au nombre singulier ou au genre masculin seulement, seront entendus comme comprenant plusieurs personnes aussi bien qu'une personne, et les femmes aussi bien que les hommes, à moins qu'il ne soit autrement et spécialement disposé, ou qu'il y ait quelque chose dans le sujet ou dans le texte d'incompatible avec cette interprétation.

550.—L'expression NOUVEL IMMIGRANT s'étend et s'applique à tout travailleur Indien du sexe masculin qui aura émigré en cette Colonie ou dans ses Dépendances depuis la publication de l'ordre de Sa Majesté en Conseil en date du 15 Janvier 1842, ou qui émigrera ainsi qu'il vient d'être dit de l'Inde Britannique après la promulgation de la présente Ordonnance, et pour l'introduction duquel des frais de passage auront été payés ou seront payés plus tard par le Gouvernement ou par un Employeur particulier, et qui n'aura pas achevé une résidence industrielle de cinq années, ainsi qu'il sera expliqué plus bas. Ord. No. 31 de 1867, Art. 1.

L'expression ANCIEN IMMIGRANT s'étend et s'applique à tout travailleur Indien du sexe masculin qui aura émigré ainsi qu'il est dit plus haut, avant la promulgation du dit Ordre en Conseil, ou pour l'introduction duquel il n'aura pas été payé de frais de passage, ou qui aura déjà achevé ou qui achèvera plus tard sa dite résidence industrielle.

L'expression RÉSIDENCE INDUSTRIELLE signifie une résidence de cinq années en cette Colonie ou ses Dépendances, en vertu d'un contrat de service écrit et après l'exécution de ce contrat.

La Résidence Industrielle sera considérée comme étant achevée :

1o.—Par le service en vertu d'un ou de plusieurs des dits contrats, pendant cinq années, certifié par la décharge du dit service signée par un Magistrat Stipendiaire.

† La "Cour d'Appel" à Maurice a été abolie par l'Ordonnance No. 2 de 1850 qui a établi la "Cour Suprême de la Colonie de Maurice."

2o.—By redemption, as hereinafter provided.

3o.—By release, as hereinafter provided.

4o.—By exemption by the Governor, as hereinafter provided.

For the purposes of the present Ordinance, the term REQUISITIONIST extends and applies to any person who shall have made requisition for the introduction of Immigrants to be specially engaged to him in India, or to be allotted to him on arrival in Mauritius, as the case may be.

For the purposes of the present Ordinance, the term SUBSTITUTED EMPLOYER extends and applies :

1o.—To any person other than the Requisitionist to whom any New Immigrant shall, on arrival in Mauritius, be engaged under Contract of Service for the whole period of his Industrial Residence.

2o.—To any person to whom any Contract of Service with a New Immigrant shall have been transferred for the unexpired residue of the Industrial Residence of such Immigrant, either by consent of parties, or under the provisions of *Article* 7 of Ordinance 16 of 1862.—(*Article* 7.—*See No.* 246.)

Indian Act, expressions in	See	No.	25.
Liberated African Slaves	„	„	163.
Verbal Contracts	„	„	208.
Sunday Labor	„	„	242.
Tierce-Opposition	„	„	334.
Laborer, in matters of Wages	„	„	344.
Gens de Service, „ „	„	„	348.
Unlawful Absence	„	„	399.
Desertion	„	„	403.
Idle and Disorderly Person	„	„	417.
Rogue and Vagabond	„	„	418.
Incorrigible Rogue	„	„	419.
Vagrancy	„	„	409 et seq.
Petty Sessions	„	„	484.

2o.—Par le rachat ainsi qu'il est expliqué ci-après.

3o.—Par la remise ainsi qu'il est expliqué ci-après.

4o.—Par l'exemption émanant du Gouverneur, ainsi qu'il est expliqué ci-après.

Pour les besoins de la présente Ordonnance le mot REQUÉRANT s'étend et s'applique à toute personne qui aura fait une réquisition pour l'introduction d'Immigrants devant s'engager spécialement avec elle dans l'Inde, ou lui être alloués à leur arrivée à Maurice, selon le cas.

Pour les besoins de la présente Ordonnance l'expression EMPLOYEUR SUBSTITUÉ s'étend et s'applique :

1o.—A toute personne autre que le Requérant, à qui un nouvel Immigrant sera, à son arrivée à Maurice, engagé par contrat de service pour tout le temps de sa résidence industrielle.

2o.—A toute personne à qui tout contrat de service avec un nouvel Immigrant aura été transféré pour le temps qui restera à courir sur la résidence industrielle de cet Immigrant, soit du consentement des parties, soit en vertu des dispositions de l'*Article* 7 de l'Ordonnance No. 16 de 1862. —(*Article 7.—Voir le No. 246.*)

ACTE DU GOUV. DE L'INDE	Voir le No.		25.
ESCLAVES AFRICAINS LIBÉRÉS	„	„	163.
ENGAGEMENT VERBAL	„	„	208.
CORVÉE DE DIMANCHE	„	„	242.
TIERCE-OPPOSITION	„	„	334.
TRAVAILLEUR, en fait de gages	„	„	344.
GENS DE SERVICE „ „	„	„	348.
ABSENCE ILLÉGALE	„	„	399.
DÉSERTION	„	„	403.
PERSONNE OISIVE ET DÉRÉGLÉE..........	„	„	417.
VAGABOND ET PERSONNE SANS AVEU......	„	„	418.
VAGABOND INCORRIGIBLE	„	„	419.
VAGABONDAGE	„	„	409 et seq.
PETTY SESSIONS....................	„	„	484.

SUPPLEMENTARY LAWS.

The laws contained in this Section having been passed while the last pages of the work were being printed, it was impossible to place these new provisions in the chapters to which they respectively belong.

Indian Act No. 6 of 1869, Sect. 1.

551.—The probable length of the voyage from Madras, to Reunion, Mauritius, or Seychelles shall, notwithstanding any thing contained in Act No. XLVI of 1860 (to authorize and regulate the emigration of native Laborers to the French Colonies) or Act No. XIII of 1864 (to consolidate and amend the law relating to the emigration of native Laborers), *section eight,* be deemed to be, between the months of November and March inclusive, six weeks.—(*Section* 8.—*See No.* 31.)

Idem, Sect. 2.

552.—For *Section* 24 of the said Act No. XIII of 1864 the following shall be substituted :—

24. " The Protector of Immigrants at each of the three ports " aforesaid, and the British Consular Agents at each of the French " Ports in India, shall license so many fit persons as shall to him " seem necessary to be recruiters of laborers, and no person shall " act or be employed as a recruiter of laborers except under a " License from such Protector of Emigrants or British Consular " Agent."—(*Section* 24.—*See No.* 47.)

Idem, Sect. 3.

553.—For *Section* 31 of the said Act No. XIII of 1864 the following shall be substituted :—

31. " For the registration of every emigrant, the recruiter shall " pay to the Magistrate a fee of one rupee. On proof of the de-" sertion of any emigrant before embarkation, the fee paid in " respect of such emigrant may be refunded by the Magistrate to " the recruiter by whom it was paid, under such rules as shall " from time to time be made in that behalf by the Governor Ge-" neral of India in Council."—(*Section* 31,—*See No.* 54.)

Idem, Sect. 4.

554.—Notwithstanding any thing contained in the same Act, *Section forty-five,* the Local Government may, in cases of emer-

LOIS ADDITIONNELLES.

Les lois contenues dans cette Section ayant été promulguées tandis que l'on imprimait les dernières pages de cet ouvrage, il a été impossible de faire figurer ces nouvelles dispositions dans les chapitres auxquels elles appartiennent.

551.—La durée probable du voyage de Madras à la Réunion, à Maurice, ou aux Seychelles sera, nonobstant toute disposition de l'Acte No. XLVI de 1860 (pour autoriser et régler l'Émigration des travailleurs indigènes aux Colonies Françaises) ou l'Acte No. XIII de 1864 (pour consolider et modifier la loi relative à l'émigration des travailleurs indigènes,) *Section huitième*, considérée être, entre les mois de Novembre et de Mars inclusivement, de six semaines.—(*Sect.* 8.—*Voir le No.* 31.) Acte du Gouv. de l'Inde No. 6 de 1869, Sect. 1.

552.—A la *Section* 24 du dit Acte No. XIII de 1864 la disposition suivante sera substitué :— Idem, Sect. 2.

" 24. Le Protecteur des Emigrants à chacun des trois Ports " ci-dessus, et l'Agent Consulaire Anglais à chacun des Ports " Français dans l'Inde, autorisera autant de personnes compé- " tentes qu'il jugera nécessaire à agir comme recruteurs de " travailleurs, et aucune personne n'agira et ne sera Employée " comme recruteur de travailleurs à moins qu'elle ne soit auto- " risée par le Protecteur des Emigrants ou par l'Agent Consulaire " Anglais ".—(*Sect.* 24.—*Voir le No.* 47.)

553.—A la *Section* 31, du dit Acte No. XIII de 1864 la suivante sera substituée :— Idem, Sect. 3.

" 31. Pour l'enregistrement de chaque Emigrant, le recruteur " paiera au Magistrat un droit d'une roupie. Sur la preuve qui " lui sera fournie qu'un Emigrant a déserté avant son embarque- " ment, le Magistrat pourra rembourser le droit payé pour le dit " Emigrant au recruteur qui l'aura payé, conformément aux " réglements qui pourront être faits de temps à autre sous ce " rapport par le Gouverneur Général de l'Inde en Conseil ".— (*Sect.* 31.—*Voir le No.* 54.)

554.—Nonobstant toute disposition du dit Acte, *section quarante-cinq*, le Gouvernement Local pourra, en cas d'urgence, Idem, Sect. 4.

gency, permit emigrants for any place West of the Cape of Good Hope to leave the port of Calcutta between the thirty-first day of July and the first day of April.—(*Section* 45.—*See No*. 68.)

Idem, Sect. 5. 555.—Notwithstanding any thing contained in the same Act, *Section forty-seven,* no compartment in an emigrant ship shall take more than one adult emigrant for every twelve superficial feet on deck, and for every cubic space of seventy-two feet, or more than one child who shall have completed two and shall not have completed ten years of age for every eight superficial feet on deck.—(*Section* 47.—*See No*. 70.)

Idem, Sect. 6. 556.—Whenever the Governor General of India in Council or the Local Government has reason to believe that in any place to which emigration is lawful, the plague or other infectious disease dangerous to human life has broken out, or that proper measures have not been taken for the protection of emigrants immediately upon their arrival in such place or during their residence therein or for their safe return to India, or to provide a return-passage to India for any such emigrants at or about the time at which they are entitled to such return-passage, the said Governor General in Council or the Local Government may, by notification published in the Gazette of India or the Local Gazette (as the case may be), declare that emigration from British India or from the territories subject to the Local Government (as the case may be) to such place shall cease and be prohibited from a certain day to be specified in the notification. Any notification issued by the Local Government under this section may be cancelled by order of the said Governor General in Council.—(*See also Nos*. 87 *to* 90.)

Idem, Sect. 7. 557.—Notwithstanding any thing contained in the said Act No. XIII of 1864, *Section sixty-three,* or in any rules made or to be made by the Governor General of India in Council pursuant thereto, the Local Government may, in cases of emergency, permit any vessel carrying emigrants to leave the port of Calcutta, although the proportion of women embarked on board such vessel is not in accordance with the said rules.—(*Section* 63.—*See No*. 86.)

Idem, Sect. 8. 558.—The third clause of *section two* of the same act is hereby repealed, and the phrases "Magistrate of such District" and

autoriser le départ d'Emigrants pour tout Port, à l'Ouest du Cap de Bonne Espérance, du Port de Calcutta, entre le 31 Juillet et le 1er Avril.—(*Sect.* 45.—*Voir le No.* 68.)

555.—Nonobstant toute disposition de la *section quarante sept* du dit Acte, aucun compartiment dans un navire à Emigrants ne contiendra plus d'un adulte par chaque douze pieds de superficie sur le pont, et par chaque espace cubique de soixante douze pieds, ou plus d'un enfant qui aura atteint l'age de deux ans et n'aura pas atteint l'age de dix ans par chaque huit pieds de superficie sur le pont.—(*Sect.* 47.—*Voir le No.* 70.) Idem, Sect. 5.

556.—Toutes les fois que le Gouverneur-Général de l'Inde en Conseil ou le Gouvernement Local aura lieu de croire que dans tout endroit, auquel l'Emigration est permise, la peste ou toute autre maladie infectieuse dangereuse pour les humains a éclaté,—ou, que des mesures convenables n'ont pas été prises pour la protection des Emigrants immédiatement à leur arrivée dans cet endroit ou pendant le temps qu'ils y séjourneront, ou pour leur retour sains et saufs dans l'Inde, ou pour procurer un passage de retour dans l'Inde aux dits Emigrants vers l'époque à laquelle ils ont droit à ce passage, le dit Gouverneur Général en Conseil ou le Gouvernement Local pourra, par un avis publié dans la Gazette de l'Inde ou la Gazette Locale (selon le cas), déclarer que l'Emigration de l'Inde Anglaise ou des territoires régis par le Gouvernement Local (selon le cas) au dit endroit cessera et sera prohibée à partir d'un jour qui sera fixé dans l'avis.—Tout avis publié par le Gouvernement Local en vertu de cette Section pourra être annullé par le dit Gouverneur Général en Conseil.—(*Voir aussi les Nos.* 87 *à* 90.) Idem, Sect. 6.

557.—Nonobstant toute disposition contenue dans la *Section soixante-trois* du dit Acte No. XIII de 1864, ou dans tous réglements faits ou qui seront faits par le Gouverneur Général de l'Inde en Conseil en vertu de cette Section, le Gouvernement Local pourra, en cas d'urgence, autoriser tout navire transportant des émigrants à quitter le port de Calcutta, quoique la proportion des femmes embarquées sur le dit navire ne soit conforme aux dits réglements.—(*Section* 63.—*Voir le No.* 86). Idem, Sect. 7.

558.—La troisième clause de la *deuxième section* du dit Acte est par le présent rapportée, et les mots " Magistrats du dit Dis- Idem, Sect. 8.

"Magistrate of the District," wherever they occur in such Act, shall be held to mean any Officer exercising in such District the full powers of a Magistrate.—(*Section 2,—See No.* 25.)

Idem, Sect. 9. **559.**— The Governor-General of India in Council may, from time to time by notification in the Gazette of India, increase any fee payable under *Sections nineteen, twenty-seven and thirty-four* of the said Act No. XIII of 1864, and may also in like manner reduce to its present amount any fee so increased. Provided that no fee shall be increased under this Section by more than double such amount.—(*Sections* 19, 27, 34,—*See Nos.* 42, 50, 57.)

Idem. Sect. 10. **560.**—Sections *fifty-five, fifty-six, fifty-seven and eighty* of the said Act No. XIII of 1864, are hereby repealed. — (*Sections* 55, 56, 57, 80,—*See Nos.* 78, 79, 80, 103.)

Idem, Sect. 11. **561.**— All persons are hereby indemnified for anything done before the passing of this Act which might lawfully have been done if this Act had been in force ; and no suit or other proceeding shall be maintained against any such person in respect of anything so done. This Section shall come into operation at once : *Section* 2 shall be deemed to have come into operation on the eighteenth day of March 1864 ; and the rest of this Act shall come into operation on the first day of May 1869.— (*Section 2,—See No,* 552.)

Govt. Notice No. 142 of 25th Aug. 1869, Art. 1. **562.**— The several additions and amendments hereinafter mentioned shall be read and construed as forming parts of the Regulations made under Ordinance No. 31 of 1867, and published by Government Notice No. 166 of 11th November 1868.

Idem, Art. 2. **563.**—The following words shall stand as an addition to *Article* 36 of the said Regulations :—

> "And any Immigrant entering into any such Contract " shall be liable to the same penalty."—(*Article* 36.—*See No.* 258.)

Idem, Art, 3. **564.**—The following clauses shall stand as an addition to *Article* 42 of the said Regulations :—

trict" et "Magistrat du District," toutes les fois qu'ils sont mentionnés dans le dit Acte seront considérés s'appliquer à tout officier exerçant dans le dit District les pleins pouvoirs d'un Magistrat.—(*Section* 2.—*Voir le No.* 25.)

559.—Le Gouverneur Général de l'Inde en Conseil pourra, de temps à autre, augmenter tout droit payable en vertu des *Sections dix-neuf, vingt-sept et trente-quatre* du dit Acte No. XIII de 1864, et pourra pareillement réduire à la somme payable actuellement tout droit qui aura été ainsi augmenté ; aucun droit néanmoins ne pourra être élevé en vertu de cette Section au double de son chiffre actuel.—(*Sections* 19, 27, 34.—*Voir les Nos.* 42, 50, 57.) Idem, Sect. 9.

560.—Les Sections *cinquante-cinq, cinquante-six, cinquante-sept* et *quatre vingt* du dit Acte No. XIII de 1864, sont par le présent rapportées.—(*Sections* 55, 56, 57, 80.— *Voir les Nos.* 78, 79, 80, 103.) Idem. Sect. 10.

561.—Toutes personnes sont par le présent indemnisées pour tous actes faits avant la promulgation de cet Acte qui auraient pu être légalement faits si cet Acte avait été en vigueur, et aucune poursuite ou instance ne pourra être maintenue contre aucune personne pour tous actes qui auront été ainsi faits. Cette Section sera mise en vigueur de suite, la *Section* 2 sera considérée comme ayant été mise en vigueur le dix-huit Mars 1864 ; et le reste de cet Acte aura force de loi à partir du 1er. Mai 1869. —(*Section* 2. —*Voir le No.* 552.) Idem, Sect. 11.

562.—Les diverses additions et modifications ci-après énumérées seront lues et interprétées comme si elles faisaient partie des Réglements passés en vertu de l'Ordonnance No. 31 de 1867 et publiés par l'avis du Gouvernement No. 166 du 11 Novembre 1868. Avis du Gouv. No. 142 du 25 Août 1869, Art. 1.

563.—Les mots suivants constitueront une addition à *l'Article* 36 des dits Réglements :— Idem, Art. 2.

> "Et tout Immigrant qui passera un contrat de cette na-"ture sera passible de la même peine."—(*Article* 36,—*Voir le No.* 258.)

564.—Les clauses suivantes constitueront une addition à *l'Article* 42 des dits Réglements :— Idem, Art. 3.

" Unless however in exceptional cases in which sickness or " other good reason be shewn for a further extension."—

" Any Old Immigrant who within eight days (or any longer " period granted by extension as aforesaid) from the date of " his discharge from a written engagement, or from the date " of the delivery to him of a Duplicate Ticket shall fail to " re-engage under written contract or to obtain a Police " Pass, shall, if unable to give a satisfactory reason for such " failure, be liable to a fine not exceeding £ 2 sterling or to " imprisonment for a period not exceeding seven days, without " prejudice to any further punishment to which he may be " liable for vagrancy or otherwise."—(*Article* 42,—*See No.* " 281.)

Idem, Art. 4. 565.—The following words shall stand as an addition to *Article* 43 of the said Regulations :—

" or to imprisonment not exceeding seven days. "—(*Article* 43.—*See No.* 287.)

Idem, Art. 5. 566.—The following clause shall stand as an addition to *Article* 44 of the said Regulations :—

" In default of such notice he shall be liable to a fine not " exceeding £ 4 sterling or to imprisonment not exceeding " fourteen days. "—(*Article* 44.—*See No.* 288.)

Idem, Art. 6. 567.—*Article* 49 of the said Regulations is hereby repealed and in lieu thereof the following provision is enacted :—

" No Job-Contractor shall employ any laborers otherwise " than under written contract of service,or beyond the District " for which any such written contract was passed ; in case of " contravention, the Job-Contractor shall be liable to a fine " not exceeding £ 2 sterling for each laborer so employed by " him."—(*Article* 49,—*See No.* 282.)

Idem, Art. 7. 568.—The following provisions shall stand as an addition to *Article* 51 of the said Regulations :—(*Article* 51.—*See No.* 305.)

" A moins, cependant, que ce ne soit dans des cas exceptionnels, où l'Immigrant fera valoir la maladie ou d'autres raisons valables et suffisantes pour obtenir une prolongation de ce délai."

" Tout ancien Immigrant qui, dans les huit jours (ou dans tout autre délai qui lui aura été accordé comme ci-dessus) qui suivront sa décharge d'un contrat de service écrit, ou qui, à partir de la date à laquelle il lui aura été délivré un duplicata de son Ticket, ne se ré-engagera pas par contrat écrit ou ne se procurera pas une Passe de Police, sera, à moins qu'il ne fournisse une excuse satisfaisante, passible d'une amende n'excédant pas £ 2 sterling ou d'un emprisonnement n'excédant pas sept jours, sans préjudice de toute autre peine dont il se sera rendu passible pour vagabondage ou toute autre cause."—(*Article* 42.—*Voir le No.* 281.)

565.—Les mots suivants constitueront une addition à l'*Article* 43 des dits Réglements :— Idem, Art. 4.

" ou d'un emprisonnement n'excédant pas sept jours."—(*Article* 43.—*Voir le No.* 287.)

566.—La clause suivante constituera une addition à l'*Article* 44 des dits Réglements :— Idem, Art. 5.

" A défaut de cet avis il sera passible d'une amende n'excédant pas £ 4 sterling ou d'un emprisonnement n'excédant pas quatorze jours."—(*Article* 44.—*Voir le No.* 288.)

567.—L'*Article* 49 des dits Réglements est par le présent rapporté, et sera remplacé par la disposition suivante :— Idem, Art. 6.

" Aucun Entrepreneur n'emploiera des travailleurs autrement que sous un Contrat de Service écrit, ou dans un autre District que celui dans lequel le dit Contrat de Service aura été passé ; dans le cas où l'Entrepreneur contreviendrait à cette disposition, il sera passible d'une amende n'excédant pas £ 2 sterling pour chaque travailleur qu'il aura ainsi employé."—(*Article* 49.—*Voir le No.* 282.)

568.—Les dispositions suivantes constitueront une addition à l'*Article* 51 des dits Réglements.—(*Article* 51.—*Voir le No.* 305.) Idem, Art. 7.

" Any Job-Contractor who may desire to engage laborers " without specifying in the Contract of Service the Estate " on which the labor is to be performed, shall be allowed to " pass a Contract in terms of the Schedule A hereunto an- " nexed, and shall furnish to the satisfaction of the Stipen- " diary Magistrate good and valid security by a Bond in " terms of Schedule B hereunto annexed, for the due execu- " tion of such contract during the whole period thereof; and " every such Job-Contractor shall be bound to maintain or " renew the said security, under the penalties provided by " the existing law, with reference to other guarantees fur- " nished by Job-Contractors.

" Besides the general security hereinbefore mentioned " every Job-Contractor employing laborers under any such " contract shall continue to be bound to furnish the spe- " cial guarantee provided by Ordinance No. 7 of 1865, of " the Owner or Lessee of each Estate on which the laborers " are next intended to work.

" Every such Job Contractor, before removing his laborers " from one Estate to another Estate, shall give notice of " such intended removal and destination to the Stipendiary " Magistrate of the District; in default thereof he shall be " liable to a fine not exceeding £ 5 sterling."

" No special guarantee aforesaid shall be signed and au- " thenticated by any Stipendiary Magistrate, unless it be " proved to his satisfaction, that the wages, guaranteed to " the laborers by the Owner or Lessee of the Estate on which " they were last employed, have been duly paid to them."

SCHEDULE A.

Be it remembered that on this day of in the year of Our Lord one thousand eight hundred and sixty , of a Job-Contractor and the Immigrants named on the list hereto subjoined, appeared before me , Stipendiary Magistrate, and in my presence signed their names or marks to the following Contract of Service.

The said agrees to hire the services of the said Immigrants, and the said Immigrants agree to render to the said their services in

" Tout Entrepreneur qui désirera engager des travailleurs, " sans spécifier, dans le Contrat de Service, l'établissement " sur lequel il doit travailler, pourra passer un contrat dans " les termes de la Cédule A ci-annexée, et devra fournir une " caution bonne et valable, à la satisfaction du Magistrat " Stipendiaire, au moyen d'une obligation dans les termes " de la Cédule B ci-jointe, garantissant l'exécution du dit " contrat pendant toute sa durée,—et l'Entrepreneur sera " tenu de maintenir ou de renouveler la dite garantie, sous " peine des pénalités prévues par la loi actuellement en vi- " gueur, relativement aux autres garanties que fournissent " les Entrepreneurs."

" Indépendamment de la garantie générale ci-dessus men- " tionnée, tout Entrepreneur employant des travailleurs en " vertu d'un contrat de cette nature, devra continuer à four- " nir la garantie spéciale prévue par l'Ordonnance No. 7 de " 1865, du propriétaire ou du locataire de chaque établis- " sement sur lequel il a l'intention de faire travailler ses " hommes."

" Tout Entrepreneur qui se trouvera dans ces conditions, " devra, avant de faire passer ses hommes d'un établissement " sur un autre, donner avis au Magistrat Stipendiaire du " District, de son intention de le faire, et de l'endroit où il " compte se rendre ; à défaut de quoi, il sera passible d'une " amende n'excédant pas £5 sterling."

" Aucune garantie spéciale ne sera signée et rendue au- " thentique par un Magistrat Stipendiaire, à moins qu'il ne " soit prouvé, à sa satisfaction, que les gages garantis aux " travailleurs par le propriétaire ou le locataire de l'établisse- " ment sur lequel ils ont été employés en dernier lieu, leur " ont été intégralement payés."

CÉDULE A.

Ce jour de mil huit cent soixante du Entrepreneur et les Immigrants nommés dans la liste ci-jointe ont paru devant moi , Magistrat Stipendiaire, et en ma présence ont apposé leurs noms ou marques au Contrat de service suivant.

Le dit consent à louer les services des dits Immigrants et les dits Immigrants consentent à rendre au dit leurs

the capacity of for Calendar months commencing on the day of in the year one thousand eight hundred and sixty .

And it is further agreed that the said shall pay to the said Immigrants the wages mentioned opposite to their respective names in the list hereto subjoined, and that such wages shall be paid monthly.

And it is also agreed that the services of the said Immigrants shall be further remunerated by the delivery to them of the various articles hereunder specified,—viz :

Rice, ...	pounds per diem.
Dholl, ...	pounds per week.
Salt Fish...	pounds per week.
Oil, ...	pounds per week.
Salt,...	pounds per week.

Proper lodgings and medical care shall be provided by the said to the said Immigrants.

And it is further agreed that if the said shall at any time employ the said laborers in any other District than the District of , then this present Contract of Service shall *ipso facto* become null and void.

The preceding agreement was signed by the above named parties in my presence the day and year above written, voluntarily, the same being, as far as I am able to judge, fully understood by them respectively.

District of , this day of one thousand eight hundred and sixty .

Stipendiary Magistrate.

Name of Immigrant.	No.	Wages.			Name of Immigrant.	No.	Wages.		
		£	s.	D.			£	s.	D.

SCHEDULE B.

Know all men by these presents that we (*names of Job-Contractor and Security*) are jointly and severally held and firmly bound unto Our Sovereign Lady the Queen in the sum of of lawful money of this Colony, for which payment to be well and faithfully made, we bind ourselves and each of us, or the same shall be levied on our and each of our goods and chattels, lands and tenements, to the use of Our Sovereign Lady the Queen, her Heirs and Successors, by way of recognizance in case default shall be made in any of the conditions of such recognizance, the conditions whereof are :—

That if the said (*name of Job-Contractor*) shall well and faithfully fulfil his part of the agreements entered into by him in a Contract of Service with certain laborers passed before the Stipendiary Magistrate of

services en qualité de pour mois, commençant le jour de mil huit cent soixante .

Et il est de plus convenu que le dit paiera aux dits Immigrants les gages mentionnés en regard de leurs noms respectifs dans la liste ci-jointe et que les dits gages seront payés mensuellement.

Et il est de plus convenu que les services des dits Immigrants seront en outre rétribués par la distribution qui leur sera faite des divers articles ci-dessous spécifiés, savoir :—

Riz	livres par jour.
Dholl	livres par semaine.
Poisson salé.	livres par semaine.
Huile	livres par semaine.
Sel.	livres par semaine.

Des logements convenables et des soins médicaux seront fournis par le dit aux dits Immigrants.

Et il est de plus convenu, que si le dit emploie jamais les dits Immigrants dans un autre district que le district de , le présent Contrat de Service deviendra nul de plein droit.

Les conventions qui précèdent ont été signées par les parties susdites en ma présence les jour et an sus-dits, volontairement, les dites parties les ayant bien comprises, autant que j'ai été capable d'en juger.

District de ce jour de mil huit cent soixante .

Magistrat Stipendiaire.

Nom de l'Immigrant.	No.	Gages.			Nom de l'Immigrant.	No.	Gages.		
		£	S.	D.			£	S.	D.

CÉDULE B.

Qu'il soit notoire par ces présentes que nous nous engageons conjointement et solidairement envers Notre Souveraine Dame la Reine au paiement fidèle de la somme de en monnaie légale de cette Colonie, laquelle sera prélevée sur nos biens, meubles et immeubles, respectivement, au profit de Notre Souveraine Dame la Reine, ses Héritiers ou Successeurs, comme étant une obligation authentique, en cas de non-exécution de notre part des conditions du présent engagement lesquelles sont ;

Que si le dit *(nom de l'Entrepreneur)* remplit fidèlement les Engagements qu'il a pris envers certains travailleurs dans un contrat de service passé devant le Magistrat Stipendiaire de le

on the day of in the year of Our Lord one thousand eight hundred and sixty then such recognizance shall be void; otherwise the same shall continue in full force.

And we hereby consent that the judgment of any Stipendiary Magistrate against the said (*name of Job-Contractor*) for a non fulfilment of any of the said agreements shall be conclusive evidence against us, in all Courts and places, of such non-fulfilment.

Idem, Art. 8. **569.**—The following clause shall stand as an addition to *Article* 54 of the said Regulations :—

" The Protector of Immigrants, with the approval of the " Governor, shall regulate from time to time, and according " to the requirements of the locality, the maximum number " of such licenses to be issued in each district."

" The holder of any such license shall be bound to accept " work as a Job-man (or day laborer) at the rates of remu- " neration contained in a tariff which shall be drawn up from " time to time by the Protector of Immigrants and published " with the approval of the Governor."—(*Article* 54.—*See No.* 283.)

Idem, Art. 9. **570.**—The following clause shall stand as an addition to *Article* 56 of the said Regulations :

" Every Job-man convicted of not being in the *bonâ fide* " exercise of the trade and calling of a Job-man shall forfeit " his license.

" Every Job-man convicted of contravening any regulation " concerning Job-men shall be liable to a fine not exceeding " £ 2 sterling or to imprisonment not exceeding seven " days."—(*Article* 56.—*See No.* 285.)

Idem, Art. 10. **571.**—The following clauses shall stand as additional paragraphs to *Article* 67 of the said Regulations :

" 4o. Any person who shall be convicted of having em- " ployed or harboured an Immigrant beyond the date spe- " cified in his permit to work shall be liable to a fine not ex- " ceeding £ 5 and not less than £ 1 sterling. "

" 5o. Any Immigrant who within three days from the ex- " piration of his permit to work or of any other permit is- " sued to him by or on behalf of the Protector of Immi-

jour de , en l'an de Notre Seigneur mil huit cent soixante , la présente obligation deviendra nulle et non avenue ; autrement elle sera maintenue et aura son plein et entier effet.

Et nous consentons par ces présentes à ce que le jugement de tout Magistrat Stipondiaire contre le dit (*nom de l'Entrepreneur*) pour non-exécution d'aucun des dits Engagements, soit dans toutes les Cours et places, preuve concluante contre nous de la non-exécution.

569.—La clause suivante constituera une addition à l'*Article* 54 des dits Réglements :— Idem. Art. 8.

" Le Protecteur des Immigrants, avec la sanction du Gou-
" verneur, fixera de temps à autre, et selon les besoins de
" chaque localité, le maximum de ces patentes qui pourra
" être délivré dans chaque District."

" Le porteur d'une de ces patentes sera tenu de travailler
" à la tâche ou comme journalier, aux prix qui seront fixés
" par un tarif qui sera préparé de temps à autre par le Pro-
" tecteur des Immigrants et publié avec l'approbation du
" Gouverneur."—(*Article* 54.—*Voir le No.* 283.)

570.—La clause suivante constituera une addition à *l'Article* 56 des dits Réglements : Idem, Art. 9.

" Tout Journalier qui sera convaincu de n'avoir pas exercé
" de bonne foi l'état ou l'emploi de Journalier aura sa pa-
" tente confisquée. Tout Journalier qui sera convaincu d'avoir
" contrevenu à aucun des réglements concernant les Journa-
" liers sera passible d'une amende qui n'excèdera pas £2
" sterling ou d'un emprisonnement n'excédant pas sept jours."
—(*Article* 56.—*Voir le No.* 285.)

571.—Les clauses suivantes seront considérées comme des paragraphes additionnels de *l'Article* 67 des dits Réglements : Idem, Art. 10.

" 4o. Toute personne qui sera convaincue d'avoir employé
" ou recelé un Immigrant au-delà de la date spécifiée dans
" son " Permis de travailler " sera passible d'une amende qui
" n'excèdera pas £5 sterling et qui ne sera pas moindre de
" £1 sterling."

" 5o. Tout Immigrant qui, dans les trois jours qui sui-
" vront l'expiration de son " Permis de travailler " ou de
" tout autre permis qui lui aura été délivré par ou au nom

" grants shall fail to deliver such permit to the Keeper of the " Immigration depot, shall be liable to imprisonment not " exceeding fourteen days."—(*Article* 67,—*See No.* 279.)

Idem. Art. 11. 572—In lieu of the fee of four shillings levied for each Jobman's license under Item 13 of the *Schedule* T annexed to the said Regulations, there shall henceforth be levied for each such license a fee of £ 1 sterling.

In lieu of the words "*under Regulation* 77", contained in Item 23 of the said *Schedule*, the following words are hereby substituted, namely "*under Regulation* 78."—(*Schedule T*,—*See No.* 487.)

Idem, Art. 12. 573.—The employer of any Old Immigrant engaged by Verbal Contract shall be bound on the termination of the Engagement to endorse on the Police-Pass of the Old Immigrant the words " Quitted me on " and the date of the cessation of the Engagement: in default whereof the employer shall be liable to a fine not exceeding £ 3 sterling.

Idem, Art. 13. 574.—Any Immigrant, who not being engaged under written Contract of Service shall fail to exhibit his Portrait-Ticket on demand to any Officer or Constable of Police, shall be liable to a fine of £ 2 sterling or to imprisonment for a period not exceeding seven days, without prejudice to any further punishment to which he may be liable for Vagrancy or otherwise.

Idem, Art. 14. 575.—It shall be lawful for any Inspector of Police on the application of any Old Immigrant to endorse on the Police-Pass of such Old Immigrant a permission to proceed to and reside in one or more foreign districts during a specified period; and such endorsement shall during such period be as effectual in each district mentioned in such permission as if the said Police-Pass had been specially issued for each such district.

Idem, Art. 15. 576.—The preceding Amendments and Additions to the Regulations under Ordinance No. 31 of 1867 shall take effect on and from the first September One thousand eight hundred and sixty-nine.

[See Appendix.

" du Protecteur des Immigrants, ne remettra pas ce permis " au Gardien du Dépôt de l'Immigration, sera passible d'un " emprisonnement n'excédant pas quatorze jours."—(*Article* 67.—*Voir le No.* 279.)

572.—Au lieu du droit de quatre schellings perçu pour chaque patente de journalier en vertu du paragraphe 13 de la *Cédule T* annexée aux dits Réglements, il sera dorénavant perçu pour chacune de ces patentes un droit de £ 1 sterling. Idem, Art. 11.

Aux mots "*en vertu du Réglement 77*" contenus dans le paragraphe 23 de la dite *Cédule* les mots suivants sont par le présent substitués, savoir : — "*en vertu du Réglement 78.*"—(*Cédule T.*—*Voir le No.* 487.)

573.—Toute personne qui emploiera un Ancien Immigrant sous Contrat Verbal sera tenue d'endosser sur la Passe de Police de cet Immigrant, à l'expiration de son engagement, les mots : " A quitté mon service le " ainsi que la date à laquelle l'Immigrant a cessé de travailler avec elle : à défaut de quoi la dite personne sera passible d'une amende n'excédant pas £ 3 sterling. Idem, Art. 12.

574.—Tout Immigrant, ne travaillant pas sous Contrat écrit, qui ne pourra pas produire un ticket contenant son portrait, sur la demande qui lui en sera faite par tout Officier ou Constable de Police, sera passible d'une amende de £ 2 sterling ou d'un emprisonnement n'excédant pas sept jours, sans préjudice de toute autre peine dont il se sera rendu passible pour vagabondage ou toute autre cause. Idem, Art. 13.

575.—Tout Officier de Police aura le droit, sur la demande qui lui en sera faite par un ancien Immigrant, d'endosser sur la Passe de Police de cet Immigrant une permission de se rendre dans un ou plusieurs autres districts et d'y demeurer pendant un temps donné, et le dit endossement sera aussi valable dans chaque district mentionné dans la dite permission que si la dite Passe de Police avait été spécialement délivrée pour chacun de ces districts. Idem, Art. 14.

576.—Les changements et les additions ci-dessus aux Réglements faits et passés en vertu de l'Ordonnance No. 31 de 1867 seront mis en vigueur à partir du 1er. Septembre mil huit cent soixante-neuf. Idem, Art. 15.

[*Voir l'Appendice.*

APPENDIX.

Order in Council 7th Sept. 1838, Preamble Par. 1.

1.—Whereas at the Court at Windsor, on the seventh day of September 1838, Her Most Excellent Majesty the Queen in Council was pleased to make an Order to the following words, that is to say :

Idem, Preamble, Par. 2.

2.—Whereas so much of the Act made in the 4th year of the Reign of His late Majesty King William the IVth, for the abolition of slavery throughout the British Colonies, for promoting the industry of the manumitted slaves, and for compensating the persons hitherto entitled to the services of such slaves as relates to the apprenticeship of such manumitted slaves, hath ceased or may shortly be expected to cease to be in force, in the Colonies of British Guiana, Trinidad, St. Lucia, and Mauritius; and whereas it is expedient that provision be made by law for regulating within the said Colonies respectively the relative rights and duties of masters and servants; it is therefore hereby ordered by the Queen's Most Excellent Majesty, by and with the advice of Her Privy Council, that within each of the said Colonies of British Guiana, Trinidad, St. Lucia, and Mauritius, the various rules and regulations hereunto subjoined and comprised in the following chapters, shall henceforth be observed, and shall have the force and effect of law.

Idem, Preamble, Par. 3.

3.—And it is further ordered, that all laws, statutes, and ordinances in force in the said Colonies, or any of them which are or shall be in any wise repugnant to or inconsistent with this present Order, shall be, and the same are hereby repealed.—(*See also No.* 11 *of this Appendix*.)

Idem, Preamble, Par. 6.

4.—And it is further ordered that the Governor of each of the said Colonies respectively shall immediately, upon the receipt by him of this present Order, publish or cause to be published a Proclamation reciting at length the whole of the present Order,

APPENDICE.

1.—Attendu qu'à la Cour de Windsor, le 7 Septembre 1838, il a plu à Sa Très Excellente Majesté la Reine en Conseil de passer un Ordre dans les termes suivants : Ordre en Conseil du 7 Sept. 1838, Préamb. Par. 1.

2.—Attendu que l'acte passé dans la quatrième année du règne de feu Sa Majesté le Roi Guillaume IV pour abolir l'esclavage dans toutes les Colonies Britanniques, pour avancer l'industrie des esclaves en manumission, et indemniser ceux qui avaient droit au service des dits esclaves, en ce qui concerne l'apprentissage des dits esclaves ainsi mis en manumission, a cessé ou doit incessamment cesser d'être en vigueur dans les Colonies de la Guiane Anglaise, Trinité, Sainte-Lucie et Maurice ; et attendu qu'il convient de prendre des mesures pour régler par une loi dans ces colonies les droits et les devoirs respectifs des maîtres et serviteurs ; il est en conséquence ordonné par Sa Très Excellente Majesté la Reine, de l'avis de son Conseil Privé, que dans chacune des dites colonies de la Guiane Anglaise, Trinité, Sainte-Lucie, et Maurice, les divers règlements ci-joints, et compris dans les chapitres suivants seront à l'avenir observés et y auront force de loi. Idem, Préambule, Par. 2.

3.—Et il est de plus ordonné que toutes lois, statuts et ordonnances en vigueur dans les dites colonies ou dans chacune d'elles, qui serait en aucune manière contraires et incompatibles avec le présent Ordre, seront et sont rapportés par le présent.—(*Voir aussi le No.* 11 *de cette Appendice.*) Idem, Préambule, Par. 3.

4.—Et il est de plus ordonné que le Gouverneur de chacune des dites colonies respectivement, à la réception du présent Ordre, publiera ou fera publier une proclamation répétant en entier le présent Ordre, et indiquant le jour du mois et de l'année qu'il Idem, Préambule, Par. 6.

and stating the day of the month and year on which the same was so received by him; and, from that day the said Order shall take effect and have the force of law in each of the said Colonies respectively. Provided, that if this Order shall arrive in any of the said Colonies before so much as aforesaid of the said recited Act of Parliament shall have ceased to be in force therein, the operation of this Order in any such Colony shall be suspended until so much as aforesaid of the said Act shall have so ceased to be in force therein, but no longer.

Idem, Préambule, Par. 7. 5.—And the Right Honorable Lord Glenelg, one of Her Majesty's Principal Secretaries of State, is to give the necessary directions herein accordingly.

Idem, Cap, 1, Sect. 1. 6.—All laws in force in any of the Colonies aforesaid, respecting contracts of apprenticeship, or service to be entered into within the limits of the said respective Colonies, between any master and servant, or respecting the rights and duties of masters and apprentices or servants, in such their relation to each other, or respecting the mode of enforcing such contracts, and the penalties to be inflicted in case of the breach or non-performance thereof, or respecting the dissolution of such contracts are repealed.

Idem, Cap. 1, Sect. 2. 7.—The before-mentioned repeal shall not annul or affect any contract entered into within any of the said Colonies previously to the taking effect therein of a certain Order made by Her Majesty in Council on the 30th day of July 1838, relating to Contracts of apprenticeship or service entered into either without or within the limits of the said respective Colonies.

Idem, Cap. 1, Sect. 3. 8.—Nevertheless any Contract of Apprenticeship or service to be performed within any of the said Colonies shall be liable to be set aside in the manner and by the authority hereinafter mentioned, whatever may have been the date thereof, upon reasonable proof being made to the satisfaction of such Petty Sessions as hereinafter mentioned, that either of the parties to such Contract was induced to enter into the same by any fraud, misapprehension, misrepresentation, or concealment.

Idem, Cap, 4, Sect. 3. 9.—For ensuring regularity and method in the exercise of this summary jurisdiction, the Governor of each Colony shall prepare forms of proceeding to be observed on lodging complaints, in issuing summonses, in the citation of witnesses, in the pronouncing

l'aura reçu ; et à dater de ce jour le dit Ordre prendra son effet et aura force de loi dans chacune des dites colonies respectivement. Pourvu que, si cet Ordre arrivait dans une des dites colonies avant que l'acte du parlement ci-dessus mentionné ait cessé d'y être en vigueur, l'effet de cet Ordre y soit suspendu jusqu'à ce que le dit acte ait cessé d'y avoir force de loi, et non au-delà.

5.—Et le très honorable Lord Glenelg, un des principaux Secrétaires d'Etat, est chargé de donner les ordres nécessaires en conséquence. Idem, Preambule Par. 7.

6.—Toutes lois en vigueur dans aucune des colonies sus-dites, relativement aux contrats d'apprentissage, ou de service, dans les limites respectives des dites colonies, entre les maîtres et serviteurs, ou relatives aux droits et aux devoirs des maîtres et des apprentis ou serviteurs dans leurs rapports sus-dits les uns envers les autres, ou touchant les moyens de forcer l'exécution de ces contrats, et les peines à appliquer en cas de violation ou de non-exécution, ou relatives à la dissolution des-dits contrats, sont abrogées. Idem, Chap. 1, Sect. 1.

7.—L'abrogation ci-dessus mentionnée n'annullera ni n'affectera aucun contrat passé dans aucune des dites colonies antérieurement à la promulgation d'un certain ordre de Sa Majesté en Conseil du treize juillet 1838, relatif aux contrats d'apprentissage ou de service passés en dehors ou dans les limites des dites Colonies respectivement. Idem, Chap. 1, Sect. 2.

8.—Néanmoins, tout contrat d'apprentissage ou de service devant être effectué dans une des dites colonies sera sujet à être annulé de la manière et par l'autorité ci-dessous désignées, quelle qu'en ait été la date, sur la preuve raisonnable qui sera fournie à la satisfaction d'une Cour de *Petty Sessions*, comme il sera dit ci-dessous, que l'une ou l'autre partie au dit contrat a été induite à le passer par quelque fraude, malentendu, surprise, ou déguisement. Idem, Chap. 1, Sect. 3.

9.—Pour assurer de la régularité et de la méthode dans l'exercice de cette juridiction sommaire, le Gouverneur de chaque colonie préparera des formes de procédure qui seront observées pour les plaintes, assignations, citations de témoins, pour la pronon- Idem, Chap. 4, Sect. 3.

awards and sentences, in issuing warrants or orders for the execution of such awards or sentences, and generally for the complete carrying of the powers of the Stipendiary Magistrates into execution; which forms shall be submitted by such Governor to the Chief Civil Judge of each such Colony respectively; and being approved by such Judge, the same shall be observed in all proceedings before the said Stipendiary Magistrates.—(*Virtually superseded by No.* 486.)

Idem, Cap. 4, Sect. 4.

10.—All such forms of proceeding shall, from time to time, be revised, repealed, or amended, by the authority, and in the manner aforesaid, as occasion may require.

Order in Council 10th June 1843.

11.—Whereas on the seventh day of September 1838, certain Orders made by the Queen's Most Excellent Majesty, by and with the advice of Her Privy Council, for promulgation in the Colonies of British Guiana, Trinidad, St. Lucia, and Mauritius, viz.: An Order for regulating the relative rights and duties of Masters and Servants, and an Order to make provision for the suppression of Vagrancy. And whereas on the sixth day of October 1838, an Order was made by Her Majesty, with the advice of Her Privy Council, for promulgation in the aforesaid Colonies, to make provision for preventing encroachments on lands therein respectively situate; and whereas the provisions of the said recited Orders may, from time to time, require amendments for the adaptation thereof to the exigencies of society within the aforesaid Colonies; and whereas it is expedient that such amendments should originate with the Local Authorities having the power of Legislation in the aforesaid Colonies;—Now, therefore, it is hereby ordered by the Queen's Most Excellent Majesty, with the advice of Her Majesty's Privy Council, that it shall, and may, be competent to the Governors, or to the Officers, for the time being, administering the Governments of the aforesaid Colonies respectively, by any Laws or Ordinances to be by them from to time made, with the advice and consent of the Legislative Councils, of the said Colonies respectively, or of the Court of Policy, in the Colony of British Guiana, to revoke, alter and amend the provisions contained in the said recited Orders; and all such laws and Ordinances so to be made as aforesaid, shall, within the Colonies aforesaid, have the same force and authority, as any other laws and Ordinances of the said Governors and Legislative Councils, or Court respectively; anything in the said Orders above recited, of the seventh day of September, and of the sixth day of October 1838, contained to the contrary notwithstanding.

Proclamation 24th April 1851.

12.—Whereas at the Court at Windsor, on the 12th day of December 1850, Her Most Excellent Majesty the Queen in Coun-

ciation des décisions et sentences, la délivrance des mandats ou ordres pour l'exécution des dites décisions ou sentences, et généralement pour l'entière exécution des pouvoirs des magistrats salariés; lesquelles formes seront soumises par le Gouverneur au Chef-Juge Civil de chaque colonie respectivement; et après avoir été approuvées par le Chef-Juge, les dites formes seront observées dans toutes les procédures devant les Magistrats Salariés.—(*Virtuellement abrogé par le No.* 486.)

10.—Toutes les dites formes de procédure seront revisées, rapportées ou amendées par l'autorité et de la manière ci-dessus indiquée, selon que les circonstances le requéreront. Idem, Cap. 4, Sect. 4.

11.—Attendu que le sept Septembre 1838, certains Ordres en Conseil ont été faits par Sa Très-Excellente Majesté la Reine, avec l'avis de Son Conseil Privé, à l'effet de promulguer dans les Colonies de la Guiane Anglaise, de la Trinité, de Ste.-Lucie et de Maurice, un Ordre en Conseil pour régler les droits et devoirs respectifs des Maîtres et des Serviteurs, et un Ordre en Conseil pour supprimer le Vagabondage, et attendu que le six Octobre 1838, un Ordre en Conseil a été fait par Sa Majesté avec l'avis de Son Conseil Privé, afin d'être promulgué dans les dites Colonies, à l'effet d'empêcher d'empiéter sur les terrains de la Couronne qui y sont situés, et attendu que les dispositions des Ordres en Conseil ci-dessus mentionnés peuvent de temps à autre avoir besoin d'être modifiées, afin de s'adapter aux exigences de la société dans les dites Colonies, et attendu qu'il est convenable que ces amendements émanent des autorités locales ayant le droit de faire des lois dans les dites Colonies, il est donc maintenant ordonné par Sa Très Excellente Majesté la Reine, avec l'avis du Conseil Privé de Sa Majesté, qu'il sera et pourra être permis aux Gouverneurs, et aux Officiers administrant pour le moment le Gouvernement des dites Colonies respectivement, par des lois ou Ordonnances faites par eux de temps à autre, avec l'avis et le consentement des Conseils Législatifs, des dites Colonies respectivement, ou de la "Court of Policy," dans la Colonie de la Guiane Anglaise, de révoquer, changer et amender les dispositions contenues dans les Ordres ci-dessus énumérés, et toutes les lois et ordonnances faites, comme il est dit ci-dessus, auront dans les Colonies ci-dessus la même force et la même autorité que toutes autres lois et ordonnances des dits Conseils Législatifs ou Gouverneurs, et de la dite Cour respectivement, nonobstant tout ce qui, dans les dits Ordres ci-dessus mentionnés du 7 Septembre et du 6 Octobre 1838, serait contraire aux présentes. Ordre en Conseil du 10 Juin 1843.

12.—Attendu qu'à la Cour de Windsor le 12 Décembre 1850, il a plu à Sa Très Excellente Majesté la Reine en Conseil de faire Procl. du 24 Avril 1851.

cil was pleased to make an order in the following words, that is to say :—Whereas by an Order in Council, bearing date the 15th day of January 1842, certain provisions were made with regard to ships or vessels carrying emigrants from India to Mauritius, and it is expedient in some respects to amend the same ; it is therefore hereby ordered by the Queen's Most Excellent Majesty, by and with advice of Her Majesty's Privy Council, that so much of the fourth article of the said Order in Council as provides that no such ships or vessels as aforesaid, having more than one deck should have less than six feet at the least between decks, and that in case any such ship or vessel should have only one deck, a platform should be laid beneath such deck, and in such manner as to afford a space of the height of six feet at the least, and that no greater number of passengers should be taken on board of such ship or vessel than should be after the rate of one such person for every 12 superficial feet of the lower deck or platform unoccupied by goods or stores not being the personal luggage of such persons, shall be and the same is hereby repealed ;— and it is further ordered that no such ship or vessel shall be of any less height between decks or shall carry any greater number of passengers in proportion to the superficial or cubical feet between decks allotted to the use of such passengers than shall be allowed by any law which may be in force in India at the time such ship or vessel shall sail therefrom ;— and it is further ordered that any infringement of this Order in Council shall be punished in like manner as any infringement of the said Order in Council of the 15th of January 1842 ;— and it is further ordered that this Order in Council shall take effect from the proclamation of the same in the said Colony of Mauritius.—And the Right Honorable Earl Grey, one of Her Majesty's Principal Secretaries of State, is to give the necessary directions accordingly.

C. C. GREVILLE.

Now, therefore, I do hereby declare that the above recited Order of Her Majesty in Council was received by me, at Mauritius, on the twenty seventh day of March 1851.

J. M. HIGGINSON.

Ord. No. 15 of 1852, Art. 24. 13.—All the provisions of the *hereinbefore cited Order in Council*, which are not contrary to the present Ordinance shall continue to have full effect.—(*Order in Council, i. e., of 7th September* 1838.)

Idem, Art. 25. 14.—Ordinance No. 26 of 1848 is hereby repealed.

Ord. No. 7 of 1856, Art. 2. 15.—In the event of any estate, upon which New Immigrants, one or more, are engaged to the proprietor thereof under

un Ordre dans les termes suivants, savoir :—Attendu que par un Ordre en Conseil en date du 15 Janvier 1842, il a été fait certaines provisions à l'égard des navires portant des Emigrants de l'Inde à Maurice, et qu'il convient, sous certains rapports, d'amender ces provisions, il est par le présent ordonné par Sa Très Excellente Majesté la Reine, avec l'avis du Conseil Privé de Sa Majesté, que la portion du quatrième article du dit Ordre en Conseil ordonnant que tous navires sus-désignés, s'ils sont à deux ponts, auront au moins six pieds d'espace entre ces deux ponts; et s'ils sont à un seul pont, qu'une plate-forme devra être placée au-dessus du dit pont, de manière à laisser libre un espace de six pieds au moins, et que le nombre des émigrants à bord des dits navires devra être réglé de manière à ce qu'il soit alloué pour chaque émigrant une superficie de douze pieds, libres de tout encombrement ou effets qui ne seraient pas ceux du dit émigrant; est et sera rapporté par le présent;—et il est de plus ordonné que tout navire sus-dit devra dans l'entrepont avoir au moins huit pieds de haut et que le nombre d'émigrants qui y seront passagers, sera, en proportion des pieds cubes ou de superficie alloués, calculés en vertu de la loi qui pourrait exister dans l'Inde lors du départ du dit navire;—et il est de plus ordonné que toute infraction au présent Ordre en Conseil sera puni de la même manière que toute infraction à l'Ordre en Conseil susmentionné du 15 Janvier 1842;—et il est de plus ordonné que le présent Ordre en Conseil aura effet à dater de la proclamation qui en sera faite dans la dite Colonie de Maurice;—et le Très Honorable Comte Grey, l'un des principaux Secrétaires d'Etat de Sa Majesté, donnera des instructions nécessaires à l'effet des présentes.

C. C. Greville.

Je déclare par le présent que l'Ordre ci-dessus de Sa Majesté en Conseil a été reçu par moi, à Maurice, le 27 Mars 1851.

J. M. Higginson.

13.—Toutes les dispositions de *l'Ordre en Conseil ci-dessus* cité, qui ne sont pas contraires à la présente Ordonnance, continueront à avoir leur plein effet.—(*Ordre en Conseil, i. e. du 7 Septembre* 1838.) Ord. No. 15 de 1852, Art. 24.

14.—L'Ordonnance No. 26 de 1848 est rapportée par le présent. Idem, Art. 25.

15.—Dans le cas où une propriété sur laquelle de nouveaux Immigrants, un ou plusieurs, sont engagés au propriétaire d'icelle Ord. No. 7 de 1858, Art. 2.

any contract of service, being acquired by a new proprietor under any lawful title of transmission, and in the event of any of the said New Immigrants being willing to engage upon such estate with the said new proprietor for the portion remaining unexpired of any contract of service subsisting at the date of such transmission, or for any period including such portion, no Stamp Duty shall be paid upon such New Engagement in so far as it relates to the said unexpired portion.*

Idem, Art. 4. 16.—*The Ordinance No.* 5 *of* 1849 shall be and the same is hereby altered and modified to the effect hereinbefore provided.—(*Ord.* 5 *of* 1849 *has been wholly repealed,—See No.* 24 *of this Appendix.*)

Ord. No. 16 of 1862, Art. 24. 17.—It shall be lawful to the Governor in Executive Council, from time to time to make regulations for carrying out the purposes of this Ordinance, and from time to time to alter the same; and all such regulations, on being published in the Government Gazette, shall have the same effect as if they had been contained *verbatim* herein; provided that they are not inconsistent with the spirit and meaning of any of the provisions hereof. — (*See also No.* 486.)

Idem, Art. 25. 18.—The following laws, vizt: Art. 3 of *Ordinance* 21 *of* 1854, Ord. 65 of 1860, are hereby repealed;—*Ord.* 30 *of* 1858 is hereby repealed in so far as it is inconsistent with the provisions of this Ordinance,—but reserving the operation of the said laws, in so far as they regard any right or interest which shall have been acquired under the same.—(*Ord. Nos.* 21 *of* 1854, *and* 30 *of* 1858 *have been wholly repealed,—See No.* 24 *of this Appendix.*)

Ord. No. 28 of 1863, Art. 1. 19.—The said Ordinance No. 11 of 1863 is hereby repealed, but reserving the effect thereof in so far as regards any proceedings which shall have been taken in virtue of its provisions while it has been in force.

Ord. No. 23 of 1865, Preamble. 20.—Whereas Ordinance No. 16 of 1862, entituled "An "Ordinance to authorize engagements of Indian Immigrants to be "made for five years, and to declare and amend, in certain "other respects, the law regarding Indian Immigrants in the "Colony," having been duly enacted by the Governor for the

---

* The foregoing provision seems to have been virtually abrogated by the subsequent law (Nos. 246 et seq) which holds New Immigrants bound to the estate for which they were engaged, notwithstanding any change in the ownership of the property.

par des contrats de service, sera acquise par un nouveau propriétaireen vertu d'un titre de transmission légal, et où les dits nouveaux Immigrants ou quelques-uns d'entre eux voudront s'engager sur la dite propriété avec le dit nouveau propriétaire pour la portion de temps non encore expirée des contrats de service à l'époque de la dite transmission, ou pour toute période comprise dans la dite portion de temps, aucun droit de timbre ne sera payé sur le nouvel engagement en tant qu'il aura rapport à la dite période non expirée.*

16.—*L'Ordonnance No.* 5 *de* 1849 sera et est par le présent amendée et modifiée aux effets prévus ci-dessus.—*L'Ord. No.* 5 *de* 1849 *a été entièrement abrogé,—Voir le No.* 24 *de cet Appendice.*) Idem, Art. 4.

17.—Le Gouverneur en Conseil Exécutif aura le droit, de temps à autre, de faire des réglements pour l'exécution des dispositions de cette Ordonnance; et de temps à autre de les modifier; et ces réglements publiés dans la Gazette du Gouvernement auront le même effet que s'ils avaient été contenus *verbatim* dans cette Ordonnance; pourvu qu'ils ne soient pas en opposition avec l'esprit et le sens de ses dispositions.—(*Voir aussi le No.* 486.) Ord. No. 16 de 1862, Art. 24.

18.—Les lois suivantes savoir: l'art. 3 de l'*Ordonnance No.* 21 *de* 1854, l'Ord. No. 65 de 1860, sont rapportées par ces présentes; l'*Ord. No.* 30 *de* 1858 est par ces présentes rapportée en tant qu'elle se trouve en opposition avec les dispositions de cette Ordonnance; mais l'effet des dites lois est préservé en tant qu'elles concernent des droits ou des intérêts qui auront été acquis en vertu d'elles.—(*Les Ord. Nos.* 21 *de* 1854 *et* 30 *de* 1858 *ont été entièrement abrogées,—Voir le No.* 24 *de cet Appendice.*) Idem, Art. 25.

19.—La dite Ordonnance No. 11 de 1863 est par ces présentes rapportée mais en réservant son effet en tant qu'elle affecte des instances qui auraient été commencées en vertu de ses dispositions pendant que l'Ordonnance était en vigueur. Ord. No. 28 de 1863, Art. 1.

20.—Attendu que l'Ordonnance No. 16 de 1862, intitulée: " Ordonnance pour autoriser à passer des engagements de cinq " ans avec des Immigrants Indiens, et pour expliquer et amender " sur certains autres points, la loi concernant les Immigrants " Indiens dans la Colonie" ayant été dûment décrété par le Gou- Ord. No. 28 de 1865, Preambule.

* La disposition ci-dessus semble avoir été virtuellement abrogée par la loi promuguée subséquemment (Nos. 246 et suiv.) et qui lie les nouveaux Immigrants à l'établissement pour lequel ils se sont engagés, nonobstant tout changement dans les propriétaires de cet établissement.

time being of Mauritius and its Dependencies, as brought into operation on the sixth day of April A. D. 1863, in virtue of a Proclamation issued by the Officer Administering the Government for the time being, and dated the second day of April A. D. 1863 ; — and whereas the said Ordinance was approved by Her Majesty's Government in England, and was brought into operation as aforesaid with the authority and approval of Her Majesty's said Government ; — and whereas, owing to its not having been proclaimed that Her Majesty approved of and confirmed the said Ordinance within three years next after the date thereof, doubts may arise as to whether the said Ordinance continued in operation after the expiry of the said three years, and it is expedient that such doubts be removed ; — be it therefore enacted and declared by His Excellency the Governor, with the advice and consent of the Council of Government, as follows :

Idem, Art. 1. 21.—The said Ordinance No. 16 of 1862 is hereby declared to be, and shall remain, in full force and effect to all intents and purposes in the same manner as if Her Majesty's approval and confirmation thereof within three years next after the date thereof, had been formally proclaimed.

Idem, Art. 2. 22.—All acts and things which shall have been done in accordance with the provisions of the said Ordinance after the expiry of the said three years, are hereby declared to be effectual to all intents and purposes in so far as the same are in accordance with the provisions of the said Ordinance.

Ord. No. 29 of 1865, Art. 1. 23.—Ordinance No. 6 of 1845 is hereby repealed, except in so far as relates to any case which shall have arisen under any of its provisions, before this Ordinance shall have come into operation.

Ord. No. 31 of 1867, Art. 78. 24.—The following Laws and parts of Laws, viz. :

Ordinance No. 2 of 1845,
" " 5 " 1849,
" " 7 " 1849,
" " 6 " 1850,
" " 16 " 1852,
" " 15 " 1854,
" " 21 " 1854,
" " 12 " 1855,

verneur de l'île Maurice et de ses Dépendances, alors en fonctions, a été mise en vigueur le dix Avril 1863, en vertu d'une Proclamation faite par l'Officier administrant alors le Gouvernement et datée le dix Avril 1863 ;—et attendu que la dite Ordonnance a été approuvée par le Gouvernement de Sa Majesté en Angleterre, et a été mise en vigueur comme il est dit plus haut avec l'autorisation et l'approbation du dit Gouvernement ;—et attendu que, en raison de ce qu'il n'a pas été proclamé que Sa Majesté a approuvé et confirmé la dite Ordonnance dans les trois ans de la date de la dite Ordonnance, des doutes peuvent s'élever quant à la question de savoir si la dite Ordonnance a continué à avoir force de loi après l'expiration des dites trois années, et attendu qu'il est convenable que ces doutes soient écartés ;—Il est en conséquence décrété par Son Excellence le Gouverneur, de l'avis et avec le consentement du Conseil du Gouvernement, ainsi qu'il suit :—

21.—La dite Ordonnance No. 16 de 1862 est déclarée par ces présentes, être, et elle restera en vigueur, et aura son plein et entier effet à tous égards, de la même manière que si son approbation et sa confirmation par Sa Majesté, dans les trois ans à partir de la date de la dite Ordonnance, avait été formellement proclamée. Idem. Art. 1.

22.—Tous les actes qui auront été faits conformément aux dispositions de la dite Ordonnance après l'expiration des dites trois années, sont par ces présentes déclarés être valables à tous égards, en tant que ces actes sont conformes aux dispositions de la dite Ordonnance. Idem, Art. 2.

23.—L'Ordonnance No. 6 de 1845 est, par ces présentes, abrogée, excepté en tant qu'elle se rapporte à toute question qui aura pu se présenter relativement à ses dispositions, avant que la présente Ordonnance n'ait été mise en vigueur. Ord. No. 29 de 1865, Art. 1.

24.—Les lois suivantes et les parties suivantes de certaines lois, savoir : Ord. No. 31 de 1867, Art. 78.

Ordonnance	No.	2	de	1845,
„	„	5	„	1849,
„	„	7	„	1849,
„	„	6	„	1850,
„	„	16	„	1852,
„	„	15	„	1854,
„	„	21	„	1854,
„	„	12	„	1855,

Ordinance No. 22 of 1857,
„ „ 30 „ 1858,
„ „ 2 „ 1859,
„ „ 18 „ 1864,
Article 14 of Ordinance No. 16 of 1852,
And Article 26 of Ordinance No. 29 of 1865,

are hereby repealed, but reserving the operation of the said Laws in so far as they regard any right or interest which shall have been acquired under the same, prior to this Ordinance coming into operation.

Govt. Notice No. 166 of 11th Nov. 1868, Art. 90.

25.—The Regulations brought into effect by the Proclamations and Government Notices hereunder mentioned are hereby revoked and abrogated :—

1. Proclamation (under Ordinance 16 of 1852) dated 31st August 1854.
2. Government Notice No. 91, dated 26th August 1857.
3. Proclamation (under Ordinance 30 of 1858) dated 12th November 1858.
4. Proclamation (under Ordinances 12 of 1855, 22 of 1857, and 30 of 1858) dated 13th December 1860.
5. Government Notice No. 96 (under Ordinance 16 of 1852) dated 8th July 1862.
6. Government Notice No. 30 (under Ordinance 16 of 1862) dated 25th February 1864.
7. Government Notice No. 100 (under Ordinance 16 of 1862) dated 29th September 1864.
8. Government Notice No. 34 (under Ordinance 16 of 1862) dated 30th March 1865.
9. Government Notice (under Ordinance 16 of 1862) dated 15th February 1867.
10. Government Notice No. 57, dated 18th October 1867.
11. Government Notice No. 16 (under Ordinance No. 16 of 1862) dated 14th January 1868.
12. Government Notice No. 72 of 1868, dated 14th May 1868.

Ordonnance No. 22 de 1857,
„ „ 30 „ 1858,
„ „ 2 „ 1859,
„ „ 18 „ 1864,
L'Article 14 de l'Ordonnance No. 16 de 1862,
Et l'Article 26 de l'Ordonnance 29 de 1865,

sont abrogés par ces présentes, mais en retenant les effets des dites lois en tant qu'elles concernent des droits ou intérêts qui auraient été acquis en vertu de ces lois avant la mise en vigueur de la présente Ordonnance.

25.—Les Réglements mis en vigueur par les Proclamations et les Avis du Gouvernement ci-dessous mentionnés sont abrogés par ces présentes : Avis du Gouv. No. 166 du 11 Nov. 1868, Art. 90.

1. Proclamation (en vertu de l'Ord. No. 16 de 1852) en date du 31 Août 1854.

2. Avis du Gouvernement No. 91, en date du 26 Août 1857.

3. Proclamation (en vertu de l'Ord. No. 30 de 1858) en date du 12 Novembre 1858.

4. Proclamation (en vertu des Ord. Nos. 12 de 1855, 22 de 1857 et 30 de 1858) en date du 13 Décembre 1860.

5. Avis du Gouvernement No. 96 (en vertu de l'Ord. No. 16 de 1852) en date du 8 Juillet 1862.

6. Avis du Gouvernement No. 30 (en vertu de l'Ord. No. 16 de de 1862) en date du 25 Février 1864.

7. Avis du Gouvernement No. 100 (en vertu de l'Ord. No. 16 de 1862) en date du 29 Septembre 1864.

8. Avis du Gouvernement No. 34 (en vertu de l'Ord. No. 16 de 1862) en date du 30 Mars 1865.

9. Avis du Gouvernement (en vertu de l'Ord. No. 16 de 1862) en date du 15 Février 1867.

10. Avis du Gouvernement No. 57 du 18 Octobre 1867.

11. Avis du Gouvernement No. 16 (en vertu de l'Ord. No. 16 de 1862) en date du 14 Janvier 1868.

12. Avis du Gouvernement No. 72 de 1868, en date du 14 Mai 1868.

Govt. Notice No. 187 of 8th Dec. 1868.

26.—*Government Scale of Wages and Allowances.*

His Excellency the Governor does hereby fix the following rates of Wages and Allowances for Ordinary Agricultural Laborers to be allotted in the Colony, and for those to be engaged in India under requisitions in which no Wages and Allowances will be stipulated.

1.—Wages per Month.

	First Year.	Second Year.	Third Year.	Fourth Year.	Fifth Year.
1.—Of New Immigrants.	Shillings	Shillings	Shillings	Shillings	Shillings
From 10 to 11 years of age, inclusive.	5	6	7	8	9
„ 12 to 14 „	6	7	8	9	10
„ 15 to 17 „	7	8	9	10	11
„ 18 upwards	8	9	10	11	12
2.—Of Immigrants who come back to Mauritius after having returned to India.					
From 14 to 17 inclusive	8	9	10	11	12
„ 18 upwards	10	11	12	13	14

2.—Allowances.

1.—Immigrants above 12 years of age, shall receive the following rations :

Rice, one pound and a half,—or two pounds of pounded maize,—or two pounds and a half of cooked manioc,—or five pounds of raw manioc. per diem.
Dholl, eight ounces...... .... per week.
Salt Fish, eight ounces .... „
Ghee or Oil, four ounces .... „
Salt, four ounces .... „

2.—Immigrants under 12 years of age, shall receive the ¾ths of the above-mentioned rations.

27.—*Act of Parliament* 6, *Geo.* 4, *Cap.* 129.—Arts. 1 and 2 have been omitted as they merely recite or repeal former Statutes.—Art. 11 is not inserted as it exclusively refers to prosecutions under the act in Scotland.

28.—The following articles have been omitted as they have been repealed.

Ordinance No. 16 of 1862, Article 14.	Repealed by Ordinance No. 31 of 1867, Art. 78.

26.—*Echelle du Gouvernement pour les Gages et Rations.*

Avis du Gouv. No. 187 du 8 Déc. 1868.

Son Excellence le Gouverneur fixe par ces présentes les taux des Gages et des Rations pour les Laboureurs ordinaires qui seront répartis dans la Colonie, et pour ceux qui seront engagés dans l'Inde sur des réquisitions dans lesquelles ne seront stipulés ni gages ni rations.

1.—GAGES MENSUELS.

	Première Année.	Deuxième Année.	Troisième Année.	Quatrième Année.	Cinquième Année.
1.—Des Nouveaux Immigrants	Schellings	Schellings	Schellings	Schellings	Schellings
De 10 à 11 ans, inclusivement.	5	6	7	8	9
„ 12 à 14 „	6	7	8	9	10
„ 15 à 17 „	7	8	9	10	11
„ 18 et au-dessus	8	9	10	11	12
2.—Des Immigrants qui reviennent à Maurice après être retournés dans l'Inde.					
De 14 à 17 ans inclusivement.	8	9	10	11	12
„ 18 ans et au-dessus	10	11	12	13	14

2.—RATIONS.

1.—Les Immigrants au-dessus de 12 ans recevront les rations suivantes :

Riz, une livre et demie, ou deux livres de maïs moulu,—ou deux livres et demie de manioc cuit, ou cinq livres de manioc cru... ...... par jour.
Dholl, huit onces ... . par semaine.
Poisson salé, huit onces .... „
Mantègue ou huile, quatre onces .... „
Sel, quatre onces ... . „

2.—Les Immigrants au-dessous de 12 ans recevront les trois-quarts des rations ci-dessus énumérées.

27.—*Acte du Parlement* 6, *Geo.* 4, *Chap.* 129.—Les articles 1 et 2 ont été omis parce qu'ils ne font qu'énumérer ou rapporter des actes précédents.—L'article 11 n'a pas été donné parce qu'il se rapporte exclusivement aux poursuites exercées en vertu de cet acte en Ecosse.

28.—Les articles suivants n'ont pas insérés parcequ'ils ont été abrogés :—

Ordonnance No. 16 de 1862, Article 14. } Abrogé par l'Ordonnance No 31 de 1867, Article 78.

Government Notice No. 111 of 4th November 1865, Article 3.	Repealed by Government Notice of 9th August 1867.
Ordinance No. 29 of 1865, Article 26.	Repealed by Ordinance No. 31 of 1867, Article 78.

29.—The following articles have not been inserted as they merely provide for the putting in force of the laws to which they belong :—

Order in Council of 7th September 1838, Cap. 6, Sect. 2.
Ordinance No. 17 of 1841, Article 3.
„ „ 42 of 1844, „ 13.
„ „ 15 of 1852, „ 26.
„ „ 7 of 1858, „ 5.
„ „ 16 of 1862, „ 26.
„ „ 28 of 1863, „ 4.
„ „ 5 of 1865, „ 4.
„ „ 7 of 1865, „ 12.
„ „ 18 of 1865, „ 12.
Government Notice No. 111 of 4th November 1865, Art. 5.
Ordinance No. 28 of 1865, Article 5.
„ „ 29 of 1865, „ 29.
„ „ 31 of 1867, „ 79.
Government Notice No. 166 of 11th November 1868, Art. 91.

Avis du Gouvernement No. 111 du 4 Novembre 1865, Article 3.	Rapporté par l'Avis du Gouverment du 9 Août 1867.
Ordonnance No. 29 de 1865, Article 26.	Rapporté par l'Ord. No. 31 de 1867, Article 78.

29.—Les articles suivants n'ont pas été insérés parcequ'ils pourvoient exclusivement à la mise en vigueur des lois auxquelles ils appartiennent :—

Ordre en Conseil du 7 Septembre 1838, Chap. 6, Sect. 2.
Ordinance No. 17 de 1841, Article 3.
„ „ 42 de 1844, „ 13.
„ „ 15 de 1852, „ 26.
„ „ 7 de 1858, „ 5.
„ „ 16 de 1862, „ 26.
„ „ 28 de 1863, „ 4.
„ „ 5 de 1865, „ 4.
„ „ 7 de 1865, „ 12.
„ „ 18 de 1865, „ 12.
Avis du Gouvernement No. 111 du 4 Novembre 1865, Art. 5.
Ordinance No. 28 de 1865, Article 3.
„ „ 29 de 1865, „ 29.
„ „ 31 de 1867, „ 79.
Avis du Gouvernement No. 166 du 11 Novembre 1868, Art. 91.

TABLE DES TITRES ET CHAPITRES.

	Page.
DE L'INTRODUCTION DES TRAVAILLEURS.	
Ch. I.—Des travailleurs de l'Inde Anglaise	2
II.—De l'introduction illégale des travailleurs de l'Inde Anglaise	97
III.—De travailleurs d'endroits autres que l'Inde Anglaise	101
IV.—Des esclaves Africains libérés...	121
DE LA RÉSIDENCE INDUSTRIELLE ET DU DROIT DE TIMBRE.	
Ch. I.—De la définition, de la remise, et de l'exemption	131
II.—Du rachat de la résidence industrielle et du droit de timbre	137
DES CONTRATS DE SERVICE.	
Ch. I.—Des engagement et des décharges...	149
II.—De la Durée, &c., du travail ... ... De l'Effet sur le contrat de l'emprisonnement " du transfert de l'établissement	179
III.—Des mauvais traitements...	183
IV.—De la Violation du Contrat de la part du maître	185
V.—De la Violation du Contrat de la part du serviteur	187
VI.—Des Causes de la résolution prématurée du Contrat...	189
VII.—De l'emploi illégal, du recèlement &c., des laboureurs	195
VIII.—De l'apprentissage des enfants	201
DES TICKETS, PASSES DE POLICE ET AUTRES PAPIERS	207
DES ENTREPRENEURS	238
DES GAGES, RATIONS ET LOGEMENT.	
Ch. I.—Des Gages et Rations	245
II.—Du Logement	267
DES SOINS MÉDICAUX ET DE L'INHUMATION.	
Ch. I.—Des Soins Médicaux...	267
II.—De l'Inhumation	301

Page.

DE LA DÉSERTION ET DU VAGABONDAGE.

Ch. I.—De l'Absence Illégale et de la Désertion ... 303

II.—Du Vagabondage 181

DE LA COALITION 339

DES COURS STIPENDIAIRES.

Ch. I.—De la Juridiction, Procédure, &c. 355

II.—Du Tarif des frais 369

III.—De la prise à partie 373

IV.—Des Appels 377

DU PROTECTEUR ET DU DEPOT D'IMMIGRATION. 383

DES MARIAGES.

Ch. I.—Des Immigrants dans l'Inde 398

II.—Des Immigrants à Maurice 399

DU DÉPART ET DE LA DÉPORTATION... 403

DES BIENS VACANTS 405

DE LA DÉFINITION DES TERMES 411

LOIS ADDITIONNELLES 417

APPENDICE 433

TABLE DES TITRES ET CHAPITRES 451

TABLE ALPHABÉTIQUE DES MATIÈRES 453

TABLE ALPHABÉTIQUE DES MATIÈRES.

(Les numéros se rapportent aux paragraphes de l'ouvrage.)

ABSENCE ILLÉGALE ET DÉSERTION.
Définition de l'absence illégale. 399.
Refus d'entrer à l'Hôpital considéré comme absence. 362.
Peine pour absence illégale. 400—402.
Emprisonnement compté comme service. 245.
Définition de la désertion.—Peines. 403.
Arrestation des déserteurs. 404. 405.
Arrestation illégale.—Peine.—Dommages. 406.
Déclaration des déserteurs au Protecteur. 407.
Publication des noms des déserteurs qui sont au Dépôt. 408.
Voir aussi Vagabondage.

AFRICAINS LIBÉRÉS.—*v.* Introduction de Travailleurs.

AGENTS D'ÉMIGRATION.—*v.* Introduction de Travailleurs.

AMENDES.—*v.* Cours Stipendiaires.

ANCIEN IMMIGRANT.
Définition du terme. 550.

ANNULATION DES CONTRATS.
Immigrants non réclamés à leur arrivée. 129.
Par consentement mutuel. 180. 182.
Pour des raisons exceptionnelles. 255.
Pour non-exécution du contrat en ce qui concerne les logements et hôpitaux. 353. 361.
Pour cause de maladie. etc., de l'Immigrant. 256.
Des Immigrants dans certains cas. 220.
Pour violation du contrat par le maître. 251.
Pour cause de non-paiement des gages. 329.
Pour contravention à la loi par les Entrepreneurs. 305. 309.
Pour cause de la minorité du serviteur. 224.
Lorsque l'engagement est fictif. 257. 258. 563.
Pour négligence, etc., de la part du serviteur. 252.
Pour violation de la loi sur la corvée du Dimanche. 242. 243.
Pour condamnation du serviteur pour crime ou délit. 259.
Pour cause d'expulsion de la Colonie par le Gouverneur. 544.

APPELS.—*v.* Cours Stipendiaires.

APPRENTISSAGE.
Des enfants entre 10 et 16 ans, par leurs parents, etc. 264. 266.
Défense d'employer les apprentis à certains travaux. 265.
Des jeunes gens de 16 ans et au-dessus. 267.
Emploi illégal, etc., d'apprentis. 260.
Loi d'Angleterre étendue à la Colonie. 268—270.
Dispositions en cas de mise en faillite du Maître. 272.
Voir aussi Mineurs.

ARBITRES.

Magistrats pris comme arbitres. 459.

BIENS VACANTS.

Successions des Immigrants qui meurent " ab intestat." 546.
Administration des biens des esclaves africains libérés. 172.
Déclaration par l'Employeur des biens du serviteur. 547.
Publication des inventaires des successions. 548.

CERTIFICATS.

Des Indiens arrivant dans la Colonie comme passagers. 208.
Faux certificats. 296. 297.
Émission illégale de certificats. 298.
Détention illégale de papiers. 234. 300.

Certificat d'Engagement.

Certificat délivré aux Immigrants nouvellement arrivés. 128.
Droit payable au Protecteur. 525.
Certificat des travailleurs sous contrat écrit. 232—234.
Droits payables d'après le tarif des Cours Stipendiaires. 487.
Signature des certificats par les Clercs des Cours Stipendiaires. 222.
Détention illégale des papiers du serviteur. Peine. 234.
Production du certificat ou d'un duplicata en cas de ré-engagement. 235.
Droit de timbre payable sur les duplicatas. 487.
Exhibition par ce travailleur du certificat sur demande. 291.

Certificat de Décharge.

Certificat donné par le maître à l'expiration du contrat. 238
Les signatures de ces certificats par les Clercs des Cours Stipendiaires. 228.
Droit de timbre. 487.
Certificats délivrés sans frais par le Magistrat. 239.
Duplicatas de ces certificats. Coût. 273. 487.
Production du certificat lors de l'engagement. 227. 232.
Cas où le Magistrat retient le Certificat. 232. 233
Retrait du certificat lorsque l'Immigrant quitte la Colonie. 541.

Certificat du Protecteur.

Certificat délivré au lieu du certicat de décharge. 273. 408.
Droit payable au Protecteur. 525.
Exemption de ce droit. 525 bis.
Production du certificat lors de l'engagement. 227.
Voir aussi MARIAGES.

CHEF JUGE CIVIL.

Définition du terme. 549.

COALITION.

Entre les maîtres ou les serviteurs. 440—442. 444.
La loi d'Angleterre s'applique à Maurice. Exception. 443. Appendice No. 27.
Réunions, cas où elles sont autorisées. 445. 446.
Délinquants, témoins de la Couronne. Indemnité. 447.
Assignation, etc., des accusés et témoins. 448. 449.
Forme de condamnation et de mandat d'emprisonnement. 450.
Appels. 451. 452.

COMPENSATION.— *v.* GAGES.

CONTRATS DE SERVICE.
Définition du terme. 549.
Engagements et décharges. 205—240.
Durée et heures du travail. Tâche. 241—244.
Effet de l'emprisonnement sur le contrat. 245.
Effet de la vente etc. de l'établissement sur le contrat. 246—248.
Mauvais traitements. 249. 250.
Violation du contrat par le maître. 251.
Violation du contrat par le serviteur. 252.
Causes de la résolution prématurée du contrat 255—259.
Emploi illégal et recèlement de travailleurs. 260—263.
Apprentissage des enfants. 264. 272.
Obligation du maître de produire le contrat. 299.
Forme des contrats passés dans l'Inde. 118. 119.
Forme des contrats passés à Maurice. 21. 131. 218.
Forme des contrats passés avec les femmes. 219.
Contrat passé par les entrepreneurs en certains cas. 568.
Contrat passé avec les esclaves africains libérés. Forme 176.

CONSTABLES SPÉCIAUX. — *v.* VAGABONDS.

CORVÉE.
Durée, etc. de la corvée du Dimanche. 242. 243.

COURS STIPENDIAIRES.

Juridiction, procédure, etc.
Nomination des Magistrats, suspension. 454.
Définition du terme " Magistrat Stipendiaire." 549.
Fonctions des Magistrats Salariés, etc. 455.
Juridiction des Cours Stipendiaires. 456. 457. 462.
Juridiction déterminée par le domicile des parties en cause. 460. 461.
Arbitrage des Magistrats Stipendiaires. 459.
Plaintes pour mauvais traitement jugées par les tribunaux ordinaires. 458.
Formes pour la procédure, etc. 486. Appendice Nos. 9 et 10.
Warrants etc. exécutés par la Police. 466.
Signification de la procédure par l'huissier de la Cour de District. 467.
Comparution des accusés avant signification de la procédure. 468.
Refus de comparaître ou de déposer en Cour. Peine. 469.
Parjure. 470.
Plaintes frivoles, mal fondées ou malicieuses. 471.
Manque de respect à la Cour. Insultes, etc. 478.
Voies de fait envers les Officiers du Tribunal. Violation de saisie. 479.
Emprisonnement de plusieurs personnes ordonnées par un seul warrant. 476. 477.
Non-paiement des amendes. Recouvrement. 474. 475.
Protection et indemnité accordées aux Magistrats. 480.
Les Magistrats de District et Stipendiaires peuvent agir les uns pour les autres. 481.
Actions en dommages-intérêts contre les Magistrats. 482. 483
Cour de " Petty Sessions ". 484. 485.

Frais de la Cour.
Tarif des droits et des frais établis par le Gouverneur. 486.
Tarif des droits et frais. 487. 572.
Documents qui ne sont pas soumis au droit de Timbre ordinaire. 488.
Paiement préalable des droits. 463.
Exemption du paiement préalable des droits. 463. 465.
Remboursement des droits dejà payés. 473.
Frais payables par la partie qui perd le procès. 472.

Prise à partie.
Prise à partie contre les Magistrats Stipendiaires. 489—501.

Appels.
Jugements attaquables par voie d'appel. 502.
Les jugements ne peuvent être cassés pour défaut de forme etc., 503.
Décisions des Magistrats agissant comme arbitres. 459.
Conditions etc., des appels ordinaires. 504. 505.
Conditions, etc., des appels formés par les Entrepreneurs. 313.
Conditions, etc., des appels des jugements rendus en vertu de la loi sur les Hôpitaux. 380.
Conditions, etc., des appels formés par les Vagabonds des jugements rendus contre eux. 422.
Conditions, etc., des appels des jugements rendus en matière de coalition. 452.
Envoi des jugements au Greffier de la Cour Suprême. 506.
Avis donné au Procureur Général.—Délai pour décider de l'appel. 507.
Intervention du Protecteur des Immigrants. 508.

CRÉANCES PRIVILÉGIÉES.— *v.* GAGES ET RATIONS.

CURATELLE.— *v.* BIENS VACANTS.

DÉCHARGES.— *v.* ENGAGEMENTS ET DÉCHARGES.

DÉPARTS.
Formalités avant de quitter la Colonie. Passeport. 540.
Forme du passeport. Retrait des papiers de l'Immigrant. 541.
Droit payable pour le passeport. 525.
Délivrance du passeport sans frais. 525 bis.
Embarquement illégal. Peine contre le Capitaine du navire. 542.
Embarquement illégal. Peine contre l'Immigrant. 543.
Passage de retour accordé gratis aux Immigrants. 183.

DÉPORTATION.
Renvoi dans l'Inde des criminels. 544. 545.

DÉPOT D'IMMIGRATION.
Réception au Dépôt des Immigrants sans emploi. 240. 516.
Réception dans le Dépôt des esclaves Africains libérés. 168.
Traitement des Immigrants indigens. 517.
" " vagabonds. 415.
Immigrants arrêtés comme vagabonds. 291. 408—413.
Immigrants reçus au Dépôt. Régime. Soins Médicaux. 518.
Immigrants reçus dans le Dépôt tenus de travailler. 519.

Rémunération pour le travail fait dans le Dépôt. 520.
Recouvrement des frais d'entretien. 521.
Conditions auxquelles l'Immigrant peut quitter le Dépôt. 522. 523.
Remise au Gardien du Dépôt des permis expirés. 571.
Evasions du Dépôt. 524.
Admission du public dans le Dépôt. 522.

Voir aussi PROTECTEUR DES IMMIGRANTS.

DÉSERTION.— *v.* ABSENCE ILLÉGALE DT DÉSERTION.

DIMANCHE (travaux du).—*v.* CORVÉE.

DROITS.— *v.* PROTECTEUR DES IMMIGRANTS.—COURS STIPENDIAIRES.—TIMBRE.

DUPLICATAS.— *v.* CERTIFICATS.—PASSES ET PERMIS.—TICKETS.

ECHELLE DES GAGES.— *v.* GAGES ET RATIONS.

EMPLOI ILLÉGAL, etc.

Recèlement, emploi, etc., illégal d'un serviteur. 260. 261.
Emploi d'un Immigrant après expiration du permis. 571.
Recèlement des Vagabonds. 262.
Emploi d'un nouvel Immigrant autrement que sous contrat écrit. 263.
Peines dont les Entrepreneurs peuvent se rendre passibles. 811. 312. 567. 568.
Peines imposées à ceux qui passent des contrats fictifs. 258. 563. 209.

EMPLOYEUR SUBSTITUÉ.

Définition du terme. 550.

EMPLOYÉS.

Privilége des employés des propriétés pour gages, 351.

EMPRISONNEMENT.

Effet sur le contrat de service. 245.

ENFANTS.—*v.* APPRENTISSAGE.—MINEURS.

ENGAGEMENTS ET DÉCHARGES.

Les contrats doivent être passés dans la Colonie. 205.
Exception à cette régle. 109. 206.

Contrats Verbaux.

Leur durée ne doit pas dépasser 4 semaines. 207.
Expiration et Renouvellement du Contrat. 208.
L'Expiration de l'engagement endossé sur la Passe. 573.
Nouvel Immigrant employé sous contrat verbal. Peine. 263.
Travailleurs employés sous Contrat verbal par des Entrepreneurs. Peine. 567.
Contrats verbaux fictifs. 209.

Contrats écrits.
Les seuls valables avec de nouveaux Immigrants. 210.
Durée des contrats écrits. 211. 212.
Conditions générales et forme. 214—218. 301.
Contrats avec des Immigrants. Conditions, forme. 219. 220.
Formalités à remplir en passant des engagements. 221.
Pouvoir des clercs de passer des Contrats. 222.
Signature du contrat par procuration. 223.
Contrats avec des entrepreneurs. 303—307. 567. 568.
Mineurs. Conditions de l'Engagement. Age. 224.
Droit du Magistrat de refuser de passer des Contrats. 225. 226.
Engagement d'Immigrants. Papiers à produire. 227. 229—231. 235.
Engagements ordinaires. Papiers nécessaires. 232.
Certificat de décharge,—cas où le Magistrat le garde. 232. 233.
Délivrance du certificat d'engagement au serviteur. 232—234.
Droit de timbre sur le certificat d'engagement. 487.
Do. do. do. les duplicatas do. 487.
Détention illégale du certificat du serviteur. 234. 300
Remise du ticket au maître. Responsabilité. 227. 228.
Annullation du contrat par consentement mutuel. 180—182.
Expiration des engagements écrits. 213.
Certificat de décharge. Note des gages dûs. Peine. 238.
Droit de timbre sur le certificat de décharge. 487.
Les décharges peuvent être certifiées par les clercs. 222.
Duplicatas des certificats de décharge.—Coût. 239. 487.
Nouveaux Immigrants déchargés d'un contrat. Obligations. 240.
Anciens Immigrants déchargés d'un contrat. Obligations. 278. 280. 564.
Transferts des contrats des Immigrants. Coût. 132. 236. 237.
Droit de timbre sur ces transferts. 487. 525.
Voir aussi ANNULATION DES CONTRATS.—CONTRATS DE SERVICE.

ENTREPRENEURS.
Patente.—Sa durée.—Obligation de la produire en engageant des hommes. 303. 304.
Contrats verbaux, avec des Entrepreneurs, illégaux. 567.
Contrats écrits limités à un seul District. 567.
Engagements généraux.—Forme.—Garantie. 567.
Engagements pour un seul établssement.—Garantie. 305.
Immigrants engagés pour les travaux des champs.—Garantie. 307.
Signature, termes et conditions de la garantie. 308. 223.
Cessation de la garantie.—Annulation du contrat.—Exception. 305. 309.
Changement de garantie en passant d'un établissement sur un autre. 310.
Emploi d'hommes sans garantie ou sans patente. 311. 312.
Recouvrement des amendes.—Appels. 313.
Manière de payer les gages garantis. Livre de paie. 315.
Les réglements entre les propriétaires et les entrepreneurs n'affectent pas les droits des travailleurs. 316.
Recouvrement des gages de la garantie. 317.

Privilége des Immigrants sur les établissements. 318.
Contrats passés avant la promulgation de la loi. 314.
Loi relative à la garantie applicable à tous les Immigrants. 306.
Loi relative à la garantie étendue aux dépendances de Maurice. 319.
Obligation de l'Entrepreneur d'avoir un Hôpital. 355. 356.

ESCLAVES AFRICAINS LIBÉRÉS.
Contrats passés à Maurice et aux Seychelles. 163.
Entretien et emploi aux Seychelles. 167.
Transfert des travailleurs de Seychelles à Maurice. 166.
Entretien à Maurice avant leur engagement. 168.
Remboursement des frais par le maître. 169. 170.
Engagement au moment de la répartition. 171.
Durée et termes du contrat. 164. 165.
Certificat de répartition. Gages et rations. 175. 176.
Ticket délivré au moment de l'engagement. 177.
Extension de certaines lois aux esclaves libérés. 172.
Nomination de tuteurs. 173.
Pouvoir accordé au Gouverneur de faire des réglements. 174.

EXPERTS.
Nomination d'experts par les Magistrats. 244.

FAILLIS.
Gages des Commis et Serviteurs.—Privilége. 352, 352 bis.
—Décharge des apprentis.—Indemnité. 272 bis.

FAUSSES PLAINTES.
Peine.—471.

FAUX TÉMOIGNAGE.
Parjure devant les Cours Stipendiaires. 470.

FAUX PAPIERS.— v CERTIFICATS.—PASSES ET PERMIS.—TICKETS.

FEMMES (Immigrantes.)
Proportion des femmes à introduire de l'Inde. 86. 122. 557.
Contrats de service.—Conditions et forme. 212. 219.
Suspension, etc., du contrat. 220.

FICTIFS.—CONTRATS.
Contrats verbaux. 209. 282.
Le Magistrat peut refuser de passer des contrats. 226.
Annulation des contrats par le Magistrat. 257. 258. 563.

FRAIS D'INTRODUCTION.— v. INTRODUCTION DE TRAVAILLEURS.

FRAIS DE LA COUR.— v. COURS STIPENDIAIRES.

GAGES ET RATIONS.
Gages etc. stipulés dans la Réquisition. 109 – 112.
Echelle du Gouvernement. Appendice No. 26.
Cette échelle peut être modifiée. 113.
Rémunération stipulée dans le Contrat. 215—219.
Paiement de la rémunération selon convention. 320.
Droits de l'Immigrant pendant la maladie. 321.

Absence illégale. Pertes des gages etc. 399—401.
Dettes contractées par le travailleur. 322.
Billets, etc. souscrits pour gages. 325.
Non-paiement des gages, etc. Recouvrement. 323. 328.
Gages arriérés. Annulation du Contrat. 329.
Recours contre la garantie de l'Entrepreneur. 317.
Paiement des gages par l'Entrepreneur. 568.
Salaires de l'Administrateur, etc. Juridiction. 324.
Serment décisoire en matière de gages, aboli. 327.
Livre de paie. Comment il doit être tenu. 326.
Gages inscrits sur certificat de décharge. 330.
Dénonciation etc. du jugement. Timbre. 331. 487.
Exécution du jugement. 332.
Responsabilité des Employeurs mineurs. 333.
Tierce Opposition. Conditions auxquelles elle est admise. 334.
Saisie des meubles. Intervention de la femme. 335.
Saisie Brandon. 336. 337.
Vente des objets saisis. 338.
Opposition, sequestre, saisie-arrêt. 339 340.
Privilége du travailleur, etc. Subrogation. Timbre. 341. 487.
Saisie des immeubles. Subrogation. 342.
Vente du bien. Privilège du travailleur, &c. 343.
Définition des termes " Travailleurs " et " Gens de Service." 344. 348.
Immigrants au service d'Entrepreneurs. Privilége. 318.
Médecins. Rémunération. Privilége. 372—375.
Salaires des Administrateurs &c. Privilège. 351.
Rang du privilège pour gages. 345—347.
Limite du privilège. 349.
Gages payés du prix de vente. Réclamation, &c. 350.
Commis ou serviteurs des Faillis. Salaires. 352.
Travailleurs, &c. au service d'un failli. Gages. 352 bis.
Gages dûs aux Immigrants, &c., décédés. 546.

GARANTIE.—v. Entrepreneurs.

GENS DE SERVICE.—v. Gages et Rations.

GOUVERNEUR.

Définition du terme. 549.

HEURES DE TRAVAIL.

Durée des travaux des champs. 241.
Travaux des Dimanches. 242. 243.

HOMMES DE JOURNÉE.—v. Journaliers.

HOPITAUX.—v. Soins Médicaux.

IMMIGRATION.— v. Dépôt d'Immigration.—Introduction de Travailleurs.

INHUMATION.

Frais d'inhumation. Responsabilité du maître. 398.

INTRODUCTION DE TRAVAILLEURS.

De l'Inde Anglaise.

Emigration autorisée.
Emigration de travailleurs, légale. 27—29.
Ports d'embarquement. 30.
Epoques fixées pour l'émigration. 8. 68. 554.
Règles et formalités à observer. 1.
L'émigration soumise à la loi de l'Inde. 26. 86. 557. 92. 133. 135.
Pouvoir du Gouvernement de l'Inde de suspendre l'émigration. 87. 90. 556.

Nomination, etc. des Fonctionnaires.
Protecteur des Immigrants à Maurice. 2.
Agents d'Emigration dans l'Inde. 2. 3. 33—35.
Protecteur des Emigrants dans l'Inde. 36—38. 45.
Inspecteur Médical des Emigrants dans l'Inde. 40. 45.

Réquisitions pour des Travailleurs.
Forme etc. des réquisitions. 109. 110.
Stipulation des gages et rations. 111—113.
Durée et annulation des réquisitions. 115. 116.
Remboursement des frais d'introduction. 114.

Recrutement des Travailleurs.
Autorisation des recruteurs. 552. 48—50. 559.
Plaque portée par les recruteurs. 51.
Production de l'autorisation. 52.
Enregistrement des Emigrants. 53. 553. 55.
Emigrants recrutés dans les villes. 56—58. 559.
Transport des émigrants au Dépôt. 59.
Contraventions par les recruteurs. Peines. 93—96.

Dépôts d'Emigration.
Etablissement, autorisation des dépôts. 41. 42. 559.
Inspection des Dépôts. 43. 44. 46.
Arrivée des Emigrants au Dépôt. 60.

Mesures Protectrices.
Examen de l'Agent d'Emigration. 4. 64. 120.
Examen du Protecteur. 39. 66. 74. 75.
Examen de l'Inspecteur Médical. 61.
Emigrans recrutés irrégulièrement, etc. 62. 63.
Emigrans refusés par l'Agent d'Emigration. 64.
Emigrans refusant de s'embarquer. 67.

Contrats de Service.
Contrats passés dans l'Inde. 117.
Conditions de ces contrats. 21.
Forme des contrats des Emigrants. 118.
" " Emigrantes. 219.
Avances de gages dans l'Inde. 119.

Embarquement.
Expédition des Emigrants de l'Inde. 121.
Proportion des femmes. 122.
Permis délivrés aux Emigrants. 65.
Production des permis à bord du navire. 76.
Embarquement illégal. 12. 77. 81. 102.

Voyage.

Inspection, etc., des navires à émigrants. 46. 69.
Emménagements du navire, etc. 5. 7. 70. 555.—Appendice No. 12.
Durée approximative du voyage. 8. 31. 551. 32.
Approvisionnement.—Soins médicaux. 7. 10. 71.
Vêtements d'hiver pour les passagers. 72.
Lois sur l'Émigration fournies au navire. 11. 84.
Certificat donné au navire. 9. 73.
Départ des navires de Calcutta. 82. 83.
Maladie à bord d'un navire allant à Seychelles. 85.
Peines prévues contre le Capitaine et le navire. 16. 17. 97—101. 134.
Exception en faveur des navires de guerre, etc. 18. 108.

Arrivée à Maurice.

Débarquement. Entretien des Émigrants. 10. 16.
Remise aux Émigrants de leurs permis. 76.
Avis de l'arrivée. Remise des listes au Protecteur, etc. 12. 13. 77.
Paiement du passage par le Trésorier. 14. 22.
Registre des Immigrants tenu par le Protecteur. 15.
Avis de l'arrivée des Immigrants. 124.
Engagements. Contrats antérieurs. 19. 20.
Paiement des frais d'introduction. 125. 127.
Recouvrement do. 126.
Remise des émigrants à leurs maîtres. 127. 128. 307.
Immigrants non réclamés à leur arrivée. 129. 131.
Transfert du Contrat à l'arrivée. 132.
Immigrants illégalement introduits. 136.

D'ENDROITS AUTRES QUE L'INDE ANGLAISE.

Immigration. Conditions auxquelles elle est légale. 137.
Autorisation accordée aux navires. 138.
Inspection du navire par le Protecteur. 141.
Mauvais traitements pendant le voyage. Peine. 150.
Débarquement des Immigrants. Rations. 142.
Introduction illégale. Peine. 139.
Immigrants illégalement introduits. 140. 145.
Prix du passage déterminé par un Comité. 147. 148.
Paiement du passage avant livraison des Immigrants. 145.
Passage. Responsabilité de l'Employeur. 149.
Engagement des Immigrants. 146.
Engagements. Contrats antérieurs. 143.
Enregistrement et Ticket. 144.
Mariage des Immigrants. 153—157.
Registres des mariages. 158.
Lois sur le travail appliquables. 152.
Sequestration illégale des Immigrants. 151.
Embauchage des femmes. 159.
Poursuites judiciaires. 161.
Pouvoir de faire des réglements. 160.
Abrogation des lois antérieures. 162.

INSULTES.

A la Cour, au Magistrat, etc. Peine. 478.

JOURNALIERS.
Patente. Passe de Police. 283.
Droit de timbre sur la patente. 487. 572.
Production, renouvellement de la patente. 284.
Plaque qu'ils doivent porter. 285.
Limitation du nombre des Journaliers. Tarif. 569.
Confiscation de la patente. 570.
Contraventions. Peine. 570.

JURIDICTION.—*v.* COURS STIPENDIAIRES.

LABOUREURS.—*v.* TRAVAILLEURS.

LÉGISLATION.
Ordre en Conseil du 7 Septembre 1838. Promulgation, etc. Appendice Nos. 1. 2. 4. 5. 3. 6. 7.
Modification du dit Ordre. Appendice No. 11.
Réglements en vertu de l'Ord. No. 16 de 1862. Appendice No. 17.
Abrogation de certaines lois. Appendice Nos. 14. 16. 18. 19. 23. 24. 25. 28.
Mise en vigueur de certaines lois. Appendice No. 29.
Confirmation de l'Ord. 16 de 1862. Appendice Nos. 20. 21. 22.

LIVRE DE PAIE.—*v.* GAGES ET RATIONS.

LOGEMENTS.
Logements des travailleurs. 353.
Visites des Inspecteurs Médicaux. 378.
Inspection du Protecteur des Immigrants. 510.

MAGISTRATS.—*v.* COURS STIPENDIAIRES.

MAITRE.
Définition du terme. 549.

MARIAGES.
Immigrants d'endroits autres que l'Inde Anglaise.—Déclaration. 153. 159.
Immigrants de l'Inde Anglaise.—Déclaration. 526—532.
Droit payable pour le certificat de mariage. 525.
Embauchage des femmes des Immigrants. 159. 533. 534.
Immigrants se mariant dans la Colonie.—Formalités. 536.
Consentement du Protecteur au mariage des Immigrants orphelins. 537—539.

MÉDECINS.— v. SOINS MÉDICAUX.

MINEURS.
Responsabilité de l'employeur mineur. 333.
Résidence industrielle des Immigrants mineurs. 123.
Contrats de service avec les mineurs. 224.
Gages des employés mineurs. Echelle. Appendice No. 26.
Tutelle des mineurs. 271. 272. 537—539.
Apprentissage. 264—272.

NOUVEL IMMIGRANT.
Définition du terme. 550.

OPPOSITIONS.— *v.* Gages et Rations.

ORPHELINS.— *v.* Mineurs.

PAPIERS.— *v.* Passes et Permis.—Certificats.—Tickets.

PARJURE.

Faux témoignage devant les Cours Stipendiaires. 470.

PASSES ET PERMIS.

Passe de Police.

Délai pour l'obtenir. Déclaration. 279—281. 564.
Immigrants trouvés sans passe. Peine. 564.
Vérification des déclarations. 292. 293.
Forme de la passe. 289. 301.
Contrat écrit. Retrait de la Passe. 230. 231.
Passe obtenue sous de faux prétextes. 209.
Expiration du contrat verbal endossé sur la Passe. 573.
Passe accordée aux Journaliers. 283.
Patente des journaliers. Coût. 283. 487. 572.
Production sur demande, &c. de la patente. 284.
Plaque que doivent porter les journaliers. 285.
Production de la passe sur demande. 291.
Changement de District. Formalités. &c. 286. 288. 566. 413.
Changement de résidence ou d'emploi. 287. 565.
Permission de demeurer dans un autre District. 575.
Duplicatas de Passes. Coût, &c. 290. 487.
Duplicatas délivrés sans frais. 290 bis. 525 bis.
Usage frauduleux de la passe. 294.
Détention illégale des passes. 300.
Retrait de la passe au départ de la Colonie. 541.

Passes et permis du Dépôt.

Permis de travailler.—Visâ. 279. 522.
Permis expiré. Peine. 571.
Permis remplaçant le certificat de décharge. 227. 273. 408.
Coût des passes et permis. 525.
Passes ou permis délivrés sans frais. 525 bis.

Fausses passes et faux permis.

Fausses passes. 296.
Faux permis. 297.
Passes délivrées illégalement. 298.

PASSEPORTS.— *v.* Départs.

PATENTES.— *v.* Entrepreneurs.—Journaliers.

PERMIS.— *v.* Passes et Permis.

PETTY SESSIONS—COUR DE.— *v.* Cours Stipendiaires.

PLAQUES.— *v.* Journaliers.

POLICE—PASSES DE.— *v.* Passes et Permis.

PORTRAITS.— *v.* Tickets.

PRISE A PARTIE.

Contre les Magistrats Stipendiaires. 489—501.

PRIVILÉGE.— v. GAGES ET RATIONS.

PROCÉDURE.— v. COURS STIPENDIAIRES.—LÉGISLATION.

PROTECTEUR DES IMMIGRANTS.

Nomination par le Gouverneur. 2.
Remplacement du Protecteur par son chef Commis. 513. 514.
Arrivée des Immigrants. Inspection etc. 12—14. 77. 81.
Registre des Immigrants. 15.
Introduction de travailleurs de l'Inde. 109—130.
Transfert des contrats à l'arrivée. 132.
Emigrants illégalement introduits de l'Inde Anglaise. 136.
Emigrants introduits d'ailleurs que l'Inde Anglaise. 141—158.
Esclaves africains libérés. 168—177.
Résidence Industrielles etc. des Immigrants. 181—200.
Ré-enregistrement des Immigrants. 274. 184. 204.
Contrats passés avec des Immigrants. 220.
Nouveaux Immigrants sans emploi. 240.
Annulation du Contrat pour cause spéciale. 255. 256.
Remise de tickets etc. aux Immigrants. 273—281. 571.
Documents livrés par le Protecteur.—Droits. 525.
Papiers délivrés sans frais. 525 bis.
Tarif et nombre des Journaliers. 569.
Garantie fournie par les Entrepreneurs. 307, 308.
Visite des établissements, camps, etc. 510.
Suspension des Médecins des établissements. 371.
Registre des Déserteurs. Avis au Maître, etc. 408.
Visites aux Dépôts des Vagabonds. 511.
Vagabonds. Emploi. Répartition. 436.
Intervention dans les cas d'appels. 508.
Do. dans les actions en dommages-intérêts. 512.
Mariage des Immigrants. 526—537.
Tutelle des Orphelins et des Aliénés. 538. 539.
Départ des Immigrants de la Colonie. 540. 542.
Successions d'Immigrants décédés. 548.
Voir aussi DÉPÔT D'IMMIGRATION.

RACHAT.— v. RESIDENCE INDUSTRIELLE.

RATIONS.— v. GAGES ET RATIONS.

RECRUTEURS.— v. INTRODUCTION DE TRAVAILLEURS.

REGISTRES.

Registres des Immigrants. 15. 144.
Registres de paie. 326.
Registres exemptés du droit de timbre. 488.
Refus de produire des livres etc. en Cour. 469.
Voir aussi SOINS MEDICAUX.

REQUERANT.

Définition du terme. 550.

REQUISITIONS.— v. INTRODUCTION DE TRAVAILLEURS.

RÉSIDENCE INDUSTRIELLE.
Définition du terme. 178.
Manière de remplir cette obligation. 179.
Exemption par l'employeur. 180.
Exemption à l'arrivée de l'Immigrant. 181.
Exemption pendant le cours du contrat. 182.
Droit payable pour l'exemption. 487. 525.
Exemption par le Gouverneur. 183.
Résidence Industrielle des enfants. 123.
Ré-enregistrement des Immigrants. 274. 184. 185.
Achévement de la Résidence Industrielle. 280. 281. 564.
Départ de la Colonie. Obligation de l'Immigrant. 540.

Rachat de la Résidence Industrielle.
Par l'Immigrant libre de tout engagement. 186. 187.
Pour des causes exceptionnelles. 188.
Paiement de l'argent de rachat. Reçu. 189.
Note sur le ticket de l'argent de rachat dû. 194.
Droit de la personne qui introduit l'Immigrant. 196.
Perte de ce droit. 197. 198.
Avis donné des sommes reçues. 200.
Paiement de l'argent de rachat à l'employeur. 199.
Dépôt au, et remboursement du, Trésor. 201. 202.
Tenue des comptes.—Reçu. 203.

RETOUR DANS L'INDE.— *v.* DEPARTS.—DEPORTATION.

SAISIE BRANDON.
Saisie des récoltes pour gages dûs. 336. 337.

SERMENT DÉCISOIRE.— *v.* GAGES ET RATIONS.

SERVITEUR.
Définition du terme. 549.

SIGNATURES.
Signatures des Magistrats, &c. 302.

SOINS MÉDICAUX.
Obligation des Maîtres d'avoir des hopitaux. 354. 356.
Faculté de se servir de l'Hôpital Civil. 354.
Formalités à observer par ceux qui s'en servent. 391. 392.
Entrepreneurs tenus d'avoir des hôpitaux, &c. 355. 356.
Situation, &c. des hôpitaux. Médicaments. Infirmiers, &c. 357.
Hôpitaux déjà construits. 358. 360.
Hôpitaux supplémentaires en temps d'épidémie. 359.
Délai pour construction &c. des hôpitaux. 360.
Contraventions à la loi sur les hôpitaux. 361.
Travailleurs malades tenus d'aller à l'hôpital. 362.
Hôpitaux communs. 363. 392. 393.
Médecins des propriétés. Avis au Magistrat. 364.
Droits des Immigrants pendant la maladie. 321.
Déclaration du nombre des serviteurs. 364. 366.
Fausses déclarations. Peines. 365.
Cessation &c. des visites du Médecin. Substitution. 367.
Visites obligatoires dn Médecin. 368.
Registre tenu par le Médecin. Certificat. 369.

Registre d'hôpital. Obligation du Maître. 370.
Fausses Entrées sur le Registre. Faux certificat. 370.
Suspension du Médecin. 371.
Rémunération des Médecins. 372.
Femmes, enfants des serviteurs. Soins Médicaux. 373.
Recouvrement des salaires du Médecin. 374.
Privilège des Médecins pour salaires. 375.
Inspecteurs Médicaux. Nomination, etc. 376. 377. 382—390.
Certificats d'hôpitaux. 390.
Inspection des hôpitaux et camps. 378. 510.
Visites trimestrielles aux hôpitaux. 386.
Rapports des Inspecteurs Médicaux. 387.
Note donnée à l'Inspecteur Médical par le Magistrat. 394. 395.
Contraventions à la loi. Juridiction. 379.
Appels. 380.
Réglements en vertu de l'Ord. 29 de 1865. 381.
Faculté de se servir des hôpitaux des Pauvres. 396.

SUBROGATION.— v. GAGES ET RATIONS.

SUBSTITUÉ.—EMPLOYEUR.
Définition du terme. 550.

SUCCESSIONS.— v. BIENS VACANTS.

TACHE.
Travaux exécutés à la tâche. 244.

TICKETS.
Des Emigrans d'endroits autres que l'Inde Anglaise. 144.
Des Esclaves Africains libérés. 177.
Des nouveaux Immigrants. 128 et page 208.
Des nouveaux Immigrants ré-enregistrés. 274.
Des anciens Immigrants. 275.
Abolition des tickets sans portrait. 278.
Production des tickets lors de l'engagement. 227. 229.
Endossement de l'engagement sur le ticket. 227.
Endossement sur le ticket du timbre dû, etc. 194. 198.
Prolongation du contrat inscrit sur le ticket. 402.
Responsabilité du Maître. 227. 228.
Production, remise du ticket par le Maître. 299. 300.
Immigrants tenus de produire leurs tickets. 574.
Rachat de la résidence. Production du ticket. 187.
Passe de Police. Production du ticket. 280.
Exemption par Protecteur du droit pour portrait. 276.
Duplicatas de tickets. Droit. 279. 525.
Usage frauduleux, etc. de tickets. 295.
Faux tickets. 296.
La forme des tickets peut être changée. 301.
Départ de la Colonie. Retrait du ticket. 541.

TIERCE OPPOSITION.— v. GAGES ET RATIONS.

TIMBRE. (DROIT DE)—
Sur les Contrats avec de Nouveaux Immigrants.
Contrats des nouveaux Immigrants. Timbre. etc. 191.
Personnes dont il ne peut être réclamé. 190.

Renouvellement de l'engagement. Timbre. 192. 193.
Endossement sur le ticket du timbre dû. 194.
Paiement du droit de timbre. 195.
Remboursement dans certains cas. 188. 204.
Droit de la personne qui introduit l'Immigrant. 196.
Perte de ce droit. 197. 298.
Publication des sommes recouvrées. 200.
Remboursement par les Caissiers de District. 199.
Remboursement par le Trésor. 201. 202.
Tenue des comptes. Reçu. 203.

Sur divers documents.

Droits perçus sur certains documents. 487. 572.
Documents, etc, exemptés du droit de timbre. 488.

TRAVAILLEUR.

Définition du terme. 344.

TUTEURS.— *v.* MINEURS.

VAGABONDS.

Passe de Police. Fausse déclaration. Enquête. 409.
Immigrants sans papiers. Arrestation. 410.
Vérification des moyens d'existence des Immigrants. 411.
Immigrants trouvés hors de leur District. 413.
Recèlement des Vagabonds. 414.
Peines infligées aux Vagabonds. 416.
Déserteurs refusant de s'employer. 415.
Condamnations réunies pour vagabondage. 476.
L'emprisonnement doit être subi dans un Dépôt. 429.
Publication des noms &c. des Vagabonds. 430. 431.
Avis donné au Maître de la condamnation. 431.
Admission des maîtres, &c. au Dépôt. 433.
Inspection des Dépôts par le Protecteur. 511.
Expiration de la peine. Emploi, &c. 432. 434—437.
Nomination de Constables spéciaux. 434. 437—439.
Personnes oisives et déréglées. Peine. 417.
Vagabonds et personnes sans aveu. Peine. 418.
Vagabonds incorrigibles. 419. 423.
Arrestation des délinquants. 420. 421. 425.
Négligence des Agents de la Police dans l'exercice de leurs fonctions. 424.
Forme du jugement prononcé contre les Vagabons. 426.
Manière d'appeler des jugements. 427.
Obligation souscrite par les témoins en cas d'appel. 422.
Abrogation des lois antérieures. 428.